This edition is dedicated to Rita Mulcahy.

Her vision made RMC the company it is today. She had a profound influence on so many people—her readers, her students, and, not least, her employees. May we all apply what we learned from her and embody her passion for improving our organizations, our communities, and our world through effective project management.

Acknowledgments

The following people made invaluable contributions to this book:

Editor
Mary Lofsness

Production Editor
Whitney Thulin

Portuguese Translation Reviewer
Roberto Pons, PMP
Executive Director, Projectlab
Rio de Janeiro, Brazil

Spanish Translation Reviewer
Isis De la Rosa de Gneco, PMP, CPIM
CEO & Founder, KIP Professional Development
Santo Domingo, Dominican Republic

Content Reviewers/Contributors
Roberto Pons, PMP
Isis De la Rosa de Gneco, PMP, CPIM
Jeffrey S. Nielsen, PMP, PgMP, PMI-RMP
Sonja Almlie, PMP
Barbara A. Carkenord, CBAP, MBA, PMP
Margo Kirwin, PMP
Roger Kent, PMP
Jean McKay, PMP, PMI-RMP

Additional Contributors
Tim Mulcahy
Eric Rudolf

Table of Contents

Introduction to *PMP® Exam Prep, Seventh Edition*

First let me take this opportunity to thank you for reading this book. For most people, opening a book doesn't have the same monumental import that it does for the author or the publisher. We realize that in reading this book you are taking a leap of faith and making an investment of your time and intellect; for that, we at RMC Publications are deeply honored.

This is the first edition of the book to be published since the passing of Rita Mulcahy. It would be an understatement to say that Rita is an icon in the project management industry. In the past, she has been called a guru. Others have said diva. Rita had a passion for project management, not only as a way of getting work done faster, better, and cheaper, but also as a way of helping people. This passion was incorporated in all of her works but, most importantly, is reflected in this book, since it was her first.

Most of the content in the book remains hers, but as with any new edition, we have added new material. The thing to realize about Rita was that, in addition to being the best project management trainer in the world, she was also one of the best project managers.

Long before Rita was diagnosed with cancer, she realized that in RMC Project Management and this book, she was creating an institution that she wanted to go beyond her life. She did what any good project manager would do. Rita performed a risk analysis and then put in place processes to mitigate those risks. What you see in this Seventh Edition is the culmination of those processes.

Rita never wrote these books in a vacuum. Well, maybe the First Edition. That one was written in our home office at a time when Rita was the only employee of RMC Project Management. Rita said she wrote the book in a week. Not true. I was there. The first draft was hammered out in a week, but the finished product took a lot longer than that.

Starting with the Fourth Edition, Rita began seeking input from her growing staff of editors and project management trainers. It started with comments and line editing but soon the scope of their contributions grew. These people not only worked for Rita, they were mentored by her as well. The trainers were taught how to train by Rita. They knew her methods and style. Our editors learned to hear Rita's voice in her work and could see areas, not many, where she went astray.

By the time the Sixth Edition came along, Rita decided it was time to pass the reins on to others to continue her work. Rita's primary role in the Sixth Edition was to review and provide comments. Don't get me wrong; she wrote large chunks of content, but she did not perform the heavy lifting for the creation of that book. That was done by Laurie Diethelm.

Laurie has been with RMC since 2005. She started out as a production editor and worked her way up through the company until today, where she is the Product Development Manager for RMC. Along the way she got her CAPM and her PMP certifications. She is now responsible for maintaining RMC's current list of products and managing the creation of new products, from RMC's e-Learning courses to our *PM FASTrack®* software and everything in between, including this book.

The most important thing you need to know about Laurie is that she was handpicked by Rita to carry on the legacy of the *PMP® Exam Prep* book. Laurie was best able to capture Rita's voice and, more importantly, her intent behind her writing.

As you read this book, you will be hard pressed to identify where content created by Rita ends and where Laurie's begins.

We hope you enjoy the book. More importantly, we hope you gain useful project management knowledge and obtain your PMP certification. After all, that's why we're all here, isn't it?

Now go get 'em.

Tim Mulcahy
President and CEO
RMC Project Management and RMC Publications

History of This Book

The first edition of Rita Mulcahy's *PMP® Exam Prep* book was published in 1999, and at the time was the first and only comprehensive resource dedicated to PMP exam preparation.

As a project manager in the late 1990s—as well as one of the world's first certified PMPs—Rita was frustrated by the lack of quality PMP preparation materials available to her and her colleagues. So combining her knowledge of accelerated learning with her extensive project management experience, Rita wrote the first draft of *PMP® Exam Prep* in less than a week. Since then, the popularity of the book has grown immensely through seven wildly successful editions, and today the book is by far the best-selling PMP exam preparation guide in the world. By the end of 2010, there were hundreds of thousands of copies in circulation worldwide in three different languages, and several more translations to come.

In September of 2005, Rita was diagnosed with Stage 4 Inflammatory Breast Cancer (IBC), just days before back-to-back speaking appearances at PMI Global Congress in Toronto, Ontario. Given only months to live, Rita spent the next five years privately fighting her disease with a continuous regimen of both Western and Holistic treatments. During that time she continued to work, authoring five more best-selling books, including *Risk Management, Tricks of the Trade® for Project Managers*, which won PMI's Professional Development Product of the Year award, and *PM Crash Course™ for IT Professionals*, co-published with Fortune 100 leader Cisco Systems. Rita also continued to deliver classes and keynote speeches across the globe and spent a great deal of time growing her business, watching RMC expand its training and product distribution to nearly 50 regions worldwide. For five years after her diagnosis, Rita worked feverishly to build RMC into one of the fastest-growing training organizations in the industry.

Tragically, Rita passed away on May 15, 2010. RMC continues her mission today with the seventh edition of the *PMP® Exam Prep* book, and with a growing line of other project-management-related courses and products that promote her vision of improving the world through effective project management. Available in English, Brazilian Portuguese, and Spanish, *PMP® Exam Prep* and its related products are used as stand-alone study tools by hundreds of thousands of project managers across the globe, and in hundreds of classroom-based prep classes at universities, training companies, and corporations large and small.

Free Updates Purchase of this book includes access to updates regarding the PMP exam, as well as additional tricks, tips, and information to help you prepare for the exam. Access this information at **www.rmcproject.com/extras**. Have this book with you when you go to the Web site.

We Need You to Help Us Stop Copyright Infringement As the publisher of the best-selling PMP exam prep book on the market, RMC is also, unfortunately, the most illegally copied. It is true that many people use our materials legally and with our permission to teach PMP exam preparation. However, from time to time, we are made aware of others who copy our exam questions, Tricks of the Trade®, and other content illegally and use them for their own financial gain.

If you recognize any of RMC's proprietary content being used in other PMP exam prep materials or courses, please notify us at copyright@rmcproject.com immediately. We will do the investigation. Please also contact us at the e-mail address above for clarification on how to use our materials in your class or study group without violating any laws.

Contact Us We love to hear your feedback. Is there anything in this book that you wish was expanded? Is there anything that we focus on too much, or is there anything not covered that you think should be here? We would love to hear from you. Send us an e-mail at pmp@rmcproject.com.

CHAPTER ONE Tricks of the Trade® for Studying for This Exam

Why Take the PMP Exam?

Preparing to take the PMP exam is a journey. If you let it, this journey can help you expand yourself and your abilities. In preparing for the exam, you have an opportunity to become a better project manager, not just pass the exam. This opportunity to learn is one of the best reasons to get your PMP certification.

To pass the PMP exam, you cannot simply cram a lot of information into your brain and retain it just long enough to get through the four-hour testing period. Instead, you need to take your knowledge to the next level. You need to truly understand the process of project management and what value that process can bring to your daily work on projects. The PMP exam is an international exam designed to prove your knowledge and experience in applying the art and science of project management. The exam focuses on situations you might encounter in the real world, rather than just asking you to repeat data you have learned. Achieving the PMP certification is a way to set yourself apart.

In addition to the opportunity to improve yourself and your abilities, there can be financial incentives for passing the exam. A salary survey by the Project Management Institute (PMI®) has found that, in the United States and some other countries, PMP-certified project managers are paid at least 10 percent more than those without this certification. RMC has had students who received a US $15,000 bonus AND a 15 percent raise when they passed the exam. Others have said they got a job over 200 others because they were PMP certified. In this economic climate, having a PMP certification can be the reason you get a job, keep your job, or are promoted. These are good incentives to finally get around to taking the exam.

Qualifying to Take the Exam

To take this exam, you must meet the requirements outlined by PMI. The current requirements are described in the following table.

Category	General Education	Project Management Education	Project Management Experience		Number of Questions
One	Bachelor's degree	35 contact hours	4,500 hours	Three years	200
Two	High school graduate	35 contact hours	7,500 hours	Five years	

RMC offers CAPM Exam Prep courses (classroom or online training) and a CAPM Exam Prep system of products to use in preparing for the CAPM exam. Visit www.rmcproject.com for more information about this series of products.

Remember, just because you might qualify on paper to take the exam does not mean you will be able to pass it! You must know project management and have experience applying it. Consider taking PMI's CAPM® exam if you do not meet the requirements in the previous table. You can find the requirements for the CAPM exam at http://www.pmi.org. Currently, test takers must document 1,500 hours of experience or 23 hours of project management education to qualify for this exam.

Are You Ready for the PMP Exam?

In RMC's experience, 50 percent of those who fail the exam do so because they have not had project management training that uses PMI terminology. This is a serious factor to consider in determining whether you are ready to take the exam. Understanding PMI's approach to managing projects is not as simple as reading the *PMBOK® Guide*. The *PMBOK® Guide* helps you improve your knowledge, but it does not teach you project management. And while this exam prep book will explain the project management process and help you understand it from PMI's perspective, if you find that many of the concepts and terms presented in this book are new to you, you probably need additional project management training before continuing to study.

Another large percentage of the people who fail this exam do not have real-world experience. They may be managing a help desk or small projects or might not even work as a project manager. This exam is designed to identify those who have not had project management training and who do not have experience. It is not an exam for a beginning project manager or for one who hopes to become a project manager. The more experience you have had working on large projects, the better prepared you will be for the exam, as the questions are written from the perspective of managing large projects.

The following are examples of large projects:

- Designing a new call center (vs. handling small call center projects)
- Designing a new manufacturing process (vs. manufacturing a standard product for a customer)
- Installing commercial software across the company (vs. installing a PC desktop operating system and associated software updates)
- Designing and constructing a new building (vs. getting an existing building repainted)

So what level are you at in your knowledge of project management? Review the following list. Do you routinely experience two or more of the following problems on projects? If so, you would benefit from learning more about project management prior to taking the exam.

- Large cost or schedule overruns
- Unrealistic schedules
- Excessive changes to the scope or schedule
- Poor communications and increased conflict
- Running out of time near the end of the project
- Unsatisfactory quality
- Low morale
- People on the team are unsure of what needs to be done
- Excessive rework and overtime
- Too many project meetings

Now think about your project management experience, particularly your experience working on large projects. Review the following list of concepts on the exam. Do you understand the following concepts and currently apply them to your real-world projects?

- The step-by-step process for managing projects, and why each step is necessary
- Roles of the project manager, sponsor, and team
- The use of historical information from previous projects
- The use of lessons learned from previous projects
- The creation of lessons learned on your projects
- Project charter
- What a work breakdown structure is (not a list or a bar chart) and how to create it
- How to manually create a network diagram
- Critical path—how to find it and what benefits it provides the project manager
- Three-point estimating

- Monte Carlo analysis
- Earned value measurement
- Schedule compression (crashing and fast tracking)
- Managing float
- A realistic schedule
- Managing the quality of both the project and the resulting product
- The risk management process (risk management is not just using a checklist)
- Expected monetary value
- Calculating budget reserves and their relationship to risk management
- A realistic and approved project management plan that you are willing to be held accountable to achieving
- Controlling the project to the project management plan
- Managing the change request process
- Controlling change
- The professional and social responsibility of the project manager

Keep in mind, on large projects the project manager does not have time to do the wrong project management activities. The project can easily get out of control if the project manager spends too much time on efforts like solving problems rather than preventing them or babysitting people instead of making sure they know what they need to do before the project starts. You need to understand what a project manager of a large project should be doing for the exam.

If you don't know (or don't do) many of the items on this list, we suggest you take our 3-day PM Tricks of the Trade® course, offered in both classroom and Live Online formats. This course will assist you in dealing with situational questions on the exam, and will also give you over half of the contact hours required to sit for the PMP exam. Please visit www.rmcproject.com or call (952) 846-4484 for more information.

Applying to Take the Exam

You must submit an application to PMI to take this exam. Applications may be submitted by mail or online. Submit online if at all possible, since PMI's response time is faster for electronic submissions. You will receive a notice authorizing you to make an appointment to take the exam. You may be subject to an audit of your application before it is approved. Be aware that an audit will delay your authorization to take the exam.

The exam is usually offered on a computer at designated testing sites, but it might be different depending on the country you are in. Your authorization notice will give you specific instructions. PMI is quickly moving to offer computerized testing around the world in many languages.

ONCE YOU RECEIVE YOUR AUTHORIZATION NOTICE, YOU MUST PASS THE EXAM WITHIN ONE YEAR! In some instances, testing centers may not have openings for several weeks.

How to Use This Book

Be Sure You Have Current Materials for the Exam Before you begin using this book, you should make sure it's the correct edition. RMC products are updated to give you the most current information available and take into account the latest changes to the exam. Previous editions of this book are out of date and should not be used to try to pass the exam. To confirm that you are using the correct edition, visit www.rmcproject.com.

How This Book Is Organized Each chapter is organized the same way: an introductory discussion, a list of Quicktest topics (listed in order of importance), Rita's Process Chart, review materials, and a practice exam. All page references in this book refer to the *PMBOK® Guide, Fourth Edition*, unless otherwise stated. The *PMP® Exam Prep* book can be used alone, but it is also designed to be part of an exam prep system with RMC's *PM FASTrack*® exam simulation software and *Hot Topics* flashcards.

Introduction to Each Chapter The introductory discussion provides an overview of the chapter and key information for understanding the material covered in the chapter.

Quicktest The list at the beginning of each chapter indicates the topics covered in the chapter and our impression as to their order of importance. Refer back to this list when you are finished with each chapter, to test your knowledge of the chapter contents and to review what is most important.

Rita's Process Chart Created in 1998 for the first edition of this book, this chart has been greatly expanded to help you understand the process of managing a project. The chart is a key trick for passing the exam with less study. You will first see this chart in chapter 3, Project Management Processes. Use the repeated chart at the beginning of each of the following chapters to know how the different knowledge areas relate to the efforts involved in the project management process.

Review Materials and Exercises This book contains extensive review materials and many exercises. These materials have been developed based on accelerated learning theory and an understanding of the difficult topics on the exam. Make sure you do the exercises, rather than jump right to the answers. Do not skip the exercises, even if their value does not seem evident to you. The exercises and activities are key benefits of this book. They will help you pass the exam.

The answers are listed immediately following the exercises. Although some readers wish the answers were shown later in the book, we have found that it is more effective to place them right after the exercises. If you want to keep yourself from seeing the answers, here is a trick: keep a blank piece of paper handy to cover the answers until you have completed each exercise and are ready to review them.

Also included in the review material are tricks to passing the exam called Tricks of the Trade® (a registered trademark of RMC). The tricks are designated by this image and will give you some extra insight on what you need to know about project management. Many of the Tricks of the Trade® first described or promoted in this book have since become industry standards.

The questions in this book are tests on the chapter content. They do not simulate the complete range and depth of the PMP exam questions. You can find such a simulation in RMC's *PM FASTrack*® PMP exam simulation software.

Our method of helping you prepare for the exam does NOT focus on rote memorization. The few things you should memorize are designated by this "memory finger" image.

Practice Exam The practice exam at the end of each chapter allows you to review the material and test your understanding. On the following pages, you will find a score sheet to use as you take the practice exams. Make a copy of it for each practice exam.

NOTE: You cannot simply practice answering questions to prepare for this exam. The questions in this book and in *PM FASTrack*® are provided to help you assess your knowledge and to get you familiar with the types of questions that are on the exam. Make sure you focus your study efforts on reading this book, doing the exercises and review activities, and filling gaps in your project management knowledge.

Notes Throughout this book, you will see superscripted note references when many project management terms are first introduced. These notes provide the historical origin of the terms or concepts and are explained in the back of the book. This information is NOT tested on the exam. It is simply provided for your interest and reference, if you choose to read the notes. For some people, understanding the development of an idea helps them remember it better. For others, such information is a distraction. If you find the notes distracting, DO NOT continue to read them. Instead, focus your study efforts on the main body of this book.

Score Sheet Use this score sheet to test your understanding. Make a copy of it for each chapter's practice exam. (Note: If you are using RMC's full PMP® Exam Prep system, please see the study plan instructions on page 13.)

Question Number	First Time	Why I Got the Question Wrong	Second Time	Why I Got the Question Wrong
1.				
2.				
3.				
4.				
5.				
6.				
7.				
8.				
9.				
10.				
11.				
12.				
13.				
14.				
15.				
16.				
17.				
18.				
19.				
20.				
21.				
22.				
23.				
24.				
25.				
26.				

Question Number	First Time	Why I Got the Question Wrong	Second Time	Why I Got the Question Wrong
27.				
28.				
29.				
30.				
31.				
32.				
33.				
34.				
35.				
36.				
37.				
38.				
39.				
40.				
41.				
42.				
43.				
44.				
45.				
Total Score	First Time		Second Time	

How will I improve how I take the exam next time?

Other Materials to Use to Study for the PMP Exam

You can use this book as a stand-alone prep tool, or it can be combined with the following products for a comprehensive exam prep experience. Do not risk overstudying or confusing yourself by using other prep books or products beyond the following resources.

Rita Mulcahy's™ *PM FASTrack®* Exam Simulation Software

(CD OR DOWNLOADABLE), BY RITA MULCAHY

Offering over 1,500 questions—including tricky situational questions with more than one "right" answer. In addition to this book, *PM FASTrack®* is the most important product for passing the exam. The software allows you to create sample exams by Knowledge Area, Process Group, Keyword, PMP Simulation, and even Super PMP Simulation. It also saves you a huge amount of time by automatically scoring and keeping records of exams with comprehensive grading and reporting capability. All questions are cross-referenced with this book or the *PMBOK® Guide*, making it easy to go back and study weak areas. Users say these questions are harder than the ones on the actual exam!

Rita Mulcahy's™ *Hot Topics* Flashcards

(HARD COPY OR AUDIO CD), BY RITA MULCAHY

Are you looking for a way to prepare for the PMP exam that fits into your busy schedule? Now you can study at the office, on a plane, or even in your car with RMC's portable and extremely valuable *Hot Topics* flashcards—in hard copy or audio CD format! Over 600 pages of the most important and difficult to recall PMP exam-related terms and definitions are now available for study as you drive, fly, or take your lunch break. Add instant mobility to your study routine.

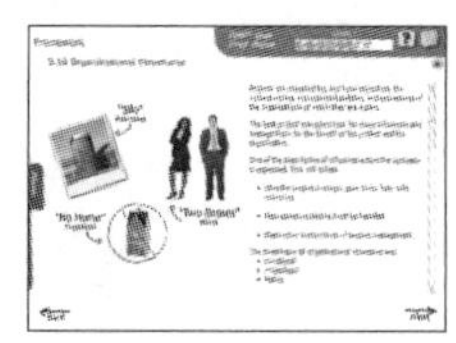

PMP® Exam Prep—Online

This self-directed e-Learning course for the new PMP exam offers over 150 video and audio clips, a 16-lesson interactive tutorial, dozens of exercises and games, multimedia flashcards, unlimited timed and scored practice exams, page number references back to the *PMBOK® Guide*, and all 35 Contact Hours necessary to apply to sit for the PMP Exam!

PMBOK® Guide, Fourth Edition

The *PMBOK® Guide, Fourth Edition* (2008), is the international standard for project management from the Project Management Institute (PMI).

What Is the PMP Exam Like?

Keep in mind three very important things about this exam. First, THE PMP EXAM IS NOT A TEST OF THE INFORMATION IN THE *PMBOK® Guide*! Second, you cannot rely only on real-world experience. Third, training in professional project management that is aligned with the *PMBOK® Guide* is critical! However, do not let any organization fool you into thinking you need weeks of training or a master's certificate in project management to take the exam.

The PMP exam includes 200 multiple-choice questions with four answer choices per question. The exam must be completed in four hours. Twenty-five of the 200 exam questions are "prerelease questions," meaning they are not included in your score for the exam. These questions will be randomly placed throughout the exam. You will not know which ones are which. They will be used by PMI to validate the questions for future inclusion in the master database. Your score will be calculated based on your response to the remaining 175 questions. The passing score on the exam has been approximately 61 percent (106 out of 175 questions answered correctly).

The questions are randomly generated from a database containing hundreds of questions. The questions may jump from topic to topic and cover multiple concepts in a single question. You get one point for each correct answer. There is no penalty for wrong answers.

The following table breaks out the percentage of scored questions currently on the exam in each process group:

Project Management Process Group	Percentage of Questions
Project initiating	13%
Project planning	24%
Project executing	30%
Project monitoring and controlling	25%
Project closing	8%

PMI occasionally makes changes to aspects of the exam, including qualification requirements, the application process, the passing score, and the breakdown of questions in each process group. For the latest information, please visit www.pmi.org and read your authorization notice carefully. Any differences between what is listed here and what is communicated by PMI should be resolved in favor of PMI's information.

The following diagram indicates the topics tested on the exam and their level of difficulty. For many people, the most difficult areas are project management processes, procurement management, risk management, and integration management.

Topics	Level of Difficulty
Project management processes	More Difficult
Procurement management	↑
Risk management	
Integration management	
Quality management	
Time management	
Cost management	
Project management framework	
Scope management	
Human resource management	↓
Communications management	Less Difficult

This next diagram indicates the level of difficulty of the process groups. Many people find project monitoring and controlling, initiating, and executing to be the most difficult. Make sure you study these carefully.

Project Management Process Group	Level of Difficulty
Project monitoring and controlling	More Difficult
Project initiating	↑
Project executing	↕
Project planning	↓
Project closing	Less Difficult

Be aware of the following for the exam:

- The PMP exam tests knowledge, application, and analysis. This makes the PMP exam more than a test of memory. You must know how to apply the information in this book and be able to analyze situations involving this information. Do not expect the exam to have all straightforward, definition-type questions.
- It is important to realize the PMP exam deals with real-world use of project management. The majority of the questions are situational (e.g., "What would you do in this situation?"). For those who have not used project management tools in the real world or whose project management efforts include common errors, these questions can be extremely difficult. You need to have been there to pass the exam.
- There may be instances on the exam where the same data is used for multiple questions, such as with network diagram questions.
- It always feels like more for the test taker, but historically, there have been only 10 to 12 questions requiring you to MEMORIZE the inputs or outputs from the *PMBOK® Guide*. (Inputs and outputs are discussed in later chapters.)
- Expect 8 to 10 formula-related calculations on the exam.
- Expect 10 to 12 earned-value questions on the exam. Not all of these require calculations using the formulas.
- Most acronyms will be spelled out (e.g., the exam typically uses the full term "work breakdown structure" rather than "WBS"), but you should know both the acronym and the full term.
- The correct answers should not include direct quotations from the *PMBOK® Guide*.
- Most people feel uncertain of only 40 or fewer of the 200 questions on the PMP exam.
- Many people need only about two and a half hours to finish the first pass through the PMP exam and then take the rest of the time to review their answers.

The questions on the exam are mostly situational, many are ambiguous and very wordy, and some even seem like they have two right answers. Be prepared for the following types of questions so you will not waste time or be caught off guard when you are taking the exam.

1. **Situational questions** These questions demonstrate why having project management experience is critical to passing this exam. Such questions require you to integrate your real-world experience and your knowledge of the exam concepts.

   Question You receive notification that a major item you are purchasing for a project will be delayed. What is the BEST thing to do?

   A. Ignore it; it will go away.
   B. Notify your boss.
   C. Let the customer know about it, and talk over options.
   D. Meet with the team and identify alternatives.

   Answer D

2. **Questions with two or more right answers** Questions that appear to have two, three, or even four right answers are a major complaint from many test takers. Many questions will list several choices that could reasonably be done, or that less-experienced or less-qualified project managers would be likely to choose.

   As you go through questions and review the answers in this book (or in *PM FASTrack®* for PMP Exam Prep system users), look for questions for which you think there is more than one right answer and try to figure out why you think multiple choices are correct. We have intentionally included such questions in our products to give you exposure to the types of questions you will see on the exam and have provided explanations to help you understand why your right answer may not be the best choice.

   Let's look again at the previous situational question. Couldn't we really do all of the choices? The right answer is certainly D, but isn't it also correct to tell the customer? Yes, but that is not the first thing to do. Essentially this question is really saying, "What is the BEST thing to do NEXT?"

3. **Questions with extraneous information** It is very important to realize that not all information included in a question will be relevant. For example, the numbers in the following question are extraneous data.

   Question Experience shows that each time you double the production of doors, unit costs decrease by 10 percent. Based on this, the company determines that production of 3,000 doors should cost $21,000. This case illustrates:

   A. Learning cycle.
   B. Law of diminishing returns.
   C. 80/20 rule.
   D. Parametric cost estimating.

   Answer D

   Some questions will be much longer than this one, possibly several paragraphs long. But again, you may not need all the information presented to answer the question. For example, imagine we changed the previous question to be wordier. It might read as follows:

   "Your company is a major manufacturer of doors, and has received numerous awards for quality. As the head of the manufacturing department, you have 230 people reporting to you on 23 different projects. Experience shows that each time you double the production of doors, unit costs decrease by 10 percent. Based on this, the company determines that production of 3,000 doors should cost $21,000. This case illustrates..."

   Can you see how the additional data does not add any value to the question? The data is a distracter. On the exam, you may see whole paragraphs of data that are not needed to answer the question. The trick is to look at each question to determine "What is this question asking about?" rather than getting lost in all the information provided. Do not get upset if you have difficulty with these long, wordy questions. Just mark them and come back to them later. If you know what to expect, you will stay calm and not lose confidence when you see such questions.

4. **Questions using made-up terms** Many people taking the exam expect that all the terms used as choices should mean something. They do not! There are often made-up terms on the exam. Perhaps the question writer needed another choice, or perhaps the made-up terms are added to trick test takers. If you consider yourself well trained and see a term you do not know on the exam, chances are it is not the right answer. For example:

   Question The ongoing definition of a project as more information becomes available to the team is called:

   A. Scope verification.
   B. Strategic planning.
   C. Progressive elaboration.
   D. Quantitative elaboration.

   Answer C

   In this question, "quantitative elaboration" in choice D is not a real project management term.

5. **Questions where understanding is important** Let's look at the following question:

   Question The process of decomposing deliverables into smaller, more manageable components is complete when:

   A. Project justification has been established.
   B. Change requests have occurred.
   C. Cost estimates can be developed for each work element.
   D. Each work element is found in the WBS dictionary.

   Answer C

   In order to answer this question, you must understand the terms, as well as the concept of decomposition and what value this technique has in the project management process. Memorization is not enough!

6. **Questions with a new approach to a known topic** There will be many instances where you understand the topic, but have never thought about it in the way the question describes. For example:

   Question In a matrix organization, information dissemination is MOST likely to be effective when:

   A. Information flows both horizontally and vertically.
   B. The communication flows are kept simple.
   C. There is an inherent logic in the type of matrix chosen.
   D. Project managers and functional managers socialize.

   Answer A

   Many people know what a matrix organization is but have not taken the time to consider how this organizational structure affects the directions in which information is shared.

7. **Questions with more than one item in each choice** Let's look at the following example:

   Question The seller on the project has presented the project manager with a formal notification that the seller has been damaged by the buyer's activities. The seller claims that the buyer's slow response to sending the seller approvals has delayed the project, and has caused the seller unexpected expense. The FIRST things the project manager should do are:

   A. Collect all relevant data, send the data to the company attorney, and consult with the attorney about legal actions.
   B. Review the contract for specific agreed-upon terms that relate to the issue, see if there is a clear response, and consult an attorney if needed.
   C. Review the statement of work for requirements, send a receipt of claim response, and meet to resolve the issue without resorting to legal action if possible.
   D. Hold a meeting with the team to review why the acceptances have been late, make a list of the specific reasons, and correct those reasons.

   Answer B

   These questions can seem hard until you apply this little trick: use the process of elimination, one item at a time. Consider the first item listed in each choice and eliminate the choices that contain an implausible first item. Then look at the second item in each remaining choice and eliminate any implausible choices. Keep going until you have only one choice remaining.

   Watch out; sometimes the items in each choice show a flow or process. See the following example:

   Question When managing a project, which of the following is the BEST order to deal with problems that arise?

   A. Go to the team, go to management, go to resource managers.
   B. Go to resource managers, go to management, go to the customer.
   C. Handle it yourself, go to the customer, go to management.
   D. Resolve problems with resources you control, go to the resource manager, go to the customer.

   Answer D

   In this case, you would need to look at each choice independently to see if the process listed is correct.

8. **Excessively wordy questions** Instead of saying "the project is behind schedule," the exam might use wordier phrasing, such as "The project float was zero and has recently gone to negative 2." Instead of saying, "The team is not reporting properly," the exam could say, "The team has lost sight of the communications management plan." The first step in answering many questions is to determine what the question is asking, and then to translate the wordy phrasing. If you are not a native English speaker, this can be an especially big problem, but it is also difficult for native English speakers. Just take your time, and practice reading wordy questions before you take the exam.

   See chapter 14 of this book for more information on the exam, and additional help in assimilating the information provided throughout this book.

How to Study for the PMP Exam

Some people believe you need to read every resource available and spend as much time as possible preparing for the PMP exam. Do not make these mistakes! You should not read every book you can find, and there is a risk in overstudying. Instead, we recommend the following approach.

The Magic Three Studies have shown that if you visit a topic three times, you will remember it. Therefore, you should read this book once and skim through it two more times, focusing most on the activities you do not do in the real world or the concepts you have trouble understanding, in addition to using our other exam preparation products.

Be in Test-Taking Mode Get used to jumping from one topic to another, and practice taking an exam for four hours. Do not underestimate the physical, mental, and emotional aspects of taking an exam lasting that long.

Your Step-by-Step Study Plan We recommend that you use one of the following study plans. Follow Plan A if you own RMC's complete PMP Exam Prep System. Follow Plan B if you do not own the entire system.

Plan A: Using This Book with the PMP Exam Prep System *(PMP® Exam Prep* book, *PM FASTrack®*, and *Hot Topics)*

1. Read this book for the first time and complete all the exercises, focusing more time on the chapters where you have the most gaps in your knowledge or real-life project management experience. Focus most on items you did not know or did not do prior to beginning this course of study. Refer to Rita's Process Chart for each chapter, and be sure you understand all the efforts involved in the knowledge areas you are working on. At the same time, skim through the corresponding chapter in the *PMBOK® Guide* to get an understanding of the flow of the processes.
2. As you finish each chapter, review the Quicktest terms listed on the first page of the chapter to make sure you know the meaning of each term or concept. Use the *Hot Topics* flashcards to improve recall and test your understanding of that chapter.
3. If it is at all possible, form a study group any time after you have read the book for the first time on your own. This will actually make your study time shorter and more effective! You will be able to ask someone questions, and the studying (and celebrating afterward) will be more fun. A study group should consist of only three or four people. (See the following discussion of "How to Use This Book in a Study Group.")
4. Once you feel confident about the material, test yourself with the first 20 questions from each knowledge area in *PM FASTrack®*. This will help you determine how much more study time you need and which chapters to read more carefully. This step will also give you a baseline against which to track your progress as you continue to study.
5. Review each question you got wrong in *PM FASTrack®*, writing down the specific reasons for each wrong answer. Assess why the correct choice is correct and why the other answers are wrong. Continue to study this book, focusing in detail on the areas in which you have gaps in your knowledge and skimming the sections or chapters in which you did well. Correct any errors in your understanding of the concepts discussed in this book. Review the *PMBOK® Guide* to focus on these same gaps.
6. Make sure you really know the material, and then take a full PMP exam simulation on *PM FASTrack®*.
   WARNING: You should limit yourself to two full PMP exam simulations before you take the actual exam. Otherwise, you diminish the value of *PM FASTrack®*.
   WARNING: If you do not score over 70 percent the first time you take a full PMP simulation (not just a knowledge area or process group exam), you may need a refresher in core project

management concepts. If you have taken a basic project management class, review the materials you received from that class. If you have not had such a class, consider taking one.

7. Review the questions you got wrong on the *PM FASTrack®* simulation. As with step 5, make sure you identify in writing the specific, not general, reason you got each question wrong on the simulation. This step is very important!
8. Use your list of why you got each question wrong (from Step 7) to determine which material to study further, and then study this material. Remember, think "large project" and how proper project management should be done, regardless of how you manage projects in your real world.
9. Take your final PMP simulation exam. You should score over 75 percent before you take the real exam. You are overusing *PM FASTrack®* if you see many of the questions repeated.
10. Use the *Hot Topics* flashcards and other materials to retain the information you have learned until you take the exam.
11. PASS THE EXAM!

Plan B: Using This Book as a Stand-Alone

1. Read this book for the first time and complete all the exercises, focusing more time on the chapters where you have the most gaps in your knowledge or real-life project management experience. Focus most on items you did not know or did not do prior to beginning this course of study. Refer to Rita's Process Chart for each chapter, and be sure you understand all the efforts involved in the knowledge areas you are working on. At the same time, skim through the corresponding chapter in the *PMBOK® Guide* to get an understanding of the flow of the processes.
2. As you finish each chapter, look at the Quicktest terms listed on the first page of the chapter and make sure you know the meaning of each term or concept. Review terms you are unsure of to improve recall and test your understanding of that chapter.
3. If it is at all possible, form a study group any time after you have read the book for the first time on your own. This will actually make your study time shorter and more effective! You will be able to ask someone questions, and the studying (and celebrating afterward) will be more fun. A study group should consist of only three or four people. (See the following discussion of "How to Use This Book in a Study Group.")
4. Once you feel confident about the material, take the practice exams at the end of each chapter in one sitting. This will give you a baseline to tell you how much you have learned after using the book. It will also help you determine how much additional study time you need and which chapters to read more carefully.
5. Review each question you got wrong in the chapter practice exams, writing down the specific reasons for each wrong answer on the Score Sheet that is provided in this chapter. Assess why the correct choice is correct and why the other answers are wrong. Continue to study this book, focusing in detail on the areas in which you have gaps in your knowledge and skimming the sections or chapters in which you did well. Correct any errors in your understanding of the concepts discussed in this book. Review the *PMBOK® Guide* to focus on these gaps.
   WARNING: If you do not score 70 percent or higher overall on the chapter practice exams, you may need a refresher in core project management concepts. If you have taken a basic project management class, review the materials you received from that class. If you have not had such a class, consider taking one. You cannot rely on these practice questions alone to prepare you for the exam.
6. Make sure you really know the material, and then retake the practice exams in the book. As with step 5, use the Score Sheet to identify in writing the specific, not general, reason you got each question wrong.
7. Use your list of why you got each question wrong (from step 6) to determine which material to study further, and then study this material. Remember, think "large project" and how proper project management should be done, regardless of how you manage projects in your real world. Make sure you are confident you have filled your gaps before taking the exam.
8. PASS THE EXAM!

How to Use This Book in a Study Group

To get started, pick someone to lead the discussion of each chapter (preferably someone who is not comfortable with the chapter, because the presenter often learns and retains the most in the group). Each time you meet, go over questions about topics you do not understand and review the hot topics on the exam using the *Hot Topics* flashcards, if you have them. Most groups meet for one hour per chapter. Either independently or with your study group, do further research on questions you do not understand or answered incorrectly.

Each member of the study group should have his or her own copy of the book, which provides exercises, homework, and even class activities. (Please note that it is a violation of international copyright laws to make copies of the material in this book or to create derivative works from this copyrighted book.)

Those leading a PMP exam preparation course using RMC's products may want to contact RMC for information on our Corporate Partnership program. Partners may be allowed to create slides or other materials using content from this book. Also, ask about other tools for study groups and independent instructors and how to receive quantity discounts on this book, *PM FASTrack®*, or *Hot Topics*.

TRICKS OF THE TRADE® Recurring Themes—PMI-isms to Know for the PMP Exam

Over the past 20 years of helping people pass the exam and become better project managers, RMC has put together the following list of things the exam emphasizes that many project managers do not know. We suggest you read it now and then remember to reread it before you take the actual exam. Rita coined the term "PMI-isms" to refer to these things uniquely emphasized on the exam. Understanding PMI-isms will help you pick the best answer from what seems like more than one correct answer. Some of the topics are listed only here, and others are summarized here and described more fully later in the book. For the exam, assume that you have or do all of the following and that these items are true for your projects.

General PMI-isms:

1. Project managers can save the universe, are "wonderful" and "great," and must be very skilled (a "Rah! Rah! for project management" topic).
2. The project manager puts the best interests of the project first, not his or her own interests.
3. The exam tests from the perspective of a large project. So assume the project manager is working on a large project that involves more than 200 people from many countries, takes at least one year, has never been done before in the organization, and has a budget of US $10 million dollars or more.
4. Project managers have all the power described in the *PMBOK® Guide* and perform all the stated activities in the real world.
5. The project manager is assigned during project initiating, not later in the life of the project.
6. The project manager understands the process of project management (i.e., what to do first, second, etc., and why!). (For more on this, see Rita's Process Chart and Rita's Process Game in the Project Management Processes chapter.)
7. Organizations have a formal project selection process, and they always choose projects based on how well those projects meet the organization's strategic goals.
8. The project manager always knows why his or her project was selected by management to be done, and makes sure those objectives are met while planning and managing the project.
9. The project manager spends time planning, managing, assessing, and controlling scope, time, cost, quality, risk, resources, and customer satisfaction.
10. Organizations have a project management office (PMO), and that office has important, clearly defined responsibilities regarding projects across the organization.
11. Organizations have project management policies, which the project manager adapts for use on his or her project. These policies may include project management methodologies, risk procedures, and quality procedures.
12. Organizations have records (historical information and lessons learned) for all previous projects that include what the work packages were, how much each work package cost, and what risks were uncovered (now referred to in the *PMBOK® Guide* as part of organizational process assets). The project manager uses this past history from other projects to plan the current project. As the project progresses, the project manager feeds historical records and lessons learned from the current project back into the organization's knowledge base.

13. The project manager works within the existing systems and culture of a company (enterprise environmental factors), and one of a project's results is to provide input to improve those systems.
14. Every project has a project charter, which authorizes the project and the role of the project manager.
15. A work breakdown structure (WBS) is used on every project.
16. A project management plan is not a bar chart, but a series of management plans. The project manager knows what is involved in creating a real project management plan.
17. The project manager creates and keeps current other documents (project documents) in addition to the project management plan to help plan, manage, and control a project.
18. Stakeholders are involved throughout the project. Their needs are taken into account while planning the project and creating the communications management plan. They may also help identify and manage risks.
19. People must be compensated for their work. (Seriously, a question about this concept has appeared on the exam.)
20. PMI does not approve of gold plating (adding extra functionality).
21. Since most projects are managed in a matrix environment, such seemingly easy topics as motivation theories or conflict resolution can be complicated on the exam.
22. The project manager has a professional responsibility to properly use the tools and processes of project management.

Planning the project:

23. Planning is very important, and all projects must be planned.
24. The project manager plans the project with input from the team and stakeholders, not on his or her own.
25. Part of planning involves deciding which processes in the *PMBOK® Guide* should be used on each project and how to tailor those processes to the project.
26. There are plans for how the knowledge areas of scope, time, cost, quality, human resources, communications, risk, and procurement will be planned, managed, and controlled. These are called management plans, and every project has one for every knowledge area.
27. If at all possible, all the required work and all the stakeholders are identified before the project work actually begins.
28. The project manager determines metrics to be used to measure quality.
29. The project manager has a plan for continually improving processes.
30. The project manager creates a system to reward team members and stakeholders.
31. All roles and responsibilities are CLEARLY documented and assigned to specific individuals on the project. These may include things like reporting responsibilities, risk management assignments, and meeting attendance, as well as project work.
32. Since the project has never been done before in the organization, the project manager focuses extensively on identifying risks.
33. The stakeholders, as well as team members, are assigned risk identification and risk management duties.
34. The project manager realizes that managing risks saves the project time and money.
35. Project cost and schedule cannot be finalized without completing risk management.
36. The project manager assesses whether the project can meet the end date and other project constraints and objectives. He or she then meets with management to resolve any differences BEFORE the project work starts. The project manager knows unrealistic schedules are his or her fault.
37. The project manager plans when and how to measure performance against the performance measurement baseline, as documented in the project management plan, but he or she also has other measurements to use to determine how the project is performing while the work is being done.
38. The project management plan is realistic, and everyone believes it can be achieved.
39. The exam defines a kickoff meeting in a way that may be different from your understanding of a kickoff meeting (see the Integration Management chapter).

While the project work is being done:

40. The project is managed to the project management plan, which is realistic and complete.
41. The project manager measures against the project management plan to help determine project status throughout the life of the project.
42. Projects are reestimated throughout the life of the project to make sure the end date and cost objectives will be met. Therefore, the project manager almost always knows if the project can meet the agreed-to end date and budget.
43. Delays must be made up by adjusting future work, rather than asking for more time.
44. The project manager has authority and power. He or she can say "No" and work to control the project for the benefit of the customer.
45. The project manager lets others know they cannot get something for nothing. A change in scope MUST be evaluated for its impacts to time, cost, quality, risk, resources, and customer satisfaction. The project manager has enough data about the project to do this analysis.
46. The project manager realizes that, over time, not everyone associated with the project will have the same understanding of what the project is and what could occur during the life of the project. Therefore, the project manager is continually looking to ensure everyone knows what is going on and has appropriate expectations.
47. The project manager understands, and takes seriously, human resource responsibilities on a project.
48. The project manager spends time on such activities as team building and ensuring team performance.
49. The project manager is proactive and finds problems early, looks for changes, and prevents problems.
50. The project manager spends more time focusing on preventing problems than dealing with problems.
51. Most problems that occur have a risk response plan already created to deal with them.
52. Risks are a major topic at every team meeting.
53. Team meetings do not focus on status. That can be collected by other means.
54. All changes to the project management plan flow through the change management process and integrated change control.
55. The project manager ensures that organizational policies are followed on the project.
56. The project manager recommends improvements to the performing organization's standards, policies, and processes. Such recommendations are expected and welcomed by management.
57. Quality should be considered whenever there is a change to any component of the project.
58. Quality should be checked before an activity or work package is completed.
59. The project manager works closely with the quality assurance/quality control department in performing some of the quality activities discussed in the *PMBOK® Guide*.
60. The project manager is actively involved with the procurement process and assists in managing procurements.
61. The project manager understands contract language.
62. The project manager makes sure all the terms of the contract are met, including those that do not seem important to him or her.

Closing the project:

63. The project manager archives all project records.
64. No project is complete unless there has been final acceptance from the customer.
65. All projects produce a final report that gives the project team a chance to announce the project objectives have been met.

Which items in this list seem different from the way you manage your real-world projects? Which of these items do you not understand? Reread this list when you think you are finished studying. Are there any items you need to think about more to make sure you will remember them when you take the exam? Knowing these PMI-isms can make a significant difference on the exam.

CHAPTER TWO Project Management Framework

Quicktest

- Stakeholder
- Stakeholder management
- Organizational structure
  - Matrix
    - Strong
    - Weak
    - Balanced
  - Functional
  - Projectized
  - Project expediter
  - Project coordinator
- Constraints
- Lessons learned
- Definition of a project
- Large project
- Operational work
- Definition of project management
- Project management office (PMO)
- Definition of a program
- Definition of a portfolio
- Product life cycle
- Project life cycle
- Project management process
- OPM3
- Tight matrix
- Objectives
- Management by objectives (MBO)

The trick to reading this chapter is to make sure you keep an open mind and specifically look for gaps in your knowledge. You will likely find a lot of small things, which can add up on the exam and can alter your understanding of more complex topics. Do not simply memorize the concepts in this chapter; instead, use this book to help you understand them and be a better project manager.

Definition of a Project PAGE 5*

(*All page number references are to the *PMBOK® Guide, Fourth Edition*)

Knowing the true definition of a project has helped many test takers get up to four questions right on the exam. Read the definition, and then read the rest of this section. Many people call their work a project when it is not.

A project:

- Is a temporary endeavor with a beginning and an end.
- Creates a unique product, service, or result.

Does the exam ask, "What is a project?" No, but it will describe situations, and part of your analysis of those situations will have to include, "Is this a project being described?"

So what is a project? If your boss walked into your office today and said, "The system is broken. Can you figure out what is wrong with it and fix it?" would this be a project?

Are you reading on before you have thought through the question? If so, please read it again, and think of your answer. This is an important concept, both for the exam and for the real world.

Of the thousands of students RMC has taught, very few came into our classes understanding that you must first take what you are given and organize the work into appropriate projects. The project planning process will produce schedules and budgets. Can you schedule "fix it" if you do not know what is wrong? Of course not, so there are at least two projects in the previous story.

Remember that a project manager must come up with a project management plan that can be agreed to, that people believe is realistic, and most importantly, that the project manager can stake his or her reputation on. It is time someone said this out loud: excluding approved changes for additional work, if the project manager does not get the project completed for the time and cost agreed to (in addition to meeting other objectives), he or she should be relieved of the position! Why so drastic? Studies conducted by the Standish Group in 2009 showed that only 32 percent of projects are successful. This means we are doing a bad job of project management and things need to change.

Are you really working on projects? For the exam, make sure the initiatives you are thinking about are truly projects. You need to imagine an initiative that would require you to use many of the tools of project management. If you work at a help desk and someone contacts you about a problem they are having, you may be able to use a WBS, but do you need a network diagram? How about management plans for scope, time, and cost? Probably not. Some activities are simply part of the company's normal operations, rather than a project.

You should have a large project in mind when you answer questions on the exam. Think of a project that is new to the organization (it has not been done before), utilizes resources from many countries, has more than 200 people on the team, lasts longer than one year, and has a budget of over US $10,000,000.

Regardless of whether you work on such projects, you will need to answer questions on the exam as if you do. There is a big difference between managing small and large projects. For example, on a small project, you walk over to the person you need to speak to when you have an issue to resolve. On a large project, you may have spent weeks planning communications. When there is an issue, you have to figure out who is involved and where they are located, look up their preferred method of communication and their contact information in the stakeholder register, and then communicate with them in that way. If you keep this large-project focus in mind as you read this book, you will see that the many different elements being described here as part of project management make sense. And if the concepts make sense to you, you do not have to memorize them—you can use logic to answer questions on the exam!

Another thing to keep in mind for the exam is that you should assume project proposals are formally reviewed and approved by management in your organization after a comparison of all possible projects. Projects are not selected arbitrarily or informally. (See the Business Case and Project Selection discussions in the Integration Management chapter.)

Operational Work PAGE 22

Most work being done in organizations can be described as either operational or project work. Operational work is ongoing, and project work ends. It is important to understand the difference for the exam. You may see instances where the real problem in the question is that someone is attempting to manage ongoing (operational) work, like manufacturing, as a project.

What Is Project Management? PAGE 6

Many people think project managers just need to know how to manage people or, even worse, that you can simply buy some software and be a project manager. The project management profession is growing rapidly. It is both a science and an art, and follows a systematic process. PMI breaks project management into process groups and knowledge areas. The process groups follow the high-level process of project management: initiating, planning, executing, monitoring and controlling, and closing. The knowledge areas are integration, scope, time, cost, quality, human resource, communications, risk, and procurement management, though PMI also gives a separate focus to the project management framework and project management processes.

Do you know what project management is? Chances are, there are some key aspects of project management you do not know. Even people with advanced degrees in project management sometimes fail this exam. The answer to "What is project management?" is described throughout this book. It can involve technical terms and processes, but it also involves roles and responsibilities and authority levels. As you read this book, you may find that project management involves more than you thought.

What Is a Program? PAGE 9

A program is a group of projects. By grouping related projects into a program, an organization can coordinate the management of those projects. The program approach may help achieve decreased risk, economies of scale, and improved management. In addition to the work required to complete each individual project, the program also includes efforts like the program manager's coordination and management activities. So when you discover that you have more than one project, if there is a benefit to it, you can manage all the projects as a program. This should be done only when the program approach adds value.

If you want to learn more about program management, visit RMC's Web site at www.rmcproject.com for information about courses on this topic.

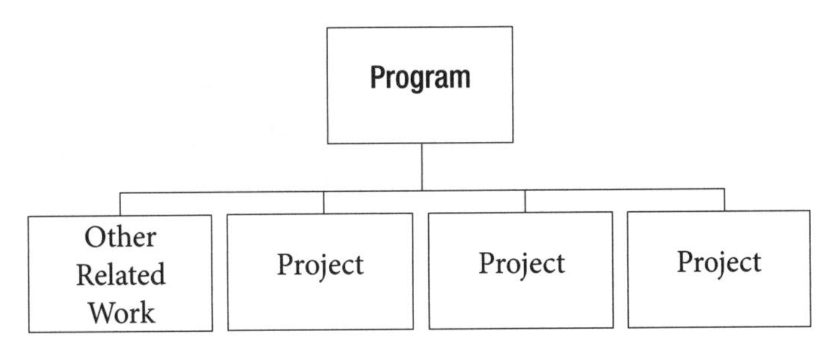

What Is a Portfolio? PAGE 8

A portfolio includes a group of programs and individual projects that are implemented to achieve a specific strategic business goal. The programs and projects that make up the portfolio may not be related other than the fact that they are helping to achieve that common strategic goal.

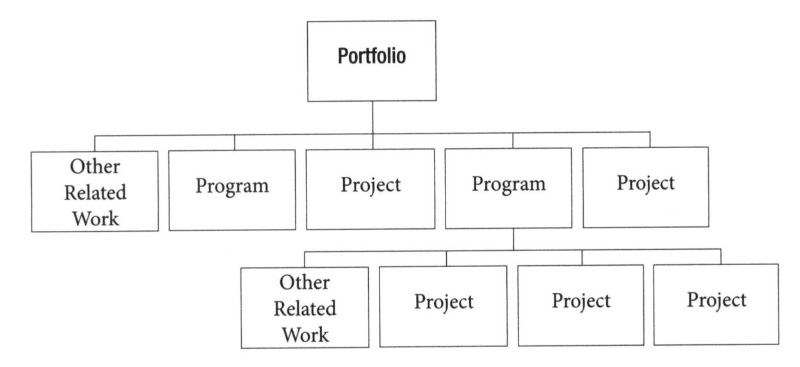

Project Management Office (PMO)[1] PAGE 11

This department centralizes the management of projects. A PMO usually takes one of three roles:

- Provides the policies, methodologies, and templates for managing projects within the organization
- Provides support and guidance to others in the organization on how to manage projects, trains others in project management and project management software, and assists with specific project management tools
- Provides project managers for different projects, and is responsible for the results of those projects; all projects, or projects of a certain size, type, or influence, are managed by this office

Be careful to understand the authority of the PMO and how it is different from the other players on a project. The PMO is a departmental unit within an organization; it is not a single person. The PMO may:

- Manage the interdependencies between projects.
- Help provide resources.
- Recommend the termination of projects.
- Monitor compliance with organizational processes.
- Help gather lessons learned and make them available to other projects.
- Provide templates (e.g., for work breakdown structures or communications management plans).
- Provide guidance.
- Provide centralized communication about the projects.
- Be more heavily involved during project initiating than later in the project.
- Be part of the change control board.
- Be a stakeholder.
- Prioritize projects.

There is a strong trend to start PMOs, but organizations should recognize the risk; if PMOs do poorly, they generate negative feelings toward professional project management that can set a company back years. To successfully implement a PMO, organizations should remember these key concepts:

- The role of the PMO must be clearly defined.
- The PMO should take one of the three roles (as previously identified), and stick to that role without trying to do everything.
- The commitment of executive management is required.
- The PMO will not improve project performance without the use of proper project management processes and techniques, so professional project management must be promoted.

Objectives

The exam may refer to different types of objectives, including both project objectives and product objectives. These questions can be a little tricky. Carefully read the following list of unique things you should know about objectives, and come back to this list after you read the rest of the book. Do you have any gaps in your knowledge?

- Project objectives are stated in the project charter.
- Projects are considered complete when the objectives have been met.
- If it is determined that the project objectives cannot be met, the project should be terminated before completion.
- A more complete understanding of the objectives may be achieved over the length of the project.
- The project manager is responsible for accomplishing the project objectives.
- The reason for quality activities is to make sure the project meets its objectives.
- Risk management enhances opportunities and reduces threats to the project objectives.
- Things that could negatively impact the project objectives, such as risk and stakeholders' influence, should be watched and tracked.
- Projects often require trade-offs between the specific requirements or scope of the project and the overall objectives the project is supposed to achieve.
- Project objectives are determined in project initiating and refined in planning.
- One of the purposes of the Develop Project Management Plan process is to determine how work will be accomplished to meet project objectives.

Management by Objectives (MBO)[2]

MBO is a management philosophy with three steps:

1. Establish unambiguous and realistic objectives.
2. Periodically evaluate whether objectives are being met.
3. Implement corrective action.

For project managers, this philosophy means that if a project is not in line with or does not support the corporate objectives, it is likely to lose resources, assistance, and attention. Also understand that MBO works only if management supports it.

Constraints[3] PAGE 6

As a project manager, you must handle or juggle many things to accomplish a project, including project constraints like time, cost, risk, scope, quality, resources, customer satisfaction, and any other factors that limit options. For example, the date a milestone is due, the date by which the project must be completed, or the maximum allowable risk a project may have are all constraints.

You use constraints to help evaluate competing demands. Management directly or indirectly sets the priority of each constraint. You then use this prioritization throughout the project to properly plan the project, evaluate the impact of changes, and prove successful project completion. It is important to realize that you need to evaluate the effect a change to one constraint has on the other constraints. In other words, you probably cannot shorten the schedule without causing a negative impact to cost, risk, etc.

Stakeholders, managers, and others will inevitably try to change something or add work to the project. As the project manager, you are responsible for analyzing these change requests and identifying the impacts on all constraints through integrated change control. Constraints will be discussed in many areas of this book. Take time to really understand the integrated change control discussion in the Integration Management chapter and how it relates to constraints.

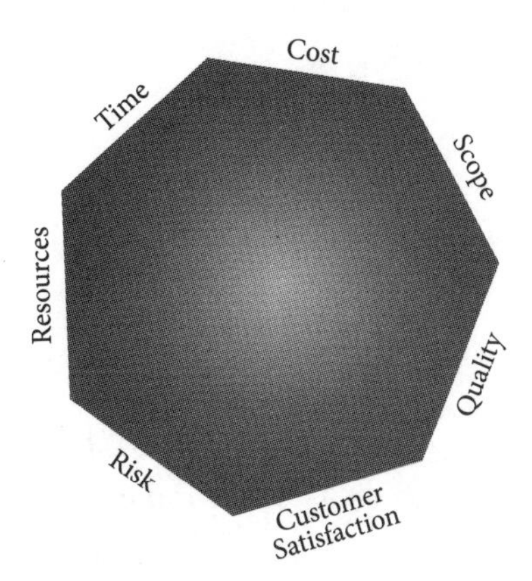

OPM3®

OPM3 is PMI's organizational project management maturity model. This model is designed to help organizations determine their level of maturity in project management. For the exam, you should be familiar with the term "OPM3" and generally know what it is.

Stakeholder,[4] Stakeholder Management[5] PAGE 23

Think about the stakeholders on your real-world projects. Do you realize that stakeholders include more than the project manager, customer, sponsor, and team? Stakeholders are any people or organizations whose interests may be positively or negatively impacted by the project or its product; they can include individuals and groups you may not have thought about before, such as the performing organization, project management team, project management office, portfolio managers, program managers, functional managers, and sellers. They may also include those who could exert positive or negative influence over the project but would not otherwise be considered stakeholders.

Now think about how you treat the stakeholders on your projects. Do you consider them to be like assistant team members? If not, this might be a gap in your knowledge that could result in getting questions wrong throughout the exam. Treating stakeholders like assistant team members means you keep them informed, solicit their input, and work to satisfy their needs and expectations. Without this effort, the project may fail.

The topic of stakeholders is discussed and expanded throughout this book, because a project manager should analyze and manage stakeholders' needs and levels of influence throughout the project. The Human Resource Management and Communications Management chapters have a special focus on the topic of stakeholders. The Human Resource Management chapter provides a way to check your understanding about the role stakeholders play on the project, and most of the stakeholder identification and management efforts are done as part of communications management.

NOTE: Several people may help complete project management activities, especially on large projects. The *PMBOK® Guide* refers to these people as the "project management team." To avoid confusion between the different types of teams, we will use only two terms in this book: "project manager" or "team." The term "project manager" refers to anyone doing project management activities on the project—this includes the lead project manager and those in supporting roles as members of the project management team. The term "team" refers to the project team—everyone who does work on the project, not just those who perform project management activities.

Organizational Structure PAGE 28

A project does not operate in a vacuum. Projects are impacted by, and have impact on, the cultural norms, management policies, and procedures of the organizations of which they are a part. The best project managers look for these influences and manage them for the benefit of the project and the organization.

One of the main forms of influence is how the company is organized. The organizational structure will dictate who the project manager goes to for help with resources, how communications must be handled, and many other aspects of project management. This influence is so important that an answer to a question on the exam can change depending on the form of organization.

Questions related to organizational theory are often phrased in terms of the project manager's level of authority and the impacts on managing projects in such environments. For example, exam questions may deal with:

- Who has the power in each type of organization—the project manager or the functional manager
- The advantages of each type of organization
- The disadvantages of each type of organization

Many people have told RMC they wished they had spent more time studying this topic. So let's get it down now. As you read through the next paragraphs defining the different organizational structures, take the time to think about how each form would impact your real-world projects.

Functional This is the most common form of organization. Such organizations are grouped by areas of specialization within different functional areas (e.g., accounting, marketing, and manufacturing). When you see "functional" on the exam, think "silo." Projects generally occur within a single department. If information or project work is needed from another department, employees transmit the request to the head of the department, who communicates the request to the other department head. Otherwise, communication stays within the project. Team members complete project work in addition to normal departmental work.

Projectized In a projectized organization, the entire company is organized by projects, and the project manager has control of the project. Personnel are assigned and report to a project manager. When you see "projectized" on the exam, remember "no home." Team members complete only project work, and when the project is over, they do not have a department to go back to. They need to be assigned to another project or get a job with a different employer. Communication primarily occurs within the project.

Matrix[6] This form is an attempt to maximize the strengths of both the functional and projectized structures. When you see "matrix" on the exam, think "two bosses." The team members report to two bosses: the project manager and the functional manager (e.g., engineering manager). Communication goes from team members to both bosses. Team members do project work in addition to normal departmental work.

In a strong matrix, power rests with the project manager. In a weak matrix, power rests with the functional manager, and the power of the project manager is comparable to that of a coordinator or expediter. In a balanced matrix, the power is shared between the functional manager and the project manager.

As stated in the previous paragraph, the project manager's role in a weak matrix (or in a functional organization) might be more of a:

- **Project Expediter**[7] The project expediter acts primarily as a staff assistant and communications coordinator. The expediter cannot personally make or enforce decisions.
- **Project Coordinator** This position is similar to the project expediter except the coordinator has some power to make decisions, some authority, and reports to a higher-level manager.

The exam typically does not identify the form of organization you are in. When it does not specify a form, assume matrix. If you remember this, you should get a few more questions right.

A tight matrix has nothing to do with a matrix organization. It simply refers to locating the offices for the project team in the same room. Because it sounds similar to the other forms of organization, it has often been used as a fourth choice for these questions on the exam.

Exercise Test yourself! You can expect questions on the exam about the advantages and disadvantages of each organizational structure. Practice by listing your answers in the spaces below.

Functional

Advantages	Disadvantages

Projectized

Advantages	Disadvantages

Matrix

Advantages	Disadvantages

Answer

Functional

Advantages	Disadvantages
Easier management of specialists	People place more emphasis on their functional specialty to the detriment of the project
Team members report to only one supervisor	No career path in project management
Similar resources are centralized, as the company is grouped by specialties	The project manager has little or no authority
Clearly defined career paths in areas of work specialization	

Projectized

Advantages	Disadvantages
Efficient project organization	No "home" when project is completed
Loyalty to the project	Lack of specialization in disciplines
More effective communications than functional	Duplication of facilities and job functions
	May result in less efficient use of resources

Matrix

Advantages	Disadvantages
Highly visible project objectives	Extra administration is required
Improved project manager control over resources	More than one boss for project teams
More support from functional areas	More complex to monitor and control
Maximum utilization of scarce resources	Resource allocation is more complex
Better coordination	Need extensive policies and procedures
Better horizontal and vertical dissemination of information	Functional managers may have different priorities than project managers
Team members maintain a "home"	Higher potential for conflict

Life Cycle PAGE 15

A life cycle is a progression through a series of developmental stages. There are two life cycles and one overall process you must know for the exam: the product life cycle, the project life cycle, and the project management process. These concepts are described in the following paragraphs.

Product Life Cycle PAGE 18 This life cycle lasts from the conception of a new product to its withdrawal. A product can require or spawn many projects over its life. For example, during a product's conception, there may be a project to determine the customer's needs. When the product is mature, there may be a project to analyze the product's competition in the marketplace.

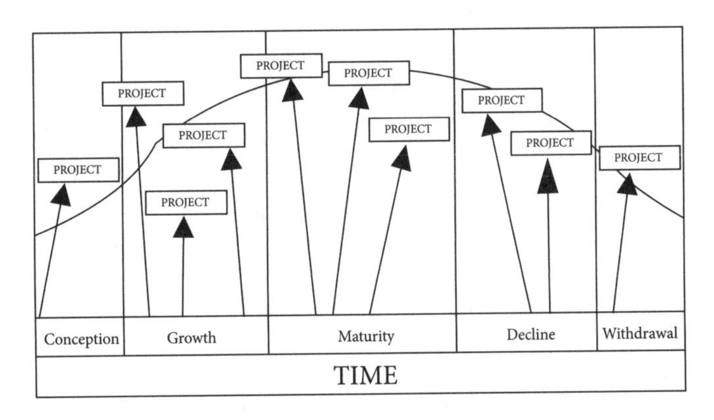

Now let's look at what is involved in completing a project. You need two methodologies. First, there is the project life cycle—what you need to do to complete the work. Second, there is the project management process—what you need to do to manage the work.

Project Life Cycle[8] PAGE 15 The project life cycle is sometimes referred to as the performing organization's or department's methodology for projects. It is what you need to do to produce the deliverables of the project. You should understand that there is such a life cycle, as you will likely see the phrase "project life cycle" on the exam. There are many different types of project life cycles, depending on the industry in which a project manager works or the organization's preferences. Examples of life cycles include:

- **Construction** Feasibility, planning, design, production, turnover, and startup
- **Information technology (IT)** High-level design, detailed design, coding, testing, installation, conversion, and turnover to operations

TRICKS OF THE TRADE® Watch out for references to life cycle phases on the exam (e.g., conception, growth, maturity, decline, withdrawal). Many test takers have seen these references and thought the exam was using alternative or outdated terms to refer to the project management process. Remember, a product or project life cycle can be described using many different terms, but there is only one way of describing the project management process on the exam.

Project Management Process The project management process includes the initiating, planning, executing, monitoring and controlling, and closing process groups. These process groups are described in more detail in the next chapter, but we will take a moment now to explore the difference between the project life cycle and the project management process. The following diagram illustrates the project management process.

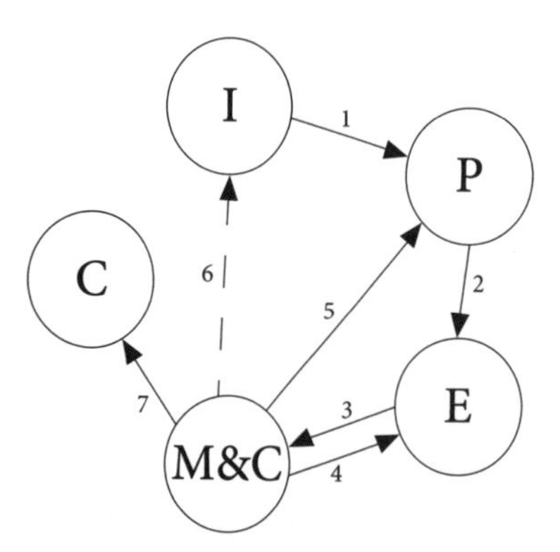

This diagram shows how the project management process groups fit together. Project initiating is necessary for the project to be officially approved. As the project manager, you do some high-level planning during initiating to verify that the project can be completed within the given constraints of scope, time, cost, etc.

Once the project has been approved, it moves from initiating into detailed planning (1), where you create the plan for how you will do planning and how you will execute and monitor and control the project.

The project then moves into executing (2), where the team completes the work according to the processes and procedures detailed in the project management plan.

While the work is being done, the work results (or work performance information) are fed into monitoring and controlling (3), to make sure the project is tracking to the baselines in the project management plan.

If there are variances from the plan that require changes but do not affect the baselines, the resulting approved changes are fed back into executing (4), and the execution of the project is adjusted to help fix the variance. But sometimes the variances require more significant changes, or there are other requested changes that require adjustments to the baselines. If these more significant changes are approved, there needs to be a planning effort (5) to identify the impact to the project baselines and revise the project management plan and project documents accordingly.

Once the changes to the baseline are identified and the plan is modified, the revised plan is fed back into executing (2), where, again, the project is executed according to the updated plan and monitored and controlled (3) to the revised baselines. If the project gets so far off the baselines that it requires an analysis of whether the project should continue at all, it moves back into initiating (6) for this decision.

Ultimately when the work is done (or the project is terminated), the project moves into project closing (7).

For small projects, you typically have one set of the project management process groups for the entire project, which can be repeated throughout the project life cycle (see Figure 2). Large projects often need to be broken into distinct phases, however, and each project phase progresses through the project management process groups (see Figure 3). At the start of a project, the project manager helps create a charter for the entire project and does high-level planning to get project charter approval. In the example of the large project shown in Figure 3, the project manager would review the project charter at the beginning of the design phase and make sure the organization wants to continue with the life cycle phase. If the organization does choose to continue, the project manager does detailed planning for the design phase, executes and monitors and controls the phase, and closes out the design phase. The project then moves to the initiating process of the code phase of the project life cycle.

Figure 2: Project Life Cycle for a Small Project

Research | Design | Code | Test | Transition

I, P, E, M&C, C

Figure 3: Project Life Cycle for a Large Project

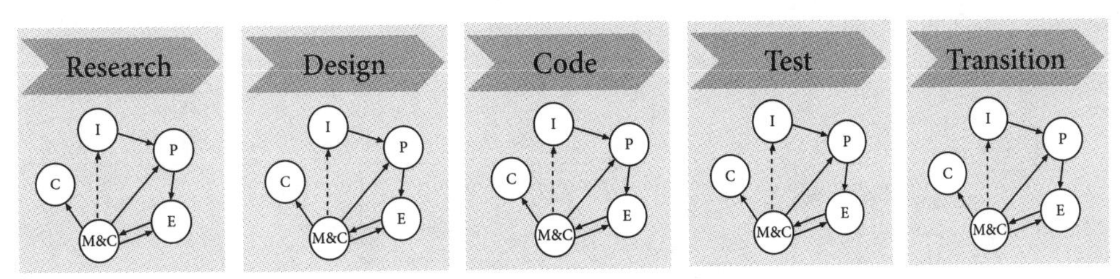

Lessons Learned (Postmortem)[9]

In the first chapter of this book, we described lessons learned (part of organizational process assets) as a PMI-ism. Lessons learned are an essential asset to managing a project; they are taken into account as well as created throughout a project. Complete the following exercise to test your understanding of lessons learned.

Exercise Test yourself! Lessons learned include what type of information?

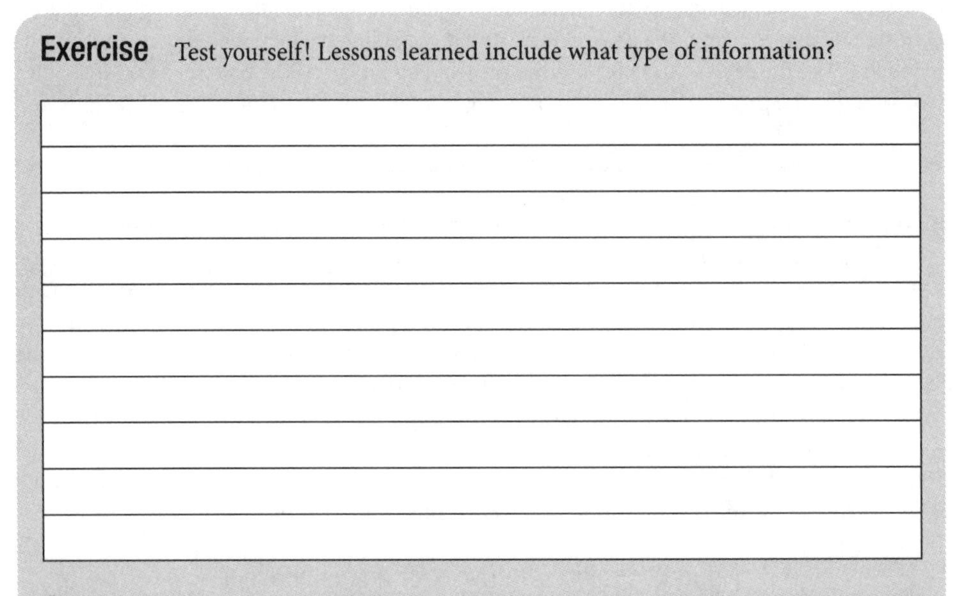

Answer The lessons learned document includes what was done right, what was done wrong, and what would be done differently if the project could be redone. Another way of saying this is that lessons learned include the causes of the issues the project has faced and the reasoning behind the changes implemented. To be as valuable as possible, lessons learned should cover three areas:

- Technical aspects of the project (What was right and wrong about how we completed the work to produce the product?)
- Project management (How did we do with WBS creation, risk planning, etc.?)
- Management (How did I do with communications and leadership as a project manager?)

TRICKS OF THE TRADE® Many project managers do not understand the role of lessons learned on projects. The following graphic helps explain their function:

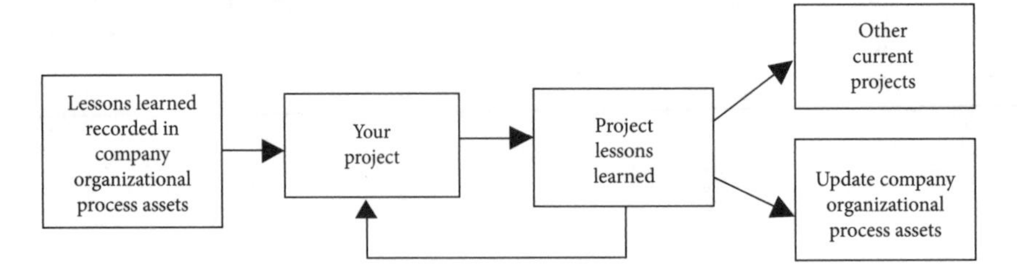

As a project manager, you need to collect and review lessons learned from similar projects before starting work on a new project. Why make the same mistakes or face the same problems others have faced? Why not benefit from others' experience? Imagine you could reach into a filing cabinet or access a database to see such data for all the projects your company has undertaken. How valuable would that be?

Once your project is underway, you are required to add lessons learned to the company database (the organizational process assets). Wait—were you paying attention to what you just read? Lessons learned are a required project management practice. They are both an input to and an output of projects. As an input, they help improve the current project. As an output, they help make the organization better. Lessons learned are realized throughout the project and should be shared with the project team to improve the current project and with the organization as part of the Distribute Information process (see the Communications Management chapter). They are then finalized during project closing or project phase closing.

Make sure you are comfortable with all the concepts in this chapter before reading on; these concepts provide a basis for understanding much of the material presented in the remainder of this book.

Practice Exam

1. Which of the following statements BEST describes how stakeholders are involved on a project?
   A. They determine the project schedule, deliverables, and requirements.
   B. They help to determine the project constraints and product deliverables.
   C. They determine the resource needs and resource constraints on the project.
   D. They help provide assumptions, the WBS, and the management plans.

2. Two project managers have just realized that they are in a weak matrix organization and that their power as project managers is quite limited. One figures out that he is really a project expediter, and the other realizes he is really a project coordinator. How is a project expediter different from a project coordinator?
   A. The project expediter cannot make decisions.
   B. The project expediter can make more decisions.
   C. The project expediter reports to a higher-level manager.
   D. The project expediter has some authority.

3. In a projectized organization, the project team:
   A. Reports to many bosses.
   B. Has no loyalty to the project.
   C. Reports to the functional manager.
   D. Will not always have a "home."

4. A project manager is trying to complete a software development project, but cannot get enough attention for the project. Resources are focused on completing process-related work, and the project manager has little authority to assign resources. What form of organization must the project manager be working in?
   A. Functional
   B. Matrix
   C. Expediter
   D. Coordinator

5. A project manager has very little project experience, but he has been assigned as the project manager of a new project. Because he will be working in a matrix organization to complete his project, he can expect communications to be:
   A. Simple.
   B. Open and accurate.
   C. Complex.
   D. Hard to automate.

6. A project team member is talking to another team member and complaining that many people are asking him to do things. If he works in a functional organization, who has the power to give direction to the team member?
   A. The project manager
   B. The functional manager
   C. The team
   D. The PMO

7. Who has the MOST power in a projectized organization?
   A. The project manager
   B. The functional manager
   C. The team
   D. They all share power

8. All of the following are characteristics of a project EXCEPT:
   A. It is temporary.
   B. It has a definite beginning and end.
   C. It has interrelated activities.
   D. It repeats itself every month.

9. All of the following are parts of the team's stakeholder management effort EXCEPT:
   A. Giving stakeholders extras.
   B. Identifying stakeholders.
   C. Determining stakeholders' needs.
   D. Managing stakeholders' expectations.

10. A manager and the head of engineering discuss a change to a major work package. After the meeting, the manager contacts you and tells you to complete the paperwork to make the change. This is an example of:
    A. Management attention to scope management.
    B. Management planning.
    C. A project expediter position.
    D. A change control system.

11. The project is in planning when three stakeholders come to the project manager asking for information on the company's new project management methodology. They want to know where it came from and why it is different from the way they currently manage projects. These stakeholders are also friends of the project manager, and the entire group has worked together for years. The project is using new terms like "corrective action" that are making some stakeholders nervous, as they are unsure whether the way the project will be managed is going to change along with new terms. What should the project manager do?
    A. Advise the stakeholders that she will keep them in the communication loop for the project.
    B. Supply a list of new terms and their definitions.
    C. Notify the project management office (PMO).
    D. Make sure she maintains her authority as the project manager even though the stakeholders are her friends.

12. A project manager is managing his second project. It started one month after the first and both are in process. Though his first project is small, this one seems to be growing in size every day. As each day passes, the project manager is beginning to feel more and more in need of help. The project manager has recently heard that there was another project in the company last year that is similar to his second project. What should he do?
    A. Contact the other project manager and ask for assistance.
    B. Obtain historical records and guidance from the project management office (PMO).
    C. Wait to see if the project is impacted by the growth in scope.
    D. Make sure the scope of the project is agreed to by all the stakeholders.

13. The project life cycle differs from the product life cycle in that the project life cycle:
    A. Does not incorporate a methodology.
    B. Is different for each industry.
    C. Can spawn many projects.
    D. Describes project management activities.

14. Management by objectives works only if:
    A. It is supported by management.
    B. The rules are written down.
    C. The project does not impact the objectives.
    D. The project includes the objectives in the project charter.

15. Your management has decided that all orders will be treated as "projects" and that project managers will be used to update orders daily, to resolve issues, and to ensure the customer formally accepts the product within 30 days of completion. Revenue from the individual orders can vary from US $100 to US $150,000. The project manager will not be required to perform planning or provide documentation other than daily status. How would you define this situation?
    A. Because each individual order is a "temporary endeavor," each order is a project.
    B. This is program management since there are multiple projects involved.
    C. This is a recurring process.
    D. Orders incurring revenue over $100,000 would be considered projects and would involve project management.

16. The previous project manager for your project managed it without much project organization. There is a lack of management control and no clearly defined project deliverables. Which of the following would be the BEST choice for getting your project better organized?
    A. Adopt a life cycle approach to the project.
    B. Develop lessons learned for each phase.
    C. Develop specific work plans for each work package.
    D. Develop a description of the product of the project.

17. A project team is working on manufacturing a new product, but they are having difficulty creating a project charter. What is the BEST description of the real problem?
    A. They have not identified the project objectives.
    B. They are working on a process and not a project.
    C. The end date has not been set.
    D. They have not identified the product of the project.

18. One of your team members informs you that he does not know which of the many projects he is working on is the most important. Who should determine the priorities between projects in a company?
    A. The project manager
    B. The project management team
    C. The project management office (PMO)
    D. The team

19. A market demand, a business need, and/or legal requirement are examples of:
    A. Reasons to hire a project manager.
    B. Reasons projects are initiated.
    C. Reasons people or businesses become stakeholders.
    D. Reasons to sponsor a project.

20. Operational work is different from project work in that it is:
    A. Unique.
    B. Temporary.
    C. Ongoing and repetitive.
    D. A part of every project activity.

21. Company procedures require the creation of a lessons learned document. Which of the following is the BEST use of lessons learned?
    A. Historical records for future projects
    B. Planning record for the current project
    C. Informing the team about what the project manager has done
    D. Informing the team about the project management plan

22. Lessons learned are BEST completed by:
    A. The project manager.
    B. The team.
    C. The sponsor.
    D. The stakeholders.

23. Consideration of ongoing operations and maintenance is crucially important to products of projects. Ongoing operations and maintenance should:
    A. Be included as activities to be performed during project closure.
    B. Have a separate phase in the project life cycle, because a large portion of life cycle costs is devoted to maintenance and operations.
    C. Not be viewed as part of a project.
    D. Be viewed as a separate project.

24. What is a program?
    A. An initiative set up by management
    B. A means to gain benefits and control of related projects
    C. A group of unrelated projects managed in a coordinated way
    D. A government regulation

25. A company is making an effort to improve its project performance and create historical records of past projects. What is the BEST way to accomplish this?
    A. Create project management plans.
    B. Create lessons learned.
    C. Create network diagrams.
    D. Create status reports.

Answers

1. **Answer** B
   Explanation The project manager determines the project schedule through schedule development. The team and other stakeholders provide the inputs. Since it is also the project manager's role to determine resource needs and create management plans, the choices including those roles cannot be best. Stakeholders are generally not involved in WBS creation either. They do, however, help in determining project constraints and product deliverables. Notice how tricky questions can be if you do not read them correctly! Watch for this in other questions, and pay close attention to the differences in wording.

2. **Answer** A
   Explanation The project coordinator reports to a higher-level manager and has authority to make some decisions. The project expediter has no authority to make decisions.

3. **Answer** D
   Explanation The main drawback of a projectized organization is that at the end of the project when the team is dispersed, they do not have a functional department ("home") to which to return.

4. **Answer** A
   Explanation In a functional organization, the project manager has the least support for the project and has little authority to assign resources. Project expediter and project coordinator are roles in a weak matrix organization.

5. **Answer** C
   Explanation Because a project done in a matrix organization involves people from across the organization, communications are more complex.

6. **Answer** B
   Explanation In a functional organization, the functional manager is the team member's boss and probably also the project manager's boss.

7. **Answer** A
   Explanation In a projectized organization, the entire company is organized by projects, giving the project manager the most power.

8. **Answer** D
   Explanation "It repeats itself every month" implies that the whole project repeats every month. Generally, the only things that might repeat in a project are some activities. The whole project does not repeat.

9. **Answer** A
   Explanation Giving stakeholders extras is known as gold plating. This is not effective stakeholder or quality management.

10. **Answer** C
    Explanation This is an example of a project expediter position because you are not evaluating the change, looking for impacts, etc. You are merely implementing others' requests.

11. **Answer** C
Explanation Some people may think this question has more than one right answer. It does not. There are many things the project manager can do, but what should be done? The company policies are managed by the project management office, and the project manager should make sure the stakeholders have clear information by sending them directly to the authority on company policies for project management.

12. **Answer** B
Explanation There are many things the project manager could do. Asking the other project manager for assistance is not the best choice, as the other project manager might not be an experienced mentor. His advice might not be adequate to help this project manager. Waiting to assess the impact on the project is reactive; a project manager should be proactive. Gaining agreement of all the stakeholders on the project scope is also not the best choice. It would be helpful, but does not specifically address the issue in this situation. If the PMO is contacted, the project manager can receive the knowledge of many project managers, historical information from many projects, and have the assistance of someone whose job it is to help.

13. **Answer** B
Explanation The project life cycle does incorporate a methodology—for doing the work. It is the product life cycle that spawns many projects. Project management activities are described in the project management process. The project life cycle is different for each industry, so that is the correct answer.

14. **Answer** A
Explanation The best answer is that it needs management support.

15. **Answer** C
Explanation Because orders are numerous and of short duration, this situation is a recurring process, not a project.

16. **Answer** A
Explanation Developing lessons learned would help improve subsequent phases, but would do nothing for control or deliverables. Having plans for each work package would help control each phase, but would not control the integration of those phases into a cohesive whole. A description of the product of the project would help, but that would not improve both control and deliverables for each phase. Effective project management requires a life cycle approach to running the project. Adopting a life cycle approach is the only answer that covers both control and deliverables.

17. **Answer** B
Explanation Manufacturing a product is an ongoing process; it is operational work, not project work. Therefore, the manufacturing team would have no reason to create a project charter and would have difficulty doing so if they tried, because of the ongoing nature of the work.

18. **Answer** C
Explanation Because the question talks about priorities between projects, this cannot be the role of the project manager, the project management team, or the project team. Determining priorities between projects is a role of the PMO.

19. **Answer** B
Explanation These are all reasons projects are initiated.

20. **Answer** C
Explanation Operational work is that which is ongoing to sustain an organization.

21. **Answer** A
Explanation Notice that this question asks about the use of a tool of project management. Many people can learn from a book what a lessons learned document is, but questions like this can more readily be answered if you actually use the tool and know from experience its value. Ask yourself about the other tools of project management. Why are they beneficial? The BEST use of lessons learned is as historical records for future projects. There are other tools that are better for accomplishing the things listed in the other choices.

22. **Answer** D
Explanation The best answer is stakeholders, as their input is critical for collecting all the lessons learned on each project. The term "stakeholders" includes all the other groups.

23. **Answer** C
Explanation Remember the definition of a project: temporary and unique. Operations and maintenance are considered ongoing activities, not temporary. Therefore, such work is not considered a project or part of a project.

24. **Answer** B
Explanation Did you select "a group of unrelated projects managed in a coordinated way"? If so, you missed the word "unrelated." Programs are groups of related projects.

25. **Answer** B
Explanation Lessons learned help to avoid future pitfalls and use the good ideas of past projects. This leads to improvements in future projects.

CHAPTER THREE Project Management Processes

Quicktest

- What is done during each of the project management process groups
  - Initiating
  - Planning
  - Executing
  - Monitoring and controlling
  - Closing
- What you do not do in your real world during each of the project management process groups

As we just discussed in the Project Management Framework chapter, the project life cycle describes what you need to do to complete the work, whereas the project management process describes what you need to do to manage the project. People often think they need to understand various industries to pass this exam, since the exam refers to many different types of projects done in many different types of industries (e.g., "You are building a bridge" or "You are creating a new system for your company"). That information is mostly background data, however. The exam does not ask you how to do the work in different industries, such as what the specific project life cycle should be or how to perform IT, construction, engineering, or any other type of projects; instead, it asks you about managing projects. The questions are general and can be answered without an understanding of the industry, if you know project management.

This chapter will examine the project management process, both at a high level and in more detail with Rita's Process Chart. Carefully review the information in the chapter, especially the process chart, and complete all the exercises. These are valuable tools for helping you identify the gaps in your knowledge and will significantly cut down your study time. Understanding the process of managing a project and knowing what should be done when provides a framework for understanding all the inputs, tools and techniques, and outputs involved in project management. If you understand the process, you can use logic on the exam, rather than having to rely on memorization. So are you ready? Read on!

First, here is the high-level look at the project management process. It includes:

- Initiating the project (Start)
- Planning the project (Plan)
- Executing the project (Do)
- Monitoring and controlling the project (Check and act)
- Closing the project (End)

As explained in the Project Management Framework chapter, for small projects, this might be exactly the process you need to use to manage your projects. For large projects that are broken into phases, this process may be repeated multiple times. For example, on a project with a research phase, you complete initiating through closing for that phase, and then do the process again for the design phase.

Now let's look at the project management process in more detail, using Rita's Process Chart.

Rita's Process Chart There have been over 70 questions on the PMP exam that directly ask about the project management process. Therefore, to pass the exam, you must understand this process. It can seem like a lot to know, but we can help you learn it without memorization.

Since the first edition of this book, people all over the world have used the following chart as a trick to learning the project management process quickly and effectively. It helps you understand what should be done when. This chart was created by Rita Mulcahy and is unique to RMC's books and products. It does not map to other project management resources; its function is simply to illustrate the efforts involved in the overall process for managing a project so you can clearly understand that process for the exam.

How to Use Rita's Process Chart

As you review Rita's Process Chart, make sure you:

- Understand the overall project management process (a PMI-ism).
- Find terms you do not know, and learn what they are by looking them up in this book.
- Understand why each item is in the column (process group) it falls into.
- Be able to replicate the specific order of the planning process by understanding what happens when, how previous work supports what comes next, and why. Knowing the planning column IN THIS ORDER can help you get a large number of questions right on the exam, because the exam often asks "What should be done next?" The work in the other process groups does not have a set order.
- Understand the project management process groups of initiating through closing and when each effort should be done on projects. The exam asks questions that present a situation and require you to know the process group the project is in.
- Understand that project planning is an iterative process. Think about how you might go back and redo (iterate) some of the items in the planning column for a large project.
- Complete Rita's Process Game that follows the chart at least three times. Going through the game will solidify your understanding of the overall project management process and help you fill gaps in your knowledge. Find your gaps before they find you on the exam!

Rita's Process Chart

INITIATING

- Select project manager
- Determine company culture and existing systems
- Collect processes, procedures, and historical information
- Divide large projects into phases
- Understand the business case
- Uncover initial requirements, assumptions, and risks
- Assess project and product feasibility within the given constraints
- Create measurable objectives
- Develop project charter
- Identify stakeholders
- Develop stakeholder management strategy

PLANNING

(This is the only process group with a set order)

- Determine how you will do planning—part of all management plans
- Determine detailed requirements
- Create project scope statement
- Assess what to purchase
- Determine team
- Create WBS and WBS dictionary
- Create activity list
- Create network diagram
- Estimate resource requirements
- Estimate time and cost
- Determine critical path
- Develop schedule
- Develop budget
- Determine quality standards, processes, and metrics
- Create process improvement plan
- Determine all roles and responsibilities
- Plan communications
- Perform risk identification, qualitative and quantitative risk analysis, and risk response planning
- Go back—iterations
- Prepare procurement documents
- Create change management plan
- Finalize the "how to execute and control" parts of all management plans
- Develop realistic and final PM plan and performance measurement baseline
- Gain formal approval of the plan
- Hold kickoff meeting

EXECUTING

- Execute the work according to the PM plan
- Produce product deliverables (product scope)
- Request changes
- Implement only approved changes
- Continuously improve
- Follow processes
- Perform quality assurance
- Perform quality audits
- Acquire final team
- Manage people
- Evaluate team and project performance
- Hold team-building activities
- Give recognition and rewards
- Use issue logs
- Facilitate conflict resolution
- Release resources as work is completed
- Send and receive information
- Hold meetings
- Select sellers

MONITORING & CONTROLLING

- Take action to control the project
- Measure performance against the performance measurement baseline
- Measure performance against other metrics determined by the project manager
- Determine variances and if they warrant a corrective action or change request
- Influence the factors that cause changes
- Request changes
- Perform integrated change control
- Approve or reject changes
- Inform stakeholders of the results of change requests
- Update the PM plan and project documents
- Manage configuration
- Create forecasts
- Gain acceptance of interim deliverables from the customer
- Perform quality control
- Report on project performance and solicit feedback
- Perform risk assessments and audits
- Manage reserves
- Administer procurements

CLOSING

- Confirm work is done to requirements
- Complete procurement closure
- Gain final acceptance of the product
- Complete financial closure
- Hand off completed product
- Solicit feedback from the customer about the project
- Complete final performance reporting
- Index and archive records
- Update lessons learned knowledge base

Notes on the Chart

- Notice in the Initiating column the phrase "Understand the business case." This could be read as "Understand the project's business case (the case for why the project is being done) to guide all other project management activities and make sure the project is worth the required investment when completed." This is a major concept on the exam that many project managers miss.

  There is a reason the project is initiated, and the project results must support that reason. It seems easy, but so many projects do not satisfy the business needs when completed. Project managers may create the project they want, rather than what was asked of them, or they may complete the project to the technical requirements and forget the reasons (stated or otherwise) the project was initiated. The problem is that many project managers do not understand the initial effort that takes place, even before the project has a charter and is therefore authorized.

  Here is what should be happening in your organization: the company should know what its strategic objectives are, and all projects should help meet those objectives. This is not what actually happens in many real-world organizations, however, to the detriment of those organizations. A company that manages itself well will have strategic objectives. It will evaluate various options for achieving those objectives. Many project ideas will be proposed, and the company will conduct an analysis to see which proposed projects meet the objectives for the least cost, time, resources, and, if it is a very well-run company, the least risk. The organization will then authorize one or more projects by issuing project charters. This is the project selection process you need to understand for the exam, and you need to know how that process affects project management activities.

  As the project manager, you should understand why the project you are assigned to was selected, and manage the project accordingly. Is the project being done to enter a new market? Is it the result of a customer request? Is it just a pet project for a company executive? Is it expected to dramatically improve the future of the company? You should know what these objectives are, including intangible objectives such as "improve the company's reputation," and keep them in mind when planning and managing the project. If you lose sight of the objectives, the project may finish on time and on budget but still fail because it does not achieve those objectives.

- Notice the phrase "Determine all roles and responsibilities" in the Planning column. You should be aware that this involves more than determining who is going to do which product-related work activities. It also includes who will be required to provide reports, who will attend meetings, who will help with risk identification, who will work with the quality department, etc. All roles and responsibilities on a project should be defined. They may be documented as part of the human resource plan, in project job descriptions, and in the management plans for each knowledge area. If this effort seems unnecessary to you, you may be thinking about it in the context of a small project that uses the same handful of resources as the last project. Remember to think in terms of large projects that have hundreds of team members.

- Notice the word "iterations" in the Planning column of Rita's Process Chart. This is an important concept. When planning a project, the project manager and the team complete each item listed in the chart above "iterations" to the best of their ability. But a project will evolve as each item is planned, and much of the earlier planning work will need to be modified or added to. For example, it is only after completing the risk management planning efforts that the WBS and the other items can be finalized. A risk response strategy (see the Risk Management chapter) might be to do additional testing. This testing will require adjusting the WBS for added scope, the network diagram to determine the order of the work, the budget for added cost, etc. The project manager might also work with discretionary dependencies (see the Time Management chapter) to decrease some risk and thereby change the network diagram. The important thing to remember is that planning should lead to a realistic, bought-into, approved, and formal project management plan that is updated throughout the project to reflect approved changes. Iterations help you create and maintain such a plan.

- Team building, risk identification, and risk response planning are focused in the process groups in which they are placed on the chart, but these activities can start in initiating and continue until closing.

- Resources can be released at any time during the project, once their work is approved and accepted and they have completed any documentation or other activities that pertain to their work. For example, the electricians on a project to build a house may test their work, get acceptance of their work, document lessons learned, suggest process improvements, and turn the work over. They can then be released from the project while the people doing drywall are still working (executing their part of the plan). Keep in mind that some team members remain on the project to its end in order to assist the project manager in creating the final lessons learned, archiving final records, and producing the final report.

- As project executing progresses, the project manager may determine that a change to the project is needed. The same could happen while monitoring and controlling the activities. That is why changes can be requested in both the executing and the monitoring and controlling process groups. The change requests are then evaluated and approved or rejected as part of the Perform Integrated Change Control process (see the Integration Management chapter).

- Many people wonder why the executing and monitoring and controlling processes occur at the same time. Let's think about it. Do the project management process groups occur sequentially? No; they all overlap. You could be using monitoring and controlling processes to monitor and control the planning of a project. The difference between project executing and project monitoring and controlling is the focus of each process group. The focus of executing is to manage people and work to accomplish the project as planned. The focus of monitoring and controlling is to measure the project's performance against the performance measurement baseline and any other established metrics. Project managers wear many hats at the same time. Look again at Rita's Process Chart, and see how the two process groups have different focuses.

TRICKS OF THE TRADE® **Rita's Process Game** The following pages contain the pieces for Rita's Process Game. Cut them out and practice putting each item into the correct process group, on your own or in a group. When you think the cards are sorted into the correct process groups, put the planning efforts in order. Lastly, check your answers using Rita's Process Chart. Play this game at least three times to ensure you understand the project management process that will be discussed throughout this chapter.

INITIATING	**PLANNING**	**EXECUTING**
MONITORING & CONTROLLING	**CLOSING**	Create measurable objectives
Determine how you will do planning—part of all management plans	Administer procurements	Execute the work according to the PM plan
Determine company culture and existing systems	Perform quality assurance	Create activity list
Go back—iterations	Develop project charter	Develop schedule

Update the PM plan and project documents	Measure performance against other metrics determined by the project manager	Collect processes, procedures, and historical information
Hand off completed product	Determine team	Request changes
Index and archive records	Determine variances and if they warrant a corrective action or change request	Gain final acceptance of the product
Create WBS and WBS dictionary	Implement only approved changes	Take action to control the project
Estimate time and cost	Create network diagram	Manage people

Evaluate team and project performance	Inform stakeholders of the results of change requests	Influence the factors that cause changes
Divide large projects into phases	Understand the business case	Produce product deliverables (product scope)
Request changes	Perform quality audits	Uncover initial requirements, assumptions, and risks
Estimate resource requirements	Determine quality standards, processes, and metrics	Use issue logs
Perform integrated change control	Create process improvement plan	Identify stakeholders

Determine critical path	Release resources as work is completed	Develop stakeholder management strategy
Perform quality control	Plan communications	Perform risk identification, qualitative and quantitative risk analysis, and risk response planning
Gain formal approval of the plan	Facilitate conflict resolution	Approve or reject changes
Hold kickoff meeting	Assess project and product feasibility within the given constraints	Prepare procurement documents
Hold team-building activities	Send and receive information	Finalize the "how to execute and control" parts of all management plans

Give recognition and rewards	Continuously improve	Develop realistic and final PM plan and performance measurement baseline
Determine all roles and responsibilities	Follow processes	Develop budget
Gain acceptance of interim deliverables from the customer	Create forecasts	Hold meetings
Complete procurement closure	Perform risk assessments and audits	Select sellers
Manage configuration	Manage reserves	Measure performance against the performance measurement baseline

Confirm work is done to requirements	Report on project performance and solicit feedback	Acquire final team
Determine detailed requirements	Assess what to purchase	Complete final performance reporting
Select project manager	Create project scope statement	Update lessons learned knowledge base
Complete financial closure	Create change management plan	Solicit feedback from the customer about the project

The What-Comes-Before Game Here is another game to help you understand the overall project management process. Playing this game after you have completed Rita's Process Game at least three times will really help solidify your understanding of these concepts.

Name the project planning effort that comes before each of the following items on Rita's Process Chart.

	Planning	What Comes Before?
1	Create network diagram	
2	Prepare procurement documents	
3	Create project scope statement	
4	Create WBS and WBS dictionary	
5	Determine critical path	
6	Develop budget	
7	Estimate time and cost	
8	Gain formal approval of the plan	
9	Hold kickoff meeting	
10	Determine quality standards, processes, and metrics	
11	Assess what to purchase	
12	Plan communications	
13	Go back—iterations	
14	Create process improvement plan	
15	Determine all roles and responsibilities	
16	Perform risk identification, qualitative and quantitative risk analysis, and risk response planning	
17	Estimate resource requirements	
18	Create activity list	

Answer

	Planning	What Comes Before?
1	Create network diagram	Create activity list
2	Prepare procurement documents	Go back—iterations
3	Create project scope statement	Determine detailed requirements
4	Create WBS and WBS dictionary	Determine team
5	Determine critical path	Estimate time and cost
6	Develop budget	Develop schedule
7	Estimate time and cost	Estimate resource requirements
8	Gain formal approval of the plan	Develop a realistic and final project management plan and performance measurement baseline
9	Hold kickoff meeting	Gain formal approval of the plan

	Planning	What Comes Before?
10	Determine quality standards, processes, and metrics	Develop budget
11	Assess what to purchase	Create project scope statement
12	Plan communications	Determine all roles and responsibilities
13	Go back—iterations	Perform risk identification, qualitative and quantitative risk analysis, and risk response planning
14	Create process improvement plan	Determine quality standards, processes, and metrics
15	Determine all roles and responsibilities	Create process improvement plan
16	Perform risk identification, qualitative and quantitative risk analysis, and risk response planning	Plan communications
17	Estimate resource requirements	Create network diagram
18	Create activity list	Create WBS and WBS dictionary

How to Use the Rest of This Chapter For many, this is the hardest chapter in the book and uncovers the most gaps in their knowledge. If this chapter is difficult for you, trust us to help you; follow along with the book, really try each exercise, and then look for gaps in your knowledge. Do not simply skip to the answers!

The exercises in this chapter are extensive and are designed to help you explore what a project manager needs to do during each of the project management process groups. Spend about 2 to 5 minutes trying to answer each exercise and about 5 to 15 minutes reviewing the answers to each exercise. Note your gaps on a separate sheet. Then spend some time making sure you research each knowledge gap and clear it from your list.

Again, we encourage you to take these exercises seriously! The exam includes common project management errors as choices and will focus on things most people do not know they should be doing. RMC has helped people all over the world find their knowledge gaps, and many of those are included in these exercises. So approach these exercises with the intent of discovering your gaps, NOT memorizing long lists of data, and make sure you are thinking of a large project when you complete the exercises.

Also note that you should read each chapter in this book more than once in preparing for the exam. When you go through this chapter the second time, focus on filling the gaps you discovered in the first pass through the chapter, rather than recreating the complete list for each exercise answer.

Initiating Process Group

The processes in the initiating process group formally start a new project or project phase. Project initiating involves officially authorizing the project and providing the project manager with the information necessary to begin the project.

In well-run organizations, there is a formal project selection process that happens before a project can be initiated. Once a project is selected, it is chartered and, therefore, authorized. In addition to creating the project charter, initiating a project involves identifying and analyzing stakeholders so their needs can be incorporated into the project. The project charter, identified stakeholders, and the strategy for managing those stakeholders are the major outputs of this process group.

Inputs to Project Initiating You do not have to memorize inputs to pass this exam. It is much better to use logic and rely on your understanding of the project management process. Try this exercise.

Exercise What do you think you would need to know or have before you initiate a project?

NOTE: You may wish the answers to exercises were not listed right after the questions. If this is distracting for you, simply keep a blank piece of paper available to cover the answers until you have completed each exercise and are ready to review it. Our analysis shows that having the answers right after the questions helps you more than it hurts.

Answer If you know what efforts are involved in project initiating, the inputs should be easy to guess. In order to initiate a project, you need to know or have the following:

- The business case for the project
- The product description or product scope description detailing the product requirements as they are known up to this point; in other words, what is the project being asked to do?
- How the project fits into or supports the company's strategic plan
- A list of likely stakeholders
- Contracts, if the work is done under a contract
- Industry standards
- The company's change control system
- Defined processes and procedures for how the company operates
- Past relationships with the sponsor of the project, likely stakeholders, and the team
- Templates from past projects
- Historical WBSs
- Historical estimates
- What is going on in the company today, the major projects, and the potential impact current and planned initiatives could have on this project
- Understanding of the company's future
- Understanding of the company's culture
- A list of people who may be good team members

Make sure you identify anything from the previous list that you did not think of, and add it to your gap list.

TRICKS OF THE TRADE® Many questions on the exam will include common errors in project management and require you to know the activities that should be done during each part of the project management process. The only way to check your knowledge is to first determine what your knowledge is and then compare it to what it should be. The following exercises are designed to help you do just that. So do not skip the exercises, and do not go right to the answers! You will need to know much more than what is in the *PMBOK® Guide* to pass the exam. The following should help you.

Exercise Let's go beyond inputs, outputs, and tools and techniques. What are the specific ACTIONS required to complete project initiating?

Answer If you are thinking only in terms of the *PMBOK® Guide*, you probably came up with the following:

- Develop Project Charter (Integration Management chapter)
- Identify Stakeholders (Communications Management chapter)

Knowing the names of these two processes will not be enough to help you pass the exam, however. While the *PMBOK® Guide* lists the processes of project management and features their inputs, tools and techniques, and outputs, it does not directly discuss the efforts involved in each process. You need to have a more detailed understanding of what really should be done (actions) in project initiating in order to pass the exam.

The following table provides a list of the actions involved in project initiating. Because the project manager is assigned to a project during initiating, some of the actions in this list are done by others in the organization, before the project manager is assigned. Remember that what needs to be done on a project varies based on the specific project and the industry, so it may not be practical to do all of these actions on every project.

As you review the list, place a checkmark next to the actions you have done on your real-world projects and leave any actions you do not know or have never done unchecked. Then make sure you study the areas that are unchecked. The items in the list are not in any particular order.

	ACTIONS Involved in Project Initiating	Place ✓ Here if You Do It; Study Areas Unchecked
1	Select the project manager.	
2	Determine the authority of the project manager.	
3	Collect historical information.	
4	Divide large projects into phases.	
5	Identify stakeholders, their influences, and their risk tolerances.	
6	Determine high-level requirements, constraints, assumptions, and risks.	
7	Turn high-level stakeholder needs, wants, and expectations into requirements.	
8	Make sure the business case and the analysis supporting the need for the project are documented and understood.	
9	Ensure the product scope is as final as practical.	
10	Understand how the project supports the organization's strategic objectives.	
11	Determine measurable project and product objectives.	
12	Facilitate the resolution of conflicting objectives.	
13	Become familiar with the company culture and structure as it relates to the project.	
14	Find existing processes, standards, and compliance requirements that affect the project.	
15	Understand how the organization does business and what procedures and policies are already in place to use on the project.	
16	Do planning using the project planning process on a high-level basis.	
17	Perform high-level estimating for the project schedule and budget.	
18	Use the high-level planning and estimating data to determine whether the product can be achieved within the given constraints.	
19	Determine what form the project charter will take, including the length and level of detail, and the reasons for the selected format.	
20	Coordinate project initiating efforts with stakeholders and the customer.	
21	Work with the customer and others to determine acceptance criteria and clarify what is and is not in the project.	
22	Determine the initial project organization.	
23	Identify any inherent or required milestones on the project.	

	ACTIONS Involved in Project Initiating	Place ✓ Here if You Do It; Study Areas Unchecked
24	Determine what specifically will constitute project success.	
25	Finalize the project charter.	
26	Obtain formal approval of the project charter.	
27	Create a stakeholder management strategy.	

The following are some points from the previous list that could use further clarification.

Progressive Elaboration You may notice that many of the items in the previous list (i.e., estimates, product scope, etc.) are begun in the initiating process group and iterated or refined later into plans that can be used to manage the project. Although the project management plan is finalized in planning, items such as the detailed estimate, project scope, and product scope may be clarified over time as the work is being done during the executing and monitoring and controlling processes. The process of continually refining estimates and scope is called progressive elaboration.

Project Manager Assigned You should notice in the previous list that the project manager is assigned early in the process. This means the project manager is involved in project initiating. Is this true in your real world? For the exam, assume you are involved this early in the project, and make sure you understand what is going on during initiating.

Business Case In the real world, do you know why your project was started? Does it matter? As described in the earlier discussion of Rita's Process Chart, the project manager needs to keep in mind throughout the project the reason the project was started. It will influence how the project is planned, what changes are allowed, and the definition of the project scope. Projects are initiated for many reasons. You need to know the reasons. (See the Develop Project Charter discussion in the Integration Management chapter for more about the importance of the business case on a project.)

High-Level Planning Is Done During Project Initiating The other important thing to notice in the previous exercise is that high-level planning is done during project initiating. Such planning may include creating a high-level WBS, performing order of magnitude estimating, and doing high-level risk identification. You use this information to determine whether the product of the project can be delivered by the end date and within the budget the organization has requested. In other words, you need to assess whether the project has a chance of being successful before the organization commits money and resources to the project. This high-level planning effort is part of creating the project charter, which then documents measurable project objectives, milestone schedules, and an initial budget for the project.

The following diagram shows reasons project initiating is begun.

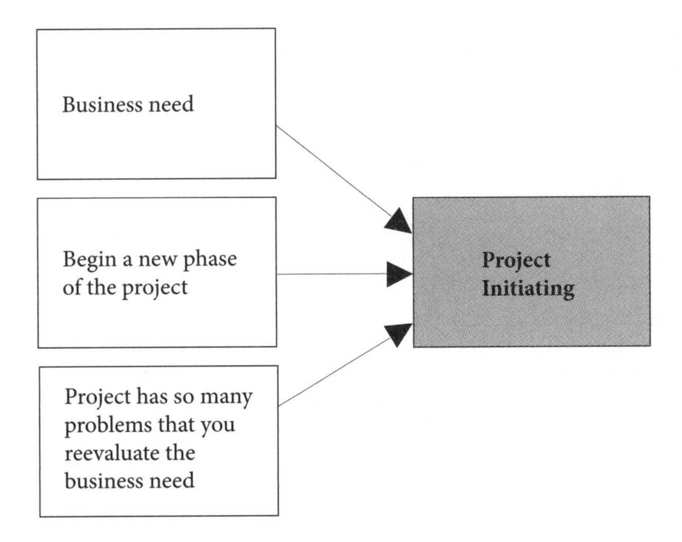

Planning Process Group

How much better would your last project be if you could magically do it over again? This is the power of planning, because it entails walking through the project and getting it organized before actually doing the work. Project planning presents a huge opportunity to save resources, time, and money.

In project planning, the project manager and the team perform a detailed analysis of whether the objectives in the project charter can be achieved. They also decide how the project will be accomplished, addressing all appropriate project management processes and knowledge areas. This means determining what processes in the *PMBOK® Guide* are appropriate for the needs of the project, to avoid wasting resources on activities that are not relevant to the particular project.

Exercise What are the specific ACTIONS required to complete project planning?

Answer If you are thinking only in terms of the *PMBOK® Guide*, you may have come up with the following:

- Develop Project Management Plan (Integration Management chapter)
- Collect Requirements (Scope Management chapter)
- Define Scope (Scope Management chapter)
- Create WBS (Scope Management chapter)
- Define Activities (Time Management chapter)
- Sequence Activities (Time Management chapter)
- Estimate Activity Resources (Time Management chapter)
- Estimate Activity Durations (Time Management chapter)
- Develop Schedule (Time Management chapter)
- Estimate Costs (Cost Management chapter)
- Determine Budget (Cost Management chapter)
- Plan Quality (Quality Management chapter)
- Develop Human Resource Plan (Human Resource Management chapter)
- Plan Communications (Communications Management chapter)
- Plan Risk Management (Risk Management chapter)
- Identify Risks (Risk Management chapter)
- Perform Qualitative Risk Analysis (Risk Management chapter)
- Perform Quantitative Risk Analysis (Risk Management chapter)
- Plan Risk Responses (Risk Management chapter)
- Plan Procurements (Procurement Management chapter)

Again, simply knowing the names of processes will not be enough to help you pass the exam. You need to have a more detailed understanding of what really should be done (actions) during project planning, and you need to find out if there are any actions you do not know or have never done.

As you check your answers against the following list, note which items you do in the real world. Make sure you understand that the following actions are done during project planning.

NOTE: Do not fall into the trap of losing focus when you are working through these long lists. This list is intended to contain a lot of information to save you the time of reading pages and pages of boring text. Spend about 15 minutes thinking through the list.

	ACTIONS Involved in Project Planning	Place ✓ Here if You Do It; Study Areas Unchecked
1	Determine how you will plan the management efforts for scope, schedule, cost, quality, human resources, communications, risk, procurement, requirements, changes, configuration, and process improvement, and put that information into the beginnings of management plans.	
2	Refine the high-level requirements from project initiating so they are more specific and detailed, and look for additional requirements.	
3	Expand on the assumptions identified in project initiating, looking for new assumptions and documenting the details of the assumptions.	
4	Refine the high-level constraints (i.e., resources, schedule, cost, etc.) from project initiating so they are more specific and detailed.	
5	Create a description of the project deliverables and the work required to complete those deliverables (project scope statement).	
6	Use the project scope statement to gain approval of the "final" scope from the stakeholders before further planning is done.	
7	Assess what may need to be purchased on the project (e.g., identify any pieces of work that may be outside the organization's abilities to complete, assess whether new equipment or technology would be needed to perform the project work, etc.).	
8	Determine who will be on the project team.	
9	Break down the work into smaller, more manageable pieces (WBS).	
10	Create descriptions of each work package in a WBS dictionary so that the work can be understood by those assigned, with little gold plating.	
11	Break down the work packages from the WBS into lists of activities.	
12	Sequence activities, and determine predecessors and successors.	
13	Estimate resource requirements (e.g., staff, facilities, equipment, etc.).	
14	Meet with managers to gain resource commitments.	
15	Decide what level of accuracy is needed for estimates.	

	ACTIONS Involved in Project Planning	Place ✓ Here if You Do It; Study Areas Unchecked
16	Have those working on the activities estimate time and cost.	
17	Determine how long the project will take without compressing the schedule.	
18	Develop a preliminary schedule, ignoring the schedule constraint contained in the project charter, and reconcile the two to come up with a final schedule for the project management plan.	
19	Develop a preliminary budget, ignoring the budget constraint contained in the project charter, and reconcile the two to come up with the final budget for the project management plan.	
20	Determine quality practices and standards, and determine which metrics will be used to measure quality performance.	
21	Determine what processes should be followed on the project to reduce the need to supervise work, and to improve quality and make use of standards.	
22	Determine how you will improve the processes in use on the project.	
23	Create a recognition and reward system.	
24	Clearly determine all roles and responsibilities so the team members and stakeholders know what their roles are on the project and what work they will need to do.	
25	Determine what information you will need from other projects and what information you can send to other projects.	
26	Plan what will be communicated on the project, to whom, by whom, when, and how.	
27	Complete detailed risk identification, qualitative and quantitative risk analysis, and risk response planning.	
28	Iterations—go back, updating project documents as necessary, in order to work toward a project management plan that is bought into, approved, realistic, and formal.	
29	Prepare procurement documents.	
30	Look for potential positive and negative interactions with other projects that can affect this project.	
31	Determine the process that will be used to request, approve, and manage changes on the project.	
32	Finalize the "execute" and "control" aspects of all management plans.	
33	Plan ways to measure project performance, the measurements to be used, when they will be taken, and how they will be interpreted.	

	ACTIONS Involved in Project Planning	Place ✓ Here if You Do It; Study Areas Unchecked
34	Determine what meetings, reports, and other activities you will use to control the project to the project management plan.	
35	Develop the final project management plan, project documents, and performance measurement baseline by performing schedule network analysis, looking for options, and confirming that project objectives can be met.	
36	Gain formal approval of the project management plan from the sponsor, team, and managers of resources.	
37	Hold a kickoff meeting with all the key stakeholders, team, team members' managers, and the customer to make sure everyone is on the same page and to gain buy-in.	

The results of the planning effort are a project management plan and project documents (described in the Integration Management chapter). Project planning is iterative. Each planning process performed may use the results of the previous processes, and each process may affect or cause changes to the previous processes. The idea, in the real world, is to attempt to complete each planning process as fully as possible. Then, after risk identification, qualitative and quantitative risk analysis, and risk response planning, you go back to finalize all the components of the project management plan and project documents. This approach to planning saves time and is efficient. Do you understand why iterations start after risk management? Because it is only after risk management is completed that the final cost and schedule can be determined. Risk management could also result in changes to the resources, when they are used, in what sequence activities are performed, and almost all other parts of the project.

Did the last two sentences make sense? If so, you are in excellent shape. If not, we encourage you to read the Risk Management chapter of this book carefully, and make sure you understand how risk management affects the entire project.

Notice the references to management plans in the previous table. As described in Chapter 1, management plans are a PMI-ism. Too often, project managers jump right into whatever they are doing without thinking about it beforehand. Such actions lead to inefficiencies, rework, mistakes, conflict, needless overtime, and just plain bad project management. Project managers are supposed to think about things before they do them. The exam assumes you take a more formal approach to considering "How will I do this?" before doing the work, and that you document this information in a management plan.

There are many components to management plans, but generally they answer the questions of "How will I go about planning scope, schedule, cost, etc.?" and "How will I manage and control scope, schedule, cost, etc., now that I have planned what needs to be done?" The answers to these questions are determined as part of project planning. For clarity, the previous table groups management plans together instead of listing each management plan separately. It also accounts for the iterations of the management plans by separating them into the planning, executing, and control pieces. The individual management plans are combined into the overall project management plan. (See more about management plans and the project management plan in the Integration Management chapter.)

Another important aspect to understand about planning is that the amount of time the team spends in project planning and the level of detail achieved in the plan should be appropriate to the needs of the project. If a high-priority project has a tight schedule that does not allow much room for variance, the project will require more planning than a low-priority project with a fairly flexible schedule.

Some projects cannot be fully planned to a detailed degree prior to starting work on the project. These projects are often organized by phases (e.g., test phase, install phase, etc.). In such cases, only the first phase may be fully planned, while the later phases are planned at a higher level until more is known about the project. Detailed planning for the next phase is then done as the previous phase nears completion. This approach is called "rolling wave planning."[1]

Who is involved in the planning processes? Everyone! The project manager compiles the project management plan and project documents with input from stakeholders. The project manager may also use information gathered from resources like historical records from previous projects, company policies, magazine articles about projects, and other such sources to plan the project.

Project planning does not just occur when the project is beginning. We also move back into planning to accommodate changes to the project, as illustrated by the following diagram.

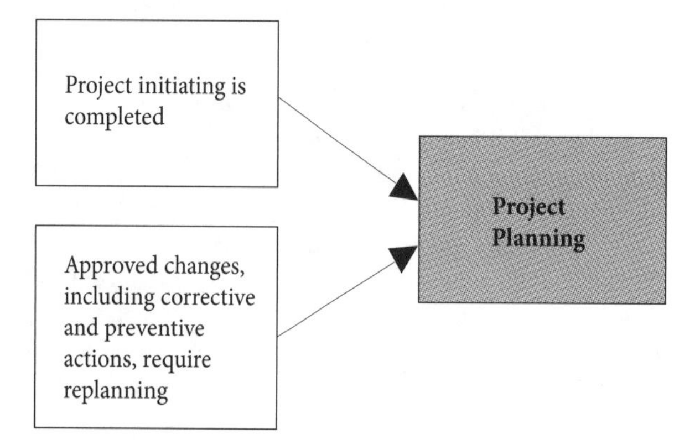

See the rest of the book for descriptions of each of the individual planning processes, particularly the Integration Management chapter, which discusses the project manager's role in creating the project management plan.

Executing Process Group

The purpose of project executing is to complete work as defined in the project management plan and to meet the project objectives. In other words, the goal is to achieve the project deliverables within the project's planned budget and schedule, and to meet any other objectives established for the project. This is the "do" step of the process defined at the beginning of this chapter (start, plan, do, check and act, end). The focus is on managing people, following processes, and distributing information. During executing, the project manager essentially has a guiding, proactive role, constantly referring back to the project management plan and project documents.

Let's think about project planning again for a moment. On your real-world projects, do you create a project management plan that is realistic and approved? Does your project management plan contain management plans for each knowledge area, as previously described? Many project managers do not create such a project management plan. Therefore, they find exam questions in this area to be extremely difficult and tricky. For the exam, get your mind around the critical difference planning makes and assume the project was properly planned before work began (unless the question indicates otherwise) as you answer the questions.

Exercise Imagine you are about to begin project executing. What type of ACTIONS must be taken?

Answer If you are thinking only in *PMBOK® Guide* terms, you may have come up with the following as part of the executing process group:

- Direct and Manage Project Execution (Integration Management chapter)
- Perform Quality Assurance (Quality Management chapter)
- Acquire Project Team (Human Resource Management chapter)
- Develop Project Team (Human Resource Management chapter)
- Manage Project Team (Human Resource Management chapter)
- Distribute Information (Communications Management chapter)
- Manage Stakeholder Expectations (Communications Management chapter)
- Conduct Procurements (Procurement Management chapter)

Again, you need to know more than the names of processes. Let's look at the actions involved in executing a project. As you check your answers against the following table, note which items you do in the real world, which items were not on your list, and if there are items you wrote that are not included here.

NOTE: This is another long list. Keep focused, and spend 15 minutes thinking through these actions. The list intentionally jumps around.

	ACTIONS Involved in Project Executing	Place ✓ Here if You Do It; Study Areas Unchecked
1	Set and manage the expectations of all stakeholders throughout the project, and ensure everyone has a common understanding of the work.	
2	Implement the original project management plan or the project management plan that was revised as a result of control activities.	
3	Complete work packages.	
4	Collect and document lessons learned.	
5	Establish and manage communication channels.	
6	Evaluate how effectively the team members function as a team.	
7	Implement approved changes, including corrective actions, preventive actions, and defect repair.	
8	Perform quality assurance to ensure the defined practices and procedures are being followed on the project.	
9	Produce project reports.	
10	Hold team-building activities.	
11	Follow ground rules at team meetings.	
12	Obtain needed training for team members.	
13	Distribute information about the project.	
14	Remove roadblocks.	
15	Achieve work results that meet requirements.	
16	Meet with managers to reconfirm resource commitments.	
17	Keep managers apprised of when their resources will be needed on the project.	
18	Commit and release project resources in accordance with the project management plan.	
19	Guide, assist, communicate, lead, negotiate, help, and coach.	
20	Utilize your technical knowledge.	
21	Hold meetings to identify or address issues, assess risks, and keep the project work moving forward.	
22	Send and receive information.	
23	Focus on preventing problems rather than just dealing with them as they arise.	

	ACTIONS Involved in Project Executing	Place ✓ Here if You Do It; Study Areas Unchecked
24	Make sure all team members have the skills, information, and equipment needed to complete their work.	
25	Focus on looking for exceptions to the approved project management plan in team members' performance, rather than checking up on every person's work or babysitting.	
26	Recommend changes to be evaluated in the Perform Integrated Change Control process.	
27	Follow organizational policies, processes, and procedures.	
28	Increase the effectiveness of processes.	
29	Create recommendations for the performing organization that increase its effectiveness.	
30	Ensure continued agreement from the stakeholders to the project management plan.	
31	Keep everyone focused on completing the project to the project charter and project management plan.	
32	Keep the project's business case in focus while managing the project, especially when problems occur.	
33	Solve problems.	
34	Stop during the project to see where changes are coming from and what you can do to eliminate the root cause of the need for change.	
35	Implement the recognition and reward system created during the planning processes.	
36	Determine team members who could not be named during the planning processes.	
37	Implement approved process improvements.	
38	Use an issue log to record project issues and details about their resolution, including who is responsible for resolving each issue and the expected timeline.	
39	Obtain seller responses to procurement documents.	
40	Review bids and quotes, and select sellers.	
41	Expend and manage project funds.	
42	Facilitate conflict resolution using conflict resolution techniques.	
43	Measure individual team member performance.	

Did your list contain items that were not in the previous table? If so, make sure those items actually should be part of executing a properly managed project. Did you include such things as getting the team to cooperate, discovering added scope, or coordinating unplanned overtime work? Although these things could (and often do) occur on a project, they are caused by a lack of proper project management. Therefore, do not expect to see them on the exam.

How about dealing with problems? Notice that "Solve problems" is only one of 43 items on the list of actions to be done during project executing. As a project manager, you should be spending time preventing problems so you do not have to spend much time dealing with them. The exam assumes problems do not occur very often, nor should they have a major impact on the project. Again, for the exam, assume proper project management was done unless the questions say otherwise!

For more information on the disadvantages of status meetings and better methods to use to collect status, visit www.rmcproject.com and read the free tips and tricks at RMC U.

Did you list meetings? Meetings are part of executing a project, but many people do not realize that proper planning can decrease the number of meetings they need, making meetings only a minor activity. If you were thinking about "go around the room and report what you have done" types of meetings, realize that status can be collected through other means. The occasions when the team gets together are too important to just collect status. How about reviewing risks and upcoming contingency plans during meetings, instead of discussing status? Status meetings can cause you to lose buy-in from your team if they feel you are wasting their time.

Make sure you have identified what you do "wrong" on your real-world projects before you take the exam!

Keep the words "work to the project management plan," "be proactive," "manage," and "guide" in mind as a way to summarize executing activities while you take the exam, to make sure you have your PMI hat on.

The processes of project management are not always performed in the same sequence. Executing means executing the latest revision of the project management plan. In other words, you are always executing to the project management plan, but the plan might change over time. The following diagram illustrates when you enter project executing.

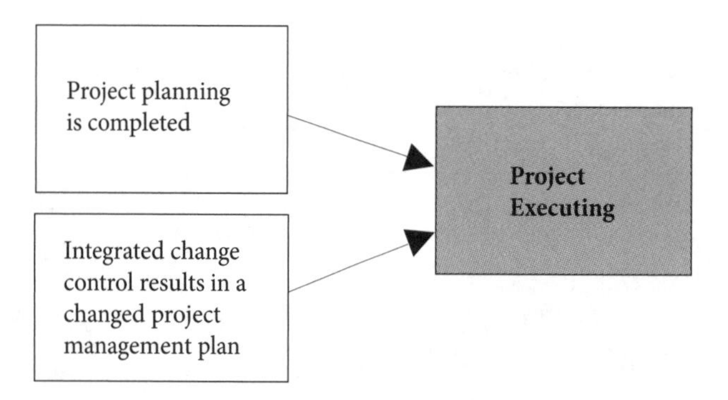

Monitoring and Controlling Process Group

Monitoring and controlling means measuring the performance of the project to the project management plan and approving change requests, including recommended corrective and preventive actions and defect repair. Project monitoring and controlling is among the worst scoring process groups on the exam for test takers. One reason for this is that you are expected to know how to control a project that has been properly planned and managed, when many people do not do this in their real world. Project managers who spend most of their time asking for percent complete, being unsure if the project will meet its performance measurement baseline, and thinking that an unrealistic schedule should simply be blamed on management typically have a great deal of trouble on the exam.

The following exercise should help you get your mind around what a project manager should do to monitor and control a project. Again, we encourage you to work through this exercise; do NOT jump right to the answers. Find the gaps in your knowledge and experience, and fill those gaps, rather than relying on memorization for the exam. As a result, you will pass the exam—and be a better project manager!

Exercise What are the specific ACTIONS required as part of project monitoring and controlling?

Answer If you are thinking only in *PMBOK® Guide* terms, you might have come up with the following:

- Monitor and Control Project Work (Integration Management chapter)
- Perform Integrated Change Control (Integration Management chapter)
- Verify Scope (Scope Management chapter)
- Control Scope (Scope Management chapter)
- Control Schedule (Time Management chapter)
- Control Costs (Cost Management chapter)
- Perform Quality Control (Quality Management chapter)
- Report Performance (Communications Management chapter)
- Monitor and Control Risks (Risk Management chapter)
- Administer Procurements (Procurement Management chapter)

The previously listed processes are described in the chapters of this book as referenced. Now let's look at what actions should be done in monitoring and controlling a project. Review the list below, and identify any you do not know or have never done. Also notice if you included items that are not listed here. Are you sure those items are part of monitoring and controlling?

NOTE: Because this is one of the worst scoring process groups on the exam, you should spend considerable time here. Do not lose focus as you read. Take a break in the middle of the list if you need to, and remember the list intentionally jumps around.

	ACTIONS Involved in Project Monitoring and Controlling	Place ✓ Here if You Do It; Study Areas Unchecked
1	Measure project performance according to the planned measures in the management plans.	
2	Measure against the performance measurement baseline.	
3	Determine variances.	
4	Exercise judgment to determine what variances are important and if they warrant recommending a change or corrective action.	
5	Recommend changes, including defect repair and preventive and corrective actions. Do not just wait for others to recommend them.	
6	Obtain a decision in integrated change control about whether changes should be approved or rejected.	
7	Manage configuration to ensure everyone knows which version of the project or product documentation is the latest version.	
8	Control scope, schedule, and cost to their baselines.	
9	Perform procurement inspections.	
10	Refine control limits as needed.	
11	Identify the root causes of problems.	

	ACTIONS Involved in Project Monitoring and Controlling	Place ✓ Here if You Do It; Study Areas Unchecked
12	Obtain formal acceptance of interim deliverables from the customer.	
13	Identify the need for replanning.	
14	Make updates to the project management plan and project documents to reflect changes to the project.	
15	Manage the time and cost reserves.	
16	Recalculate how much the project will cost and how long it will take, and create forecasts.	
17	Obtain additional funding if needed.	
18	Hold periodic inspections.	
19	Make decisions to accept or reject work.	
20	Evaluate the effectiveness of implemented corrective actions.	
21	Reassess the effectiveness of project control systems.	
22	Spend time trying to improve quality.	
23	Get information from stakeholders to determine if project controls need to be updated.	
24	Identify and analyze trends.	
25	Evaluate the effectiveness of risk responses in a risk audit.	
26	Look for newly arising risks.	
27	Reanalyze existing risks.	
28	Use milestones as a project control tool.	
29	Observe.	
30	Report on performance to all stakeholders and solicit their feedback to ensure the project still meets the business need.	
31	Use variance reports to help correct small problems before they become serious.	
32	Calculate estimate to complete.	
33	Use and interpret earned value calculations.	
34	Use quality control tools—inspection, Pareto charts, cause and effect diagrams, etc.	
35	Authorize work on work packages using a work authorization system.	
36	Control changes.	
37	Ensure that only approved changes are implemented.	
38	Work with the change control board.	
39	Evaluate customer satisfaction.	
40	Administer procurements.	
41	Validate defect repair.	

	ACTIONS Involved in Project Monitoring and Controlling	Place ✓ Here if You Do It; Study Areas Unchecked
42	Stop during the project to see where changes are coming from and what you can do to eliminate the root cause of the need for change.	
43	Consider the project's business case when analyzing change requests.	

For the exam, assume:

- You have a project management plan that is realistic and complete.
- You have plans already in place for how and when you will measure time, cost, and scope performance against the performance measurement baseline.
- You are accountable for meeting the performance measurement baseline.
- You also measure against the metrics you have determined for the project and included in the project management plan to see how the project is performing.
- You take action to correct any variances that warrant action.
- Any deviations from the plan should be made up, rather than requesting a change to the project to accommodate them. Submitting a change request should be the very last resort and only used if there is no other way to make up the deviation.

The exam assumes a project manager spends time and focused effort controlling scope, time, communications, risks, etc. Do you do this? These concepts overlap and repeat themselves throughout the knowledge areas. Since people score so poorly in this process group, we have included the following information about many of the control processes to provide a better overall understanding of project monitoring and controlling. These control processes are only briefly discussed in the other chapters of this book, so read the following carefully to get a better sense of what control is.

Control Scope

- Follow the change management plan
- Measure performance against the performance measurement baseline
- Control actual changes
- Control the impacts of scope changes
- Analyze variances
- Request changes
- Adjust the scope baseline and requirements documentation
- Document lessons learned

Control Schedule

- Follow the change management plan
- Measure schedule performance against the performance measurement baseline
- Control actual changes
- Control the impacts of schedule changes
- Request changes
- Analyze variances
- Document lessons learned
- Update the project management plan and project documents

- Manage the time reserve
- Use earned value analysis

Control Costs

- Follow the change management plan
- Measure cost performance against the performance measurement baseline
- Control actual changes
- Control the impacts of cost changes
- Request changes
- Analyze variances
- Document lessons learned
- Update the project management plan and project documents
- Recalculate the estimate at completion
- Obtain additional funding when needed
- Manage the budget reserve
- Use earned value analysis

Perform Quality Control

- Hold periodic inspections
- Ensure the deliverables are meeting the standards
- Request changes or improvements to work and processes
- Make decisions to accept or reject work
- Evaluate the effectiveness of implemented changes
- Reassess the effectiveness of project control systems

Report Performance

- Hold performance reviews
- Identify and analyze trends and variances
- Report project performance based on variance or trend analysis and earned value analysis
- Issue change requests

Monitor and Control Risks

- Create and implement workarounds
- Implement contingency and fallback plans
- Evaluate the effectiveness of risk response plans
- Work in accordance with the risk management plan
- Update lists of risks and risk response plans
- Use risk management procedures
- Issue change requests

Administer Procurements

- Monitor to make sure both parties to the contract meet contractual obligations
- Protect your legal rights
- Authorize work
- Report performance
- Inspect and verify the product
- Manage changes
- The buyer makes payments

The process of project management does not always go from initiating to planning to executing to monitoring and controlling to closing. The following diagram illustrates when you might enter project monitoring and controlling. It also shows that you might go from monitoring and controlling to any of the other process groups (i.e., initiating, planning, executing, or closing), depending on the needs of the project.

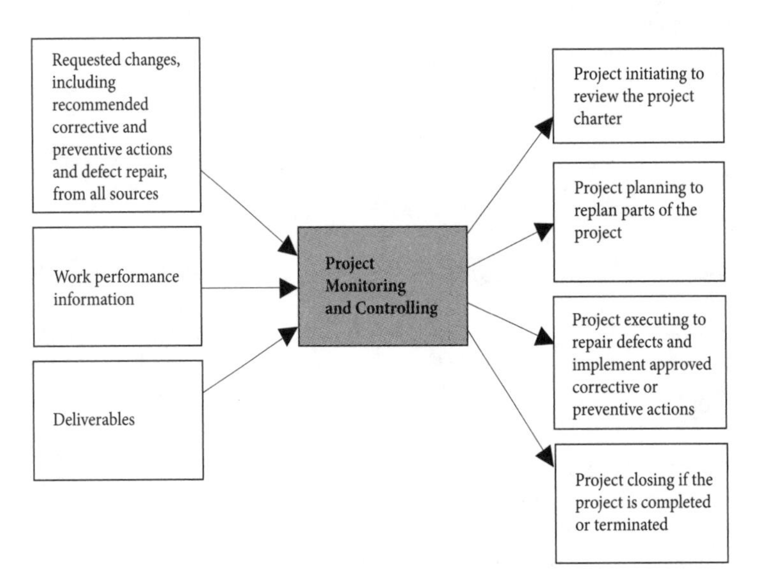

Closing Process Group

You have completed all the product scope. Is the project finished? No, work remains to be done. Project closing is where the project is finished. This is one of the most ignored parts of the project management process. If you take time now to understand the concepts that we discuss in this section, the 14 scored questions about closing on the exam should be easy.

Remember that a project is not complete when the final product scope is done; it is completed only when closure is completed. This effort will include administrative activities such as collecting and finalizing all the paperwork needed to complete the project, and technical work to verify that the final product of the project is acceptable. It will also include any work needed to transfer the completed project to those who will use it and to solicit feedback from the customer about the product and the project.

In many real-world situations, projects never seem to officially finish. Sometimes the project manager just goes on to do other things; sometimes work on the project just stops; sometimes the project priority decreases. There are no official titles for the ways projects can end, but they should all be completed using the closing processes.

In any situation, ignoring the closing processes is a real mistake, as the work to be done during closure is extremely important to the performing organization and to the customer. The exam asks questions in this area to see if you know what those valuable activities are and when a project is really done. Try this!

Exercise What are the specific ACTIONS required to complete project closing?

Answer The *PMBOK® Guide* lists the following processes:

- Close Project or Phase (Integration Management chapter)
- Close Procurements (Procurement Management chapter)

Now review the list of closing actions in the following table and identify any that you do not know or have never done. Look for gaps in your knowledge.

	ACTIONS Involved in Project Closing	Place ✓ Here if You Do It; Study Areas Unchecked
1	Confirm that all the requirements in the project have been met.	
2	Verify and document that the project, or project phase, meets completion or exit criteria set in place during project planning.	
3	Obtain formal (legal) sign-off and final acceptance of the product of the project from the customer.	
4	If the project was terminated before completion, document the reasons for termination and the status of the project.	
5	Make final payments, and complete cost records.	
6	Gather final lessons learned.	
7	Update project records.	
8	Ensure all the project management processes are complete.	
9	Update corporate processes, procedures, and templates based on lessons learned.	
10	Add new skills acquired to team members' human resource records.	

	ACTIONS Involved in Project Closing	Place ✓ Here if You Do It; Study Areas Unchecked
11	Complete procurement closure and project (or phase) closure.	
12	Analyze and document the success and effectiveness of the project.	
13	Create and distribute a final report of project (or phase) performance.	
14	Index and archive project records.	
15	Evaluate customer satisfaction regarding the project and the deliverables.	
16	Hand off the completed project deliverables to the assigned stakeholders (e.g., the customer, operations and maintenance, etc.).	
17	Celebrate!	

Does this list of actions make sense? Take a moment to go back and look again at the previous table, and make sure you envision how each item is done in the real world. Read this and the lists for the other process groups well to help you on the exam and to provide a solid understanding of the project management process as you read the rest of this book.

There is a very valuable action listed in the previous table that many people miss. Some project managers consider the end celebration and the final project performance report to be unimportant parts of the project. But there is a reason these points are tested on the exam. Having some form of celebration and a final report that shows, beyond a shadow of a doubt, the project's success sends a strong message to all stakeholders that your team finished the project. Isn't that a good thing? Would you sign your name to the last few projects you completed? If not, why not? What about having a party where the entire team autographs the project?

Confirming that all the requirements have been met is another item on the previous list that seems unimportant to some project managers. Most studies show that many requirements are not met on projects, especially on projects with numerous pages of requirements. This confirmation needs to happen.

What about handing off the completed project deliverables to operations and maintenance? Did you realize there is work to be done as part of the project to complete such a transfer? The work could include meetings to explain the project nuances, training, and other activities as needed.

We noted in the first chapter of this book that historical records are a PMI-ism. Make sure you understand the value of these records for the exam and the project manager's and team's responsibility for creating them. Historical information is collected throughout the project, but it is during project closing that the final versions of the lessons learned are compiled and made available to other projects and the project management office. In addition, project closing involves a concerted effort to index all files, letters, correspondence, and other records of the project into an organized archive that is stored for use on future projects.

Now let's think about formal sign-off and formal acceptance. These are important because they indicate the customer considers the project completed and accepts the whole project. Formal sign-off in a procurement situation constitutes legal acceptance. Without that acceptance, you cannot be sure the project was finished. Imagine the team never gains formal acceptance on a project for an external customer, but moves on to other projects. Then the customer calls for additional scope to be added to the project. How difficult would it be to regroup the team to perform the new work? Gaining formal acceptance helps ensure this is not necessary.

In addition to obtaining formal acceptance, another important part of project closing is measuring customer satisfaction. Have you ever had a customer accept your work although they were not happy with the project? This is a common occurrence. Smart project managers will solicit feedback from the customer about both the project and the product and evaluate the customer's satisfaction level during project closing. Just like lessons learned, measuring customer satisfaction should be ongoing throughout the project, but it MUST occur during project closing.

Once the administrative pieces of project closure are completed and formal sign-off that the product of the project is acceptable is received from the customer, other stakeholders, and/or the sponsor, the project is closed. At that point, the project manager can release any resources who had been helping to close the project or project phase.

The following diagram illustrates when we might enter project closing.

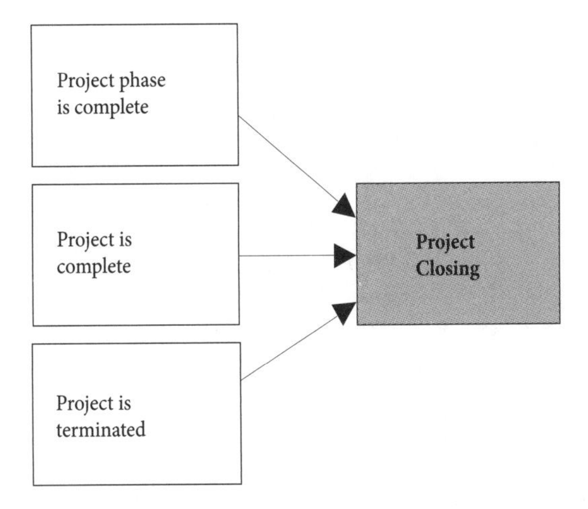

TRICKS OF THE TRADE® **The Project Management Scramble Game** The following exercise is an extension of Rita's Process Game and should help you see how well you understood what you have read. This exercise will look at more specific actions, rather than the generalized ones stated in Rita's Process Chart. For each item listed in the following table, simply determine if it is done in initiating, planning, executing, monitoring and controlling, or closing.

	Actions	During Which Process Group Is This Done?
1	Use the project scope statement to gain approval of the "final" scope from stakeholders before further planning is done.	
2	Determine high-level requirements, constraints, assumptions, and risks.	
3	Measure against the performance measurement baseline.	

	Actions	During Which Process Group Is This Done?
4	Implement approved changes, including corrective actions, preventive actions, and defect repair.	
5	Reanalyze existing risks.	
6	Use the high-level planning and estimating data to determine whether the product can be achieved within the given constraints.	
7	Verify and document that the project, or project phase, meets completion or exit criteria set in place during project planning.	
8	Hold team-building activities.	
9	Evaluate the effectiveness of risk responses in a risk audit.	
10	Determine how you will plan the management efforts for scope, schedule, cost, quality, human resources, communications, risk, procurement, requirements, changes, configuration, and process improvement, and put that information into the beginnings of management plans.	
11	Obtain formal (legal) sign-off and final acceptance of the product of the project from the customer.	
12	Increase the effectiveness of processes.	
13	Recalculate how much the project will cost and how long it will take, and create forecasts.	
14	Plan what will be communicated on the project, to whom, by whom, when, and how.	
15	Spend time trying to improve quality.	
16	Make sure the business case and the analysis supporting the need for the project are documented and understood.	
17	Evaluate how effectively the team members function as a team.	
18	Determine how you will improve the processes in use on the project.	
19	Determine measurable project and product objectives.	
20	Manage the time and cost reserves.	
21	Focus on looking for exceptions to the approved project management plan in team members' performance, rather than checking up on every person's work or babysitting.	
22	Develop the final project management plan, project documents, and performance measurement baseline by performing schedule network analysis, looking for options, and confirming that project objectives can be met.	
23	Gather final lessons learned.	
24	Keep everyone focused on completing the project to the charter and project management plan.	
25	Calculate estimate to complete.	
26	Understand how the project supports the organization's strategic objectives.	
27	Implement approved process improvements.	
28	Identify stakeholders, their influences, and their risk tolerances.	

	Actions	During Which Process Group Is This Done?
29	Determine variances.	
30	Add new skills acquired to team members' human resource records.	
31	Meet with managers to gain resource commitments.	
32	Use and interpret earned value calculations.	
33	Ensure the product scope is as final as practical.	
34	Create and distribute a final report of project (or phase) performance.	
35	Recommend changes to be evaluated in the Perform Integrated Change Control process.	
36	Finalize the "execute" and "control" aspects of all management plans.	
37	Index and archive project records.	
38	Keep managers apprised of when their resources will be needed on the project.	
39	Evaluate customer satisfaction regarding the project and the deliverables.	
40	Determine who will be on the project team.	
41	Create recommendations for the performing organization that increase its effectiveness.	
42	Perform procurement inspections.	
43	Turn high-level stakeholder needs, wants, and expectations into requirements.	
44	Look for newly arising risks.	
45	Determine what processes should be followed on the project to reduce the need to supervise work and to improve quality and make use of standards.	
46	Obtain formal acceptance of interim deliverables from the customer.	
47	Identify the need for replanning.	
48	Determine what specifically will constitute project success.	
49	Measure individual team member performance.	
50	Obtain a decision in integrated change control about whether changes should be approved or rejected.	
51	Perform quality assurance to ensure the defined practices and procedures are being followed on the project.	
52	Evaluate the effectiveness of implemented corrective actions.	
53	Plan ways to measure project performance, the measurements to be used, when they will be taken, and how they will be interpreted.	
54	Reevaluate the project's business case when a severe problem occurs.	
55	Determine the process that will be used to request, approve, and manage changes on the project.	

Answer

	Actions	During Which Process Group Is This Done?
1	Use the project scope statement to gain approval of the "final" scope from stakeholders before further planning is done.	Planning
2	Determine high-level requirements, constraints, assumptions, and risks.	Initiating
3	Measure against the performance measurement baseline.	Monitoring and controlling
4	Implement approved changes, including corrective actions, preventive actions, and defect repair.	Executing
5	Reanalyze existing risks.	Monitoring and controlling
6	Use the high-level planning and estimating data to determine whether the product can be achieved within the given constraints.	Initiating
7	Verify and document that the project, or project phase, meets completion or exit criteria set in place during project planning.	Closing
8	Hold team-building activities.	Executing
9	Evaluate the effectiveness of risk responses in a risk audit.	Monitoring and controlling
10	Determine how you will plan the management efforts for scope, schedule, cost, quality, human resources, communications, risk, procurement, requirements, changes, configuration, and process improvement, and put that information into the beginnings of management plans.	Planning
11	Obtain formal (legal) sign-off and final acceptance of the product of the project from the customer.	Closing
12	Increase the effectiveness of processes.	Executing
13	Recalculate how much the project will cost and how long it will take, and create forecasts.	Monitoring and controlling
14	Plan what will be communicated on the project, to whom, by whom, when, and how.	Planning
15	Spend time trying to improve quality.	Monitoring and controlling
16	Make sure the business case and the analysis supporting the need for the project are documented and understood.	Initiating
17	Evaluate how effectively the team members function as a team.	Executing
18	Determine how you will improve the processes in use on the project.	Planning
19	Determine measurable project and product objectives.	Initiating
20	Manage the time and cost reserves.	Monitoring and controlling
21	Focus on looking for exceptions to the approved project management plan in team members' performance, rather than checking up on every person's work or babysitting.	Executing

	Actions	During Which Process Group Is This Done?
22	Develop the final project management plan, project documents, and performance measurement baseline by performing schedule network analysis, looking for options, and confirming that project objectives can be met.	Planning
23	Gather final lessons learned.	Closing
24	Keep everyone focused on completing the project to the charter and project management plan.	Executing
25	Calculate estimate to complete.	Monitoring and controlling
26	Understand how the project supports the organization's strategic objectives.	Initiating
27	Implement approved process improvements.	Executing
28	Identify stakeholders, their influences, and their risk tolerances.	Initiating
29	Determine variances.	Monitoring and controlling
30	Add new skills acquired to team members' human resource records.	Closing
31	Meet with managers to gain resource commitments.	Planning
32	Use and interpret earned value calculations.	Monitoring and controlling
33	Ensure the product scope is as final as practical.	Initiating
34	Create and distribute a final report of project (or phase) performance.	Closing
35	Recommend changes to be evaluated in the Perform Integrated Change Control process.	Executing, Monitoring and controlling
36	Finalize the "execute" and "control" aspects of all management plans.	Planning
37	Index and archive project records.	Closing
38	Keep managers apprised of when their resources will be needed on the project.	Executing
39	Evaluate customer satisfaction regarding the project and the deliverables.	Closing
40	Determine who will be on the project team.	Planning
41	Create recommendations for the performing organization that increase its effectiveness.	Executing
42	Perform procurement inspections.	Monitoring and controlling
43	Turn high-level stakeholder needs, wants, and expectations into requirements.	Initiating
44	Look for newly arising risks.	Monitoring and controlling
45	Determine what processes should be followed on the project to reduce the need to supervise work and to improve quality and make use of standards.	Planning
46	Obtain formal acceptance of interim deliverables from the customer.	Monitoring and controlling
47	Identify the need for replanning.	Monitoring and controlling

	Actions	During Which Process Group Is This Done?
48	Determine what specifically will constitute project success.	Initiating
49	Measure individual team member performance.	Executing
50	Obtain a decision in integrated change control about whether changes should be approved or rejected.	Monitoring and controlling
51	Perform quality assurance to ensure the defined practices and procedures are being followed on the project.	Executing
52	Evaluate the effectiveness of implemented corrective actions.	Monitoring and controlling
53	Plan ways to measure project performance, the measurements to be used, when they will be taken, and how they will be interpreted.	Planning
54	Keep the project's business case in focus while managing the project, especially when problems occur.	Executing
55	Determine the process that will be used to request, approve, and manage changes on the project.	Planning

Inputs and Outputs Why worry about inputs and outputs? Here is a trick to help you gain confidence in your understanding of the project management processes.

An input means:
- "What do I need before I can. . ."

An output means:
- "What will I have when I am done with. . ."
- Or, "What am I trying to achieve when I am doing. . ."

Inputs and outputs are logical. If you really know project management, they should not require memorization. So what is an input to a WBS? If you cannot answer right now, you may need more basic training before preparing for the exam. Make sure you read the Create WBS discussion carefully in the Scope Management chapter and pay attention throughout this book to when and how the WBS is used.

Do not expect all the inputs tested on the exam to be clearly listed in the *PMBOK® Guide*. For example, you know you need the project team (or at least an initial version of the project team) to create a work breakdown structure, yet the team is not specifically listed as an input to creating the work breakdown structure in the *PMBOK® Guide*. The remaining chapters of this book will help you understand the processes of project management and the inputs and outputs so you can see the logic behind them.

Practice Exam

1. In which project management process group is the detailed project budget created?
   A. Initiating
   B. Before the project management process
   C. Planning
   D. Executing

2. The project charter is created in which project management process group?
   A. Executing
   B. Planning
   C. Closing
   D. Initiating

3. The project team has just completed the initial project schedule and budget. The NEXT thing to do is to:
   A. Identify risks.
   B. Begin iterations.
   C. Determine communications requirements.
   D. Create a bar (Gantt) chart.

4. A detailed project schedule can be created only after creating the:
   A. Project budget.
   B. Work breakdown structure.
   C. Project management plan.
   D. Detailed risk assessment.

5. The person who should be in control of the project during project planning is the:
   A. Project manager.
   B. Team member.
   C. Functional manager.
   D. Sponsor.

6. Which of the following is NOT an input to the initiating process group?
   A. Company processes
   B. Company culture
   C. Historical WBSs
   D. Project scope statement

7. The project sponsor has just signed the project charter. What is the NEXT thing to do?
   A. Begin to complete work packages.
   B. Verify scope.
   C. Start integrated change control.
   D. Start to create management plans.

8. The high-level project schedule constraints have just been determined. What project management process group are you in?
   A. Initiating
   B. Planning
   C. Executing
   D. Monitoring and controlling

9. The WBS and WBS dictionary are completed. The project team has begun working on identifying risks. The sponsor contacts the project manager, requesting that the responsibility assignment matrix be issued. The project has a budget of US $100,000 and is taking place in three countries using 14 human resources. There is little risk expected for the project, and the project manager has managed many projects similar to this one. What is the NEXT thing to do?
   A. Understand the experience of the sponsor on similar projects.
   B. Create an activity list.
   C. Make sure the project scope is defined.
   D. Complete risk management and issue the responsibility assignment matrix.

10. A project manager does not have much time to spend planning before the mandatory start date arrives. He therefore wants to move through planning as effectively as possible. Which of the following would you recommend?
    A. Make sure you have a signed project charter and then start the WBS.
    B. Create an activity list before creating a network diagram.
    C. Document all the known risks before you document the high-level assumptions.
    D. Finalize the quality management plan before you determine quality metrics.

11. The BEST time to assign a project manager to a project is during:
    A. Executing.
    B. Closing.
    C. Initiating.
    D. Planning.

12. A project manager gets a call from a team member notifying him that there is a variance between the speed of a system on the project and the desired or planned speed. The project manager is surprised because that performance measurement was not identified in planning. If the project manager then evaluates whether the variance warrants a response, he is in which part of the project management process?
    A. Initiating
    B. Executing
    C. Monitoring and controlling
    D. Closing

13. A team member notifies the project manager that the activities comprising a work package are no longer appropriate. It would be BEST for the project manager to be in what part of the project management process?
    A. Corrective action
    B. Integrated change control
    C. Monitoring and controlling
    D. Project closing

14. During a team meeting, a team member asks about the measurements that will be used on the project to judge performance. The team member feels that some of the measures related to activities assigned to him are not valid measurements. The project is BEST considered to be in what part of the project management process?
    A. Closing
    B. Monitoring and controlling
    C. Executing
    D. Initiating

15. Which of the following would be the MOST appropriate thing to do during the initiating process group?
    A. Create a detailed description of the project deliverables.
    B. Get familiar with the company culture and structure as it relates to the project.
    C. Identify the root cause of problems.
    D. Ensure all project management processes are complete.

16. Which of the following is a characteristic of project management processes?
    A. Iterative
    B. Unique
    C. Unnecessary
    D. Standardized

17. Which project management process group generally takes the MOST project time and resources?
    A. Planning
    B. Design
    C. Integration
    D. Executing

18. All of the following must be performed during project initiating EXCEPT:
    A. Identify and document business needs.
    B. Create a project scope statement.
    C. Divide a large project into phases.
    D. Accumulate and evaluate historical information.

19. Closure includes all of the following EXCEPT:
    A. Determining performance measures.
    B. Turning over the product of the project.
    C. Documenting the degree to which each project phase was properly closed after its completion.
    D. Updating the company's organizational process assets.

20. The first phase of your project has come to an end. What should you ensure is done BEFORE beginning the next phase?
    A. Verify that the resources are available for the next phase.
    B. Check the project's progress compared to its baselines.
    C. Confirm that the phase has reached its objectives, and have its deliverables formally accepted.
    D. Recommend corrective action to bring the project results in line with project expectations.

21. During which process group does the team measure and analyze the work being done on the project?
    A. Initiating
    B. Executing
    C. Monitoring and controlling
    D. Closing

22. Which process groups must be included in every project?
    A. Planning, executing, and closing
    B. Initiating, planning, and executing
    C. Initiating, planning, executing, monitoring and controlling, and closing
    D. Planning, executing, and monitoring and controlling

23. Control Schedule, Report Performance, and Administer Procurements are in which process group?
    A. Initiating
    B. Planning
    C. Executing
    D. Monitoring and controlling

24. Which process group focuses on completing the requirements of the project?
    A. Initiating
    B. Planning
    C. Executing
    D. Closing

25. All of the following occur during the planning process group EXCEPT:
    A. Develop Project Charter.
    B. Create WBS.
    C. Estimate Costs.
    D. Sequence Activities.

Answers

1. **Answer** C
   Explanation Notice the use of the word "detailed." Such a budget is created during project planning.

2. **Answer** D
   Explanation The project charter is needed before planning and execution of the work can begin.

3. **Answer** C
   Explanation Communications requirements and quality standards are needed before risks (especially risks relating to communications and quality) can be determined. Iterations cannot begin until the risks are identified, qualified, and quantified and responses are developed. Through iterations, the WBS and other parts of the project management plan are revised. A bar chart would have been done during the creation of the schedule, so it cannot be the next thing. Of the choices listed, determine communications requirements is the best option.

4. **Answer** B
   Explanation In the project management process, the project budget, project management plan, and detailed risk assessment come after the schedule. The only answer that could be an input is the work breakdown structure.

5. **Answer** A
   Explanation The project manager should be named early in the project, during project initiating if possible. It is then his or her responsibility to control the project throughout its life.

6. **Answer** D
   Explanation Notice the question asks which is NOT an input to project initiating. Did you read it correctly? Companies should have processes in place for hiring resources, reporting, and managing risks on projects (to name only a few). These are inputs to project initiating, as are company culture and historical WBSs. The project scope statement is an output of project planning.

7. **Answer** D
   Explanation To answer this type of question, look for the choice that occurs closest to the process group you are in. The project charter is created during project initiating. Completing work packages is done during project executing. Verifying scope and performing integrated change control are done during project monitoring and controlling. Starting to create management plans is the best choice, as it is part of project planning.

8. **Answer** A
   Explanation High-level constraints are identified in the project charter, which is created during project initiating.

9. **Answer** B
   Explanation Look at the order of planning the project that the team has chosen. Although understanding the experience of the sponsor might sound like a good idea, the sponsor is a stakeholder and understanding the stakeholders is part of stakeholder analysis. That should have occurred before the creation of a WBS. In planning the project, the project scope is defined, and must come before creating a WBS. Completing risk management and issuing the responsibility assignment matrix cannot be best, as that work does not come next in the process. Other work

must be done before risk management can effectively be completed. Creating an activity list comes next after the WBS and WBS dictionary.

10. **Answer** B
    Explanation This question is asking which of the choices is the most effective way to move through project planning. Starting the WBS immediately after obtaining a project charter skips the important steps of defining the scope and other activities. High-level assumptions are determined in project initiating. Quality metrics are determined as part of the quality management plan, not after it. The activity list is created before the network diagram, so that is the best option.

11. **Answer** C
    Explanation The project manager should be assigned during project initiating.

12. **Answer** C
    Explanation Even though the measurement was not identified in planning, the project manager would still have to investigate the variance and determine if it is important. Therefore, the project manager is in project monitoring and controlling.

13. **Answer** C
    Explanation If you chose another part of the project management process, you probably forgot that the situation needs to be evaluated by the project manager before recommending a change or beginning integrated change control.

14. **Answer** C
    Explanation This situation does not describe an actual measurement (a monitoring and controlling activity) but rather a meeting occurring during project executing.

15. **Answer** B
    Explanation A detailed description of the project deliverables is created during project planning, as part of creating the project scope statement. Root cause analysis occurs during project monitoring and controlling, not initiating. Ensuring all project management processes are complete occurs during project closing. It is important for a project manager to become familiar with the company culture and structure as it relates to the project as early in the project as possible. This is the most appropriate choice to do in project initiating.

16. **Answer** A
    Explanation As the project life cycle progresses, more information becomes available, allowing the team to manage the project to a more detailed level.

17. **Answer** D
    Explanation Doing the actual work will generally take the most project time and resources.

18. **Answer** B
    Explanation A project scope statement is created during project planning.

19. **Answer** A
    Explanation Performance measures are determined earlier in the project so they can be used to measure progress during the project, making determining performance measures the only correct answer to this question.

20. **Answer** C
    Explanation A phase or project must be formally closed and accepted.

21. **Answer** C
    Explanation During project monitoring and controlling, project performance is measured and needed changes are identified and approved.

22. **Answer** C
    Explanation All five process groups are addressed in each project. It is the responsibility of the project manager to determine the level of attention to give to each process group.

23. **Answer** D
    Explanation All of these processes are parts of project monitoring and controlling.

24. **Answer** C
    Explanation Project executing is where work is done to produce the product of the project.

25. **Answer** A
    Explanation Develop Project Charter occurs during project initiating.

CHAPTER FOUR Integration Management

Quicktest

- Integration management process
- Integrated change control
- Process for making changes
- Project management plan
  - Management plans
  - Baselines
  - Requirements management plan
  - Change management plan
  - Configuration management plan
  - Process improvement plan
- Project charter
- Business case
- Project selection
- Project documents
- Change requests
- Corrective action
- Preventive action
- Defect repair
- Project manager's role as integrator
- Enterprise environmental factors
- Organizational process assets
  - Processes, procedures, policies
  - Corporate knowledge base
  - Historical information
  - Lessons learned
- Constraints and assumptions
- Project management plan and project document updates
- Configuration management system
- Change control system
- Change control board
- Cost benefit analysis
- Kickoff meeting
- Work authorization system
- Project statement of work
- Net present value
- Internal rate of return
- Payback period
- Present value
- Project management information system (PMIS)
- Economic value added
- Opportunity cost
- Sunk costs
- Law of diminishing returns
- Working capital
- Depreciation

If you were asked, "What is a project manager's main role?" what would you say? The answer is to perform integration management—to pull all the pieces of a project together into a cohesive whole. This is so much a part of a project manager's job that it is arguably the reason for the project manager's existence in an organization and on a project.

Many people who have trouble with this knowledge area on the exam either do not currently perform integration management on their projects or they do not think about integration management from a large-project perspective. While the work of the project is being done, the team members are concentrating on completing the work packages, the project sponsor should be protecting the project from changes and loss of resources, and the project manager is responsible for integration—putting all the pieces of the project together into one cohesive whole that gets the project done faster, cheaper, and with fewer resources, while meeting the project objectives.

Think about integration as balancing all the processes in the knowledge areas (scope, time, cost, quality, human resource, communications, risk, and procurement management) with each other. Project management processes do not happen independently. In order to complete a cost estimate, for example, the number of resources on the project, the scope being estimated, the risk reserves, etc., should be taken into account. In another example, adding a new resource to the project may require cost or schedule changes. In dealing with each situation that comes up on a project, the project manager is integrating the processes of project management.

This chapter is about the high-level work a project manager needs to do. The other knowledge area chapters in this book explain the detailed work. Read this chapter carefully—integration management is a difficult area on the exam, and there may be up to 14 questions on this topic!

Rita's Process Chart—Integration Management

Where are we in the project management process?

INITIATING

- **Select project manager**
- **Determine company culture and existing systems**
- **Collect processes, procedures, and historical information**
- **Divide large projects into phases**
- **Understand the business case**
- **Uncover initial requirements, assumptions, and risks**
- **Assess project and product feasibility within the given constraints**
- **Create measurable objectives**
- **Develop project charter**
- Identify stakeholders
- Develop stakeholder management strategy

PLANNING

(This is the only process group with a set order)

- **Determine how you will do planning—part of all management plans**
- Determine detailed requirements
- Create project scope statement
- Assess what to purchase
- **Determine team**
- Create WBS and WBS dictionary
- Create activity list
- Create network diagram
- Estimate resource requirements
- Estimate time and cost
- Determine critical path
- Develop schedule
- Develop budget
- Determine quality standards, processes, and metrics
- Create process improvement plan
- **Determine all roles and responsibilities**
- Plan communications
- Perform risk identification, qualitative and quantitative risk analysis, and risk response planning
- **Go back—iterations**
- Prepare procurement documents
- **Create change management plan**
- **Finalize the "how to execute and control" parts of all management plans**
- **Develop realistic final PM plan and performance measurement baseline**
- **Gain formal approval of the plan**
- **Hold kickoff meeting**

EXECUTING

- **Execute the work according to the PM plan**
- **Produce product deliverables (product scope)**
- **Request changes**
- **Implement only approved changes**
- **Continuously improve**
- **Follow processes**
- Perform quality assurance
- Perform quality audits
- Acquire final team
- Manage people
- Evaluate team and project performance
- Hold team-building activities
- Give recognition and rewards
- Use issue logs
- Facilitate conflict resolution
- Release resources as work is completed
- Send and receive information
- Hold meetings
- Select sellers

MONITORING & CONTROLLING

- **Take action to control the project**
- **Measure performance against the performance measurement baseline**
- **Measure performance against other metrics determined by the project manager**
- **Determine variances and if they warrant a corrective action or change request**
- **Influence the factors that cause changes**
- **Request changes**
- **Perform integrated change control**
- **Approve or reject changes**
- **Inform stakeholders of the results of change requests**
- **Update the PM plan and project documents**
- **Manage configuration**
- Create forecasts
- Gain acceptance of interim deliverables from the customer
- Perform quality control
- Report on project performance and solicit feedback
- Perform risk assessments and audits
- Manage reserves
- Administer procurements

CLOSING

- **Confirm work is done to requirements**
- Complete procurement closure
- **Gain final acceptance of the product**
- **Complete financial closure**
- **Hand off completed product**
- **Solicit feedback from the customer about the project**
- **Complete final performance reporting**
- **Index and archive records**
- **Update lessons learned knowledge base**

The following should help you understand how each part of integration management fits into the overall project management process:

The Integration Management Process	Done During
Develop Project Charter	Initiating process group
Develop Project Management Plan	Planning process group
Direct and Manage Project Execution	Executing process group
Monitor and Control Project Work	Monitoring and controlling process group
Perform Integrated Change Control	Monitoring and controlling process group
Close Project or Phase	Closing process group

Integration management cannot be understood without a solid understanding of the process of project management. Therefore, if you have limited project management training or experience, you might want to do a high-level review of this chapter the first time, read the rest of this book, and then come back and read this chapter again. It will make more sense the second time. Remember that integration management is the primary role of the project manager. You must understand integration from a real-world, large-project perspective.

The following diagram shows the relationship between the knowledge areas and the process groups. All of the knowledge areas include processes that occur in planning, and most include monitoring and controlling processes. Integration management is the only knowledge area that has processes occurring in all process groups, throughout the project management process. The project manager is always integrating.

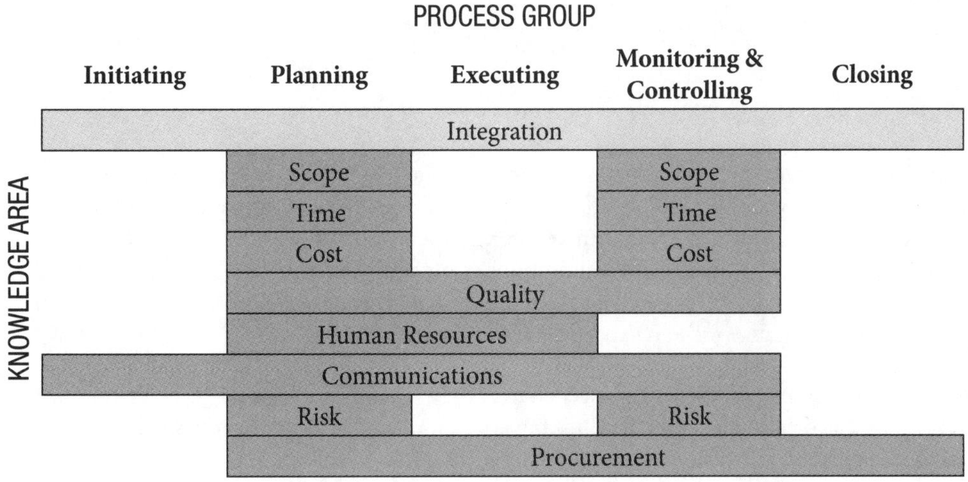

PROCESS GROUP

KNOWLEDGE AREA

<table>
<tr><th>Initiating</th><th>Planning</th><th>Executing</th><th>Monitoring & Controlling</th><th>Closing</th></tr>
<tr><td colspan="5">Integration</td></tr>
<tr><td></td><td>Scope</td><td></td><td>Scope</td><td></td></tr>
<tr><td></td><td>Time</td><td></td><td>Time</td><td></td></tr>
<tr><td></td><td>Cost</td><td></td><td>Cost</td><td></td></tr>
<tr><td></td><td colspan="3">Quality</td><td></td></tr>
<tr><td></td><td colspan="2">Human Resources</td><td></td><td></td></tr>
<tr><td colspan="4">Communications</td><td></td></tr>
<tr><td></td><td>Risk</td><td></td><td>Risk</td><td></td></tr>
<tr><td></td><td colspan="4">Procurement</td></tr>
</table>

Develop Project Charter[1] PAGE 73

> **Process:** Develop Project Charter
> **Process Group:** Initiating
> **Knowledge Area:** Integration Management

The first part of integration management is coming up with a project charter. The exam could include up to eight questions that reference a project charter. You should understand what a project charter is, why it is important, and how it is used throughout the life of the project.

Exercise Test yourself! Answer the following question.

What Is Included in a Project Charter?

Answer Unfortunately, many companies expect project charters to include information such as a detailed schedule and a full risk analysis. Such information is not available at this point in the project management process, however. A project charter is not a project management plan! Read the rest of this section to learn what is included in a project charter and to see examples.

Creating the project charter does involve planning the project at a high level to assess whether it is feasible within the given constraints, but detailed planning does not happen until after the charter is signed. In project initiating, you may meet with key stakeholders and define the high-level objectives, constraints, requirements, scope, risks, and assumptions in an effort to assess the feasibility of the project. But detailed planning takes time and costs money, and this time and money cannot be spent until the project is officially authorized by approval of the project charter.

The following is a brief example of what a project charter for a small project may include. It does not represent the scale of projects you should be thinking about for the exam, but it should help you to understand the elements of a project charter. You will see a sample charter for a large project later in this chapter. These charter examples focus on what is done in the real world and what you need to know for the exam. They go beyond what is listed as part of the project charter in the *PMBOK® Guide*.

NOTE: The following project charter example refers to attached documents. These documents are not shown as part of this example.

Project Charter

Project Title and Description *(What is the project?)* **Customer Satisfaction Fix-It Project**
Over the last few months, the quality assurance department has discovered many of our customers' orders for our XYZ equipment have taken the customer ten times longer to place through our computer network than our competitors' networks. The purpose of this project is to investigate the reasons for the problem and propose a solution. The solution will be authorized as a subsequent project. Quality Control has detailed records of their findings that can be used to speed up this project.

Project Manager Assigned and Authority Level *(Who is given authority to lead the project, and can he/she determine, manage, and approve changes to budget, schedule, staffing, etc.?)*
Jan Navratil shall be the project manager for this project and have authority to select team members and determine the final project budget.

Business Case *(Why is the project being done? On what financial or other basis can we justify doing this project? Describe the project purpose and justification.)*
This project is being completed in order to prevent a further breakdown of customer satisfaction. We expect that improved customer satisfaction will increase revenue to the company in the first year by at least $200,000 due to a decrease in service calls. As a side benefit, we hope the project will generate ideas on improving customer satisfaction while fixing this problem.

Resources Preassigned *(How many or which resources will be provided?)*
Steve Peterson and Rich Conniff are already dedicated to the project because of their expertise in computer networks of this type. Other resources will be determined by the project manager.

Stakeholders *(Who will affect or be affected by the project (influence the project), as known to date?)*
Stakeholders include Jason Craft representing Quality Control, Jennie Rutter in Customer Service, and Eric Rudolf in Marketing. These resources are available to assist the project as needed by the project manager.

Stakeholder Requirements As Known *(Requirements related to both project and product scope)*
Attached to this document are the detailed specifications for the existing system, the requirements the existing system was designed to meet. It is expected that this project will not change how the system affects the existing requirements.

The project must include utilizing the data available from Quality Control.

Product Description/Deliverables *(What specific product deliverables are wanted, and what will be the end result of the project?)*

1. A report that outlines what can be changed, how much each change will cost, and the expected decrease in the time it takes to place an order resulting from each change. Few words are necessary in the report, but it must be created electronically and be agreed to by the representatives of Quality Control, Customer Service, and Marketing, in addition to the project team.
2. A list of the interactions with our customers necessary to complete the changes.
3. A work breakdown structure, due within two weeks, that outlines what will be involved in the project, followed one week later by a list of risks in completing the project.

Measurable Project Objectives *(How does the project tie into the organization's strategic goals? What project objectives support those goals? The objectives need to be measurable and will depend on the defined priority of the project constraints.)*
The objective of this project is to improve customer satisfaction by reducing the time customers spend placing orders via the computer network to 10 percent of the current time. Scope and customer satisfaction are the top priorities on this project, closely followed by schedule and then cost.

- **Summary milestone schedule:** Due no later than September 1, 20XX.
- **Summary budget:** $50,000.

Project Approval Requirements *(What items need to be approved for the project, and who will have sign-off? What designates success?)*
Approvals for this project include:

- The sponsors will approve the WBS before planning efforts continue.
- The sponsors will approve the list of risks before planning efforts continue.

Final project approval will be provided by the sponsors.

High-Level Project Risks *(Potential threats and opportunities for the project)*

- Because this project analyzes customer satisfaction, the project may help generate ideas to improve customer satisfaction, resulting in higher levels of customer retention.
- Because we have little experience in this area, implementing an inadequate solution could cause more frustration and more time delays for customers, resulting in additional lost business.
- Because this problem is greatly troubling to our customers, project delay could result in lost customers, jeopardizing the likelihood of meeting this year's sales goals.
- Because assessment of this system is difficult, changes to the system could affect the requirements the system was designed to meet, resulting in impacts to other business functions.

Project Sponsors Authorizing This Project:

Connor Mulcahy, Executive Vice President	Kerry Mulcahy, Vice President

Exercise Test yourself! Answer the question below.

What Does the Project Charter Do for the Project Manager?

Answer Do not underestimate the value of the project charter! The project charter is such an important document that a project cannot be started without one. If the project charter is your target for the project and serves as a definition of how success will be measured, then without a project charter, the project and project manager cannot be successful! Know the following for the exam.

The project manager may create the project charter, but it is issued by the sponsor as part of project initiating. The project charter should be broad enough so it does not NEED to change as the project progresses. It provides, at a minimum, the following benefits:

- The project charter formally recognizes (authorizes) the existence of the project, or establishes the project. This means that a project does not exist without a project charter.
- It gives the project manager authority to spend money and commit corporate resources to the project. On the exam, this is the most commonly described benefit or use of the project charter. In most project situations, the project team does not report to the project manager in the corporate structure. This reporting structure can lead to cooperation and performance issues. The project charter helps resolve these issues.
- The project charter provides the objectives and high-level requirements for the project.
- The project charter identifies the constraints and high-level risks for the project.
- The process of creating the charter uncovers assumptions about the project, which the project manager can later address in the detailed requirements gathering, scope definition, and risk management efforts.
- The project charter links the project to the ongoing work of the organization.

Any change to the project charter should call into question whether the project should continue.

Can you see that the creation of a project charter is influenced by all the project management knowledge areas (i.e., scope, time, cost, quality, human resource, communications, risk, and procurement management)? This is why Develop Project Charter is an integration process.

Large Projects As we discussed in earlier chapters, you need to maintain a large-project perspective when answering questions on the exam. To help you understand this critical concept, review the following project charter for a large project, and then complete the following exercise.

NOTE: The following charter example refers to attached documents. These documents are not shown as part of this example.

Project Charter

Project Title and Description *(What is the project?)* **The First Personal Assistant**
Design a prototype and create the manufacturing plan for the first consumer product that can act as a personal assistant. This product would be worn on the ear, respond to voice commands, and do everything that a human personal assistant can do.

Project Manager Assigned and Authority Level *(Who is given authority to lead the project, and can he/she determine, manage, and approve changes to budget, schedule, staffing, etc.?)*
Mary Lofsness shall be the project manager for this project. She may select any team member she sees fit and has signature authority up to $10,000. Dave Pedersen is assigned as assistant project manager, and Whitney Thulin is assigned as project administrator.

Business Case *(Why is the project being done? On what financial or other basis can we justify doing this project?)*
We consider ourselves to be the premier consumer products company in the world, and we want to continue that lead with a new product that could start a whole new industry. Our analysis shows a potential return on investment for this product to be 175%: 85% of that return will be in the first year and 45% in years two and three.

Resources Preassigned *(How many or which resources will be provided?)*
The entire research and development department in our Tokyo office consisting of 90 people is assigned to this team. In addition, the attached list gives the names of 87 dedicated people from 6 countries covering the fields of marketing, consumer metals, software design, and manufacturing. We will be working with a design firm in the Netherlands we have used before. We need to find a firm that can manufacture casing parts for the end product. English will be the project language. Other resources needed must be identified and negotiated for by the project manager.

Stakeholders *(Who will affect or be affected by the project (influence the project), as known to date?)*
The attached document lists 303 stakeholders who might be impacted by this project. They consist of representatives from the public, our largest buyers of our consumer products, and company management.

Stakeholder Requirements As Known *(Requirements related to both project and product scope)*
Attached to this document are the detailed specifications for the personal assistant as gathered by marketing research and as determined by potential customers of this product. The product should be able to perform Internet searches; make hotel, flight, and restaurant reservations; take dictation and fax or e-mail the results; and be able to make phone calls itself using its own voice. It must be small enough to be worn on the ear and respond to voice-only commands. The scope of this project does not call for typed entry into the system. It will be entirely voice activated and managed. The technical requirements consisting of acceptable weight ranges, acceptable materials, and other needs are attached. The applicable regulatory and compliance requirements are also attached. Creating marketing, advertising, and promotional plans are not part of this project; however, this work is authorized under a separate project, requiring the project team to provide the needed information. A list of that information and the schedule for its availability is also attached, but it is expected to change as the project progresses.

Product Description/Deliverables *(What specific product deliverables are wanted and what will be the end result of the project?)*

1. A working prototype that meets the requirements
2. A plan for manufacturing
3. A plan for transitioning this project to the manufacturing environment

Measurable Project Objectives *(How does the project tie into the organization's strategic goals? What project objectives support those goals? The objectives need to be measurable and will depend on the defined priority of the project constraints.)*

The objective of this project is to introduce a radically new product into the marketplace, giving our corporation the eight-month advantage of being the sole vendor in this industry. The product must integrate not only with our existing products but also those of our competitors so as to pull market share away from them. The marketing plan must take advantage of our corporate support of the national sports league. Initially our main customer will be the early adaptor, who is used to some minor issues with products. Time to market will be most important, with reducing risk a secondary constraint. Cost and scope will be lowest in priority, with quality falling somewhere in the middle.

- Summary milestone schedule: Due no later than October 6, 20XX
- Summary budget: US $3,450,000

Project Approval Requirements *(What items need to be approved for the project, and who will have sign-off? What designates success?)*

Approvals for this project include:

- Recommended materials list
- Prototype options (to be reduced to two approved prototypes)
- Final prototype design
- Manufacturing plan

Final project approval will be provided by the sponsors.

High-Level Project Risks *(Potential threats and opportunities for the project)*

- Because there may be changes in the international marketplace, the project requirements may change, potentially resulting in delays, wasted effort, or rework.
- Because the value of the US dollar impacts the return on investment for this project, a greater than 10 percent change to inflation rates or the value of the US dollar could possibly result in termination of the project prior to completion.
- Because this is an entirely new and untested product for our company, we may have difficulty achieving the high standards of quality and reliability in the initial release that our customers have come to expect of our products, resulting in damage to our company's reputation and potentially decreasing customer's receptiveness to this type of product in the future.
- Because we are in a highly competitive industry, we may have information leaks, resulting in our competitors learning about the product and potentially losing four to six months of product advantage.
- Because this is a new type of product in the marketplace, a successful product may launch a new industry, resulting in our company being at the forefront of the industry.

Project Sponsors Authorizing This Project:

______________________________	______________________________
Timothy Mulcahy, Executive Vice President	Rick Kolb, Vice President

Exercise Make a list of what is different about managing the large project described in this charter versus managing the small project described in the earlier charter example.

What Would Be Different about Managing the Large Project vs. the Small Project?

Answer The following are some possible answers to this question, though there are certainly other correct answers. The large project:

- Has a larger stakeholder group
- Has a more diverse team composition
- Requires a broader and more complex communications management plan to deal with the number of stakeholders and language issues
- Contends with multiple nations, cultures, time zones, languages, and laws
- Will be affected by money exchange rates
- Requires a more formal change management process to handle the possible scope changes
- Has thousands of activities to track
- Has larger activities, making it more difficult to get good time and cost estimates
- Will have a more complex network diagram with many discretionary and external dependencies
- Requires a more robust tracking system for all the project metrics
- Involves multiple contracts, requiring more management of the sellers
- Has much more risk, requiring a more detailed risk management process

Regardless of whether you are creating a charter for a large or small project, developing the project charter requires the following actions:

- Identifying stakeholders
- Meeting with key stakeholders to confirm high-level requirements, project scope, risks, assumptions, and issues
- Defining product scope
- Defining project objectives, constraints, and success criteria
- Documenting risks

The following influence the creation of the project charter.

Business Case[2] PAGE 75 Stop for a minute, and think about your real world. How is one project selected over another in your organization? Do you know? In some companies, the selection is arbitrary, based on what a manager feels like doing. If this is your real world, make sure you understand that the exam assumes there is a defined business case for every project and that it is unacceptable to select a project based on anything but a sound business case. The business case captures the business need; it explains why the project was selected and how it fits into the organization's strategic goals.

Imagine you are an executive of a very large company. The departments within your company present you with ideas about many different initiatives (potential projects) to spend money on. Arbitrarily picking one project over another may result in a waste of available resources. Your organization should instead have a method to determine which of the possible projects or programs will provide the greatest benefit or, in *PMBOK® Guide* terms, will best support your company's strategic plan. There might even be a project selection committee in place to put all the data together on the various project ideas. For the exam, you should be familiar with project selection methods (described next), but understanding these methods is not as important as knowing (or assuming) that such activities occur prior to initiating a project. Although project managers are not typically involved in project selection, they need to keep the business case in mind throughout the project to make sure the project achieves the results for which it was selected.

Let's look at an example of how a business case can affect the way a project is managed. A company has selected a particular project because the project will contribute to its strategic plan of entering a new area of business. The project manager has a project management plan that includes an approved schedule and budget. The project manager finds that the approved budget is a constraint that could inhibit the company's successful entrance into the new market. She asks for a change in budget, rather than cutting costs on the project to stay within the project management plan. If the project manager did not ask for the budget increase, the company may have missed its objective of successfully launching itself into the new area of business.

So project managers must know why their project was selected and how it fits into the organization's strategic plan. They then have to make sure the project meets those needs. The business case described in the project charter explains the business need and the analysis used to justify the project.

Project Selection There are various ways to select which projects to initiate from among many possible choices. As we just discussed, the project manager is not typically involved in project selection, but the projects the organization considered before a particular initiative was chosen, as well as the process the company used to select that project, influence how the project manager will plan and manage the project. Therefore, you should be familiar with project selection terms and concepts.

The following are two categories of project selection methods and examples of approaches that can be used with each method. Simply know that these terms relate to project selection:

1. **Benefit measurement methods (Comparative approach)**[3]
   - Murder board (a panel of people who try to shoot down a new project idea)
   - Peer review
   - Scoring models
   - Economic models (described next)
2. **Constrained optimization methods (Mathematical approach)**[4]
   - Linear programming
   - Integer programming
   - Dynamic programming
   - Multi-objective programming

Economic Models for Project Selection

The following are economic models for selecting a project. As noted previously, such economic models take a comparative approach and fall into the category of benefit measurement methods.

- Present value
- Net present value
- Internal rate of return
- Payback period
- Cost benefit analysis

We will briefly discuss each of these concepts. Again, keep in mind as you read this section that the reasons a project is selected and the value it is expected to bring to an organization indicate its significance to the company. The project manager needs to know if the project will establish a new area of business, if it is being implemented to meet regulatory or compliance requirements, or if it was chosen because it was the least expensive or most feasible solution to a problem. These reasons can impact what constraints are most flexible, and knowing this information will influence the way the project manager plans and manages the project.

Present Value (PV)[5]

PLEASE NOTE: Historically, present value has only been mentioned once or twice on the exam. You will not have to calculate it, nor know the formula; just understand the concept.

Present value means the value today of future cash flows and can be found using the following formula:

$PV = \frac{FV}{(1 + r)^n}$	FV = future value r = interest rate n = number of time periods

Watch out! The acronym PV is also used for planned value (described in the Cost Management chapter). Avoid confusing these two terms.

In a simple example, without using the formula, see if you can guess the answer to the following question:

> **Question** *What is the present value of $300,000 received three years from now if we expect the interest rate to be 10 percent? Should the answer be more or less than $300,000?*
>
> **Answer** *Less. You can put an amount of money less than $300,000 in the bank and in three years have $300,000. To solve the problem, if you were inclined to do so:* $300/(1 + 0.1)^3 = 300/1.331 =$ *$225,394.*

Net Present Value (NPV)[5]

You will not have to calculate NPV; just know that it is the present value of the total benefits (income or revenue) minus the costs over many time periods. Calculating the NPV of each possible project provides a means for the organization to compare many projects and select the best project to initiate. Generally, if the NPV is positive, the investment is a good choice unless an even better investment opportunity exists. The project with the greatest NPV is typically selected.

Do you already have a good understanding of this topic? Test yourself with the following question.

Question *An organization has two projects to choose from. Project A will take three years to complete and has an NPV of $45,000. Project B will take six years to complete and has an NPV of $85,000. Which one is a better investment?*

Answer *Project B. The number of years is not relevant, as it would have been taken into account in the calculation of the NPV. See the following sample calculation if you are confused. If you understand the concept of NPV already, skip the example.*

To calculate NPV, you need to calculate the present value of both income and cost figures using the present value formula. You then add the present values as shown in the following table.

Time Period	Income/Revenue	Present Value of Income at 10% Interest Rate	Costs	Present Value of Cost at 10% Interest Rate
0	0	0	200	200
1	50	45	100	91
2	100	83	0	0
3	300	225	0	0
Total		**353**		**291**

Therefore, NPV = 353 – 291 = 62.

Internal Rate of Return (IRR)[5]

To understand this concept, think of a bank account. You put money in a bank account and expect to get a return of 2 percent. You can think of a project in the same way. If a company has more than one project in which to invest, the company may look at the returns of the different projects and then select the project with the highest return.

IRR does get confusing when you give it a formal definition: The rate (read it as "interest rate") at which the project inflows ("revenues") and project outflows ("costs") are equal. Calculating IRR is complex and requires the aid of a computer. You will not have to perform any IRR calculations on the exam. Simply know the higher the IRR number, the better.

Question *An organization has two projects from which to choose: Project A with an IRR of 21 percent or Project B with an IRR of 15 percent. Which one is a better option?*

Answer *Project A*

Payback Period

This term refers to the length of time it takes for the organization to recover its investment in the project before it starts accumulating profit. For example:

Question *There are two projects from which to choose: Project A with a payback period of six months or Project B with a payback period of 18 months. Which one should the organization select?*

Answer *Project A*

Cost Benefit Analysis[5]

Cost benefit analysis compares the expected costs of the project to the potential benefits it could bring the organization. (For project selection purposes, benefits are the same as revenue. Remember that revenue is not the same as profit.) This analysis results in the calculation of a benefit cost ratio, which can be expressed as a decimal or a ratio. A benefit cost ratio of greater than 1 means the benefits are greater than the costs. A benefit cost ratio of less than 1 means the costs are greater than the benefits. A benefit cost ratio of 1 means the costs and benefits are the same.

Question *What does a benefit cost ratio of 1.7 mean?*
A. *The costs are greater than the benefits*
B. *Revenue is 1.7 times the costs*
C. *Profit is 1.7 times the costs*
D. *Costs are 1.7 times the profit*

Answer *B. The benefits, or revenue, the project brings to the organization are 1.7 times the cost of the initiative. Remember, the benefit cost ratio calculation is looking at revenue, not the smaller figure of profits.*

Please note that although the organization may use the benefit cost ratio to help it choose from among many potential projects, a project manager may also perform cost benefit analysis to determine the best way to implement a project once it is selected. The project manager may perform the analysis at a high level during project initiating and at a more detailed level during project planning. This information helps determine things like what level of quality efforts are appropriate for the project, what equipment or technology should be purchased, and whether it would be best to outsource certain pieces of work.

Exercise Remember, you do not have to be an accountant to pass this exam. You do NOT have to use accounting formulas or even remember formulas like present value for the exam. But you may need to have a general understanding of what the terms mean. So test yourself! For each row on the following chart, enter the letter of the project you would select if the following information was provided.

	Project A	Project B	Which Project Would You Pick?
Net present value	$95,000	$75,000	
IRR	13 percent	17 percent	
Payback period	16 months	21 months	
Benefit cost ratio	2.79	1.3	

Answer

	Project A	Project B	Which Project Would You Pick?
Net present value	$95,000	$75,000	A
IRR	13 percent	17 percent	B
Payback period	16 months	21 months	A
Benefit cost ratio	2.79	1.3	A

The following are some additional accounting terms related to project selection that you should be familiar with for the exam.

Economic Value Added (EVA)

In terms of project selection, this concept is concerned with whether the project returns to the company more value than the initiative costs. (Note that this is a different concept than earned value analysis, which can also have the acronym of EVA. Earned value, discussed in the Cost Management chapter, is frequently mentioned on the exam, whereas economic value added should rarely appear in questions or choices.)

Opportunity Cost[5]

This term refers to the opportunity given up by selecting one project over another. This does NOT require any calculation. See the example below.

Question *An organization has two projects to choose from: Project A with an NPV of $45,000 or Project B with an NPV of $85,000. What is the opportunity cost of selecting project B?*

Answer *$45,000*

The opportunity cost is the value of the project not selected.

Sunk Costs[5]

Sunk costs are expended costs. People unfamiliar with accounting standards might have trouble with the following question:

Question *You have a project with an initial budget of $1,000,000. You are halfway through the project and have spent $2,000,000. Do you consider the fact that it is already $1,000,000 over budget when determining whether to continue with the project?*

Answer *No. The money spent is gone.*

Be aware that accounting standards say that sunk costs should not be considered when deciding whether to continue with a troubled project.

Law of Diminishing Returns[5, 6]

This law states that after a certain point, adding more input (e.g., programmers) will not produce a proportional increase in productivity (e.g., modules per hour). A single programmer may produce at a rate of 1 module per hour. With a second programmer, the two may produce at a rate of 1.75 modules per hour (.75 increase). With a third programmer, the group may produce at a rate of 2.25 modules per hour (.5 increase). This disparity may be due to many factors. For example, added coordination is required between programmers.

Working Capital

This term refers to current assets minus current liabilities for an organization. In other words, it is the amount of money the company has available to invest, including investment in projects.

Depreciation[5]

Large assets (e.g., equipment) purchased by a company lose value over time. Accounting standards call this depreciation. Several methods are used to account for depreciation. The exam may ask you what they are. You do not have to perform any calculations. (See, we said we could make this easy for you!) The following information is all you need to know.

There are two forms of depreciation:

1. **Straight Line Depreciation** The same amount of depreciation is taken each year.
   Example: A $1,000 item with a 10-year useful life and no salvage value (how much the item is worth at the end of its life) would be depreciated at $100 per year.

2. **Accelerated Depreciation** For many years, the exam has not asked detailed questions on this topic. Just know the following for the exam:
   - There are two forms of accelerated depreciation. (You do not have to understand what these two forms mean or do any calculations.)
     - Double Declining Balance
     - Sum of the Years Digits
   - Accelerated depreciation depreciates faster than straight line depreciation.
     Example: A $1,000 item with a 10-year useful life and no salvage value (how much the item is worth at the end of its life) would be depreciated at $180 the first year, $150 the second, $130 the next, etc.

The exam may present questions about project selection in the following ways.

- Easier questions may be direct, such as "What type of project selection technique is linear programming?" The answer is "a constrained optimization method." The exam has not required test takers to know what "constrained optimization method" or the other project selection methods mean. Instead, just know what category the methods fall into.
- The exam may also ask more challenging questions relating to business cases and project selection methods. You need to understand that there is a selection process for a project, to know what that process is, and to know that the project must support the company's strategic goals.
- The exam may use project selection concepts like internal rate of return as distracters. Such information may be provided in the question when you do not need the data to answer the question. Read the questions carefully to pick out which data is relevant.

Now that we've discussed the importance of the business case and understanding why the organization selected the project, let's look at other aspects of the Develop Project Charter process.

Constraints and Assumptions PAGES 115-116 AND THROUGHOUT

It is important to identify and document high-level project constraints and assumptions that are uncovered in discussions with stakeholders during project initiating. Constraints are factors that limit the team's options, such as limits on resources, budget, schedule, and scope (e.g., management saying the project must be completed with only five resources). Assumptions are things that are assumed to be true but that may not be true (e.g., it is assumed that we will not need engineering department approval before we start the activity).

Constraints and assumptions are inputs to many project management processes. They are identified at a high level in project initiating and are then refined and documented in detail as part of the Define Scope process in project planning.

Once they are identified, constraints and assumptions need to be managed. The sponsor, the team, and other stakeholders may help identify constraints and assumptions and review them for validity throughout the life of the project. If the constraints change or the assumptions are proven wrong, the project management plan may need to change. Assumptions analysis is part of the risk management process.

Project Statement of Work[7] (SOW) PAGE 75 The project statement of work is created by the customer or sponsor and describes their needs, the product scope, and how the project fits into the strategic plan. If you have worked with contracts, think of this as the long wordy document the buyer sends the seller. This document may not be complete when received as an input to the Develop Project Charter process. It is further defined in the project scope statement during project planning. (See the diagram later in this chapter.)

Charters with Work Under Contract All projects should have charters. When the work is being done for an outside organization, the seller still needs to create a project charter from their own perspective. Therefore, on projects where there are buyers and sellers, both organizations would create project charters that have different points of view. The buyer's reason for the project, as stated in their project charter, might be to achieve a particular product scope while meeting project constraints. The seller's reason for working on the project, as stated in their project charter, might be to increase revenue, enhance their reputation, or gain additional work from the buyer.

TRICKS OF THE TRADE® **Enterprise Environmental Factors** PAGE 14 AND THROUGHOUT Since the beginning of time, project managers have had to deal with and make use of company culture and existing systems. The *PMBOK® Guide* calls these "enterprise environmental factors." They are inputs to Develop Project Charter and many other processes. The trick is to think of them as what they really are—company culture and existing systems that the project will have to deal with or can make use of. They could also be thought of as the company "baggage" that comes with the project. Use this trick to more easily understand the meaning of questions or the choices on the exam, no matter how the term "enterprise environmental factors" is used.

Project Management Information System (PMIS)

An organization's project management information system is part of its enterprise environmental factors. The PMIS includes automated tools, such as scheduling software, a configuration management system, shared workspaces for file storage or distribution, and other such systems.

TRICKS OF THE TRADE® **Organizational Process Assets** PAGE 32 AND THROUGHOUT Since the beginning of time, project managers have also been dealing with existing processes, procedures, and historical information. The *PMBOK® Guide* calls these organizational process assets. They help the project benefit from past company experience. The trick is to think of organizational process assets as what they really are—processes, procedures, and historical information. The following are some examples of organizational process assets.

Processes, Procedures, and Policies

Why reinvent the wheel? Over time, organizations develop processes, procedures, and policies that have proven to be best practices. Such information is a key part of organizational process assets.

Corporate Knowledge Base[8]

When answering questions on the exam, assume the organization has information such as historical records and lessons learned from previous projects and that the company has incorporated those records into an indexed corporate knowledge base available to all. Does your organization do this?

Many project managers do not even have their own historical databases from previous projects, and so they essentially plan, estimate, and schedule each project from scratch. The creation of a corporate knowledge database of historical information and lessons learned is an organizational responsibility that can contribute to continuous improvement. For the exam, assume you have such historical information from all company projects readily accessible.

Historical Information

Historical information (or data) is a record of past projects. It is used to plan and manage future projects, thereby improving the process of project management. Historical information can include:

- Activities
- Lessons learned (described next)
- WBSs
- Benchmarks
- Reports
- Risks
- Estimates
- Resources used
- Project management plans
- Correspondence

Lessons Learned

Project initiating involves looking up past lessons learned for use on the current project. A detailed discussion of lessons learned is included in the Project Management Framework chapter of this book.

Develop Project Management Plan PAGE 78

Process: Develop Project Management Plan
Process Group: Planning
Knowledge Area: Integration Management

Project managers must plan before they act. Let's first look at what management plans are, and then move on to discuss the project management plan.

Management Plans The concept of management plans is very important to understand for the exam. Management plans document the strategy for managing the project and the processes related to the knowledge areas of scope, schedule, cost, quality, human resources, communications, risk, and procurement. Therefore, there is a management plan for each knowledge area. When creating a management plan, you ask yourself, "How will I define, plan, manage, and control scope (or schedule, cost, quality, etc.) for the project?" In other words, you think ahead and document how you will plan the project based on its particular needs, how you will manage the project, and how you will control it. This effort to think through the project in advance should cover all aspects of the project management process. For example, you need to think about how you will identify risks for this project. You also need to think about the people involved in the project and how you will manage those people. Management plans are, of necessity, unique to each project in order to address the project's particular needs.

The format and level of detail of management plans should be customized to fit the needs of the project, the style of the project manager, and the organizational influences. For example, a scope management plan might address such topics as who will be involved in figuring out what the final scope will be, how that effort will happen (meetings, expert opinions, etc.), how to make sure all the scope is completed, and how to measure the work against the plan for scope.

The creation of management plans is an integral part of a project manager's job. If you are not familiar with management plans and have no experience creating them, do not just study this concept. Before you read further, spend some time imagining what management plans for scope, schedule, cost, quality, human resources, communications, risk, and procurement might contain for a large project. Many project managers don't realize how big their knowledge gap is regarding management plans until it finds them on the exam. Don't let this happen to you!

To reiterate, a management plan records how you will define, plan, manage, and control the project. Note the inclusion of "control." While in project planning, the project manager must determine how scope, risk, etc., will be measured to the scope management plan or the risk management plan; how variances will be found; and how changes, including corrective and preventive actions, will be requested, approved, and implemented. Do you do this? If not, make sure you spend some time thinking about management plans.

Here is a trick to understanding the topic of management plans for the exam. Know that management plans look forward in time, and that there are management plans all for the knowledge areas. There are also the following management plans:

- Change management plan
- Configuration management plan
- Requirements management plan
- Process improvement plan

Assume the project manager has created management plans when taking the exam. For example, if a question talks about a problem on a project, the answer might be for the project manager to look at the management plan to see how the plan says to handle such a problem. Or when the work is being done, the project manager might refer to the cost management plan to see how costs are supposed to be measured on the project.

Project Management Plan[9] What do you currently think of as a project management plan or project plan? If you think of such a plan as a schedule, then you need to significantly expand your understanding of this concept.

A project management plan serves an integration function—it integrates all the knowledge area management plans into a cohesive whole. The overall project management plan also includes the baselines for the project. Do you remember the discussion in the Project Management Processes chapter about the iterations in project planning leading to a realistic project management plan? This means a project management plan is a series of plans and baselines (not just a schedule). The project management plan includes:

- **The project management processes that will be used on the project** Think about the science of project management for a moment. Would you want to use everything in the *PMBOK® Guide* for every project? No; a project manager should determine what processes need to be used, based on the needs of the project. This activity is part of developing the project management plan.
- **The knowledge area management plans (scope, schedule, cost, quality, human resources, communications, risk, and procurement)**
- **Scope, schedule, and cost baselines** Baselines are described next.
- **A requirements management plan** This is a plan for how requirements will be managed and controlled on the project. It is described later in this section.
- **A change management plan** This is a plan for managing changes on the project. It is described later in this section.

- **A configuration management plan** This is a plan for managing changes to the deliverables of the project. It is described later in this section.
- **A process improvement plan** This is a plan for how processes to complete the work that are used on the project will be improved. It is described later in this section.

Baselines (Performance Measurement Baseline)[10]

The project management plan includes scope, schedule, and cost baselines, against which the project manager will report project performance. These baselines are created during planning.

- **Scope baseline** The project scope statement, work breakdown structure (WBS), and WBS dictionary
- **Schedule baseline** The agreed-upon schedule, including the start and stop dates
- **Cost baseline** The time-phased cost budget (i.e., the spending plan indicating how much money is available for the project and when the funds are available)

Together these baselines are called the **performance measurement baseline**.

What do baselines mean for the project manager and team? The project manager must be able to clearly, completely, and realistically define the scope, schedule, and cost budget to derive the baselines. That is not all, however. The project performance, and the performance of the project manager, will be measured against the baselines. The project manager will look for deviations from the baselines while the work is being done. If a deviation is discovered, he or she needs to assess whether adjustments can be made to the project to deal with the problem. If adjustments will not correct the deviation, a formal change request to the baselines might be necessary. A substantial part of project control is making sure the baselines are achieved, which in turn helps ensure the sponsor and the organization get the complete benefits of the project they chartered. Therefore, as a project manager, not only is your ability to plan a project important, but your ability to control the project and to get the project completed as planned is also very important.

Baselines can be changed, but it should not be an easy thing to do. Changes to the baselines can be formally requested during project executing and monitoring and controlling. These requests are evaluated and approved in the Perform Integrated Change Control process. Baseline changes are so serious that the evolution of the baselines should be documented to show why and when changes were made.

TRICKS OF THE TRADE® The exam tests you at an expert level. So how would you like to get a sophisticated question right without studying? You need to understand the following: deviations from baselines are often due to incomplete risk identification and risk management. Therefore, if the exam asks what to do when a project deviates significantly from established baselines, the correct answer is likely the one about reviewing the project's risk management process. Many project managers do not understand that such an effort should be done. Does it make sense to you now that we've pointed it out?

Baselines are mentioned frequently on the exam. Make sure you understand the concepts described here and have the right attitude about them.

Requirements Management Plan

Part of the scope management process (which we will describe in the next chapter) involves analyzing stakeholders' needs, wants, expectations, and assumptions to determine the requirements for the project. A requirements management plan describes how this effort will be done to identify, analyze, and document the requirements, as well as how the requirements will be managed and controlled throughout the project.

Change Management Plan

Controlling a project to the baselines and the rest of the project management plan is so important that the project manager needs to think in advance about where there might be changes and what to do to limit the negative effects of changes. Are you this focused on change management on your real-world projects? Regardless of whether you work on small or large projects, your role is not to just facilitate the making of changes by others. Instead, you need to stand as a barrier to prevent unnecessary changes and to plan the project in a way that minimizes the need for changes. Changes are much more costly than if the work was included from the beginning. Changes should not be undertaken lightly.

The change management plan describes how changes will be managed and controlled and may include:

- Change control procedures (how and who)
- The approval levels for authorizing changes
- The creation of a change control board to approve changes (described later in this chapter)
- A plan outlining how changes will be managed and controlled
- Who should attend meetings regarding changes
- The organizational tools to use to track and control changes

Change Control System

Many organizations have a change control system as part of their project management information system (PMIS). This system includes standardized forms, reports, processes, procedures, and software to track and control changes. It is part of an organization's enterprise environmental factors.

Configuration Management Plan

With all the product and project documentation that is part of managing a project and all the changes to this documentation that will occur throughout the life of the project, wouldn't it be wise to have a plan for making sure everyone knows what version of the scope, schedule, and other components of the project management plan are the latest version? This is the purpose of the configuration management plan. It defines how you will manage changes to the deliverables and the resulting documentation, including which organizational tools you will use in this effort (part of the configuration management system).

Configuration Management System[11]

Like the change control system, the configuration management system is part of the project management information system (PMIS). It contains the organization's standardized configuration management tools, processes, and procedures that can be used to track and control the evolution of the project documentation.

Process Improvement Plan

As part of planning, you need to identify existing processes to use on the project and may create some processes of your own. You also need to plan in efforts to improve these processes during the project. The focus on improvement is important because good processes help the team complete work faster, cheaper, and with higher quality. Imagine that a project includes installing software on hundreds of computers. Because there is a lot of repetitive work on the project, the project manager should find or create a process for doing the work. After a few installations are completed, and then again after more installations are completed, the project manager should look for ways to improve the process. This effort will help the team complete higher quality work more efficiently and at a lower cost.

The project management plan, including the individual management plans and the scope, schedule, and cost baselines, is created by completing the activities described in the planning column of Rita's Process Chart. Once the project management plan is complete, the sponsor or key stakeholders review and approve it. The Develop Project Management Plan process must result in a project management plan that is bought into, approved, realistic, and formal. In other words, the project management plan needs to be agreed to by those involved in the project, it needs to be formally approved, everyone needs to believe the project can be done according to plan, and it needs to remain a formal document that is controlled and used throughout the project. If this is a new concept to you, make sure you spend time thinking about how to accomplish this in the real world.

Let's see how everything connects so far by looking at the following diagram.

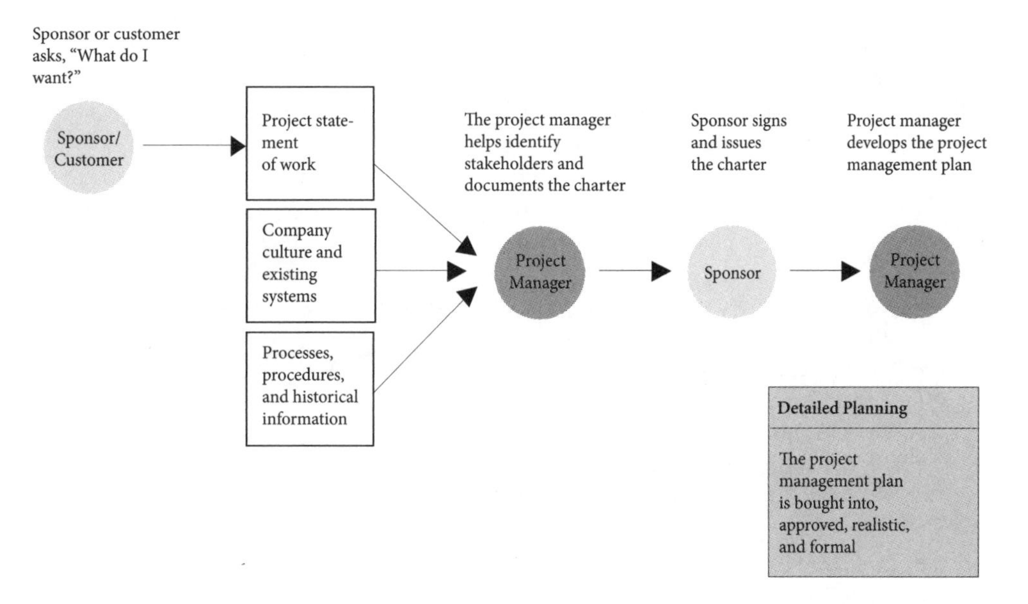

Once completed, the project manager uses the project management plan as a tool to help manage the project on a daily basis. It is not just a document created for the sponsor or other key stakeholders. Though it may evolve and even change over the life of the project, the project management plan is designed to be as complete as possible when project executing begins.

Exercise Test yourself! Make a list of the specific ACTIONS required to create a project management plan that is bought into, approved, realistic, and formal.

Answer Some of the possible answers to this exercise include:

- Determine a methodology for creating the project management plan.
- Agree on reporting formats and communications plans.
- Agree on processes to report, control, and incorporate changes.
- Analyze the stakeholders' needs, wants, expectations, and assumptions.
- Capture the project requirements as completely as possible.
- Analyze the skills and knowledge of all the stakeholders, and determine how you will use them on the project.
- Meet with stakeholders to define their roles on the project.
- Meet with resource managers to get the best resources possible.
- Give team members a chance to approve the final schedule that converts the team's activity estimates into a calendar schedule.
- Get resource managers to approve the schedule and when their resources will be used.
- Work through iterations of the plan (e.g., update the work breakdown structure after you complete risk analysis).
- Create the necessary project documents.
- Apply risk reserves to the project schedule and budget.
- Look for impacts on your project from other projects.
- Hold meetings or presentations to let the sponsor know if any of the project requirements or constraints that were outlined in the project charter cannot be met.
- Perform schedule compression (i.e., crash, fast track) and present options to the sponsor.

If you included most of the answers in the previous list, you are in good shape. But why is it so important to have a project management plan that is realistic, and that everyone believes can be done? Because later in the project management process, you will need to constantly measure progress against the project management plan to see how the project is going. The end date, end cost, and other constraints in the project MUST be met. There is no excuse. You use the project management plan (including the scope, schedule, and cost baselines contained in the plan) as a measurement tool to make sure the project meets these constraints.

So, when you think of the project management plan, think of all the meetings, sign-offs, interactions with other projects, negotiations, schedule compressions, juggling, begging, crying, etc., that will be required to bring the plan to the point of being bought into, approved, realistic, and formal.

Project Documents PAGE 350 There is a lot of information that needs to be captured on a project, and not all of that information is recorded in the project management plan. "Project documents" is the term the *PMBOK® Guide* uses to refer to any project-related documents that are not part of the project management plan. They include the project charter, statement of work, contracts, the stakeholder register, requirements documentation, the activity list, quality metrics, the risk register, the issue log, the change log, and other such documentation (see page 350 in the *PMBOK® Guide* for a complete list). While the sponsor or key stakeholders will see and approve the project management plan, most project documents are created by the project manager for his or her own needs and typically are not shown to the sponsor, except for the charter, contracts, and statement of work.

Due to the iterative nature of planning, updates to project documents are frequently needed. For the exam, know that project document updates are an output of many of the project management processes, though this book will not cover it each time.

Project Management Plan Approval Since the project management plan is a formal document that defines how the project will be managed, executed, and controlled and includes items like the project completion date, milestones, costs, etc., it typically requires formal approval by management, the sponsor, the project team, and other key stakeholders. Formal approval means sign-off (signatures). If the project manager has identified all the stakeholders and their requirements and objectives, included the resulting project and product scope in the plan, and dealt with conflicting priorities in advance, getting the project management plan approved will be less difficult.

Kickoff Meeting Before the Develop Project Management Plan process can really be completed and project executing can begin, a kickoff meeting should be held. This is a meeting of the key parties involved in the project (e.g., customers, sellers, the project team, senior management, functional management, the sponsor). The purpose of this meeting is to announce the start of the project and to ensure everyone is familiar with its details and with the people working on it. In other words, the meeting is held to make sure everyone is on the same page. In addition to introducing those involved in the project, the meeting may review such items as project milestones, project risks, the communications management plan, and the meetings schedule.

Direct and Manage Project Execution PAGE 83

Process: Direct & Manage Project Execution
Process Group: Executing
Knowledge Area: Integration Management

This process represents the integration part of project executing.
In Direct and Manage Project Execution, the project manager integrates all the executing work into one coordinated effort to accomplish the project management plan and produce the deliverables. In addition to completing the activities and deliverables in the project management plan, Direct and Manage Project Execution involves requesting changes and completing the work necessitated by approved change requests.

Please note the confusing terms. If the exam talks about directing and managing project execution, it may NOT be talking about the entire executing process group. Instead, it may just be referring to the integration piece of executing.

The *PMBOK® Guide* does not say much about the Direct and Manage Project Execution process, but this and the Monitor and Control Project Work process make up the majority of the project work. Make sure you remember that the Direct and Manage Project Execution process involves managing people, doing the work, improving the processes involved in the work, and implementing approved changes. It is about being of service to the team to help them get the work completed, and ensuring a common understanding of the project among stakeholders to keep everyone focused and informed. In other words, the project manager needs to do things like facilitate technical discussions, make sure the stakeholders whose scope was not included in the project understand they will not receive that scope, keep the team and functional managers informed of the next month's schedule, increase efficiency by following the process improvement plan, and inform other departments within the organization how the project may affect their work.

Take a moment to remember what is in the executing column of Rita's Process Chart, and think about what has to be integrated into a cohesive whole through this process.

There is another piece of the Direct and Manage Project Execution process that you need to be aware of for the exam. PMI assumes that when executing the project, the project manager takes time to focus on managing the schedule, managing the budget, managing risks, managing quality, and managing all the other knowledge areas. This way of thinking about project executing is not an approach that many project managers take. We just manage the project as a whole, rather than giving individual attention to each knowledge area. This can also mean we do not take the time to properly look at how issues relating to one knowledge area affect other knowledge areas (e.g., scope management issues can affect quality and human resource management). Inevitably we forget to even think about some of the knowledge areas. Integration management requires project managers to keep all the knowledge areas in mind at all times.

The work of Direct and Manage Project Execution can be illustrated as follows:

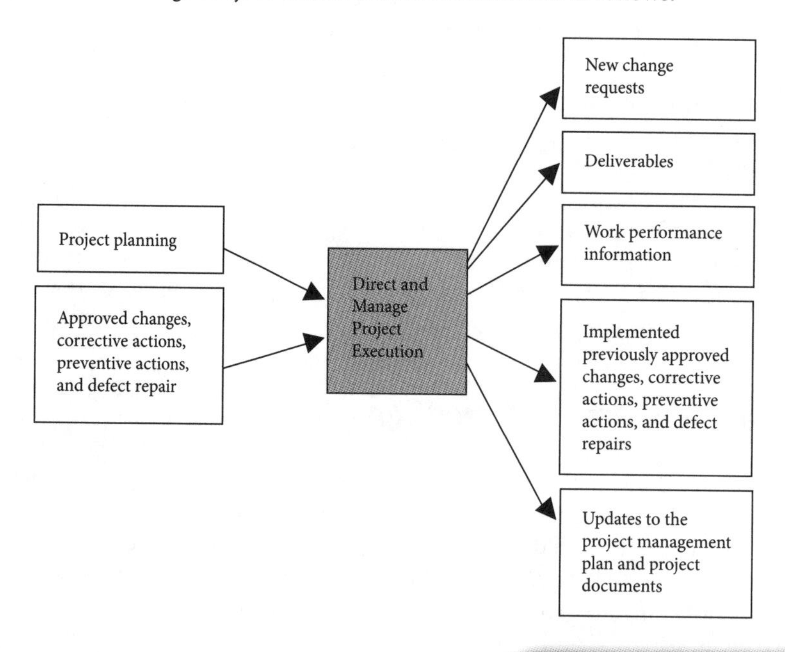

Monitor and Control Project Work PAGE 89

Process: Monitor & Control Project Work
Process Group: Monitoring & Controlling
Knowledge Area: Integration Management

Monitoring and controlling project work involves looking at what is actually happening on the project and comparing that performance to what was planned. It is a control function that is done from project initiating through project closing. When you think of a large project, it makes sense that the project manager would need a formal effort to monitor and control how the processes are going, because he or she would not be personally involved in performing the project work. The results of Monitor and Control Project Work are change requests (including recommended corrective and preventive actions and defect repairs), as well as updates to the project management plan and project documents. The change requests from this and other processes are evaluated and approved or rejected in the Perform Integrated Change Control process, described later in this chapter.

Please note the confusing terms. If the exam talks about monitoring and controlling project work, it may NOT be talking about the entire monitoring and controlling process group. Instead, it may just be referring to the integration process.

Remember that monitoring and controlling means measuring against the project management plan.

As you already know, scope may be completed on a project but the quality may not be acceptable, or the schedule might be met but at excessive costs. Monitor and Control Project Work is an integration function because the project manager must balance the demands of the different knowledge areas to control the project. This process also involves monitoring any other performance measures that the project manager has created for the project.

Keep in mind that a project must be controlled. This effort all too often does not happen in the real world. Many project managers do not control their projects to the project management plan. If the exam asks what you should do if a work activity on the project takes longer than estimated, the answer is to take corrective action (discussed later in this section) to make up for the delay. Such action keeps the project on or close to schedule and allows the project manager to feel comfortable that the scope will be completed according to the budget and schedule agreed to. This knowledge is the value of controlling the project. What do you do in your real world?

The integration function of monitoring and controlling project work also includes activities like analyzing and tracking risks, performing quality control activities, forecasting, and reviewing changes and corrective actions made on the project to see if they were effective. The following concepts are important to the process of Monitor and Control Project Work.

Work Authorization System[12] This is the project manager's system for authorizing the start of work packages or activities. It is part of the project management information system, which in turn is part of the enterprise environmental factors that are an input to this process.

If you have never used such a system, imagine a large construction project with hundreds of people working on the project. Can you have a plumber and an electrician show up to work in one small area at the same time? No. Remember that a project is planned to the level of detail needed for that particular project. There might be instances where the project manager needs to manage to a more detailed level, however, as in the case of the plumber and the electrician. To handle these types of situations, a work authorization system is put in place to make sure work is only started when a formal authorization is given. In many cases, this tool for authorizing work is a company-wide system used on the project, not created just for the project. There will likely only be one question about this on the exam, but the term may be included frequently as a choice.

Change Requests PAGE 92 No matter how well you plan a project, there will always be changes. Some changes are additions to the project or even changes to the policies and procedures used on the project. Other changes are identified as you manage the execution of the project or as part of monitoring and controlling when you measure project performance against the performance measurement baseline. See the Perform Integrated Change Control section for more about changes.

Corrective Action PAGE 92 A corrective action is any action taken to bring expected future project performance in line with the project management plan. Stop! Do not read on until you read the last sentence again. Most project managers do not have a realistic performance measurement baseline to measure against, so they cannot determine where corrective action is needed on the project. Those who have serious problems with this in their real world have problems on the exam. What do you do now on your project? Do you have predetermined areas to measure and have you identified an acceptable range in which the measurements can fall (control limits) to determine if the project is on schedule and on budget?

You cannot simply jump in and start implementing corrective actions. Instead, you need to:

- Have a purposeful focus rather than a random focus in identifying areas that need corrective action.
- Look for problems rather than just wait for them to be brought to your attention.
- Create metrics during project planning that cover all aspects of the project.
- Have a realistic project management plan to measure against.
- Continue to measure throughout the project.
- Know when the project is off track, and know when to recommend corrective action.
- Find the root cause of the deviation rather than the surface cause.

- Measure project performance after a corrective action is implemented to evaluate the effectiveness of the corrective action.
- Determine whether there is a need to recommend further corrective action.

Any corrective actions that would change the project management plan, baselines, policies or procedures, charter, contract, or statement of work require a formal change request, to be reviewed and approved or rejected as part of the Perform Integrated Change Control process.

As you can see, a significant portion of the project manager's time while the work is being done is spent measuring performance (to determine the need for corrective action) and implementing corrective actions. Therefore, you can expect many questions about this topic on the exam. Do not expect all of these questions to use the words "corrective action," however. Some questions may just describe a situation and ask you, "What is the BEST thing to do?" In order to answer those questions, you need to know when to look for corrective actions. Try the next exercise to see if you understand when you might identify the need for such actions.

Exercise

When in the Project Management Process Would You Identify the Need to Recommend Corrective Actions?

Answer There are two approaches to take in answering this question. A general answer to this question would say that recommended corrective actions are determined during (are outputs of) the following processes. (Notice that corrective actions can be recommended in executing and monitoring and controlling processes.)

- Direct and Manage Project Execution (Integration Management chapter)
- Monitor and Control Project Work (Integration Management chapter)
- Verify Scope (Scope Management chapter)
- Control Scope (Scope Management chapter)
- Control Schedule (Time Management chapter)
- Control Costs (Cost Management chapter)
- Perform Quality Assurance (Quality Management chapter)
- Perform Quality Control (Quality Management chapter)
- Manage Project Team (Human Resource Management chapter)
- Manage Stakeholder Expectations (Communications Management chapter)
- Report Performance (Communications Management chapter)
- Monitor and Control Risks (Risk Management chapter)
- Administer Procurements (Procurement Management chapter)

A more specific way to answer the question would be to think about particular situations that may arise on a project. Some of the possible answers are listed below.

When	*PMBOK® Guide* Title
When meeting with the customer to obtain acceptance of interim deliverables	Verify Scope
When measuring project performance against the performance measurement baseline	Control Scope, Control Schedule, Control Costs
When making sure people are using the correct processes	Perform Quality Assurance
When creating performance reports	Report Performance
When working with the project team	Manage Project Team
When you notice that there are many unidentified risks occurring	Monitor and Control Risks
When you discover that the seller's performance is not meeting expectations	Administer Procurements
When you discover that a team member is not performing	Manage Project Team
When making sure deliverables meet quality standards	Perform Quality Control
When communicating with stakeholders to resolve issues and manage their perceptions about the project	Manage Stakeholder Expectations

Because this topic is so important, here is a trick. If you are a member of PMI and have access to an electronic version of the *PMBOK® Guide*, search for the term "corrective action." Seeing how it is used will improve your understanding of the topic.

Preventive Action PAGE 92 AND THROUGHOUT Whereas taking corrective action involves dealing with actual deviations from the performance measurement baseline, taking preventive action means dealing with anticipated or possible deviations from the performance measurement baseline. The process for taking preventive actions is not as clear as it is for taking corrective actions. Knowing when preventive action is needed requires more experience than calculation. Examples of preventive actions include:

- Adjusting the project to prevent the same problem from occurring again later in the project.
- Changing a resource because the resource's last activity nearly failed to meet its acceptance criteria.
- Arranging for team members to gain training in a certain area because there is no one with the necessary skills to back up a team member who may unexpectedly get sick.

Any preventive actions that would change the project management plan, baselines, policies or procedures, charter, contract, or statement of work require a formal change request, to be reviewed and approved or rejected as part of the Perform Integrated Change Control process.

You will see preventive action mentioned throughout the *PMBOK® Guide*. Preventive action can be implemented at any time for any project management process, but recommended preventive actions are specifically mentioned in the *PMBOK® Guide* as being an output of the following processes:

- Direct and Manage Project Execution (Integration Management chapter)
- Monitor and Control Project Work (Integration Management chapter)
- Control Scope (Scope Management chapter)
- Control Schedule (Time Management chapter)
- Control Costs (Cost Management chapter)
- Perform Quality Assurance (Quality Management chapter)
- Perform Quality Control (Quality Management chapter)
- Manage Project Team (Human Resource Management chapter)
- Manage Stakeholder Expectations (Communications Management chapter)
- Report Performance (Communications Management chapter)
- Monitor and Control Risks (Risk Management chapter)

Defect Repair PAGE 92 AND THROUGHOUT Defect repair is another way of saying "rework." Defect repair may be requested when a component of the project does not meet specifications. As with corrective and preventive actions, any defect repairs that would change the project management plan, baselines, policies or procedures, charter, contract, or statement of work require a formal change request, to be reviewed and approved or rejected as part of the Perform Integrated Change Control process.

The need for defect repairs is discovered during (or, defect repairs are outputs of) the following processes.

- Direct and Manage Project Execution (Integration Management chapter)
- Monitor and Control Project Work (Integration Management chapter)
- Verify Scope (Scope Management chapter)
- Control Scope (Scope Management chapter)
- Perform Quality Assurance (Quality Management chapter)
- Perform Quality Control (Quality Management chapter)

Perform Integrated Change Control[13] PAGE 93

Process: Perform Integrated Change Control
Process Group: Monitoring & Controlling
Knowledge Area: Integration Management

During project executing and monitoring and controlling, changes to any part of the project may be requested. Keep in mind that just because a change is requested, however, it does not mean the change has to be—or even should be—implemented. Changes are evaluated and accepted or rejected in the Perform Integrated Change Control process. A key focus of integrated change control is to look at the impact of each change on all of the project constraints. For example, any scope change needs to be assessed for its impact on quality, risk, time, cost, resources, and customer satisfaction.

Integrated change control can be a difficult topic on the exam for people who do not work on projects that have formal change procedures. It can also be difficult for project managers who simply estimate the cost of a change and stop there, rather than looking for the impacts of a change on the other parts of the project. You can check your understanding of this topic with the following example:

> *A stakeholder wants to add scope to the project. You estimate that the change will add two weeks to the project duration. What do you do next?*

Do not simply read on; try to answer the question. Understanding the Perform Integrated Change Control process is very important. There can be up to 20 questions on this topic on the exam.

So what is your answer? Is it to look for ways to save time so the change can be accommodated? Or should you get the change approved? How about asking for an extension of time to accommodate the change?

None of the previous choices are the correct answer. Instead, the NEXT thing to do would be to see how the proposed change impacts the project cost, quality, risks, resources, and possibly customer satisfaction. Whenever the exam mentions changes, keep in mind that a change to one of the project constraints should be evaluated for impacts on all of the other constraints.

In order to evaluate the impacts of a change, it is necessary to have:

- A realistic project management plan to measure against
- A complete product scope and project scope (see the definitions in the Scope Management chapter)

Are changes bad? This can be a controversial question in many industries. Changes can have negative effects. In fact, changes can be very expensive and disrupt the project. Some studies show that changes made late in the project can be up to 100 times more expensive than if they were made early in the project. The function of each process within the monitoring and controlling process group is to control changes. If there are a lot of changes on a project, it can become impossible for a project manager to coordinate the work, because it is constantly shifting. Team members who are trying to complete work packages are frequently pulled off that work to help create or evaluate changes.

Change is inevitable on projects, but a project manager should work to prevent the root cause of changes whenever possible. And in many cases, the root cause is that the project manager did not properly plan the project. The need for changes may indicate that the project manager did not fully identify stakeholders and uncover their requirements or that he or she did not properly complete other project management actions. Although changes can happen, they are not encouraged, and the handling of possible changes must be planned, managed, and controlled.

To control changes on the project, the project manager should make sure to:

- Work to obtain final requirements as soon as possible.
- Spend enough time on risk management to comprehensively identify the project's risks.
- Establish time and cost reserves (see the discussion of reserve analysis in the Time, Cost, and Risk Management chapters).
- Have a process in place to control changes.
- Follow the process to control changes.
- Have a process and templates in place for creating change requests.
- Have clear roles and responsibilities for approving changes.
- Reevaluate the business case (in the project charter) if the number of changes becomes excessive.
- Consider terminating a project that has excessive changes and starting a new project with a more complete set of requirements.
- Allow only approved changes to be added to the project baselines.

Changes can be grouped into two broad categories—those that affect the project management plan, baselines, policies and procedures, charter, contract, or statement of work and those that do not.

The *PMBOK® Guide* can be confusing in how it describes changes, so let's clarify the issue. It is expected that companies have established procedures for managing and controlling changes, including authority levels for approving changes. The project manager must follow these procedures; the *PMBOK® Guide* does not attempt to supersede them.

Change Control Board[14] PAGE 98 Why should the project manager always have to be the one to deny a change request? He or she might not even have the knowledge or expertise to analyze a change request. Depending on the project manager's level of authority, his or her role might be to facilitate decisions about some changes, rather than actually make the decisions. For these reasons, many projects have change control boards. The board is responsible for reviewing and analyzing change requests. It then approves or rejects the changes. The board may include the project manager, the customer, experts, the sponsor, functional managers, and others. For the exam, assume that all projects have change control boards.

Process for Making Changes The exam has many situational questions that deal with how to make changes. For example:

A functional manager wants to make a change to the project. What is the first thing a project manager should do?

Or, someone wants to make a change to the project scope. What is the best thing to do first?

The answers are the same in either case. A trick for answering questions that ask about the process for making changes is to know that, on a high-level basis, the project manager should follow these steps:

1. **Evaluate the impact** Evaluate (assess) the impact of the change to the project (e.g., this change will add three weeks to the project length, require $20,000 additional funding, and have no effect on resources).
2. **Create options** This can include cutting other activities, compressing the schedule by crashing or fast tracking, or looking at other options. For example, you may be able to decrease the potential effect of the change on the project by spending more time decreasing project risk, or by adding another resource to the project team.
3. **Get the change request approved internally**
4. **Get customer buy-in** (if required)

The process of handling changes is often tested on the exam. Note in the previous steps that changes are always evaluated first. In most cases, "evaluate" involves considering all of the project constraints. "Options" are created based on crashing, fast tracking, reestimating, and playing "what if" using project management software. (See the Time Management chapter for questions about crashing, fast tracking, and reestimating.)

Do you remember the following question from earlier in the chapter? It is an example of the type of question you may see on the exam.

A stakeholder wants to add scope to the project. You estimate that the change will add two weeks to the project duration. What do you do next?

Now notice how the following question is different.

A change in scope has been determined to have no effect on the project constraints. What is the BEST thing to do?

Be careful when reading these questions. Expect the right answer to "What is the best thing to do?" about a change to depend on how the question is written and the situation involved. Sometimes evaluation has been done, so the best thing to do is to look for options. Sometimes evaluation AND looking for options have been done and the best thing to do is to meet with the sponsor or change control board. In the second question, evaluation has been done. The answer would be to look for options and then meet with the sponsor or change control board to discuss the change and its lack of impact to the project constraints. After informing the sponsor or change control board, the project manager may inform the customer according to the process defined in the communications management plan.

Detailed Process for Making Changes

Now that you know the high-level process, let's look at a more detailed process for making changes.

1. **Prevent the root cause of changes** The project manager should not just focus on managing changes, but proactively eliminate the need for changes.
2. **Identify change** Changes can come from the project manager, as a result of measuring against the performance measurement baseline, or from the sponsor, the team, management, the customer, or other stakeholders. The project manager should actively be looking for changes from all these sources, because discovering a change early will decrease the impact of the change.
3. **Look at the impact of the change** If it is a scope change, how will it affect the rest of the scope of the project? If it is a time change, how will it affect the rest of the schedule for the project?
4. **Create a change request** Changes can be made to the product scope, any part of the project management plan, the contract, charter, statement of work, policies and procedures, or even the performance measurement baseline. The process of making a change should follow the change management plan.
5. **Perform integrated change control** How will the change affect all the other project constraints?
   a. **Assess the change** Does the change fall within the project charter? If not, it should not be a change to your project; it may be an entirely different project. Wait! Did you catch that? Many project managers have never really thought about this. Is the change beneficial to the project? Is it needed? If the answer to any of these questions is no, the change should not be approved. However, any change that already had a reserve created for it (a previously identified risk event) should be handled as part of risk management (see the Risk Management chapter), rather than through the change management process.
   b. **Look for options** Options include actions to decrease threats further, increase opportunities, compress the schedule through crashing or fast tracking, change how the work is performed, adjust quality, or cut scope so that the effect of the change will be minimized. Be careful—it is not wise to decrease the impact of every change. In doing so, the project manager could decrease the overall probability of success on the project. Sometimes an additional two weeks' worth of scope added to the project should receive a two-week extension of time to the project, if the work occurs on the critical path. (See the Time Management chapter for a discussion of the critical path.)
   c. **The change is approved or rejected** If a change does not affect the project management plan, baselines, company policies and procedures, the charter, the contract, or the statement of work, the company's change management policies may allow the project manager to approve the change. If the change does affect these key documents, the change typically needs to go to a change control board. Project documents may be updated as a result of approved changes. The approved changes are then implemented in the Direct and Manage Project Execution process.
   d. **Update the status of the change in the change control system** This helps everyone know the status of the change. If a change is not approved, the reasons it was rejected should also be documented.
6. **Adjust the project management plan, project documents, and baselines** Approved changes need to be incorporated into the project baselines. The changes could affect other parts of the project management plan or project documents or affect the way the project manager will manage the project, and the project documentation must be updated to reflect the changes. For example, if there is a change in scope, the scope baseline (the WBS, WBS dictionary, and project scope statement), the project management plan, and the requirements traceability matrix should be updated. If that change in scope affects other areas of the project, the associated documentation (e.g., the activity list, human resource plan and other resource documentation, schedule, budget, risk register, etc.) also needs to be updated.
7. **Manage stakeholders' expectations by communicating the change to stakeholders affected by the change** How often do you remember to do this? This could be thought of as

configuration management (version control to make sure everyone is working off the same project documentation).

8. **Manage the project to the revised project management plan and project documents**

Exercise Test yourself! Describe common changes on projects, and determine what you would do to handle each. An example is provided. Because of the wide variety of possible changes, this exercise does not have an "answer," but it will help you prepare for questions related to change on the exam.

Common Change	How to Handle It
Customer wants to add scope	Make sure you know what the specific scope is and why it is necessary. Make sure all the data needed in the change request is filled out. Assess the change, including whether reserves were allocated on the project to accommodate the addition of the scope. Look at the impact of the change. Look for options. Have the change reviewed by the change control board if necessary.

Common Change	How to Handle It

Close Project or Phase PAGE 99

Process: Close Project or Phase
Process Group: Closing
Knowledge Area: Integration Management

(See also the Project Management Processes chapter of this book for a discussion of the closing process group.)

Many of the high-level concepts of closing have already been discussed in the Project Management Processes chapter. In terms of the Close Project or Phase process, you need to understand that this effort finalizes all activities across all process groups to formally close out the project or project phase.

Is your project really done when the technical work is done? Not if you don't close it out! The Close Project or Phase process is one part of project closing. The other part is the Close Procurements process, described in the Procurement Management chapter. Together, these two processes are addressed in about 14 questions on the exam.

TRICKS OF THE TRADE® Watch out; people with limited project management training and experience have difficulty with this section on the exam. Many do not seem to understand the significance of closure and what it does for both the project manager and the project. A project manager must get formal acceptance of the project, issue a final report that shows the project has been successful, issue the final lessons learned, and index and archive all the project records. Do you understand the importance of the items included in Rita's Process Chart? Make sure you become familiar with all the concepts here and imagine completing these activities in the real world on large projects if you do not currently do this for your projects.

Be sure to remember for the exam that "You always close out a project, no matter the circumstances under which it stops, is terminated, or is completed!"

There are financial, legal, and administrative efforts involved in closing. Let's look again at the activities presented in Rita's Process Chart. (This list includes efforts in both the Close Project or Phase and Close Procurements processes.)

- Confirm work is done to requirements
- Complete procurement closure
- Gain final acceptance of the product
- Complete financial closure
- Hand off completed product
- Solicit feedback from the customer about the project
- Complete final performance reporting
- Index and archive records
- Update lessons learned knowledge base

Note that the Close Project or Phase process involves getting the final formal acceptance of the project or phase as a whole from the customer, whereas the Verify Scope process in scope management (a monitoring and controlling process) involves getting formal acceptance from the customer for many interim deliverables. The project needs both processes.

Does it make sense to you that the Close Project or Phase process is an integration management function? If not, think of the example of final performance reporting. Can you see how you would have to report on all knowledge areas? How about the example of indexing and archiving project records? Wouldn't you need to do so for records from all the knowledge areas? Take some time to think about project closing and how it applies to proper project management for large projects before you take the exam.

Practice Exam

1. Effective project integration usually requires an emphasis on:
   A. The personal careers of the team members.
   B. Timely updates to the project management plan.
   C. Effective communication at key interface points.
   D. Product control.

2. The need for ____ is one of the major driving forces for communication in a project.
   A. Optimization
   B. Integrity
   C. Integration
   D. Differentiation

3. Which of the following describes the BEST use of historical records from previous projects?
   A. Estimating, life cycle costing, and project planning
   B. Risk management, estimating, and creating lessons learned
   C. Project planning, estimating, and creating a status report
   D. Estimating, risk management, and project planning

4. When it comes to changes, the project manager's attention is BEST focused on:
   A. Making changes.
   B. Tracking and recording changes.
   C. Informing the sponsor of changes.
   D. Preventing unnecessary changes.

5. A project manager has managed four projects for the company and is being considered to join the project management office team. The following is discovered during the evaluation of his performance. The project manager's first project had an ending cost variance of -500, used two critical resources, needed to rework the project charter during project executing, and was ranked 14th in priority within the company. The second project finished with a schedule variance of +100, was completed with a vastly compressed schedule, and received a letter of recommendation from the sponsor, but the product of the project was not used. The third project had 23 percent more changes than expected, had an SPI of 0.90, and 25 open items in the issue log when the project was completed.

   Each of these projects had a cost budget of $10,000 and 20 to 28 percent more changes than others of its size. The project management office decided not to add this project manager to the team. Which of the following BEST describes why this might have happened?
   A. The project manager has only managed low-priority projects, and he had to compress the schedule, showing that he does not have the skill to work in the project management office.
   B. Issue logs should not be used on projects of this size, showing that the project manager does not have the knowledge to work in the project management office.
   C. The project manager did not effectively involve the stakeholders, showing that he does not have the knowledge to work in the project management office.
   D. The project manager had two critical resources on his team and still needed to rework the project charter, showing that he does not have the discipline to work in the project management office.

6. All of the following are parts of an effective change management plan EXCEPT:
   A. Procedures.
   B. Standards for reports.
   C. Meetings.
   D. Lessons learned.

7. A work authorization system can be used to:
   A. Manage who does each activity.
   B. Manage when and in what sequence work is done.
   C. Manage when each activity is done.
   D. Manage who does each activity and when it is done.

8. A project is plagued by changes to the project charter. Who has the primary responsibility to decide if these changes are necessary?
   A. The project manager
   B. The project team
   C. The sponsor
   D. The stakeholders

9. Integration is done by the:
   A. Project manager.
   B. Team.
   C. Sponsor.
   D. Stakeholders.

10. Which of the following BEST describes the project manager's role as an integrator?
    A. Help team members become familiar with the project.
    B. Put all the pieces of a project into a cohesive whole.
    C. Put all the pieces of a project into a program.
    D. Get all team members together into a cohesive whole.

11. Approved corrective actions are an input to which of the following processes?
    A. Verify Scope
    B. Direct and Manage Project Execution
    C. Develop Project Charter
    D. Develop Schedule

12. Double declining balance is a form of:
    A. Decelerated depreciation.
    B. Straight line depreciation.
    C. Accelerated depreciation.
    D. Life cycle costing.

13. You are a new project manager who has never managed a project before. You have been asked to plan a new project. It would be BEST in this situation to rely on ______ during planning in order to improve your chance of success.
    A. Your intuition and training
    B. Stakeholder analysis
    C. Historical information
    D. Configuration management

14. Which of the following BEST describes a project management plan?
    A. A printout from project management software
    B. A bar chart
    C. Risk, staffing, process improvement, and other management plans
    D. The project scope

15. Which of the following is TRUE about the development of a project charter?
    A. The sponsor creates the project charter, and the project manager approves it.
    B. The project team creates the project charter, and the PMO approves it.
    C. The executive manager creates the project charter, and the functional manager approves it.
    D. The project manager creates the project charter, and the sponsor approves it.

16. A project management plan should be realistic in order to be used to manage the project. Which of the following is the BEST method to achieve a realistic project management plan?
    A. The sponsor creates the project management plan based on input from the project manager.
    B. The functional manager creates the project management plan based on input from the project manager.
    C. The project manager creates the project management plan based on input from senior management.
    D. The project manager creates the project management plan based on input from the team.

17. You are taking over a project during project planning and discover that six individuals have signed the project charter. Which of the following should MOST concern you?
    A. Who will be a member of the change control board
    B. Spending more time on configuration management
    C. Getting a single project sponsor
    D. Determining the reporting structure

18. The project charter for a project was approved for planning and you have just been assigned as project manager. Realizing that project planning is an ongoing effort throughout the project, which processes are you MOST likely to combine?
    A. Create WBS and Define Activities
    B. Estimate Activity Durations and Develop Schedule
    C. Develop Human Resource Plan and Estimate Costs
    D. Estimate Costs and Determine Budget

19. All of the following are parts of the Direct and Manage Project Execution process EXCEPT:
    A. Identifying changes.
    B. Using a work breakdown structure.
    C. Implementing corrective actions.
    D. Setting up a project control system.

20. A project manager is appointed to head a highly technical project in an area with which this person has limited familiarity. The project manager delegates the processes of Develop Schedule, Estimate Costs, Define Activities, and Estimate Activity Resources to various project team members, and basically serves as an occasional referee and coordinator of activities. The results of this approach are likely to be:
    A. A team functioning throughout the project at a very high level, demonstrating creativity and commitment.
    B. A team that initially experiences some amounts of confusion, but that after a period of time becomes a cohesive and effective unit.
    C. A team that is not highly productive, but that stays together because of the work environment created by the project manager.
    D. A team that is characterized by poor performance, low morale, high levels of conflict, and high turnover.

21. You are in the middle of executing a major modification to an existing product when you learn that the resources promised at the beginning of the project are not available. The BEST thing to do is to:
    A. Show how the resources were originally promised to your project.
    B. Replan the project without the resources.
    C. Explain the impact if the promised resources are not made available.
    D. Crash the project.

22. You have been assigned to manage the development of an organization's first Web site. The site will be highly complex and interactive, and neither your project team nor the client has much experience with Web site development.

    The timeline is extremely aggressive. Any delay will be costly for both your firm and the client. You have a project sponsor and have achieved agreement and sign-off on both the project charter and the project management plan. Client personnel have been kept fully informed of the project's progress through status reports and regular meetings. The project is on schedule and within budget, and a final perfunctory review has been scheduled.

    Suddenly you hear that the entire effort may be cancelled because the product developed is totally unacceptable. What is the MOST likely cause of this situation?
    A. A key stakeholder was not adequately involved in the project.
    B. The project charter and project management plan were not thoroughly explained or adequately reviewed by the client.
    C. Communications arrangements were inadequate and did not provide the required information to interested parties.
    D. The project sponsor failed to provide adequate support for the project.

23. The project manager has just received a change from the customer that does not affect the project schedule and is easy to complete. What should the project manager do FIRST?
    A. Make the change happen as soon as possible.
    B. Contact the project sponsor for permission.
    C. Go to the change control board.
    D. Evaluate the impacts on other project constraints.

24. Your company just won a major new project. It will begin in three months and is valued at US $2,000,000. You are the project manager for an existing project. What is the FIRST thing you should do once you hear of the new project?
    A. Ask management how the new project will use resources.
    B. Resource level your project.
    C. Crash your project.
    D. Ask management how the new project will affect your project.

25. You are a project manager who was just assigned to take over a project from another project manager who is leaving the company. The previous project manager tells you that the project is on schedule, but only because he has constantly pushed the team to perform. What is the FIRST thing you should do as the new project manager?
    A. Check risk status.
    B. Check cost performance.
    C. Determine a management strategy.
    D. Tell the team your objectives.

26. You are assigned as the project manager in the middle of the project. The project is within the baselines, but the customer is not happy with the performance of the project. What is the FIRST thing you should do?
    A. Discuss it with the project team.
    B. Recalculate baselines.
    C. Renegotiate the contract.
    D. Meet with the customer.

27. It is the middle of the project when the project manager is informed by her scheduler that the project control limits are secure. That same morning she receives a note from a team member about a problem he is having. The note says, "This activity is driving me crazy, and the manager of the accounting department won't help me until the activity's float is in jeopardy." In addition, the project manager has e-mails from a minor stakeholder and 14 e-mails from team members. While she is reading the e-mails, a team member walks into the project manager's office to tell her a corrective action was implemented by a team member from the project management office, but was not documented. What should the project manager do NEXT?
    A. Report the documentation violation to the project management office, evaluate the security of the control limits, and review the e-mailing rules in the communications management plan.
    B. Clarify the reasoning behind documentation being a problem, get the accounting department to assist the team member, and respond to the minor stakeholder.
    C. Add the implemented corrective action to the historical records, discuss the value of documentation at the next team meeting, and smooth the team member with the accounting department problem.
    D. Find out who caused the problem with the accounting department, respond to the minor stakeholder before responding to the other e-mails, and review the process listed in the communications management plan for reporting concerns with the team member having the documentation problem.

28. The client demands changes to the product specification that will add only two weeks to the critical path. Which of the following is the BEST thing for the project manager to do?
    A. Compress the schedule to recover the two weeks.
    B. Cut scope to recover the two weeks.
    C. Consult with the sponsor about options.
    D. Advise the client of the impact of the change.

29. During project executing, the project manager determines that a change is needed to material purchased for the project. The project manager calls a meeting of the team to plan how to make the change. This is an example of:
    A. Management by objectives.
    B. Lack of a change management plan.
    C. Good team relations.
    D. Lack of a clear work breakdown structure.

30. The project was going well when all of a sudden there were changes to the project coming from multiple stakeholders. After all the changes were determined, the project manager spent time with all the stakeholders to find out why there were changes and to discover any more.

    The project work has quieted down when a team member casually mentions to the project manager that he added functionality to a product of the project. "Do not worry," he says, "I did not impact time, cost, or quality!" What should the project manager do FIRST?
    A. Ask the team member how the need for the functionality was determined.
    B. Hold a meeting to review the team member's completed work.
    C. Look for other added functionality.
    D. Ask the team member how he knows there is no time, cost, or quality impact.

31. You are asked to prepare a budget for completing a project that was started last year and then shelved for six months. All the following would be included in the project budget EXCEPT:
    A. Fixed costs.
    B. Sunk costs.
    C. Direct costs.
    D. Variable costs.

32. Which of the following sequences represents straight line depreciation?
    A. $100, $100, $100
    B. $100, $120, $140
    C. $100, $120, $160
    D. $160, $140, $120

33. This project is chartered to determine new ways to extend the product life of one of the company's medium-producing products. The project manager comes from the engineering department, and the team comes from the product management and marketing departments.

    The project scope statement and project planning are completed when a stakeholder notifies the team that there is a better way to complete one of the work packages. The stakeholder supplies a technical review letter from his department proving that the new way to complete the work package will actually be faster than the old way.

    The project manager has had similar experiences with this department on other projects, and was expecting this to happen on this project. What is the FIRST thing the project manager should do?
    A. Contact the department and complain again about their missing the deadline for submission of scope.
    B. Look for how this change will impact the cost to complete the work package and the quality of the product of the work package.
    C. See if there is a way to change from a matrix organization to a functional organization so as to eliminate all the interference from other departments.
    D. Ask the department if they have any other changes.

34. Project A has an internal rate of return (IRR) of 21 percent. Project B has an IRR of 7 percent. Project C has an IRR of 31 percent. Project D has an IRR of 19 percent. Which of these would be the BEST project?
    A. Project A
    B. Project B
    C. Project C
    D. Project D

35. An output of the Close Project or Phase process is the creation of:
    A. Project archives.
    B. A project charter.
    C. A project management plan.
    D. A risk management plan.

36. All of the following occur during the Close Project or Phase process EXCEPT:
    A. Creating lessons learned.
    B. Formal acceptance.
    C. Performance reporting.
    D. Performing cost benefit analysis.

37. Which of the following is included in a project charter?
    A. A risk management strategy
    B. Work package estimates
    C. Detailed resource estimates
    D. The business case for the project

38. A project manager is trying to convince management to use more formal project management procedures and has decided to start improving the company's project management by obtaining a project charter for each of his projects. Which of the following BEST describes why a project charter would help the project manager?
    A. It describes the details of what needs to be done.
    B. It lists the names of all team members.
    C. It gives the project manager authority.
    D. It describes the project's history.

39. Linear programming is an example of what type of project selection criteria?
    A. Constrained optimization
    B. Comparative approach
    C. Benefit measurement
    D. Impact analysis

40. You have created the project charter, but could not get it approved. Your manager and his boss have asked that the project begin immediately. Which of the following is the BEST thing to do?
    A. Set up an integrated change control process.
    B. Show your manager the impact of proceeding without approval.
    C. Focus on completing projects that have signed project charters.
    D. Start work on only the critical path activities.

41. The engineering department has uncovered a problem with the cost accounting system and has asked the systems department to analyze what is wrong and fix the problem. You are a project manager working with the cost accounting programs on another project. Management has issued a change request to the change control board to add the new work to your project.

    Your existing project has a cost performance index (CPI) of 1.2 and a schedule performance index (SPI) of 1.3, so you have some room to add work without delaying your existing project or going over budget. However, you cannot see how the new work fits within the project charter for your existing project. After some analysis, you determine that the new work and existing work do not overlap and can be done concurrently. They also require different skill sets. Which of the following is the BEST thing to do?
    A. Develop a project charter.
    B. Reestimate the project schedule with input from the engineering department.
    C. Verify the scope of the new work with the help of the stakeholders.
    D. Identify specific changes to the existing work.

42. All technical work is completed on the project. Which of the following remains to be done?
    A. Verify Scope
    B. Plan Risk Responses
    C. Create a staffing management plan
    D. Complete lessons learned

43. Your company can accept one of three possible projects. Project A has a net present value (NPV) of US $30,000 and will take six years to complete. Project B has an NPV of US $60,000 and will take three years to complete. Project C has an NPV of US $90,000 and will take four years to complete. Based on this information, which project should the company choose?
    A. They all have the same value.
    B. Project A
    C. Project B
    D. Project C

Answers

1. **Answer** C
   Explanation This question is asking for the most important of the choices. Think about what is involved in integration: project management plan development, project management plan execution, and integrated change control. Updates and product control are parts of project monitoring and controlling, while integration includes more than control. Advancing the careers of team members falls under project executing (the Develop Project Team process). In order to integrate the project components into a cohesive whole, communication is key whenever one activity will interface with another or one team member will interface with another, and when any other form of interfacing will occur.

2. **Answer** C
   Explanation The project manager is an integrator. This is a question about your role as an integrator and communicator.

3. **Answer** D
   Explanation Historical records are not generally used for life cycle costing, lessons learned, or creating status reports. They are useful in estimating, risk management, and overall project planning.

4. **Answer** D
   Explanation Project managers should be proactive. The only proactive answer here is preventing unnecessary changes.

5. **Answer** C
   Explanation This is a very confusing question. Did you notice all the distracters that may or may not be relevant? Most project schedules are compressed by the project manager during project planning, so that is not a logical reason and cannot be the best choice. Issue logs can be used on smaller projects, which means the project manager's use of issue logs is not the best choice. The number of critical (or hard-to-get) resources noted has no bearing on the need to rework the project charter. Therefore, that cannot be the best choice. Take another look at the second and third projects. In the second project, the product of the project was not used. This implies many things, including the possibilities that either the project manager did not identify the requirements of all the stakeholders or that the business need for the project changed dramatically and the project manager did not notice. This indicates a major flaw in the project manager's abilities. In the third project, there were 25 concerns of the stakeholders that were not addressed before the project was completed. Again, this shows a major lack of project management knowledge. The needs of the stakeholders and not just the sponsor must be taken into account on all projects. This makes the project manager's failure to effectively involve the stakeholders the best choice.

6. **Answer** D
   Explanation A change management plan includes the processes and procedures that allow smooth evaluation and tracking of changes. Lessons learned are reviews of the processes and procedures after the fact, to improve them on future projects.

7. **Answer** B
   Explanation Who does each activity is managed with the responsibility assignment matrix. When each activity is done is managed with the project schedule. A work authorization system is used to coordinate when and in what order the work is performed so that work and people may properly interface with other work and other people.

8. **Answer** C
   Explanation The sponsor issues the project charter and so he or she should help the project manager control changes to the charter. The primary responsibility lies with the sponsor.

9. **Answer** A
   Explanation Integration is a key responsibility of the project manager.

10. **Answer** B
    Explanation Integration refers to combining activities, not team members.

11. **Answer** B
    Explanation Direct and Manage Project Execution is the only correct response.

12. **Answer** C
    Explanation Double declining balance is a form of depreciation. That eliminates the choice of life cycle costing. The choices of decelerated depreciation and straight line depreciation are also incorrect because double declining balance is a form of accelerated depreciation.

13. **Answer** C
    Explanation Because you have no experience, you will have to look at the experience of others. This information is captured in the historical records from previous projects.

14. **Answer** C
    Explanation The project management plan contains more than just a bar chart and the project manager's plan for completing the work. It includes all the management plans for the project.

15. **Answer** D
    Explanation The project manager creates the project charter, but it is approved and authorized by the project sponsor, giving the project manager authority to proceed with the project.

16. **Answer** D
    Explanation If we were to rephrase the question, it is asking, "Who creates the project management plan?" The best answer is that the project management plan is created by the project manager but requires input from the team.

17. **Answer** B
    Explanation Determining who will be on the change control board and determining the reporting structure may have already been done. In any case, these choices are not directly impacted by the number of sponsors who have signed the charter. Having a single project sponsor is not necessary. This situation implies that there are six areas concerned with this project. In addition to added communications requirements, you should be concerned with competing needs and requirements impacting your efforts on configuration management.

18. **Answer** A
    Explanation The Create WBS process consists of subdividing major project deliverables (scope) into smaller, more manageable work packages. The Define Activities process defines the activities that must take place to produce those deliverables. Therefore, it would be the most practical choice to combine those processes.

19. **Answer** D
    Explanation A WBS is created in project planning, but can be used to help manage the project during project executing. The wording here was not "creating a WBS," but "using a WBS." A project control system is set up during project planning, not during project executing, and therefore is the exception.

20. **Answer** D
    Explanation A project manager must manage a project. If all activities are delegated, chaos ensues and team members will spend more time jockeying for position than completing activities.

21. **Answer** C
    Explanation Crashing and replanning are essentially delaying the situation. Instead, the project manager should try to prevent the situation by showing the consequences if the resources are not available. This is a more effective strategy than saying, "But you gave them to me."

22. **Answer** A
    Explanation A single high-level executive can end an entire project if he or she is not satisfied with the results, even if that person has, by choice, been only tangentially involved in the project. It is critical to ensure that all of the final decision makers have been identified early in a project in order to ensure that their concerns are addressed.

23. **Answer** D
    Explanation The other impacts to the project should be evaluated first. Such impacts include scope, cost, quality, risk, resources, and customer satisfaction. Once these are evaluated, the change control board, if one exists, can approve or deny the change.

24. **Answer** D
    Explanation You do not have enough information to consider resource leveling or crashing this project. As you work on any project, you need to constantly reevaluate the project objectives and how the project relates to other concurrent projects. Is your project still in line with corporate objectives? If the other project will impact yours, you need to be proactive and work on options now.

25. **Answer** C
    Explanation Before you can do anything else, you have to know what YOU are going to do. Developing the management strategy will provide the framework for all the rest of the choices presented and the other activities that need to be done.

26. **Answer** D
    Explanation First, you need to find out why the customer is not happy. Then meet with the team and determine options.

27. **Answer** C
    Explanation Notice how many situations are thrown at you in this question. It is important to practice reading through questions to discover what is important and what is just background information. In this question, the only thing relevant was the corrective action taken. Once you discover what the primary issue is, look at the choices to find out which is best for addressing that issue. What is the primary issue here? Did you realize the team member's note is about a noncritical path activity? ("Until the project float is in jeopardy" means there is float and, thus, it is not on the critical path.) So is the issue the noncritical path activity or the documentation? You might disagree with the logic, but in this case the answer is the documentation. In the real world, problems often repeat. Without a record of what was done, there is no opportunity to consider the same solution for future problems. Documentation is critical to projects. Because documentation

becomes part of the historical records database, it is best to first record the corrective action taken, then discuss the value of documentation at the next team meeting, and smooth the team member with the accounting department problem.

28. **Answer** C
Explanation Do you remember what to do when there is a change? Evaluate first. You wouldn't take action before getting approval, so compressing the schedule or cutting scope would happen after consulting the sponsor and/or advising the client of the impact of the change. You would not go to the customer before going to your internal management, so advising the client is not the correct thing to do next. The next step is to discuss options with the sponsor.

29. **Answer** B
Explanation The project manager is asking how to make a change. Such a question cannot be resolved using management by objectives, team relations, or a work breakdown structure. The procedures, forms, sign-offs, and other similar requirements for handling changes should have already been determined in the change management plan. Because they were not, the project manager will waste valuable work time trying to figure it out after the fact.

30. **Answer** D
Explanation Notice that the first paragraph is extraneous. Also notice that the question states that the change has already been made. The project manager's actions would be different if the change had not been made. It is the project manager's job to investigate impacts, as the project manager is the only one who can tell how a change impacts the project as a whole. Asking the team member how he knows there is no impact on time, cost, or quality is the best answer. This begins the project manager's analysis of the impacts to the project as a whole by finding out what analysis has already been done. He can then determine how he must finalize the analysis as it applies to the entire project.

31. **Answer** B
Explanation Sunk costs are expended costs. The rule is that they should not be considered when deciding whether to continue with a troubled project.

32. **Answer** A
Explanation Straight line depreciation uses the same amount each time period.

33. **Answer** B
Explanation Complaining about the missed deadline could be done, but it is not proactive. It would be helpful to get to the root cause of why this department always comes up with such ideas or changes after the project begins. However, this is not the immediate problem; the change is the immediate problem, and therefore complaining is not best. The type of project organization described is a matrix organization. There is not anything inherently wrong with such an organization, nor is there anything in this particular situation that would require it to be changed, so changing way the company is organized cannot be best. The department's history indicates that asking if the department has other changes is something that should definitely be done, but the proposed change needs more immediate attention. Looking at impacts of the change begins integrated change control.

34. **Answer** C
Explanation Remember, the internal rate of return is similar to the interest rate you get from the bank. The higher the rate, the better the return.

35. **Answer** A
Explanation The project charter is created in initiating. The project management plan and risk management plans are outputs of project planning. Project records are archived in the Close Project or Phase process.

36. **Answer** D
Explanation Cost benefit analysis is done earlier in the project to help select between alternatives. All the other choices are done during the Close Project or Phase process. Therefore, performing cost benefit analysis must be the best answer.

37. **Answer** D
Explanation A risk management strategy and work package estimates are not created until project planning, but the project charter is created in initiating. A project charter may include the names of some resources (the project manager, for example), but not detailed resource estimates. Of the choices given, only the business case for the project is included in the project charter.

38. **Answer** C
Explanation The exam will ask questions like this to make sure you know the benefits you should be getting out of the processes and tools of project management. The details of what needs to be done are found in the WBS dictionary. The names of team members are included in the responsibility assignment matrix and other documents. Project history is found in the lessons learned and other historical records. A major benefit of a project charter is that it documents the authority given to the project manager.

39. **Answer** A
Explanation Constrained optimization uses mathematical models. Linear programming is a mathematical model.

40. **Answer** B
Explanation The best thing to do would be to show the impact. This is the only choice that prevents future problems—always the best choice. The other choices just pretend the problem does not exist.

41. **Answer** A
Explanation How long did it take you to read this question? Expect long-winded questions on the exam. Take another look at the choices before you continue reading. Did you notice that each of the choices occurs during a different part of the project management process?

This question is essentially asking if the new work should be added to the existing project. There may be many business reasons to try to do this, but from a project management perspective, major additions to the project are generally discouraged. In this case, the new work is a self-contained unit of work, has no overlap with the existing work, does not fit within the project charter, and needs a different skill set. Therefore, it is best to make it a new project.

The first step to answering this question is to realize that the work should be a separate project. The second step is to look at the choices and see which relates to initiating a new project. Reestimating the project sounds like the best choice only if you did not realize that the new work should be a separate project. Verifying scope is done during project monitoring and controlling, and does not relate to the decision of whether to add work to the project. Identifying scope changes also implies that the new work has been accepted as an addition to the existing project. Developing a project charter is among the first steps of initiating a new project, and the best choice in this situation.

42. **Answer** D
Explanation Did you pick Verify Scope? Then you may have forgotten that the Verify Scope process is done during project monitoring and controlling, not project closing. Planning the risk responses and creating the staffing management plan are done earlier in the project. The lessons learned can only be completed after the work is completed.

43. **Answer** D
Explanation Remember, project length is incorporated when computing NPV, so the references to how long the projects will take is extraneous information. You would choose the project that provides the most value, in this case the project with the highest NPV.

CHAPTER FIVE Scope Management

Quicktest

- Scope management process
- Scope baseline
- Work breakdown structure (WBS)
- Project scope statement
- WBS dictionary
- Requirements documentation
- Requirements traceability matrix
- How to create a WBS
- Benefits of a WBS
- Uses of a WBS
- Requirements management plan
- Scope management plan
- Work package
- Activity
- Decomposition
- Product scope
- Project scope
- Data collection techniques
  - Focus groups
  - Facilitated workshops
  - Brainstorming
  - Nominal group technique
  - Delphi technique
  - Mind maps
  - Affinity diagrams
  - Observation
  - Prototypes
  - Group decision-making (unanimous, dictatorship, majority, plurality, consensus)
- Control account
- Product analysis
- Validated deliverables

Scope management is the process of defining what work is required and then making sure all of that work—and only that work—is done. This is generally an easy topic, but we all have gaps in our knowledge, even regarding things like scope management that we deal with daily. The following are gaps that many people do not know they have. Read through this list and see if it helps you uncover any gaps in your knowledge.

TRICKS OF THE TRADE® Things to Know about Scope Management for the Exam

- You must plan, in advance, how you will determine the scope, as well as how you will manage and control scope. This is part of your scope management plan.
- Scope must be defined, clear, and formally approved before work starts.
- Requirements are gathered from all the stakeholders, not just the person who assigned the project.
- Requirements gathering can take a substantial amount of time, especially on large projects that may involve obtaining requirements from hundreds of people.
- A work breakdown structure (WBS) is used on all projects. A side benefit of this tool is that you may find additional scope and be able to clarify identified scope when you create the WBS.
- While the project is being completed, you must check to make sure you are doing all the work but only the work included in the project management plan.
- Gold plating a project (adding extras) is not allowed.
- Any change to scope must be evaluated for its effect on time, cost, risk, quality, resources, and customer satisfaction.
- No changes to scope are allowed without an approved change request.
- Scope changes should not be approved if they relate to work that does not fit within the project charter.
- You need to continuously determine what is and is not included in the project.

Please note that creating a WBS is a REQUIRED part of project management. A WBS is not a list! If you have never created one or do not currently use a WBS on your projects, this chapter will help you understand how highly beneficial this tool is and what it can do for you. Remember, the exam asks questions from an expert level and assumes you have experience using the tools of project management. Therefore, you need to know how the WBS can help you clearly define requirements, plan how you will manage scope, and control scope.

Rita's Process Chart—Scope Management

Where are we in the project management process?

INITIATING

- Select project manager
- Determine company culture and existing systems
- Collect processes, procedures, and historical information
- Divide large projects into phases
- Understand the business case
- Uncover initial requirements, assumptions, and risks
- Assess project and product feasibility within the given constraints
- Create measurable objectives
- Develop project charter
- Identify stakeholders
- Develop stakeholder management strategy

PLANNING

(This is the only process group with a set order)

- **Determine how you will do planning—part of all management plans**
- **Determine detailed requirements**
- **Create project scope statement**
- Assess what to purchase
- Determine team
- **Create WBS and WBS dictionary**
- Create activity list
- Create network diagram
- Estimate resource requirements
- Estimate time and cost
- Determine critical path
- Develop schedule
- Develop budget
- Determine quality standards, processes, and metrics
- Create process improvement plan
- **Determine all roles and responsibilities**
- Plan communications
- Perform risk identification, qualitative and quantitative risk analysis, and risk response planning
- **Go back—iterations**
- Prepare procurement documents
- Create change management plan
- **Finalize the "how to execute and control" parts of all management plans**
- **Develop realistic and final PM plan and performance measurement baseline**
- Gain formal approval of the plan
- Hold kickoff meeting

EXECUTING

- Execute the work according to the PM plan
- Produce product deliverables (product scope)
- Request changes
- Implement only approved changes
- Continuously improve
- Follow processes
- Perform quality assurance
- Perform quality audits
- Acquire final team
- Manage people
- Evaluate team and project performance
- Hold team-building activities
- Give recognition and rewards
- Use issue logs
- Facilitate conflict resolution
- Release resources as work is completed
- Send and receive information
- Hold meetings
- Select sellers

MONITORING & CONTROLLING

- **Take action to control the project**
- **Measure performance against the performance measurement baseline**
- **Measure performance against other metrics determined by the project manager**
- **Determine variances and if they warrant a corrective action or change request**
- **Influence the factors that cause changes**
- **Request changes**
- Perform integrated change control
- Approve or reject changes
- Inform stakeholders of the results of change requests
- Update the PM plan and project documents
- Manage configuration
- Create forecasts
- **Gain acceptance of interim deliverables from the customer**
- Perform quality control
- Report on project performance and solicit feedback
- Perform risk assessments and audits
- Manage reserves
- Administer procurements

CLOSING

- Confirm work is done to requirements
- Complete procurement closure
- Gain final acceptance of the product
- Complete financial closure
- Hand off completed product
- Solicit feedback from the customer about the project
- Complete final performance reporting
- Index and archive records
- Update lessons learned knowledge base

The following should help you understand how each part of scope management fits into the overall project management process:

Scope Management Process	Done During
Collect Requirements	Planning process group
Define Scope	Planning process group
Create WBS	Planning process group
Verify Scope	Monitoring and controlling process group
Control Scope	Monitoring and controlling process group

You should understand the following concepts for the exam.

Product Scope PAGE 103 Product scope is another way to say "requirements that relate to the product of the project." It answers the question of "What end result is wanted?" There may be a separate, preliminary project to determine product scope, or you may define the requirements as part of your project.

Let's look at an example of product scope. On a project to build a new train terminal, the product scope is "a new train terminal that meets these technical specifications." To determine if the project successfully achieved the product scope, the resulting product (the new train terminal) is compared to the product requirements, which are recorded in the requirements documentation and the project scope statement for the project.

Project Scope PAGE 103 The project scope is the work the project will do to deliver the product of the project (i.e., the product scope). In the train terminal example, the project scope is the work that needs to be done to deliver the train terminal. This work includes the planning, coordination, and management activities (such as meetings and reports) that ensure the product scope is achieved. These efforts become part of the scope management plan, which is part of the project management plan. To determine if the project scope has been successfully completed, the work accomplished is measured against the scope baseline in the project management plan.

Scope management involves managing both product scope and project scope. Be careful to notice which word is used in questions on the exam. The answer to a question about product scope is different than the answer to a question about project scope.

Scope Management Plan Each of the knowledge areas has a management plan. For scope, this plan answers the questions of, "How will I achieve the scope? What tools should I use to plan how the project will accomplish the scope? What enterprise environmental factors and organizational process assets (described in the Integration Management chapter) come into play?" It also addresses how the scope will be managed and how it will be controlled to the project management plan. The scope management plan essentially contains three parts: how scope will be planned, executed, and controlled. The *PMBOK® Guide* does not identify the creation of this document as a separate scope management process. Instead, the plan is created as part of the Develop Project Management Plan process.

Although very few companies have templates, forms, or standards for scope management, these are valuable assets to have on a project. Each project's scope management plan is unique, but it may cover topics that can be standardized for the company or for the type of project. Once completed, the scope management plan becomes part of the project management plan, and the project manager uses it to guide and measure the project until closing.

The scope management plan can be developed in stages, or iterated, during project planning. The first step is to determine how scope will be defined. Once the rest of the project is planned, the project manager will have enough information to decide how the scope will be executed and controlled. Those decisions will then become part of the scope management plan. Another aspect of iterations is that later parts of project planning, such as the Plan Risk Responses process, can add new scope to the project, thereby changing the scope management plan.

Stop; do not just read on. Instead, read this section over again. Notice that you need a good understanding of the project scope in order to create a scope management plan. The idea behind the creation of this and all management plans is "if you cannot plan it, you cannot do it." Yet many people make the mistake of starting to work on a project before the product and project scope are finalized and before they have properly planned how they will manage scope. Do you? As we've previously explained, you need to assume proper project management is being done on the project when you take the exam, unless the question says otherwise. Remember, creating a scope management plan is a required part of project management.

The Scope Management Process To avoid the risk that you will read the rest of this chapter and miss an important issue, let's make this point clear right away: How PMI says scope should be managed and how you manage it in the real world might be different. There are a lot of acceptable ways to manage scope. If you do it differently than described here, you are not necessarily wrong; you may just be managing scope differently based on the needs of your projects. The *PMBOK® Guide* describes the scope management process as:

1. Determine requirements, making sure all requirements support the project's business case as described in the project charter.
2. Sort and balance the needs of the stakeholders to determine product scope and project scope.
3. Create a WBS to break the scope down to smaller, more manageable pieces.
4. Verify that the completed scope of work is acceptable to the customer.
5. Measure scope performance, and adjust as needed.

Again, this may not be what you do in the real world. For example, many organizations establish a separate project to handle the requirements gathering process and determine what the project will be. This is especially true for work that demands a large requirements gathering effort and when the people involved in determining requirements are different than those who will perform the work. Past editions of the *PMBOK® Guide* assumed the requirements were determined before the project began. The *PMBOK® Guide, Fourth Edition* includes gathering and determining requirements as part of project work, however. In the real world, the decision of whether to gather requirements as a separate project should be made based on the needs of the project and the organization.

While taking the exam, assume that you will need to determine requirements as part of the project.

If you work as a seller, your process might begin with the receipt of a large technical description (possibly 300 pages) of what the customer wants. Since the product requirements are supplied in such cases, the requirements step is more about clarifying product requirements than determining them. The project requirements would still need to be determined, however.

Assume that you are the project manager for the BUYER for all questions on the exam that involve procurement, unless the question specifically states otherwise.

Here is something else to notice about PMI's scope management process. Do you realize what the phrase "making sure all requirements support the project's business case, as described in the project charter" means in the real world? It means that no one can request or add work that is not related to the reason documented in the charter for initiating the project. Yet, in your real world, do you see people who want work done and try to attach it to any project they can to get the work accomplished? Do you see scope on projects that does not support the company's business objectives? It happens all the time. Therefore, a project manager must be assertive. This is also the attitude you should have when you take the exam. You must be able to say no and not allow such activities to take place on your project. Unnecessary scope adds time, cost, and risk to the project that you just do not need. You have to be able to say, "That sounds like it is its own project. It should go through the project approval process, instead of being added to my project." Understanding this attitude that a project manager needs to properly plan and protect the project is essential for passing the exam.

Now let's look in more detail at the process promoted by PMI.

Collect Requirements PAGE 105

Process: Collect Requirements
Process Group: Planning
Knowledge Area: Scope Management

Requirements are what stakeholders need from a project or product. Work should not be included in a project just because someone wants it. Instead, the requirements should relate to solving problems or achieving objectives. Requirements may include requests about how the work is managed ("You cannot shut down our systems on a Friday") or capabilities stakeholders would like to see in the product of the project ("The new software should allow multiple users to access it at the same time"). They also may be related to quality ("There can be no more than one day of unexpected down time"), business processes ("You must track and report the project's expenses in this way"), compliance ("By law, we have to meet this safety standard"), or even project management ("We require risk management procedure X to be used on the project"). The Collect Requirements process looks for all requirements, not just those related to the product of the project.

The high-level project and product requirements should have already been defined in the project charter during initiating. The Collect Requirements process involves gathering more specific input on those requirements and any related assumptions from all stakeholders. This process is critical to project success, as a missed requirement could mean significant changes and conflict throughout the remainder of the project and even project failure.

So how do you collect requirements? First, know who your stakeholders are. This information is recorded in the stakeholder register. Then get the stakeholders to give you requirements! It may sound simple, but it is not. For large projects, there could be hundreds of stakeholders, and no single method of collecting requirements will work for all stakeholders. Since missing a needed requirement can be very expensive and time consuming and cause other problems later, an extensive and concerted effort needs to be made to find all the requirements before work starts on a project. This effort may involve reviewing lessons learned and other historical records and using various data gathering techniques (described next). The project manager needs to choose the techniques that are most appropriate for the project and the stakeholders. Many of these techniques can also be used as part of other data gathering efforts, such as identifying risks during the risk management process.

Reviewing Historical Records Historical records and lessons learned can indicate what the requirements were on similar projects and help identify relevant processes and expectations. For example, historical records may provide data about reporting requirements, project management requirements, system compatibility requirements, compliance requirements, etc. Lessons learned from other projects may also identify commonly overlooked areas of scope to help ensure such requirements are not missed on the current project.

Interviewing This technique may also be called "expert interviewing" on the exam. The team or project manager interviews project stakeholders to identify their requirements for a specific element of the product or project work, or for the overall project. These interviews can take place between two individuals or in group settings. Interviews can also be conducted via e-mail, phone calls, letters, or other methods.

Focus Groups The focus group technique helps get a specific set of stakeholders' or subject matter experts' opinions and requirements for the product or an aspect of the project. The members of the focus group can discuss their ideas with each other, but the conversation is directed by a moderator.

Facilitated Workshops Facilitated workshops bring together stakeholders with different perspectives (e.g., product designers and end-users) to talk about the product and, ultimately, define requirements.

Brainstorming Be careful here—many people think brainstorming is just a meeting where people discuss ideas, but it is more than that. The purpose of brainstorming is not to get individual thoughts; instead this technique strives for "group think." One person mentions an idea to solve a problem or, in this case, determine scope. That idea generates an idea from another participant, which leads to yet another idea, and so on. This technique does not assure that all the participants' ideas are captured. Instead, it produces ideas that were generated from each other.

As with any group technique, the results of brainstorming sessions vary depending on who the participants are. It can be highly beneficial to include people with different perspectives or backgrounds. The participants may be internal or external to the project or the organization.

Nominal Group Technique[1] This technique is usually, but not always, done during the same meeting as brainstorming. The meeting participants rank the most useful ideas generated during the brainstorming session.

Delphi Technique With this technique, a request for information is sent to experts who participate anonymously, their responses are compiled, and the results are sent back to them for further review until consensus is reached.

Mind Maps[2] A mind map is a diagram of ideas or notes to help generate, classify, or record information. It looks like several trees radiating out of a central core word (see the following diagram). Colors, pictures, and notations can be used to make the diagram more readable.

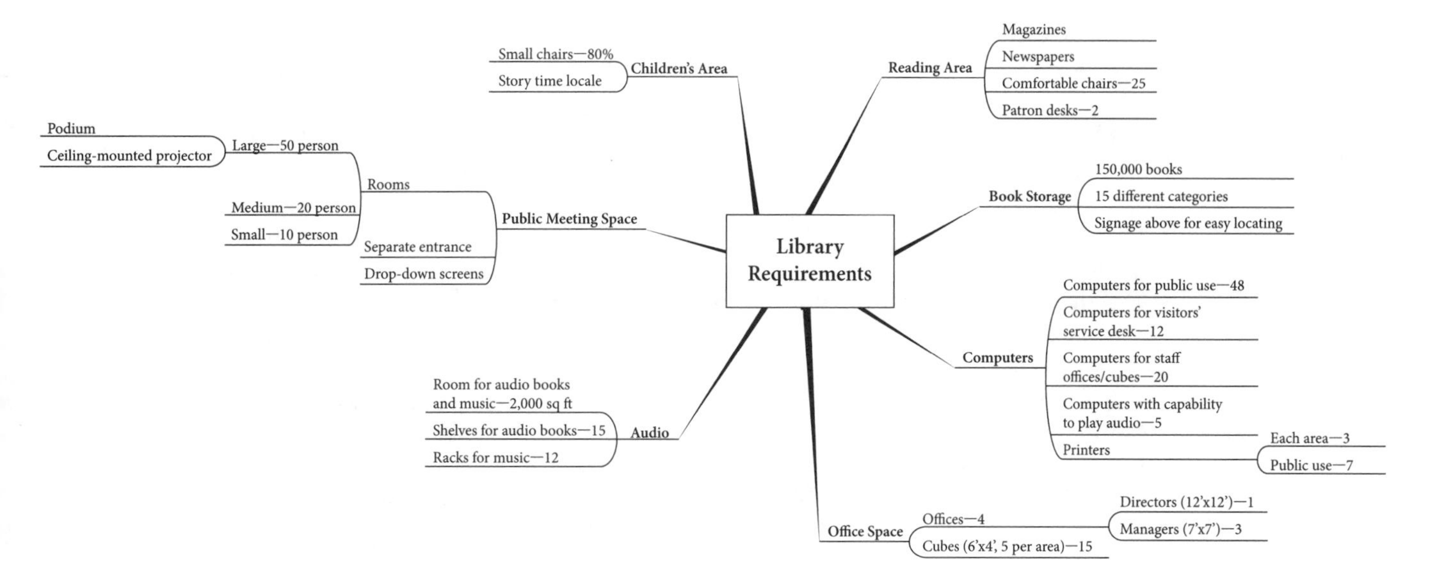

Affinity Diagrams[3] In this technique, the ideas generated from any other requirements gathering techniques are grouped by similarities. Each group of requirements is then given a title. This sorting makes it easier to see additional areas of scope (or risks) that have not been identified.

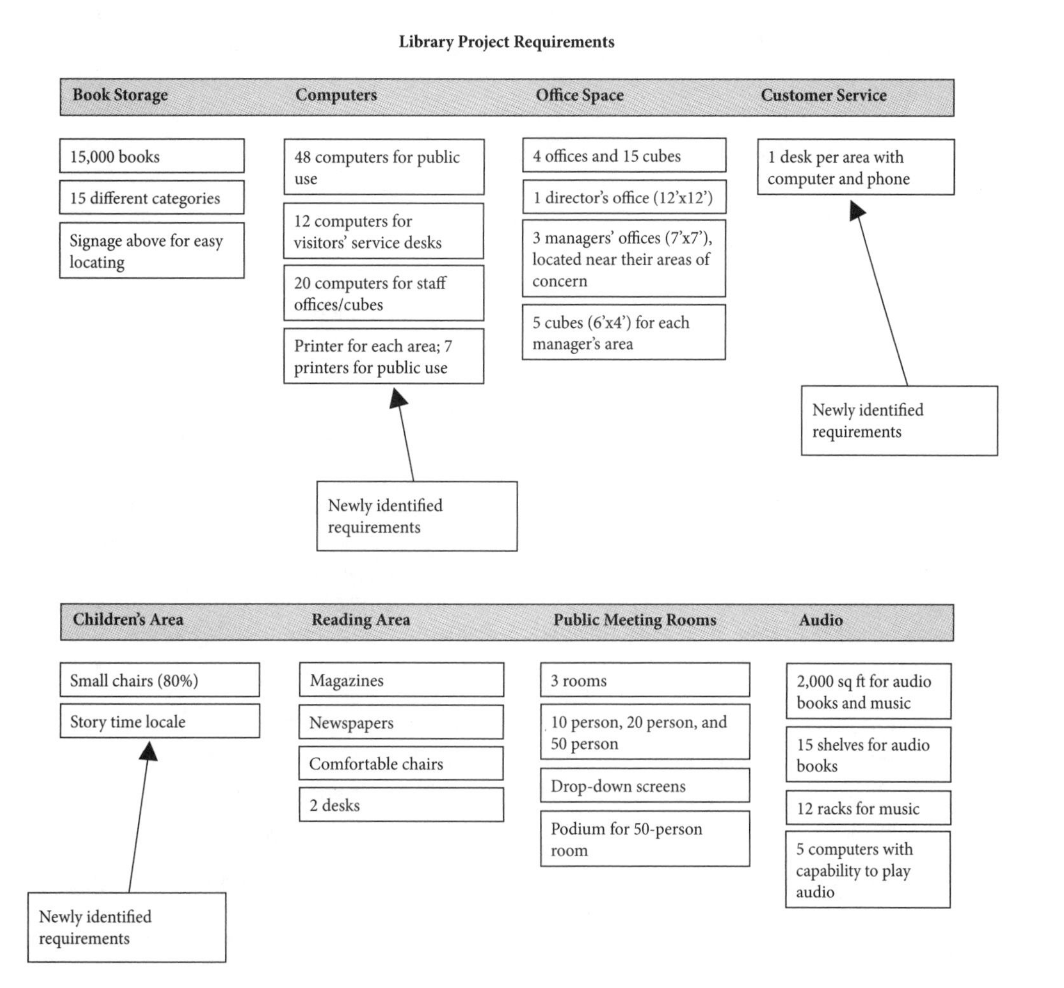

Questionnaires and Surveys Questionnaires or surveys are typically used for large groups. The questions are asked in such a way as to elicit requirements from the respondents.

Observation This technique involves job shadowing—watching a potential user of the product at work and, in some cases, participating in the work to help identify requirements.

Prototypes A prototype is a model of the proposed product. In this technique, the prototype is presented to stakeholders for feedback. The prototype may be updated multiple times to incorporate the feedback until the requirements have been solidified for the product.

Group Decision-Making Soliciting input on requirements from all stakeholders may result in too many or conflicting requirements. These need to be reviewed, analyzed, accepted or rejected, and prioritized before recording them in project documents. There are different ways to make decisions in a group setting. If the group agrees on a requirement **unanimously** (i.e., everyone agrees), the decision is easy. The decision-making process can also be easy if a single person is assigned to make the decision for the entire group. This technique, known as the **dictatorship** technique, can have negative impacts on the project if the stakeholders do not buy into the decision, however.

When there are conflicting opinions, groups may take a **majority** approach. With this technique, the group chooses the decision that more than half of its members support. If there is no majority opinion, the group may go with the decision that has the largest number of supporters. This is known as the **plurality** technique. The final technique is the **consensus** approach, which achieves general agreement about a decision; those who would prefer another option are willing to accept the decision that most members of the group support.

Requirements Documentation After the requirements have been collected and finalized, they are documented. Imagine you have suggested requirements from hundreds of people. Can you see how documenting those requirements would be useful? This documentation is an output of the Collect Requirements process and helps make sure the requirements are clear and unambiguous.

The requirements documentation can contain various types of information, but there is one thing you should be sure to include. You will have a lot of requirements that could easily be misunderstood. Therefore, one of the great questions to ask stakeholders is, "How will we know if the work we do will meet this requirement?" Not only is this a great way to make sure you understand the stakeholder's requirement, but it also helps ensure the work being done will be acceptable.

Balancing Stakeholders' Requirements This effort is an important aspect of the Collect Requirements process. Part of balancing stakeholders' requirements involves making sure the requirements can be met within the project objectives. If they cannot, then you need to look for options to adjust the competing demands of scope, time, cost, quality, resources, risk, and customer satisfaction. Balancing stakeholders' requirements also involves prioritizing requirements and resolving any conflicts between them.

There is a need to balance stakeholders' requirements beyond the Collect Requirements process. It may only become apparent later in the project that some stakeholders' requirements do not match those of the project or those of other stakeholders. Whenever this occurs, you need to balance the requirements against the interests of the project and resolve any conflicts.

Balancing stakeholders' requirements is never easy or fast, but it can become an impossible effort if you do not have clear project objectives and if you do not identify and prioritize ALL the requirements from ALL of the stakeholders during the Collect Requirements process. Do you spend the effort in your real-world to get as close to final requirements as possible? Are your requirements ranked by order of importance? If not, think about how such actions could improve your real-world projects. When you take the exam, assume the project manager has expended the effort necessary to determine all the requirements and that those requirements are ranked by order of importance.

Exercise This exercise outlines some of the key actions involved in balancing stakeholders' requirements. It goes beyond the Collect Requirements process and looks at this effort throughout the project life cycle. Spend some time thinking about balancing stakeholders' requirements while getting ready for the exam. This exercise will help you determine if you really understand the process summarized here. Go through each topic and put a checkmark next to the ones you understand. Put an X next to the ones you are able to apply in the real world. Then spend time thinking about the unmarked topics.

ACTION	Understand ✓	Can Do X
Identify who all the stakeholders are on the project, and understand their needs, wants, assumptions, and expectations related to the project.		
Work to get the requirements as clear and complete as possible before starting the project work.		
Use information about stakeholders and their requirements to resolve competing requirements while the work is being done on the project.		
Look for competing interests during project planning; don't just wait for them to show up during project executing.		
Look for possible options to resolve competing interests and alternative ways of completing the project activities. This may involve using techniques like brainstorming, schedule compression, reestimating, and other project management and management-related practices.		
Resolve stakeholders' competing requirements based on how the requirements affect the project. (See the guidelines listed in the following discussion.)		
Give priority to the customer. (For the exam, know that if any needs conflict with those of the customer, the customer's needs normally take precedence.)		
Use quality management to ensure the project will satisfy the needs for which it was undertaken.		
Deal with problems and conflicts as soon as they arise through the use of team-building, problem-solving, and conflict-management techniques.		
Say "No" to some of the competing interests. (For the exam, assume the project manager has the authority to say "No" when necessary to protect the project.)		

ACTION	Understand ✓	Can Do X
Call on management to help resolve competing interests when the project manager and the team cannot come up with a fair and equitable solution.		
Fix the project when the project starts to deviate from the requirements, rather than changing or lowering the requirements to meet the results of the project.		
Work toward fair resolution of disputes that consider all stakeholders' interests as well as the needs of the project.		
Hold meetings, interviews, and discussions to facilitate the resolution of competing requirements.		
Use negotiation techniques to resolve disputes between stakeholders.		
Plan and implement effective communication. (Do not just read this item and move on! Take some time to think about what effective communication is.)		
Gather, assess, and integrate information into the project.		

Resolving Competing Requirements Many project managers have no idea how to weight requirements. What if the engineering department wants the project to focus on decreasing defects and the accounting department wants the project costs to be lower? Can both needs be met? What if the engineering department is the primary stakeholder or even the sponsor of the project? Do that department's needs outweigh the needs of the accounting department? What if the needs of the engineering department actually hurt the accounting department?

Some issues are so complex they cannot be resolved by the project manager alone and require management intervention. There are some standard guidelines for balancing competing requirements, however. One trick is to walk through the following list for each requirement.

You should help resolve competing requirements by accepting those that best comply with the following:

- The business case stating the reason the project was initiated (market demand, legal requirement, etc.)
- The project charter
- The project scope statement (if this is available at the time of the conflict)
- The project constraints

So a stakeholder's request to do or add something to the project that is not related to the reason the project was initiated should be rejected. If the requirement is related to the reason the project was initiated but it does not fall within the project charter, this request should also be rejected. Any suggested changes to the project charter need to be brought to the sponsor's attention for approval. When considering constraints, if the most important constraint is schedule, then any requirements that would delay the schedule would not likely be accepted. Those that enhance the schedule (without serious impact on the other project constraints) would more likely be accepted. Requests that do not fall within these guidelines could become part of a future project instead.

Requirements Management Plan Remember that PMI-ism to plan before you do? The requirements management plan falls into that category. It is an output of the Collect Requirements process. In addition to describing the methods you intend to use to identify requirements, the plan should answer the following questions: "Once I have all the requirements, what will I do to analyze, prioritize, manage, and track changes to them? What should I include in the requirements traceability matrix (described next)?"

Requirements Traceability Matrix[4] Have you ever worked on a project in which some requirements got lost in the details? The process of determining requirements (especially on large projects) can easily involve one requirement leading to more refined requirements and clarifications. It can be difficult to remember where a requirement came from and its significance to the project. Losing focus on the reason for a requirement can result in a major strategic or project objective not being met. The requirements traceability matrix, another output of the Collect Requirements process, helps link the requirements to the objectives and/or other requirements to ensure the strategic goals are accomplished. The matrix is used throughout the project in analyzing proposed changes to project or product scope.

The following is an example of a requirements traceability matrix.

	Reading Area				Book Storage			Public Meeting Space			Children's Area		Audio			Office Space		Computers				
Objectives	Magazines	Newspapers	Comfortable chairs – 25	Patron desks – 2	150,000 books	15 different categories	Signage above for easy locating	Rooms	Separate entrance	Drop-down screens	Small chairs – 80%	Story time locale	Room for audio books and music	Shelves for audio books – 15	Racks for music – 12	Offices – 4	Cubes – 15	For public use – 48	For visitor's service desk – 12	For staff – 20	With audio capability – 5	Printers
Improve access to job resources by 20%.		X		X				X		X								X	X			X
Improve local children's reading levels by two grade levels in one year.			X		X		X					X						X				
Provide a pleasant place for community members to meet.	X	X	X					X	X		X		X	X	X							
Replace the existing library by end of next quarter.	X	X	X		X	X	X					X		X		X	X	X		X	X	X

Information like requirement identification numbers, the source of each requirement, who is assigned to manage the requirement, and the status of the requirement should also be recorded. The *PMBOK® Guide* suggests documenting this information in the requirements traceability matrix. For large projects, however, including all this information in the matrix would make it cumbersome and difficult to use. Another option is to store this data in a separate repository, preserving the matrix as an easy-to-reference tool. For the exam, simply understand that the requirements traceability matrix links requirements to objectives and/or other requirements, and that the requirement attributes (i.e., identification numbers, source, status, etc.) also need to be documented.

Did you notice in the previous paragraph that each requirement is assigned to someone to manage, or own? This concept is similar to that of risk owners, described in the Risk Management chapter. An owner helps ensure the customer receives what they asked for and the objectives are met. Assigning team members to manage requirements also helps free up the project manager's time. The role of requirement owner is another example of the type of work team members may do on a project beyond their efforts to produce the product.

Define Scope PAGE 112

Process: Define Scope
Process Group: Planning
Knowledge Area: Scope Management

The Define Scope process is primarily concerned with what is and is not included in the project and its deliverables. This process uses the requirements documentation created in the Collect Requirements process, the project charter, and any additional information about project risks, assumptions, and constraints to define the project and product scope.

Remember that planning is iterative. When the requirements have been determined, the project manager follows the project management planning process outlined in Rita's Process Chart to determine the schedule and budget. If the resulting schedule and budget do not meet the sponsor's or management's expectations for the project, the project manager needs to balance the requirements (scope) against the budget, schedule, and other constraints in the project. The iteration process involves coming up with options for meeting the scope, time, and cost objectives of the project and presenting those options to management for a decision. This work may include compressing the schedule, identifying alternative ways to perform the work on the project, or adjusting the budget or scope. The result is a realistic schedule and budget that can achieve the project's scope.

The Define Scope process is summarized in this book. The following are two key reasons this process is important on the exam:

- Many project managers complain about unrealistic schedules, but you need to understand for the exam that unrealistic schedules are the project managers' fault because they have not done planning in an iterative way, as described in the previous paragraph.
- Project managers spend a large portion of their time, while the work is being done, looking for options to adjust the project and still make the project schedule or budget. Therefore, all the tools used in planning to come up with a realistic schedule and budget, such as negotiating scope and fast tracking, are also major activities while the work is being done.

The process of Define Scope will continue as the project progresses and will be iterated. Regardless of when it is performed, its purpose is always to determine what scope is and is not in the project.

Product Analysis As noted at the beginning of this section, part of defining scope is determining what the deliverables of the project are. The purpose of product analysis is to analyze the objectives and description of the product stated by the customer or sponsor and turn them into tangible deliverables. For the exam, realize you may need to determine and define deliverables as part of the project, rather than receiving a complete list from the customer.

Project Scope Statement[5] The primary result, or output, of the Define Scope process is the project scope statement. This document in effect says "Here is what we will do on this project" or "Here is the approved project and product scope for this project." The development of the project scope statement can take a lot of time and involve the expert judgment of many stakeholders and even experts from outside the organization. While defining requirements and defining scope, you should identify areas where people requested scope but it was not approved to be included in the project. You should also clarify areas where the scope could easily be misunderstood. It is a waste of project time and money to create scope that is not needed or approved, yet it is easy for this to occur. A trick to avoiding this problem is to identify in the project scope statement what is not in the project to make it clear that such additions are not allowed.

The project scope statement, along with the WBS and WBS dictionary (described later in this chapter), comprise the scope baseline, which is part of the project management plan. The project scope statement may include:

- Product scope
- Project scope
- Deliverables
- Product acceptance criteria
- What is not part of the project
- Constraints and assumptions

Create Work Breakdown Structure (WBS)[6] PAGE 116 & THROUGHOUT

Process: Create Work Breakdown Structure
Process Group: Planning
Knowledge Area: Scope Management

Before you go any further, ask yourself, "What is a WBS?" It is essential to correctly understand this project management tool for the exam.

Exercise Test yourself! What is a WBS?

Answer This question should be easy if you currently use WBSs on your projects. You may be in trouble on the exam if you do not create these in the real world, however. Why? The WBS is a required element in project management. This organizational tool shows all the scope on the project, broken down to manageable deliverables. Without a WBS, the project will take longer, elements will slip through the cracks, and the project will be negatively impacted. So there is no choice. All projects, even small ones, need a WBS. Read the rest of this section to learn more about what a WBS is and how it adds value to the project.

Questions on the exam are designed to identify those who know what WBSs are but who do not use them in the real world. What if a question described details of a project to you and then asked, "You are in the middle of planning this project and creating a WBS. Which of the following would you most likely need to worry about?" It is difficult to answer such questions with only academic knowledge. You need to have been there! You need experience using this tool.

Let's work through the topic of the WBS together. Try the following exercise.

Exercise Many people simply make a list of things to do as their method of defining the activities on a project. This is a mistake; there are enormous advantages to using a WBS instead. Test yourself. Can you explain why the image on the right side (a list) is not as good as the diagram on the left (a WBS)?

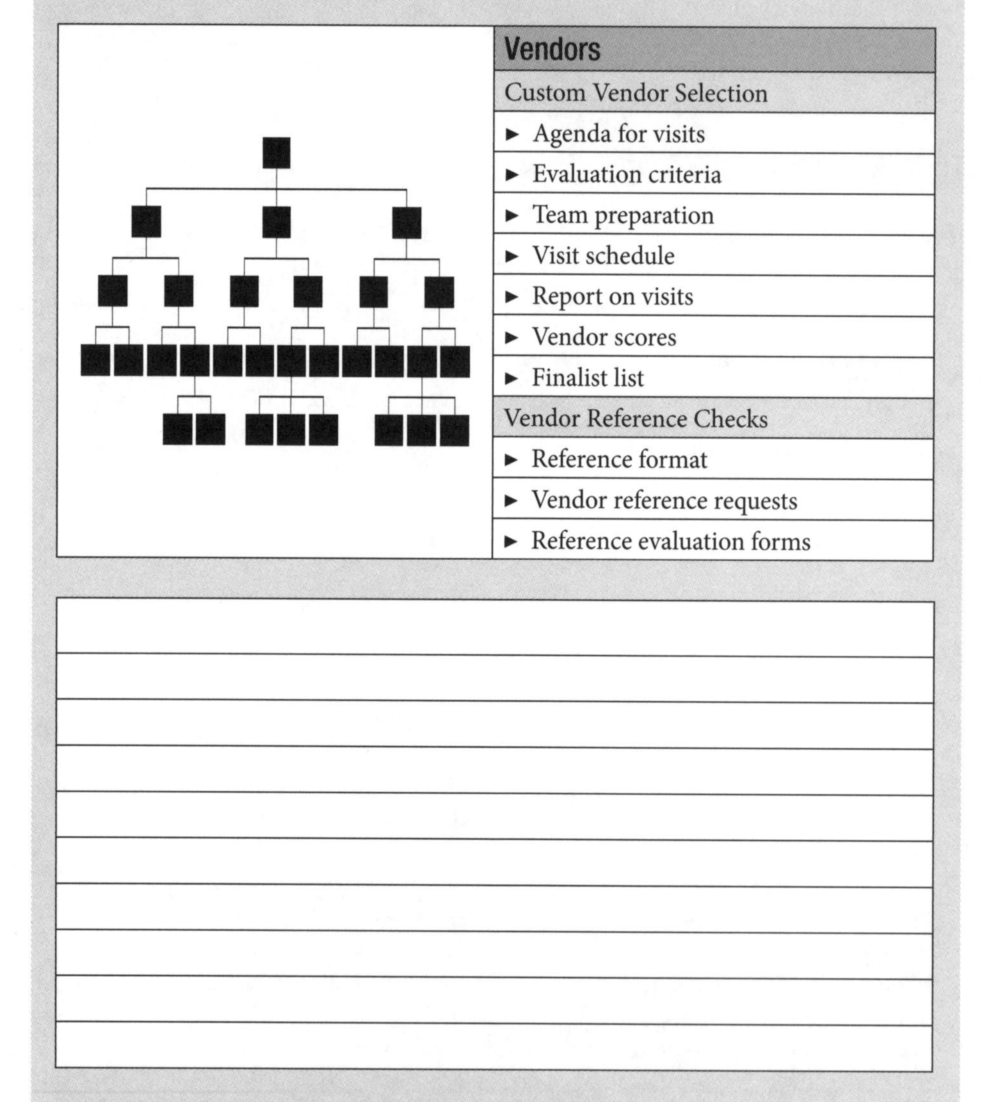

Vendors
Custom Vendor Selection
► Agenda for visits
► Evaluation criteria
► Team preparation
► Visit schedule
► Report on visits
► Vendor scores
► Finalist list
Vendor Reference Checks
► Reference format
► Vendor reference requests
► Reference evaluation forms

Answer Here are just a few answers to why a WBS is better than a list:

- The way a list, the method on the right, is created and the way it displays information make it easy to overlook some deliverables. In contrast, the construction of the WBS chart on the left helps to ensure that nothing slips through the cracks.
- A list can be cumbersome and does not allow you to clearly break down a large project into small enough pieces. With a WBS, you can easily break down

the work into work packages, and the WBS shows how the work packages are derived.

- A list is usually created by one person, whereas the WBS is created with input from the team and stakeholders. Involving the team and stakeholders helps gain their buy-in, and increased buy-in leads to improved performance. In contrast, a list often makes people wary of the project because they do not understand the project by looking at the list, nor do they know how it was created.
- The process of creating a WBS allows the team to walk through the project in their minds and thus improves the project plan. The execution of the project is typically easier and less risky as a result.
- Being involved in the creation of the WBS helps people better understand the project and makes it feel more achievable.
- A WBS shows a complete hierarchy of the project, making it easier to see how one deliverable relates to another. A list is just a list.

So will this be on the exam? Not directly, but you will need to fully understand a WBS, and this discussion describes aspects of using a WBS that many people do not understand.

The following is a sample WBS.

A WBS (on a Summary Level) for a Hardware/Software Creation and Installation Project

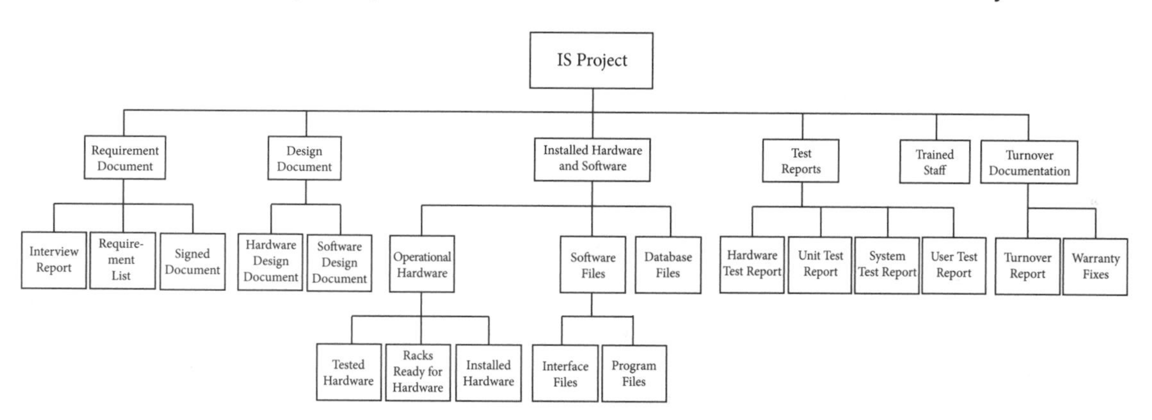

Most commonly, the project title goes at the top of the WBS. The first level is typically the same as the project life cycle (for example, for the IS project shown in the previous diagram: requirements documentation, design, installation, testing, training, turnover). The later levels break the project into smaller pieces. Such decomposition continues until the project manager reaches the level appropriate to manage the project.

Although the WBS may look like a corporate organizational chart, it is not! It serves a different function. The WBS allows you to break down a seemingly overwhelming project into pieces you can plan, organize, manage, and control. The creation of the WBS is a top-down effort to decompose the deliverables, and the work required to produce them, into smaller pieces called work packages.

For the exam, note that each work package consists of nouns—things, rather than actions. A WBS is deliverable-oriented. This does not mean that only customer deliverables are included in the WBS. The complete scope of the project, including product scope, project scope, and project management efforts, are included.

Watch out for the word "task." What many people refer to as a "task" in the real world is often called an "activity" on the exam.

Understand that there are few set rules for creating a WBS. WBSs created by two people for the same project will look different. That is fine, as long as these rules are followed:

- The WBS is created with the help of the team.
- The first level is completed before the project is broken down further.
- Each level of the WBS is a smaller piece of the level above.
- The entire project is included in each of the highest levels of the WBS. Eventually some levels will be broken down further than others.
- The WBS includes only deliverables that are required for the project.
- Deliverables not in the WBS are not part of the project.

The team breaks down the WBS until work packages are reached. This occurs when the deliverables:

- Can be realistically and confidently estimated
- Can be completed quickly
- Can be completed without interruption (without the need for more information)
- May be outsourced or contracted out

Once they are determined, you might enter the work packages—the items at the lowest level of the WBS—into project scheduling software. You would not try to derive the list of work packages by using this software, however. That list comes from the creation of the WBS.

The levels in the WBS are often numbered for ease of location later. When the WBS is complete, identification numbers are assigned to help distinguish where a work package is in the WBS. There are many different numbering systems you can use. The following image provides an example:

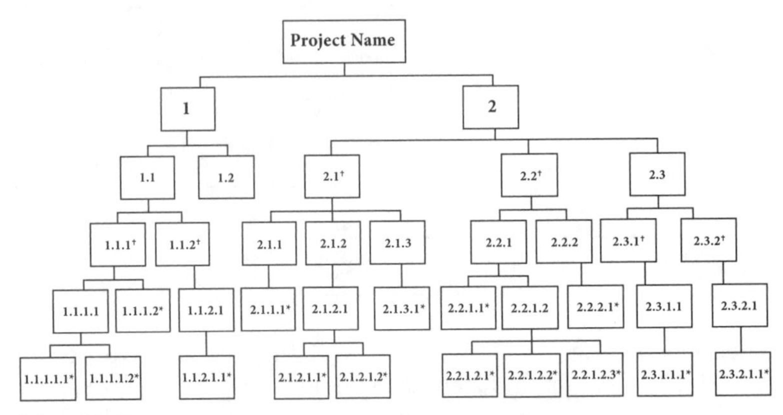

You may see the term "control account" (shown in the previous image) on the exam. For some projects, you might not want to manage costs at the work package level. Instead, you would manage them at a higher level in the WBS, called the control account.

As the planning process progresses, the team breaks down the work packages from the WBS into the schedule activities (or "activities" for short) that are required to produce the work packages. Note that this further breakdown of the WBS into an activity list is done as part of the time management process of Define Activities. The team uses the project scope statement, WBS, and WBS dictionary (described later in this chapter) to help define which activities are required to produce the deliverables.

On small projects, the WBS is often broken down into work packages that involve from 4 to 40 hours of work. On large projects, however, the work packages may be much larger than this; for example, they could involve 300 hours of work. Therefore, the Define Activities process is especially important on large projects. Can you imagine how this effort is different on a large project than on a small project?

If your company works on many similar projects, it is important to realize that the WBS from one project may be used as the basis for the next. Therefore, the project management office should collect WBS examples and encourage the creation of templates.

Great project managers do not only see the value of the information provided in the WBS; they also recognize the value that the effort involved in creating the WBS adds to the project. Do you really understand what a WBS is? Try the next exercise. If you miss many of the answers, review this section again and rethink your knowledge of WBSs before taking the exam.

Exercise Test yourself! What are the benefits of using a WBS?

Answer This exercise may seem redundant of the previous exercise, but it is important to clearly understand the value of the WBS for the exam. The following are benefits of using a WBS:

- Helps prevent work from slipping through the cracks
- Provides the project team members with an understanding of where their pieces fit into the overall project management plan and gives them an indication of the impact of their work on the project as a whole
- Facilitates communication and cooperation between and among the project team and other stakeholders
- Helps prevent changes
- Focuses the team's experience on what needs to be done, resulting in increased quality and a project that is easier to manage
- Provides a basis for estimating resources, cost, and time
- Provides PROOF of the need for resources, funds, and time
- Gets team buy-in and builds the team
- Helps people get their minds around the project

The WBS is the foundation of the project. This means almost everything that occurs in planning after the creation of the WBS is related to the WBS. For example, project costs and time are estimated at the work package or activity level, not for the project as a whole. Risks are identified by work package, not just for the project as a whole. Work packages are assigned to individuals or parts of the performing organization, depending on the size of the project. Does the following diagram make sense to you? Are you getting the full value of the WBS on your projects?

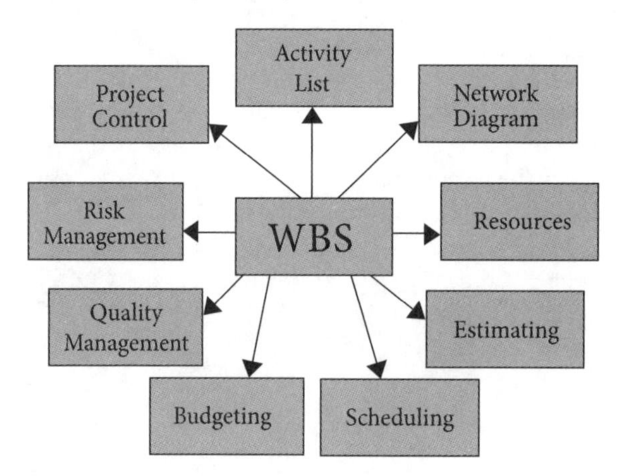

Let's think about the project control element in the previous diagram. Many people forget to use the project management tools from project planning while the work is being done. They may create a WBS as a required activity but then forget about it. As a result, they do not get all the tool's benefits. If the exam asks what you do with the WBS once you have created it, what will you answer?

Exercise What do you do with a WBS once you have created it?

Answer If you were going to test someone's knowledge, would you test the basics like "What is a WBS?" or would you test knowledge about how a WBS helps better manage a project? The exam strongly weighs toward the latter. So take some time to really think about this question.

When completed, the WBS can be used any time the scope of the project needs to be reevaluated. For example, you can use a WBS:

- When there is a scope-related change request to the project. The WBS, along with the project scope statement, can help you see if the request is within the planned scope of the project.
- As part of integrated change control to evaluate any impacts of other changes on scope.

- As a way to control scope creep (i.e., scope increasing or varying from what was planned on the project) by reminding everyone what work is to be done.
- As a communications tool.
- To help new team members see their roles.

There can be many references to the WBS on the exam. In short, remember the following. A WBS:
- Is a graphical picture of the hierarchy of the project.
- Identifies all the deliverables to be completed—if it is not in the WBS, it is not part of the project.
- Is the foundation upon which the project is built.
- Is VERY important.
- Should exist for every project.
- Forces you to think through all aspects of the project.
- Can be reused for other projects.
- Does NOT show dependencies.

The previous list should help you get a few more tricky questions right on the exam. Now, would you like to get one more right? Many people confuse the terms "WBS" and "decomposition." The best way to think of decomposition is that decomposition is what you are doing, and the WBS is the means to do it. In other words, you can decompose the project using a WBS.

The exam may use the term "deconstruction" instead of "decomposition." Both terms mean the same thing.

Like tricks? Here is another one. Use the following diagram to keep the relationships straight in your mind.

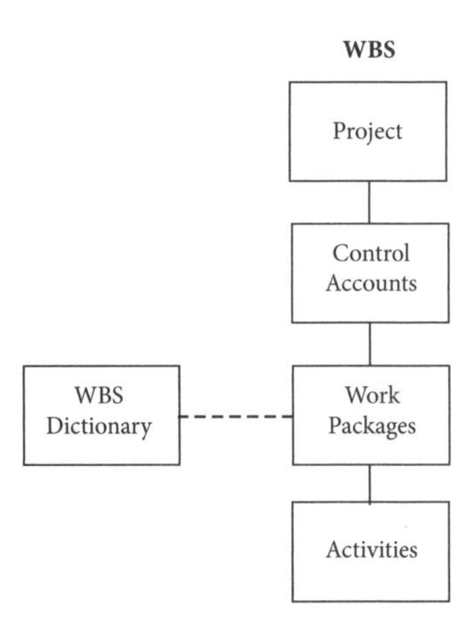

WBS Dictionary PAGE 121 Do you want to hear about a really great idea? Think about how a work package is identified in a WBS. It is usually described in a few words, such as "casing design" or "module XYZ code." But giving such a brief description of the deliverable to a team member allows for too much possible variation from what the deliverable was intended to be; it allows for scope creep. A WBS dictionary is the solution to this problem. This document provides a description of the work to be done for each WBS work package and helps make sure the resulting work better matches what is needed. Therefore, a project manager can use the WBS dictionary to prevent scope creep before work even starts on the project, rather than dealing with scope creep while the work is being done through the use of management skills and constant inspection.

The WBS dictionary is an output of the Create WBS process. This document may be used as part of a work authorization system, which informs team members of when their work package is going to start. The WBS dictionary describes the schedule milestones, the acceptance criteria, and other information about the work package. You can also use it to control what work is done when, to prevent scope creep, and to increase stakeholders' understanding of the effort required for each work package. The WBS dictionary essentially puts boundaries on what is included in the work package (similar to the way the project charter puts boundaries on what is included in the project). NOTE: Some of the entries in the WBS dictionary are filled in during iterations, rather than when it is first drafted (i.e., durations, interdependencies, etc.).

A WBS dictionary may contain information similar to the following:

WBS Dictionary			
Control Account ID #	Work Package Name/ Number	Date of Update	Responsible Organization/ Individual
Work Package Deliverable Description			
Work Involved			
Acceptance Criteria (How to know if the deliverable/work is acceptable)			
Assumptions			
Risks			
Resources Assigned			
Duration			
Schedule Milestones			
Cost			
Due Date			
Interdependencies Before this work package ___________ After this work package ___________			
Approved By: Project Manager ______________________________			Date: ______________

Scope Baseline PAGE 122 Think about the word "baseline." We discussed baselines in the Integration Management chapter and will continue to mention baselines throughout this book. Some people who do not currently use baselines to help control their projects have a hard time understanding this concept. Baselines are simply the final, approved version of certain pieces of the project management plan. For scope, the baseline is the version of the WBS, WBS dictionary, and project scope statement that was approved at the end of planning, before the project work began. As the work on the project progresses, the project manager looks at where the project is at compared to where the baseline says it should be. In other words, what scope has been completed on the project? Does it match what is defined in the WBS, WBS dictionary, and project scope statement?

If scope is needed that is not in the baseline, a change has to be formally approved through the integrated change control process, and a new item (or items) then needs to be added to the WBS, WBS dictionary, and project scope statement to show the scope addition. This updated documentation becomes the new scope baseline for the project. Any other components of the project management plan and project documents that are affected by the change in scope also need to be updated (e.g., parts of the project management plan or project documents related to schedule, budget, resources, quality, risk, etc.).

A project's (and project manager's) measurements of success include whether the project has met the requirements and whether the scope baseline has been met. And because a project manager's performance is evaluated along with the success of the project, it is essential to use the tools, techniques, and practices of project management in the real world. These assets make it so much easier to achieve success on a project and to get a great evaluation of your own performance as the project manager.

Verify Scope[7] PAGE 123

Process: Verify Scope
Process Group: Monitoring & Controlling
Knowledge Area: Scope Management

Many people are confused about what it means to verify scope. Are you one of them? If so, we can help you get up to five more questions right on the exam by clarifying this process.

TRICKS OF THE TRADE® First, think about the name of the process. Many people think Verify Scope means making sure you documented the right scope during project planning. This is incorrect, however. The Verify Scope process actually involves frequent, planned-in meetings with the customer or sponsor to gain formal acceptance of deliverables during project monitoring and controlling. That's a big difference, isn't it?

Let's look at the inputs to this process. Try this exercise.

Exercise What would you expect the inputs to Verify Scope to be? (Remember that the word "input" means, "What do I need before I can. . .?")

Answer

- Work must be completed and checked each time before you meet with the customer; therefore, you must have what are called **validated deliverables** from the Perform Quality Control process.
- It might be helpful to have the approved scope with you when you meet with the customer, so you need the **project management plan** (specifically, the **scope baseline**).

- You might also need the **requirements traceability matrix** for the meeting, so you can track where requirements came from and prove that requirements were achieved and in what work.
- In addition, you should have the **requirements documentation** to refresh your memory about the full details of the requirements.
- You would previously have agreed to what the deliverables are and the need for the customer to formally accept deliverables while planning the project (part of the **scope management plan**).

Can you see how important having experience working on projects is for the exam, and how you can use logic to answer many questions correctly, even input questions? Now let's try the dreaded outputs.

Exercise Name the outputs of Verify Scope. (Remember that output means, "What will I have when I am done with. . .?")

Answer Another way of looking at an output is to think about why you are bothering doing this and what the results should be. Verify Scope is done to help ensure the project is on track from the customer's point of view during the project, rather than just hoping to get the final acceptance in project closure. It is better to find changes and issues during the project than at the end. The customer will either accept deliverables or make change requests. In either case, the project documents will need to be updated to reflect completion or changes. Therefore, the outputs are:

- Accepted deliverables
- Change requests
- Project document updates

TRICKS OF THE TRADE® Beyond the potentially misleading name, there are a few more tricky aspects of the Verify Scope process. First, it can be done at the end of each project phase in the project life cycle (to verify the phase deliverables along the way) and at other points throughout the project as part of monitoring and controlling (to verify any deliverables that require approval in the middle of the phase or project). Therefore, you verify scope with the customer multiple times in one project. The difference between the Verify Scope and the Close Project or Phase processes can also be a little tricky. Whereas the Verify Scope process results in formal acceptance by the customer of interim deliverables, remember that part of the reason for the Close Project or Phase process is to get final acceptance or sign-off from the customer for the project or phase as a whole.

The third tricky area is how Verify Scope relates to Perform Quality Control. See the following diagram.

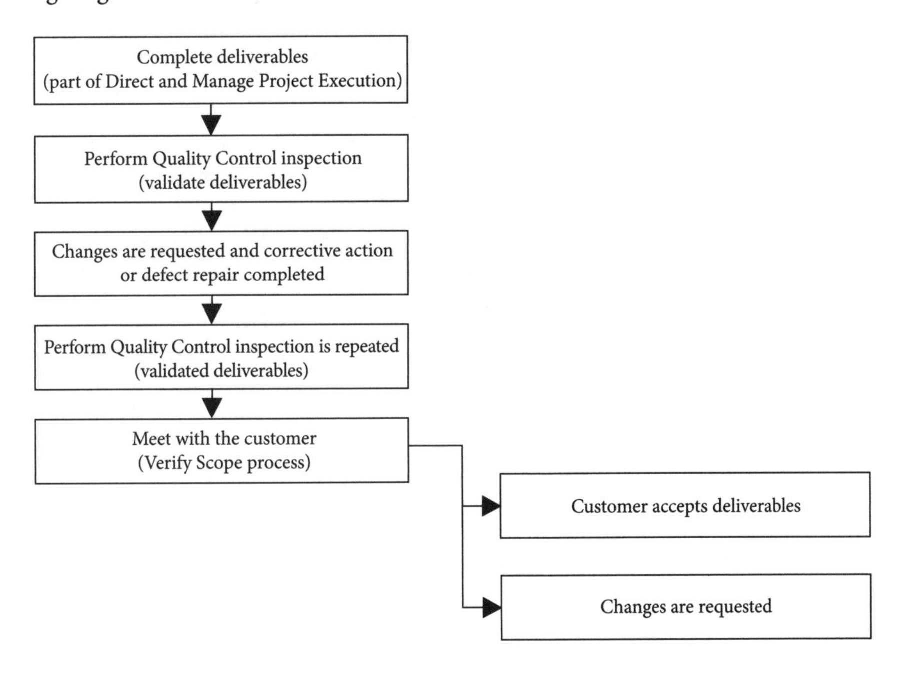

Although Perform Quality Control is generally done first (to make sure the deliverable meets the requirements before it is shown to the customer), the two processes are very similar in that both involve checking for the correctness of work. The difference is the focus of the effort and who is doing the checking. In Perform Quality Control, the quality control department checks to see if the requirements specified for the deliverables are met and makes sure the work is correct. In Verify Scope, the customer checks and hopefully accepts the deliverables.

Control Scope PAGE 125

Process: Control Scope
Process Group: Monitoring & Controlling
Knowledge Area: Scope Management

Many project managers do not really control their projects. If this is true for you, you might have some gaps in your knowledge of this process. Control Scope involves measuring project and product scope performance and managing scope baseline changes. How do you measure scope now? Are you doing it frequently, so that you are sure at any point in the project that the scope is being completed according to plan? As you take the exam, assume that the project manager is controlling scope in this way. Assume proper project management is being done on the project unless the question states otherwise.

To control scope, you first need to have a clear definition of what the scope should be (the scope baseline from the project management plan) and you need to have work completed on the project. You also need to be aware of the original requirements recorded in the requirements documentation and the requirements traceability matrix (inputs to this process). You then have to measure scope performance (the work completed) against the scope baseline to analyze any variances and decide if corrective action or preventive action is required. Once you have that information, you determine if you need to make any updates to the scope baseline, other parts of the project management plan, or the project documents, and what changes you need to request. At the same time, you look for the impact any scope changes would have on all aspects of the project (through the Perform Integrated Change Control process).

Remember that the Control Scope process is extremely proactive. It includes thinking about where changes to scope are coming from on the project, and what can be done to prevent or remove the need for any more changes from that source. If you properly use project management tools, techniques, and practices, it saves you from having to deal with unnecessary problems. As a result, you have time to do such analysis.

As a project manager, your job is not to just process other people's changes; it is to control the project to the project management plan and to meet all baselines. Therefore, you should not be easily swayed or influenced and should not let others add scope or change scope without following the approved change management process and without the suggested changes being within the planned scope of the project. As discussed earlier, people who want work to be done will try to add it to the project whether it is logically part of the project or not. So you must control the project scope.

Practice Exam

1. A work breakdown structure numbering system allows the project team to:
   A. Systematically estimate costs of work breakdown structure elements.
   B. Provide project justification.
   C. Identify the level at which individual elements are found.
   D. Use it in project management software.

2. The work breakdown structure can BEST be thought of as an effective aid for _____ communications.
   A. Team
   B. Project manager
   C. Customer
   D. Stakeholder

3. Which of the following is a KEY output of the Verify Scope process?
   A. A more complete scope management plan
   B. Customer acceptance of project deliverables
   C. Improved schedule estimates
   D. An improved project management information system

4. During project executing, a team member comes to the project manager because he is not sure what work he needs to accomplish on the project. Which of the following documents contain detailed descriptions of work packages?
   A. WBS dictionary
   B. Activity list
   C. Project scope statement
   D. Scope management plan

5. During which part of the project management process is the project scope statement created?
   A. Initiating
   B. Planning
   C. Executing
   D. Monitoring and controlling

6. The program was planned years ago, before there was a massive introduction of new technology. While planning the next project in this program, the project manager has expanded the scope management plan because, as a project becomes more complex, the level of uncertainty in the scope:
   A. Remains the same.
   B. Decreases.
   C. Decreases then increases.
   D. Increases.

7. During a meeting with some of the project stakeholders, the project manager is asked to add work to the project scope. The project manager had access to correspondence about the project before the project charter was signed and remembers that the project sponsor specifically denied funding for the scope mentioned by these stakeholders. The BEST thing for the project manager to do is to:
   A. Let the sponsor know of the stakeholders' request.
   B. Evaluate the impact of adding the scope.
   C. Tell the stakeholders the scope cannot be added.
   D. Add the work if there is time available in the project schedule.

8. A new project manager is being mentored by a more experienced PMP-certified project manager. The new project manager is having difficulty finding enough time to manage the project because the product and project scope are being progressively elaborated. The PMP-certified project manager advises that the basic tools for project management, such as a work breakdown structure, can be used during project executing to assist the project manager. For which of the following can a work breakdown structure be used?
   A. Communicating with the customer
   B. Showing calendar dates for each work package
   C. Showing the functional managers for each team member
   D. Showing the business need for the project

9. During a project team meeting, a team member suggests an enhancement to the scope that is beyond the scope of the project charter. The project manager points out that the team needs to concentrate on completing all the work and only the work required. This is an example of:
   A. Change management process.
   B. Scope management.
   C. Quality analysis.
   D. Scope decomposition.

10. When should the Verify Scope process be done?
    A. At the end of the project
    B. At the beginning of the project
    C. At the end of each phase of the project
    D. During the planning processes

11. The project is mostly complete. The project has a schedule variance of 300 and a cost variance of -900. All but one of the quality control inspections have been completed and all have met the quality requirements. All items in the issue log have been resolved. Many of the resources have been released. The sponsor is about to call a meeting to obtain product verification when the customer notifies the project manager that they want to make a major change to the scope. The project manager should:
    A. Meet with the project team to determine if this change can be made.
    B. Ask the customer for a description of the change.
    C. Explain that the change cannot be made at this point in the process.
    D. Inform management.

12. You have just joined the project management office after five years of working on projects. One of the things you want to introduce to your company is the value of creating and utilizing work breakdown structures. Some of the project managers are angry that you are asking them to do "extra work." Which of the following would be the BEST thing you could tell the project managers to convince them to use work breakdown structures?
    A. Work breakdown structures will prevent work from slipping through the cracks.
    B. Work breakdown structures are only needed on large projects.
    C. Work breakdown structures are required only if the project involves contracts.
    D. Work breakdown structures are the only way to identify risks.

13. A new project manager has asked you for advice on creating a work breakdown structure. After you explain the process to her, she asks you what software she should use to create the WBS and what she should do with it when it is completed. You might respond that it is not the picture that is the most valuable result of creating a WBS. It is:
    A. A bar chart.
    B. Team buy-in.

C. Activities.
D. A list of risks.

14. To manage a project effectively, work should be broken down into small pieces. Which of the following does NOT describe how far to decompose the work?
A. Until it has a meaningful conclusion
B. Until it cannot be logically subdivided further
C. Until it can be done by one person
D. Until it can be realistically estimated

15. A project manager may use ______ to make sure the team members clearly know what work is included in each of their work packages.
A. The project scope statement
B. The product scope
C. The WBS dictionary
D. The schedule

16. A project manager has just been assigned to a new project and has been given the approved project charter. The FIRST thing the project manager must do is:
A. Create a project scope statement.
B. Confirm that all the stakeholders have had input into the scope.
C. Analyze project risk.
D. Begin work on a project management plan.

17. The construction phase of a new software product is near completion. The next phases are testing and implementation. The project is two weeks ahead of schedule. Which of the following processes should the project manager be MOST concerned with before moving on to the final phase?
A. Verify Scope
B. Perform Quality Control
C. Report Performance
D. Control Costs

18. You are managing a six-month project and have held bi-weekly meetings with your project stakeholders. After five-and-a-half months of work, the project is on schedule and budget, but the stakeholders are not satisfied with the deliverables. This situation will delay the project completion by one month. The MOST important process that could have prevented this situation is:
A. Monitor and Control Risks.
B. Control Schedule.
C. Define Scope.
D. Control Scope.

19. All of the following are parts of the scope baseline EXCEPT the:
A. Scope management plan.
B. Project scope statement.
C. Work breakdown structure.
D. WBS dictionary.

20. One of the stakeholders on the project contacts the project manager to discuss some additional scope they would like to add to the project. The project manager asks for details in writing and then works through the Control Scope process. What should the project manager do NEXT when the evaluation of the requested scope is complete?
    A. Ask the stakeholder if there are any more changes expected.
    B. Complete integrated change control.
    C. Make sure the impact of the change is understood by the stakeholder.
    D. Find out the root cause of why the scope was not discovered during project planning.

21. During the completion of project work, the sponsor asks the project manager to report on how the project is going. In order to prepare the report, the project manager asks all the team members what percent complete their work is. There is one team member who has been hard to manage from the beginning. In response to being asked what percent complete he is, the team member asks, "Percent complete of what?" Being tired of such comments, the project manager reports to the team member's boss that the team member is not cooperating. Which of the following is MOST likely the real problem?
    A. The project manager did not get buy-in from the manager for the resources on the project.
    B. The project manager did not create an adequate reward system for team members to improve their cooperation.
    C. The project manager should have had a meeting with the team member's boss the first time the team member caused trouble.
    D. The project manager did not assign work packages.

22. The development of the scope baseline can BEST be described as involving:
    A. The functional managers.
    B. The project team.
    C. All the stakeholders.
    D. The project expediter.

23. Which of the following is an output of the Collect Requirements process?
    A. Requirements traceability matrix
    B. Project scope statement
    C. Work breakdown structure
    D. Change requests

24. A scope change has been suggested by one of the stakeholders on the project. After careful consideration and a lot of arguing, the change control board has decided to reject the change. What should the project manager do?
    A. Support the stakeholder by asking the board for the reason for the rejection.
    B. Suggest to the stakeholder that the next change they request will be approved.
    C. Record the change request and its result.
    D. Advise the change control board to make sure they create approval processes before the next change is proposed.

25. The cost performance index (CPI) on the project is 1.13, and the benefit cost ratio (BCR) is 1.2. The project scope was created by the team and stakeholders. Requirements on the project have been changing throughout the project. No matter what the project manager has tried to accomplish in managing the project, which of the following is he MOST likely to face in the future?
    A. Having to cut costs on the project and increase benefits
    B. Making sure the customer approved the project scope
    C. Not being able to measure completion of the product of the project
    D. Having to add resources to the project

26. Verify Scope is closely related to:
    A. Perform Quality Control.
    B. Sequence Activities.
    C. Perform Quality Assurance.
    D. Time Management.

27. Which of the following can create the MOST misinterpretation of the project scope statement?
    A. Imprecise language
    B. Poor pattern, structure, and chronological order
    C. Small variations in size of work packages or detail of work
    D. Too much detail

28. Which of the following is CORRECT in regard to the Control Scope process?
    A. Effective scope definition can lead to a more complete project scope statement.
    B. The Control Scope process must be done before scope planning.
    C. The Control Scope process must be integrated with other control processes.
    D. Controlling the schedule is the most effective way of controlling scope.

29. Which of the following BEST describes the Verify Scope process?
    A. It provides assurances that the deliverable meets the specifications, is an input to the project management plan, and is an output of Perform Quality Control.
    B. It ensures the deliverable is completed on time, ensures customer acceptance, and shows the deliverable meets specifications.
    C. It ensures customer acceptance, shows the deliverable meets specifications, and provides a chance for differences of opinion to come to light.
    D. It is an output of Perform Quality Control, occurs before Define Scope, and ensures customer acceptance.

30. Which of the following BEST describes product analysis?
    A. Working with the customer to determine the product description
    B. Mathematically analyzing the quality desired for the project
    C. Gaining a better understanding of the product of the project in order to create the project scope statement
    D. Determining whether the quality standards on the project can be met

Answers

1. **Answer** C
   Explanation The numbering system allows team members to quickly identify the level in the work breakdown structure where the specific element is found. It also helps to locate the element in the WBS dictionary.

2. **Answer** D
   Explanation The term "stakeholder" encompasses all the other choices. In this case, it is the best answer since the WBS can be used (but does not need to be used) as a communications tool for all stakeholders to "see" what is included in the project.

3. **Answer** B
   Explanation The output of the Verify Scope process is customer acceptance of project deliverables. The other choices all happen during project planning, well before the time the Verify Scope process takes place.

4. **Answer** A
   Explanation Activity lists may identify the work package they relate to, but they do not contain detailed descriptions of the work packages. The project scope statement defines the project scope, but it does not describe the work a team member is assigned. The scope management plan describes how scope will be planned, managed, and controlled. It does not include a description of each work package. The WBS dictionary defines each element in the WBS. Therefore, descriptions of the work packages are in the WBS dictionary.

5. **Answer** B
   Explanation The project scope statement is an output of the Define Scope process, which occurs during project planning.

6. **Answer** D
   Explanation Not all questions will be difficult. The level of uncertainty in scope increases based on the scale of effort required to identify all the scope. For larger projects, it is more difficult to "catch" everything.

7. **Answer** C
   Explanation Though one could let the sponsor know about the stakeholders' request, the best choice listed would be to say no. An even better choice would be to find the root cause of the problem, but that choice is not listed here.

8. **Answer** A
   Explanation A WBS does not show dates or responsibility assignments. The business need is described in the project charter. In this situation, the product and project scope are being fine tuned. It would save the project manager time in effectively managing progressive elaboration if the WBS was used as a communications tool. Using the WBS helps ensure everyone (including the customer) understands the scope of the work.

9. **Answer** B
   Explanation The team member is suggesting an enhancement that is outside the scope of the project charter. Scope management involves focusing on doing the work and only the work in the project management plan that meets the objectives of the project charter. The project manager is performing scope management.

10. **Answer** C
Explanation The Verify Scope process occurs during project monitoring and controlling. It is done at the end of each project phase to get approval for phase deliverables, as well as at other points to get approval for interim deliverables.

11. **Answer** B
Explanation Do not jump into the problem without thinking. The customer only notified the project manager that they want to make a change. They did not describe the change. The project manager should not say no until he or she knows more about the potential change, nor should the project manager go to management without more information. The project manager must understand the nature of the change and have time to evaluate the impact of that change before doing anything else. Of these choices, the first thing to do is to determine what the change is. The project manager might then analyze the potential change with the team, but only if their input is required.

12. **Answer** A
Explanation Work breakdown structures are required on projects of every size, regardless of whether contracts are involved. Work breakdown structures can be used to help identify risks, but risks can be identified using other methods as well. Preventing work from being forgotten (slipping through the cracks) is one of the main reasons the tool is used, and is the best choice offered here.

13. **Answer** B
Explanation The WBS is an input to all of these choices. However, team buy-in is a direct result of the WBS creation process, while the other choices use the WBS to assist in their completion. Involving the team in creating the WBS provides project team members with an understanding of where their pieces fit into the overall project management plan and gives them an indication of the impact of their work on the project as a whole.

14. **Answer** C
Explanation The lowest level of the WBS is a work package, which can be completed by more than one person. The other choices are aspects of a work package.

15. **Answer** C
Explanation The project scope statement describes work on a high-level basis. Work packages need to be specific to enable team members to complete their work without gold plating. The product scope does not tell team members what work is assigned to them. The team should have a copy of the schedule, but a schedule does not show them what work is included in each of their work packages. Work packages are described in the WBS dictionary. NOTE: Do not think of the WBS dictionary as a dictionary of terms.

16. **Answer** B
Explanation This question can be tricky, especially if you have spent so much time studying that you have forgotten some good project management practices. A quick look at Rita's Process Chart in this book might lead you to conclude that the first thing to do would be to start planning. However, the question indicates that the project manager was not involved until after the charter was created and approved. Therefore, wouldn't it be smart to make sure the project charter is clear and complete before moving on? This is why it is best for the project manager to confirm the stakeholders had input into the scope.

17. **Answer** A
Explanation The Verify Scope process deals with acceptance by the customer. Without this acceptance, the project manager will not be able to move into the next project phase.

18. **Answer** C
Explanation Monitor and Control Risks, Control Schedule, and Control Scope are monitoring and controlling processes. This situation asks how to prevent the problem, which would have been done during planning. The project deliverables are defined in the Define Scope process, which is a part of project planning. Good planning reduces the likelihood of a situation like the one described, by including the right people and spending adequate time clarifying the project scope.

19. **Answer** A
Explanation The scope baseline includes the WBS, WBS dictionary, and the project scope statement. The scope management plan is not part of the scope baseline.

20. **Answer** B
Explanation Notice that there are many things the project manager could do listed in the choices. The question asks what is the BEST thing to do NEXT. Management of the change is not complete when the Control Scope process is completed. It is important to look at the impact of the change on other parts of the project, such as time and cost. Therefore, performing integrated change control is the best thing to do next. This would probably be followed by making sure the impact of the change is understood by the stakeholder, then determining why this scope was not identified in planning, and asking the stakeholder if there are more changes expected.

21. **Answer** D
Explanation The project manager is not losing resources (which is implied by not getting the manager's buy-in). Although a reward system would help with cooperation, the real problem here is not cooperation. Meeting with the team member and his boss cannot be the answer because it also does not solve the problem at hand (the team member not knowing what he is to do). If you selected this choice, be very careful! You can get 10 to 20 questions wrong on the exam simply because you do not see the real problem! The whole discussion of the team member and his actions is a distracter. The real problem in this scenario is not that the team member is being uncooperative. He is asking a question that many team members want to ask in the real world. "How can I tell you how things are going if I do not know what work I am being asked to do?" The real problem is the lack of a WBS and work packages. If there were a WBS and work packages for the project, the team member would not have to ask such a question.

22. **Answer** B
Explanation After obtaining input from the customer and other stakeholders, the project team is responsible for developing the scope baseline. Remember that the scope baseline includes the WBS, WBS dictionary, and project scope statement.

23. **Answer** A
Explanation The project scope statement is an output of the Define Scope process. The work breakdown structure is an output of the Create WBS process. Scope change requests are outputs of the Verify Scope and Control Scope processes. The requirements traceability matrix is an output of the Collect Requirements process, and is used to track the requirements throughout the life of the project.

24. **Answer** C
Explanation There is no reason to think that the board's rejection would not contain an explanation already, since providing that information is commonly done. Suggesting a change

process that circumvents the change control board's authority is not ethical. There is no reason to think that approval processes are not already in place. A rejected change should be recorded for historical purposes, in case the idea is resurrected later, and for other reasons.

25. **Answer** C
Explanation There are many pieces of data in this question that are distracters from the real issue. Though it is common to have to cut costs and add resources to a project, nothing in the question should lead you to think these will be required in this situation. Customers do not generally approve the project scope (what you are going to do to complete their requirements); instead, they approve the product scope (their requirements). Since requirements are used to measure the completion of the product of the project, not having complete requirements will make such measurement impossible.

26. **Answer** A
Explanation Perform Quality Control checks for correctness, and Verify Scope checks for acceptance.

27. **Answer** A
Explanation Much of the work on the project is dictated by the project scope statement. Any imprecision in such a key document will lead to differing interpretations.

28. **Answer** C
Explanation Though it is correct that effective scope definition can lead to a more complete project scope statement, this cannot be the answer, because it does not deal with control. Scope planning occurs before the Control Scope process, not after it. Controlling the schedule is not the best way to control scope, so that is not the best answer. The control processes do not act in isolation. A change to one will most likely affect the others. Therefore the need to integrate the Scope Control process with other control processes is the best answer.

29. **Answer** C
Explanation The project management plan is completed before the Verify Scope process. The Verify Scope process does not deal with time, but rather acceptance. The Verify Scope process does not occur before the Define Scope process. The choice stating that the Verify Scope process ensures customer acceptance, shows the deliverable meets specifications, and provides a chance for differences of opinion to come to light is entirely correct, making that the best answer.

30. **Answer** C
Explanation You need to have a product description before you can do product analysis. Analyzing the level of quality desired is related to the Plan Quality process. Determining whether the quality standards on the project can be met is done in the Perform Quality Assurance process. Product analysis includes gaining a better understanding of the product of the project, in order to create the project scope statement.

CHAPTER SIX Time Management

Quicktest

- Time management process
- Schedule baseline
- Schedule compression
  - Crashing
  - Fast tracking
- Activity list
- Network diagram
- Dependencies
  - Mandatory
  - Discretionary
  - External
- Precedence diagramming method (PDM)
- Critical path
- Float (Slack)
  - Free float
  - Total float
  - Project float
- Three-point estimating
- Monte Carlo analysis
- Bar charts
- Milestone charts
- Schedule management plan
- Resource leveling
- Leads and lags
- Heuristics
- GERT
- Variance
- Milestones, milestone list
- Resource breakdown structure
- One-point estimate
- Reserve analysis
- Padding
- Analogous estimating
- Parametric estimating
- Critical path method
- Near-critical path
- Critical chain method
- Activity attributes
- Activity resource requirements
- Reestimating

Some people find this chapter intimidating because they do not know how to manually create network diagrams. Don't worry; we can help you with that. But this chapter is often very difficult for those who do not realize that an unrealistic schedule is the project manager's fault. Yes, it's true! One of the key responsibilities of a project manager is to see if the needed end date for a project can be met and to create options to make it happen, all BEFORE project executing starts. If you know the many options for compressing a project schedule, and understand that a project schedule must be realistic before project executing begins, this chapter should not be difficult for you.

In order to answer time management questions correctly, you should thoroughly understand the process of scheduling a project. Although most project managers use some type of software to assist with scheduling, the exam has required test takers to manually draw network diagrams to answer questions about network diagrams and scheduling. Therefore, you need to know some things that normally go on behind the scenes when using "project management software."

Watch out! Although we just used the term "project management software," make sure you realize there is no such thing as true project management software. The software available can be extremely helpful for scheduling, analyzing "what if" scenarios, and performing status reporting functions, but it does not tell you how to manage a project. You cannot simply follow the software; you must adapt it to your needs. Software cannot do a project manager's job.

Many existing software programs suggest planning a project in ways that do not conform to proper project management methods: first make a list of the activities, next assign them to calendar dates, and then the project management plan is finished. These programs do not address all aspects of project management and may have changed some of the basic components of the tools of project management (such as what is in a bar chart) in ways that could cause you to get questions wrong on the exam. Make sure you understand the full project management process and keep that process in mind for the exam.

Read this chapter carefully, and check your knowledge as you go.

Rita's Process Chart—Time Management

Where are we in the project management process?

INITIATING

- Select project manager
- Determine company culture and existing systems
- Collect processes, procedures, and historical information
- Divide large projects into phases
- Understand the business case
- Uncover initial requirements, assumptions, and risks
- Assess project and product feasibility within the given constraints
- Create measurable objectives
- Develop project charter
- Identify stakeholders
- Develop stakeholder management strategy

PLANNING

(This is the only process group with a set order)

- **Determine how you will do planning—part of all management plans**
- Determine detailed requirements
- Create project scope statement
- Assess what to purchase
- Determine team
- Create WBS and WBS dictionary
- **Create activity list**
- **Create network diagram**
- **Estimate resource requirements**
- **Estimate time and cost**
- **Determine critical path**
- **Develop schedule**
- Develop budget
- Determine quality standards, processes, and metrics
- Create process improvement plan
- **Determine all roles and responsibilities**
- Plan communications
- Perform risk identification, qualitative and quantitative risk analysis, and risk response planning
- **Go back—iterations**
- Prepare procurement documents
- Create change management plan
- **Finalize the "how to execute and control" parts of all management plans**
- **Develop realistic and final PM plan and performance measurement baseline**
- Gain formal approval of the plan
- Hold kickoff meeting

EXECUTING

- Execute the work according to the PM plan
- Produce product deliverables (product scope)
- Request changes
- Implement only approved changes
- Continuously improve
- Follow processes
- Perform quality assurance
- Perform quality audits
- Acquire final team
- Manage people
- Evaluate team and project performance
- Hold team-building activities
- Give recognition and rewards
- Use issue logs
- Facilitate conflict resolution
- Release resources as work is completed
- Send and receive information
- Hold meetings
- Select sellers

MONITORING & CONTROLLING

- **Take action to control the project**
- **Measure performance against the performance measurement baseline**
- **Measure performance against other metrics determined by the project manager**
- **Determine variances and if they warrant a corrective action or change request**
- **Influence the factors that cause changes**
- **Request changes**
- Perform integrated change control
- Approve or reject changes
- Inform stakeholders of the results of change requests
- **Update the PM plan and project documents**
- Manage configuration
- **Create forecasts**
- Gain acceptance of interim deliverables from the customer
- Perform quality control
- Report on project performance and solicit feedback
- Perform risk assessments and audits
- Manage reserves
- Administer procurements

CLOSING

- Confirm work is done to requirements
- Complete procurement closure
- Gain final acceptance of the product
- Complete financial closure
- Hand off completed product
- Solicit feedback from the customer about the project
- Complete final performance reporting
- Index and archive records
- Update lessons learned knowledge base

The following should help you understand how each part of time management fits into the overall project management process:

The Time Management Process	Done During
Define Activities	Planning process group
Sequence Activities	Planning process group
Estimate Activity Resources	Planning process group
Estimate Activity Durations	Planning process group
Develop Schedule	Planning process group
Control Schedule	Monitoring and controlling process group

Schedule Management Plan PAGE 130 Though specifically listed in most other chapters, the management plan for scheduling is not defined as a separate part of the scheduling process. Instead, it is created as part of the Develop Project Management Plan process in integration management. Know for the exam that a time management planning process exists, and that you must create a schedule management plan. This process answers the following questions: "Who will be involved, and what approach will we take to plan the schedule for the project?" "What organizational processes and procedures will I use to create the schedule?" (Note: The scheduling methodology may already be defined and recorded as part of the organizational process assets.) "What tools will I use for scheduling?" (Note: The tools approved for use within the organization may already be documented as part of enterprise environmental factors.) And then, "How will I effectively manage and control the project to the schedule baseline, and manage schedule variances?" Did you notice that such a plan requires thinking in advance about how you will manage the schedule? This is a concept that many project managers miss on their real-world projects.

The schedule management plan includes:

- The scheduling methodology and scheduling software to be used on the project.
- Rules for how estimates should be stated. For example, should estimates be in hours, days, or weeks? Should estimators identify both the effort (the amount of labor involved in completing an activity; e.g., 12 hours) and duration (the amount of work periods the effort will span; e.g., 1.5 days) needed to complete an activity?
- Establishment of a schedule baseline for measuring against as part of project monitoring and controlling.
- Identification of the performance measures that will be used on the project, to identify variances early.
- Planning for how schedule variances will be managed.
- Identification of schedule change control procedures.
- Reporting formats to be used.

Does this list make you think? Do you currently do this for your projects? Notice the identification of performance measures. Many project managers just work on the project and hope they meet the deadline. But a proper schedule management plan requires you to measure progress along the way. So you determine in advance what the measures of performance will be and how you will capture the data you need to measure. The schedule management plan answers questions like, "How will I measure schedule performance during the project?" "Will I measure once a month or once a week?" "What calculations will I use?" "What data will I collect?"

The schedule management plan can be formal or informal, but it is part of the project management plan. It helps make the schedule estimating process faster by providing guidelines on how estimates should be stated (e.g., in hours, days, or weeks). During monitoring and controlling, the schedule management plan can help determine if a variance is over the allowable threshold and therefore must be acted upon. The schedule management plan can also help determine the types of reports required on the project relating to schedule.

Define Activities PAGE 133

Process: Define Activities
Process Group: Planning
Knowledge Area: Time Management

This process involves taking the work packages created in the WBS and breaking them down into the activities that are required to produce the work package deliverables. The activities should be at a level small enough to estimate, schedule, monitor, and manage. These activities are then sequenced in the next process, Sequence Activities. (Note that the creation of the work packages in the WBS is part of scope management, and the identification of activities is part of time management.)

TRICKS OF THE TRADE® Defining activities is not always done as a separate process in the real world. Many project managers combine this effort with creating a WBS; they take their WBS down one more level to show activities, rather than stopping at work packages. Other project managers say they cannot work with a network diagram created at the activity level because it becomes too large. Instead, they create the network diagram to the work package level. Neither of these practices is wrong; just know this for the exam—the *PMBOK® Guide* states that in the Define Activities process, the WBS work packages are decomposed into activities (schedule activities), and in the Sequence Activities process (described next), those activities are sequenced to create the network diagram.

So what do you need in order to define activities? (That question is all there really is to the concept of inputs.) You need your scope baseline (scope statement, WBS, and WBS dictionary), and you need your team, because involving the team helps define the activities completely and accurately and therefore makes the estimates, created later in the planning process, more accurate.

Have you ever felt a project had too many unknown components to adequately break down the work and schedule it? Be careful—when that is the case, you might really have more than one project (see the earlier discussion of the defintion of a project in the Project Management Framework chapter). Or, you might just have found it better to not plan to the lowest detail in advance, but instead to plan to a higher level and then wait until the project work has begun and the work is clearer to plan the lower levels. This practice is called "rolling wave planning." With this method, you plan activities to the detail needed to manage the work only when you start that phase of the project life cycle. But remember—the options of rolling wave planning and planning to a higher level than a work package are not excuses for improperly planning a project or for not making sure all the scope that can be known is known before starting work!

When completed, the Define Activities process results in an **activity list** and documentation of the details of the activities (**activity attributes**). The Define Activities process also involves determining the milestones to use on the project.

Milestones Milestones are significant events within the project schedule. They are not work activities. For example, a completed design, certain deliverable due dates from the customer, or a company-required checkpoint could be milestones. The sponsor may impose milestones, and a summary of these milestones would be included in the project charter. What many people do not understand is that the project manager can also impose additional milestones during the Sequence Activities or Develop Schedule processes, as checkpoints to help control the project. If a checkpoint in the schedule arrives and any of the planned work has not been completed, it indicates the project is not progressing as planned. Part of the Define Activities process involves creating a list of appropriate milestones to use on the project. This milestone list becomes part of the project management plan and is added to the project scope statement and WBS dictionary as part of iterations in planning.

Sequence Activities PAGE 136

Process: Sequence Activities
Process Group: Planning
Knowledge Area: Time Management

The next process involves taking the activities and milestones and sequencing them in the order in which the work will be performed. The result is a network diagram (also referred to as a project schedule network diagram), which can look like the following image. Some people incorrectly call a network diagram a PERT chart. There are several exercises to help you draw and interpret network diagrams later in this chapter.

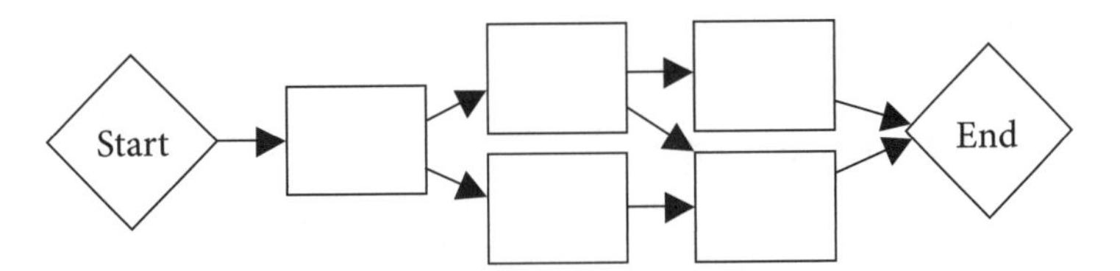

For the exam, know that in its pure form, the network diagram shows just dependencies (logical relationships). If activity duration estimates (estimates) are added to the diagram, it can also show the critical path. If plotted out against time (or placed against a calendar-based scale), the network diagram is a time-scaled schedule network diagram.

If you feel you need extra help understanding how to create and interpret network diagrams, please visit the Web site that accompanies the book: www.rmcproject.com/extras.

Methods to Draw Network Diagrams[1]

In the past, the Precedence Diagramming Method (PDM)[2], the Arrow Diagramming Method (ADM)[3], and the Graphical Evaluation and Review Technique (GERT)[4] method were commonly used to draw network diagrams. Today most network diagrams are created using PDM.

Precedence Diagramming Method (PDM) or Activity-on-Node (AON)

In this method, nodes (or boxes) are used to represent activities, and arrows show activity dependencies, as follows:

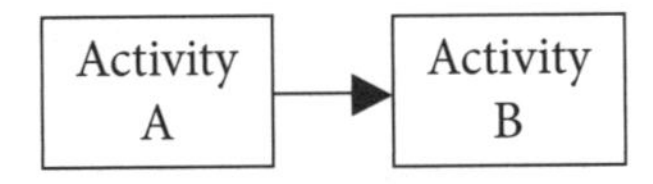

This type of drawing can have four types of logical relationships between activities:

- **Finish-to-start (FS)** An activity must finish before the successor can start. This is the most commonly used relationship. Example: You must finish digging a hole before you can start the next activity of planting a tree.
- **Start-to-start (SS)** An activity must start before the successor can start. Example: You must start designing and wait for two weeks lag in order to have enough of the design completed to start coding.
- **Finish-to-finish (FF)** An activity must finish before the successor can finish. Example: You must finish testing before you can finish documentation.
- **Start-to-finish (SF)** An activity must start before the successor can finish. This dependency is rarely used.

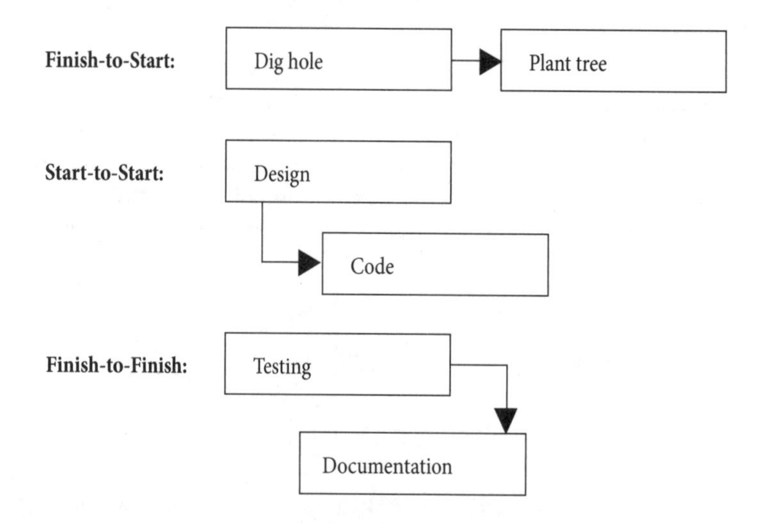

Graphical Evaluation and Review Technique (GERT)

GERT is a modification to the network diagram drawing method. It is a computer simulation technique that allows loops between activities. The easiest example is when you have an activity to design a component and then test it. After testing, it may or may not need to be redesigned. GERT is rarely on the exam, and when it does appear, it is most often just an incorrect answer choice.

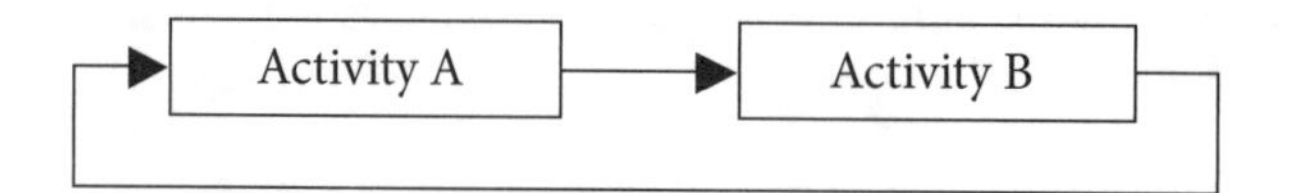

Types of Dependencies The sequence of activities is determined based on the following dependencies:[5]

- **Mandatory Dependency (Hard Logic)** A mandatory dependency is inherent in the nature of the work being done (e.g., you must design before you can construct) or is required by the contract.
- **Discretionary Dependency (Preferred, Preferential, or Soft Logic)** The project manager or team determines this dependency. You can change a discretionary dependency if needed, while you cannot easily change the other types of dependencies. Discretionary dependencies are important when analyzing how to compress the schedule to decrease the project duration (fast track the project).
- **External Dependency** This dependency is based on the needs or desires of a party outside the project (e.g., government or suppliers).

Leads and Lags PAGE 140 A lead may be used to indicate that an activity can start before its predecessor activity is completed. For example, coding might be able to start five days before the design is finished. A lag is inserted waiting time between activities, such as needing to wait three days after pouring concrete before constructing the frame for the house.

Now it's time to test your knowledge. Instead of just asking what a network diagram is, the exam will ask harder, more sophisticated questions like "How can the network diagram help you?" You need to have worked with network diagrams to accurately answer such questions. See how you do with the next exercise.

Exercise Describe how the network diagram can help you on the project.

Answer You should know that network diagrams can be used to:

- Help justify your time estimate for the project.
- Aid in effectively planning, organizing, and controlling the project.
- Show interdependencies of all activities.
- Show workflow so the team will know what activities need to happen in a specific sequence.
- Identify opportunities to compress the schedule in planning and throughout the life of the project (defined later in this chapter).
- Show project progress (when used for controlling the schedule and reporting).

In addition to a network diagram, the Sequence Activities process may result in updates to project documents such as the activity list and the activity attributes. Sequencing the activities can also reveal new risks, resulting in changes to the risk register.

Things About Estimating to Know for the Exam

The next two time management processes (Estimate Activity Resources and Estimate Activity Durations) and the Estimate Costs process (see the Cost Management chapter) all involve estimating. The following are important points to understand about time and cost estimating for the exam.

- Estimating should be based on a WBS to improve accuracy.
- Estimating should be done by the person doing the work whenever possible to improve accuracy.
- Historical information from past projects (part of organizational process assets) is key to improving estimates.
- Schedule, cost, and scope baselines should be kept and not changed except for approved project changes.
- The project schedule should be managed to the schedule baseline for the project.
- The project budget should be managed to the cost baseline for the project.
- Changes are approved in integrated change control.
- Estimates are more accurate if smaller-size work components are estimated.
- Changes should be requested when problems with schedule, cost, scope, quality, or resources occur.
- A project manager should never just accept constraints from management, but should instead analyze the needs of the project, come up with his or her own estimates based on input from the team members doing the work when possible, and reconcile any differences to produce realistic objectives. (Yes, this should be true in the real world!)
- The project manager may periodically recalculate the estimate to complete (ETC) for the project in order to make sure adequate time, funds, resources, etc., are available for the project.

- Plans should be revised during completion of the work as necessary with approved changes.
- There is a process for creating the most accurate estimate possible.
- Padding is not an acceptable project management practice.
- The project manager must meet any agreed-upon estimates.
- Estimates must be reviewed when they are received to see if they are reasonable and to check for padding and risks.
- Estimates must be kept realistic through the life of the project by reestimating and reviewing them periodically.
- Estimates can be decreased by reducing or eliminating risks.
- A project manager has a professional responsibility to provide estimates that are as accurate as feasible and to maintain the integrity of those estimates throughout the life of the project.

In the past, the exam has focused on the practices required to produce good estimates, more than it has found on calculations. Therefore, make sure you take some time to think about these points. Remember, incorrect project management practices will be listed as choices on the exam. Project managers who do not adequately understand and manage their projects in this way have difficulty on the exam and do not even know why.

Now let's look at an important topic related to estimating. Really try to answer the following question before reading on. It will help you assume the right perspective for studying this topic.

Exercise Why should you welcome management giving you an end date for the project or a total cost constraint?

If you need more help with scheduling or handling unrealistic schedules, visit www.rmcproject.com for free tips and information about courses on these topics.

Answer In the real world, many of us struggle with unrealistic schedules or budgets. As we have now stated a few times in this book, the project manager is responsible for making sure the schedule or budget is realistic. This is a difficult concept to get past for many people. Project managers often complain about unrealistic schedules and budgets and put the blame on senior management, but they do not realize that a major reason for having a project manager on a project is to make the schedule and budget realistic. So how do you go about achieving a realistic schedule or budget?

Let's think about the process logically. First, you look at the work needed to complete a project. You then estimate the time and cost of the work and come up with a calculated end date and budget for the project. You try to optimize that date and budget, and then compare your results to the end date and budget required by management. If there is a difference, you analyze the project and provide options on how to change it to meet management's time and cost requirements or negotiate a change to the end date or budget (in other words, you balance the constraints).

An unrealistic schedule or budget is the project manager's fault because he or she should be performing such activities in planning and while the project is underway to keep the project on track. This is an essential concept to understand for the exam. Do you follow the process we just described? If not, take some time now to truly understand it and think about how you can implement these practices in your real world.

So the quick answer to the question in this exercise is that you should welcome management providing an end date or total cost constraint because it gives you an opportunity to reconcile what management wants to what can be done BEFORE committing resources, wasting company time and money on projects that will not be successful, and damaging your reputation. As a project manager (especially as a PMP-certified project manager), you have a professional responsibility to properly manage the schedule.

Estimate Activity Resources PAGE 141

Process: Estimate Activity Resources
Process Group: Planning
Knowledge Area: Time Management

Once the activities are sequenced, the type and quantity of needed resources are determined. Remember that resources include equipment and materials, as well as people. The project manager must plan and coordinate resources in order to avoid common problems such as a lack of resources and resources being taken away from the project. This process results in defined activity resource requirements and a resource breakdown structure (RBS), which shows the resources to be used, organized by their category and type. The following exercise looks at the actions involved in the Estimate Activity Resources process.

Exercise Which of the following actions are involved in the Estimate Activity Resources process? Simply put a yes or no in the right-hand column. Then check your answers against the following table. (Assume the full project management process is being used on a large project as you complete this exercise.)

	Action	Is It Part of Estimate Activity Resources?
1	Review resource availability.	
2	Get one time estimate per activity.	
3	Complete an analysis of the reserves needed on the project.	
4	Create a company calendar identifying working and non-working days.	
5	Create milestones.	
6	Review the WBS and activity list.	
7	Develop a risk register.	

	Action	Is It Part of Estimate Activity Resources?
8	Identify potentially available resources.	
9	Review historical information about the use of resources on similar projects.	
10	Review organizational policies on resource use.	
11	See how leads and lags affect the time estimate.	
12	Solicit expert judgment on what resources are needed and available.	
13	Analyze alternative equipment or methods to use in completing the work and whether different approaches help to better utilize resources.	
14	Show network dependencies per activity.	
15	Identify areas of the project that cannot be completed internally or would otherwise be more efficiently achieved through outsourcing (make-or-buy decisions).	
16	Crash the project.	
17	Break the activity down further if the activity is too complex to estimate resources (bottom-up estimating).	
18	Quantify resource requirements by activity.	
19	Create a hierarchical image that organizes the planned resources by their category and type (a resource breakdown structure).	
20	Fast track the project.	
21	Develop the schedule.	
22	Develop a plan as to what types of resources will be used.	
23	Update project documents.	

Answer The Estimate Activity Resources process involves:

	Action	Is It Part of Estimate Activity Resources?
1	Review resource availability.	Yes
2	Get one time estimate per activity.	No
3	Complete an analysis of the reserves needed on the project.	No
4	Create a company calendar identifying working and non-working days.	No
5	Create milestones.	No
6	Review the WBS and activity list.	Yes
7	Develop a risk register.	No

	Action	Is It Part of Estimate Activity Resources?
8	Identify potentially available resources.	Yes
9	Review historical information about the use of resources on similar projects.	Yes
10	Review organizational policies on resource use.	Yes
11	See how leads and lags affect the time estimate.	No
12	Solicit expert judgment on what resources are needed and available.	Yes
13	Analyze alternative equipment or methods to use in completing the work and whether different approaches help to better utilize resources.	Yes
14	Show network dependencies per activity.	No
15	Identify areas of the project that cannot be completed internally or would otherwise be more efficiently achieved through outsourcing (make-or-buy decisions).	Yes
16	Crash the project.	No
17	Break the activity down further if the activity is too complex to estimate resources (bottom-up estimating).	Yes
18	Quantify resource requirements by activity.	Yes
19	Create a hierarchical image that organizes the planned resources by their category and type (a resource breakdown structure).	Yes
20	Fast track the project.	No
21	Develop the schedule.	No
22	Develop a plan as to what types of resources will be used.	Yes
23	Update project documents.	Yes

Estimate Activity Durations PAGE 146

Process: Estimate Activity Durations
Process Group: Planning
Knowledge Area: Time Management

Once the activities are defined and sequenced and the type and quantity of resources required for each activity are identified, the next step is to estimate how much time each activity will take. This is the Estimate Activity Durations process. The estimators should be those who will be doing the work, when possible; for large projects, however, the estimators are more often the members of the project team, as it is known during planning, who are most familiar with the work that needs to be done. To come up with realistic time estimates, these individuals need to have access to activity resource requirements, resource calendars, organizational process assets (historical data and lessons learned about activity durations, past project calendars, and the defined scheduling methodology), and enterprise environmental factors (company culture and existing systems that the project will have to deal with or can make use of, such as estimating software and productivity metrics). Later in project planning, during the risk management efforts, the time estimates and any other information gathered during this estimating process are considered when creating the risk register.

Now let's think about estimating in your real world for a moment. Do your team members feel like this?

The previous image is an example of padding. Do you consider this practice normal or appropriate? It is not. Many project managers rely on this practice, but padding undermines the professional responsibility of a project manager to develop a realistic schedule and budget. This is another point that is essential to understand for the exam.

So, what is wrong with padding? A pad is extra time or cost added to an estimate because the estimator does not have enough information. Shouldn't the project manager be providing that information? In cases where the estimator has many unknowns and the information is not available to clarify the unknowns, the potential need for additional time or funds should be addressed with reserves through the risk management process. Through risk management, the uncertainties are turned into identifiable opportunities and threats (risks). They should not remain hidden; instead, estimators need to identify and openly address uncertainties with the project manager.

What happens if all or many of your estimates are padded? Quite simply, you have a schedule or budget that no one believes. And if that is the case, why even bother creating a schedule or a budget? In the real world, we need the schedule and the budget to manage the project against, so we need them to be as believable and realistic as possible and we need to adhere to them. To be a successful project manager, you need to be able to meet the agreed-upon project completion date or cost. It is important to understand that padding is a sign of poor project management and that it can damage your reputation and the credibility of the project management profession as a whole.

In a properly managed project, the estimators have a WBS and may even have helped create it. They also have a description for each work package (the WBS dictionary) and may have helped create that as well. They may even have helped create the activity list from the work packages, and they know there will be time and cost reserves on the project that will be determined through actual calculations—not arbitrary guesses—to address identified risks or unknowns. With all that information, they should not need to pad their estimates!

If you allow padding on your projects now and consider it to be an appropriate practice, please make sure you reread this section and carefully review the Risk Management chapter. You need to understand the difference between padding and creating reserves and how padding can be detrimental to your project. The exam questions in this area are designed to identify those who make common project management errors like padding.

How Is Estimating Done? As stated earlier in this chapter, those who will be doing the work or those most familiar with the activities to be done should be the ones creating the activity estimates. They may use techniques such as analogous estimating, parametric estimating, three-point estimating, or reserve analysis, which we will describe next. But first let's look at the project manager's role in this process. If other people are creating the estimates, then what is the project manager doing?

The role of the project manager in estimating is to:

- Provide the team with enough information to properly estimate each activity.
- Let those doing the estimating know how refined their estimates must be.
- Complete a sanity check of the estimates.
- Prevent padding.
- Formulate a reserve (more on this later in the reserve analysis discussion in this section and in the Risk Management chapter).
- Make sure assumptions made during estimating are recorded for later review.

Now let's look at several different estimating techniques that may be used on a project.

One-Point Estimating

When estimating time using a one-point estimate, the estimator submits one estimate per activity. For example, the person doing the estimating says that the activity will take five weeks. The time estimate may be based on expert judgment or historical information, or it could be just a guess. As a result, this technique can be problematic.

One-point estimating can have the following negative effects on the project:

- It can force people into padding their estimates.
- It hides important information about risks and uncertainties from the project manager that the project manager needs to better plan and control the project.
- It can result in a schedule that no one believes in, thus decreasing buy-in to the project management process.
- When a person estimates that an activity will take 20 days and it is completed in 15 days, it can make the person who provided the estimate look untruthful and untrustworthy.
- It often results in the estimators working against the project manager to protect themselves, rather than with the project manager to help all involved in the project.

One-point estimates should only be used for projects that do not require a detailed, highly reliable schedule. For most projects, however, three-point estimates (described later in this section) are preferable. If one-point estimates are used, it is critical for the project manager to provide the estimator with as much information as possible, including the WBS, WBS dictionary, and activity list, or the estimate will likely be unreliable.

NOTE: You will frequently see a one-point estimate per activity used on the exam, as shown in the exercises later in this chapter. Although one-point estimating is often not the best method to use, it provides an easier way to improve your understanding of how to find critical paths and draw network diagrams. Using one-point estimates also allows for quick calculation on the exam and proof that you understand concepts such as the critical path.

Analogous Estimating[6] (Top-down) PAGE 149

Analogous estimating can be done for a project (e.g., the last five projects similar to this one each took eight months, so this one should also) or an activity (e.g., the last two times this activity was completed each took three days; since we have no other information to go on, we will use three days as the estimate for this activity and review the estimate when more details become available). Analogous estimating uses expert judgment and historical information to predict the future. In the past, the exam seemed to take an analogous estimate to mean only the overall project estimate given to the project manager from management or the sponsor. Take care to interpret these questions correctly.

Parametric Estimating PAGE 150

Parametric estimating looks at the relationships between variables on an activity to calculate estimates. The data can come from historical records from previous projects, industry requirements, standard metrics, or other sources. For example, the estimator may use measures like time per line of code, time per linear meter, or time per installation. (When used in cost estimating, the measures include cost as one of the variables. So the measures would be cost per line of code, cost per linear meter, etc.)

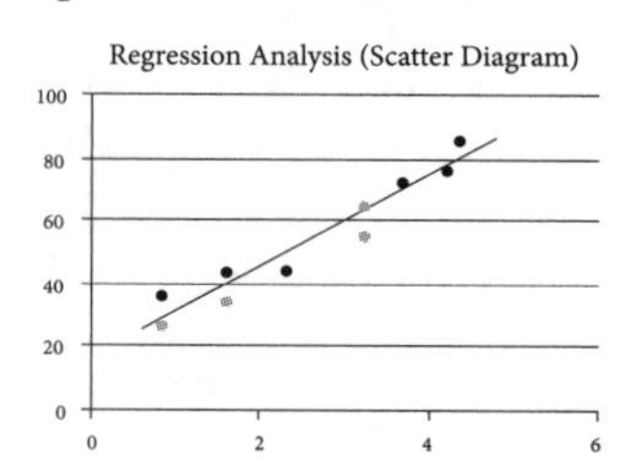

There are two ways an estimator might create parametric estimates:

- **Regression analysis (scatter diagram)**[7] This diagram tracks two variables to see if they are related and creates a mathematical formula to use in future parametric estimating.
- **Learning curve** Example: The 100th room painted will take less time than the first room because of improved efficiency.

Heuristics[8] A heuristic means a rule of thumb. An example of a heuristic is the 80/20 rule. This rule, applied to quality, suggests that 80 percent of quality problems are caused by 20 percent of potential sources of problems. A schedule heuristic might be, "Design work is always 15 percent of the total project length." The results of parametric estimating can become heuristics.

Three-Point Estimating[9] (PERT analysis, Program Evaluation and Review Technique[10]) PAGE 150

Statistically, there is a very small probability of completing a project on exactly any one date. As we know, things do not always go according to plan. Therefore, it is often best to state estimates in a range using three-point estimates. Analyzing what could go right and what could go wrong can help estimators determine an expected range for each activity, and if they state this range using three time (or cost) estimates, the project manager can better understand the potential variation of the activity estimates and the overall project estimate. With the three-point technique, estimators give an optimistic (O), pessimistic (P), and most likely (M) estimate for each activity. This ultimately provides a risk-based expected duration estimate by taking either the average or a weighted average (using PERT analysis) of the three estimates. See the following formulas.

You must MEMORIZE these formulas and know that they can be used for both time and cost estimates.

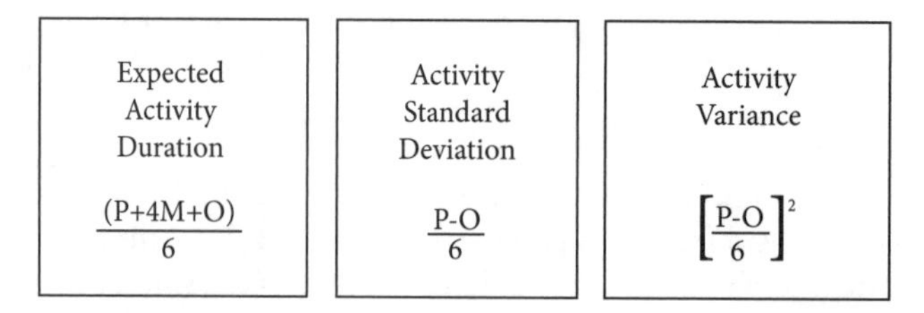

Legend: P = Pessimistic, M = Most Likely, O = Optimistic

Know the formula for activity variance as simply, "Standard deviation squared."

The exam may ask you to calculate a range for an individual activity estimate. To do this, you need to know the PERT expected activity duration (EAD) and the activity standard deviation (SD)[11]. You calculate the range using EAD +/– SD. The start of the range is EAD – SD, and the end of the range is EAD + SD. The following exercise will give you a chance to practice the calculations.

Exercise 1 Complete the chart using the previously described formulas. All estimates are in hours. It is best to calculate to three decimal places and round to two decimal places when you are ready to check your answers on the real exam.

Activity	P	M	O	Expected Activity Duration (or PERT)	Activity Standard Deviation	Activity Variance	Range of the Estimate
A	47	27	14				
B	89	60	41				
C	48	44	39				
D	42	37	29				

Answer See the table below for the answers. Remember that a number squared is not the number times two, but the number times itself.

Activity	P	M	O	Expected Activity Duration (or PERT)	Activity Standard Deviation	Activity Variance	Range of the Estimate
A	47	27	14	28.167	5.500	30.250	22.667 to 33.667, or 28.167 +/- 5.500
B	89	60	41	61.667	8.000	64.000	53.667 to 69.667, or 61.667 +/- 8.000
C	48	44	39	43.833	1.500	2.250	42.333 to 45.333, or 43.833 +/- 1.500
D	42	37	29	36.500	2.167	4.696	34.333 to 38.667, or 36.500 +/- 2.167

Note that the previous formulas relate to activities, rather than the overall project, and that the exam concentrates on using three-point estimating to find ranges for activity estimates. But as a project manager, you need to know more than just the ranges of individual activity duration estimates to manage a project successfully; you need to understand how these ranges affect the estimate of the overall project duration. You can then use this knowledge to effectively address variations on your project.

Finding the range for the overall project duration estimate is not as simple as finding the range for an individual activity estimate. You start by finding the expected project duration; this is the sum of the expected activity durations (EADs, or PERT estimates) for all activities on the critical path. You then find the standard deviation for the project. You cannot simply add the standard deviations for each activity on the critical path. Instead, you must calculate the variances for each critical path activity, add those variances, and then take the square root of the sum of the activity variances. So the project duration estimate range is the expected project duration (the sum of the EADs) plus or minus the project standard deviation (the square root of the sum of the activity variances).

Did you get lost in the last paragraph? Don't worry; it is further explained in Exercise 2. For the exam, you need to be able to do simple calculations using the formulas, understand that estimates of time (or cost) should be in a range, and know the concept of three-point time (or cost) estimates per activity. You may also see a PERT total project duration used in questions not requiring calculation (e.g., the project duration is 35 months plus or minus 3 months). The following exercise will help you get more prepared.

Exercise 2 Assuming that the activities listed in Exercise 1 make up the entire critical path for the project, how long should the project take?

Project	Expected Project Duration (or PERT)	Project Standard Deviation	Project Variance	Range of the Estimate
Project Duration Estimate				

Answer Again, please note that this question is provided for understanding and does not represent the complexity of questions on the exam. Most of the questions on the exam relating to three-point estimating are as simple as the ones at the end of this chapter.

See the table and the following explanation of the answer.

Project	Expected Project Duration (or PERT)	Project Standard Deviation	Project Variance	Range of the Estimate
Project Duration Estimate	170.167	10.060	101.196	160.107 to 180.227 *or* 170.167 +/- 10.060

The answer is 170.167 hours +/- 10.06 hours at one standard deviation.

The expected duration of the project, 170.167, is found by adding the EAD estimates for each of the critical path activities (in this case, all the activities listed). The +/- 10.06 represents the standard deviation of the estimate (the range of the estimate) and is found by adding the variances of the critical path activities, total of 101.196, and calculating the square root to get 10.060.

In order to find the standard deviation of a series of items, remember this rule: you cannot add standard deviations; you must convert standard deviations into variances, add the variances, and then take the square root of the total to convert back into standard deviation. This calculation means adding 30.250 + 64.000 + 2.250 + 4.696 and taking the square root to find 10.06. Therefore, if we add one standard deviation to the expected project duration total (for a 68.27 percent confidence level; see the discussions of standard deviation, or sigma, in the Quality Management chapter), the project would not be estimated to take 170.167 hours, but between 160.107 hours and 180.227 hours. If we add two standard deviations (for a 95.45 percent confidence level), the project would be estimated to take between 150.047 hours and 190.287 hours (170.167 +/- 20.12).

So why do project managers need to understand expected durations, range estimates, and standard deviations? The main purpose is to use these concepts to better control projects. These calculations help you know the potential variances on your project and determine appropriate courses of action. See the following example.

You have estimated that a portion of your project will cost $1 million with a standard deviation of $200,000. You need to decide whether to use a fixed price contract to outsource that piece of the project work. The standard deviation indicates there is a 40 percent range in the cost estimate for the work. Therefore, you would not likely choose a fixed-price contract, since there is not a firm definition of the scope of the work to be done. (See the Procurement Management chapter for information about different types of contracts.)

You can also use estimate ranges and standard deviation to assess risk. Looking at the answers for the previous Exercise 1, which activity has the most risk? The answer is Activity B. It has the widest range, the highest standard deviation, and the largest variation. These calculations are based on the pessimistic, optimistic, and most likely estimates for an activity. The further away from the mean these estimates are, the more that could go right and wrong to affect the activity. Therefore, you can assess and compare the risk of various activities by looking at activity ranges, standard deviations, and variances.

The exam addresses standard deviation and variance in many different ways. Make sure you have a general understanding of these concepts. If you are still struggling with this topic, review this section again.

Reserve Analysis

We've discussed padding and how detrimental this practice is, and how three-point estimates for an activity (or a project) will have a wider range the more risk they have. Now let's connect the topics of estimating and risk management. Estimating will help identify more risks, and completing the risk management process will reduce the range of time and cost estimates and make them more accurate by addressing those risks. Risk management saves the project time and money!

Project managers have a professional responsibility to establish a reserve to accommodate for the risks that remain in the project after the risk management planning processes have been completed. Often in the risk management process, an initial reserve is estimated, the Plan Risk Responses process is performed to reduce the risk, and then a revised reserve is created. Project planning is iterative.

As the Risk Management chapter describes, there can be two types of reserves added to the project: contingency reserves (also called time reserves or buffers) and management reserves. The contingency reserves are for the risks remaining after the Plan Risk Responses process. The management reserves are additional funds set aside to cover unforeseen risks. The Risk Management chapter explains how these reserves are calculated. You should understand for the exam the major difference between the practice of creating reserves and the practice of padding; in creating reserves, the project manager has the information necessary to reliably calculate what additional time or funds the project may need, whereas with padding, team members arbitrarily determine how much of a pad they want to attach to their estimates.

When the Estimate Activity Durations process is completed, you will of course have estimates. But also remember that you may update or change parts of the project documents as a result of this process.

Develop Schedule PAGE 152

Process: Develop Schedule
Process Group: Planning
Knowledge Area: Time Management

Once a network diagram and activity duration estimates are completed, it is time to put the information into a schedule. Remember that the difference between a time estimate and a schedule is that the schedule is calendar-based. Think about what is involved in creating a schedule and complete the following exercises.

Exercise Let's start at the beginning. What do you need before you can develop a schedule for your project?

Answer In order to develop a schedule, you need to have:

- An understanding of the work required on the project, including the project assumptions, milestones, and constraints (project scope statement)
- Defined activities (activity list)
- The order of how the work will be done (network diagram)
- An estimate of the duration of each activity (activity duration estimates)
- An estimate of the resources needed (activity resource requirements)
- An understanding of the availability of resources (resource calendars)
- A company calendar identifying what are working and nonworking days

Exercise As a project manager, you need to use the estimating data and other inputs to create a schedule that you will be able to stake your reputation on meeting. What do you need to do to create such a finalized schedule?

Answer Let's go beyond the *PMBOK® Guide*. The Develop Schedule process really includes everything you need to do to develop a finalized schedule that is bought into, approved, realistic, and formal. This is what developing the schedule is all about. What do you need to do to get it to that level?

- Work with stakeholders' priorities
- Look for alternative ways to complete the work
- Look for impacts on other projects
- Meet with managers to negotiate for resource availability
- Apply leads and lags to the schedule
- Compress the schedule by crashing, fast tracking, and reestimating
- Adjust components of the project management plan as necessary (e.g., change the WBS because of planned risk responses)
- Input the data into a scheduling tool (project management software) and perform calculations to determine the optimum schedule
- Simulate the project using Monte Carlo analysis to determine the likelihood of completing the project as scheduled
- Level resources if necessary
- Give the team a chance to approve the final schedule; they might have estimated an activity, but they should also look at the calendar allocation of their estimates to see if they are still feasible
- Conduct meetings and conversations to gain stakeholder buy-in and formal management approval

The schedule is a major output of the project management process. Think carefully about all that is involved in creating the project schedule before you continue reading. Then review the list of actions for the Develop Project Management Plan process in the Integration Management chapter. Many of those actions are also performed as part of the Develop Schedule process.

The Develop Schedule process is iterative and can occur many times over the life of the project (at least once per project life cycle phase on a large project). A schedule is one of the tools of project management that virtually every project manager has real-world experience using. However, the Develop Schedule process is a source of problems on the exam for many project managers. Read this entire section carefully. The exam will test you as an expert in handling schedule development during project planning and whenever there are changes to the project.

Schedule Network Analysis Once you have an initial schedule, you begin schedule network analysis to create the final schedule. This analysis may take the form of one or more of the following techniques:

- Critical path method
- Schedule compression
- What-if scenario analysis
- Resource leveling
- Critical chain method

Critical Path Method[12]

The critical path method involves determining the longest path through the network diagram (the critical path), the earliest and latest an activity can start, and the earliest and latest it can be completed. To use this method, you need to understand the following basic concepts.

Critical Path The critical path is the longest duration path through a network diagram and determines the shortest time it could take to complete the project.

Exercise Test yourself! How does the critical path help you as a project manager?

Answer The critical path:

- Helps prove how long the project will take.
- Helps you determine where best to focus your project management efforts.
- Helps determine if an issue needs immediate attention.
- Provides a vehicle to compress the schedule during project planning and whenever there are changes.
- Provides a vehicle to determine which activities have float and can therefore be delayed without delaying the project.

The easiest way to find the critical path is to identify all paths through the network and add the activity durations along each path. The path with the longest duration is the critical path.

Near-Critical Path[13] In addition to the critical path, you should be familiar with the concept of a near-critical path. This path is close in duration to the critical path. Something could happen that shortens the critical path or lengthens the near-critical path to the point where the near-critical path becomes critical. The closer in length the near-critical and critical paths are, the more risk the project has. You need to focus time and effort monitoring and controlling activities on both the critical and near-critical paths so there is no delay to project completion.

Float (Slack)[14] You should understand float and be able to calculate it manually for the exam. The three types of float to know for the exam are:

- **Total float (slack)** Total float is the amount of time an activity can be delayed without delaying the project end date or an intermediary milestone. This is the primary type of float, but there are others. Please note that the terms "float" and "slack" mean the same thing. You may see either or both on the exam.
- **Free float (slack)** This is the amount of time an activity can be delayed without delaying the early start date of its successor(s).
- **Project float (slack)** Project float is the amount of time a project can be delayed without delaying the externally imposed project completion date required by the customer or management, or the date previously committed to by the project manager.

Activities on the critical path have zero float. Critical path activities that are delayed or have dictated dates can result in negative float.

Float is an asset on a project. If you know where you have float, you can use it to help organize and manage the project. Do you do this in your real world? If not, study this section carefully.

How is float an asset? Once you know the critical path and any near-critical paths, you can use float as a way to focus your management on a project and to achieve better allocation of resources. For example, if you have a resource who is not very experienced but whom you must use for the project, you can assign him (assuming he has the skill set) to work on the activity with the most float. This gives you some level of security; even if his activity takes longer, the project is less likely to be delayed.

Knowing float also helps team members juggle their work on multiple projects. They of course need to get approval from the project manager for any delays from the plan, but the amount of float tells them how much time flexibility they may have for each activity they are working on.

Sometimes the exam questions are presented in such a way that you can simply see the amount of float, but other times you will need to calculate it. Float is calculated using either of the following equations: Float = Late Start (LS) – Early Start (ES), or Float = Late Finish (LF) – Early Finish (EF). Either formula gets you the same answer. Do you want to remember them without any further study? Just know the following:

"There is a start formula and a finish formula, and we always begin late." Notice that the formula uses either two starts or two finishes and each begins with late.

Start Formula	Finish Formula
Float = LS – ES	Float = LF – EF

You determine whether to use the start or finish formula based on the information available. For example, if an exam question states that you have a late start of 30, an early start of 18, and a late finish of 34, how do you find the float? Using the previous trick, you know to subtract the two starts or the two finishes. Since you do not have two finishes, you subtract 30 – 18 to get 12.

Using the Critical Path Method Now that we have discussed the basic concepts, let's look at how the critical path method works. We'll use the following network diagram as an example:

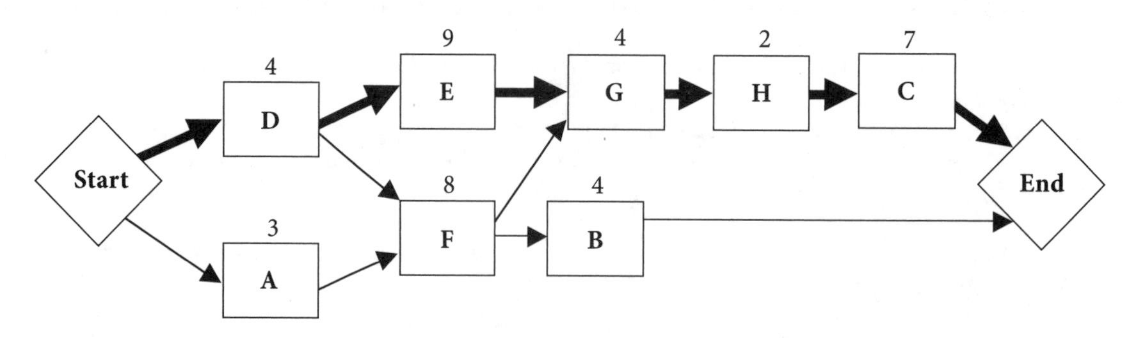

To determine the earliest and latest each activity can start and the earliest and latest each activity can be completed, you need to perform a forward and backward pass through the network diagram. The "early" figures are found by calculating from the beginning of the project to the end of the project, following the dependencies in the network diagram—a forward pass through the network diagram. The "late" figures are found by moving from the end of the project, following the dependencies to the beginning of the project—a "backward" pass.

You can also access free tricks and tools, including an article about finding float by calculating the forward and backward passes in a network diagram, at www.rmcproject.com.

The first activity in the diagram normally has an early start of zero. Some people, however, use 1 as the early start of the first activity. There is no right way to start calculating through network diagrams for the early and late starts; either method will get you the right answer. Just pick one method, and use it consistently.

Let's start with the forward pass. You need to move through the activities from the start until you reach the end, determining the early starts and early finishes, as illustrated in the following diagram. This example uses zero as the early start for the first activities.

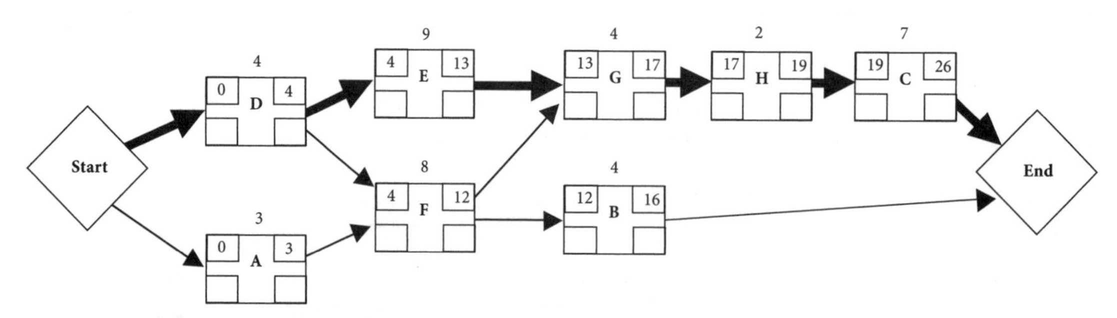

Key for the previous diagram:

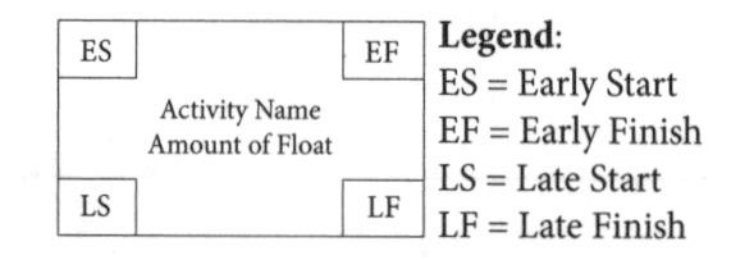

It is important to look at where paths converge (path convergence). To compute the early start and the early finish in a forward pass, you have to take into account all the paths that lead into that activity (see activity F and activity G in the previous diagram). The same concept applies to the backward pass; to compute the late finish and late start you need to consider all the paths that flow backward into an activity (see activity D and activity F in the previous diagram). In this diagram, paths converge during the forward pass at activity F and at activity G. So you need to do the forward pass on both paths leading up to activity F, calculating the early finishes for activities D (EF = 4) and A (EF = 3). You then select the later early finish of activities D and A to use as the early start for activity F, since activity F cannot start until both activities D and A are complete. Therefore, the early start of activity F is 4. You use the same process for calculating the early finish of activities E (EF = 13) and F (EF = 12) before determining the early start of activity G (ES = 13).

Once you have completed the forward pass, you can begin the backward pass, computing the late finish and late start for each activity. The backward pass uses the duration of the critical path (in this case, 26) as the early finish of the last activity or activities in the network. See the following diagram for the late start and late finish data.

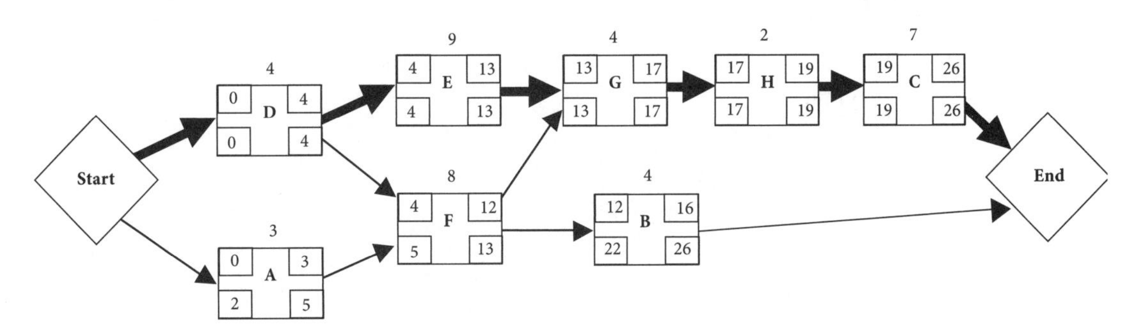

If you want additional practice, there are more questions on float and critical path in RMC's *PM FASTrack®* exam simulation software.

Key for the previous diagram:

Duration

ES | EF

Activity Name
Amount of Float

LS | LF

Legend:
ES = Early Start
EF = Early Finish
LS = Late Start
LF = Late Finish

Again, you need to be careful at points of convergence as you move through the network diagram. There is convergence at activity F and at activity D. You work from the end back to these by first computing the late start of activities B (LS = 22) and G (LS = 13). Select the earlier late start to use for the late finish of activity F, since activity F must be finished before either activity B or G can start. Therefore, the late finish of activity F is 13. This same process should be used on activities E (LS = 4) and F (LS = 8) before calculating the late finish for activity D (LF = 4).

Once you finish calculating the starts and finishes, you have the data required to calculate float. It's time to use those formulas. What was that trick again? "There is a start formula and a finish formula, and we always begin late." Therefore, the formulas are:

Start Formula	Finish Formula
Float = LS – ES	Float = LF – EF

The activities with zero float are on the critical path (identified by the bold arrows). See the following diagram for the float of each activity:

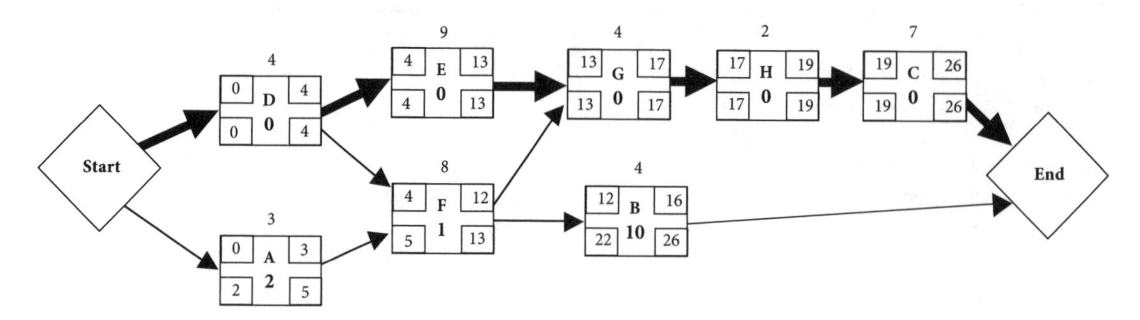

Key for the previous diagram:

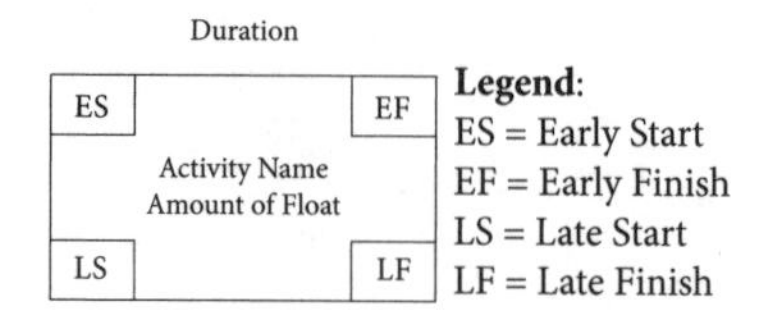

The next few exercises should help you better understand these concepts. As you do the exercises, think about how knowing float helps you in managing your real-world projects.

Exam questions may be substantially similar to the following exercises, or they may be more situational and wordy, without requiring you to draw a network diagram. Be prepared for both types.

Exercise Test yourself. Draw a network diagram, and answer the following questions.

You are the project manager for a new project and have figured out the following dependencies:

- Activity 1 can start immediately and has an estimated duration of 3 weeks.
- Activity 2 can start after activity 1 is completed and has an estimated duration of 3 weeks.
- Activity 3 can start after activity 1 is completed and has an estimated duration of 6 weeks.
- Activity 4 can start after activity 2 is completed and has an estimated duration of 8 weeks.
- Activity 5 can start after activity 4 is completed and after activity 3 is completed. This activity takes 4 weeks.

1. What is the duration of the critical path?

2. What is the float of activity 3?

3. What is the float of activity 2?

4. What is the float of the path with the longest float?

5. The resource working on activity 3 is replaced with another resource who is less experienced. The activity will now take 10 weeks. How will this affect the project?

6. After some arguing between stakeholders, a new activity 6 is added to the project. It will take 11 weeks to complete and must be completed before activity 5 and after activity 3. Management is concerned that adding the activity will add 11 weeks to the project. Another stakeholder argues the time will be less than 11 weeks. Who is correct? Use the original information (without the change to activity 3 listed in the previous question) to answer this question.

7. Based on the information in question 6, how much longer will the project take?

Answer There are many ways to answer these questions. If you learned another way in your project management training and are comfortable with that method, use it. Here is a simple way to compute the answers.

1. The length of the critical path is 18. There are two paths here:

Paths	Duration
Start, 1, 2, 4, 5, End	18
Start, 1, 3, 5, End	13

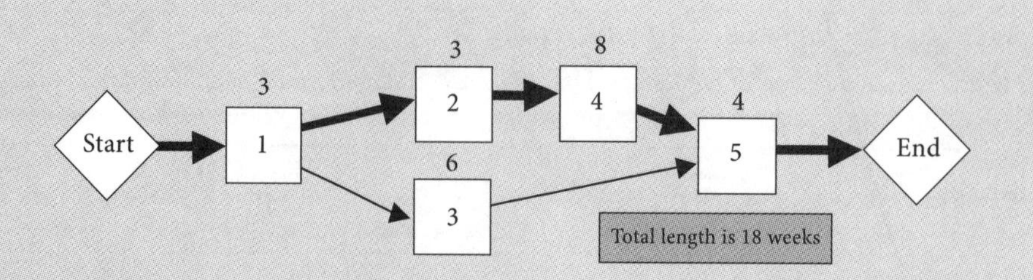

Start, 1, 2, 4, 5, End (shown with the bold arrows in the previous diagram) is the longest duration path and is therefore the critical path. The durations of the activities add up to 18, so the critical path is 18 weeks long.

2. The float is 5 weeks, per the following diagram. This diagram shows how to calculate float using the forward and backward pass.

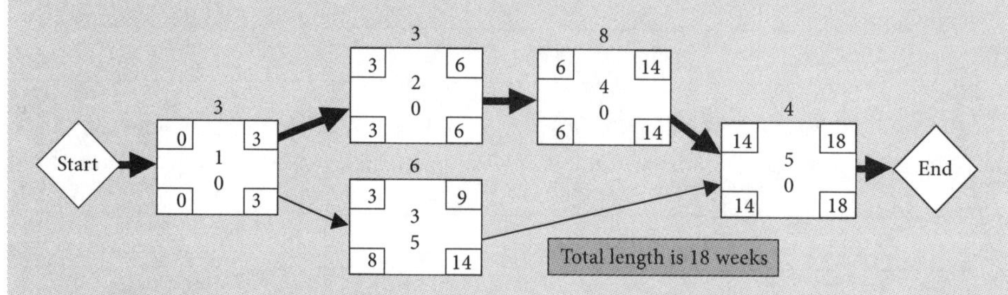

Key for the previous diagram:

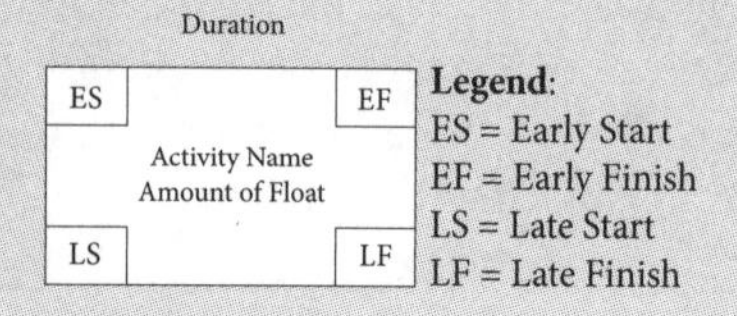

You can use either float formula to compute float. Late Finish – Early Finish = 14 – 9 = 5, or Late Start – Early Start = 8 – 3 = 5.

3. The float is zero; it is on the critical path. An activity on the critical path generally has no float.

4. The float is 5 weeks. There are only two paths in this example: Start, 1, 2, 4, 5, End and Start, 1, 3, 5, End. The length of the non-critical path (Start, 1, 3, 5, End) is 13. The length of the project is 18, and 18 – 13 is 5. The total float of the path with the longest float is 5.

5. It will have no effect. The length of path activities 1, 3, and 5 is 13. Adding 4 more weeks to the length of activity 3 will make that path 17. Since that path is still shorter than the critical path, the critical path does not change. The length of the critical path is still 18 weeks because activity 3 is not on the critical path.

6. The stakeholder who says the time will be less than 11 weeks is correct. The new activity will be added to a non-critical path that has a float of 5 weeks. Therefore, adding 11 weeks will make this path the new critical path. The overall effect of adding an activity that takes 11 weeks will be a delay to the project of 6 weeks.

7. The project will take 6 weeks longer. (NOTE: If you answered 24, you did not read the question correctly!) Follow the bold arrows in the following diagram.

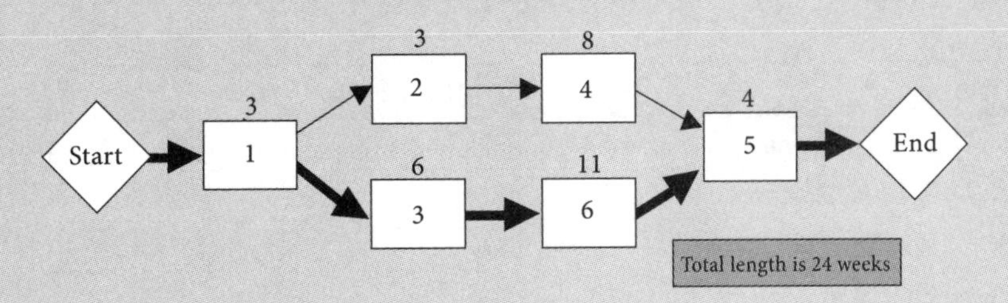

Exercise Considering the following data:

Activity	Preceding Activity	Estimate in Months
Start		0
D	Start	4
A	Start	6
F	D, A	7
E	D	8
G	F, E	5
B	F	5
H	G	7
C	H	8
End	C, B	0

1. What is the duration of the critical path?

2. What is the float of activity B?

3. What is the float of activity E?

4. What is the float of activity D?

5. To shorten the length of the project, the sponsor has offered to remove the work of activity E from the project, making activity D the predecessor to activities G and F. What will be the effect?

Answer

1. The critical path (project duration) is 33 months.

Paths	Duration
Start, D, E, G, H, C, End	32
Start, D, F, G, H, C, End	31
Start, D, F, B, End	16
Start, A, F, G, H, C, End	33
Start, A, F, B, End	18

2. The float is 15 months, per the following diagram.

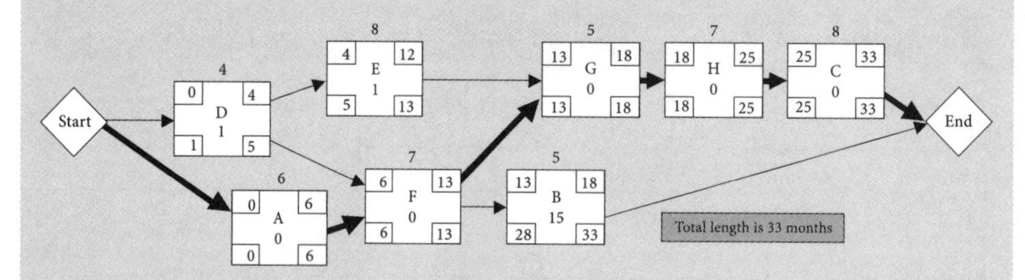

Key for the previous diagram:

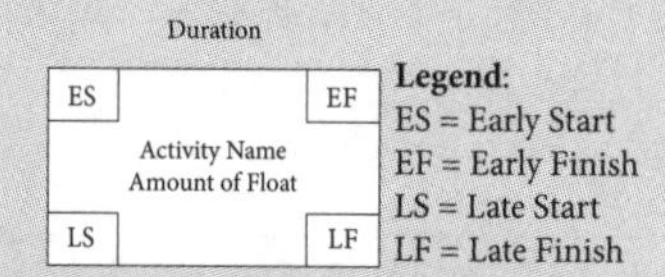

3. The float is one month. Once you have finished calculating using the long way, all the other answers are usually quick. Just look at the diagram to see the float of any activity.

   Watch out here for the float of activity E. The project must be completed by the end of month 33. Activity E must be completed before activities G, H, and C can start. So the late finish for E is 33 – 8 – 7 – 5, or 13.

   Activity E must be completed after Activity D. So the early finish is 4 + 8, or 12.

   Float = Late Finish – Early Finish, so 13 – 12 = 1

4. The float is one month; just look at the network diagram.

   Now let's look at using a calculation to get the float for activity D. The project must be completed by the end of month 33. Activity D must be completed before activities E, F, G, H, C, and B can start. Looking backward through the dependencies, the late finish is 33 – 8 – 7 – 5, but then we run into a problem. Normally we would go along the critical path, but look at activities E and F. Activity E is longer than activity F, so we must go along the longest duration path, from activity G to activity E, making the late finish 33 – 8 – 7 – 5 – 8, or 5.

Early finish is easier. There are no predecessors, so the early finish is the end of month 4.

Float = 5 – 4, or 1 month.

5. There is no effect on the critical path. The paths are now:

Paths	Duration
Start, D, G, H, C, End	24
Start, D, F, G, H, C, End	31
Start, D, F, B, End	16
Start, A, F, G, H, C, End	33
Start, A, F, B, End	18

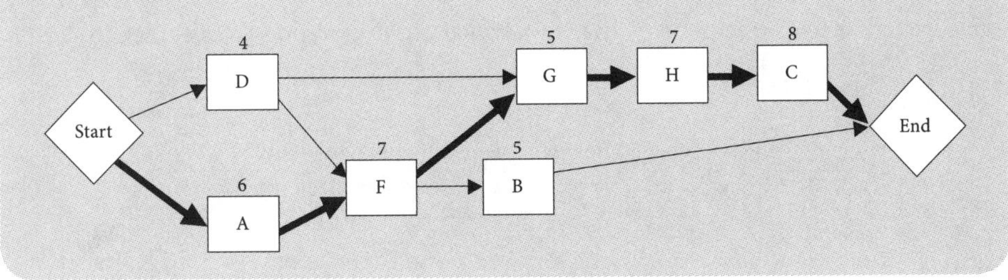

You survived! Hopefully it was not too hard.

The following are good questions to test your knowledge about critical paths, float, etc.:

- **Can there be more than one critical path?** Yes, you can have two, three, or many critical paths.
- **Do you want there to be?** No; it increases risk.
- **Can a critical path change?** Yes.
- **Can there be negative float?** Yes; it means you are behind.
- **How much float does the critical path have?** In planning, the critical path has zero float. During project executing, if an activity on the critical path is completed earlier or later than planned, the critical path may then have positive or negative float. Negative float on the critical path requires corrective actions or changes to the project to bring it back in line with the plan.
- **Does the network diagram change when the end date changes?** No, not automatically, but the project manager should investigate schedule compression options such as fast tracking and crashing the schedule to meet the new date. Then, with approved changes, the project manager should change the network diagram accordingly.
- **Would you leave the project with negative float?** No; you would compress the schedule.

If you encounter multiple questions on the exam that require you to draw a network diagram, you may be able to reuse the same network diagram to answer more than one question. Look to see if this is true before you spend time redrawing the diagram.

Schedule Compression[15] PAGE 156; SEE ALSO RESOURCE LEVELING, PAGE 156

One of the most common problems on projects is an unrealistic timeframe. This problem can arise during project planning when management or the customer requires a completion date that cannot be met, or during project executing when the project manager needs to bring the project back in line with the schedule baseline or adjust the project for changes. As we discussed earlier, many project managers blame their sponsors or executives for unrealistic schedules, but project managers have a professional responsibility to push back, present options, and make sure the project is achievable by properly planning the project and using schedule network analysis techniques like schedule compression.

During project planning, schedule compression can help a project manager determine if the desired completion date can be met and, if not, what can be changed to meet the requested date. This technique is also used during integrated change control to look at the impacts changes to other parts of the project (i.e., cost, scope, risk, resources, quality, etc.) have on the schedule. The objective is to compress the schedule without changing project scope.

Fast Tracking This technique involves doing critical path activities in parallel that were originally planned in a series (see the following diagram). Fast tracking often results in rework, usually increases risk, and requires more attention to communication.

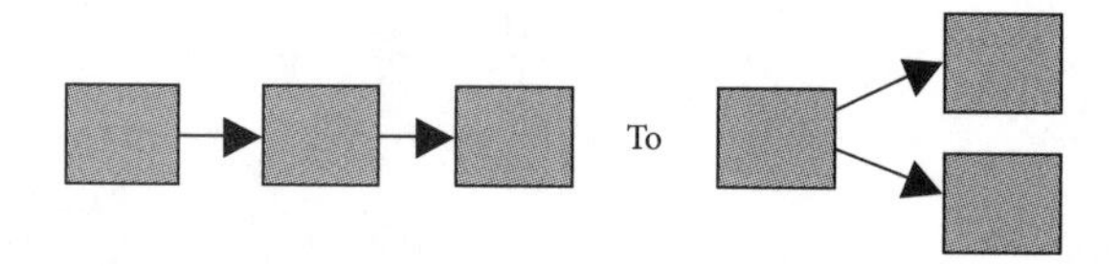

For example, using the following network diagram, which activity would you fast track to shorten the project length?

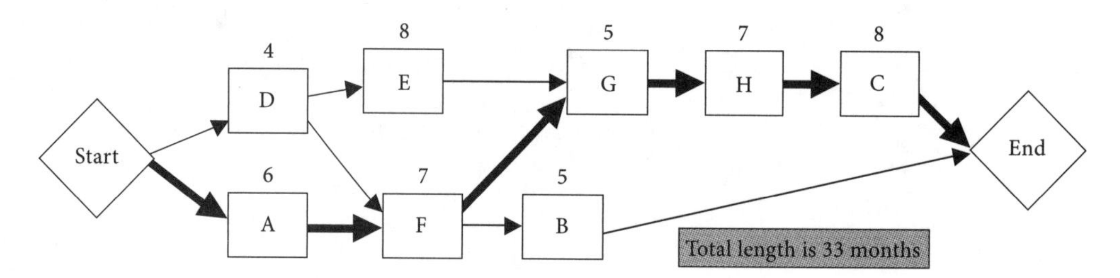

Assuming the dependencies are discretionary, activity H could be fast tracked by making it occur at the same time, or in parallel with, activity G. Any other pair of activities on the critical path could be fast tracked. Activities C and H could also be fast tracked by having part of activity C done concurrently with activity H.

Crashing This technique involves making cost and schedule trade-offs to determine how to compress the schedule the most for the least cost while maintaining project scope. In other words, if time must change, what option will cause the least impact on cost? Crashing, by definition, always results in increased costs. It trades time for money.

For example, using the network diagram shown in the previous fast tracking discussion, a contract resource could supplement the internal resource's efforts on a critical path activity (assuming this is logical, based on the nature of the work). Another option to crash the project might be to buy a software application; the purchase adds cost to the project but helps the team work more efficiently, thus saving time.

If you have negative project float (meaning the estimated completion date is after the desired date), would your first choice be to tell the customer the date cannot be met and to ask for more time? No; the first choice would be to analyze what could be done about the negative float by compressing the schedule. In crashing or fast tracking, it is best to see all potential choices and then select the option or options that have the least negative impact on the project. For the exam, remember that you need to identify all the possible options and, if given a choice between crashing or fast tracking options, select the choice or combination of choices with the least negative impact on the project. This tip can help you on exam questions that seem to have two right answers.

In the real world, many project managers use the network diagram to manage the day-to-day operation of the project and to make adjustments when changes occur. You should expect this to be reflected on the exam by the number of questions on network diagrams, calculations, and "What do you do in this situation?" type of questions.

Let's make sure you are prepared to deal with unrealistic schedules on the exam. This issue is so important that you can expect to see more than 10 questions about it. Most project managers have some gaps in their knowledge in this area, and it shows on their score sheets. To remedy this, let's try an exercise.

Exercise During project planning, the project duration is estimated to be 33 months. However, you have been given a completion date of 30 months. Using the following network diagram, identify options for shortening the schedule to 30 months.

This is a general exercise with little detail. Make any assumptions you need to make in order to come up with as many options as possible.

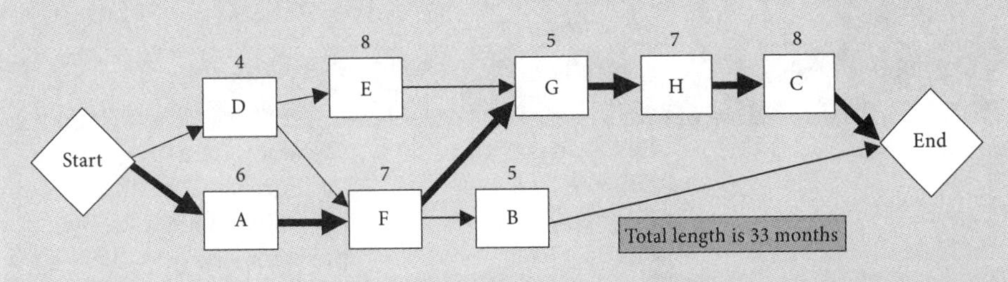

Option	How to Achieve It	Explanation (Including Assumptions Made)

Option	How to Achieve It	Explanation (Including Assumptions Made)

Answer Did this situation make sense? If it did, you are in good shape. If not, you should study a little more. Notice how this effort allows the project manager to proactively deal with the reality of the project and take action to be sure the project completion date can be met. The following options and methods are explained in the next few pages.

Option	How to Achieve It	Explanation (Including Assumptions Made)
Reestimate	Review risks	Now it is time to look at the estimates and see which contain hidden risks. By reducing the risks, the estimate can be lowered and the project finished faster. It is never an option to just cut 10 percent off of the estimate.
Execute activities H and C in parallel	Fast track (schedule compression)	We assume that the dependency between activities H and C is a discretionary one.
Add resources from within the organization (at additional cost to the project) to activity G.	Crash (schedule compression)	We assume that adding resources to activity G would, in fact, be practical and that there are resources available.
Cut activity H	Reduce scope	Though not the first choice, as it likely will affect the customer, reducing scope should be considered an option.
Hire consultants to assist on activity G, H, or C	Crash (schedule compression)	We assume that adding external resources to these activities would be practical and that there are resources available.

Option	How to Achieve It	Explanation (Including Assumptions Made)
Move more experienced people to activities on the critical path (i.e., activities G, H, or C)	Schedule compression	We assume that some of the critical path activities are being done by less experienced people.
Cut time	Lower quality standards (schedule compression)	Do not get excited. Quality is a project constraint and is an option. In this case, it would probably be easier and thus faster to complete the project with the lowered quality standards.
Say no; the project must have 33 months	Stand your ground	This is not a viable option until other alternatives are exhausted.
Get more work done with the same amount of resources	Work overtime	This is not an option during project planning. There are too many other ways to compress the schedule that do not have the negative effects of overtime. Save it for a last resort.

Which of the options listed is the best? To answer the question, think of the impacts to the project of each one. Is the best option to cut time by lowering quality standards? What are the impacts of cutting quality? Is there another option? Why not do what many project managers do—ask for more resources? But adding resources may also add cost. Why not work overtime? If you have not realized overtime should be one of the last choices, you have a large gap in your knowledge. Most organizations are working at close to 100 percent capacity. Your project working overtime limits the possibility of resources responding to emergencies for any other project they are working on, thereby putting other projects at risk. Besides, how much overtime can a person take? Overtime is not free.

The first and possibly the best choice is to look at risks and then reestimate. Once it is known that the schedule (or budget) must be reduced, a project manager can investigate the activity estimates that contain the most unknowns, eliminate or reduce these risks, and thus decrease the estimate. Eliminate risks in the risk management process, and everyone wins!

Let's look at these concepts again with a few more exercises.

Exercise What are the impacts of the schedule shortening options listed in the following table?

Option	General Impacts to the Project
Fast track	
Crash	
Reduce scope	
Cut quality	

Answer

Option	General Impacts to the Project
Fast track	▸ Always adds risk ▸ May add management time for the project manager
Crash	▸ Always adds cost ▸ May add management time for the project manager
Reduce scope	▸ May save cost, resources, and time ▸ May negatively impact customer satisfaction
Cut quality	▸ May save cost, resources, and time ▸ May increase risk ▸ Requires good metrics ▸ May negatively impact customer satisfaction

Exercise Here is another chance to test yourself on schedule compression.

Activity	Original Duration (in Months)	Crash Duration (in Months)	Time Savings	Original Cost (in Dollars)	Crash Cost (in Dollars)	Extra Cost (in Dollars)	Cost per Month
J	14	12	2	$10,000	$14,000	$4,000	$2,000
K	9	8	1	$17,000	$27,000	$10,000	$10,000
N	3	2	1	$25,000	$26,000	$1,000	$1,000
L	7	5	2	$14,000	$20,000	$6,000	$3,000
M	11	8	3	$27,000	$36,000	$9,000	$3,000

1. Imagine that this project has a project float of -3 months. Which activity or activities presented above would you crash to save 3 months on the project, assuming that the activities listed above represent critical path activities?

2. How much would it cost to crash this project?

Answer

1. The options to save 3 months are:

Activities	Cost
J and K	$14,000
J and N	$5,000
K and L	$16,000
L and N	$7,000
M	$9,000

Crashing activities J and N is the least expensive option and there is nothing in the question to eliminate it, so the choice of activities J and N is the best answer. Any time you have negative project float, it means that the project is not going to meet its deliverable date. The answer, depending on how the question is worded, involves crashing or fast tracking the project and coming up with options, or telling the customer the date cannot be met.

2. Crashing activities J and N would result in the least added cost—only $5,000. The "Cost per Month" column in this exercise is a distracter; you can answer this question with just the "Activity," "Time Savings," and "Extra Cost" columns. Don't assume you will need all the data provided to you in questions on the exam.

Exercise Consider the following:

Management has told you to get the project completed two weeks early. What is the BEST thing for you to do?

A. Consult the project sponsor
B. Crash
C. Fast track
D. Advise management of the impact of the change

Answer Did you get fooled by this question? Did you think you had to choose between crashing and fast tracking? There is no information provided to help you determine which one is better. Therefore, the best choice presented is D, inform management of the impact of the change.

The exam will ask many such questions requiring you to know that a project manager needs to analyze first and then let management, the sponsor, the customer, or other parties know the impact of their requests (see the four-step process for handling changes in the Integration Management chapter). A project manager does NOT just say yes! Instead, after analyzing the change for its impact to all areas of the project (cost, risk, resources, etc.), he or she could say something like, "Yes, I would be happy to make the change, BUT the project will be delayed two weeks, I will need two more resources, or the project will cost $25,000 more."

WARNING: For questions about changes to the network diagram, make sure you look for shifts to new critical paths caused by the changes to the network diagram or to activity durations.

What-If Scenario Analysis PAGE 156

In creating a finalized, realistic schedule, it is helpful to ask "What if a particular factor changed on the project? Would that produce a shorter schedule?" The assumptions for each activity can change and, therefore, the activity durations can also change. One of the ways to calculate the effect of these changes is through a Monte Carlo analysis.

Monte Carlo Analysis[16] PAGE 156 This technique uses computer software to simulate the outcome of a project, based on the three-point estimates (optimistic, pessimistic, and most likely) for each activity and the network diagram. The simulation can tell you:

- The probability of completing the project on any specific day.
- The probability of completing the project for any specific amount of cost.
- The probability of any activity actually being on the critical path.
- The overall project risk.

Monte Carlo analysis is another way of putting together the details of a three-point estimate into a project estimate. It is more accurate than other methods because it simulates the actual details of the project and calculates probability.

Monte Carlo analysis can help deal with "path convergence," places in the network diagram where multiple paths converge into one or more activities, thus adding risk to the project (see the following diagram). Monte Carlo analysis is also used as a risk management tool to quantitatively analyze risks (see the Risk Management chapter).

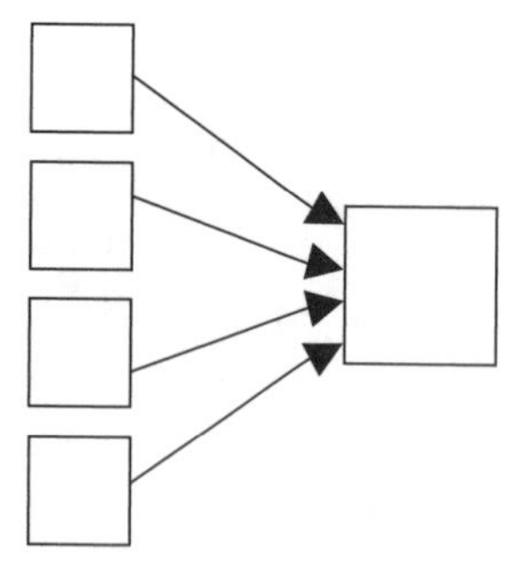

Resource Leveling[17] PAGE 156

Resource leveling is used to produce a resource-limited schedule. Leveling lengthens the schedule and increases cost in order to deal with a limited amount of resources, resource availability, and other resource constraints. A little-used function in project management software, this technique allows you to level the peaks and valleys of the schedule from one month to another, resulting in a more stable number of resources used on your project.

You might level the resources if your project utilized 5 resources one month, 15 the next, and 3 the next, or some other up-and-down pattern that was not an acceptable use of resources. Leveling could also be used if you do not have 15 resources available and would prefer to lengthen the project (which would be a result of leveling) instead of hiring more resources.

Critical Chain Method[18] PAGE 155

The critical chain method is another way to develop a bought-into, approved, realistic, and formal schedule. Unlike the other schedule network analysis techniques, it takes into account both activity and resource dependencies. There are many variations of this method, so be careful here.

For more exercises that involve network diagrams, visit www.rmcproject.com/extras or use RMC's *PM FASTrack®* exam simulation software.

The critical chain method uses a network diagram and develops a schedule by assigning each activity to occur as late as possible to still meet the end date. You add resource dependencies to the schedule, and then calculate the critical chain. Starting at the end date, you build duration buffers into the chain at critical milestones (think of this as your time reserves from risk response planning). These reserves, spread throughout the project, will provide cushions for delays in the scheduled activities. You manage these buffers so that you meet each individual milestone date and thus the project milestone completion date as well.

Do not get carried away with studying this technique; it should not be mentioned on the exam more than three times. And remember, when it is "mentioned" on the exam, this does not necessarily mean there are three questions about it—it could just be an incorrect choice in a question.

Project Schedule The project schedule is the result of the previous planning processes and the schedule network analysis that is performed as part of the Develop Schedule process. As planning progresses, the schedule will be iterated in response to risk management and other parts of project planning until an acceptable and realistic schedule can be agreed upon. The iterated and realistic schedule that results from this effort is called the schedule baseline and becomes part of the project management plan.

The schedule can be shown with or without dependencies (logical relationships) and can be shown in any of the following formats, depending on the needs of the project:

- Network diagram
- Milestone chart
- Bar chart

Milestone Charts[19]

These are similar to bar charts (described next), but they only show major events. Remember that milestones have no duration; they simply represent the completion of activities. Milestones may include "requirements are complete" or "design is finished" and are part of the inputs to the Sequence Activities process. Milestone charts are good tools for reporting to management and to the customer.

ID	Milestone	December	January	February	March	April
1	Start	◆12/14				
2	Requirements Gathered		◆12/31			
3	Design Complete		◆1/17			
4	Coding Complete			◆2/15		
5	Testing Complete				◆3/15	
6	Implementation Complete					◆4/4
7	End					◆4/15

Bar Charts (also called Gantt Charts)[20]

Bar charts are weak planning tools, but they are effective for progress reporting and control. They are not project management plans. The following is a sample bar chart:

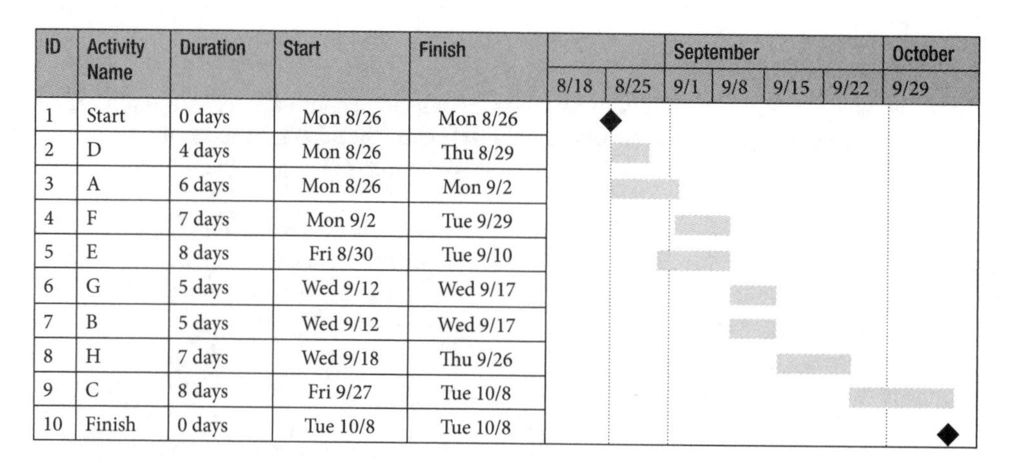

ID	Activity Name	Duration	Start	Finish
1	Start	0 days	Mon 8/26	Mon 8/26
2	D	4 days	Mon 8/26	Thu 8/29
3	A	6 days	Mon 8/26	Mon 9/2
4	F	7 days	Mon 9/2	Tue 9/29
5	E	8 days	Fri 8/30	Tue 9/10
6	G	5 days	Wed 9/12	Wed 9/17
7	B	5 days	Wed 9/12	Wed 9/17
8	H	7 days	Wed 9/18	Thu 9/26
9	C	8 days	Fri 9/27	Tue 10/8
10	Finish	0 days	Tue 10/8	Tue 10/8

Notice that there are no lines between activities to show interdependencies, nor are assigned resources shown. Bar charts do not help organize the project as effectively as a WBS and network diagram do. They are completed after the WBS and the network diagram in the project management process.

Understanding the Benefits of Different Formats

No matter how much you know about project management, there are always questions on the exam that will be tricky if you have never thought of them before. The different types of schedule formats can be one of those areas. Think through the next exercise. Make sure you look for anything you did not know, and organize your knowledge according to the exercise answers. You can get quite a few questions right on the exam if you know what each of the schedule formats is used for.

Exercise Test yourself! Answer the following questions in the spaces provided.

Under what circumstances would you use a network diagram instead of a bar chart?	
Under what circumstances would you use a milestone chart instead of a bar chart?	
Under what circumstances would you use a bar chart instead of a network diagram?	

Answer See the answers in the following table.

Under what circumstances would you use a network diagram instead of a bar chart?	To show interdependencies between activities
Under what circumstances would you use a milestone chart instead of a bar chart?	To report to senior management
Under what circumstances would you use a bar chart instead of a network diagram?	To track progress To report to the team

Schedule Baseline PAGE 159 The schedule baseline is the version of the schedule used to manage the project and that the project team's performance is measured against. Remember that the baseline can only be changed as a result of formally approved changes. Meeting the schedule baseline is one of the measures of project success. If the project can be done faster than the customer requested, there may be a difference between the schedule baseline and the end date required by the customer. This difference is called project float.

The process of creating a final and realistic schedule could cause changes to project documents, including the activity resource requirements and activity attributes, as well as the risk register.

Control Schedule PAGE 160

Process: Control Schedule
Process Group: Monitoring & Controlling
Knowledge Area: Time Management

Controlling the project was discussed in the Project Management Processes chapter, but we will spend a little more time talking about it here. Control means measure, which means you measure against the plan. You need to stay in control of your project and know how it is performing compared to the plan. Do you do this now in your real world? If not, pay particular attention to the concept of control in this chapter and throughout this book. Make sure you understand that such actions are done as part of basic project management. When answering exam questions, you need to assume proper project management was done unless the questions state otherwise. On properly managed projects, a project manager does not have to spend all of his or her time dealing with problems, because most of those problems were prevented through risk management. Project managers are measuring, measuring, measuring against the plan and controlling the project!

The project (and the project manager) will be considered a failure if the schedule baseline—the end date agreed to in planning and adjusted for approved changes—is not met. So control efforts go beyond measuring; they also involve taking corrective and preventive action over and over again during the life of the project to keep the project in line with the plan. Do you do this? If not, why not? Without such work, all the efforts in planning to create a realistic schedule could be wasted effort.

Schedule control also means looking for the things that are causing changes and influencing the sources of the changes. For example, if there is one person or one piece of work causing a lot of changes, the project manager must do something about it, rather than let the issues and the high number of changes continue. A project manager must be proactive.

If the project can no longer meet the agreed-upon completion date (the schedule baseline), the project manager might recommend the termination of the project before any more company time is wasted. In other words, the project manager might have to influence higher up the organization to control the project. Schedule control is more than just issuing updated schedules!

Make sure you really understand what is involved in schedule control. Think of someone protecting the hard work of all those involved in planning to make sure what was planned occurs as close to the plan as possible. Think of someone who is constantly on the lookout for anything that might be affecting the schedule. This is what it means to control the schedule, and the project.

The following are some additional activities involved in controlling the schedule:

- Reestimate the remaining components of the project partway through the project (see the following discussion).
- Conduct performance reviews by formally analyzing how the project is doing (see the Earned Value Measurement discussion in the Cost Management chapter).
- Adjust future parts of the project to deal with delays, rather than asking for a time extension.
- Measure variances against the planned schedule, and determine if those variances warrant attention.

- Consider leveling resources to distribute work more evenly among the resources.
- Continue to play "What if…?" with the project schedule to better optimize it.
- Adjust metrics that are not giving the project manager the information needed to properly manage the project.
- Adjust progress reports and reporting as needed to capture the information necessary to control and manage the project (see the Progress Reporting discussion in the Cost Management chapter).
- Identify the need for changes, including preventive actions.
- Follow the change control process.

Reestimating Did you notice the activity of reestimating in the previous list? One of the roles of a project manager is to make sure the project meets the project objectives. Realize that the project was estimated while in planning and, although you might have done your best to understand the project well enough to estimate it accurately, it is extremely difficult to estimate well. Therefore, it is standard practice to reestimate the entire remaining part of the project at least once during the life of the project to make sure you can still meet the end date, budget, and other project objectives and to adjust the project if you cannot. Again, assume proper project management was done when answering questions on the exam unless the question provides specific information to indicate it was not.

The Control Schedule process results in work performance measurements, changes to the schedule baseline or schedule management plan, and changes to any other part of the project. For example, a change to the schedule might require additional resources or a change in scope. Such changes must be handled as part of the Perform Integrated Change Control process. Make sure you review this important process in the Integration Management chapter and realize the exam assumes that you perform it as part of your basic project management activities.

Practice Exam

1. To control the schedule, a project manager is reanalyzing the project to predict project duration. She does this by analyzing the sequence of activities with the least amount of scheduling flexibility. What technique is she using?
   A. Critical path method
   B. Flowchart
   C. Precedence diagramming
   D. Work breakdown structure

2. A dependency requiring that design be completed before manufacturing can start is an example of a(n):
   A. Discretionary dependency.
   B. External dependency.
   C. Mandatory dependency.
   D. Scope dependency.

3. Which of the following are GENERALLY illustrated BETTER by bar charts than network diagrams?
   A. Logical relationships
   B. Critical paths
   C. Resource trade-offs
   D. Progress or status

4. If the optimistic estimate for an activity is 12 days, and the pessimistic estimate is 18 days, what is the standard deviation of this activity?
   A. 1
   B. 1.3
   C. 6
   D. 3

5. A heuristic is BEST described as a:
   A. Control tool.
   B. Scheduling method.
   C. Planning tool.
   D. Rule of thumb.

6. Lag means:
   A. The amount of time an activity can be delayed without delaying the project finish date.
   B. The amount of time an activity can be delayed without delaying the early start date of its successor.
   C. Waiting time.
   D. The product of a forward and backward pass.

7. Which of the following is the BEST project management tool to use to determine the longest time the project will take?
   A. Work breakdown structure
   B. Network diagram
   C. Bar chart
   D. Project charter

8. Which of the following is CORRECT?
   A. The critical path helps prove how long the project will take.
   B. There can be only one critical path.
   C. The network diagram will change every time the end date changes.
   D. A project can never have negative float.

9. What is the duration of a milestone?
   A. It is shorter than the duration of the longest activity.
   B. It is shorter than the activity it represents.
   C. It has no duration.
   D. It is the same length as the activity it represents.

10. Which of the following BEST describes the relationship between standard deviation and risk?
    A. There is no relationship.
    B. Standard deviation tells you if the estimate is accurate.
    C. Standard deviation tells you how uncertain the estimate is.
    D. Standard deviation tells you if the estimate includes a pad.

11. The float of an activity is determined by:
    A. Performing a Monte Carlo analysis.
    B. Determining the waiting time between activities.
    C. Determining lag.
    D. Determining the length of time the activity can be delayed without delaying the critical path.

12. A project has three critical paths. Which of the following BEST describes how this affects the project?
    A. It makes it easier to manage.
    B. It increases the project risk.
    C. It requires more people.
    D. It makes it more expensive.

13. If project time and cost are not as important as the number of resources used each month, which of the following is the BEST thing to do?
    A. Perform a Monte Carlo analysis.
    B. Fast track the project.
    C. Perform resource leveling.
    D. Analyze the life cycle costs.

14. When would a milestone chart be used instead of a bar chart?
    A. Project planning
    B. Reporting to team members
    C. Reporting to management
    D. Risk analysis

15. Your project management plan results in a project schedule that is too long. If the project network diagram cannot change but you have extra personnel resources, what is the BEST thing to do?
    A. Fast track the project.
    B. Level the resources.
    C. Crash the project.
    D. Perform Monte Carlo analysis.

16. Which of the following is the BEST thing to do to try to complete a project two days earlier?
    A. Tell senior management that the project's critical path does not allow the project to be finished earlier.
    B. Tell your boss.
    C. Meet with the team to look at options for crashing or fast tracking the critical path.
    D. Work hard and see what the project status is next month.

17. In attempting to complete the project faster, the project manager looks at the cost associated with crashing each activity. The BEST approach to crashing would also include looking at the:
    A. Risk impact of crashing each activity.
    B. Customer's opinion of which activities to crash.
    C. Boss's opinion of which activities to crash and in which order.
    D. Project life cycle phase in which the activity is due to occur.

18. Which of the following processes includes asking team members about the time estimates for their activities and reaching agreement on the calendar date for each activity?
    A. Sequence Activities
    B. Develop Schedule
    C. Define Scope
    D. Develop Project Charter

19. A project manager is in the middle of executing of a very large construction project when he discovers the time needed to complete the project is longer than the time available. What is the BEST thing to do?
    A. Cut product scope.
    B. Meet with management and tell them the required date cannot be met.
    C. Work overtime.
    D. Determine options for schedule compression and present management with his recommended option.

20. During project planning, you estimate the time needed for each activity and then add the estimates to create the project estimate. You commit to completing the project by this date. What is wrong with this scenario?
    A. The team did not create the estimate, and estimating takes too long using that method.
    B. The team did not create the estimate, and a network diagram was not used.
    C. The estimate is too long and should be created by management.
    D. The project estimate should be the same as the customer's required completion date.

21. You are a project manager on a US $5,000,000 software development project. While working with your project team to develop a network diagram, you notice a series of activities that can be worked in parallel but must finish in a specific sequence. What type of activity sequencing method is required for these activities?
    A. Precedence diagramming method
    B. Arrow diagramming method
    C. Critical path method
    D. Operational diagramming method

22. You are a project manager on a US $5,000,000 software development project. While working with your project team to develop a network diagram, your data architects suggest that quality could be improved if the data model is approved by senior management before moving on to other design elements. They support this suggestion with an article from a leading software development journal. Which of the following BEST describes this type of input?
    A. Mandatory dependency
    B. Discretionary dependency
    C. External dependency
    D. Heuristic

23. Based on the following, if you needed to shorten the duration of the project, what activity would you try to shorten?

Activity	Preceding Activity	Duration in Weeks
Start	None	0
A	Start	1
B	Start	2
C	Start	6
D	A	10
E	B, C	1
F	C	2
G	D	3
H	E	9
I	F	1
End	G, H, I	0

    A. Activity B
    B. Activity D
    C. Activity H
    D. Activity C

24. You have a project with the following activities: Activity A takes 40 hours and can start after the project starts. Activity B takes 25 hours and should happen after the project starts. Activity C must happen after activity A and takes 35 hours. Activity D must happen after activities B and C and takes 30 hours. Activity E must take place after activity C and takes 10 hours. Activity F takes place after Activity E and takes 22 hours. Activities F and D are the last activities of the project. Which of the following is TRUE if activity B actually takes 37 hours?
    A. The critical path is 67 hours.
    B. The critical path changes to Start, B, D, End.
    C. The critical path is Start, A, C, E, F, End.
    D. The critical path increases by 12 hours.

25. A project manager has received activity duration estimates from his team. Which of the following does he need in order to complete the Develop Schedule process?
    A. Change requests
    B. Schedule change control system
    C. Recommended corrective actions
    D. Reserves

26. A project manager is taking over a project from another project manager during project planning. If the new project manager wants to see what the previous project manager planned for managing changes to the schedule, it would be BEST to look at the:
    A. Communications management plan.
    B. Update management plan.
    C. Staffing management plan
    D. Schedule management plan.

27. A project manager is using weighted average duration estimates to perform schedule network analysis. Which type of mathematical analysis is being used?
    A. Critical path method
    B. PERT
    C. Monte Carlo
    D. Resource leveling

28. The WBS, estimates for each work package, and the network diagram are completed. Which of the following would be the NEXT thing for the project manager to do?
    A. Sequence the activities.
    B. Verify that they have the correct scope.
    C. Create a preliminary schedule and get the team's approval.
    D. Complete risk management.

29. A new product development project has four levels in the work breakdown structure and has been sequenced using the precedence diagramming method. The activity duration estimates have been received. What should be done NEXT?
    A. Create an activity list.
    B. Begin the work breakdown structure.
    C. Finalize the schedule.
    D. Compress the schedule.

30. You are the project manager for a new product development project that has four levels in the work breakdown structure. The network diagram and duration estimates have been created, and a schedule has been developed and compressed. What time management activity should you do NEXT?
    A. Control Schedule.
    B. Estimate Activity Resources.
    C. Analogously estimate the schedule.
    D. Gain approval.

31. A team member from research and development tells you that her work is too creative to provide you with a fixed single estimate for the activity. You both decide to use the average labor hours per installation from past projects to predict the future. This is an example of which of the following?
    A. Parametric estimating
    B. Three-point estimating
    C. Analogous estimating
    D. Monte Carlo analysis

32. An activity has an early start (ES) of day 3, a late start (LS) of day 13, an early finish (EF) of day 9, and a late finish (LF) of day 19. The activity:
    A. Is on the critical path.
    B. Has a lag.
    C. Is progressing well.
    D. Is not on the critical path.

33. The project is calculated to be completed four days after the desired completion date. You do not have access to additional resources. The project is low risk, the benefit cost ratio (BCR) is expected to be 1.6, and the dependencies are preferential. Under these circumstances, what would be the BEST thing to do?
    A. Cut resources from an activity.
    B. Make more activities concurrent.
    C. Move resources from the preferential dependencies to the external dependencies.
    D. Remove an activity from the project.

34. A project manager for a small construction company has a project that was budgeted for US $130,000 over a six-week period. According to her schedule, the project should have cost US $60,000 to date. However, it has cost US $90,000 to date. The project is also behind schedule, because the original estimates were not accurate. Who has the PRIMARY responsibility to solve this problem?
    A. Project manager
    B. Senior management
    C. Project sponsor
    D. Manager of the project management office

35. Senior management is complaining that they are not able to easily determine the status of ongoing projects in the organization. Which of the following types of reports would help provide summary information to senior management?
    A. Detailed cost estimates
    B. Project management plans
    C. Bar charts
    D. Milestone reports

36. Rearranging resources so that a constant number of resources is used each month is called:
    A. Crashing.
    B. Floating.
    C. Leveling.
    D. Fast tracking.

37. Which of the following is a benefit of an analogous project estimate?
    A. It will be closer to what the work will actually require.
    B. It is based on a detailed understanding of what the work requires.
    C. It gives the project team an understanding of management's expectations.
    D. It helps the project manager determine if the project will meet the schedule.

38. During project executing, a large number of changes are made to the project. The project manager should:
    A. Wait until all changes are known and print out a new schedule.
    B. Make approved changes as needed, but retain the schedule baseline.
    C. Make only the changes approved by management.
    D. Talk to management before any changes are made.

Answers

1. **Answer** A
   Explanation There are only two choices related to scheduling; critical path method and precedence diagramming. Precedence diagramming, however, is a diagramming technique that deals with the relationship between activities, not schedule flexibility. The project manager is analyzing the critical path.

2. **Answer** C
   Explanation No mention is made that the dependency comes from a source outside the project, so this is not an external dependency. Scope dependency is not a defined term. The key word in the question is "requires." Since the dependency is required, it could not be discretionary and therefore must be mandatory. The question defines a mandatory dependency.

3. **Answer** D
   Explanation The bar chart (or Gantt chart) is designed to show a relationship to time. This is best used when demonstrating progress or status as a factor of time.

4. **Answer** A
   Explanation The standard deviation is computed by [P – O]/6. Therefore, the answer is [18 – 12]/6 = 6/6 = 1.

5. **Answer** D
   Explanation A heuristic is a rule of thumb. Examples are cost per line of code, cost per square foot of floor space, etc.

6. **Answer** C
   Explanation Total float and free float are the time an activity can be delayed without impacting the entire project or the next activity. A forward or backward pass refers to a network analysis technique, not waiting time. Waiting time is the correct definition of lag.

7. **Answer** B
   Explanation The bar chart may show an end date, but it is not used to determine dates. The project charter also may include a required end date, but not a logical determination of how long the project will take. The network diagram takes the work packages from the work breakdown structure and adds dependencies. The dependencies allow us to look at the various paths through the diagram to determine the longest duration (critical) path. The network diagram is the best answer.

8. **Answer** A
   Explanation This question tests your knowledge about a number of topics. There can often be more than one critical path, but you might adjust the plan in order to decrease risk and have only one critical path. The network diagram may or may not change when the end date changes, depending on the amount of schedule reserve and the reason for the change to the schedule. You can have negative float if you are behind schedule. The critical path helps prove how long the project will take. This is the only correct statement of the choices given.

9. **Answer** C
   Explanation A milestone shows the completion of a series of activities or work packages. Therefore, it takes no time of its own.

10. **Answer** C
Explanation An estimate can have a wide range and still be accurate if the item estimated includes identified risks. There is no such thing as a pad in proper project management. An estimate might be inflated, but it is a calculated reserve to account for risks, not arbitrary padding. The standard deviation tells you the amount of uncertainty or risk involved in the estimate for the activity.

11. **Answer** D
Explanation The float of an activity is the length of time the activity can be delayed without delaying the critical path.

12. **Answer** B
Explanation Though having three critical paths COULD require more people or cost more, the answer that is definitely and always true is that it increases project risk. Because you need to manage three critical paths, there is more risk that something could happen to delay the project.

13. **Answer** C
Explanation Fast tracking affects both time and cost but may not help even out resource usage. Monte Carlo analysis and analysis of life cycle costs do not directly deal with resources. Leveling is the only choice that will definitely affect resources.

14. **Answer** C
Explanation Both types of charts are used in project planning. Team members need to see details and so they need a bar chart rather than a milestone chart. Risk analysis COULD make use of both charts. A milestone chart is used instead of a bar chart for any situation where you want to report in a less detailed way. Since bar charts can scare people with their complexity and often show too much detail to be worthwhile on a management level, milestone charts are more effective for reporting to management.

15. **Answer** C
Explanation Leveling resources generally extends the schedule. Monte Carlo analysis does not directly address the constraints of this situation. To compress the schedule, you could either crash or fast track. However, the situation says that the network diagram cannot change. This eliminates the fast tracking option, leaving crashing the project as the best answer.

16. **Answer** C
Explanation This is another question that asks about problem solving. Telling the boss or waiting to see the status next month do not try to solve the real problem. It would be inaccurate to report that the project cannot be finished earlier. Only meeting with the team to look for options for crashing or fast tracking the critical path relates to problem solving.

17. **Answer** A
Explanation You may or may not need your customer's or your boss's input, but you will definitely need to include an analysis of risk.

18. **Answer** B
Explanation By the time this process is taking place, Develop Project Charter, Sequence Activities, and Define Scope and would be completed. The team members would have provided estimates in the Estimate Activity Durations process, but the project manager may talk to them about those estimates as part of developing the project schedule. The process defined in the question is Develop Schedule.

19. **Answer** D
    Explanation This question again tests whether you know how to solve problems. Cutting product scope negatively affects the customer, and is therefore not best. A project manager's job is to determine options for meeting any end date; therefore, simply telling management the required date cannot be met is not correct. Working overtime is expensive and unnecessary when there are many other choices that could be selected first. Determining options for schedule compression would have the least negative effect on the project.

20. **Answer** B
    Explanation Time estimates for the activities should be created by the team and should not be added together to create the project estimate. Some activities may take place concurrently; these would be identified in the network diagram.

21. **Answer** A
    Explanation The question implies a finish-to-finish relationship between activities. The arrow diagramming method does not support that type of relationship. Critical path is not a diagramming method, and operational diagramming method is a made-up term. The precedence diagramming method is most appropriate in this case.

22. **Answer** B
    Explanation The situation is neither mandatory nor driven by an external source. A heuristic is a rule of thumb that can be used consistently. This situation is a unique occurrence for which a preferred method is being suggested. Therefore, this is a discretionary dependency.

23. **Answer** D
    Explanation This is an example of a two-stage question you may find on the exam. First you need to draw the network diagram and find the critical path, and then make a decision. The network diagram would be:

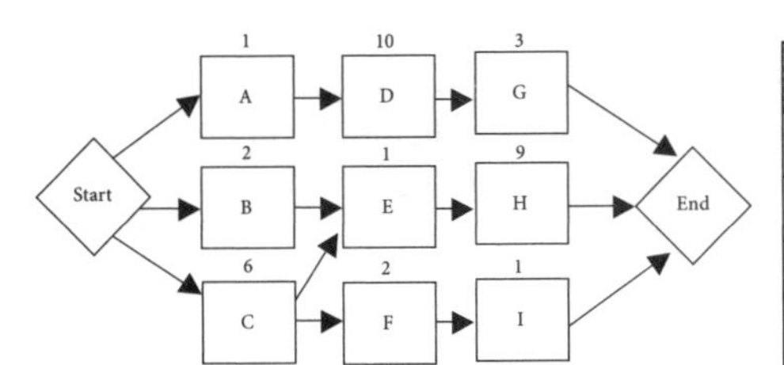

Paths	Duration in Weeks
Start, A, D, G, End	14
Start, B, E, H, End	12
Start, C, E, H, End	16
Start, C, F, I, End	9

The critical path is 16 (Start, C, E, H, End). Many people immediately look for the longest duration activity on the project to cut. Here activity D is the longest, at 10 weeks. However, that activity is not on the critical path, and cutting it would not shorten the project's duration. You must change the critical path. In this case, both activity C and activity H are on the critical path. If you have a choice, all things being equal, choose the earlier option. Therefore, activity C is the best answer.

24. **Answer** C
    Explanation Did you notice how difficult this question was to read? Such wording is intentional, to prepare you for interpreting questions on the real exam. Looking at this situation, you see there are three paths through the network as shown in the following table. If the duration of activity B changes from 25 to 37, the activity will take 12 hours longer. As the activity is only on the third path, it will only change the duration of that path from 55 to 55 + 12, or 67 hours. Since the duration of the critical path is 107 hours, the delay with activity B will have no impact on the project timeline or the current critical path.

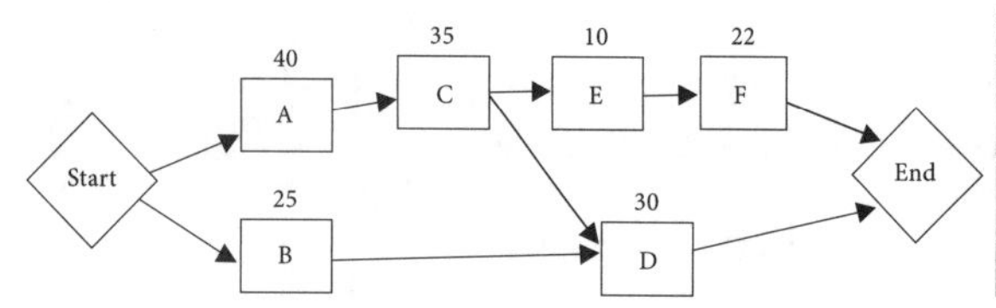

Paths	Duration in Hours
Start, A, C, E, F, End	107
Start, A, C, D, End	105
Start, B, D, End	55

25. **Answer** D
Explanation The Develop Schedule process includes all work and uses all inputs needed to come up with a finalized, realistic schedule. Reserves are created to cover identified and unknown schedule risks. All the other items are parts of Control Schedule and occur after the Develop Schedule process.

26. **Answer** D
Explanation The schedule management plan is the most correct answer. It is created as part of the Develop Project Management Plan process and is the repository for plans for schedule changes.

27. **Answer** B
Explanation PERT uses weighted averages to compute activity durations.

28. **Answer** C
Explanation Sequencing the activities is the same thing as creating a network diagram, so that has already been done. The Verify Scope process is done during project monitoring and controlling, not during project planning. Since a schedule is an input to risk management, risk management comes after the creation of a preliminary schedule, and so that is not the "next thing to do." Creating the preliminary schedule is next.

29. **Answer** D
Explanation The question is really asking, "What is done after the Estimate Activity Durations process?" The work breakdown structure and activity list are done before Estimate Activity Durations. The schedule is not finalized until after schedule compression. Therefore compressing the schedule is done next.

30. **Answer** D
Explanation Notice how this question and the previous one seem very similar. This is intended to prepare you for similar questions on the exam. Estimating activity resources and analogously estimating the schedule should have already been completed. The situation described is within the Develop Schedule process of time management. Control Schedule is the next time management process after Develop Schedule, but the Develop Schedule process is not yet finished. Final approval of the schedule by the stakeholders is needed before one has a project schedule.

31. **Answer** A
Explanation Monte Carlo relates to what-if analysis. Three-point estimating uses three time estimates per activity. One could use data from past projects to come up with the estimate (analogous estimating) but the best answer is parametric estimating because past history is being used to calculate an estimate. An estimate such as hours per installation is a characteristic of this form of estimating.

32. **Answer** D
    Explanation There is no information presented about lag or progress. The activity described has float, because there is a difference between the early start and late start. An activity that has float is probably not on the critical path.

33. **Answer** B
    Explanation Cutting resources from an activity would not save time, nor would moving resources from the preferential dependencies to the external dependencies. Removing an activity from the project is a possibility, but since the dependencies are preferential and the risk is low, the best choice would be to make more activities concurrent, as this would have less impact on the project.

34. **Answer** A
    Explanation Did you get lost looking at all the numbers presented in this question? Notice that there are no calculations required, simply an understanding of what the problem is. This question describes schedule management, which is a responsibility of the project manager.

35. **Answer** D
    Explanation Detailed cost estimates have nothing to do with the situation described. Project management plans include more detail than is necessary for the situation described, and may distract from the conversation if used in this situation. Bar charts are most effective for reporting to the team. The best answer is milestone reports, which present the right level of detail for upper management.

36. **Answer** C
    Explanation The key to this question is the phrase "constant number used each month." Only leveling has such an effect on the schedule.

37. **Answer** C
    Explanation Remember for the exam that analogous estimates are considered to be top-down, high-level estimates. Therefore, they are not based on a detailed understanding of what the work will require. The project manager needs more than an analogous (high-level) estimate to determine whether or not the project will meet the schedule. The benefit of an analogous project estimate is that it is management's expectations of what the project will cost. Any differences between the analogous estimate and the detailed bottom-up estimate can be reconciled in the planning processes.

38. **Answer** B
    Explanation Waiting until all changes are known, and then printing out a new schedule, is a common error many project managers make. Instead, the project manager should be controlling the project throughout its completion. The situation in the question does not provide a reason to believe the schedule baseline must be changed. A project manager must be in control of the project, rather than consulting with management before making any changes. Whenever a large number of changes occur on a project, it is wise to confirm that the business case, as stated in the project charter, is still valid.

CHAPTER SEVEN Cost Management

Quicktest

- Cost management process
- Earned value measurement
  - PV
  - EV
  - AC
  - CPI
  - SPI
  - BAC
  - EAC
  - ETC
  - VAC
  - CV
  - SV
  - TCPI
- Cost baseline
- Cost budget
- Performance measurement baseline
- Three-point estimating
- Analogous estimating
- Bottom-up estimating
- Parametric estimating
- Inputs to estimating costs
- Cost management plan
- Rough order of magnitude estimate
- Definitive estimate
- Budget estimate
- Reserve analysis
- Cost risk
- Variable/fixed costs
- Direct/indirect costs
- Life cycle costing
- Value analysis
- Progress reporting
- 50/50 rule
- Cost of quality
- Project management software

Do you create a budget for your projects? Do you have practical experience managing and controlling project costs? The questions on the exam are written to test whether you have such experience. If these efforts are not part of how you manage your real-world projects, make sure you read this chapter carefully and fully understand the concepts discussed.

Many people are nervous about questions relating to earned value. This chapter should help ease your mind. There have typically been about 12 questions on earned value on the exam. Only about six of these questions have required earned value calculations. With a little study, such questions should be easy.

There is a strong connection between cost management and time management on the exam. Some topics (including planning, estimating, and monitoring and controlling) covered here in the Cost Management chapter also apply to the Time Management chapter. Do not assume that because a topic is listed here it cannot be used for planning, estimating, and monitoring and controlling time. Earned value management is a good example of a tool that can be used for both time and cost.

The Time Management chapter talks about the identification of activities as smaller components of work packages. For many projects, activities are used to create cost estimates. On some large projects, however, it might be more practical to estimate and control costs at a different level. This level is called a control account. It is higher than the work package level in the WBS.

Rita's Process Chart—Cost Management

Where are we in the project management process?

INITIATING

- Select project manager
- Determine company culture and existing systems
- Collect processes, procedures, and historical information
- Divide large projects into phases
- Understand the business case
- Uncover initial requirements, assumptions, and risks
- Assess project and product feasibility within the given constraints
- Create measurable objectives
- Develop project charter
- Identify stakeholders
- Develop stakeholder management strategy

PLANNING

(This is the only process group with a set order)

- **Determine how you will do planning—part of all management plans**
- Determine detailed requirements
- Create project scope statement
- Assess what to purchase
- Determine team
- Create WBS and WBS dictionary
- Create activity list
- Create network diagram
- Estimate resource requirements
- **Estimate time and cost**
- Determine critical path
- Develop schedule
- **Develop budget**
- Determine quality standards, processes, and metrics
- Create process improvement plan
- **Determine all roles and responsibilities**
- Plan communications
- Perform risk identification, qualitative and quantitative risk analysis, and risk response planning
- **Go back—iterations**
- Prepare procurement documents
- Create change management plan
- **Finalize the "how to execute and control" parts of all management plans**
- **Develop realistic and final PM plan and performance measurement baseline**
- Gain formal approval of the plan
- Hold kickoff meeting

EXECUTING

- Execute the work according to the PM plan
- Produce product deliverables (product scope)
- Request changes
- Implement only approved changes
- Continuously improve
- Follow processes
- Perform quality assurance
- Perform quality audits
- Acquire final team
- Manage people
- Evaluate team and project performance
- Hold team-building activities
- Give recognition and rewards
- Use issue logs
- Facilitate conflict resolution
- Release resources as work is completed
- Send and receive information
- Hold meetings
- Select sellers

MONITORING & CONTROLLING

- **Take action to control the project**
- **Measure performance against the performance measurement baseline**
- **Measure performance against other metrics determined by the project manager**
- **Determine variances and if they warrant a corrective action or change request**
- **Influence the factors that cause changes**
- **Request changes**
- Perform integrated change control
- Approve or reject changes
- Inform stakeholders of the results of change requests
- Update the PM plan and project documents
- Manage configuration
- **Create forecasts**
- Gain acceptance of interim deliverables from the customer
- Perform quality control
- Report on project performance and solicit feedback
- Perform risk assessments and audits
- Manage reserves
- Administer procurements

CLOSING

- Confirm work is done to requirements
- Complete procurement closure
- Gain final acceptance of the product
- Complete financial closure
- Hand off completed product
- Solicit feedback from the customer about the project
- Complete final performance reporting
- Index and archive records
- Update lessons learned knowledge base

The following should help you understand how each part of cost management fits into the overall project management process:

The Cost Management Process	Done During
Estimate Costs	Planning process group
Determine Budget	Planning process group
Control Costs	Monitoring and controlling process group

Cost Management Plan PAGE 165 As with scope and time, the management plan for cost is not listed as part of the formally defined cost management process. The plan is a required part of project management, however. The cost management plan is referred to in the introduction to the Cost Management chapter in the *PMBOK® Guide*, but it is created as part of the Develop Project Management Plan process in integration management. On the exam, the cost management plan may also be called the "budget management plan" or "budget plan." Whatever term is used, just know the step of creating this management plan exists. The cost management planning process answers the questions, "How will I go about planning cost for the project?" and "How will I effectively manage the project to the cost baseline (a.k.a., the cost performance baseline), control costs, and manage cost variances?"

The cost management plan is similar to other management plans (a PMI-ism). It can be formal or informal, but it is part of the project management plan. Once again, you can see that such a plan requires thinking in advance about how you will manage costs. This is a concept that many project managers miss.

The cost management plan includes:

- Specifications for how estimates should be stated (in what currency)
- The level of accuracy needed for estimates
- Reporting formats to be used
- Rules for measuring cost performance
- Whether costs will include both direct costs (those costs directly attributable to the project) and indirect costs (costs not directly attributable to any one project, such as overhead costs)
- Establishment of a cost baseline for measuring against as part of project monitoring and controlling
- Control thresholds
- Cost change control procedures

Notice the inclusion of control thresholds. The creation of the cost management plan (like any other management plan in project management) requires thinking ahead about how you will control costs. If an actual cost comes in higher than expected, will you need to take action? What if it's a two dollar difference? Control thresholds are the amount of variation allowed before you need to take action. You determine these thresholds in planning while creating the cost management plan.

You should also know the following cost management concepts:

Life Cycle Costing[1] Remember the product life cycle we discussed earlier? Would it be wise to design the project so that the project costs are low but the maintenance costs are higher than the project cost savings? For example, you plan the project to produce the product at a lower level of quality and save $9,000. After the project is completed, the maintenance costs are $100,000 over the product's life, instead of the $20,000 in maintenance and repair that it could have cost. Your $9,000 "savings" cost the company $80,000 (or $71,000 additional cost). This is the concept of life cycle costing—looking at the cost of the whole life of the product, not just the cost of the project.

Value Analysis[2] This concept is sometimes referred to as value engineering in the real world. Its focus is to find a less costly way to do the same work. In other words, this technique asks, "How can we decrease cost on the project while maintaining the same scope?" When performing value analysis, you systematically identify the required project functions, assign values to these functions, and provide functions at the lowest overall cost without loss of performance.

Cost Risk[3] Some topics cross the boundaries between knowledge areas. For example, the concept of cost risk involves risk, procurement, and cost management. This term means just what its name implies—cost-related risk. Since such topics cross knowledge areas, so do the questions on the exam about the topics. See the following example question:

Question *Who has the cost risk in a fixed price contract—the buyer or the seller?*

Answer *The seller*

Estimate Costs PAGE 168

Process: Estimate Costs
Process Group: Planning
Knowledge Area: Cost Management

The Estimate Costs process involves coming up with cost estimates for each activity. This process does not combine all the estimates into one time-phased spending plan (the cost budget). That happens in the next process, Determine Budget.

In the Time Management chapter, we discussed "Things About Estimating to Know for the Exam." As noted in that chapter, these concepts apply to both time and cost estimating. Take some time now to review that discussion on page 183. It is helpful to have those concepts fresh in your mind before continuing to read about the Estimate Costs process.

So what costs should you estimate? To put it simply, the costs involved in all the efforts needed to complete the project. These include:

- Costs of quality efforts
- Costs of risk efforts
- Costs of the project manager's time
- Costs of project management activities
- Costs directly associated with the project, including labor, materials, training for the project, computers, etc.
- Office expenses for physical office spaces used directly for the project
- Profit, when applicable
- Overhead costs, such as management salaries and general office expenses

Types of Cost There are several ways to look at costs when creating an estimate. In the past, the exam has only asked a few questions regarding types of cost. The following information should help you answer such questions.

A cost can be either variable or fixed:

- **Variable Costs** These costs change with the amount of production or the amount of work. Examples include the cost of material, supplies, and wages.
- **Fixed Costs** These costs do not change as production changes. Examples include the cost of set-up, rent, etc.

A cost can be either direct or indirect:

- **Direct Costs** These costs are directly attributable to the work on the project. Examples are team travel, team wages, recognition, and costs of material used on the project.
- **Indirect Costs** Indirect costs are overhead items or costs incurred for the benefit of more than one project. Examples include taxes, fringe benefits, and janitorial services.

Inputs to Estimating Costs (or "What do you need before you estimate costs?")

These inputs help you create estimates more quickly and more accurately. For example, imagine having access to a repository that contains all the previous WBSs for projects similar to yours, along with the estimates and actual costs for each activity. Can you see how that might be helpful in creating more accurate estimates on your own project? Having highly accurate estimates will help you better control the project later and, therefore, save you effort. So read through the following list of inputs (do not just skim over this list!), and think through why each might help you in estimating costs.

- **The scope baseline** In order to create an estimate, you need to know the details of what you are estimating; this includes knowing what is out of scope and what constraints have been placed on the project. This information can be found by looking at all the components of the scope baseline (the project scope statement, WBS, and WBS dictionary).
- **Project schedule** This is one of the key inputs to cost management, as the schedule contains the activities, the resources assigned to complete the work, and when the work will occur. Keep in mind that you need a schedule before you can come up with a budget. There are two reasons for this: first, the timing of when you buy something affects its cost; second, you need to develop a time-phased spending plan to control project expenditures (a budget) so that you know how much money will be spent during specific periods of time (January, next month, etc.). But know that it goes both ways; costs will also affect the schedule. For example, the price of material or a piece of equipment may vary due to factors like availability, seasonal pricing fluctuations, new model releases, etc. If you know that something will be more expensive to buy at the time when it is scheduled to be purchased, you may want to change the schedule to be able to purchase the material or equipment at a different time, for a lower price. This is the process of iterative planning, as shown in Rita's Process Chart.
- **Human resource plan** Reward systems (part of the human resource plan) can increase productivity and save money, but they are still a cost item and need to be estimated. Another part of the human resource plan that needs to be considered is labor rates. The project manager should have access to the rates paid to everyone who works on the project. Is this different from your real world? If so, take note of this for the exam. The human resource plan also lists the human resources (including the quantity of resources needed and their skills) intended to be used for the project. Of course, these resources have costs associated with them.
- **Risk register** Like reward systems, risk management will save time and money, but there are costs associated with the efforts to control risks. It is important to remember that these costs, in turn, will result in more risks (cost risks). In other words, risks are both an input to the Estimate Costs process and an output. Again, planning is iterative.
- **Policies and historical records related to estimating, templates, processes, procedures, lessons learned, and historical information (i.e., organizational process assets)** As noted earlier, historical records from past projects can be highly beneficial in creating estimates for a current project. Organizational policies and standardized templates related to estimating can also make this effort faster and easier.
- **Company culture and existing systems that the project will have to deal with or can use (i.e., enterprise environmental factors)** For cost estimating, this includes marketplace conditions and commercial cost databases. While estimating, you might review the different sources from which supplies might be procured and at what costs as part of estimating.
- **Project management costs** If you are unfamiliar with cost estimating, understand that part of the expense of the project comes from the costs associated with project management activities.

Although project management efforts save money on projects overall, they do incur costs and should be included in the project cost estimates. These include not only costs associated with the efforts of the project manager but also those associated with status reports, change analysis, etc.

Exercise Do you think you really understood the discussion of cost estimating inputs? Test yourself! Try to recreate the list of inputs to estimating in the space below. Spend some time thinking about any inputs you forgot, to make sure you really understand these inputs for the exam.

How Is Estimating Done?

Costs can be estimated using the same techniques described in the Time Management chapter: one-point estimating, analogous estimating, parametric estimating, and three-point (PERT) estimating. Costs can also be estimated using a bottom-up estimating technique.

Bottom-Up Estimating[4] PAGE 172

This technique involves creating detailed estimates for each part of an activity (if available) or work package (if activities are not defined). The estimates are then rolled up into control accounts and finally into an overall project estimate. To do this well requires an accurate WBS.

Exercise Test yourself! See if you understand the differences between analogous and bottom-up estimating by identifying the advantages and disadvantages of each technique. (Analogous estimating was described in the Time Management chapter.)

What Are the Advantages of Analogous Estimating?	What Are the Disadvantages of Analogous Estimating?

What Are the Advantages of Bottom-Up Estimating?	What Are the Disadvantages of Bottom-Up Estimating?

Answer There are many possible answers to these questions. The purpose of this exercise is to get you thinking about the differences so that you can answer any questions on the topic, no matter how they may be worded.

Advantages of Analogous Estimating	Disadvantages of Analogous Estimating
Quick	Less accurate
Activities need not be identified	Estimates are prepared with a limited amount of detailed information and understanding of the project
Less costly to create	Requires considerable experience to do well
Gives the project manager an idea of the level of management's expectations (for a project analogous estimate)	There may be infighting to gain the biggest piece of the budget without being able to justify the need
Overall project costs will be capped (for a project analogous estimate)	Extremely difficult for projects with uncertainty
	Does not take into account the differences between projects

Advantages of Bottom-up Estimating	Disadvantages of Bottom-up Estimating
More accurate	Takes time and expense to use this estimating technique
Gains buy-in from the team because the team creates estimates they can live with	Tendency for the team to pad estimates unless they understand the use of reserves
Based on a detailed analysis of the project	Requires that the project be defined and well understood before estimating begins
Provides a basis for monitoring and controlling, performance measurement, and management	Requires time to break the project down into smaller pieces

The following are used in the process of creating estimates:

Project Management Software Remember there is no such thing as one software package to tell you how to manage a project. The software referred to here might be any software used for estimating. If a project has hundreds or thousands of activities, each of which has similar cost components added like overhead, software can significantly speed up the calculations.

Determining Resource Cost Rates Although many project managers do not have access to this information on their projects, the exam assumes that a project manager knows the actual cost of labor when performing detailed cost estimating. Remember that resources are not just internal human resources. This work might also involve estimating the work of consultants, vendors, and suppliers. When the project includes plans to outsource pieces of work, the Estimate Costs and Plan Procurements processes impact each other and require iterations as planning progresses. This same relationship exists between Plan Procurements and the other estimating processes (i.e., Estimate Activity Resources and Estimate Activity Durations). Planning is iterative.

Reserve Analysis It is required project management to use reserves to accommodate the cost and time risk in a project estimate. This involves identifying which activities on the project have significant risks and determining how much time and money to set aside to account for the risks if they occur. Contingency reserves are used for known risks, which are specifically identified risks. A lump sum management reserve is used to accommodate unknown risks, or unidentified risks. See the Risk Management chapter to learn how these reserves are calculated. Reserve analysis should include making sure individual activity estimates are not padded.

Cost of Quality The cost of work added to the project to accommodate quality efforts should be included in the project estimate.

Accuracy of Estimates Think about someone walking into your office now and asking you to estimate the total cost of a new project. The first question you would probably ask is, "How accurate do you want me to be?" Estimates made in the early part of the project will be less accurate than those made later, when more is known about the project. Estimates should be in a range, as it is very unlikely that an activity will be completed for exactly any particular amount of money. In the early part of the project, you typically provide wide-ranging estimates. Then over time, as you determine more information about the project during planning, you can narrow the estimate range.

Organizations often have different standards for different ranges, from preliminary to conceptual to feasibility to order of magnitude to definitive estimates. The standard ranges of the order of magnitude estimate, budget estimate, and definitive estimate are shown below. Such ranges tell you how much time and effort needs to go into estimating to make sure the actual cost is within the range of the estimate.

These ranges often show up on the exam. Make sure you memorize them.

- **Rough Order of Magnitude (ROM) Estimate**[5] This type of estimate is usually made during project initiating. A typical range for ROM estimates is +/-50 percent from actual, but this range can vary depending on how much is known about the project when creating the estimates.
- **Budget Estimate** This type of estimate is usually made during project planning and is in the range of -10 to +25 percent from actual.
- **Definitive Estimate** As the project progresses, the estimate will become more refined. Some project managers use the range of +/-10 percent from actual, while others use -5 to +10 percent from actual.

When completed, the Estimate Costs process results in activity cost estimates and an explanation of how those estimates were derived (basis of estimates). It can also result in changes or updates to the risk register and other parts of the project management plan and project documents.

Determine Budget PAGE 174

Process: Determine Budget
Process Group: Planning
Knowledge Area: Cost Management

In this part of cost management, the project manager calculates the total cost of the project in order to determine the amount of funds the organization needs to have available for the project. The result of this calculation is called the budget. Meeting the cost baseline will be a measure of project success, so the budget should be in a form the project manager can use while the work is being done to control costs and, therefore, control the overall project.

In estimating the total cost of a project (i.e., determining the project's budget), a project manager MUST perform risk management activities and include reserves in that estimate! Make sure you note this for the exam if you do not formally manage risks on your real-world projects. There are two types of reserves that can be added to the estimate: contingency reserves and management reserves.[6] Contingency reserves address the cost impacts of the risks remaining during risk response planning. Management reserves are additional funds set aside to cover unforeseen risks or changes to the project. The cost baseline includes the contingency reserves; it represents the funds the project manager has authority to manage and control. The cost budget is the cost baseline plus the management reserves. The cost budget is how much money the company should have available for the project.

To create a budget, activity costs are rolled up to work package costs. Work package costs are then rolled up to control account costs and finally to project costs. This process is called cost aggregation. Contingency reserves are added to achieve the cost baseline. In the final step, the management reserves are added. See the following diagram.

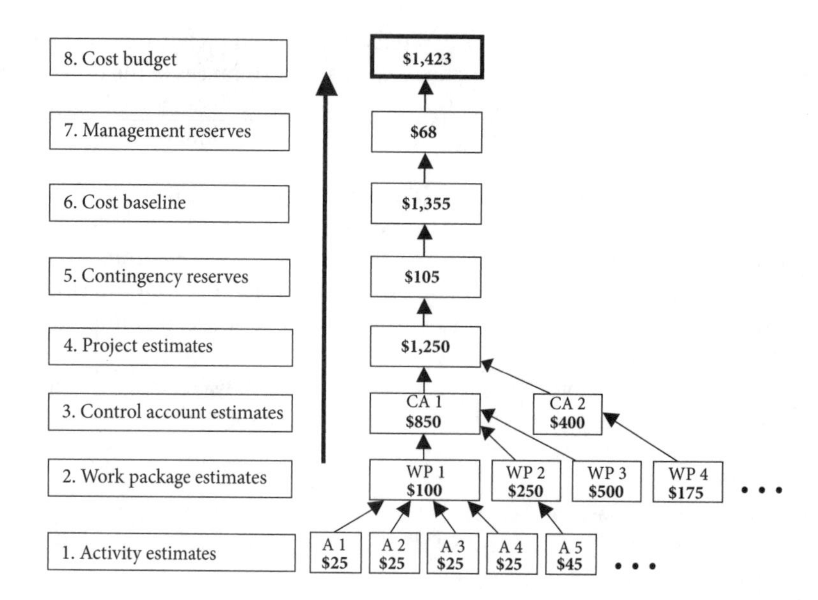

After the cost baseline and cost budget are estimated, the project manager may compare these numbers to parametric estimates, expert judgment, or historical records as a sanity check. For example, a rule of thumb for a high-level parametric estimate in some industries is that design should be 15 percent of the cost of construction. Other industries consider the cost of design to be 60 percent of the project budget. The project manager needs to investigate and justify any significant differences between the project estimates and the reference data to ensure the estimates are correct.

The next thing to check is cash flow (part of funding limit reconciliation[7]). Funding may not be available when it is needed on the project, causing changes to the other parts of the project and iterations of the project documents or project management plan. For example, if equipment costing $500,000 is scheduled to be purchased on June 1 but the money for the purchase is not available until July 1, the activities dependent on that equipment will have to be moved to later points in the schedule. The cost baseline, therefore, is time-phased and may be shown as an S-curve[8].

The project manager needs to perform another reconciliation before the proposed cost baseline and cost budget can become final: reconciliation with any cost constraints in the charter. If the project estimate exceeds the constraints, the project manager has to meet with management, explain why their cost cannot be met, and propose options to decrease costs. Pay particular attention to that last sentence. If such actions are a required part of project management, then an unrealistic budget is the project manager's fault! As with the schedule, project managers have a professional responsibility to reconcile the budget in this way. This reconciliation is done as part of integration management.

When the Determine Budget process is complete, the cost baseline, including all funding requirements, is established. As in the other processes we have discussed, the efforts involved in determining the budget may create the need for updates to other project documentation, including cost estimates, the risk register, and the project schedule.

Control Costs PAGE 179

Process: Control Costs
Process Group: Monitoring & Controlling
Knowledge Area: Cost Management

The Control Costs process is similar to the control part of any other knowledge area, with a focus on cost. That being said, complete the following exercise and imagine how this would work on real-world projects.

Exercise What ACTIONS should a project manager take to control costs? (This is an important topic, so really take the time to think about this question, even if you are tired of exercises.)

Answer Was one of your answers "follow the cost management plan"? This is an excellent answer! The cost management plan includes your plan for how you will control the costs of the project, such as meetings on cost, reports, measurements that will be made, and their frequency. The control part of the management plan is customized to the needs of the project.

If you understand the idea behind PMI-isms, you might also have answered something like "look at any organizational process assets that are available." This is also a good answer. You need to consider any policies, procedures, tools, or reporting formats related to controlling costs that are available or required by your company.

Was another one of your answers "manage changes"? This is generally correct, but make sure you understand the complexity of this effort. What about preventing unnecessary changes and influencing the things that are causing costs to rise? What about letting people know which changes are approved and which are not so that everyone is working on the same project? You need to have an "attitude" of control. It is your project and your career. You must be assertive and make sure the project goes according to the plan. Oversight and CONTROL are essential for the success of both the project and your career as a project manager. It is important to understand that this attitude of control applies to all parts of the project, not just cost. Think of yourself as a detective looking for anything that can get in the way of project success, and you will choose the better answer choice for questions that seem to have more than one "correct" answer.

Also keep in mind that control means measure. When taking the exam, assume that the project manager is measuring, measuring, measuring on the project, even if you do not do this on your real-world projects. Measurement helps you see if there are any variances. You can then determine if those variances require changes, including corrective or preventive actions. The cost management plan should include what you will measure, when, and what amount of variation between planned and actual will require action (your control limits). In other words, you plan what you will do to control the project before you get started. Do you do this in your real world? Assume that you do, and assume that all proper project management is being done when you take the exam unless the question tells you (directly or indirectly) that proper project management was not done.

Progress Reporting PAGE 185 The project manager can use information about project progress to help control the schedule and costs and to assess whether the project is on track through earned value measurement (described next). Many project managers determine progress by asking team members for an estimate of percent complete for each work package or activity. On projects where work is not objectively measured, the estimate the team members provide is simply a guess. The method of asking for percent complete is time-consuming and generally a waste of time when the estimate is a guess, because it does not provide a realistic estimate of the project's progress.

If a project has been planned using a WBS and it is broken down to the level of work packages that require about 80 hours of work, there are alternatives to asking for percent complete. Because such work packages are completed relatively quickly and frequently, the project manager can use one of the following practices to report progress:

50/50 Rule

An activity is considered 50 percent complete when it begins and gets credit for the last 50 percent only when it is completed.

20/80 Rule

An activity is considered 20 percent complete when it begins and gets credit for the last 80 percent only when it is completed.

0/100 Rule

An activity does not get credit for partial completion; it only gets credit for full completion.

Earned Value Measurement[9] PAGE 181 Okay, let's pause for a moment. You probably know earned value is on the exam. Are you worried about it? Don't be. We are going to make it easier.

First, think about this: how valuable would it be to KNOW how your project is really going? Could you sleep better at night? Would you be able to spend your time in more productive ways than worrying? These are the benefits of earned value. If you currently rely on hope, guesses, or a general percent complete estimate to assess how your project is going, you probably know from experience that these methods do not tell you much, nor are they very accurate. And they may regularly result in the need to work overtime at the end of the project because of the lack of control along the way. Keep the benefits of earned value in mind as you read this section, and go through it slowly if it seems confusing. Make sure you "get it" the first time you read it.

Earned value is used to measure project performance against the scope, schedule, and cost baselines. Please note that the earned value technique calls the combination of these three baselines the performance measurement baseline. The measurements resulting from an earned value analysis of the project indicate whether there are any potential deviations from the scope, schedule, and cost baselines (the performance measurement baseline). Many project managers manage their project's performance by comparing planned to actual results. With this method, however, you could easily be on time but overspend according to your plan. Using earned value measurement is better, because it integrates cost, time, and the work done (or scope) and can be used to forecast future performance and project completion dates and costs.

Using the data gathered through earned value analysis, a project manager can create reports, including budget forecasts, and other communications related to the project's progress (see the Communications Management chapter for more on earned-value-related reports). Earned value measurements may also result in change requests to the project.

Here are the earned value terms you need to know.

Terms to Know

Acronym	Term	Interpretation
PV	Planned Value	As of today, what is the estimated value of the work planned to be done?
EV	Earned Value	As of today, what is the estimated value of the work actually accomplished?
AC	Actual Cost (total cost)	As of today, what is the actual cost incurred for the work accomplished?
BAC	Budget at Completion (the budget)	How much did we BUDGET for the TOTAL project effort?
EAC	Estimate at Completion	What do we currently expect the TOTAL project to cost (a forecast)?
ETC	Estimate to Complete	From this point on, how much MORE do we expect it to cost to finish the project (a forecast)?
VAC	Variance at Completion	As of today, how much over or under budget do we expect to be at the end of the project?

Formulas and Interpretations to Memorize

The exam focuses not just on calculations, but also on knowing what the numbers mean. Therefore, you should know all the following formulas. (Note: The ^{C} in the following table stands for "cumulative.")

Name	Formula	Interpretation
Cost Variance (CV)	EV – AC	NEGATIVE is over budget; POSITIVE is under budget.
Schedule Variance (SV)	EV – PV	NEGATIVE is behind schedule; POSITIVE is ahead of schedule.
Cost Performance Index (CPI)[10]	$\frac{EV}{AC}$	We are getting $_____ worth of work out of every $1 spent. Funds are or are not being used efficiently.
Schedule Performance Index (SPI)	$\frac{EV}{PV}$	We are (only) progressing at ____ percent of the rate originally planned.

Name	Formula	Interpretation
Estimate at Completion (EAC)		As of now, how much do we expect the total project to cost? $ ______. (See the formulas to the left, below.)
NOTE: There are many ways to calculate EAC, depending on the assumptions made. Notice how the purpose of the formulas really is to create forecasts based on past performance on the project.	AC + Bottom-up ETC	This formula calculates actual plus a new estimate for the remaining work. It is used when the original estimate was fundamentally flawed.
	$\frac{BAC}{CPI^C}$	This formula is used if no variances from the BAC have occurred or you will continue at the same rate of spending.
	AC + (BAC – EV)	This formula calculates actual to date plus remaining budget. It is used when current variances are thought to be atypical of the future. It is essentially AC plus the remaining value of work to perform.
	$AC + \frac{(BAC - EV)}{(CPI^C \times SPI^C)}$	This formula calculates actual to date plus the remaining budget modified by performance. It is used when current variances are thought to be typical of the future. It assumes poor cost performance and a need to hit a firm completion date.
To Complete Performance Index (TCPI)	$\frac{(BAC - EV)}{(BAC - AC)}$	This formula divides the work remaining to be done by the money remaining to do it. It answers the question of "In order to stay within budget, what rate must we meet for the remaining work?"
Estimate to Complete (ETC)	EAC – AC	How much more will the project cost?
	Reestimate	Reestimate the remaining work from the bottom up.
Variance at Completion (VAC)	BAC – EAC	How much over or under budget will we be at the end of the project?

The CPI in the previous table is a cumulative CPI because it is using costs to date. It could be written as $CPI^C = EV^C/AC^C$ with the ^{C} standing for cumulative. This cumulative formula is the same as that in the previous table, but it more clearly states that the data used is cumulative. CPI can also be calculated for costs incurred during a specific period of time (week, month, or quarter) rather than over all the time to date.

Make sure you understand and MEMORIZE the following:

- EV comes first in every formula. Remembering this one fact alone should help you get about half the earned value questions right. (Aren't you glad you purchased this book?)
- If it is a variance, the formula is EV minus something.
- If it is an index, it is EV divided by something.
- If the formula relates to cost, use AC.
- If the formula relates to schedule, use PV.

- For variances interpretation: negative is bad and positive is good. Thus a –200 cost variance means that you are behind (over budget).
- For indices interpretation: greater than one is good; less than one is bad.

One type of earned value question people often answer incorrectly requires that you differentiate between EAC and ETC and the other terms. The following table may help you understand this difference. Notice that planned value (PV; what the value was expected to be at this point in the project according to the plan) and actual cost (AC; what the cost has actually been on the project prior to this point) look backward at the project. Budget at completion (BAC), estimate to complete (ETC), and estimate at completion (EAC) look forward. BAC simply states the project's planned budget; it indicates what the end cost of the project would be if everything went according to plan. ETC and EAC forecast future performance based on what has actually occurred on the project, taking into account any variances from the plan the project has already experienced. ETC is an estimate of how much more the remaining part of the project will cost to complete. EAC indicates what the total project cost is forecasted to be.

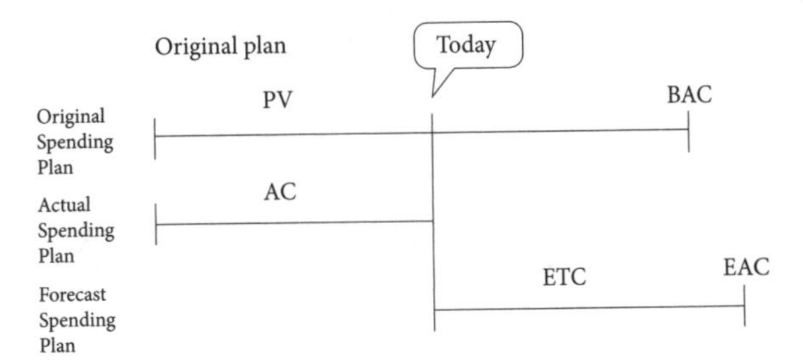

Are you still worried about earned value? Not for long. Read the following pages and do the exercises; you might end up appreciating earned value questions over some of the more ambiguous and confusing questions on this exam.

Earned Value in Action

Earned value is an effective tool for measuring performance and determining the need to request changes. The following is a sample team meeting conversation on this subject:

> Olaf, the project manager, calls a team meeting and says, "We are six months into this million dollar project, and my latest analysis shows a CPI of 1.2 and an SPI of 0.89. This means that we are getting 1.2 dollars for every dollar we put into the project, but only progressing at 89 percent of the rate originally planned. Let's look for options to correct this problem."
>
> "We could remove me from the project team and replace me with someone less expensive. I must be the most expensive team member," Ashley says.
>
> "Not only would it sadden me to lose you, but your suggestion would improve costs, not schedule. You are the company's best network specialist. Someone else would not be as proficient as you in completing the work."
>
> "We could remove the purchase of the new computers from the project," says Tony. "Or, we could just tell the customer the project will be two weeks late."
>
> "Canceling the new computers would save us money, not time. We need to focus on time," Olaf says. "Nor can we just change the project schedule baseline arbitrarily. That would be unethical."

"Since we are doing well on cost, why don't we bring in another programmer from the IT department to work on this project? We can get the next two activities completed faster," Deborah suggests.

"That sounds like the most effective choice in this situation. Let's see if we can find someone who will improve performance, at the lowest cost. Thanks for your help," Olaf says.

The best way to learn the earned value analysis technique is to use it. The following exercises are designed to give you a chance to practice both calculations AND interpretation. Earned value questions on the exam have generally required fewer calculations for each question than these exercises.

Exercise

The cost performance index (CPI) and the schedule performance index (SPI) can be charted each month to show the project trends. Based on the diagram, what would you be more concerned about—cost or schedule—if you were taking over this project from another project manager?

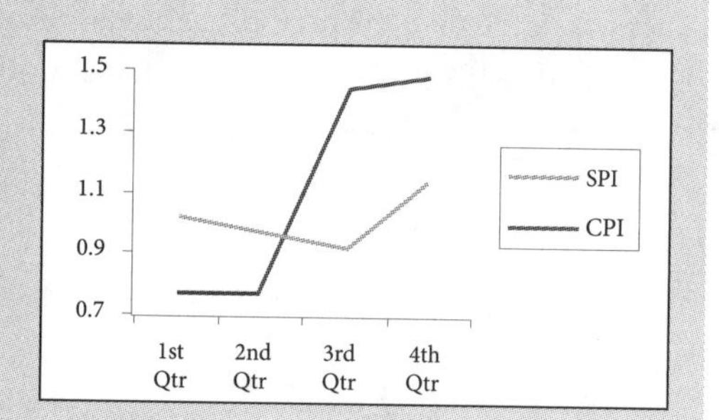

Answer Since these calculations were made in the past, the data in the chart is historical data. The last, most current measurement was in the fourth quarter, which shows both SPI and CPI being above one (good). Therefore, the answer is schedule. As of the fourth quarter (the most current information available), the SPI is lowest. An easy way to answer performance index questions that ask whether cost or schedule should concern you most is to pick the option with the lowest index.

Exercise The Fence #1

You have a project to build a new fence. The fence is four sided as shown. Each side is to take one day to build and is budgeted for $1,000 per side. The sides are planned to be completed one after the other. Today is the end of day three.

Using the following project status chart, calculate PV, EV, etc., in the spaces provided. When completed, check your answers. Interpretation is also important on the exam. Can you interpret what each answer means?

Do the calculations to three decimal place accuracy on the exercises. On the real exam, round the results of your calculations to two decimal places when you are ready to check your answers against the choices provided.

Activity	Day 1	Day 2	Day 3	Day 4	Status End of Day 3
Side 1	S---------F				Complete, spent $1,000
Side 2		S--------PF	----F		Complete, spent $1,200
Side 3			PS--S---PF		50% done, spent $600
Side 4				PS--------PF	Not yet started

Key S = Actual Start, F = Actual Finish, PS = Planned Start, and PF = Planned Finish

	What Is:	Calculation	Answer	Interpretation of the Answer
1	PV			
2	EV			
3	AC			
4	BAC			
5	CV			
6	CPI			
7	SV			
8	SPI			
9	EAC			
10	ETC			
11	VAC			

Answer **The Fence #1**

	What Is:	Calculation	Answer	Interpretation of the Answer
1	PV	$1,000 plus $1,000 plus $1,000	$3,000	We should have done $3,000 worth of work.
2	EV	Complete, complete, half done or $1,000 plus $1,000 plus $500	$2,500	We have actually completed $2,500 worth of work.
3	AC	$1,000 plus $1,200 plus $600	$2,800	We have actually spent $2,800.
4	BAC	$1,000 plus $1,000 plus $1,000 plus $1,000	$4,000	Our project budget is $4,000.
5	CV	$2,500 minus $2,800	-$300	We are over budget by $300.

	What Is:	Calculation	Answer	Interpretation of the Answer
6	CPI	$2,500 divided by $2,800	$0.893	We are only getting about 89 cents out of every dollar we put into the project.
7	SV	$2,500 minus $3,000	-$500	We are behind schedule.
8	SPI	$2,500 divided by $3,000	$0.833	We are only progressing at about 83 percent of the rate planned.
9	EAC	$4,000 divided by $.893	$4,479	We currently estimate that the total project will cost $4,479.
10	ETC	$4,479 minus $2,800	$1,679	We need to spend $1,679 to finish the project.
11	VAC	$4,000 minus $4,479	-$479	We currently expect to be $479 over budget when the project is completed.

NOTE: If your answers differ, check your rounding. Again, it is best to calculate to three decimal places and then round to two decimal places when you are ready to compare your results against the choices provided on the exam.

Exercise The Fence #2

You have a project to build a new fence. The fence is four sided as shown. Each side is to take one day to build and is budgeted for $1,000 per side. The sides are planned to be completed one after the other. In this case, ASSUME THAT THE SIDES HAVE A FINISH-TO-FINISH RELATIONSHIP INSTEAD OF A FINISH-TO-START RELATIONSHIP, so more than one side can be worked on at the same time (in parallel).

Using the following project status chart, calculate PV, EV, etc., in the spaces provided. When completed, check your answers.

Activity	Day 1	Day 2	Day 3	Day 4	Status End of Day 3
Side 1	S----------F				Complete, spent $1,000
Side 2		S----F----PF			Complete, spent $900
Side 3		S----	PS-------PF		50% done, spent $1,000
Side 4			S----	PS-------PF	75% done, spent $300

Key S = Actual Start, F = Actual Finish, PS = Planned Start, and PF = Planned Finish

	What Is:	Calculation	Answer	Interpretation of the Answer
1	PV			
2	EV			
3	AC			
4	BAC			
5	CV			
6	CPI			
7	SV			
8	SPI			
9	EAC			
10	ETC			
11	VAC			

Answer The Fence #2

	What Is:	Calculation	Answer	Interpretation of the Answer
1	PV	$1,000 plus $1,000 plus $1,000	$3,000	We should have done $3,000 worth of work.
2	EV	Complete, complete, half done, 75% done or $1,000 plus $1,000 plus $500 plus $750	$3,250	We have actually completed $3,250 worth of work.
3	AC	$1,000 plus $900 plus $1,000 plus $300	$3,200	We have actually spent $3,200.
4	BAC	$1,000 plus $1,000 plus $1,000 plus $1,000	$4,000	Our project budget is $4,000.
5	CV	$3,250 minus $3,200	$50	We are under budget by $50.
6	CPI	$3,250 divided by $3,200	$1.016	We are getting about $1.02 out of every dollar we put into the project.
7	SV	$3,250 minus $3,000	$250	We are ahead of schedule.
8	SPI	$3,250 divided by $3,000	$1.083	We are progressing at about 108 percent of the rate planned.

	What Is:	Calculation	Answer	Interpretation of the Answer
9	EAC	\$4,000 divided by \$1.016	\$3,937	We currently estimate that the total project will cost \$3,937.
10	ETC	\$3,937 minus \$3,200	\$737	We need to spend \$737 to finish the project.
11	VAC	\$4,000 minus \$3,937	\$63	We currently expect to be \$63 under budget when the project is completed.

In this example, you are looking for the value of the work that has actually been done. The finish-to-finish relationship allowed the team to work on more than one side at the same time. In this case, work is being done on both sides 3 and 4 at the same time. Since the value of each side is \$1,000, we look at how much of each side is complete and apply that percent to the value. Here sides one and two are completed; thus, each receives a value of \$1,000. (It doesn't matter what it actually cost—just the value.) Side three is 50 percent done and receives a value of \$500 (50 percent of \$1,000). Side four is 75 percent done and receives a value of \$750 (75 percent of \$1,000). The earned value to date is \$3,250.

Understanding the meaning of the results of each calculation is as important as knowing how to calculate them.

Expect questions on the exam that say things like, "The CPI is 0.9, and the SPI is 0.92. What should you do?" You will need to interpret this and other data in the question and then be able to determine which choice would address the issue(s) described. In this example, there are both cost and schedule problems.

You may also get questions on the exam that require you to back into an answer. Try the following exercise.

Exercise Your project is running well. In the latest earned value report, you see the CPI = 1.2, the SPI = 0.8, the PV = \$600,000, and the SV = -\$120,000. You can't find the CV in the report, so you calculate it based on the information given. What is the CV?

Answer The formula for CV is CV = EV – AC. Therefore, you need to find EV and AC to calculate CV. Since SV = EV – PV, and we know the values for SV (-\$120,000) and PV (\$600,000), we can find EV.

$$\begin{aligned} -\$120{,}000 &= EV - \$600{,}000 \\ +\$600{,}000 &\qquad\quad +\$600{,}000 \\ \hline \$480{,}000 &= EV \end{aligned}$$

Now we need AC, which we can get from the CPI (1.2).

The formula is $CPI = \frac{EV}{AC}$ or $1.2 = \frac{\$480{,}000}{AC}$

So you start by multiplying both sides of the equation by AC:

$$1.2 \times AC = \frac{\$480{,}000}{AC} \times AC$$

The resulting equation is:

$1.2 \times AC = \$480{,}000$

Now you divide both sides by 1.2:

$$\frac{(1.2 \times AC)}{1.2} = \frac{\$480{,}000}{1.2}$$

The resulting equation is:

$$AC = \frac{\$480{,}000}{1.2}$$

So AC = $400,000

Therefore, $CV = EV - AC$
$CV = \$480{,}000 - \$400{,}000$
$CV = \$80{,}000$

The Control Costs process provides measurements that indicate how the work is progressing and that allow the project manager to create reliable forecasts and take action to control the project, This process also results in change requests, including recommended corrective or preventive actions, and updates to the project management plan and project documents. The project manager needs to make sure these changes and updates are communicated to stakeholders and the team to ensure they understand the revisions to the project and are implementing them correctly.

Practice Exam

1. One common way to compute estimate at completion (EAC) is to take the budget at completion (BAC) and:
   A. Divide by SPI.
   B. Multiply by SPI.
   C. Multiply by CPI.
   D. Divide by CPI.

2. Estimate at completion (EAC) is a periodic evaluation of:
   A. The cost of work completed.
   B. The value of work performed.
   C. The anticipated total cost at project completion.
   D. What it will cost to finish the project.

3. If earned value (EV) = 350, actual cost (AC) = 400, planned value (PV) = 325, what is cost variance (CV)?
   A. 350
   B. -75
   C. 400
   D. -50

4. The customer responsible for overseeing your project asks you to provide a written cost estimate that is 30 percent higher than your estimate of the project's cost. He explains that the budgeting process requires managers to estimate pessimistically to ensure enough money is allocated for projects. What is the BEST way to handle this?
   A. Add the 30 percent as a lump sum contingency fund to handle project risks.
   B. Add the 30 percent to your cost estimate by spreading it evenly across all project activities.
   C. Create one cost baseline for budget allocation and a second one for the actual project management plan.
   D. Ask for information on risks that would cause your estimate to be too low.

5. Analogous estimating:
   A. Uses bottom-up estimating techniques.
   B. Is used most frequently during project executing.
   C. Uses top-down estimating techniques.
   D. Calculates estimates using actual detailed historical costs.

6. All of the following are outputs of the Estimate Costs process EXCEPT:
   A. An understanding of the cost risk in the work that has been estimated.
   B. The prevention of inappropriate changes from being included in the cost baseline.
   C. An indication of the range of possible costs for the project.
   D. Documentation of any assumptions made during the Estimate Costs process.

7. The main focus of life cycle costing is to:
   A. Estimate installation costs.
   B. Estimate the cost of operations and maintenance.
   C. Consider installation costs when planning the project costs.
   D. Consider operations and maintenance costs in making project decisions.

8. Cost performance measurement is BEST done through which of the following?
   A. Asking for a percent complete from each team member and reporting that in the monthly progress report
   B. Calculating earned value and using the indexes and other calculations to report past performance and forecast future performance
   C. Using the 50/50 rule and making sure the life cycle cost is less than the project cost
   D. Focusing on the amount expended last month and what will be expended the following month

9. A cost performance index (CPI) of 0.89 means:
   A. At this time, we expect the total project to cost 89 percent more than planned.
   B. When the project is completed, we will have spent 89 percent more than planned.
   C. The project is progressing at 89 percent of the rate planned.
   D. The project is getting 89 cents out of every dollar invested.

10. A schedule performance index (SPI) of 0.76 means:
   A. You are over budget.
   B. You are ahead of schedule.
   C. You are progressing at 76 percent of the rate originally planned.
   D. You are progressing at 24 percent of the rate originally planned.

11. Which of the following is NOT needed in order to come up with a project estimate?
   A. A WBS
   B. A network diagram
   C. Risks
   D. A change control system

12. Which of the following is an example of a parametric estimate?
   A. Dollars per module
   B. Learning bend
   C. Bottom-up
   D. CPM

13. A rough order of magnitude estimate is made during which project management process group?
   A. Planning
   B. Closing
   C. Executing
   D. Initiating

14. A cost baseline is an output of which cost management process?
   A. Estimate Activity Resources
   B. Estimate Costs
   C. Determine Budget
   D. Control Costs

15. During which project management process group are budget forecasts created?
   A. Monitoring and controlling
   B. Planning
   C. Initiating
   D. Executing

16. Which type of cost is team training?
    A. Direct
    B. NPV
    C. Indirect
    D. Fixed

17. Project setup costs are an example of:
    A. Variable costs.
    B. Fixed costs.
    C. Overhead costs.
    D. Opportunity costs.

18. Value analysis is performed to get:
    A. More value from the cost analysis.
    B. Management to buy into the project.
    C. The team to buy into the project.
    D. A less costly way of doing the same work.

19. Which estimating method tends to be MOST costly for creating a project cost estimate?
    A. Bottom-up
    B. Analogous
    C. Parametric
    D. 50/50

20. Which of the following represents the estimated value of the work actually accomplished?
    A. Earned value (EV)
    B. Planned value (PV)
    C. Actual cost (AC)
    D. Cost variance (CV)

21. Which of the following are ALL items included in the cost management plan?
    A. The level of accuracy needed for estimates, rules for measuring cost performance, specifications for how duration estimates should be stated
    B. Specifications for how estimates should be stated, rules for measuring cost performance, the level of accuracy needed for estimates
    C. Rules for measuring team performance, the level of accuracy needed for estimates, specifications for how estimates should be stated
    D. Specifications for how estimates should be stated, the level of risk needed for estimates, rules for measuring cost performance

22. Your project has a medium amount of risk and is not very well defined. The sponsor hands you a project charter and asks you to confirm that the project can be completed within the project cost budget. What is the BEST method to handle this?
    A. Build an estimate in the form of a range of possible results.
    B. Ask the team members to help estimate the cost based on the project charter.
    C. Based on the information you have, calculate a parametric estimate.
    D. Provide an analogous estimate based on past history.

23. The cost contingency reserve should be:
    A. Hidden to prevent management from disallowing the reserve.
    B. Added to each activity to provide the customer with a shorter critical path.
    C. Maintained by management to cover cost overruns.
    D. Added to the base costs of the project to account for risks.

24. You are having difficulty estimating the cost of a project. Which of the following BEST describes the most probable cause of your difficulty?
    A. Inadequate scope definition
    B. Unavailability of desired resources
    C. Lack of historical records from previous projects
    D. Lack of company processes

25. Your cost forecast shows that you will have a cost overrun at the end of the project. Which of the following should you do?
    A. Eliminate risks in estimates and reestimate.
    B. Meet with the sponsor to find out what work can be done sooner.
    C. Cut quality.
    D. Decrease scope.

26. A new store development project requires the purchase of various equipment, machinery, and furniture. The department responsible for the development recently centralized its external purchasing process and standardized its new order system. In which document can these new procedures be found?
    A. Project scope statement
    B. WBS
    C. Staffing management plan
    D. Organizational policies

27. Early in the life of your project, you are having a discussion with the sponsor about what estimating techniques should be used. You want a form of expert judgment, but the sponsor argues for analogous estimating. It would be BEST to:
    A. Agree to analogous estimating, as it is a form of expert judgment.
    B. Suggest life cycle costing as a compromise.
    C. Determine why the sponsor wants such an accurate estimate.
    D. Try to convince the sponsor to allow expert judgment because it is typically more accurate.

28. You have just completed the initiating processes of a small project and are moving into project planning when a project stakeholder asks you for the project's budget and cost baseline. What should you tell her?
    A. The project budget can be found in the project charter, which has just been completed.
    B. The project budget and baseline will not be finalized and accepted until the planning processes are completed.
    C. The project management plan will not contain the project's budget and baseline; this is a small project.
    D. It is impossible to complete an estimate before the project management plan is created.

29. The project manager is allocating overall cost estimates to individual activities to establish a baseline for measuring project performance. What process is this?
    A. Cost Management
    B. Estimate Costs
    C. Determine Budget
    D. Control Costs

30. Monitoring cost expended to date in order to detect variances from the plan occurs during:
    A. The creation of the cost change management plan.
    B. Recommending corrective actions.
    C. Updating the cost baseline.
    D. Project performance reviews.

31. A cost management plan contains a description of:
    A. The project costs.
    B. How resources are allocated.
    C. The budgets and how they were calculated.
    D. The WBS level at which earned value will be calculated.

32. A manufacturing project has a schedule performance index (SPI) of 0.89 and a cost performance index (CPI) of 0.91. Generally, what is the BEST explanation for why this occurred?
    A. The scope was changed.
    B. A supplier went out of business and a new one needed to be found.
    C. Additional equipment needed to be purchased.
    D. A critical path activity took longer and needed more labor hours to complete.

33. Although the stakeholders thought there was enough money in the budget, halfway through the project the cost performance index (CPI) is 0.7. To determine the root cause, several stakeholders audit the project and discover the project cost budget was estimated analogously. Although the activity estimates add up to the project estimate, the stakeholders think something was missing in how the estimate was completed. Which of the following describes what was missing?
    A. Estimated costs should be used to measure CPI.
    B. SPI should be used, not CPI.
    C. Bottom-up estimating should have been used.
    D. Past history was not taken into account.

34. Earned value measurement is an example of:
    A. Performance reporting.
    B. Planning control.
    C. Ishikawa diagrams.
    D. Integrating the project components into a whole.

35. Identified risks are:
    A. An input to the Estimate Costs process.
    B. An output of the Estimate Costs process.
    C. Not related to the Estimate Costs process.
    D. Both an input to and an output of the Estimate Costs process.

36. The difference between the cost baseline and the cost budget can be BEST described as:
    A. The management reserves.
    B. The contingency reserves.
    C. The project cost estimate.
    D. The cost account.

37. You provide a project cost estimate for the project to the project sponsor. He is unhappy with the estimate, because he thinks the price should be lower. He asks you to cut 15 percent off the project estimate. What should you do?
    A. Start the project and constantly look for cost savings.
    B. Tell all the team members to cut 15 percent from their estimates.
    C. Inform the sponsor of the activities to be cut.
    D. Add additional resources with low hourly rates.

38. Cost risk means:
    A. There are risks that will cost the project money.
    B. The project is too risky from a cost perspective.
    C. There is a risk that project costs could go higher than planned.
    D. There is a risk that the cost of the project will be lower than planned.

39. A project manager needs to analyze the project costs to find ways to decrease costs. It would be BEST if the project manager looks at:
    A. Variable costs and fixed costs.
    B. Fixed costs and indirect costs.
    C. Direct costs and variable costs.
    D. Indirect costs and direct costs.

Answers

1. **Answer** D
   Explanation This question is asking for the formula for EAC, which is BAC/CPI^C. You have to remember the formula to get the answer correct.

2. **Answer** C
   Explanation When you look at earned value, many of the terms have similar definitions. This could get you into trouble. EAC means the estimate at completion. What it will cost to finish the project is the definition of ETC, or estimate to complete.

3. **Answer** D
   Explanation The formula is CV = EV – AC. Therefore, CV = 350 – 400, or CV = -50.

4. **Answer** D
   Explanation Presenting anything other than your original estimate (allocating more to the budget) is inaccurate and calls into question your competence and integrity as a project manager. The customer should list potential changes and risks related to your estimate. If the costs and risks are justified, you can increase the budget.

5. **Answer** C
   Explanation Analogous estimating is used most frequently during project planning, not project executing. Parametric estimating involves calculations based on historical records. Analogous estimating uses top-down estimating techniques.

6. **Answer** B
   Explanation This question is asking, "When you finish estimating costs, what do you have?" Many people who do not realize that estimates should be in a range pick that option. Documentation of assumptions is referring to the basis of estimates, which are an output of Estimate Costs. The prevention of inappropriate changes is more correctly part of the cost management plan and the change control system.

7. **Answer** D
   Explanation Life cycle costing looks at operations and maintenance costs and balances them with the project costs to try to reduce the cost across the entire life of the project.

8. **Answer** B
   Explanation Asking percent complete is not a best practice since it is usually a guess. Often the easiest work is done first on a project, throwing off any percentage calculations of work remaining. The life cycle cost cannot be lower than the project cost, as the life cycle cost includes the project cost. Focusing on the amount spent last month and what will be spent in the next month is often done by inexperienced project managers who know of nothing else. Not only does this provide little information, but the data cannot be used to predict the future. Using earned value and other calculations is the best answer since this choice looks at the past and uses that information to estimate future costs.

9. **Answer** D
   Explanation The CPI is less than one, so the situation is bad. The project is only getting 89 cents out of every dollar invested.

10. **Answer** C
    Explanation Earned value questions ask for a calculation or an interpretation of the results. In this case, the project is progressing at 76 percent of the rate planned.

11. **Answer** D
    Explanation A change control system is not required to obtain estimates, but without the other three choices, you cannot develop the estimates. You need the WBS to define the activities, the network diagram to see the dependencies, and the risks to determine contingencies. NOTE: These are high-level risks, not the detailed risks we identify later in project planning.

12. **Answer** A
    Explanation Parametric estimates use a mathematical model to predict project cost or time.

13. **Answer** D
    Explanation This estimate has a wide range. It is done during project initiating, when very little is known about the project.

14. **Answer** C
    Explanation A cost baseline is an output of the Determine Budget process.

15. **Answer** A
    Explanation Budget forecasts are an output of Control Costs, which is part of monitoring and controlling.

16. **Answer** A
    Explanation You are training the team on skills required for the project. The cost is directly related to the project and thus a direct cost.

17. **Answer** B
    Explanation Setup costs do not change as production on the project changes. Therefore, they are fixed costs.

18. **Answer** D
    Explanation Notice that you need to know the definition of value analysis to answer this question. Also notice that the other choices could be considered correct by someone who does not know the definition. Value analysis seeks to decrease cost while maintaining the same scope.

19. **Answer** A
    Explanation Because you need project details to estimate this way, the effort expended will be greater with bottom-up estimating.

20. **Answer** A
    Explanation It can be confusing to differentiate earned value terms from each other. The estimated value of the work actually completed is the definition of EV, or earned value.

21. **Answer** B
    Explanation Notice how one item in each of the incorrect options makes the entire choice incorrect. Duration estimates are created during time management, and measuring team performance is a part of human resource management. There is no level of risk required for estimates. Specifications for how estimates should be stated, rules for measuring cost performance, and the level of accuracy needed for estimates are all parts of the cost management plan.

22. **Answer** A
Explanation With such limited information, it is best to estimate in a range. The range can be narrowed as planning progresses and risks are addressed.

23. **Answer** D
Explanation Hiding the reserve is an inappropriate action. Adding cost to each activity will not shorten the critical path, and thus is an incorrect statement. Management reserves, not contingency reserves, are maintained by management to cover cost overruns. During the risk management process, you determine appropriate contingency reserves to cover the cost of identified risks.

24. **Answer** A
Explanation Although all choices could cause difficulty, only inadequate scope definition makes estimating impossible.

25. **Answer** A
Explanation Look for the choice that would have the least negative impact in this situation. You would not need to meet with the sponsor to determine which work can be done sooner. Cutting quality and decreasing scope always have negative effects. The choice with the least negative impact is to eliminate risks in estimates and reestimate.

26. **Answer** D
Explanation Procedures for the rental and purchase of supplies and equipment are found in the organizational policies, part of organizational process assets.

27. **Answer** A
Explanation This is a tricky question. Determining why the sponsor wants such an accurate estimate sounds like a good idea at first. However, analogous estimates are less accurate than other forms of estimating, as they are prepared with a limited amount of detailed information. Reading every word of this choice helps eliminate it. In order to pick the best answer, you need to realize that analogous estimating is a form of expert judgment.

28. **Answer** B
Explanation The overall project budget may be included in the project charter but not the detailed costs. Even small projects should have a budget and schedule. It is not impossible to create a project budget before the project management plan is created. However, it is not wise to do so, as the budget will not be accurate. The project budget and baseline are not finalized and accepted until the planning processes are completed.

29. **Answer** C
Explanation Cost Management is too general. The estimates are already created in this situation, so the answer is not Estimate Costs. The answer is not Control Costs, because the baseline has not yet been created. The work described is the Determine Budget process.

30. **Answer** D
Explanation The correct choice is project performance reviews. Recommending corrective actions and possible updates to the cost baseline result from project performance reviews; they are not concurrent with them. Monitoring costs is part of change control, but not part of creating the change control system.

31. **Answer** D
Explanation The exam will ask you what the tools of project management contain in order to test whether you really understand them. The cost management plan identifies the WBS level at which earned value will be calculated.

32. **Answer** D
Explanation To answer this question, you must look for a choice that would take longer and cost more. Notice one of the choices says scope was changed, but it was not necessarily added to. If the change was to reduce the scope, it might also have reduced cost. Though it would take time to handle the issue of the need to find a new supplier, the impacted activity might not be on the critical path and thus might not affect time. Purchasing additional equipment definitely adds cost, but not necessarily time. A critical path activity taking longer and requiring more labor hours to complete would negatively affect both time and cost.

33. **Answer** C
Explanation Actual costs are used to measure CPI, and there is no reason to use SPI in this situation. Using past history is another way of saying "analogous." The best way to estimate is bottom-up. Such estimating would have improved the overall quality of the estimate.

34. **Answer** A
Explanation Earned value measurement is a great reporting tool. With it, you can show where you stand on budget and schedules, as well as provide forecasts for the rest of the project.

35. **Answer** D
Explanation Identified risks are both an input to and an output of the Estimate Costs process.

36. **Answer** A
Explanation Cost accounts are included in the project cost estimate, and the contingency reserves are added to that to come up with the cost baseline. Thereafter, the management reserves are added to come up with the cost budget. The management reserves make up the difference between the cost baseline and the cost budget.

37. **Answer** C
Explanation This question is full of choices that are not correct project management actions. To answer the question, you must first realize that it is never appropriate for a project manager to just cut estimates across the board. You should have created a project estimate based on realistic work package estimates that do not include padding. Then, if costs must be decreased, you can look to cut quality, decrease risk, cut scope, or use cheaper resources (and at the same time closely monitor the impact of changes on the project schedule).

One of the worst things a project manager can do is to start a project knowing that the time or cost for the project is unrealistic. Did you notice the choice of adding additional resources? Even though they have low hourly rates, that would add cost. Evaluating, looking for alternatives, and then reporting the impact of the cost cutting to the sponsor is the best action to take.

38. **Answer** C
Explanation While it is true that risk will cost the project money, that is not the definition of cost risk. Stating that the project is too risky from a cost perspective assumes that the risk is too great to do the project. Cost risk is the risk that project costs could go higher than planned.

39. **Answer** C
Explanation Direct costs are directly attributable to the project, and variable costs are costs that vary with the amount of work accomplished. It is best to look at decreasing these costs on the project.

The Numbers Game

The following game is designed to improve your ability to correctly answer questions on the exam that deal with numbers (including formulas, analysis techniques, estimates, critical paths, accounting terms related to project selection, etc.). These questions are based on information in the Integration, Time, and Cost Management chapters. The game is best done verbally with more than one person. The second person can be a spouse, child, or someone else studying for the PMP exam.

Cut out the cards along the lines provided. Try to answer as many questions as you can in 10 minutes. If you answer 10 questions correctly in ten minutes, this should prove to you that you will not have a time problem taking the exam. (The exam allows about 1 minute, 15 seconds per question.) GOOD LUCK!

- **For One Participant** Ask yourself the question and then turn the card over to see the answer.
- **For Two Participants** One person asks the questions, and the other answers.
- **For More Than Two Participants** One person asks the questions, and the others answer. One of those answering should also keep track of the number of correct answers.

Question: What is a formula for estimate at completion?	**Question:** What estimating method would use optimistic time estimates?	**Question:** "How much work should be done" has what earned value name?
Question: What is the critical path?	**Question:** The types and quantities of resources required are calculated in what part of time management?	**Question:** What does the schedule variance tell you?
Question: What schedule network analysis technique involves crashing?	**Question:** What does a finish-to-start relationship mean?	**Question:** What does the estimate at completion tell you?
Question: Why would you want to crash a project?	**Question:** The "what-if" scenario method of schedule network analysis primarily makes use of what technique?	**Question:** What are sunk costs?
Question: What does a milestone chart show?	**Question:** What is the duration of a milestone?	**Question:** What is analogous estimating?

Answer: Planned value	**Answer:** Three-point estimate	**Answer:** BAC/Cumulative CPI
Answer: How far you are behind or ahead of schedule	**Answer:** Estimate Activity Resources	**Answer:** The longest duration path in the network; The shortest time to complete the project
Answer: What we now expect the total project to cost	**Answer:** One activity must finish before the next can start	**Answer:** Schedule compression
Answer: Expended costs	**Answer:** Monte Carlo analysis	**Answer:** To shorten the project duration
Answer: Top-down estimating	**Answer:** Zero	**Answer:** Dates of significant events on the project

Question: What are fixed costs?	**Question:** What are direct costs?	**Question:** What is the earned value name for "how much you have spent to date?"
Question: What is value analysis?	**Question:** What is a management reserve?	**Question:** What is the cost variance formula?
Question: Cost risk is greater for the buyer in what type of contract?	**Question:** What schedule network analysis technique uses buffers?	**Question:** What does present value mean?
Question: What is the formula for total float?	**Question:** Why would a project manager want to use resource leveling?	**Question:** What does a benefit cost ratio of 2.5 mean?
Question: A critical path activity will generally have how much float?	**Question:** What is parametric estimating?	**Question:** What is the range of accuracy with a definitive estimate?

Answer: Actual cost	**Answer:** Costs incurred directly by the project	**Answer:** Costs that do not change with project activity
Answer: EV – AC	**Answer:** An amount of time or money set aside to cover unforeseen risks	**Answer:** Finding a less costly way to complete the work without affecting quality
Answer: The value today of future cash flows	**Answer:** Critical chain	**Answer:** Cost reimbursable
Answer: The benefits are 2½ times the costs	**Answer:** To smooth the peaks and valleys of monthly resource usage consumed by the project	**Answer:** LS – ES, or LF – EF; This is the amount of time an activity can be delayed without delaying the project
Answer: +/-10 percent	**Answer:** Using mathematical relationships found in historical information to create estimates (e.g., dollars per foot)	**Answer:** Zero

CHAPTER EIGHT Quality Management

Quicktest

- Quality management process
- Definition of quality
- Metrics
- Quality management plan
- Process improvement plan
- Continuous improvement
- Process analysis
- Quality tools
  - Control chart
    - Special cause variation
    - Control limits
    - Mean
    - Specification limits
    - Out of control
    - Rule of seven
  - Pareto chart
    - 80/20 principle
  - Cause and effect diagram
  - Benchmarking
  - Design of experiments
  - Checklist
  - Statistical sampling
  - Flowchart
  - Run chart
  - Scatter diagram
  - Histogram
- Prevention over inspection
- Gold plating
- Just in time
- Quality audits
- Quality standards (ISO, CISG, OSHA)
- Total quality management
- Responsibility for quality
- Impact of poor quality
- Costs of conformance and nonconformance
- Cost benefit analysis
- Cost of quality
- Marginal analysis
- Population
- Sample
- Normal distribution
- Mutually exclusive
- Probability
- Statistical independence
- Standard deviation
- 3 or 6 sigma
- Quality theorists (Juran, Deming, Crosby)

Before you read this chapter, think about the quality management plan on your project. Do you have one? If your answer is yes, you probably only need to give this chapter a brief review. If you do not have a quality management plan or if you do not manage quality now, however, this could be a difficult topic for you on the exam. This chapter will help you get familiar with what quality is and understand its role in the project management process.

Some people argue that project managers do not have time to spend managing quality, and many organizations do not require their project managers to have quality management plans. But think about what you stand to gain by managing quality on your projects. A lack of attention to quality means more rework or defects. The more rework you have to do, the more time and money you are wasting, and the less likely you are to meet the project time and cost baselines. But with a focus on quality, you can spend time preventing, rather than dealing with, problems. You can actually save time on the project that you would have otherwise spent in rework and problem-solving.

If asked, "Is it better to plan in quality, or inspect to find quality problems?" almost everyone will answer correctly that it is better to plan in quality. However, that is not how most of the quality-related questions are presented on the exam. Instead, they focus on situations to see if you know what to do. For example:

The project manager finds that one of his team members has created her own process for installing hardware. What should the project manager do?

Beginning project managers might choose a response that relates to thanking the team member for the effort. More experienced project managers might select a choice that relates to finding out if the process was a good one. The top project managers select the choice that relates to investigating the quality management plan to determine if a standard process should have been provided.

People without quality management experience generally have a hard time with such questions. Fortunately, not all the quality questions on the exam are that difficult. Expect to see questions that talk about manufacturing environments (e.g., the project manager works for a manufacturer of tables) on the exam. Also, expect questions about the process of quality management and how quality relates to the project constraints, as defined in this book.

Rita's Process Chart—Quality Management

Where are we in the project management process?

INITIATING

- Select project manager
- Determine company culture and existing systems
- Collect processes, procedures, and historical information
- Divide large projects into phases
- Understand the business case
- Uncover initial requirements, assumptions, and risks
- Assess project and product feasibility within the given constraints
- Create measurable objectives
- Develop project charter
- Identify stakeholders
- Develop stakeholder management strategy

PLANNING

(This is the only process group with a set order)

- **Determine how you will do planning—part of all management plans**
- Determine detailed requirements
- Create project scope statement
- Assess what to purchase
- Determine team
- Create WBS and WBS dictionary
- Create activity list
- Create network diagram
- Estimate resource requirements
- Estimate time and cost
- Determine critical path
- Develop schedule
- Develop budget
- **Determine quality standards, processes, and metrics**
- **Create process improvement plan**
- **Determine all roles and responsibilities**
- Plan communications
- Perform risk identification, qualitative and quantitative risk analysis, and risk response planning
- **Go back—iterations**
- Prepare procurement documents
- Create change management plan
- **Finalize the "how to execute and control" parts of all management plans**
- **Develop realistic and final PM plan and performance measurement baseline**
- Gain formal approval of the plan
- Hold kickoff meeting

EXECUTING

- Execute the work according to the PM plan
- Produce product deliverables (product scope)
- **Request changes**
- Implement only approved changes
- **Continuously improve**
- **Follow processes**
- **Perform quality assurance**
- **Perform quality audits**
- Acquire final team
- Manage people
- Evaluate team and project performance
- Hold team-building activities
- Give recognition and rewards
- Use issue logs
- Facilitate conflict resolution
- Release resources as work is completed
- Send and receive information
- Hold meetings
- Select sellers

MONITORING & CONTROLLING

- **Take action to control the project**
- Measure performance against the performance measurement baseline
- **Measure performance against other metrics determined by the project manager**
- **Determine variances and if they warrant a corrective action or change request**
- **Influence the factors that cause changes**
- **Request changes**
- Perform integrated change control
- Approve or reject changes
- Inform stakeholders of the results of change requests
- Update the PM plan and project documents
- Manage configuration
- Create forecasts
- Gain acceptance of interim deliverables from the customer
- **Perform quality control**
- Report on project performance and solicit feedback
- Perform risk assessments and audits
- Manage reserves
- Administer procurements

CLOSING

- Confirm work is done to requirements
- Complete procurement closure
- Gain final acceptance of the product
- Complete financial closure
- Hand off completed product
- Solicit feedback from the customer about the project
- Complete final performance reporting
- Index and archive records
- Update lessons learned knowledge base

Imagine a project to build a stadium that is mostly made of concrete. The concrete part of the stadium is two-thirds poured when the buyer arrives one day and tests the strength of the concrete. The buyer finds that the concrete does not meet the clearly stated quality requirements for concrete strength in the contract. You can imagine the problems when the buyer says, "Rip out the concrete; it is not acceptable." Whose fault is this? Why did this occur?

Could we say it is the buyer's fault for not testing the concrete sooner? You might argue that case, but isn't the real fault with the seller for not testing the quality themselves? Where was their quality plan? They should have noted the requirement and determined when and how they would confirm that they met it. Lack of attention to quality in this scenario needlessly added considerable risk to the project, which resulted in a tremendous amount of rework and added expense.

Here is something else to consider. Have any of your customers ever said one of your deliverables was not acceptable, although they had not previously provided you with a definition of what was acceptable? It is important to know—in advance—what acceptable quality is and how it will be measured on the project. You can then determine what you will do to make sure the project meets those requirements. If you do not take these steps, you will have unclear acceptance criteria such as "the customer likes it." Performing the quality management process well helps you avoid many issues later in the project.

The following should help you understand how each part of quality management fits into the overall project management process:

The Quality Management Process	Done During
Plan Quality	Planning process group
Perform Quality Assurance	Executing process group
Perform Quality Control	Monitoring and controlling process group

Before we start discussing these three processes in detail, let's look at some basic quality management concepts that you should understand for the exam.

Definition of Quality What is quality? Know the short definition for the exam. Quality is defined as the degree to which the project fulfills requirements. MEMORIZE this phrase; there have been about four questions on this topic on the exam.

Now here is a story about quality. A student in one of RMC's classes looked out the window during class and noticed someone painting the limestone of an old building white. The student said, "That is not quality!" Let's think about the student's statement for a moment. Why would such painting not "be quality"? If the painting contract required the painter to use a certain kind of paint and follow painting standards, and he was doing so, the work met the quality requirements. The issue the student really had was that the wonderful old stone was being painted instead of cleaned. In other words, this was a disagreement with the requirements, not the quality of the work.

Let's review the definition of quality again: the degree to which the project fulfills requirements. Can you achieve quality if you do not have all the stated and unstated requirements defined in the project scope statement? Of course not. This makes the requirements gathering effort (from scope management) and the project scope statement very important to the quality management effort.

Definition of Quality Management PAGE 189 Quality management includes creating and following policies and procedures to ensure that a project meets the defined needs it was intended to meet from the customer's perspective. We could also say it means ensuring a project is completed with no deviations from the project requirements. Quality management includes the processes of Plan Quality, Perform Quality Assurance, and Perform Quality Control.

Quality Theorists

The following people are known for their theories on quality:

- **Joseph Juran** He developed the 80/20 principle, advocated top management involvement, and defined quality as "fitness for use."
- **W. Edwards Deming** He developed 14 points to total quality management and advocated the Plan-Do-Check-Act cycle[1] as the basis for quality improvement.
- **Philip Crosby** He popularized the concept of the cost of poor quality and advocated prevention over inspection and "zero defects." He believed that quality is "conformance to requirements."

TRICKS OF THE TRADE®

Quality-Related PMI-isms

Quality-related questions can be confusing because many of the topics on the exam are not in the *PMBOK® Guide* and because PMI's quality philosophy may be different from that of your company. Some companies refer to what PMI calls Perform Quality Assurance as quality planning. Some companies believe in giving the customer extras, while PMI wants us to focus on meeting the requirements. It is important to understand PMI's philosophy to answer exam questions correctly. Therefore, know the following PMI-isms related to quality:

- The project manager should recommend improvements to the performing organization's standards, policies, and processes. Such recommendations are expected and welcomed by management.
- Quality should be considered whenever there is a change to any of the project constraints.
- Quality should be checked before an activity or work package is completed.
- The project manager must spend time trying to improve quality.
- The project manager must determine metrics to be used to measure quality before the project work begins.
- The project manager must put in place a plan for continually improving processes.
- The project manager must make sure authorized approaches and processes are followed.
- Some quality activities may be done by a quality assurance or quality control department.

Do you think you understand PMI's philosophy and how quality management fits into the project management process? Test yourself by doing the following exercise.

Exercise

List the specific ACTIONS required to ensure quality on the project.

Answer There are a lot of possible answers. Did you come up with these?

- Review the project charter and project scope statement.
- Make sure you have asked the customer what their definition of quality is.
- Identify the desired levels of performance in the product and components of the product.
- Identify at what level you should control the project (e.g., the work package, activity, or more detailed level).
- Identify any quality standards and processes that are applicable to the project.
- Determine the quality standards and processes to use, when, and on what parts of the project.
- Set standards to reach the level of desired performance for activities and the project.
- Set metrics to measure quality from the customer's and the organization's perspective.
- Decide what you will do to make sure the processes are followed and the standards are met—your quality control system.
- Determine how you will improve the processes on the project—your process improvement plan.
- Test the validity of assumptions before they result in problems.
- Make sure team members understand what quality is for their work.
- Collect problems, errors, and complaints, and review what can be done to prevent them from reoccurring on the project.
- Have teams "roaming" the project looking for quality improvements.
- Inspect work as it is being done, not after.
- Perform quality reviews.
- Measure performance against standards.
- Hold meetings, issue reports, take measurements, and perform calculations.
- Perform quality assurance.
- Perform quality control.
- Reassess the quality standards.
- Evaluate the effectiveness of the quality control system.
- Manage quality with the same effort as time, cost, or scope.
- Request changes, including corrective and preventive actions and defect repairs.
- Include quality issues in lessons learned.
- Feed lessons learned back into the project.

Gold Plating[2] Gold plating refers to giving the customer extras (e.g., extra functionality, higher-quality components, extra scope, or better performance). Although you might have a policy promoting gold plating at work (such as "meeting and exceeding customers' expectations"), advanced quality thinking does not recommend this practice and neither does PMI. Gold plating is often the team's impression of what is valued by the customer, and the customer might not agree. It is also a problem because so few projects provide what the customer wanted. Since most projects have difficulty meeting the project objectives, all available effort should go into achieving those objectives, instead of gold plating.

Sometimes gold plating is not planned, but arises out of a team member's efforts to do the best he or she can. The project might not call for the best, however, just what was asked for. Therefore, the project manager must be on the lookout for team members providing extra functionality, extra work, or higher quality than what is part of the project.

Prevention over Inspection Is it better to inspect work to find problems or to prevent them in the first place? Which takes less effort? Remember that QUALITY MUST BE PLANNED IN, NOT INSPECTED IN! This concept has frequently come up on the exam.

Marginal Analysis[3] Marginal analysis refers to looking for the point where the benefits or revenue to be received from improving quality equals the incremental cost to achieve that quality. This is an important concept that you probably already understand. Sometimes added attention to something such as quality does not produce added value. When that point is reached, you should stop trying to improve quality.

Continuous Improvement (or Kaizen)[4] Continuous improvement involves continuously looking for small improvements in quality. These two terms ("continuous improvement" and "*Kaizen*") are taken to mean the same thing on the exam; however, in Japan, *Kaizen* means to alter (*Kai*) and make better or improve (*Zen*). *Kaizen* is a general term, while continuous improvement is a quality movement. In the United States and most of Western Europe, improvements are thought of as BIG improvements. In Japan, improvements are thought of as small improvements.

Just in Time (JIT)[5] Many companies are finding that holding raw materials in inventory is too expensive and is unnecessary. Instead, they have their suppliers deliver raw materials just when they are needed or just before they are needed, thus decreasing inventory to close to zero. A company using JIT must achieve a high level of quality in their practices; otherwise, there will not be enough raw materials to meet production requirements because of waste and rework. A JIT system forces attention on quality.

Total Quality Management (TQM)[6] This philosophy encourages companies and their employees to focus on finding ways to continuously improve the quality of their products and their business practices at every level of the organization.

Responsibility for Quality The entire organization has responsibilities relating to quality. Therefore, read questions on this topic carefully. Determine to whom in the organization questions on the exam are referring. The project manager has the ultimate responsibility for the quality of the product of the project, but each team member must check his or her work by inspecting it themselves. It is not acceptable for team members to simply complete the work and then turn it over to the project manager or their manager to be checked. Work should meet the project requirements, and testing should be done whenever appropriate before submitting the work.

Senior management has the ultimate responsibility for quality in the organization as a whole. According to W. Edwards Deming (a quality expert), 85 percent of the quality problems on a project are attributable to the management environment and the system in which the team works.

Impact of Poor Quality Everyone knows intuitively that spending time on quality produces value, but the exam will test your knowledge about what the effects of quality efforts, or the lack thereof, are. So what is the impact of poor quality? If you have poor quality, you might also have:

- Increased costs
- Low morale
- Low customer satisfaction
- Increased risk
- Rework
- Schedule delays

In contrast, increases in quality can result in increased productivity, higher morale, increased customer satisfaction, increased cost and schedule effectiveness, and decreased cost risk.

Understanding the Difference between Plan Quality, Perform Quality Assurance, and Perform Quality Control One of the major challenges people have while studying is understanding the difference between Plan Quality, Perform Quality Assurance, and Perform Quality Control. This confusion can be due to the difference between what your company calls these processes and what the exam does. It can also be due to the confusing nature of the questions in this knowledge area.

For purposes of the exam, here is a brief description of the three processes: Plan Quality focuses on defining quality for the project and identifying how it will be achieved. Perform Quality Assurance is an executing process, so its focus is on the work being done on the project; its purpose is to ensure the team is following the processes as planned to produce the project's deliverables. In contrast, Perform Quality Control (a monitoring and controlling process) examines the actual deliverables produced on the project; its purpose is to ensure the deliverables are correct and that they meet the planned level of quality.

TRICKS OF THE TRADE® The following chart is a trick for correctly answering questions about these three processes on the exam. But be aware that even if you spend a great deal of time studying this section, you may still see confusing questions about the differences between the quality management processes. Make sure you read such questions carefully.

<table>
<tr><th>Plan Quality</th><th>Perform Quality Assurance</th><th>Perform Quality Control</th></tr>
<tr><td colspan="3">High-Level Description of What Each Process Focuses On</td></tr>
<tr><td>What is quality? How will we ensure it?</td><td>Are we following the procedures and processes as planned?</td><td>Are the results of our work meeting the standards?</td></tr>
<tr><td colspan="3">More Detailed Description of What Each Process Focuses On</td></tr>
<tr><td>► Find existing quality practices, standards, and requirements for product and project management
► Create additional project-specific practices, standards, and metrics
► Determine what work you will do to meet the standards
► Determine how you will measure to make sure you meet the standards
► Balance the needs of quality with scope, cost, time, risk, resources, and customer satisfaction
► Create a process improvement plan and a quality management plan as part of the project management plan</td><td>► Use measurements from quality control to assess whether the correct processes are being followed
► Perform continuous improvement to increase efficiency and effectiveness
► Determine if project activities comply with organizational and project policies, processes, and procedures—quality audit
► Find good practices
► Share good practices with others in the organization
► Submit change requests
► Update the project management plan and project documents</td><td>► Measure the quality of deliverables
► Identify the need for quality improvements
► Validate deliverables
► Complete checklists
► Update lessons learned
► Submit change requests
► Update the project management plan and project documents</td></tr>
<tr><td colspan="3">Process Group</td></tr>
<tr><td>Project planning</td><td>Project executing</td><td>Project monitoring and controlling</td></tr>
</table>

Plan Quality PAGE 192

Process: Plan Quality
Process Group: Planning
Knowledge Area: Quality Management

In addition to organizational process assets and enterprise environmental factors, the project manager needs the stakeholder register, scope baseline (project scope statement, WBS, and WBS dictionary), schedule baseline, cost baseline, and risk register to perform the Plan Quality process. These items serve as a guide to planning the project's quality efforts because they include stakeholder information, the major project deliverables, thresholds, and acceptance criteria.

The objective of the Plan Quality process is to identify all relevant organizational or industry practices, standards, and requirements for the quality of the project, the product of the project, and the project management efforts. The main result of this process is a quality management plan.

Notice the discussion of organizational and industry practices in the previous paragraph. On many projects and in many organizations, practices are not standardized. If this is true in your real world, take some time now to imagine what such standardized practices would be for your projects and how they might be helpful to you. For example, there can be a standardized practice for installing wallpaper on home construction projects. Imagine all the wallpaper installers within an organization putting together their best ideas to make the work of installing wallpaper easier for everyone in the future. That would be a valuable effort, wouldn't it? As another example, the *PMBOK® Guide* is a practice standard for project management. Standardization can come from within the organization or from government or professional associations. The performing organization or the project may adopt these practices as they apply to the work of the project. As part of the Plan Quality process, the project manager needs to look for any such standards that might help the project avoid "reinventing the wheel," so to speak, and that help achieve higher quality. Some available standards include:

- **The United Nations Convention on Contracts for International Sale of Goods (CISG)**[7] The CISG is the standard that governs international sales transactions.
- **ISO 9000**[8] This family of standards was created by the International Organization for Standardization (ISO) to help ensure that organizations have quality procedures and that they follow them. Many people incorrectly believe that ISO 9000 tells you what quality should be, or describes a recommended quality system.
- **Occupational Safety and Health Administration (OSHA)** OSHA sets standards for the safety of American workers.

The project must comply with any required external standards and practices (enterprise environmental factors) as well as organizational and departmental policies, standards, and procedures (organizational process assets). Organizational process assets are the result of lessons learned on previous projects and the performing organization's idea of the best way to accomplish work.

In addition, the project manager must plan the project so it meets the customer's quality standards. Examples of such standards are the acceptable number of software bugs per module, the strength of concrete, or the average time per installation. These types of measures of quality will help the project manager know when the project is out of control and when to then request changes, including corrective actions as well as preventive actions (to prevent the problem from reoccurring).

Once existing practices and standards are identified, the project manager must create any additional project-specific standards and procedures that are needed. Wait; did you notice what you just read? The project manager must define standards and procedures or practices as part of planning the project. Do you do this now?

A project manager may create standards and procedures based on how quality is defined for each piece of work. A tricky thing to know for the exam is that this effort could also include defining processes for how project management activities should be done. The new practices cannot violate other relevant standards.

After the standards and procedures have been identified or created, the project manager needs to determine what work is required to meet those standards. Perhaps additional testing will need to be added to the project, resources will need to be moved around, or the descriptions of products to be purchased will need to be changed. The project manager should also determine the specific measurements that will be made each week, each month, or for each deliverable to ensure compliance with all standards.

The Plan Quality process will result in additions or changes (i.e., iterations) to the project management plan and project documents. For example, work may be added to the WBS, resources may be changed, or extra project management efforts may be added to the project management plan.

It is important to keep in mind that the level of quality efforts should be appropriate to the needs of the project. There is no reason to negatively impact project scope, time, or cost if higher quality is not required on the project. Quality must be balanced with the other project constraints. That sounds easy, right? Often times, it is not. Do you remember all the times on your projects that team members delivered more than was needed? Do you remember how hard it has been at times to keep a project from producing the Taj Mahal when all you needed was a garage? The project scope statement, WBS, and WBS dictionary (the scope baseline) help the project manager maintain the proper perspective and plan quality to the appropriate level. The resulting quality management plan becomes part of the project management plan.

The following tools and techniques are used in the Plan Quality process. Remember that the objective of using these tools and techniques in Plan Quality is to determine what the requirements, procedures, and standards for the project and product are. If these topics are new to you, keeping this objective in mind will help you understand them. Also remember that some tools and techniques are repeated in other parts of the quality management process. If they are used in Plan Quality, the tools and techniques help determine requirements, procedures, and standards. If they are used later, they may help measure whether practices and procedures are being followed (Perform Quality Assurance) or requirements and standards have been met (Perform Quality Control). This concept is similar to creating a form in planning and then using the form later in the project.

Cost Benefit Analysis[9] PAGE 195 Using this technique, the project manager weighs the benefits versus the costs of quality efforts to determine the appropriate quality level and requirements for the project. As noted in the Integration Management chapter, this technique can also be used in project selection and in other planning efforts, including assessing the costs and benefits of potential procurements.

Cost of Quality (COQ)[10] PAGE 195 We have talked about understanding that quality must be planned in and that not performing quality management activities is detrimental to a project. While these are important concepts, the idea behind cost of quality seems in some ways to be the opposite concept. Looking at the cost of quality means making sure the project is not spending too much to achieve a particular level of quality. This involves looking at what the costs of conformance and nonconformance[11] to quality will be on the project and creating an appropriate balance. The following table provides some examples of such costs.

Cost of Conformance	Cost of Nonconformance
Quality training	Rework
Studies	Scrap
Surveys	Inventory costs
Efforts to ensure everyone knows the processes to use to complete their work	Warranty costs
	Lost business

The costs of conformance should be lower than the costs of nonconformance. Otherwise, why spend time improving quality? The exam has asked about three questions on this simple topic alone. Not all questions are difficult!

Control Charts[12] PAGE 196 Much of what the exam focuses on regarding control charts is not in the *PMBOK® Guide*. But do not worry; the following explanation and exercise will help you understand this tool, even if control charts are new to you. Once you understand control charts, it is generally easy to get questions about them right on the exam.

Control charts are SET UP in Plan Quality as part of the effort to define quality on the project. They are UTILIZED in Perform Quality Control to help determine if the results of a process are within acceptable limits.

To better understand the need for control charts and what they are used for, think of a manufacturer of doors. Would each door be the same exact height? Weight? Not likely. Instead there is a range, however small, that is acceptable. Each door should be within the range of normal and acceptable limits. During the Perform Quality Control process, samples are taken and plotted on the chart (the small squares shown on the control chart in the following exercise). The control chart shows whether the samples are within those limits.

You should note that a control chart can also be used to monitor things like project performance figures, such as cost and schedule variances. Most commonly, however, a control chart helps monitor production and other processes to see if the results are within acceptable limits (i.e., "in control"), or if there are any actions required (i.e., the process, results, or whatever is being measured is "out of control"). A "special cause variation" means the process is out of control.

Now that we have discussed the basic concept of a control chart, let's look at some of the related terms you should know for the exam. You will see questions on this topic, but they will be fairly straightforward and, therefore, relatively easy. The following can be indicated on a control chart:

Upper and Lower Control Limits

Control limits are often shown as two dashed lines on a control chart. These limits are the acceptable range of variation of a process's results. Every process is expected to have some variation in its results (e.g., each door manufactured will not be exactly the same size). The acceptable range of measurements between the upper and lower control limits is set by the project manager and stakeholders based on the organization's quality standard. Normally this range is calculated based on +/- 3 sigma, or standard deviations (described in the Perform Quality Control discussion later in this chapter). Data points within this range are generally thought of as "in control," excluding the rule of seven (described later in this section), and are an acceptable range of variation. Data points outside this range indicate the process is out of control.

The concept of control limits is also important outside of a control chart. A project manager can have control limits for many things. How about for a work package? Is one hour late in its delivery a problem? How about one day? Such control limits help the project manager know when to take action.

Mean (Average)

The mean is indicated by a line in the middle of the control chart. It shows the middle of the range of acceptable variation.

Specification Limits

While control limits represent the performing organization's standards for quality, specification limits represent the customer's expectations or contractual requirements for performance and quality on the project. Specification limits are characteristics of the measured process and are not inherent. In other words, specification limits are not calculated based on the control chart; instead, they are inputs from the customer. Therefore, they can appear either inside or outside of the control limits. To meet the customer's specification limits, the performing organization's standards for quality (control limits) must be stricter than those of the customer. Agreeing to do a project when your work does not meet the customer's quality standards adds waste and extra management to the project to sort out acceptable items. Therefore, on the exam, assume that specification limits are outside the upper and lower control limits.

Out of Control

The process is out of a state of statistical control under either of two circumstances:

- A data point falls outside of the upper or lower control limit.
- There are nonrandom data points; these may be within the upper and lower control limits, such as the rule of seven (described next).

Think of "out of control" as a lack of consistency and predictability in the process or its results.

Rule of Seven[13]

The rule of seven is a rule of thumb, or heuristic. It refers to a group or series of nonrandom data points that total seven on one side of the mean. The rule of seven tells you that, although none of these points are outside of the control limits, they are not random and the process may be out of control. The project manager should investigate this type of situation and find a cause.

Assignable Cause/Special Cause Variation[14]

If there is an assignable cause or special cause variation, it means a data point or series of data points (as discussed with the rule of seven) require investigation to determine the cause of the variation.

Exercise Now try this exercise. On the following charts, label the examples of each of the ten listed items by placing the item number next to its location on the chart(s). If you are unsure, take a guess and then review the control chart discussion. The pictures represent two different control charts.

When you are able to pick out all the items on the control charts, you should be ready to answer questions about control charts on the exam.

NOTE: The questions on the exam relating to control charts may be easier to answer if you can picture a control chart in your mind. It is unlikely one will be shown to you on the exam. Instead, the exam will use the terms in situational questions, and you will need to know what they mean (e.g., A team member tells you that one sample is outside the lower control limit. What do you do?). This exercise is designed to help you visualize control charts and make sure you understand these tools so you can answer questions about them.

Find the following on the charts:

1. Upper control limit
2. Lower control limit
3. Assignable cause/Special cause
4. The process is out of control
5. Normal and expected variation in the process
6. Rule of seven
7. Specification limits
8. Three sigma
9. Six sigma
10. Normal distribution curve

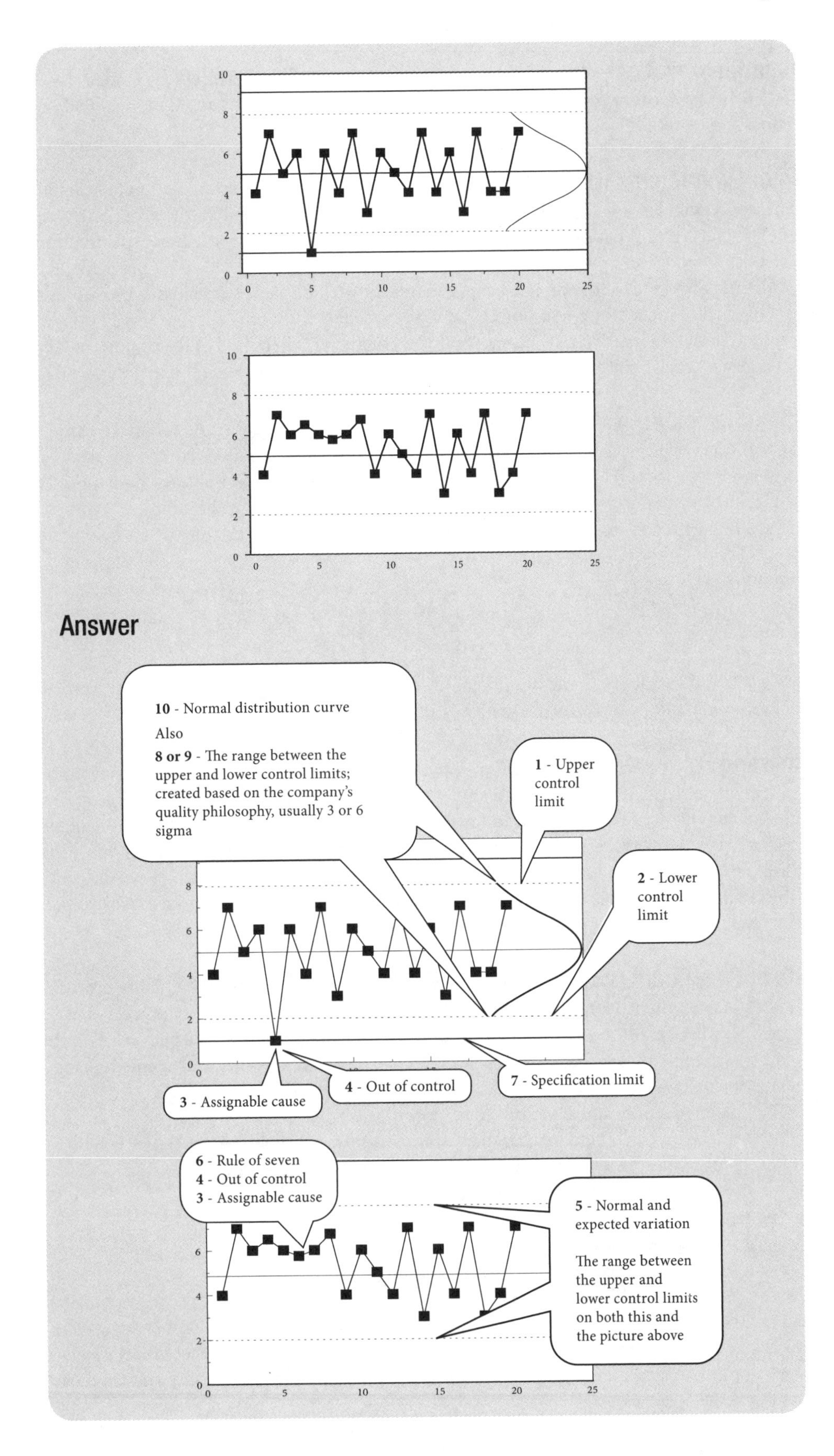

10 - Normal distribution curve
Also
8 or 9 - The range between the upper and lower control limits; created based on the company's quality philosophy, usually 3 or 6 sigma
1 - Upper control limit
2 - Lower control limit
3 - Assignable cause
4 - Out of control
7 - Specification limit
6 - Rule of seven
4 - Out of control
3 - Assignable cause
5 - Normal and expected variation
The range between the upper and lower control limits on both this and the picture above

Answer

Benchmarking[15] PAGE 197

This technique involves looking at other projects to get ideas for improvement on the current project and to provide a basis (or benchmark) to use in measuring quality performance.

Design of Experiments (DOE)[16] PAGE 197

This technique uses experimentation to statistically determine what variables will improve quality. For example, you could analyze the effect on overall quality of using different processes for software development while leaving all other aspects of the effort unchanged. As another example, you could change the type of wood used on a desk but leave all other variables the same. Conducting individual experiments for each possible variable in a process to assess its impact on quality can be time-consuming. DOE is a valuable technique because it is a faster and more accurate statistical method that allows you to systematically change all of the important factors in a process and see which combination has a lower impact on the project.

Statistical Sampling

Let's think again about the manufacture of doors. As discussed earlier, there would be some allowable variation in the height and weight of the doors. Even so, the doors must be checked to see if they meet quality standards on the project. What if inspecting each door would cause damage or take too much time? Then you may need to take a statistically valid sample. It is best to take a sample of a population if you believe there are not many defects, or if studying the entire population would:

- Take too long
- Cost too much
- Be too destructive

The sample size and frequency of measurements are determined as part of the Plan Quality process, and the actual sampling is done in Perform Quality Control.

Flowcharting[17]

A flowchart shows how a process or system flows from beginning to end and how the elements interrelate. In the Plan Quality process, this tool can be used to "see" a process and find potential quality problems. It is used in the Perform Quality Control process to analyze quality problems. Imagine that work results are passed to four departments for approval. Might this lead to decreased quality? What about an unfinished fragile product in a manufacturing environment? Would the quality of the product be reduced if it needed to be passed by hand from person to person? Flowcharts can be used in many parts of project management.

Outputs of Plan Quality PAGE 200

The following are the results of the Plan Quality process:

- **Quality Management Plan** Remember that the purpose of the Plan Quality process is to determine what quality is and to put a plan in place to manage quality. This plan is called the quality management plan. There are many different examples of quality management plans. Most include the following:
  - The quality practices and standards that apply to the project
  - Who will be involved in managing quality, when, and what their specific duties will be
  - Review of earlier decisions to make sure those decisions are correct
  - The meetings to be held addressing quality
  - The reports that will address quality
  - What metrics will be used to measure quality
  - What parts of the project or deliverables will be measured and when
- **Quality Metrics** There is an underlying theme throughout this book that the project manager must know how the project is going and be able to determine when to request changes. The only way to effectively do this is to determine metrics in advance. This means the project manager needs to think through the areas on the project that are important to measure and (in most

cases) decide what measurement is acceptable. (See also Control Limits.) The following are some examples of quality metrics:
- The number of changes (to help measure the quality of the project management planning process)
- The number of resources used
- The number of items that fail inspection
- The variance of the weight of a product produced by the project compared to the planned weight
- The number of bugs found in the software that is being developed as part of the project

- **Checklist** A quality checklist is a list of items to inspect, a list of steps to be performed, or a picture of the item to be inspected, with space to note any defects found. In Plan Quality, these checklists are created. In Perform Quality Control, they are used when checking the quality of the deliverables.
- **Process Improvement Plan** As a project manager, not only must you know what the processes are on the project and create additional processes as necessary, you must also improve the processes that are currently in use on the project. This plan for improvement is called the process improvement plan and becomes part of the project management plan. The process improvement plan helps save time by increasing efficiency and preventing problems. It also saves money and increases the probability that the customer will be satisfied.
- **Project Management Plan and Project Document Updates** Updates to the project management plan and project documents are needed throughout the project management process. Have you understood that planning quality (or any other knowledge area) can affect the existing project documentation? Planning is iterative. As a result of quality planning, you might go back and change information about the roles assigned on the project, the stakeholders who are significant to the quality management effort, the work to be done in the scope baseline, the cost associated with the work, and the risks on the project. Does this make sense?

Perform Quality Assurance[18] PAGE 201

Process: Perform Quality Assurance
Process Group: Executing
Knowledge Area: Quality Management

Perform Quality Assurance, an executing process, is performed while the project work is being done. A group outside the project, such as a quality assurance department, usually handles this assessment on a project. This group uses the measurements gathered as part of the Perform Quality Control process to answer the following two questions:
- Are we following the procedures and processes as planned?
- Can we improve the way we are doing the work?

The Peform Quality Assurance process uses the following tools and techniques:

Plan Quality and Perform Quality Control Tools and Techniques

The tools and techniques of the Plan Quality and Perform Quality Control processes are also used as part of the Perform Quality Assurance process. As noted earlier, when these tools are used in Plan Quality, they help determine requirements, procedures, and standards. When they are used in Perform Quality Assurance, they help assess whether the practices and procedures are being followed as planned. In Perform Quality Control, they are used to measure whether the deliverables meet the planned requirements and standards.

Quality Audits PAGE 204

Imagine a team of auditors walking into your office one day to check up on you and the project. Their job is to see if you are complying with company policies, standardized practices, and procedures and to determine whether the policies, practices, and procedures being used are efficient and effective. This scenario represents a quality audit, and it serves as an example of how seriously companies take quality. Do not think of a quality audit as a negative event. Instead, a good quality audit will look for new lessons learned and effective practices that your project can contribute to the performing organization. So the work of a project is not only to produce the product of the project; it could also be said that a project should contribute to the best practices within the organization and, therefore, make the organization better. If you do not have a team of auditors from the quality assurance department coming to see you on your real-world projects, do you take on the responsibility of looking for opportunities to identify lessons learned and best practices on your projects? Although quality audits are usually done by the quality assurance department, the project manager can lead this effort if the performing organization does not have such a department.

Process Analysis[19] PAGE 204 Have you ever worked on a project where some of the activities or work packages were repeated? This often happens when projects have multiple installations, such as a project to install software onto hundreds of computers. The lessons learned on the first few installations are used to improve the process on the remaining ones. Though this often happens naturally, formal process analysis should be planned in at certain points in the project (e.g., after every 10 installations). Process analysis is a part of the continuous improvement effort on a project and focuses on identifying improvements that might be needed in processes.

Outputs of Perform Quality Assurance PAGE 205 To understand the value of the Perform Quality Assurance process, you need to know that it leads to the following outputs:

- Change requests, including recommended corrective and preventive actions and defect repair
- Updated standards and processes
- Updated project management plan and project documents

Perform Quality Control PAGE 206

Process: Perform Quality Control
Process Group: Monitoring & Controlling
Knowledge Area: Quality Management

Perform Quality Control is the process of ensuring a certain level of quality in a deliverable, whether it be a product or service. Control means measure, and that is the major function of the Perform Quality Control process. It measures products or services to determine whether they meet the quality standards.

Although a project manager must be involved and concerned about quality control, a quality control department may complete much of this work in large companies. The department then informs the project manager about quality issues through change requests, which are accompanied by any necessary documentation and reports to detail the quality issues. The project manager must be able to read and understand quality measurement reports.

Quality control occurs throughout the life of the project. For example, during project planning, quality control might measure how long it takes to plan the project, or measure other areas of planning performance. Much of quality control occurs as part of monitoring and controlling the project, however.

It is during Perform Quality Control that the height of doors in a manufacturing process or the number of bugs per module will be measured. Quality control helps answer the following questions: "Are the results of our work meeting the standards?" and "What changes in the project should be considered?" Perform Quality Control results in change requests, including recommended corrective and preventive actions and defect repair. The project manager then acts on these change requests to help improve quality.

You may see manufacturing situations described on the exam. This does not mean you have to learn about all industries. The exam may highlight manufacturing because quality is an important factor in this industry, and manufacturing examples tend to be understandable to all. Do not let the industry featured in a question confuse you. Instead, focus on the situation that is being described.

To better understand questions relating to quality control, you should be familiar with the following terms. You will likely see these as choices or even as part of questions on the exam.

Mutual Exclusivity The exam may reference statistical terms. One such term that often confuses people is "mutual exclusivity." Two events are said to be mutually exclusive if they cannot both occur in a single trial. For example, flipping a coin once cannot result in both a head and a tail.

Probability This term refers to the likelihood that something will occur. Probability is usually expressed as a decimal or a fraction, on a scale of zero to one.

Normal Distribution A normal distribution is the most common probability density distribution chart. It is in the shape of a bell curve and is used to measure variations.

Statistical Independence Another confusing statistical term often showing up on the exam is "statistical independence." This means the probability of one event occurring does not affect the probability of another event occurring. For example, the probability of rolling a six on a die is statistically independent from the probability of getting a five on the next roll.

Standard Deviation (or Sigma) A measure of a range is its standard deviation. This concept is also sometimes stated as a measure of how far you are from the mean (not the median). (Remember (P – O)/6 is the three-point estimate formula for standard deviation, using optimistic, pessimistic, and most likely estimates, as described in the Time Management chapter.)

3 or 6 Sigma[20] Sigma is another name for standard deviation. 3 or 6 sigma represents the level of quality that a company has decided to try to achieve. At 6 sigma, less than 1.5 out of 1 million doors produced will have a problem. At 3 sigma, approximately 2,700 will have a problem. Therefore, 6 sigma represents a higher quality standard than 3 sigma. 3 or 6 sigma are also used to calculate the upper and lower control limits in a control chart, described earlier in this chapter.

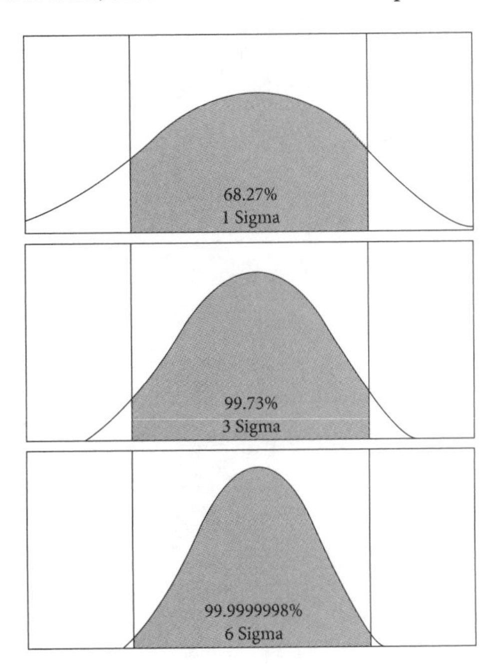

Know the following for the exam:

- Sigma is taken on both sides of the mean. Half the curve is to the right of the mean, and half the curve is to the left of the mean.
- +/- 1 sigma (or one standard deviation) is equal to 68.27%, which is the percentage of occurrences to fall between the two control limits.
- +/- 2 sigma (or 2 standard deviations) equals 95.45%.
- +/- 3 sigma (or 3 standard deviations) equals 99.73%.
- +/- 6 sigma (or 6 standard deviations) equals 99.9999998%

Seven Basic Tools of Quality PAGE 208

The following tools are known as Ishikawa's seven basic tools of quality. Each is used during the Perform Quality Control process.

- Cause and effect diagram
- Flowchart (see the description of this tool in the Plan Quality section of this chapter)
- Histogram
- Pareto chart
- Run chart
- Scatter diagram
- Control chart (see the description of this tool in the Plan Quality section of this chapter)

Cause and Effect Diagram (Fishbone Diagram, Ishikawa Diagram)[21]

Is it better to fix a defect or get to the root cause of the defect? Think about this question for a moment. The answer is that you should do both, and a cause and effect diagram can help you. In the following example, the diagram shows the defect of "system will not install" on the right and then lists the potential causes, such as hardware issues, software issues, etc. Various subcauses of each potential cause are also listed in an effort to find the root cause of the defect.

A project manager can create cause and effect diagrams to look backwards at what may have contributed to quality problems on the project. The exam has used the following type of phrasing to describe cause and effect diagrams:

1. A creative way to look at the causes of a problem
2. Helps stimulate thinking, organize thoughts, and generate discussion
3. Can be used to explore the factors that will result in a desired future outcome

The following is an illustration of a fishbone diagram:

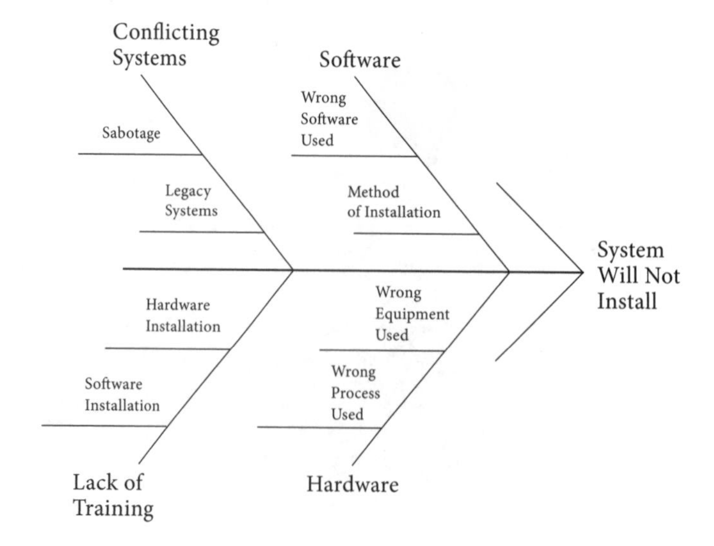

Histogram[22]

You have probably seen many histograms but never realized they were called histograms. A histogram displays data in the form of bars or columns. This tool shows what problems are worth dealing with. A typical histogram presents data in no particular order.

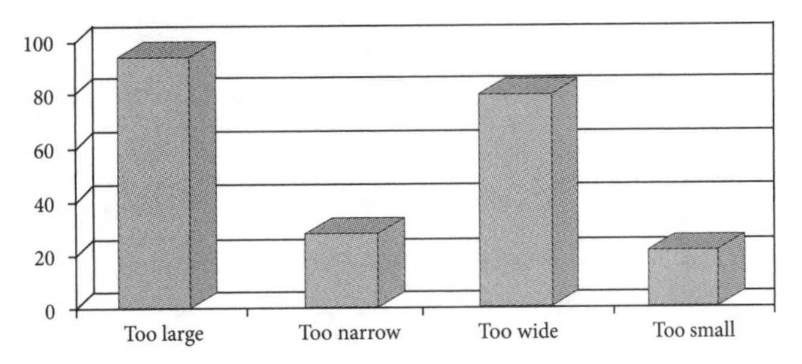

Pareto Chart (Pareto Diagram)[23]

A Pareto chart or Pareto diagram is a type of histogram, but it arranges the results from most frequent to least frequent to help identify which root causes are resulting in the most problems. Joseph Juran adapted Vilfredo Pareto's 80/20 rule to create the 80/20 principle (also known as the Pareto Principle), which states that 80 percent of problems are due to 20 percent of the root causes. Imagine you have very little time to spend improving quality on the project. If you took all the problems you have had and stacked them into piles of like problems, which root cause would you address, that of the large pile or that of the small pile? The answer is of course the root cause of the large pile. Addressing the root cause of the most frequent problems makes the greatest impact on quality.

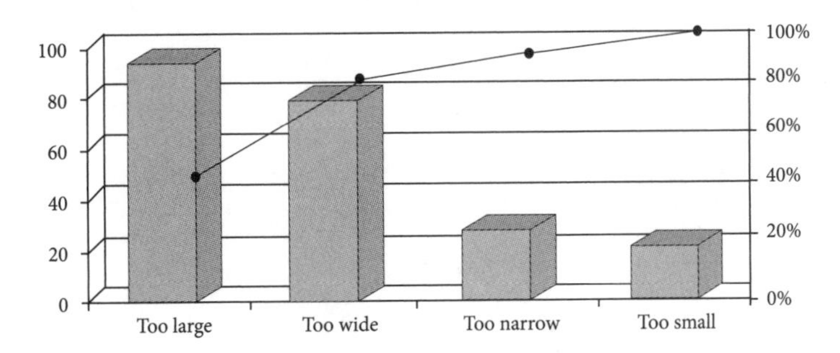

The exam asks about Pareto charts in many ways and sometimes uses unfamiliar words instead of the more common phrases. Remembering the following about Pareto charts should help you on the exam.

Pareto charts:

- Help focus attention on the most critical issues
- Prioritize potential "causes" of the problems
- Separate the critical few from the uncritical many

Run Chart[24]

A run chart is a useful tool for controlling quality because it allows you to look at history to see if there is a pattern of variation. If you have ever charted progress and looked for trends, then you have likely used run charts. The following is an example of a run chart.

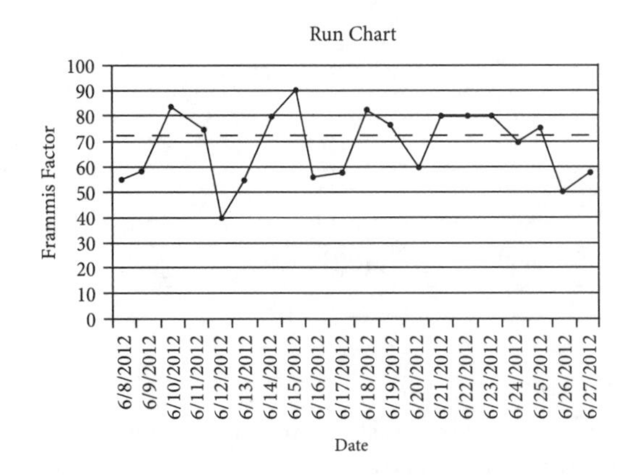

Scatter Diagram[25]

This diagram tracks two variables to see if they are related. For example, if in the manufacture of doors, the quality of the wood used has changed and so has the strength of the doors, a scatter diagram might be used to see if the two are related.

The following is an example of a scatter diagram.

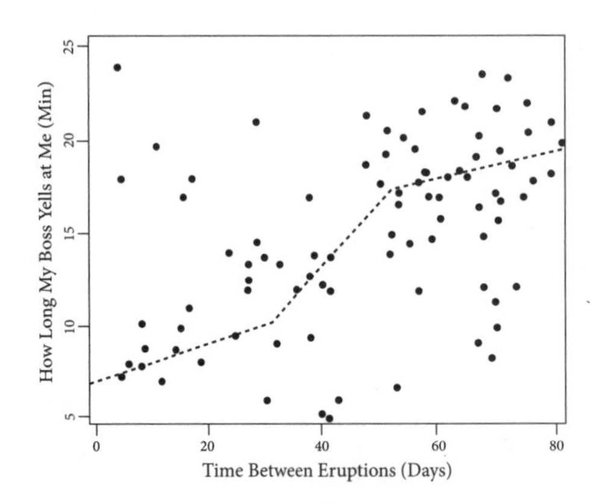

Outputs of Perform Quality Control PAGE 213 When you have completed the Perform Quality Control process, you will have the following outputs:

- Measurements
- Validated changes
- Updates to the project management plan and project documents
- Change requests, including recommended corrective and preventive actions and defect repair
- Lessons learned
- Validated deliverables

Putting It All Together

Do you feel like you understand quality management now? If not, don't worry; we are not done with this chapter yet. The following descriptions and exercises will help you review the information you have learned. Take this opportunity to solidify your understanding of what quality management is and how it fits into the overall project management process.

Quality Management in the Real World Many people getting ready for this exam have limited quality management experience, so they struggle with envisioning how these efforts fit into managing a project in the real world. The following scenario and diagram serve as an example to help clarify these concepts.

1. The customer determines their requirements.
2. The project team clarifies those requirements.
3. The project team determines what work will be done to meet those requirements.
4. The project manager determines the existing standards, policies, plans, and procedures that might be available for the project. He or she might approach a quality assurance or quality control department for help in finding the standards.
5. The project manager creates other standards and processes that may be needed.
6. Quality becomes one of the knowledge areas that the project manager must integrate.
7. Project planning work and project execution get underway by the team.

8a. The quality control department:
- Measures the performance of the project by looking at the quality of its deliverables.

8b. The quality assurance department:
- Audits the project work periodically as part of the executing process, looking at the quality control measurements to see if there is any indication that the standards, policies, plans, and procedures are not being followed.
- Looks for best practices that can be used throughout the organization.
- Looks to improve processes being used throughout the organization.

9. Change requests are issued, including notification of areas that need preventive actions, corrective actions, or defect repair.
10. The change control board:
    - Evaluates all change requests (in Perform Integrated Change Control).
11. The team adjusts plans and work as needed and returns to step seven until done.

The results:
- The project is completed, quality targets are reached, and the customer is happy.
- The organization has improved processes.

The diagram on the following page illustrates this scenario.

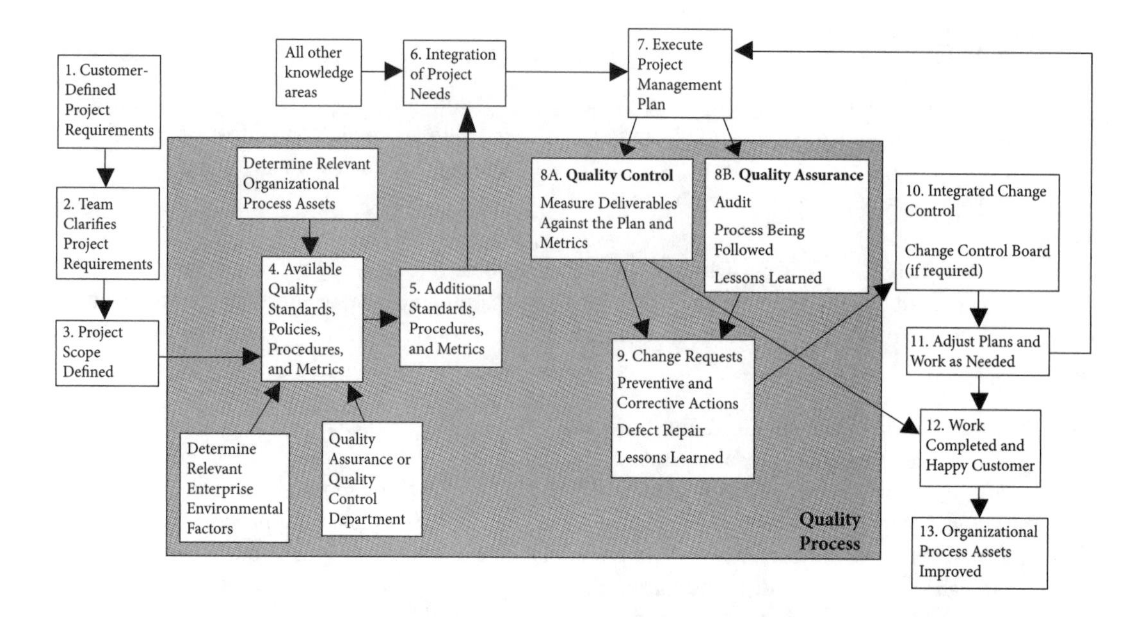

TRICKS OF THE TRADE®

Understanding the Tools and Techniques Used in Quality Management

As you have read through this chapter, have you found yourself asking questions like, "Now when are all these tools and techniques used?" or "What are the differences between the three parts of the quality management process again?" Although there are not a lot of questions on the exam on these topics, people tend to struggle with these concepts. The following exercises will help.

Exercise Take a moment to research in this book the different tools and techniques that are created or used in each of the quality management processes. Write the name of the tools and techniques in the following table under the header of the appropriate quality management process. Notice similarities and repeated occurrences of these items, and think about how the repeated tools and techniques might be used for different purposes.

Plan Quality	Perform Quality Assurance	Perform Quality Control

Plan Quality	Perform Quality Assurance	Perform Quality Control

Answer

Plan Quality	Perform Quality Assurance	Perform Quality Control
Control charts (set up in planning)	Any tools from Plan Quality and Perform Quality Control can be used to check if proper processes were followed or if processes need to be improved	Control charts (used to assess or evaluate the project results in quality control)
Statistical sampling (sample size and process determined in planning)	Quality audits	Statistical sampling (samples taken in quality control)
Flowcharts (used to "see" processes in planning)	Process analysis	Flowcharts (used to analyze problems in quality control)
Checklists (created in planning)		Checklists (used to check quality in quality control)
Cost benefit analysis		Cause and effect diagrams
Cost of quality		Histogram
Benchmarking		Pareto chart
Design of experiments		Run chart
		Scatter diagram

Exercise Now take what you have learned and see if you can apply it in a different way. This exercise should help prepare you for questions on the exam, regardless of how they are written.

TRICKS OF THE TRADE® Here is a trick: If the situation is looking forward in time, it is most likely a planning function. If it is looking back in time at project results, it is most likely part of quality control. If it is looking back in time at processes and procedures, it is most likely part of quality assurance.

	Situation	What Tool/ Technique Is Being Referred To?	What Part of the Quality Management Process Are You In?
1	Looking at the project practices of comparable projects		
2	Measuring 4 of the doors produced, rather than all 400		
3	Identifying the factors that influence particular variables of a product or process		
4	Analyzing a chart of problems to find the most frequent one in order to determine if processes need to be improved		
5	Comparing the expense of quality efforts to the return on that investment		
6	Determining what will be acceptable upper and lower thresholds of variance		
7	Comparing what was done to what was documented as needing to be done		
8	Selecting 3 projects to refer to out of a total possible 12		
9	Graphically representing a process to determine where a process that is achieving low-quality results might be failing		
10	Taking measurements and comparing them to the upper and lower thresholds of variance		
11	Graphically representing a process to determine where quality problems might arise		
12	Analyzing a graphic with an organized series of lines displaying issues that might have led to a defect to examine if the proper process was followed		

	Situation	What Tool/ Technique Is Being Referred To?	What Part of the Quality Management Process Are You In?
13	Showing data in the form of bars to measure and plot how frequently a problem occurred		
14	Collecting many data points to look at the pattern of relationships or correlation between two variables		
15	Using a bar chart to show how many problems occurred for each cause and arranging them according to the frequency at which the problems occurred		
16	Creating a list of items to be checked during inspections		
17	Reviewing a graphic with an organized series of lines displaying issues or potential issues that might have led to a defect or problem		

Answer Remember that the tools and techniques can be described in many ways on the exam. Get used to the idea that the exam will ask questions indirectly, and be able to differentiate between the tools or techniques and their uses.

	Situation	What Tool/ Technique Is Being Referred To?	What Part of the Quality Management Process Are You In?
1	Looking at the project practices of comparable projects	Benchmarking	Plan Quality
2	Measuring 4 of the doors produced, rather than all 400	Statistical sampling	Perform Quality Control
3	Identifying the factors that influence particular variables of a product or process	Design of experiments	Plan Quality
4	Analyzing a chart of problems to find the most frequent one in order to determine if processes need to be improved	Pareto chart	Perform Quality Assurance
5	Comparing the expense of quality efforts to the return on that investment	Cost benefit analysis	Plan Quality
6	Determining what will be acceptable upper and lower thresholds of variance	Control chart	Plan Quality

	Situation	What Tool/ Technique Is Being Referred To?	What Part of the Quality Management Process Are You In?
7	Comparing what was done to what was documented as needing to be done	Checklists	Perform Quality Control
8	Selecting 3 projects to refer to out of a total possible 12	Statistical sampling	Plan Quality
9	Graphically representing a process to determine where a process that is achieving low-quality results might be failing	Flowcharting	Perform Quality Control
10	Taking measurements and comparing them to the upper and lower thresholds of variance	Control chart	Perform Quality Control
11	Graphically representing a process to determine where quality problems might arise	Flowcharting	Plan Quality
12	Analyzing a graphic with an organized series of lines displaying issues that might have led to a defect to examine if the proper process was followed	Cause and effect diagram	Perform Quality Assurance
13	Showing data in the form of bars to measure and plot how frequently a problem occurred	Histogram	Perform Quality Control
14	Collecting many data points to look at the pattern of relationships or correlation between two variables	Scatter diagram	Perform Quality Control
15	Using a bar chart to show how many problems occurred for each cause and arranging them according to the frequency at which the problems occurred	Pareto chart	Perform Quality Control
16	Creating a list of items to be checked during inspections	Checklists	Plan Quality
17	Reviewing a graphic with an organized series of lines displaying issues or potential issues that might have led to a defect or problem	Cause and effect diagram	Perform Quality Control

TRICKS OF THE TRADE®

Understanding the Differences between the Three Parts of the Quality Management Process

Are you still unsure about the difference between Plan Quality, Perform Quality Assurance, and Perform Quality Control? Think through what you have learned in this chapter, and see if you can recreate the quality chart shown earlier by filling in the following table. When you are finished, check your answers against the chart on page 268.

Plan Quality	Perform Quality Assurance	Perform Quality Control
High-Level Description of What Each Process Focuses On		
More Detailed Description of What Each Process Focuses On		
Process Group		

Practice Exam

1. When a product or service completely meets a customer's requirements:
   A. Quality is achieved.
   B. The cost of quality is high.
   C. The cost of quality is low.
   D. The customer pays the minimum price.

2. To what does the following definition refer? "The point where the benefits or revenue to be received from improving quality equals the incremental cost to achieve that quality."
   A. Quality control analysis
   B. Marginal analysis
   C. Standard quality analysis
   D. Conformance analysis

3. Who is ultimately responsible for quality management on the project?
   A. The project engineer
   B. The project manager
   C. The quality manager
   D. The team member

4. A project has faced major difficulties in the quality of its deliverables. Management now states that quality is the most important project constraint. If another problem with quality were to occur, what would be the BEST thing for the project manager to do?
   A. Fix the problem as soon as possible.
   B. Allow the schedule to slip by cutting cost.
   C. Allow cost to increase by fixing the root cause of the problem.
   D. Allow risk to increase by cutting cost.

5. A manager notices that a project manager is holding a meeting with some of the team and some stakeholders to discuss the quality of the project. The project schedule has been compressed, and the CPI is 1.1. They have worked hard on the project, the team has been rewarded according to the reward system the project manager put in place, and there is a strong sense of team. The manager suggests that the project manager does not have enough time to hold meetings about quality when the schedule is so compressed. Which of the following BEST describes why the manager is wrong?
   A. Improved quality leads to increased productivity, increased cost effectiveness, and decreased cost risk.
   B. Improved quality leads to increased productivity, decreased cost effectiveness, and increased cost risk.
   C. Improved quality leads to increased productivity, increased cost effectiveness, and increased cost risk.
   D. Improved quality leads to increased productivity, decreased cost effectiveness, and decreased cost risk.

6. From the project perspective, quality attributes:
   A. Determine how effectively the performing organization supports the project.
   B. Provide the basis for judging the project's success or failure.
   C. Are specific characteristics for which a product is designed and tested.
   D. Are objective criteria that must be met.

7. Quality is:
   A. Meeting and exceeding the customer's expectations.
   B. Adding extras to make the customer happy.
   C. The degree to which the project meets requirements.
   D. Conformance to management's objectives.

8. All the following are tools of Perform Quality Control EXCEPT:
   A. Inspection.
   B. Cost of quality.
   C. Pareto chart.
   D. Fishbone diagram.

9. Pareto charts help the project manager:
   A. Focus on the most critical issues to improve quality.
   B. Focus on stimulating thinking.
   C. Explore a desired future outcome.
   D. Determine if a process is out of control.

10. A control chart helps the project manager:
    A. Focus on the most critical issues to improve quality.
    B. Focus on stimulating thinking.
    C. Explore a desired future outcome.
    D. Determine if a process is functioning within set limits.

11. Testing the entire population would:
    A. Take too long.
    B. Provide more information than wanted.
    C. Be mutually exclusive.
    D. Show many defects.

12. All of the following are examples of the cost of nonconformance EXCEPT:
    A. Rework.
    B. Quality training.
    C. Scrap.
    D. Warranty costs.

13. Standard deviation is a measure of how:
    A. Far the estimate is from the highest estimate.
    B. Far the measurement is from the mean.
    C. Correct the sample is.
    D. Much time remains in the project.

14. What percentage of the total distribution is 3 sigma from the mean equal to?
    A. 68.27 percent
    B. 99.9999998 percent
    C. 95.45 percent
    D. 99.73 percent

15. All of the following result from quality audits EXCEPT:
    A. Determination of whether project activities comply with organizational policies.
    B. Improved processes to increase productivity.
    C. Creation of quality metrics.
    D. Confirmation of the implementation of approved change requests.

16. A control chart shows seven data points in a row on one side of the mean. What should be done?
    A. Perform a design of experiments.
    B. Adjust the chart to reflect the new mean.
    C. Find an assignable cause.
    D. Nothing. This is the rule of seven and can be ignored.

17. You are managing a project in a just-in-time environment. This will require more attention, because the amount of inventory in such an environment is generally:
    A. 45 percent.
    B. 10 percent.
    C. 12 percent.
    D. 0 percent.

18. In planning your project, which would generally have the highest priority: quality, cost, or schedule?
    A. Cost is most important, quality next, and then schedule.
    B. Quality is more important than cost or schedule.
    C. Schedule is most important, quality next, and then cost.
    D. It should be decided for each project.

19. There are several executing activities underway on your project. You are beginning to get concerned about the accuracy of the progress reporting your team members are doing. How could you verify whether there is a problem?
    A. Quality audits
    B. Risk quantification reports
    C. Regression analysis
    D. Monte Carlo analysis

20. A project manager and team from a firm that designs railroad equipment are tasked to design a machine to load stone onto railroad cars. The design allows for two percent spillage, amounting to over two tons of spilled rock per day. In which of the following does the project manager document quality control, quality assurance, and quality improvements for this project?
    A. Quality management plan
    B. Quality policy
    C. Control charts
    D. Project management plan

21. During a team meeting, the team adds a specific area of extra work to the project because they have determined it would benefit the customer. What is wrong in this situation?
    A. The team is gold plating.
    B. These efforts shouldn't be done in meetings.
    C. Nothing. This is how to meet and exceed customer expectations.
    D. Nothing. The project manager is in control of the situation.

22. The project team has created a plan for how they will implement the quality policy. It addresses the organizational structure, responsibilities, procedures, and other information about plans for quality. If this plan changes during the project, WHICH of the following plans will also change?
    A. Quality assurance plan
    B. Quality management plan
    C. Project management plan
    D. Quality control plan

23. You are a project manager for a major information systems project. Someone from the quality department comes to see you about beginning a quality audit of your project. The team, already under pressure to complete the project as soon as possible, objects to the audit. You should explain to the team that the purpose of a quality audit is:
    A. To satisfy part of an ISO 9000 investigation.
    B. To check if the customer is following the quality process.
    C. To identify inefficient and ineffective policies.
    D. To check the accuracy of costs submitted by the team.

24. You are in the middle of a major new facility construction project. The structural steel is in place and the heating conduits are going into place when a senior manager informs you that he is worried the project will not meet the quality standards. What should you do in this situation?
    A. Assure senior management that during the Plan Quality process, it was determined that the project would meet the quality standards.
    B. Analogously estimate future results.
    C. Form a quality assurance team.
    D. Check the results from the last quality management plan.

25. You are asked to select tools and techniques to implement a quality assurance program to supplement existing quality control activities. Which of the following would NOT be appropriate for this purpose?
    A. Quality audits
    B. Statistical sampling
    C. Pareto charts
    D. Focus groups

26. The new software installation project is in progress. The project manager is working with the quality assurance department to improve stakeholders' confidence that the project will satisfy the quality standards. Which of the following MUST they have before they start this process?
    A. Quality problems
    B. Quality improvement
    C. Quality control measurements
    D. Rework

27. The project you are working on has an increase in cost effectiveness, increased productivity, and increased morale. What might be the reason for these changes?
    A. Project objectives are in line with those of the performing organization
    B. Increased quality
    C. Management's focus on cost containment
    D. Rewards presented for individual efforts

28. A project manager has just taken over the project from another project manager during project executing. The previous project manager created a project budget, determined communications requirements, and went on to complete work packages. What should the new project manager do NEXT?
    A. Coordinate completion of work packages.
    B. Identify quality standards.
    C. Begin the Identify Risks process.
    D. Execute the project management plan.

29. Design of experiments:
    A. Identifies which variables will have the most influence on a quality outcome.
    B. Identifies which variables will have the least influence on a quality outcome.
    C. Determines what a quality outcome is.
    D. Determines methods to be used for research and development.

30. At the end of a project, a project manager determines the project has added four areas of functionality and three areas of performance. The customer has expressed satisfaction with the project. What does this mean in terms of the success of the project?
    A. The project was an unqualified success.
    B. The project was unsuccessful because it was gold plated.
    C. The project was unsuccessful because the customer being happy means they would have paid more for the work.
    D. The project was successful because the team had a chance to learn new areas of functionality and the customer was satisfied.

31. During project executing, a project team member informs the project manager that a work package has not met the quality metric, and that she believes it is not possible to meet it. The project manager meets with all parties concerned to analyze the situation. Which part of the quality management process is the project manager involved in?
    A. Perform Quality Assurance
    B. Project Control
    C. Perform Quality Control
    D. Plan Quality

32. The project manager notices that project activities being completed by one department are all taking slightly longer than planned. To date, none of the activities in the work packages have been on the critical path, nor have they affected the critical chain planning that has occurred. The project manager is bothered by the problem, since four of the next five critical path activities are being completed by this department.

    After making three calls, the project manager is finally able to converse with the department manager to determine what is going on. The conversation is slow, because both speak different native languages and they are trying to converse in French, a shared language. To make communication easier, the project manager frequently asks the department manager to repeat back what has been said.

    The department manager communicates that his staff is following a company policy that requires two levels of testing. During the conversation, the department manager also makes a comment that leads the project manager to believe that the policy may include excessive work. This is the fourth time the project manager has heard such a comment. What is the BEST thing to do?

A. Create a better communications management plan that requires only one language to be the universal language on the project and have translators readily available on a moment's notice.
B. Contact someone else in the department who speaks the project manager's native language better to confirm the department manager's opinion.
C. Find out if the upcoming activities should be reestimated.
D. Work on increasing the effectiveness of the performing organization by recommending continuous improvement of the policy in question.

33. As the project manager, you are preparing your quality management plan. You are looking for a tool that can demonstrate the relationship between events and their resulting effects. You want to use this tool to depict the events that cause a negative effect on quality. Which of the following is the BEST choice for accomplishing your objective?
A. Histogram
B. Pareto chart
C. Ishikawa diagram
D. Control chart

34. Which of the following explains why quality is planned in and not inspected in?
A. It reduces quality and is less expensive.
B. It improves quality and is more expensive.
C. It reduces quality and is more expensive.
D. It improves quality and is less expensive.

35. Work on a project is ongoing when the project manager overhears two workers arguing over what a set of instructions means. The project manager investigates and discovers that the instructions for the construction of the concrete footings currently being poured were poorly translated between the different languages in use on the project. Which of the following is the BEST thing for the project manager to do FIRST?
A. Get the instructions translated by a more experienced party.
B. Look for quality impacts of the poor translation of the instructions for the footings.
C. Bring the issue to the attention of the team and ask them to look for other translation problems.
D. Inform the sponsor of the problem in the next project report.

Answers

1. **Answer** A
   Explanation As a general rule, one cannot say that quality (as defined in the question) is either of high or low cost. It provides what the customer wanted, which may not be the lowest or highest cost. When a product or service completely meets a customer's needs, quality is achieved.

2. **Answer** B
   Explanation This is the definition of marginal analysis. Know the term so you will be able to answer questions that deal with this concept. The other choices may sound good, but they are made-up terms.

3. **Answer** B
   Explanation Although each person working on the project should check their own work, the project manager ultimately has the responsibility for quality on the project as a whole.

4. **Answer** C
   Explanation If a problem with quality were to occur again, many people would opt to fix the problem as soon as possible. It is proactive, but some other project constraint(s) must change to accommodate fixing the root cause of the problem. It may not be necessary to allow the schedule to slip, because the project manager might be able to compress the schedule in other areas. Cutting cost does not necessarily cause the schedule to slip, nor would that necessarily fix the problem at hand. Allowing risk to increase by cutting cost is not the best choice, because a quality problem is most likely to create additional cost, rather than cut cost. Allowing the cost to increase by fixing the root cause of the problem addresses both finding the cause and the probable impact of dealing with the problem.

5. **Answer** A
   Explanation Did you notice there is a lot of data not relevant to answering the question? Expect distracters to appear in many questions on the exam.

   Quality efforts should produce a decrease rather than an increase in cost risk as a result of less rework. Quality efforts should also provide increased cost effectiveness due to less rework. This leaves the only best answer: Improved quality leads to increased productivity, increased cost effectiveness, and decreased cost risk.

6. **Answer** C
   Explanation Quality attributes are the measurements that determine if the product is acceptable. They are based on the characteristics of the product for which they were designed.

7. **Answer** C
   Explanation There can be a cost impact (or time, risk, etc.) of exceeding expectations or adding extras. Quality is the degree to which the project meets requirements.

8. **Answer** B
   Explanation Inspection, Pareto charts, and fishbone diagrams are tools of Perform Quality Assurance or Perform Quality Control (depending on how they are used). Cost of quality is part of Plan Quality, making sure the project is not spending too much to achieve a particular level of quality.

9. **Answer** A
   Explanation Fishbone diagrams are often used to stimulate thinking and to explore a desired future outcome. Determining whether a process is out of control is a function of control charts. Only focusing on critical issues to improve quality relates to Pareto charts.

10. **Answer** D
    Explanation Focusing on the most critical issues to improve quality relates to Pareto charts. Stimulating thinking and exploring a desired future outcome relate to fishbone diagrams. Only determining if a process is functioning within set limits relates to control charts.

11. **Answer** A
    Explanation The length of time it takes to test a whole population is one of the reasons to take a sample.

12. **Answer** B
    Explanation Quality training is a cost of conformance to quality. All the other choices are costs of nonconformance to quality.

13. **Answer** B
    Explanation Standard deviation is the measurement of a range around the mean.

14. **Answer** D
    Explanation You should know the numbers for 1, 2, 3, and 6 sigma for the exam.

15. **Answer** C
    Explanation Quality metrics are an output of the Plan Quality process. They are an input to the Perform Quality Assurance process, which is the process in which quality audits take place.

16. **Answer** C
    Explanation The rule of seven applies here. If you have seven data points in a row on the same side of the mean, statistically the mean has shifted, calling for action to correct the problem.

17. **Answer** D
    Explanation With a just-in-time environment, supplies are delivered when you need them and not before. Therefore, you have little or no inventory.

18. **Answer** D
    Explanation This can be a tricky question, in that most project managers dismiss the need to focus on quality. Quality, cost, and schedule should be considered of equal importance unless specific project objectives make any one of them most important. Quality, cost, schedule, scope, risk, and other factors may be prioritized differently on each project.

19. **Answer** A
    Explanation Quality audits are a necessary part of the Perform Quality Assurance process. They help you assess whether the processes are being followed correctly on the project.

20. **Answer** A
    Explanation The quality policy and control charts are components of a quality management plan. Although the quality management plan is part of the project management plan, the best answer is the quality management plan.

21. **Answer** A
Explanation This is an example of gold plating. You should provide ONLY what the customer asked for. The team does not know if their change will provide benefit to the customer. The team should focus its efforts on fulfilling the requirements.

22. **Answer** C
Explanation The plan described is the quality management plan. Since the quality management plan is included in the project management plan, changing the quality management plan will also change the project management plan.

23. **Answer** C
Explanation Perform Quality Assurance, of which an audit is part, focuses on processes, procedures, and standards. Though ISO 9000 is a standard, that is not the only reason an audit would be conducted. The seller cannot generally control or review the customer's quality process. Checking accuracy of costs submitted by the team is more representative of a cost audit than a quality audit, so that option cannot be the best choice. One purpose of a quality audit is to identify inefficient and ineffective policies.

24. **Answer** C
Explanation Assuring management that it was determined in planning that the project would meet quality standards is not productive, since it does not solve the problem. An analogous estimate looks at the past history of other projects. This would not be appropriate to determine how the current project is going. The quality management plan does not provide results. A quality assurance team could help to determine whether the team is following the correct proces to satisfy the relevant quality standards.

25. **Answer** D
Explanation Quality audits, statistical sampling, and Pareto charts are tools and techniques used in the Perform Quality Assurance and Perform Quality Control processes. Focus groups are a tool of the Collect Requirements process, and would not be useful in the Perform Quality Assurance process.

26. **Answer** C
Explanation Though quality problems MAY lead to quality assurance efforts, they are not a MUST. Quality improvement is a result of Perform Quality Assurance, not an input. Rework (or defect repair) can be an output of Perform Quality Control. That leaves only quality control measurements, which are inputs to the Perform Quality Assurance process.

27. **Answer** B
Explanation This question is similar to others in this book, but it is not exactly the same. You may also see this occur on your exam. Carefully read the questions! As you increase quality, there will be associated benefits for the project. Some of these benefits are increased productivity, increased cost effectiveness, decreased cost risk, and improved morale.

28. **Answer** B
Explanation Completion of work packages is done after project planning. Since the previous project manager did not finish planning, continuing to execute the project management plan should not be next. Identify Risks sounds like a good choice; however, identifying quality standards occurs before the Identify Risks process. This is the best answer, as planning must be completed on a project.

29. **Answer** A
Explanation The design of experiments technique allows you to find those factors that have the most impact on quality. It allows the project manager to focus attention on the factors that are most important.

30. **Answer** B
Explanation Gold plating a project wastes time and probably cost. It makes the project unsuccessful.

31. **Answer** C
Explanation Measuring is part of the Perform Quality Control process. Did you select project control? The question asked what part of the quality process are you in, not what part of the project management process are you in.

32. **Answer** D
Explanation Changing the communications management plan might be a good idea, but this choice has two problems. It may not be needed on the project, and it does not deal with the problem at hand, the policy that is slowing things down. Confirming the department manager's opinion with someone else in the department is not the best choice, as the project manager already has heard the opinion on many other occasions. It is already confirmed. Determining whether upcoming activities should be reestimated is just being reactive. A good project manager will find the root cause and deal with that, even if it means attempting to improve the company's policies and processes. Yes, recommending improvement of the policy is the best answer. This is continuous improvement. Because there are several activities affected by the policy, it would best serve the project to get to the root cause of the problem and solve it.

33. **Answer** C
Explanation All reports and diagrams are communications tools. This question asks you to pick the most appropriate quality tool to help communications. An Ishikawa diagram, also called a cause and effect diagram, is more appropriate than a Pareto chart since you are trying to determine the causes. Once causes are known and you have data on occurrences, the data can be displayed in a Pareto chart.

34. **Answer** D
Explanation Look for the proactive approach. When we plan for quality, it improves quality, which is less expensive over the long run. NOTE: You may spend more initially for increased quality, but you will save through reduced rework and other such benefits.

35. **Answer** B
Explanation Although all of these choices are correct things to do, the question asks what to do first. What is the most immediate problem? Getting the instructions translated by a more experienced party could be done, but it does not address the immediate concern. Asking the team to look for other translation issues is an excellent idea. However, it does not address the immediate problem. Informing the sponsor is also not taking action to solve the problem. Isn't it most urgent to find out whether the concrete footings meet your project requirements? Are they adequate? Only the option of looking for quality impacts of the poor translation will help you determine that.

CHAPTER NINE

Human Resource Management

Quicktest

- Human resource management process
- Role of:
  - Project manager
  - PM team
  - Sponsor
  - Team
  - Stakeholders
  - Functional manager
  - Portfolio manager
  - Program manager
- HR responsibilities for project managers
- Human resource plan
- Staffing management plan
- Recognition and reward systems
- Team building
- Powers of the project manager
- Conflict resolution techniques
- Sources of conflict
- Team performance assessment
- Project performance appraisals
- Ground rules
- Issue log
- Responsibility assignment matrix
  - RACI chart
- Organizational breakdown structure
- Resource breakdown structure
- Position descriptions
- Resource histogram
- Motivation theory
  - McGregor's theory of X and Y
  - Maslow's hierarchy of needs
  - McClelland's theory of needs
  - Herzberg's theory
- Training
- Halo effect
- Co-location/war room
- Management and leadership styles
- Problem-solving method
- Expectancy theory
- Arbitration
- Perquisites
- Fringe benefits
- Preassignment
- Negotiation
- Virtual teams
- Stages of team formation and development
- Observation and conversation

You might be thinking this chapter will be an easy one. Many parts of it are easy, but you still need to look for gaps in your project management knowledge. The following are the most common knowledge gaps people have about human resource management. Review these, and look for others that apply to you as you read the rest of this chapter.

- Creating recognition and reward systems is an important human resource function, and such systems are a required part of project management.
- The project manager is responsible for improving the team members' competencies.
- Human resource management is primarily done in the executing process group.
- The project manager's human resource activities are formal and require documentation.
- There should be formal roles and responsibilities on the project, and these include assisting the project manager, responsibilities at meetings, and other non-activity-related work.
- The exam assumes (unless stated otherwise) that the project is operating in a matrix environment. Therefore, such topics as motivation theories and powers of the project manager are more serious than you might otherwise expect.
- Projects are planned by the team and coordinated by the project manager.
- The project manager must continually confirm resource availability.
- The project is so large that the project manager might have some of the team help with project management activities. These people are called the project management team. So the team consists of the project manager, the project management team, and the other members of the project team.
- The project manager formally plans team-building activities in advance; these activities are a required part of project management.
- The project manager must track team member performance.

If you manage small projects (those lasting only a few months or those that involve fewer than 20 people), keep in mind that human resource responsibilities increase as the size of the project team increases. The human resource management process takes time and effort to plan how you will use people, identify the team members you will need, define everyone's roles, create reward systems, improve team members' performance individually and as a team, and track performance. It is much more involved than working with the same four people who already know each other.

Rita's Process Chart—Human Resource Management

Where are we in the project management process?

INITIATING

- Select project manager
- Determine company culture and existing systems
- Collect processes, procedures, and historical information
- Divide large projects into phases
- Understand the business case
- Uncover initial requirements, assumptions, and risks
- Assess project and product feasibility within the given constraints
- Create measurable objectives
- Develop project charter
- Identify stakeholders
- Develop stakeholder management strategy

PLANNING

(This is the only process group with a set order)

- **Determine how you will do planning—part of all management plans**
- Determine detailed requirements
- Create project scope statement
- Assess what to purchase
- **Determine team**
- Create WBS and WBS dictionary
- Create activity list
- Create network diagram
- Estimate resource requirements
- Estimate time and cost
- Determine critical path
- Develop schedule
- Develop budget
- Determine quality standards, processes, and metrics
- Create process improvement plan
- **Determine all roles and responsibilities**
- Plan communications
- Perform risk identification, qualitative and quantitative risk analysis, and risk response planning
- **Go back—iterations**
- Prepare procurement documents
- Create change management plan
- **Finalize the "how to execute and control" parts of all management plans**
- **Develop realistic and final PM plan and performance measurement baseline**
- Gain formal approval of the plan
- Hold kickoff meeting

EXECUTING

- Execute the work according to the PM plan
- Produce product deliverables (product scope)
- **Request changes**
- Implement only approved changes
- Continuously improve
- Follow processes
- Perform quality assurance
- Perform quality audits
- **Acquire final team**
- **Manage people**
- **Evaluate team and project performance**
- **Hold team-building activities**
- **Give recognition and rewards**
- **Use issue logs**
- **Facilitate conflict resolution**
- **Release resources as work is completed**
- Send and receive information
- Hold meetings
- Select sellers

MONITORING & CONTROLLING

- Take action to control the project
- Measure performance against the performance measurement baseline
- Measure performance against other metrics determined by the project manager
- Determine variances and if they warrant a corrective action or change request
- Influence the factors that cause changes
- Request changes
- Perform integrated change control
- Approve or reject changes
- Inform stakeholders of the results of change requests
- Update the PM plan and project documents
- Manage configuration
- Create forecasts
- Gain acceptance of interim deliverables from the customer
- Perform quality control
- Report on project performance and solicit feedback
- Perform risk assessments and audits
- Manage reserves
- Administer procurements

CLOSING

- Confirm work is done to requirements
- Complete procurement closure
- Gain final acceptance of the product
- Complete financial closure
- Hand off completed product
- Solicit feedback from the customer about the project
- Complete final performance reporting
- Index and archive records
- Update lessons learned knowledge base

TRICKS OF THE TRADE® Human resources can be divided into administrative and behavioral management topics. Most of the answers to human resource questions should come from your everyday knowledge and work experience. Though you will see a lot of different topics described in this chapter, these concepts do not amount to a lot of questions on the exam. To study, read this chapter two or three times and simply make a list of the gaps in your knowledge as you read. After a couple of passes through this chapter, you will likely remember the information well enough for the high-level questions you will find on the exam.

The following should help you understand how each part of human resource management fits into the overall project management process:

The Human Resource Management Process	Done During
Develop Human Resource Plan	Planning process group
Acquire Project Team	Executing process group
Develop Project Team	Executing process group
Manage Project Team	Executing process group

Roles and Responsibilities PAGE 220 A project manager must clearly identify the roles and responsibilities of management, team members, and other stakeholders on the project, using tools like a responsibility assignment matrix to do so. Roles and responsibilities are discussed throughout this book, but this chapter summarizes many of the roles mentioned in other chapters. It is important to understand for the exam what different people involved in the project should be doing. Some who fail the exam do so because they do not really know what a project manager is, or at least do not understand how PMI defines the role of a project manager. They may also have problems differentiating between what the team, project manager, and management should be doing.

Exercise Test yourself! Describe the role of the project sponsor/initiator.

Answer

The Role of the Project Sponsor/Initiator A basic definition of a sponsor is one who provides the financial resources for the project, but the exam has attributed more duties to the sponsor than just providing the financial resources. If the project is being done for an outside customer (meaning you are the seller), the customer may be both the sponsor and the customer. In this case, some of the functions otherwise associated with the sponsor may be taken over by senior management in the performing organization. (Management is anyone senior to the project manager in the organization, including program or portfolio managers.)

Think about your company's management as you read this. Do they know what their role is on projects? Do you? How can you help them better understand their role? Without having the sponsor or someone in management performing the following functions, the project will suffer, wasting time and resources. Management must serve as a protector of the project.

Read over the following list carefully to understand the role and characteristics of the sponsor and/or senior management in an organization. Since the list is so long and since many project managers have gaps in their knowledge here, we have organized this section by process groups.

- During or prior to project initiating, the sponsor:
  - Has requirements that must be met.
  - Is a project stakeholder.
  - Advocates for or champions the project, especially while the project concept is being put together.
  - Serves as a voice of the project or spokesperson to those who do not know about the project, including upper management.
  - Gathers the appropriate support for the project.
  - Ensures buy-in throughout the organization.
  - Provides funding.
  - Provides the project statement of work (if not done by the customer).
  - Provides information regarding the initial scope of the project.
  - May dictate milestones, key events, or the project end date (along with the customer).
  - Determines the priorities between the constraints (if not done by the customer).
  - Provides information that helps develop the project charter.
  - Gives the project manager authority as outlined in the project charter.
  - Helps organize work into appropriate projects.
  - Sets priorities between projects.
  - Encourages the finalization of high-level requirements and scope by the stakeholders.
  - Guides the process to get the project approved and formalized, assisted by the project manager as necessary.
- During project planning, the sponsor:
  - Provides the project team with time to plan.
  - May review the WBS.
  - Supplies lists of risks.
  - Determines the reports needed by management to oversee the project.
  - Provides expert judgment.

    - Helps evaluate trade-offs during crashing, fast tracking, and reestimating.
    - Approves the final project management plan.
- During project executing and project monitoring and controlling, the sponsor:
    - Protects the project from outside influences and changes.
    - Enforces quality policies.
    - Provides expert judgment.
    - Helps evaluate trade-offs during crashing, fast tracking, and reestimating.
    - Resolves conflicts that extend beyond the project manager's control.
    - Approves or rejects changes or authorizes someone representing him or her to do so (change control board).
    - May direct that a quality assurance review be performed.
    - Clarifies scope questions.
    - Works with the project manager to monitor progress.
- During project closing, the sponsor:
    - Provides formal acceptance of the deliverables (if he or she is the customer).
    - Supports the collection of historical records from past projects.

Exercise Test yourself! Describe the role of the team.

Answer

The Role of the Team The team is a group of people who will complete work on the project. The team members can change throughout the project as people are added to and removed from the project.

Generally it is the team's role to help plan what needs to be done by creating the WBS and creating time estimates for their work packages or activities. During project executing and monitoring and controlling, the team members complete work packages or activities and help look for deviations from the project management plan. More specifically, the team may help:

- Identify and involve stakeholders.
- Identify requirements.

- Identify constraints and assumptions.
- Create the WBS.
- Decompose work packages for which they are responsible into schedule activities.
- Help identify dependencies between activities.
- Provide time and cost estimates.
- Participate in the risk management process.
- Comply with quality and communications plans.
- Help enforce ground rules.
- Execute the project management plan to accomplish work defined in the project scope statement.
- Attend project team meetings.
- Conduct process improvement.
- Recommend changes to the project, including corrective actions.

Some team members may have project management responsibilities in addition to responsibilities for implementing the work. If so, they are considered part of the project management team. See the role of the project manager for more about the project management team's responsibilities.

Exercise Test yourself! Describe the role of the stakeholders as a group.

Answer

The Role of the Stakeholders As described in the Project Management Framework chapter, a stakeholder is anyone who can positively or negatively influence the project, including the customer or users, the project manager and team, the project's sponsor, program and portfolio managers, the PMO, functional managers within the organization, and external sellers that provide services or materials for the project. The role of stakeholders and how they should be managed appears throughout the exam.

The stakeholders' role on a project is determined by the project manager and the stakeholders. Stakeholders should be involved in planning the project and managing it more extensively than many people are used to on their real-world projects. For example, stakeholders:

- May be involved in:
  - The creation of the project charter and the project scope statement.
  - Project management plan development.
  - Approving project changes and being on the change control board.
  - Identifying constraints.
  - Identifying requirements.
  - Risk management.
- May become risk response owners.

Exercise Test yourself! Describe the role of the functional manager.

Answer

The Role of the Functional Manager A functional manager manages and "owns" the resources in a specific department, such as IT, engineering, public relations, or marketing, and generally directs the technical work of individuals from that functional area who are working on the project.

The degree to which functional managers are involved in a project depends on the form of organizational structure. In a matrix organization, the functional managers share responsibility for directing the work of individuals with the project manager. In a projectized organization, the project manager does all of the directing. In contrast, the project manager does little directing in a functional organization, where that responsibility falls to functional managers. To avoid conflict, the project manager and functional managers must coordinate their respective needs regarding the use of resources to complete project work. It is generally the responsibility of the project manager to manage this relationship.

The specific activities performed by functional managers on a project vary greatly based on the type of organizational structure, as well as the type of project. They MAY include:

- Assign specific individuals to the team, and negotiate with the project manager regarding resources.
- Let the project manager know of other projects that may impact the project.
- Participate in the initial planning until work packages or activities are assigned.
- Provide subject matter expertise.
- Approve the final schedule during schedule development.
- Approve the final project management plan during project management plan development.
- Recommend changes to the project, including corrective actions.
- Manage activities within their functional area.
- Assist with problems related to team member performance.
- Improve staff utilization.

Exercise Test yourself! Describe the role of the project manager.

Answer

The Role of the Project Manager To put it simply, the project manager is responsible for managing the project to meet project objectives. Think about your role on projects. Do you do the things listed throughout this book? Do you have the knowledge, abilities, and authority described? Do you fully plan and control your projects? Are you the one person really in charge of the project?

In today's project environments, many people managing projects do not realize they lack knowledge of what proper project management involves, and many companies do not understand what project management is and why it is so important. People with the title of project manager are often not really project managers at all; instead, their role is more like a project coordinator (see the Project Management Framework chapter). Before taking the exam, it is important that you not only understand the project manager's role but also all the roles of other people involved in projects.

As we have discussed at other points in this book, there may be too much project management work for one person to perform on large projects. Therefore, the project manager may select some project team members to help perform the project management activities. The *PMBOK® Guide* refers to these people as the project management team. In order to assume this role, members of this team must have project management training. Keep this in mind when the exam uses the term "project management team" versus "project team" or just "team."

To avoid confusion, this book refers only to the project manager (meaning both the project manager and the project management team) or team (meaning everyone on the project team, not just those who perform project management activities).

The project manager's role is described throughout this book. As noted in the previous exercise about the functional manager's role, the project manager's level of authority can vary depending on the form of organization. On this exam, however, such authority has generally meant the project manager:

- Is assigned to the project no later than project initiating.
- Helps write the project charter.
- Is in charge of the project, but not necessarily the resources.
- Does not have to be a technical expert.
- Influences the project team and the atmosphere in which the team works by promoting good communication, insulating the team from having to deal with politics (both internal and external to the project), enhancing the positive aspects of cultural differences, and resolving team issues.
- Ensures professional interactions between the project team and other stakeholders.
- Coordinates interactions between the project and key stakeholders.
- Selects appropriate processes for the project.
- Identifies and analyzes constraints and assumptions.
- Leads and directs the project planning efforts.
- Identifies dependencies between activities.
- Must understand how to handle unrealistic schedule requirements to produce a realistic schedule.
- Understands and enforces professional and social responsibility.
- Identifies and delivers required levels of quality.
- Assists the team and other stakeholders during project executing.
- Defines the project change management plan.
- Maintains control over the project by measuring performance and determining if there are any variances from the plan.
- Determines the need for change requests, including recommended corrective and preventive actions and defect repair, and either approves or rejects changes as authorized or submits the change requests to the change control board.
- Uses metrics to see variances and trends in project work.
- Works with team members to resolve variances from the project management plan.
- Keeps the team members focused on risk management and possible responses to the risks.
- Develops time and cost reserves for the project.
- Must have the authority and accountability necessary to accomplish the project management work.
- Must say "no" when necessary.
- Is the only one who can integrate the project components into a cohesive whole that meets the customer's needs.
- Spends more time being proactive than dealing with problems (being reactive).

- Is accountable for project success or failure.
- Performs project closing at the end of each phase and for the project as a whole.
- Performs or delegates most of the activities outlined in this book.
- Overall, applies project management knowledge and uses personal and leadership skills to achieve project success.

Exercise Test yourself! Describe the role of the portfolio manager.

Answer

The Role of the Portfolio Manager The portfolio manager is responsible for governance at an executive level of the projects or programs that make up a portfolio. A project is included in a portfolio based on the value of the project, the potential return on investment, whether it meets the corporate strategy, whether the level of risk associated with the project is acceptable, and other factors critical to organizational success.

The role of the portfolio manager may include:

- Managing various projects or programs that may be largely unrelated to each other.
- Ensuring selected projects provide value to the organization.
- Working with senior executives to gather support for individual projects.
- Getting the best return from resources invested.

Exercise Test yourself! Describe the role of the program manager.

Answer

The Role of the Program Manager The program manager is responsible for managing a group of related projects. Projects are combined into programs to provide coordinated control, support, and guidance. The program manager works to meet project and program goals.

The role of the program manager may include:

- Managing related projects to achieve results not obtainable by managing each project separately.
- Ensuring selected projects support the strategic goals of the organization.
- Providing oversight to adjust projects for the program's benefit.
- Guiding and supporting individual project manager's efforts.

Exercise Test yourself! This exercise is designed to help you answer the situational questions on the exam dealing with project roles and responsibilities. If you disagree with some of the answers, make sure you are not reading something into the question (a bad habit you should discover before you take the exam) and assess whether it could indicate a gap in your project management knowledge.

Considering the previous discussion of roles, write the initials of the key person responsible for solving each of the problems in the following chart. Since much of the confusion of roles is between the team members (T), the project manager (PM), the sponsor (SP), and the functional manager (FM), this exercise is limited to those people. Remember, since the exam questions are typically based on what would happen in a matrix environment, keep matrix organizations in mind when considering these situations.

	Situation	Key Person
1	Two project team members are having a disagreement.	
2	There is a change to the overall project deliverable.	
3	A functional manager is trying to pull a team member off the project to do other work.	
4	The project manager does not have the authority to get things done.	
5	There are not enough resources to complete the project.	
6	The team is unsure of what needs to happen when.	
7	An activity needs more time and will cause the project to be delayed.	
8	An activity needs more time without causing the project to be delayed.	
9	A team member is not performing.	
10	The team is not sure who is in charge of the project.	
11	There is talk that the project may no longer be needed.	
12	The sponsor provides an unrealistic schedule objective.	
13	The team is in conflict over priorities between activities.	
14	The project is behind schedule.	
15	A team member determines that another method is needed to complete an activity.	
16	The project is running out of funds.	
17	Additional work is added to the project that will add cost and was not identified during the risk management process.	

Answer

	Situation	Key Person
1	Two project team members are having a disagreement. *The people involved in the conflict should attempt to solve it themselves.*	T
2	There is a change to the overall project deliverable. *This is a change to the project charter. Only the sponsor can approve changes to the project charter.*	SP
3	A functional manager is trying to pull a team member off the project to do other work. *The project manager must give team members enough information (e.g., schedule, network diagram, project management plan, risks) so that they can manage their own workloads. Because the word "trying" is used, we know this situation is occurring at the present time. If the question had used the words "has pulled," the answer would be project manager. Read situational questions carefully.*	T
4	The project manager does not have the authority to get things done. *It is the sponsor's role to give the project manager authority via the project charter.*	SP
5	There are not enough resources to complete the project. *The sponsor and functional manager control resources.*	SP/FM
6	The team is unsure of what needs to happen when. *It is the project manager's role to take the individual estimates, combine them into the project schedule, and communicate that schedule to team members.*	PM
7	An activity needs more time and will cause the project to be delayed. *Notice the word "will." This means the evaluation by the team is completed and there is no available reserve since the project completion date is most likely included in the project charter. Any such changes are changes to the project charter and require sponsor involvement.*	SP
8	An activity needs more time without causing the project to be delayed. *Think about integrated change control here. It is the project manager's role to look for impacts to the other project constraints.*	PM
9	A team member is not performing. *In a matrix environment, both the project manager and the functional manager share responsibility for directing resources.*	PM/FM
10	The team is not sure who is in charge of the project. *The sponsor designates the project manager in the project charter.*	SP
11	There is talk that the project may no longer be needed. *It is the sponsor's role to protect the project from changes, including such a large change as termination.*	SP

	Situation	Key Person
12	The sponsor provides an unrealistic schedule objective. *Only the sponsor can make a change to the project charter (including schedule objectives). The project manager must provide evidence that the schedule is unrealistic.*	SP
13	The team is in conflict over priorities between activities. *It is the project manager's role to settle any such conflicts between activities and to provide a network diagram and critical path. It is the sponsor's or program/portfolio manager's role to set priorities between projects.*	PM
14	The project is behind schedule. *Only the project manager can control the overall project schedule.*	PM
15	A team member determines that another method is needed to complete an activity. *The team member has control over his or her activities as long as the team member meets the time, quality, cost, and scope objectives set up with the project manager. The team member must keep the project manager informed of these changes so the project manager can integrate them into the rest of the project and look for any impacts.*	T
16	The project is running out of funds. *It is the sponsor's role to provide funding for the project.*	SP
17	Additional work is added to the project that will add cost and was not identified during the risk management process. *The fact that the change was not identified in the risk management process and is additional work means it was not included in the original project budget (or the budget reserve). Therefore, the sponsor must be involved in providing additional funds.*	SP

If you got many of the answers wrong, you should reread the roles and responsibilities discussions and the exact wording of the situations presented here. With such a brief description, you could easily have thought the question meant something different than was intended. You may have preferred the word "decide" or the words "make the final decision" in place of "solve" in some of these questions. This exercise should help prepare you to interpret questions on the exam. It is meant to make you think!

Human Resource Responsibilities for Project Managers This chapter and the Professional and Social Responsibility chapter discuss how a project manager needs to manage and interact with team members. Make sure you connect the ideas in these two chapters in your mind. The Professional and Social Responsibility chapter presents a high-level discussion, while this chapter gets into more detail.

TRICKS OF THE TRADE® The trick to correctly answering exam questions about this topic is to realize that, as a project manager, you have responsibilities regarding team members. Some of these are ethical responsibilities described in the Professional and Social Responsibility chapter, while others are administrative. The best way to approach administrative responsibilities is to think of your team as if they are employees who report directly to you. Project managers have some responsibilities similar to those of a manager or "owner" of the resources.

The following is a list of the responsibilities project managers most often do not know about before preparing for this exam. Read the list carefully for PMI-isms. (Do you recognize any of the points from the first chapter of this book? If so, good—you read it well. It is important to understand PMI-isms!)

- Determine what resources you will need.
- Negotiate with resource managers for the optimal available resources.
- Create a project team directory.
- Create project job descriptions for team members and other stakeholders.
- Make sure all roles and responsibilities on the project are clearly assigned.
- Understand the team members' needs for training related to their work on the project, and make sure they get the training.
- Create a formal plan covering such topics as how the team will be involved in the project and what roles they will perform—a human resource plan.
- Insert reports of team members' performance into their official company employment record.
- Send out letters of commendation to team members and their bosses.
- Make sure team members' needs are taken care of.
- Create recognition and reward systems—described in the Human Resource Plan section of this chapter.

Develop Human Resource Plan PAGE 218

Process: Develop Human Resource Plan
Process Group: Planning
Knowledge Area: Human Resource Management

A common complaint of team members is that roles and responsibilities are not clearly defined on a project. The definition of roles and responsibilities should happen as part of the Develop Human Resource Plan process. Project work often includes more than just completing work packages. It may also include responsibilities like assisting with risk, quality, and project management activities. Team members need to know what work packages and activities they are assigned to, what skills they need to have, when they are expected to report, what meetings they will be required to attend, and any other "work" they will be asked to do on the project.

The Develop Human Resource Plan process involves using or creating the following items.

Enterprise Environmental Factors PAGE 219 Before you develop a human resource plan, you need to understand what enterprise environmental factors can come into play. Remember that this term means company culture and existing systems the project will have to deal with or can make use of. For this process, you should take into account factors such as:

- What organizations will be involved in the project?
- Are there hidden agendas?
- Is there anyone who does not want the project?
- What is the availability of contract help?
- What is the availability of training for project team members?

For most experienced project managers, this is common sense. They already consider such things on their projects, even if they have not called them enterprise environmental factors.

Organizational Process Assets PAGE 219 You also need to consider organizational process assets (processes, procedures, and historical information) in developing the human resource plan. Wouldn't it be great to have a template that describes the common responsibilities on projects like yours so that you do not forget to assign those responsibilities? How about having historical information from past projects? These assets can help increase the efficiency of the Develop Human Resource Plan process, as well as the effectiveness of the resulting plan.

Organization Charts and Position Descriptions PAGE 220-221 WITH ILLUSTRATIONS As stated earlier, any roles and responsibilities that are expected of team members, such as project management team assignments, reporting requirements, or meeting attendance, need to be clearly assigned, in addition to the project activities the team members are expected to complete. In other words, all efforts the project team might expend should be determined in advance. If you work on small projects, you might never have taken the time to do this. Spend a moment now thinking about how much time this effort (and other efforts in this book) might take on a large project. There are a lot of ways to record and communicate roles and responsibilities, including responsibility assignment matrices, organizational breakdown structures, resource breakdown structures, and position descriptions. Know these options for the exam and the information each tool displays so that you can answer questions like the following:

Question *A responsibility assignment matrix does not show _____.*

Answer *When people will do their jobs (time)*

Responsibility Assignment Matrix[1] PAGE 220

This chart cross-references team members with the activities or work packages they are to accomplish. Here is an example:

Activity	Team Member			
	Jeri	Mary	Erica	Jude
A	P		S	
B		S		P

Key: P = Primary responsibility, S = Secondary responsibility

RACI Chart (Responsible, Accountable, Consult, and Inform) PAGE 221 This chart is a type of responsibility assignment matrix that defines role assignments more clearly than the previous example. Instead of the P and S shown in the previous matrix, the letters R for Responsible, A for Accountable, C for Consult, and I for Inform are used.

Organizational Breakdown Structure[2]

This chart shows responsibilities by department. See the following diagram.

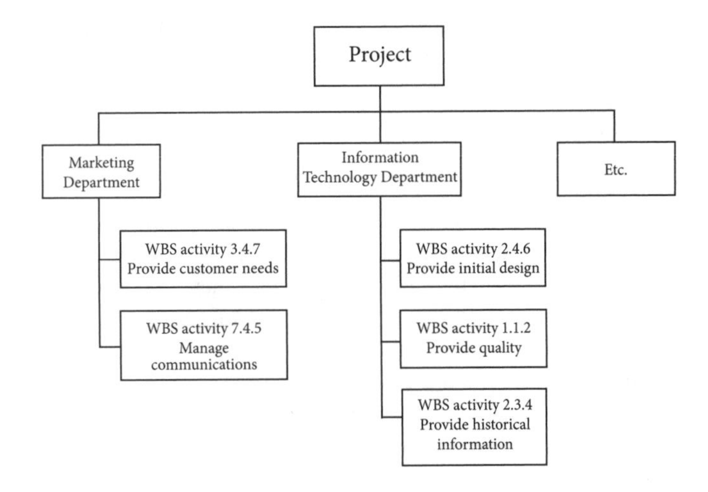

Resource Breakdown Structure

The resource breakdown structure breaks the work down by type of resource. See the following diagram.

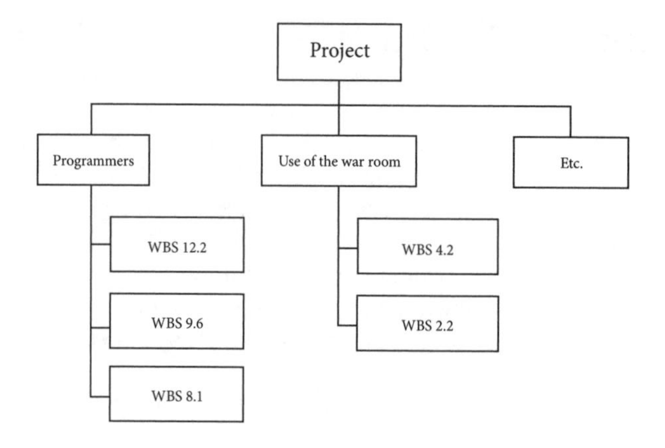

Position Descriptions

Position descriptions are usually documented in text format. If you haven't used these on your projects, imagine a common job description, but created only for project work.

Human Resource Plan PAGE 222 The result (output) of the Develop Human Resource Plan process is, of course, a human resource plan. If you manage small projects, think for a moment about what the human resource management effort would involve on a large project that has 300 human resources assigned to it. Would it take more work than you are doing now to manage human resources on your project? Large projects require a plan for when and how team members will be added, managed, controlled, and released from the project. This is what the human resource plan does.

The human resource plan includes:

- Roles and responsibilities (described earlier in this chapter)
- Project organization charts (described earlier in this chapter)
- Staffing management plan (described next)

Staffing Management Plan[3]

Large projects with hundreds of resources require a staffing management plan. This plan, which is part of the human resource plan, includes:

- Your plan for staff acquisition (Where will they come from?)
- Resource calendars (When are people available? When will they be used?)
- Staff release plan (When will resources be released and no longer be charged to the project?)
- Staff training needs (What training do the resources need?)
- Recognition and rewards (What are they? What are the criteria for their use?)
- Compliance (How will the project comply with any rules related to human resources?)
- Safety (What policies protect the resources?)

The exam does not often ask questions as simple as, "What is included in…?" Rather, the questions jump right into more sophisticated issues to test if you really understand and use an item on your projects. You might have trouble with such questions if you have never created a staffing management plan. Take some time to imagine what this plan would look like and how it would be used.

Recognition and Reward Systems Recognition and reward systems, which are part of the staffing management plan, are something that many project managers have never thought of on their real-world projects, but this concept is tested on the exam. Planning a system to reward resources on a large project can be a significant effort.

A project manager must be able to motivate the team, especially when working on a project in a matrix organization. Have you ever wondered, "How do I get improved performance from people who do not report directly to me in the organization?" If your team members are not motivated, it is nearly impossible to be effective as a project manager. This is not to say that great project managers do not have issues with motivating people, but they have the tools and knowledge to prevent and to deal with such problems. A recognition and reward system is one of these tools. It is one of the most effective ways to motivate and gain cooperation from your team, regardless of the reporting relationship. (Motivation concepts are discussed in more detail later in this chapter.)

To create a recognition and reward system, ask yourself how you will motivate and reward not the team, but each team member individually. This involves asking what your team members and stakeholders want to get out of the project, on a professional and personal level. They might respond with such things as, "I want to learn more about XYZ," "I want to decrease the time I am allocated to this project," "I want to make sure I leave work on time on Tuesday nights because I have a family obligation," or "I want to be assigned a certain piece of the project work." Asking such questions about what a team member hopes to gain from a project is a required, not optional, part of managing a project.

The project manager takes his or her knowledge of the needs of the stakeholders and then creates a recognition and reward system. Such a system might include the following actions:

- Say "thank you" more often.
- Award prizes such as Team Member of the Month recognition.
- Award prizes for performance.
- Recommend team members for raises or choice work assignments, even though such actions by the project manager may not officially be part of the team members' performance reviews.
- Send notes to team members' managers about great performance.
- Plan milestone parties or other celebrations.
- Acquire training for team members, paid for out of the project budget.
- Adjust the project to assign people to activities they have been wanting to work on or remove them from disliked activities as a reward.
- Work with the boss to have a team member removed from the project as a reward if they feel they want or need to, and if other resources are available.
- Assign a team member to a non-critical path activity so that he or she can gain more knowledge in that area.

The list can go on and on, but ask yourself, "Do I do any of these things? Do I do them systematically?" Creating a recognition and reward system requires planning in advance of starting the project work.

Resource Histogram PAGE 224 The staffing management plan, as part of the human resource plan, may also include visual representations of information, like a resource histogram. This bar chart shows the number of resources used per time period and where there is a spike in the need for resources. With such information, the project manager can arrange for the resources necessary at that time or change the project to minimize the peaks and valleys of resource usage (level the resources). The following diagram is an example of a resource histogram.

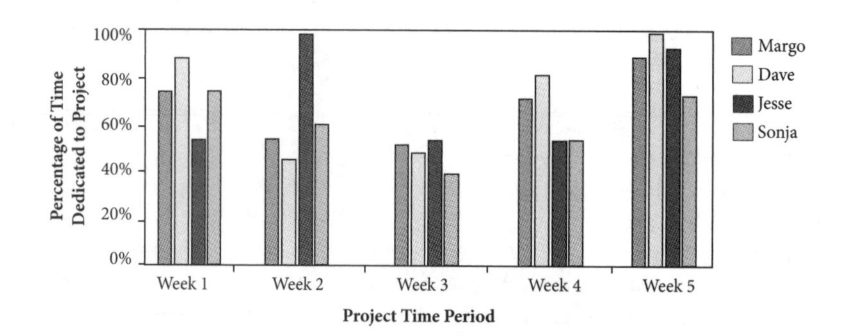

Acquire Project Team PAGE 225

Process: Acquire Project Team
Process Group: Executing
Knowledge Area: Human Resource Management

You have been working hard and are now half asleep. WAKE UP! The Acquire Project Team process can be confusing, especially since it occurs during project executing. "What?" you might say, "That does not make sense!" The team is required to plan the project, and the team is acquired early in planning, so how can this be an executing process? Once again, remember the *PMBOK® Guide* is referring to large projects. When hundreds of resources are needed for a project, the actual people who will be doing some of the work may not be selected until shortly before the work is to begin. The final team might include contractors or sellers, or people who will work on the project years into the future and may not even be employed by the company until needed.

You should read the phrase "acquire project team" as "acquire final project team."

Remember that on a properly managed project, team members need to have input into the project, including what work needs to be done, when, at what cost, what the risks may be, etc., no matter when they get involved in the project. Great project managers will invite new team members to review their part of the project for changes before they start work. People perform better when they have input, rather than simply being told what to do.

The inputs to the Acquire Project Team process include:

- **Project management plan** Or more specifically, the human resource plan that is part of the project management plan
- **Enterprise environmental factors** Including who is available, whether they work well together, if they want to work on the project, how much they cost, and outsourcing policies
- **Organizational process assets** Including policies for using staff on projects and hiring procedures

Acquiring the project team involves the following:

- Knowing which resources are preassigned to the project and confirming their availability
- Negotiating for the best possible resources
- Hiring new employees
- Hiring resources through the contracting process from outside the performing organization—outsourcing
- Understanding the possibilities and problems with using virtual teams—teams made up of people who never or rarely meet
- Managing the risk of resources becoming unavailable

Preassignment As noted in the previous list, sometimes resources are assigned in advance to the project. A project manager has to work with the resources he or she is given as part of the team.

Negotiation PAGE 227 When resources are not preassigned, they may be acquired through negotiation. You will see negotiation frequently referenced on the exam as it relates to gaining resources from within your organization and in procurement situations. To negotiate for resources from within the organization, the project manager should do the following:

- Know the needs of the project and its priority within the organization.
- Be able to express how the resource's manager will benefit from assisting the project manager.
- Understand that the resource's manager has his or her own work to do and that the individual may not gain benefits from supporting the project.
- Do not ask for the best resources if the project does not need them.
- Be able to prove, by using project management tools such as the network diagram and project schedule, why the project requires the stated quantity and quality of resources.
- Use the negotiation as an opportunity to discover what the resource's manager will need from the project manager in order to manage his or her own resources.
- Build a relationship so the project manager can call on the resource's manager's expertise later in the project if necessary.
- Work with the resource's manager to deal with situations as they arise.

Notice the previous list goes beyond traditional negotiation strategy and includes elements of professional responsibility. Although chapter 13 focuses on professional and social responsibility, the topic is discussed throughout this book and is relevant in every part of a project manager's job.

Resources can also be acquired from outside the organization from external vendors, suppliers, contractors, etc. Your organization or the other parties' organizations may have procurement and negotiating polices and procedures for the acquisition of resources. (See the Procurement Management chapter for information related to procuring resources from outside sources.)

Virtual Teams Not all teams meet face to face. Teams that do not meet face to face are called virtual teams. Think of the opportunity for the project if you can reach out to the whole world to find the best team members! The exam may ask why virtual teams might be helpful and describe some situations that involve virtual teams, but do not expect this topic to be as significant a concern on the exam as it may be on your projects.

Halo Effect[4] The "halo effect" is something to be aware of when dealing with team members. There can be a tendency to rate team members high or low on all factors due to the impression of a high or low rating on some specific factor. This can mean, "You are a great programmer. Therefore, we will make you a project manager and expect you to be great at that as well." Since these people may not, in fact, be qualified for the new position, such assumptions can have a negative impact on the project schedule, cost, and quality and should be avoided.

The results or outputs of the Aquire Project Team process include project staff or work assignments, resource calendars that show the resources' availability, and changes to the human resource plan and other components of the project management plan resulting from acquiring additional staff.

Develop Project Team PAGE 229

Process: Develop Project Team
Process Group: Executing
Knowledge Area: Human Resource Management

The Develop Project Team process is done as part of project executing. This process should result in decreased turnover, improved individual knowledge and skills, and improved teamwork.

Exercise What do you think the project manager needs to do to develop a project team?

Answer Did you try to do this exercise, or did you plan to skip over it to look at the answer? The only effective way to find gaps in your knowledge is to test your knowledge before you look at the answers.

You may do some of the following things on your real-world projects, but you might not plan them in or do them consistently or consciously. These activities are part of proper project management. Keep them in mind for the exam to help you understand the situations described. Remember to assume that proper project management was done unless the exam says otherwise.

A major role of the project manager is to ensure the project team is working together as effectively and efficiently as possible. Your answer could include:

- Use many soft skills, including mentoring, leadership, empathy, communication, etc.
- Encourage teamwork.
- Communicate honestly, effectively, and in a timely manner with the people assigned to your team. (See more on this topic in the Communications Management chapter.)
- Establish and maintain trust between the project manager and each team member, and between all stakeholders.
- Collaborate with the team to make good, bought-into decisions and to find mutually beneficial solutions to problems.

- Capitalize on cultural differences.
- Hold team-building activities from project initiating through project closing.
- Provide training for team members where needed.
- Establish ground rules for team member behavior.
- Create and give recognition and rewards.
- Place team members in the same location (co-location).
- Assess team member performance.
- Improve team performance.
- Motivate.
- Improve team members' knowledge.
- Create a team culture.

Team-Building Activities Team-building activities can play a major role in team development. Such activities help form the project team into a cohesive group working for the best interest of the project, to enhance project performance. Make sure you know:

- It is the project manager's job to guide, manage, and improve the interactions of team members.
- The project manager should improve trust and cohesiveness among the team members.
- The project manager should incorporate team-building activities into all project activities.
- Team building requires a concerted effort and continued attention throughout the life of the project.
- WBS creation is a team-building tool.
- Team building should start early in the life of the project.

Let's go back to the concept of trust. First think of project problems you have recently experienced. Now ask yourself the following questions: "Could these problems be caused by a lack of trust? Do team members trust each other? Do they trust me?" Your team needs to feel that you are working in the best interest of the project, the company, and them, rather than for your own best interest. Trust is gained or lost from the minute you meet each team member for the first time. If the team does not trust you, you cannot easily be successful; the team will not take your direction or follow your instructions, and the project will suffer. Once you have trust, it can easily be lost if you are not honest and consistent. Many project managers never think of trust. Imagine you work in a matrix organization. How do you get people to cooperate if you do not have the ability to give them a raise or a promotion? Trust, as well as a recognition and reward system, are the answers.

Trust also affects and is affected by your reputation. Do you know what your reputation is? Many of the people you meet know. Why not ask, so you can deal with any changes you need to make?

Team building is a concept that appears throughout the exam. It is an attitude, as well as an action. Do you have the attitude of helping to build the team, or do you think of the team members as just workers to do things for you? Some project managers think team building is a minor activity; they bring in lunch for the team once during their three-year project and believe they have done team building.

Team building, like many parts of project management, is in part a science. There are even formally identified stages of team formation and development. These stages are:[5]

- **Forming** People are brought together as a team.
- **Storming** There are disagreements as people learn to work together.
- **Norming** Team members begin to build good working relationships.
- **Performing** The team becomes efficient and works effectively together. This is the point when the project manager can give the most attention to developing individual team members.
- **Adjourning** The project ends, and the team is disbanded.

New teams may go through each step, while teams that have worked together before may experience a shortened version or skip some of the early steps.

Team building is an ongoing activity that you should be thinking about before you even have a team, and it does not end until project closure. Project managers who feel they do not have time for team building typically are not using proper project management on their projects. Practices like properly planning a project and managing risks and quality save significant amounts of time on a project and free up the project manager to do other important things, like team-building activities. When you take the exam, assume the project manager featured in the questions has an extensive team-building plan.

Team-building activities can include:

- Taking classes together.
- Milestone parties.
- Holiday and birthday celebrations.
- Outside-of-work trips.
- Creating the WBS.
- Getting everyone involved in some way in planning the project.

Training Any training needed by team members in order to perform on the project or to enhance their performance is a project cost. It should be paid for by the project and documented in the human resource plan. The project manager should look for such opportunities not only to help team members, but also to decrease the overall project cost and schedule by increasing efficiency.

Ground Rules PAGE 233 What about trying to do something about the negative impacts of bad behavior? Think about your real-world projects. What behavior is acceptable and what is not acceptable on your project? What standards of behavior do you expect for team members' interactions with each other? What are the project's rules? Ground rules help establish standards and expectations for the team. These rules can address things such as:

- Honesty in all communications.
- The way a team member should resolve a conflict with another team member.
- When a team member should notify the project manager that he or she is having difficulty with an activity.
- Whether it is allowable for people to interrupt one another in a meeting.
- What are acceptable ways to interrupt someone talking during a meeting.
- How to prevent people from taking over a meeting inappropriately or talking too much.
- Whether people can join a meeting late, and the consequences for late attendance.
- Whether people can take other phone calls, look at e-mails, or read text messages during the meeting.
- Who is allowed to talk to the vice president about the project.
- Who is authorized to give direction to contractors.
- When and how to provide status to the project manager.
- The methods to coordinate and approve changes to team members' calendars, both in normal and emergency situations.

Setting ground rules can help eliminate conflicts or problems with the team during the project because everyone knows what is expected of them. Ground rules are especially important when the team is managed virtually.

Co-location (or War Room) PAGE 234 A project manager might try to arrange for the entire team in each city to have offices together in one place or one room. This is called co-location and helps improve communication, decreases the impact of conflict (since all parties are right there), and improves project identity for the project team and for management in a matrix organization. A war room is a central location for project coordination, usually with the WBS, network diagram, schedule, etc., posted on the walls.

Recognition and Rewards In the Develop Project Team process, the project manager appraises performance and gives out team-member-appropriate recognition and rewards, as defined in the human resource plan.

Team Performance Assessment The project manager completes formal and informal team performance assessments as part of developing the project team. These assessments are meant to evaluate and enhance the effectiveness of the team as a whole. They may include an analysis of how much team members' skills have improved; how well the team is performing, interacting, and dealing with conflict; and the turnover rate.

Think of team performance assessment as looking at "team effectiveness."

Manage Project Team PAGE 236

Process: Manage Project Team
Process Group: Executing
Knowledge Area: Human Resource Management

The Manage Project Team process is also done during project executing. It involves all the day-to-day management of people that you are likely already doing on your projects. Managing the project team is different from developing the team. The Manage Project Team process involves the following actions to help challenge team members to be part of a superior performing team:

- Encouraging good communication (see the Communications Management chapter)
- Working with other organizations
- Using negotiation skills
- Using leadership skills
- Observing what is happening
- Using an issue log
- Keeping in touch
- Completing project performance appraisals (described later in this section)
- Making good decisions
- Influencing the stakeholders
- Being a leader
- Actively looking for and helping resolve conflicts that the team members cannot resolve on their own

Although the concepts here are not hard, you may still have some gaps in your knowledge about this topic. Think about your real-world projects. Do you have your team help create the project management plan? Does it seem realistic to do so? What happens if you do not use the team's help? Does that make it harder to manage the team? Of course, and the difference can be astronomical! Now let's think about professional responsibility. Is it ethical to reprimand or penalize someone for not performing when they were not given clear roles or a clear WBS dictionary? If someone did not agree to a time, cost, or even scope limitation, they are not likely to support it or meet it. That is why, on a properly managed project, the project team helps to create the project management plan. Because they are involved in developing the plan, the team members can take on the attitude of, "I helped create this plan, so I do not mind being held to what I agreed to." If, on your real-world projects, you have ever had difficulty gaining cooperation, could it have been due to a lack of trust, a poor (or nonexistent) recognition and reward system, or the team and stakeholders not being involved in creating the plan?

There are many concepts that can appear on the exam about managing people. The following is a summary.

Observation and Conversation Do you have a tendency to sit in your office and issue reports, rather than watch what is going on? Even though your team might be virtual, paying attention to the tone of e-mails and phone conversations, for example, will tell you more about what is going on than simply looking at reports. A project manager should watch what is happening and specifically talk to people to understand how things are going.

Project Performance Appraisals Project performance appraisals are evaluations of employees' performance by those who supervise them. This is a common business practice around the world. Such evaluations should include the employees' work on projects. The project manager may adjust the project to handle changes in performance based on these appraisals.

A new and sophisticated way to complete a performance appraisal is to include the input of coworkers and subordinates, as well as supervisors. This may result in a clearer picture of actual performance and is called a 360-degree review.

NOTE: The concept of project performance appraisals assumes supervisors separately evaluate performance on projects in addition to the day-to-day work of their employees. Unfortunately, this level of support may not be present in your organization. In addition, it assumes the team member is also being supervised by someone other than the project manager (a matrix organization).

TRICKS OF THE TRADE® There are two similar concepts in this chapter that can be confusing: team performance assessment and project performance appraisals. Project performance appraisals are a technique of the Manage Project Team process. In this effort, the project manager collects information from team members' supervisors and adjusts the project accordingly. The focus is on the individual. In contrast, team performance assessment, a technique of the Develop Project Team process, focuses on team performance, not the individual. Team performance assessment is done by the project manager in order to evaluate and improve the effectiveness of the team as a whole.

Issue Log Issue logs can be used in managing team members and stakeholders. Such a register indicates to people that their needs will be considered, even if they are not addressed at the time the issue arises. Effective project managers control issues so they do not impact the project.

An issue log might look like the following:

Issue #	Issue	Date Added	Raised By	Person Assigned	Resolution Due Date	Status	Date Resolved	Resolution

The *PMBOK® Guide* lists issue logs as a tool and technique of Manage Project Team, but many project managers use this tool on a broader scale, for issues that arise across the project, not just those related to human resources. An issue log, also known as an issue register, can be used to communicate what the issues are on the project, as well as assess the causes of the issues, their impacts on the project (e.g., on scope, time, cost, risk, etc.), and corrective actions that could be taken. Issue resolutions should be recorded in the register, including the results of corrective actions.

The exam may use words or phrases that are unfamiliar to you when it describes situations and the people involved in them. Read over the following section to make sure you are generally familiar with the terms listed. This will help you understand what it means when the exam states such things as, "The project manager was delegating," "The project manager was being consultative-autocratic," or "What leadership style should be used in this situation?"

Powers of the Project Manager This section could be titled, "How to get cooperation from the team and stakeholders." Project managers almost always have difficulty getting people to cooperate and perform, especially if they are working in a matrix organization. Understanding the following types of power can help:

- **Formal (Legitimate)** This power is based on your position. Example: "You need to listen to me when I tell you to do this work, because I have been put in charge!"
- **Reward** This power stems from giving rewards. Example: "I understand that you want to participate in the acceptance testing of this project. Because of your performance, I will assign you as part of that team."
- **Penalty (Coercive)** This power comes from the ability to penalize team members. Example: "If this does not get done on time, I will remove you from the group going to Hawaii for the customer meeting."
- **Expert** This power comes from being the technical or project management expert. Example: "I hear the project manager has been very successful on other projects. Let's give her a chance!"
- **Referent** This power comes from another person liking you, respecting you, or wanting to be like you. It is the power of charisma and fame. Example: The most liked and respected project manager in the organization says, "I think we should change the content of our standard project charter."

NOTE: The best forms of power are EXPERT and REWARD. Penalty is the worst form. FORMAL, REWARD, and PENALTY are powers derived from your position in the company. EXPERT power is earned on your own.

On the exam, expect questions that describe a situation and then ask what you should do. The options have included solutions using various forms of power. To answer these questions, know that penalty is generally an incorrect choice, but make sure it isn't the most appropriate choice for the particular situation described.

Management and Leadership Styles The exam talks about management, leadership, and leadership styles by using the terms discussed in this section. However, there is no one "right" way to lead or manage that fits all situations or all project managers. Project managers should know the science of project management and make educated decisions about what they are doing, even when it comes to interacting with and managing people. To choose the most effective approach, you must consider your personal style; the skill levels, experience, and needs of your team members; and the complexity of the project work you are managing.

TRICKS OF THE TRADE® You will likely need to use many leadership approaches throughout the life of a project. The term "situational leadership" refers to a manager using different leadership styles, based on the people and project work he or she is dealing with. For example, there is a general consensus that a project manager needs to provide more direction (directing leadership style) at the beginning of the project, because only the project manager knows the project management work that must be done to plan the project. During project executing, the project manager needs to do more coaching, facilitating, and supporting.

You should be aware of the following terms related to leadership and management styles. Read the following definitions two or three times so you are familiar with the terms before you see them on the exam.

- **Directing** This style involves telling others what to do.
- **Facilitating** When facilitating, the project manager coordinates the input of others.
- **Coaching** In coaching, the manager helps others achieve their goals.

- **Supporting** A supporting leadership style means the project manager provides assistance along the way.
- **Autocratic** This is a top-down approach where the manager has power to do whatever he or she wants. The manager may coach or delegate, but everyone does what the manager wants them to do.
- **Consultative** This bottom-up approach uses influence to achieve results. The manager obtains others' opinions and acts as the servant for the team.
- **Consultative-Autocratic** In this style, the manager solicits input from team members, but retains decision-making authority for him- or herself.
- **Consensus** This style involves problem solving in a group, and making decisions based on group agreement.
- **Delegating** With a delegating style, the manager establishes goals and then gives the project team sufficient authority to complete the work. For basic project management, the manager involves the team in the planning process and assigns or delegates planning work and executing work to team members. Delegating can be hard for some people, because they feel they can do the work better themselves. Using proper project management practices should help a project manager feel comfortable that others know what needs to be done and that the project can be successful.
- **Bureaucratic** This style focuses on following procedures exactly. The bureaucratic style may be appropriate for work in which details are critical or in which specific safety or other regulations must be strictly adhered to.
- **Charismatic** Charismatic managers energize and encourage their team in performing project work. With this style, project success may become dependent on the presence of the charismatic leader, and the team relies on the leader for motivation.
- **Democratic or Participative** This style involves encouraging team participation in the decision-making process. Team members "own" the decisions made by the group, which results in improved teamwork and cooperation.
- ***Laissez-faire*** The French term "*laissez-faire*" has been translated as meaning "allow to act," "allow to do," or "leave alone." A *laissez-faire* manager is not directly involved in the work of the team, but manages and consults as necessary. This style can be appropriate with a highly skilled team.
- **Analytical** This style depends on the manager's own technical knowledge and ability. Analytical managers often make the technical decisions for the project, which they communicate to their teams. Interview-style communication, in which the project manager asks questions to get the facts, is common with this management style.
- **Driver** A manager with a driver style is constantly giving directions. His or her competitive attitude drives the team to win.
- **Influencing** This style emphasizes teamwork, team building, and team decision making. These managers work with their teams to influence project implementation.

Conflict Management PAGE 239 As discussed earlier, most of the questions on the exam are situational. Many of those situations involve conflicts. Therefore, to be able to pick the best choice from many "right" answers, you should understand different conflict resolution techniques and be able to determine which one is best for the situation.

First, let's think about conflict. Is it bad? Should we spend time preventing the root causes of conflict? Who should resolve the conflict?

Try to answer the questions just posed. Get them right, and you are likely to do well on this part of the exam. The answers are no; yes; and those who have the conflict, possibly assisted by the project manager.

Although we often think conflict is bad, it actually presents opportunities for improvement. This is another situation where many people have a different understanding of a concept than what is stated in currently accepted research. Make sure your basic thinking about conflict is on the new side and not the old.

Changing Views of Conflict	
Old	**New**
Conflict is dysfunctional and caused by personality differences or a failure of leadership.	Conflict is an inevitable consequence of organizational interactions.
Conflict is to be avoided.	Conflict can be beneficial.
Conflict is resolved by physical separation or the intervention of upper management.	Conflict is resolved through openness, identifying the causes, and problem solving by the people involved and their immediate managers.

Conflict is INEVITABLE because of the:

- Nature of projects trying to address the needs and requirements of many stakeholders
- Limited power of the project manager
- Necessity of obtaining resources from functional managers

The project manager has a professional responsibility as part of basic project management to attempt to avoid conflicts through the following actions:

- Informing the team of:
  - Exactly where the project is headed
  - Project constraints and objectives
  - The contents of the project charter
  - All key decisions
  - Changes
- Clearly assigning work without ambiguity or overlapping responsibilities
- Making work assignments interesting and challenging
- Following good project management and project planning practices

Note what we just stated: many conflicts can be avoided. Do you do the things on the previous list? Did you ever realize the project manager has a professional responsibility to do such things? They are not optional; they are good project management.

Many people think the main source of conflict on a project is personality differences. They may be surprised to learn that this is rarely the case. It only becomes personal if the root cause of the problem is not resolved. The following describes the seven sources of conflict in order of frequency. MEMORIZE the top four, and remember that personality is last:

1. Schedules
2. Project priorities
3. Resources
4. Technical opinions
5. Administrative procedures
6. Cost
7. Personality

Conflict is best resolved by those involved in the conflict. The project manager should generally try to resolve problems and conflict as long as he or she has authority over those in conflict or the issues in conflict. If not, the sponsor or functional managers may be called in to assist. There is one exception. In instances of professional and social responsibility (breaking laws, policies, ethics), the project manager must go over the head of the person in conflict.

When you have questions on the exam relating to conflict management, make sure you first think, "Who generally has authority over the situation described in this question?" Another good phrase to remember is, "What resolution of this problem would best serve the customer's interests?"

The following are the main conflict resolution techniques to know for the exam. Notice that some have more than one title; you should know both.

- **Confronting (Problem Solving)** First, did you notice that this technique has two names? Did you realize that both names mean the same thing? This has confused many people because, at first glance, these two terms do not seem to mean the same thing. Confronting means solving the real problem so that the problem goes away. Confronting leads to a win-win situation.
- **Compromising** This technique involves finding solutions that bring some degree of satisfaction to both parties. This is a lose-lose situation, since no party gets everything. Did you know that compromise is not the best choice, but rather second to confronting?
- **Withdrawal (Avoidance)** In this technique, the parties retreat or postpone a decision on a problem. Dealing with problems is a PMI-ism; therefore, withdrawal is not usually the BEST choice for resolving conflict.
- **Smoothing (Accommodating)** This technique emphasizes agreement rather than differences of opinion.
- **Collaborating** In this technique, the parties try to incorporate multiple viewpoints in order to lead to consensus.
- **Forcing** This technique involves pushing one viewpoint at the expense of another.

Remember to look for confronting or problem-solving choices as generally the best answers, and forcing as the worst, but realize the answer depends on the situation described. There could be situations where withdrawal is the best option.

Exercise Read the description of a conflict resolution, and try to determine which of the techniques is being used.

	Description	Form of Conflict Resolution This Represents
1	"It seems the real problem here is not a lack of communication, but a lack of knowledge of what needs to be done and when. Here is a copy of the project schedule. It should help you understand what you need to know."	
2	"Do it my way!"	
3	"Let's calm down and get the job done!"	
4	"Let us do a little of what both of you suggest."	
5	"Let's deal with this issue next week."	
6	"Carly and Amanda, both of you want this project to cause as little distraction to your departments as possible. With that in mind, I am sure we can come to an agreement on the purchase of equipment and what is best for the project."	
7	"We have talked about new computers enough. I do not want to get the computers, and that is it!"	

	Description	Form of Conflict Resolution This Represents
8	"Carly, you say the project should include the purchase of new computers, and Amanda, you say the project can use existing equipment. I suggest we perform the following test on the existing equipment to determine if it needs to be replaced."	
9	"Let's see what everyone thinks, and try to reach a consensus."	
10	"Since we cannot decide on the purchase of new computers, we will have to wait until our meeting next month."	
11	"Carly, what if we get new computers for the design activity on the project and use the existing computers for the monitoring functions?"	

Answer

	Description	Form of Conflict Resolution This Represents
1	"It seems the real problem here is not a lack of communication, but a lack of knowledge of what needs to be done and when. Here is a copy of the project schedule. It should help you understand what you need to know."	Confronting
2	"Do it my way!"	Forcing
3	"Let's calm down and get the job done!"	Smoothing
4	"Let us do a little of what both of you suggest."	Compromising
5	"Let's deal with this issue next week."	Withdrawal
6	"Carly and Amanda, both of you want this project to cause as little distraction to your departments as possible. With that in mind, I am sure we can come to an agreement on the purchase of equipment and what is best for the project."	Smoothing
7	"We have talked about new computers enough. I do not want to get the computers, and that is it!"	Forcing
8	"Carly, you say the project should include the purchase of new computers, and Amanda, you say the project can use existing equipment. I suggest we perform the following test on the existing equipment to determine if it needs to be replaced."	Confronting
9	"Let's see what everyone thinks, and try to reach a consensus."	Collaborating

	Description	Form of Conflict Resolution This Represents
10	"Since we cannot decide on the purchase of new computers, we will have to wait until our meeting next month."	Withdrawal
11	"Carly, what if we get new computers for the design activity on the project and use the existing computers for the monitoring functions?"	Compromising

Problem Solving Method Like many other topics in this chapter, you likely have some experience with problem solving methods, but you may not use the terms or processes tested on the exam and you might not have learned the methods as a science. Many people solve problems using an incorrect method. Try the next exercise to test your problem solving knowledge.

Exercise What steps would you use to solve a problem?

Answer The important thing to realize about problems is if they are not solved completely, they just return again and again. Many people prefer to avoid conflict (withdraw) instead of solving the problem. Imagine a senior manager who is arbitrarily adding work to your project that does not fit within its charter. Would you deal with it, or delay action? Would you deal directly with the person or try to avoid doing so? Questions in this area are not always easy. Before you read on, keep in mind that people have failed the exam because they did not "see" the problems explained in questions or they solved the problems the wrong way. So let's look at the right method:

1. Define what is the real or root problem, not what is presented to you or what appears to be the problem.
2. Analyze the problem.
3. Identify solutions.
4. Pick a solution.
5. Implement a solution.
6. Review the solution, and confirm that the solution solved the problem.

As you have been studying, you might be saying to yourself, "I do not have time to do that!" The issue may not be that you do not have time, but that you are spending your time in the wrong areas . Think about step 6 from the previous list. If you do not make sure the problem is resolved, it will just return and take up more of your valuable time.

When questions on the exam require you to solve problems, ask yourself, "What is the real problem behind the situation presented?" Here is an example:

> *During project executing, a project manager discovers that the seller did not supply the report required by the contract for the last four weeks. What should he do?*

If you have *PM FASTrack®*, look up this question on the software by doing a search for question number 1145. *PM FASTrack®* gives you more information on this and many similarly difficult problem-solving questions.

What would you do? Would you call the seller and investigate why it was late? If so, you would get the answer wrong on the exam. In a contract situation, the seller has breached the contract by not doing something required in the contract. The required legal action for a breach is to send written notification of the breach, not call the seller. You need to understand the real problem.

Making sure you are solving the right problem is extremely important, because it is a significant issue for many people who take the exam, especially those who have never managed projects that are more than a few months long or who have not had formal training in project management. There can be many questions that, in a manner of speaking, describe that there is a fire and ask you what to do. You might choose the answer that amounts to "find out why there is a fire" when you should choose the choice that relates to "get out of the danger zone."

TRICKS OF THE TRADE®

Other Important Terms, Topics, and Theories One of the things that drives people crazy about the exam is that they see terms they do not know. You should realize the exam does have made-up terms and processes as answer choices. The following should help you get more familiar with some real terms that have been on the exam that you may not have run across previously. But remember, if you are well trained in project management and you see a term on the exam that you do not recognize, chances are it is not the right answer!

Expectancy Theory[6] Employees who believe their efforts will lead to effective performance and who expect to be rewarded for their accomplishments will remain productive as rewards meet their expectations.

Arbitration In arbitration, a neutral party hears and resolves a dispute.

Perquisites (Perks) Some employees receive special rewards, such as assigned parking spaces, corner offices, and executive dining.

Fringe Benefits[7] These are the "standard" benefits formally given to all employees, such as education benefits, insurance, and profit sharing.

Motivation Theory[8] **(Or "What Do People Really Want?")** Were you going to skim through this topic? Caught you! If most projects are operated in a matrix environment, then one of the few things a project manager can do to gain cooperation of team members is to understand how to motivate them. This section provides answers.

Why would this topic be on the exam? As you have read in this chapter, one of the best ways to gain cooperation is to give rewards. How can we reward people if we do not understand what motivates them? Questions on the exam in this area do not always directly quote motivation theorists. The questions may simply describe situations and ask you what to do. The answer might depend on understanding that the person in the situation is a Theory X manager, or that the project manager was motivating people in the wrong way. Take this section seriously, and look for practice questions that demonstrate such situations.

Here are four motivation theories you need to understand for the exam.

McGregor's Theory of X and Y[9]

McGregor believed that all workers fit into one of two groups, X and Y. The exam may describe this concept in many different ways. It can be confusing to determine which answer is correct or even what the choices are saying. For those of you with strong visual memories, here is a trick to answering questions on these theories.

Theory X Based on the picture, take a guess as to what Theory X is.

Managers who accept this theory believe that people need to be watched every minute. They believe employees are incapable, avoid responsibility, and avoid work whenever possible.

Theory Y Based on the picture, take a guess as to what Theory Y is.

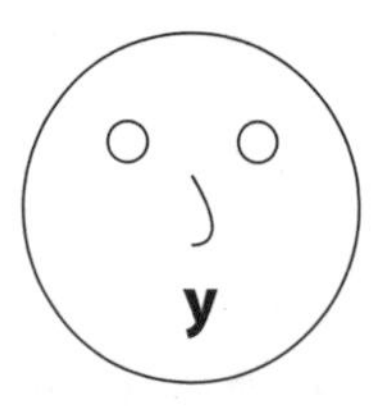

Managers who accept this theory believe that people are willing to work without supervision, and want to achieve. They believe employees can direct their own efforts.

Maslow's Hierarchy of Needs[10]

Maslow's message is that people are not most motivated to work by security or money. Instead, the highest motivation is to contribute and to use their skills. Maslow calls this "self-actualization." He created a pyramid to show how people are motivated and said one cannot ascend to the next level until the levels below are fulfilled.

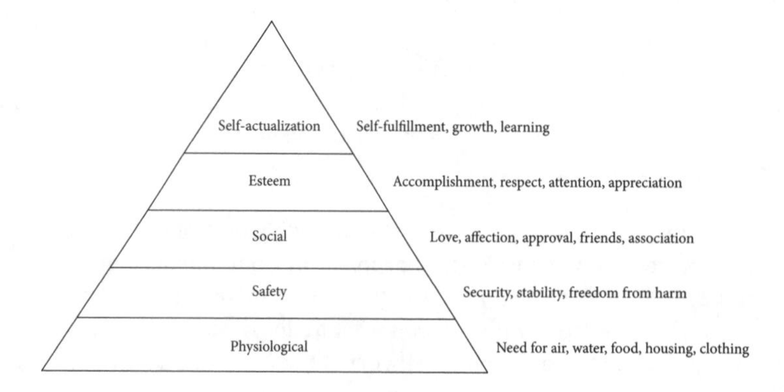

David McClelland's Theory of Needs (or Acquired Needs Theory)[11]

This theory states that people are most motivated by one of the three needs listed in the following table. A person falling into one category would be managed differently than a person falling into another category.

Primary Need	Behavioral Style
Achievement	▶ These people should be given projects that are challenging but are reachable. ▶ They like recognition.
Affiliation	▶ These people work best when cooperating with others. ▶ They seek approval rather than recognition.
Power	▶ People whose need for power is socially oriented, rather than personally oriented, are effective leaders and should be allowed to manage others. ▶ These people like to organize and influence others.

Herzberg's Theory[12]

Herzberg's theory deals with hygiene factors and motivating agents.

Hygiene Factors Poor hygiene factors may destroy motivation, but improving them, under most circumstances, will not improve motivation. Hygiene factors are not sufficient to motivate people.

Examples of hygiene factors are:

- Working conditions
- Salary
- Personal life
- Relationships at work
- Security
- Status

Motivating Agents What motivates people is the work itself, including such things as:

- Responsibility
- Self-actualization
- Professional growth
- Recognition

So the lesson here is that motivating people is best done by rewarding them and letting them grow. Giving raises is not the most effective motivator. This is generally good news for project managers, as they often do not have any influence over the pay raises of their team members.

This brings us to the end of the Human Resource Management chapter. The work that is done as part of creating the human resource plan on a project and acquiring, developing, and managing the team greatly impacts the next knowledge area, communications management.

Practice Exam

1. All of the following are forms of power derived from the project manager's position EXCEPT:
   A. Formal.
   B. Reward.
   C. Penalty.
   D. Expert.

2. The highest point of Maslow's hierarchy of needs is called:
   A. Physiological satisfaction.
   B. Attainment of survival.
   C. Need for association.
   D. Esteem.

3. The halo effect refers to the tendency to:
   A. Promote from within.
   B. Hire the best.
   C. Move people into project management because they are good in their technical fields.
   D. Move people into project management because they have had project management training.

4. The sponsor's role on a project is BEST described as:
   A. Helping to plan activities.
   B. Helping to prevent unnecessary changes to project objectives.
   C. Identifying unnecessary project constraints.
   D. Helping to develop the project management plan.

5. Which of the following conflict resolution techniques will generate the MOST lasting solution?
   A. Forcing
   B. Smoothing
   C. Compromise
   D. Problem solving

6. The MOST common causes of conflict on a project are schedules, project priorities, and:
   A. Personality.
   B. Resources.
   C. Cost.
   D. Management.

7. What conflict resolution technique is a project manager using when he says, "I cannot deal with this issue now!"
   A. Problem solving
   B. Forcing
   C. Withdrawal
   D. Compromising

8. What does a resource histogram show that a responsibility assignment matrix does not?
   A. Time
   B. Activities
   C. Interrelationships
   D. The person in charge of each activity

9. You have just been assigned as project manager for a large telecommunications project. This one-year project is about halfway done. The project team consists of 5 sellers and 20 of your company's employees. You want to understand who is responsible for doing what on the project. Where would you find such information?
   A. Responsibility assignment matrix
   B. Resource histogram
   C. Bar chart
   D. Project organization chart

10. During project planning in a matrix organization, the project manager determines that additional human resources are needed. From whom would he request these resources?
    A. The PMO manager
    B. The functional manager
    C. The team
    D. The project sponsor

11. A project manager must publish a project schedule. Activities, start/end times, and resources are identified. What should the project manager do NEXT?
    A. Distribute the project schedule according to the communications management plan.
    B. Confirm the availability of the resources.
    C. Refine the project management plan to reflect more accurate costing information.
    D. Publish a bar chart illustrating the timeline.

12. During every project team meeting, the project manager asks each team member to describe the work he or she is doing, and the project manager assigns new activities to team members. The length of these meetings has increased because there are many different activities to assign. This could be happening for all the following reasons EXCEPT:
    A. Lack of a WBS.
    B. Lack of a responsibility assignment matrix.
    C. Lack of resource leveling.
    D. Lack of team involvement in project planning.

13. You are a project manager leading a cross-functional project team in a weak matrix environment. None of your project team members report to you functionally and you do not have the ability to directly reward their performance. The project is difficult, involving tight date constraints and challenging quality standards. Which of the following types of project management power will likely be the MOST effective in this circumstance?
    A. Referent
    B. Expert
    C. Penalty
    D. Formal

14. A team member is not performing well on the project because she is inexperienced in system development work. There is no one else available who is better qualified to do the work. What is the BEST solution for the project manager?
    A. Consult with the functional manager to determine project completion incentives for the team member.
    B. Obtain a new resource more skilled in development work.
    C. Arrange for the team member to get training.
    D. Allocate some of the project schedule reserve.

15. A project manager has just found out that a major subcontractor for her project is consistently late delivering work. The project team member responsible for this part of the project does not get along with the subcontractor. To resolve the problem, the project manager says, "You both will have to give up something to solve this problem." What conflict resolution method is she using?
   A. Confrontation
   B. Compromise
   C. Smoothing
   D. Communicating

16. A project has several teams. Team C has repeatedly missed deadlines in the past. This has caused team D to have to crash the critical path several times. As the team leader for team D, you should meet with:
   A. The leader of team C.
   B. The project manager.
   C. The project manager and management.
   D. The project manager and the leader of team C.

17. The new project is exciting to both the project manager and the team. This is the project manager's first assignment as project manager. The team feels they will be able to complete work that has never been tried before. There are 29 people contributing to the product description, and the team consists of 9 highly experienced experts in their field.

   Part of the way through planning, three highly technical team members are disagreeing about the scope of two of the deliverables. One is pointing to the draft WBS and saying that two additional work packages should be added. Another is saying that a particular work package should not even be done. The third team member agrees with both of them. How should the project manager BEST deal with the conflict?
   A. He should listen to the differences of opinion, determine the best choice, and implement that choice.
   B. He should postpone further discussions, meet with each individual, and determine the best approach.
   C. He should listen to the differences of opinion, encourage logical discussions, and facilitate an agreement.
   D. He should help the team focus on agreeable aspects of their opinions and build unity by using relaxation techniques and common-focus team building.

18. The project is just starting out and consists of people from 14 different departments. The project charter was signed by one person and contains over 30 major requirements that must be met on the project. The sponsor has informed the project manager that the SPI must be kept between 0.95 and 1.1. A few minutes of investigation resulted in the identification of 34 stakeholders, and the schedule objectives on the project are constrained. The project manager has just been hired. Which of the following types of project management power will BEST help the project manager gain the cooperation of others?
   A. Formal
   B. Referent
   C. Penalty
   D. Expert

19. A project manager is trying to settle a dispute between two team members. One says the systems should be integrated before testing, and the other maintains each system should be tested before integration. The project involves over 30 people, and 12 systems need to be integrated. The sponsor is demanding that integration happen on time. What is the BEST statement the project manager can make to resolve the conflict?
    A. Do it my way.
    B. Let's calm down and get the job done.
    C. Let's deal with this again next week after we all calm down.
    D. Let's do limited testing before integration and finish testing after integration.

20. A project is in the middle of the executing effort when a stakeholder suggests a major new change. This change will cause the third major overhaul of the project. At the same time, the project manager discovers that a major work package was not completed because a team member's boss moved him to another project that had a higher priority. Which of the following is the BEST person for the project manger to address these issues with?
    A. The team
    B. Senior management
    C. The customer
    D. The sponsor

21. What theory proposes that employees' efforts will lead to effective performance and the employees will be rewarded for accomplishments?
    A. Conditional reinforcement
    B. Maslow's hierarchy
    C. McGregor's
    D. Expectancy

22. Conflict resolution techniques that may be used on a project include confronting, smoothing, forcing, and:
    A. Withdrawing.
    B. Directing.
    C. Organizing.
    D. Controlling.

23. The installation project has a CPI of 1.03 and an SPI of 1.0. There are 14 team members, and each team member had input into the final project management plan. The customer has accepted the three deliverables completed so far without complaint and the responsibility assignment matrix has not changed since the project began. The project is being completed in a matrix environment and there are no contracts needed for the project.

    Although the sponsor is happy with the status of the project, one of the team members is always complaining about how much time his project work is taking. Which of the following would be the BEST thing for the project manager to do?
    A. Review the reward system for the project.
    B. Try to improve schedule performance of the project.
    C. Meet with the customer to try to extend the schedule.
    D. Gain formal acceptance in writing from the customer.

24. The project has been challenging to manage. Everyone has been on edge due to pressure to complete the project on time. Unfortunately, the tension has grown to the point where team meetings have become shouting matches and little work is accomplished during the meetings. One team member asks to be excused from future team meetings, as all the shouting upsets him. Meanwhile, the sponsor has expressed interest in attending future team meetings in order to better understand how the project is going and the issues involved in completing the project, and the customer has started discussions about adding scope to the project. In this situation, it would be BEST for the project manager to:
    A. Ask the sponsor if the information needed could be sent in a report rather than have her attend the meetings.
    B. Inform the team member who asked to be excused from the meetings of the value of communication in such meetings.
    C. Create new ground rules for the meetings and introduce them to the team.
    D. Hold a team-building exercise that involves all the team members.

25. Project performance appraisals are different from team performance assessments in that project performance appraisals focus on:
    A. How an individual team member is performing on the project.
    B. An evaluation of the project team's effectiveness.
    C. A team-building effort.
    D. Reducing the staff turnover rate.

26. A project manager had a complex problem to solve and made a decision about what needed to be done. A few months later, the problem resurfaced. What did the project manager MOST likely NOT do?
    A. Proper risk analysis
    B. Confirm the decision solved the problem
    C. Have the project sponsor validate the decision
    D. Use an Ishikawa diagram

27. The project cost performance index (CPI) is 1.02, the benefit cost ratio (BCR) is 1.7, and the latest round of performance reviews identified few needed adjustments. The project team was co-located into a new building when the project started. Everyone commented on how excited they were to have all new facilities. The sponsor is providing adequate support for the project, and few unidentified risks have occurred. In an attempt to improve performance, the project manager spends part of the project budget on new chairs for the team members and adds the term "senior" to each team member's job title.

    Which of the following is the MOST correct thing that can be said of this project or the project manager?
    A. The project manager has misunderstood Herzberg's theory.
    B. The project is slowly spending more money than it should. The project manager should begin to watch cost more carefully.
    C. The performance review should be handled better to find more adjustments.
    D. The project manager should use good judgment to determine which variances are important.

28. You just found out that a major subcontractor for your project consistently provides deliverables late. The subcontractor approaches you and asks you to continue accepting late deliverables in exchange for a decrease in project costs. This offer is an example of:
    A. Confronting.
    B. Compromise.
    C. Smoothing.
    D. Forcing.

29. The management theory which states that people can direct their own efforts is:
    A. Theory Y.
    B. Herzberg's theory.
    C. Maslow's hierarchy.
    D. Theory X.

30. Which of the following aspects of leadership is MOST important for a project manager?
    A. Communication
    B. Team building
    C. Technical expertise
    D. Project control

31. During the first half of the project, five team members left for other projects without being replaced, two team members went on vacation without informing you, and other team members expressed uncertainty about the work they were to complete. In this situation, it is BEST if you create a __________ for the second half of the project.
    A. Work breakdown structure
    B. Resource histogram
    C. Staffing management plan
    D. Responsibility assignment matrix

32. The project manager is looking at the project's resource needs and lessons learned from past projects. This information causes the project manager to be concerned about the ability to acquire enough resources for the project in six months. Which of the following would be the LEAST effective preventive action?
    A. Make sure functional managers have a copy of the resource histogram.
    B. Show the sponsor the data, and explain the project manager's concern.
    C. Determine metrics to use as an early warning sign that resources will not be available.
    D. Ask functional managers for their opinions.

33. A large project is underway when one of the team members reviews the project status report. He sees the project is currently running late. As he looks at the report further, he notices the delay will cause one of his activities to be scheduled during a time he will be out of the country and cannot work on the activity. This is of great concern to the team member because he is very committed to the success of the project and he does not want to be the cause of the project being further delayed. What is the BEST THING for him to do?
    A. Contact the project manager immediately to provide the project manager with his schedule.
    B. Include the information in his next report.
    C. Request that the issue be added to the project issue log.
    D. Recommend preventive action.

34. There have been many work packages completed successfully on the project, and the sponsor has made some recommendations for improvements. The project is on schedule to meet an aggressive deadline when the successor activity to a critical path activity suffers a major setback. The activity has 14 days of float and is being completed by four people. There are two other team members with the skill set to assist the troubled activity, if needed.

    The project manager receives a call that three other team members are attempting to be removed from the project because they do not feel the project can be successful. When the project manager pursues this, he discovers that those team members have issues that have not been addressed. Which of the following is the BEST thing to do to improve the project?

    A. Have the team members immediately assist the troubled activity.
    B. Investigate why the project schedule is aggressive.
    C. See who can replace the three team members.
    D. Create an issue log.

Answer

1 **Answer** D
Explanation When someone is given the job of project manager, they will have formal, reward, and penalty power. But just having the position does not make the project manager either a technical or project management expert. Expert power has to be earned.

2. **Answer** D
Explanation This question is asking which of the FOLLOWING is the highest. Self-actualization is not listed, so the next best choice is esteem.

3. **Answer** C
Explanation The halo effect refers to the tendency to move a person into project management because they are good in their technical field. Just because a person is good in a technical field does not mean he or she will also be a good project manager.

4. **Answer** B
Explanation Though the sponsor may help plan some of the activities, it is not his exclusive duty. Some project constraints come from the sponsor, but they should be considered necessary. The project management plan is created by the team and approved by the sponsor and other management. Since the project objectives are stated in the project charter, and it is the sponsor who issues the project charter, helping to prevent unnecessary changes to project objectives is the correct answer.

5. **Answer** D
Explanation Problem solving normally takes more time, but it gets buy-in from everyone, generating a more lasting solution.

6. **Answer** B
Explanation Know the top four sources of conflict on projects (schedules, project priorities, resources, and technical opinions) so you can answer questions such as this one. Don't be fooled because "personality" is on the list. It is not a major cause of conflict.

7. **Answer** C
Explanation Delaying the issue is called withdrawal.

8. **Answer** A
Explanation The responsibility assignment matrix maps specific resources to the work packages from the WBS. On a resource histogram, the use of resources is shown individually or by groups over time.

9. **Answer** A
Explanation The resource histogram shows the number of resources used in each time period. In its pure form, a bar chart shows only activity and calendar date. The organizational chart shows who reports to whom. The responsibility assignment matrix shows who will do the work.

10. **Answer** B
Explanation In a matrix organization, power is shared between the functional manager and the project manager, so the project manager needs to negotiate with the functional manager for the resources.

11. **Answer** B
    Explanation The project schedule remains preliminary until resource assignments are confirmed.

12. **Answer** C
    Explanation The lack of a WBS, responsibility assignment matrix, or team involvement in planning could contribute to excessively long meetings to assign resources to activities. Resource leveling refers to maintaining the same number of resources on the project for each time period and would not impact the length of meetings.

13. **Answer** B
    Explanation Reward and expert are the best types of power to use in such a circumstance. Reward is not listed as a choice, and the question says the project manager has limited ability to reward the team members.

14. **Answer** C
    Explanation The job of the project manager includes providing or obtaining project-specific training for team members. This kind of training is a direct cost of the project.

15. **Answer** B
    Explanation Confrontation leads to a win-win situation. Smoothing emphasizes agreement, rather than differences. The act of both parties giving up something defines compromise.

16. **Answer** D
    Explanation Those involved in the problem should resolve the problem. Having had to crash the critical path several times implies that team D has already tried to deal with this problem. In this case, the two team leaders need to meet. The extent of this situation requires the project manager's involvement as well.

17. **Answer** C
    Explanation Do not get confused by the wordiness of the question. Ask yourself what is the best way to resolve any conflict, and you can get the answer. Most of the situation is a distracter. Problem solving (confronting) and compromising are the two most important conflict resolution techniques. Conflict management is a key general management skill.

18. **Answer** A
    Explanation Generally, the best forms of power are reward or expert. The project manager has not had time to become a recognized expert in the company and reward power is not included as a choice here. This leaves formal power as the only logical answer.

19. **Answer** D
    Explanation Doing limited testing before integration and finishing testing after integration is an example of compromising. This is the best way for the project manager to resolve the conflict in this situation.

20. **Answer** D
    Explanation It is the sponsor's role to prevent unnecessary changes and to set priorities between projects. The situation described in this question implies that such work is not being done and the project manager must therefore go to the root of the problem: the sponsor.

21. **Answer** D
    Explanation Expectancy theory states that employees who believe their efforts will lead to effective performance and who expect to be rewarded for their accomplishments will stay productive as rewards meet their expectations.

22. **Answer** A
Explanation There is always the option to simply postpone dealing with the issue until later. This is withdrawing.

23. **Answer** A
Explanation Improving schedule performance relates to getting the project completed sooner. Although it would seem to be a good idea to improve schedule performance, this project's performance is fine. The schedule has been approved as it is. It would be better for the project manager to spend more time controlling the project to make sure it finishes according to plan than to improve schedule performance.

    If you chose attempting to extend the schedule, look at the SPI. There is nothing wrong with the schedule performance of the project that would require an extension.

    Gaining formal acceptance from the customer will need to be done, as it provides an opportunity for the team to check if everything is going well. This action will not affect the problem of the team member's dissatisfaction however.

    The only real problem presented in this situation is that the team member is complaining. If you read the situation completely, you will notice that the team member was involved and approved the project management plan, including his own involvement in the project. Since the responsibility assignment matrix has not changed, the team member has not even been assigned different duties since the project began. There must be something else causing the team member to complain. The project manager should investigate and find out if the reward system is ineffective.

24. **Answer** C
Explanation Here is a situation where all four choices could be done, but there is one best answer. Asking the sponsor if the information could be sent in a report does not solve the root cause of the problem described. Informing the team member of the value of communication in meetings merely dismisses the concerns of the team member and might cause anger. A team-building exercise would take planning and so could not be done right away. Remember, the sponsor might be attending the next meeting and at least one team member might not attend because of past problems. The best thing to do would be to set up new ground rules governing team behavior and then plan a team-building exercise.

25. **Answer** A
Explanation Questions like this can drive people crazy on the exam because it is easy to get confused. The best thing to do is to look at the two terms used here (project performance appraisals and team performance assessments) and review in your mind what each means BEFORE looking at the choices. Team performance assessments evaluate the project team's effectiveness as a whole. Project performance appraisals deal with how each team member is performing on the project.

26. **Answer** B
Explanation Notice the phrasing of this question, "most likely NOT do." Expect to see questions worded on the exam in ways that can cause you to misinterpret them. You will also see questions about things we forget to do in the real world. "Who has time," you might say, "to determine if each problem is really solved?" One could respond with, "Who has time not to do this? Who has time to deal with the same problem twice?" The final steps of problem solving include: implement a decision, review it, and confirm that the decision solved the problem.

27. **Answer** A
Explanation The option of the project manager watching cost more closely includes the concept of cost to trick you into selecting it if you are unsure of the real answer. There is no indication that the costs are trending in any particular direction. There is no reason to think that performance reviews should turn up more adjustments. The project manager should always use good judgment but nothing in this question talks about judgment regarding variances, so this cannot be the best choice. In this situation, the project manager is making great working conditions better. According to Herzberg's theory, fixing bad working conditions will help you motivate the team, but making good ones better will not improve motivation. The project manager needs to focus on the motivating agents and not the hygiene factors.

28. **Answer** B
Explanation Both parties are giving up something. This is a compromise.

29. **Answer** A
Explanation Theory Y is the belief that people can direct their own efforts. Know the difference between Theory X and Theory Y for the exam.

30. **Answer** A
Explanation As project managers can spend 90 percent of their time communicating, the correct choice must be communication.

31. **Answer** C
Explanation The resource histogram shows the resources used per time period, but would provide limited benefits in this situation. The responsibility assignment matrix cross-references resources with the activities or work packages they are to accomplish, but it does not show when they will be required to do their work. The staffing management plan describes when resources will be brought onto and taken off the project, and would provide the most benefit for this project.

32. **Answer** A
Explanation Sending data without pointing out the issue does not mean the communication will be adequately decoded by the recipient. The other choices describe more effective communication in this instance.

33. **Answer** D
Explanation Notice that this question asks what the team member should do. It is important for the project manager to understand the team member's role and possibly even instruct team members on how to work on projects and what is expected of them. Providing the project manager with his schedule, including the information in a report, and requesting that the issue be added to the issue log have one thing in common. They involve the team member asking the project manager to do something. In reality, it may very well be the team member who will come up with a solution (such as decreasing the scope of the activity, fast tracking, or specific suggestions about changes to predecessor activities). Therefore, recommending preventive action is the best choice for the team member. Note that recommended corrective or preventive actions can come from the team or stakeholders in addition to the project manager.

34. **Answer** D
Explanation Sometimes complex problems are caused by not doing simple things. The data in the first paragraph, once you read the choices, is completely extraneous. The troubled activity has float and so does not need immediate attention. It may not be necessary for additional team members to assist the troubled activity, but none of the choices suggest investigating whether the

amount of float is enough to cover any delay caused by the trouble. Rather, the choices take you in different directions.

Investigating why the schedule is so aggressive should have been done before the project began. Replacing team members does not solve the root cause of the problem. Could there be something the project manager is doing wrong, or could be doing that he is not, that would solve the problem without losing resources? Wouldn't it be more effective to discover the root cause of those team members' concerns so the problem does not surface again later? The creation of an issue log will let the troubled team members know their concerns have been heard, are noted, and will be resolved. This might be enough to stop them from leaving and avoid the resultant project delays and confusion if new team members must be added.

CHAPTER TEN Communications Management

Quicktest

- Communications management process
- Stakeholders
- Communications management plan
- Stakeholder analysis
- Stakeholder register
- What should be reported
- Types of reports
- Information distribution
- Importance of managing stakeholders' expectations
- Stakeholder management strategy
- Communication models
  - Effective communication
  - Nonverbal
  - Percent of communication that is nonverbal
  - Paralingual
  - Active listening
  - Effective listening
  - Feedback
  - Noise
- Communication types
  - Formal/informal written
  - Formal/informal verbal
- Communication technology
- Communication methods
  - Interactive communication
  - Push communication
  - Pull communication
- Communication channels
- Rules for meetings
- Communication blockers
- Control of communications

How many times have you deleted a voice mail without listening to the very end of the message? Is your inbox flooded with e-mails? How many times have you not read all the way through an e-mail? These types of occurrences happen all too often on projects and indicate a need to better plan and manage communications. Think about your real-world projects. How much time do you spend planning and managing communications?

In almost every study, communication-related issues are the most frequent problems a project manager has on a project. Project managers spend up to 90 percent of their time communicating. With communication being such an incredibly important part of managing a project, shouldn't we do something to plan, structure, and control our messages?

Many beginning project managers do nothing to address communications on their projects beyond issuing status reports. As project managers gain experience, they often recognize the need for a structured communications management plan, and their official communications about the project become more involved than simply reporting status. Highly experienced and effective project managers also create a communications management plan and go beyond status reports, but they do the following as well: they ask stakeholders what they need communicated to them, identify what communications they need from stakeholders, and frequently revisit communications at team meetings to limit the potential for communication problems. This is the type of mindset you should have about communicating on projects to pass the exam.

Although it is not particularly difficult, make sure you take this chapter seriously and find your gaps regarding communications. Communications questions are frequently combined with other topics. For example, a WBS could be used as a communications tool (see the Scope Management chapter), and risk response strategies should be communicated to the stakeholders (see the Risk Management chapter).

Rita's Process Chart—Communications Management

Where are we in the project management process?

INITIATING

- Select project manager
- Determine company culture and existing systems
- Collect processes, procedures, and historical information
- Divide large projects into phases
- Understand the business case
- Uncover initial requirements, assumptions, and risks
- Assess project and product feasibility within the given constraints
- Create measurable objectives
- Develop project charter
- **Identify stakeholders**
- **Develop stakeholder management strategy**

PLANNING

(This is the only process group with a set order)

- **Determine how you will do planning—part of all management plans**
- Determine detailed requirements
- Create project scope statement
- Assess what to purchase
- Determine team
- Create WBS and WBS dictionary
- Create activity list
- Create network diagram
- Estimate resource requirements
- Estimate time and cost
- Determine critical path
- Develop schedule
- Develop budget
- Determine quality standards, processes, and metrics
- Create process improvement plan
- **Determine all roles and responsibilities**
- **Plan communications**
- Perform risk identification, qualitative and quantitative risk analysis, and risk response planning
- **Go back—iterations**
- Prepare procurement documents
- Create change management plan
- **Finalize the "how to execute and control" parts of all management plans**
- **Develop realistic and final PM plan and performance measurement baseline**
- Gain formal approval of the plan
- Hold kickoff meeting

EXECUTING

- Execute the work according to the PM plan
- Produce product deliverables (product scope)
- **Request changes**
- Implement only approved changes
- Continuously improve
- Follow processes
- Perform quality assurance
- Perform quality audits
- Acquire final team
- Manage people
- Evaluate team and project performance
- Hold team-building activities
- Give recognition and rewards
- Use issue logs
- Facilitate conflict resolution
- Release resources as work is completed
- **Send and receive information**
- **Hold meetings**
- Select sellers

MONITORING & CONTROLLING

- **Take action to control the project**
- Measure performance against the performance measurement baseline
- **Measure performance against other metrics determined by the project manager**
- **Determine variances and if they warrant a corrective action or change request**
- **Influence the factors that cause changes**
- **Request changes**
- Perform integrated change control
- Approve or reject changes
- **Inform stakeholders of results of change requests**
- **Update the PM plan and project documents**
- Manage configuration
- **Create forecasts**
- Gain acceptance of interim deliverables from the customer
- Perform quality control
- **Report on project performance and solicit feedback**
- Perform risk assessments and audits
- Manage reserves
- Administer procurements

CLOSING

- Confirm work is done to requirements
- Complete procurement closure
- Gain final acceptance of the product
- Complete financial closure
- Hand off completed product
- Solicit feedback from the customer about the project
- Complete final performance reporting
- Index and archive records
- Update lessons learned knowledge base

The following should help you understand how each part of communications management fits into the overall project management process:

The Communications Management Process	Done During
Identify Stakeholders	Initiating process group
Plan Communications	Planning process group
Distribute Information	Executing process group
Manage Stakeholder Expectations	Executing process group
Report Performance	Monitoring and controlling process group

Stakeholders

Sometimes there are topics on the exam that seem easy, and you might tend to skip studying them. Does the topic of stakeholders fall into this category for you? Before you dismiss the importance of this concept, take note of the example of one person who failed the exam because he did not understand the proper management of stakeholders. His method of managing projects was simply to tell people what to do, and he always worked with the same four people. He forgot to think in terms of large projects (those that utilize hundreds of people, not just four) and how having so many stakeholders involved would greatly impact how they are managed. In his real world, he believed project management was about the project manager being the expert and basically bossing everyone around. Who cared about or needed the stakeholders? During the exam, he thought only in terms of his small team and did not consider all the different types of stakeholders described in the Project Management Framework and Human Resource Management chapters.

In reality, the project manager needs to be the expert in project management, while the stakeholders serve as the technical experts in what needs to be done and how it needs to be done. The project manager is the orchestra leader, and work cannot be done well without stakeholder involvement. As a result of not thinking in this way, the person described in the previous paragraph answered questions incorrectly across all knowledge areas on the exam. This one concept of identifying, using, and managing stakeholders had a huge impact on his understanding of project management. What about you? Do you properly involve stakeholders on your projects?

Let's think about another scenario. Imagine you are assigned as the project manager for a project. Your boss provides you with a 200-page scope of work and a charter and tells you to get started on the project work. What do you do next? Do you just get started? If you said yes, then you need to understand a very important concept before taking the exam: proper project management requires you to identify the stakeholders; determine their requirements, expectations, and influence; and then incorporate that information into the product and project scope as needed. You cannot simply accept a scope of work or project charter handed to you without considering the stakeholders involved in the project and their requirements and expectations. Is this different from your real world? Remember that requirements must be gathered as completely as possible from all stakeholders before starting work!

If you have access to an electronic copy of the *PMBOK® Guide* as a member of PMI, search for the word "stakeholders." You will see over 200 references. Think about whether the requisite involvement of stakeholders is different from your real world, and make note of your gaps.

In the next section of this chapter, we will discuss the Identify Stakeholders process, which occurs during project initiating with the Develop Project Charter process. This does not mean you only have to worry about stakeholders at the beginning of the project, however. Stakeholders are extremely important throughout the project. You need to identify them as early as possible, during project initiating, and continue to manage their expectations, involvement, and influence throughout the project.

Because the concept of stakeholder management can be troublesome on the exam for those who do not do it on their real-world projects, let's look at the entire stakeholder management process. Identifying stakeholders, planning communications, distributing information, managing their expectations, and reporting performance are important aspects of stakeholder management. (These topics are described again later in this chapter in their own sections.)

So, what should you do with stakeholders throughout the project?

- **Identify ALL of them.** Why is identifying all stakeholders so important? (If you get the answer right, you could answer two more questions correctly on the exam.) Any stakeholders who are missed will likely be found later. When they are discovered, they will probably request changes, which may cause delays. Changes made later in the project are much more costly and harder to integrate than those made earlier. Identifying all the stakeholders helps create a better organized project that considers all the stakeholders' interests. A list of stakeholders is included in the stakeholder register. Stakeholders are first identified as part of initiating the project, and this list is reassessed during project planning and executing.
- **Determine ALL of their requirements.** This is neither easy nor fast, but the project manager must make every effort to obtain ALL the requirements before the work begins. Do you try to do this? How hard do you really try? Many project managers do not even attempt it.

  To realize why this is important, think about the effects of starting a project without all the requirements. Those effects would likely include changes, delay, and possible failure. How would it look if you had to say to your manager, "I did not know Kerry was a stakeholder on this project. Now that I know this, I need to extend the schedule to accommodate her needs or cut out of the project another stakeholder's needs." This is just bad project management.

  Some people claim, "The nature of my project is that we will not know what we need for the second part until the first part is done." If this is the case, they likely have two or more projects, not one, and they should be managing them as such.

  There are many ways to make sure you have all the requirements—from just asking if you do, to conducting requirements reviews, to telling people the negative consequences to the company and the project if a requirement is found later.

  The requirements should not just relate to how stakeholders want the product of the project to function, but should also include their communications requirements: what do stakeholders want communicated to them, when, in what form, how frequently?
- **Determine their expectations.** These expectations include what stakeholders think will happen to them, their department, and the company as a whole as a result of the project. Expectations tend to be much more ambiguous than stated requirements, or they may be undefined requirements. They may be intentionally or unintentionally hidden. Expectations include such things as, "I expect that this project will not interrupt my department's work" or "I expect the system will be dramatically improved as a result of the project." Naturally, expectations that go unidentified will have major impacts across all constraints. Expectations are converted to requirements and become part of the project.
- **Determine their interests.** Stakeholders may be particularly interested in working on some part of the project, getting a chance to learn new skills, getting a chance to prove their skills, or even getting out of working on certain parts of the project. A great project manager will determine each stakeholder's interests related to the project and attempt to either build these interests into the project or implement them as a reward.

- **Determine their level of influence.** To some degree, each stakeholder will be able to negatively or positively affect a project. This is their level of influence, and it should be identified and managed.
- **Plan how you will communicate with them.** Project management focuses on planning before taking action. Since communications are the most frequent cause of problems on projects, planning communications is critical.
- **Communicate with them.** Stakeholders are included in project presentations and receive project information, including progress reports, updates, changes to the project management plan, and changes to the project documents, when appropriate.
- **Manage their expectations and influence.** Managing stakeholders doesn't end during initiating or planning. They must be managed throughout the life of the project.

TRICKS OF THE TRADE® A key to your success as a project manager is how you handle stakeholders. Stakeholders must be involved, and their involvement must be managed by the project manager. That involvement may range from minor to extensive, depending on the needs of the project and the performing organization. Therefore, a list of where the stakeholders can be involved may also be limited or extensive. The following are the areas the exam focuses on. The table spans the entire Communications Management process, from Identify Stakeholders to Report Performance. If you are unable to check two or more of the following items, you should spend more time researching this topic.

	How the Project Manager Should Involve Stakeholders on the Project	Place ✓ Here if You Do It; Study Areas Unchecked
1	Determine all the stakeholders by name.	
2	Determine all of the stakeholders' requirements.	
3	Determine stakeholders' interest in being involved in the project.	
4	Determine stakeholders' level of influence on the project.	
5	Determine stakeholders' expectations, and turn them into requirements.	
6	Determine when stakeholders will be involved in the project and how much.	
7	Get stakeholders to sign off that the requirements are finalized.	
8	Assess stakeholders' knowledge and skills.	
9	Analyze the project to make sure stakeholders' needs will be met.	
10	Let stakeholders know what requirements will and what requirements will not be met and why.	
11	Get and keep stakeholders involved in the project by assigning them project work, such as the role of risk response owners.	
12	Manage and influence the stakeholders' involvement.	
13	Use stakeholders as experts.	
14	Make sure the project communicates to stakeholders what they need to know, when they need to know it.	
15	Involve stakeholders, as necessary, in change management and approval.	
16	Involve stakeholders in the creation of lessons learned.	
17	Get stakeholders' sign-off and formal acceptance during project or project phase closing.	
18	Reassess stakeholders' involvement during project executing.	

	How the Project Manager Should Involve Stakeholders on the Project	Place ✓ Here if You Do It; Study Areas Unchecked
19	Manage stakeholders' expectations (discussed later in this chapter).	
20	Ensure a common understanding of the work.	

Identify Stakeholders PAGE 246

Process: Identify Stakeholders
Process Group: Initiating
Knowledge Area: Communications Management

Identify Stakeholders has been moved into its own process in initiating in the *PMBOK® Guide*, thus giving stakeholder management more focus. As you read through this section, compare it to what you do in the real world.

The following are performed or created as part of the Identify Stakeholders process:

Stakeholder Analysis This technique involves both identifying stakeholders and analyzing their impact or influence on the project. The project manager can use the initial list of stakeholders from the project charter and, if applicable, any contracts related to the project as a starting point (or input) for identifying the project's stakeholders. Records from past projects and data gathering techniques such as interviewing and brainstorming (see the Scope Management and Risk Management chapters) can also help determine and analyze stakeholders. As new stakeholders are identified, they may be able to suggest other stakeholders to add to the list.

In addition to analyzing each stakeholder's potential impact or influence, the project manager needs to identify ways to manage those impacts effectively. Classification tools such as power/interest grids and salience models can be used to group stakeholders by qualifications like authority level, impact or influence, or requirements. These classifications can then help the project manager determine how, what, and when to communicate with each stakeholder.

Stakeholder Register All the information about stakeholders is compiled in the stakeholder register, an output of the Identify Stakeholders process. For example, the stakeholder register may include each stakeholder's name, title, supervisor, project role, contact information, requirements and expectations, impact and influence, attitude about the project, the classifications the individual falls into, and other relevant information. The following is an example of a stakeholder register.

Stakeholder Register										
Project Title						Project Number				
ID	Name	Title	Department(s)/ Supervisor	Contact Information	Impact					
					Major Requirements	Main Expectations	Influence (1 to 5)	Role(s) in Project	Responsibilities in Project	Classification
1										
2										
3										

Stakeholder Management Strategy As described throughout this book, much of project management focuses on thinking ahead before taking action. Therefore, the other major output of this process is a strategy for how stakeholders will be managed. The Identify Stakeholders process can result in a register of hundreds of stakeholders, and managing the influence and impact of this many people can take a lot of time. The project manager needs to develop a stakeholder management strategy to determine how to manage all of these individuals. Stakeholders can be managed individually, or they can be grouped and then managed in those groups if such an approach would be easier and less time consuming. Some stakeholders will require more management and some less. The project manager needs to think ahead about how to manage stakeholders, because stakeholders can be an asset or a problem on the project, depending on how well it is planned. Both the negative and positive aspects of the stakeholders' involvement in the project should be managed.

Think about this for a moment. Consider how you would manage the following people. Notice that these are generalized descriptions and answers, but if you do not work on large projects in your real world, reviewing the following information will help you better understand the work that needs to happen for large projects.

Stakeholder Description	Some Options for Managing the Stakeholder
High interest in the project, low influence, highly knowledgeable expert on high risk areas	Invite the stakeholder to participate in the risk management process
Low interest, the source of major requirements on the project (high influence), not easy to work with	Make sure requirements are clear Send reports
High interest, high influence, not a supporter of the project	Make sure you know why the stakeholder is not a supporter and base your plan for managing this stakeholder on dealing with those reasons
High interest, high influence, a supporter of the project	Involve the stakeholder in team meetings, report to this person, and include the information the stakeholder requested
Moderate interest, high influence, completing many activities on the project, a project supporter	Invite the stakeholder to officially join the project management team
Moderate interest, high influence because he or she has identified a large number of potential risks for the project, a supporter of the project	Plan to meet with the stakeholder periodically throughout the project to see if he or she has identified any more risks
Moderate interest, nervous about completing his or her assigned activities	Plan to find and forward relevant literature to help the stakeholder and arrange for training if necessary

Plan Communications PAGE 251

Process: Plan Communications
Process Group: Planning
Knowledge Area: Communications Management

The *PMBOK® Guide* often suggests work be done in a more structured way than many project managers have previously thought to do, and that efforts on projects need to be planned before they are done. Communication is no exception. In order to create an effective plan, you must consider the performing organization's environment (enterprise environmental factors), including its culture and expectations. You must understand and take a structured approach to using communications technology, methods, and models. You must also take into account the performing organization's established processes and procedures for communicating about projects, its historical records and lessons learned from previous projects, and other stored information (organizational process assets), as well as the stakeholder register and stakeholder management strategy described previously. The result is the communications management plan, which becomes part of the project management plan.

The Plan Communications process is focused on the information and communication needs of the stakeholders. While the effort to identify stakeholders and their communication requirements and preferences began in project initiating, the planning effort determines how to apply that information. The Plan Communications process looks at how to maximize the effectiveness and efficiency of communications on the project, including what should be communicated, to whom, when, with what method, and how frequently.

If you work on a small project, you might believe you can simply spend a few minutes thinking about what information the four people on your team need. Taking this attitude for the exam is a mistake, however. Imagine a team of 300 people spread throughout the world, speaking many different languages with many different cultural ways of communicating, and you can better see how much work planning communications takes and how worthwhile the effort is. Many project managers fail to recognize how much impact communications have on a project and how complex they can get. When we teach communication in our Project Management Tricks of the Trade® class, this topic is one that most people are not initially interested in, yet they find the communication activities we offer in class to be some of the most valuable.

This topic is important on the exam, but luckily it is not difficult as long as you think in terms of large projects. A basic concept of communications is that they should be efficient (providing only the information needed) and effective (providing information in the right format at the right time). Think about your real-world communications. Do you do the following?

- Ask people what information they need and when.
- Plan communications to all the stakeholders.
- Customize standardized communication practices within your organization to the needs of the project.
- Use multiple methods of communicating.
- Confirm communication is actually received and understood.
- Realize that communication is two-sided, to and from a stakeholder.
- Plan communication with each stakeholder based on the individual's needs and interests.
- Remember to include such people as team members' bosses in the list of stakeholders.

Exercise Test yourself! What information and documents need to be communicated on a project?

Answer Some possible answers are:

- Project charter
- Project management plan and project documents
- Impacts to and from other projects
- WBS
- When resources will be needed
- Meeting schedule
- Work assignments
- Status
- New risks uncovered
- Uncertainties
- Problems
- Successes
- Changes to project scope and product scope
- Schedule of planned reviews of the project management plan and when updates are likely to be issued
- Updates to the project management plan or project documents
- Results of change requests
- Upcoming work
- Delays
- The date of the next milestone completion party
- Performance reports
- Lessons learned
- Issue logs
- Configuration management issues
- What types of e-mails will be sent to each stakeholder
- Contact information for all stakeholders
- Method of updating the communications management plan

Communications occur internally and externally to the core project team, vertically (up and down the levels of the organization), and horizontally (among peers). Make sure your planning includes communicating in all of the following directions.

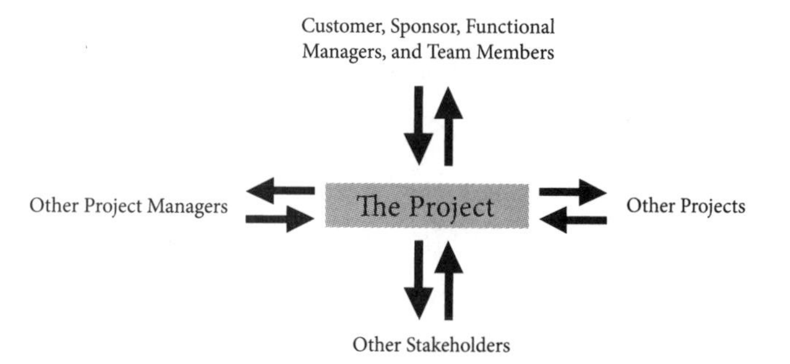

Many people forget communications between projects, as if there were no other projects that could take resources, cause delays, or cause some other such problem on the project.

In order to have clear, concise communications, you need to handle communications in a structured way and choose the best type of communication for the situation. Information can be expressed in different ways—formally or informally, written or verbal. You need to decide what approach to use for each instance of communication. Make sure you understand the following chart:

Communication Types	When Used
Formal written	Complex problems, project management plan, project charter, memos, communicating over long distances
Formal verbal	Presentations, speeches
Informal written	E-mail, handwritten notes, text messages, instant messaging
Informal verbal	Meetings, conversations

Exercise Test yourself! What is the best type of communication in the following situations?

Situation	Communication Types
Updating the project management plan	
Giving presentations to management	
Trying to solve a complex problem	
Making notes regarding a telephone conversation	
Making changes to a contract	
Informing a team member of poor performance (first notice)	
Informing a team member of poor performance (second notice)	
Scheduling a meeting	
Clarifying a work package	
Requesting additional resources	
Trying to discover the root cause of a problem	
Sending an e-mail to ask for clarification of an issue	
Holding a milestone party	
Conducting a bidder conference	

Answer Imagine these as situational questions. Exam questions may have more words, but they will boil down to straightforward situations like the ones described in the following table.

Situation	Communication Types
Updating the project management plan	Formal written
Giving presentations to management	Formal verbal
Trying to solve a complex problem	Formal written
Making notes regarding a telephone conversation	Informal written
Making changes to a contract	Formal written

Situation	Communication Types
Informing a team member of poor performance (first notice)	Informal verbal
Informing a team member of poor performance (second notice)	Formal written
Scheduling a meeting	Informal written
Clarifying a work package	Formal written
Requesting additional resources	Formal written
Trying to discover the root cause of a problem	Informal verbal
Sending an e-mail to ask for clarification of an issue	Informal written
Holding a milestone party	Informal verbal
Conducting a bidder conference	Formal verbal

Communication Models Many of us make the mistake of not ensuring that messages are properly sent and received. We do not think scientifically about our communications. We just send an e-mail and hope it is read and interpreted properly without checking to see if important communications are understood. But as noted earlier, project management requires a more structured approach to communications. You should therefore understand communication models.

Communication models are comprised of three parts: the sender, the message, and the receiver. Each message is encoded by the sender and decoded by the receiver. Factors like the receiver's education, experience, language, and culture affect the way the receiver decodes a message. Communication models often call these types of factors "noise."

Effective Communication

The sender should encode a message carefully, determine which communication method to use to send it, and confirm that the message is understood. When encoding the message, the sender needs to be aware of the following communication factors:

- **Nonverbal** About 55 percent of all communication is nonverbal (i.e., based on physical mannerisms). Therefore, most of what is communicated is nonverbal.
- **Paralingual** Pitch and tone of voice also help to convey a message.

To confirm the message is understood, the sender should ask for feedback, saying things like, "Do you understand what I have explained?"

Effective Listening

The receiver should decode the message carefully and confirm the message is understood. This includes watching the speaker to pick up physical gestures and facial expressions, thinking about what to say before responding, and using active listening, in which the receiver confirms he or she is listening, expresses agreement or disagreement, or asks for clarification.

Even if a message is not understood, the receiver should still acknowledge the message (i.e., saying things such as, "I am not sure I understand; can you explain that again?"). Like the sender, the receiver needs to keep in mind the potential effects of nonverbal and paralingual communication when giving feedback.

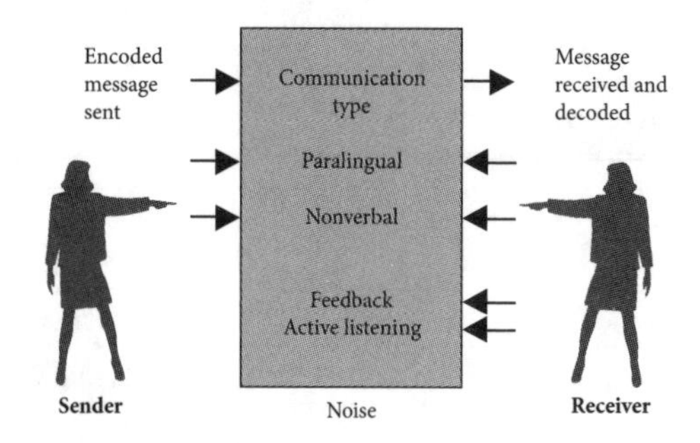

Communication Technology PAGE 254 Another aspect of planning communications is determining the specifics of how to communicate each item. Communications can take place in many ways. A few examples are face-to-face interactions; by telephone, fax, mail, or e-mail; through virtual or in-person meetings; and through intranet- or Internet-based forums for information. These different means of communicating are referred to as communication technology. To determine the appropriate technology to use, ask questions such as:

- Would it be better to communicate the information through an e-mail or telephone call?
- What technology is the team familiar and comfortable with (e.g., online forums, data reports, telephone conferences)?
- How quickly do I need to communicate the information?
- Should I send a letter through the mail in order for it to get real attention?

TRICKS OF THE TRADE® As you read this chapter, you may be seeing many new terms. You can figure out most of these terms without memorization as long as you understand the concept that communications must be planned and thought through to include all stakeholders in many countries. For example, can you guess what a push communication might be without reading the next paragraph? You will see these terms on the exam, but do not waste time memorizing them. Just read this chapter over once or twice, and you should understand the concepts for the exam.

Communication Methods PAGE 256 When planning communications, it is also important to determine the communication method. These methods can be grouped into the following categories:[1]

- **Interactive Communication** This method is reciprocal and can involve two people or many people. One person provides information; others receive it and then respond to the information. Examples of interactive communication include conversations, meetings, and conference calls.
- **Push Communication** This method involves a one-way stream of information. The sender provides the information to the people who need it but does not expect feedback on the communication. Examples of push communication are status reports, e-mailed updates, and company memos.
- **Pull Communication** In this method, the project manager places the information in a central location. The recipients are then responsible for retrieving, or "pulling," the information from that location. This method is used to distribute large documents or to send information to many people.

In choosing a communication method, the project manager should consider whether feedback is needed or if it is enough to simply provide the information.

Control of Communications The exam may also ask:

- **Can the project manager control all communications?** The answer is, "No!" That would be impossible.
- **Should the project manager try to control communications?** Yes, otherwise changes, miscommunications, unclear directions, and scope creep can occur.
- **What percentage of the project manager's time is spent communicating?** About 90 percent.

Meetings Project managers may have many different types of meetings. Meetings are a problem in the real world, because many project managers manage by doing everything in meetings and most meetings are not efficient.

Expect questions about the following rules for meetings: (But then we already know these and follow them, right?)

- Set a time limit, and keep to it.
- Schedule recurring meetings in advance.
- Meet with the team regularly, but not too often.
- Have a purpose for each meeting.
- Create an agenda with team input.
- Distribute the agenda beforehand.
- Stick to the agenda.
- Let people know their responsibilities in advance.
- Bring the right people together.
- Chair and lead the meeting with a set of rules.
- Assign deliverables and time limits for all work assignments that result from meetings.
- Document and publish meeting minutes.

Communication Channels When you add one more person to the team, does the number of communication channels simply increase by one? No. There is a substantial increase, and communication needs can grow rapidly with each added stakeholder.

Communication channels can be calculated using the following formula:

$\frac{N(N-1)}{2}$	N = the number of people

You should understand this formula for the exam. Are you thinking, "What? Another formula to know?" Don't worry. You should have no problem knowing this formula without memorization. Just practice it. How about some tricks?

The only formula with the letter "N" in it on the exam is communication channels.

If you have a question like, "You have a team of four people; how many channels of communication are there?" simply draw the lines or channels of communication, as shown, to get six channels of communication.

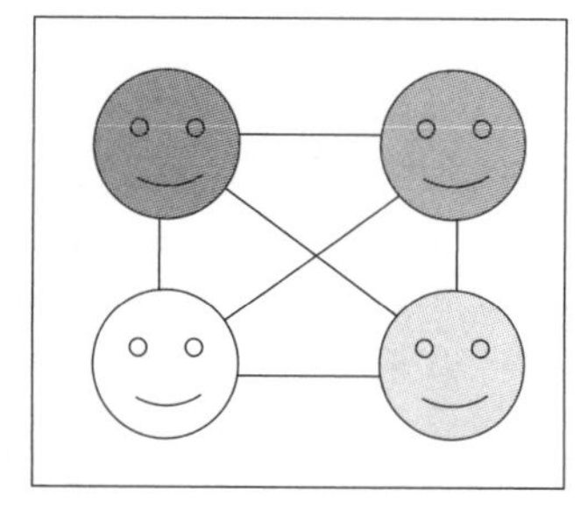

Now let's use the formula to the answer to the previous question. Calculate 4 times 3 (which is N−1) to get 12, and then divide by 2 to reach the answer, which is 6.

Now try it on your own. If you have four people on your project and you add one more, how many more communication channels do you have?

The answer is 10 of course, right? Wrong! The question asked how many more. Do you know how many people get a question wrong because they read it incorrectly?

To use the trick described previously, simply draw a new person and draw lines from the new person to all the other people to see that there are four more channels of communication, as shown.

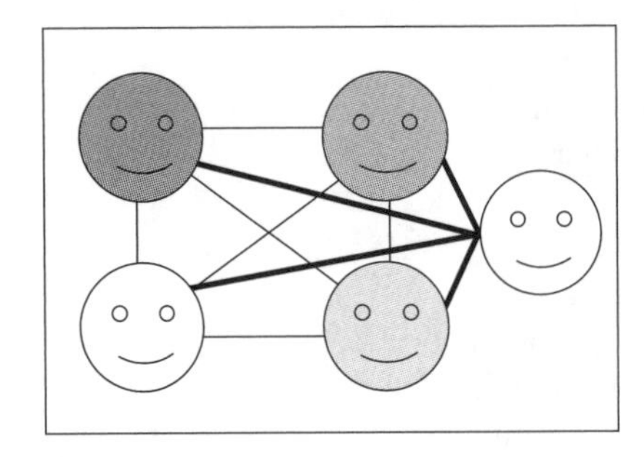

To get the answer using the formula, you would have to calculate the communication channels with a team of four and with a team of five and then subtract the difference. We already did the calculation for four people to find six channels. The calculation for five team members is 5 times 4 equals 20; 20 divided by 2 equals 10; 10 minus 6 equals 4.

Communications Management Plan PAGE 256

The primary output of the Plan Communications process is a communications management plan.

A communications management plan documents how you will manage and control communications. Many people do not realize the extent of the information that must be distributed. The following is just one sample of what a communications management plan might look like.

What Needs to Be Communicated	Why	Between Whom	Best Method for Communicating	Responsibility for Sending	When and How Often

Because communications are so complex, a communications management plan should be in writing for most projects. It must address the needs of all the stakeholders. The communications management plan becomes part of the project management plan. If you have communications problems on your projects, spending more time in this area can help resolve them.

Distribute Information PAGE 258

Process: Distribute Information
Process Group: Executing
Knowledge Area: Communications Management

While the project is being executed, many stakeholders will need to receive information about the project. The project manager is responsible for providing this information. The idea of communicating information to stakeholders is likely not a new concept to you, but what some project managers do not understand is that different stakeholders need to receive different information in various formats, and the project manager should have determined in advance what each stakeholder needs to know, how, and when. So the Distribute Information process involves implementing the communications management plan, which is part of the project management plan. Not only do you send information in this process, but you also need to make sure the communications are received, effective, and efficient.

Manage Stakeholder Expectations PAGE 261

Process: Manage Stakeholder Expectations
Process Group: Executing
Knowledge Area: Communications Management

Managing stakeholder expectations is a communications function. Stakeholders' needs must continue to be met and their issues resolved throughout the project. When was the last time you did something like the following scenario?

> *A project manager knows a stakeholder felt strongly that a certain scope should have been part of the project. Anticipating that the stakeholder will continue pressing to get the scope added, the project manager communicates the following: "I know that during project planning you wanted a certain scope to be part of the project. The entire group of sponsors on this project agreed to remove that scope from the project. It would not be worth your time to try to get it added now."*

How about this situation?

> *During requirements gathering, a stakeholder expressed concern about how much the project would impact her department's other work. The project manager contacts her to say, "I have kept your concern in mind while planning the project. You know there is little probability we could do this project without impacting your department, but because you were so concerned, I have put a report together telling you when we will impact your department's regular work. I will update the report on a monthly basis."*

Why bother doing such work? Such actions are proactive and make the stakeholders feel that their needs and concerns are at least being considered, even if they are not agreed to. These efforts also serve the valuable role of keeping open communication channels with the stakeholders so they can inform the project manager of potential changes, added risks, and other information.

Do you think you don't have time in your real world to do these things? As with many other areas of project management, such efforts can actually help you save time, rather than take more of your time. These types of actions help reduce the amount of time project managers are forced to spend dealing with problems. When taking the exam, assume the project manager has followed the practices of proper project management and done everything right. Therefore, the project manager has time to spend making sure communications are appropriate and stakeholder expectations are managed.

So how important is it to manage stakeholder expectations? Think about what expectations are. They are beliefs about (or mental pictures of) the future. Can you see how stakeholders all having different pictures of the future could cause problems? A difference between what a stakeholder thinks will happen and what actually happens might cause conflicts, rework, and those dreaded changes. Why wait for a change? Why not prevent changes as much as possible by asking stakeholders what they expect and clarifying any expectations that are not accurate? Managing stakeholder expectations might involve walking them through what will occur to make sure they do not have unrealistic expectations.

The project manager reviews the stakeholder register, stakeholder management strategy, communications management plan, issue logs, and changes to determine what to do to manage stakeholder expectations. Managing expectations requires attention to the stakeholders' needs while the work is being done and making sure trust is built, conflicts are resolved, and problems are prevented.

Communication Blockers You planned well; now what can get in the way of good communications? Many project managers unknowingly introduce communication blockers into their projects. Communication blockers include such phrases as "What is your game plan?" "Getting down to the nitty gritty," or "Zero in on problems." These phrases can cause miscommunication with people from other cultures. Such comments as "What a bad idea!" also hamper effective communication. The exam has often had one or two questions that ask, "What can get in the way of communications?" or "The following has occurred; what is wrong?" The answer may include:

- Noisy surroundings
- Distance between those trying to communicate
- Improper encoding of messages
- Making negative statements
- Hostility
- Language
- Culture

The Manage Stakeholder Expectations process can result in documentation of lessons learned, change requests including recommended corrective and preventive actions, updates to issue logs to inform stakeholders about issues and any corrective actions taken to resolve them, and changes to the communications management plan, stakeholder management strategy, and stakeholder register.

Report Performance PAGE 266

Process: Report Performance
Process Group: Monitoring & Controlling
Knowledge Area: Communications Management

Reporting performance is yet another communications management process. This effort involves collecting work performance information, analyzing it, and sending it to stakeholders. It also involves asking for feedback on the reports from stakeholders to ensure the project still meets the business case for which it was selected and supports the organization's strategic goals. There is not much here that you probably do not already know, but make sure you understand the following:

- Reports should provide the kinds of information and the level of detail required by stakeholders.
- Reports should be designed for the needs of the project.
- The best way to have a report read and acted on is to use the most appropriate communication method in sending it. Do you expect people to notice your e-mail when they receive hundreds in a day? Would it be better to mail the report overnight? Make sure you consider such factors when reporting information.
- You should not spend all your time reporting. Remember that many reports are just about the past. Finding information about the past means it is too late to prevent the problem. You need to keep managing the project, rather than just reporting on it, to make a project successful. Many people new to project management make the mistake of spending too much time reporting and not enough time managing.
- Reports should include measurements against the performance measurement baseline set in the project management plan. Remember, you should have a performance measurement baseline (the combined scope, schedule, and cost baselines) that can be measured. Those measurements are an indication of how successful you are as a project manager.
- Reports must be truthful and not hide what is really going on. This seems logical, but there may be a few questions on the exam that describe such situations because of recent company scandals around the world regarding untruthful reporting.
- You should report cost, schedule, scope, and quality performance, not just schedule.
- Reports help the team members know where they need to recommend and implement corrective actions.
- The process of Report Performance includes looking into the future. The team and sponsor can use forecasts to determine what preventive actions are needed.

- You should get feedback from the people who receive the reports as part of this process. This feedback is essential to ensure the project still meets the business needs and aligns with the organization's strategic goals.
- There are different types of performance reports, not just one that might come out of some software application. Think in terms of a large project and realize a project manager might be issuing the following types of reports:
  - **Status Report** This report describes where the project now stands regarding the performance measurement baseline.
  - **Progress Report** A progress report describes what has been accomplished.
  - **Trend Report** This report examines project results over time to see if performance is improving or deteriorating.
  - **Forecasting Report** This report predicts future project status and performance.
  - **Variance Report**[2] A variance report compares actual results to baselines.
  - **Earned Value Report**[3] An earned value report integrates scope, cost, and schedule measures to assess project performance, using the terms described in the Cost Management chapter (i.e., PV, EV, AC, etc.).
  - **Lessons Learned Documentation** Reports on performance are used as lessons learned for future projects.

This concludes the Communications Management chapter. For the exam, keep in mind that communications are essential to success and affect all areas of a project. Poor communications can cause major problems and rework. Therefore, a project manager should spend the time in the early stages of the project to identify ALL the stakeholders and take a structured approach to communications by creating a communications management plan. As the project work is being done, the project manager needs to manage stakeholder expectations and follow the communications management plan to distribute information about the project. In addition, when reporting project status and forecasted performance, the project manager should solicit feedback on those reports to verify they are being read and to ensure the project still meets the business need.

Practice Exam

1. A project manager has a problem with a team member's performance. What is BEST form of communication for addressing this problem?
   A. Formal written communication
   B. Formal verbal communication
   C. Informal written communication
   D. Informal verbal communication

2. Extensive use of ___ communication is most likely to aid in solving complex problems.
   A. Verbal
   B. Written
   C. Formal
   D. Nonverbal

3. The work breakdown structure can be an effective aid for communication in which setting(s)?
   A. Internal within the project team
   B. Internal within the organization
   C. External with the customer
   D. Internal and external to the project

4. The MOST likely result of communication blockers is that:
   A. The project is delayed.
   B. The trust level is enhanced.
   C. Conflict occurs.
   D. Senior management is displeased.

5. Communications are often enhanced when the sender ___ the receiver.
   A. Speaks up to
   B. Uses gestures when speaking to
   C. Speaks slowly to
   D. Shows concern for the perspective of

6. Formal written correspondence with the customer is required when:
   A. Defects are detected.
   B. The customer requests additional work not covered under contract.
   C. The project has a schedule slippage that includes changes to the critical path.
   D. The project has cost overruns.

7. When a project manager is engaged in negotiations, nonverbal communication skills are of:
   A. Little importance.
   B. Major importance.
   C. Importance only when cost and schedule objectives are involved.
   D. Importance only to ensure he wins the negotiation.

8. A large, one-year telecommunications project is about halfway done when you take the place of the previous project manager. The project involves three different sellers and a project team of 30 people. You would like to see the project's communications requirements and what technology is being used to aid in project communications. Where will you find this information?
   A. The project management plan
   B. The information distribution plan
   C. The bar chart
   D. The communications management plan

9. Changes to some project deliverables have been documented in the project management plan. These changes, and other project information, have been distributed according to the communications management plan. One stakeholder expressed surprise to the project manager upon hearing of a documented change to a project deliverable. All stakeholders received the communication containing notification of the change. What should the project manager do?
   A. Determine why the stakeholder did not receive the information and let him know when it was published.
   B. Ask the functional manager why the stakeholder did not understand his responsibility.
   C. Review the communications management plan and make revisions if necessary.
   D. Address the situation in the next steering committee meeting so others do not miss published changes.

10. The project status report is an example of which form of communication?
    A. Formal written communication
    B. Formal verbal communication
    C. Informal written communication
    D. Informal verbal communication

11. Communication is key to the success of a project. As the project manager, you had three stakeholders with whom you needed to communicate. Therefore, you had six channels of communication. A new stakeholder has been added with whom you also need to communicate. How many communication channels do you have now?
    A. 7
    B. 10
    C. 12
    D. 16

12. Two people are arguing about what needs to be done to complete a work package. If the project manager wants to know what is going on, she should pay MOST attention to:
    A. What is being said and when.
    B. What is being said, who is saying it, and the time of day.
    C. Physical mannerisms and what is being said.
    D. The pitch and tone of the voices, and physical mannerisms.

13. A project manager has a project team consisting of people in four countries. The project is very important to the company, and the project manager is concerned about its success. The length of the project schedule is acceptable. What type of communication should he use?
    A. Informal verbal communication
    B. Formal written communication
    C. Formal verbal communication
    D. Informal written communication

14. The project status meeting is not going well. Many attendees are talking at the same time, there are people who are not participating, and many topics are being discussed at random. Which of the following rules for effective meetings is NOT being adhered to?
    A. Demonstrate courtesy and consideration of each other, and control who is allowed to speak.
    B. Schedule meetings in advance.
    C. Have a purpose for the meeting, with the right people in attendance.
    D. Create and publish an agenda and a set of rules for controlling the meeting.

15. You have just been assigned as project manager for a large manufacturing project. This one-year project is about halfway done. It involves 5 different sellers and 20 members of your company on the project team. You want to quickly review where the project now stands. Which of the following reports would be the MOST helpful in finding such information?
    A. Work status
    B. Progress
    C. Forecast
    D. Communications

16. A team member is visiting the manufacturing plant of one of the suppliers. Which of the following is the MOST important thing to be done in any telephone calls the project manager might make to the team member?
    A. Ask the team member to repeat back what the project manager says.
    B. Review the list of contact information for all stakeholders.
    C. Ask the team member to look for change requests.
    D. Review the upcoming meeting schedule.

17. A project manager overhears a conversation between two stakeholders who are discussing how unhappy they are with the impacts of the project on their own departments. Stakeholder A asks if the project is on time, and stakeholder B replies that the SPI is 1.05. Stakeholder A asks if the project manager for the project knows of stakeholder B's concern. Stakeholder B responds that he is not sure. What is the BEST thing for the project manager to do?
    A. Make sure the stakeholders see that the project manager overheard. Then ask them to direct any questions in writing to the project manager.
    B. Make a presentation to all the stakeholders regarding the status of the project.
    C. Send both stakeholders a copy of the issue log and ask for additional comments.
    D. Arrange a meeting with both stakeholders to allow them to voice any concerns they may have.

18. A project manager wants to more extensively involve the stakeholders on the project. Which of the following would be the BEST way to accomplish this?
    A. Have the stakeholders periodically review the list of project requirements.
    B. Invite the stakeholders to attend project status meetings.
    C. Send status report to the stakeholders.
    D. Update the stakeholders on the status of all project changes.

19. During the middle of the project, things have been going well. The work authorization system has allowed people to know when to start work, and the issue log has helped keep track of stakeholders' needs. The sponsor has expressed his appreciation for the team members' efforts by hosting a milestone party. The project manager gets a call from a team member saying the results from the completion of her activity's predecessor are two days late. Which of the following reasons would BEST describe why this occurred?
    A. The project manager was focusing on the sponsor's needs.
    B. Functional management was not included in the communications management plan.
    C. The successor activities should have been watched, not the predecessors.
    D. The right people were not invited to the milestone party.

20. A project manager has just been assigned a team that comes from many countries including Brazil, Japan, the US, and Britain. What is her BEST tool for success?
    A. The responsibility assignment matrix (RAM)
    B. The teleconference
    C. Team communication with the WBS
    D. Communication and well-developed people skills

21. The project has 13 team members and affects more than 15 departments in the organization. Because the project is 20 percent complete to date and the team has had successful performance reports from five of the affected departments, the project manager holds a party to celebrate. The project manager invites key stakeholders from all of the departments to the party, in order to give those providing good reviews an informal opportunity to communicate good things to those departments that have not yet been affected by the project. At the party, the project manager walks around to try to discover any relevant information that would help him make the project even more successful. He happens to hear a manager of one of the departments talking about setting up more regular meetings on the project.

    The BEST thing for the project manager to do would be to FIRST:
    A. Record the effectiveness of the party in the project lessons learned.
    B. Review the information distribution methods on the project.
    C. Hold a meeting of all the stakeholders to discuss their concerns.
    D. Make sure the manager has a copy of the communications management plan so he is reminded that such concerns should be sent to the project manager.

22. The purpose of status meetings is to:
    A. Exchange information about the project.
    B. Have team members report on what they are doing.
    C. Issue work authorizations.
    D. Confirm the accuracy of the costs submitted by the team.

23. The requirements of many stakeholders were not approved for inclusion in your project. Therefore, you had a difficult time receiving formal approval of the project management plan. The stakeholders argued and held up the project while they held meeting after meeting about their requirements. The project was finally approved and work began six months ago. All of the following would be good preventive actions to implement EXCEPT:
    A. Keep a file of what requirements were not included in the project.
    B. Make sure the change control process is not used as a vehicle to add the requirements back into the project.
    C. Maintain an issue log.
    D. Hold meetings with the stakeholders to go over the work that will not be added to the project.

24. The project manager is expecting a deliverable to be submitted by e-mail from a team member today. At the end of the day, the project manager contacts the team member to notify him that it has not been received. The team member apologizes and explains that he was not able to e-mail the deliverable, and it was sent through the mail instead. The team member goes on to remind the project manager that he had informed the project manager, during a phone conversation, that this would occur. "Was that the conversation we had when I told you I could not hear you well due to poor cell phone coverage?" asks the project manager. "Yes," replies the team member. What could have been done to avoid this problem?
    A. Paralingual communication
    B. Adding to the issue log after the phone call
    C. Better attention to determining communications requirements
    D. Feedback during the communication

25. When do stakeholders have the MOST influence on a project?
    A. At the beginning of the project
    B. In the middle of the project
    C. At the end of the project
    D. Throughout the project

26. The project has been going well, except for the number of changes being made. The project is being installed into seven different departments within the company and will greatly improve departmental performance when operational. The team has selected the appropriate processes for use on the project. The project manager is a technical expert as well as having been trained in communications and managing people. Which of the following is the MOST likely cause of the project problems?
    A. The project manager was not trained in understanding the company environment.
    B. The project should have more management oversight since it will result in such great benefits to the company.
    C. The project should have used more of the project management processes.
    D. Some stakeholders were not identified.

27. Stakeholders can be identified in which project management process groups?
    A. Initiating, planning, executing, monitoring and controlling, and closing
    B. Initiating and planning
    C. Planning and monitoring and controlling
    D. Monitoring and controlling and closing

28. If a project manager wants to report on the actual project results vs. planned results, she should use a:
    A. Trend report.
    B. Forecasting report.
    C. Status report.
    D. Variance report.

29. A particular stakeholder has a reputation for making many changes on projects. What is the BEST approach a project manager can take at the beginning of the project to manage this situation?
    A. Say "No" to the stakeholder a few times to dissuade him from submitting more changes.
    B. Get the stakeholder involved in the project as early as possible.
    C. Talk to the stakeholder's boss to find ways of directing the stakeholder's activities to another project.
    D. Ask that the stakeholder not be included in the stakeholder listing.

30. Communications under a contract should tend toward:
    A. Formal written communication.
    B. Formal verbal communication.
    C. Informal written communication.
    D. Informal verbal communication.

Answers

1. **Answer** D
   Explanation The best choice is informal verbal communication. This does not mean you do not keep records of the problem, but it is best to start this discussion informally. If informal communication does not solve the problem, formal written communication is the next choice.

2. **Answer** B
   Explanation Written communication allows your words to be documented, and they will go to everyone in the same form. When there are complex problems, you want everyone to receive the same information.

3. **Answer** D
   Explanation The work breakdown structure can be used for communication vertically and horizontally within the organization, as well as outside the project.

4. **Answer** C
   Explanation The major result of communication blockers and miscommunication as a whole is conflict.

5. **Answer** D
   Explanation Understanding the receiver's perspective allows the sender to direct the communication to meet the receiver's needs.

6. **Answer** B
   Explanation Everything we do is more formal in a procurement environment than in other project activities. Therefore, formal written communication is required when the customer requests work not covered under the contract.

7. **Answer** B
   Explanation Nonverbal communication carries 55 percent of the message you send. With this much at stake, nonverbal communication is of major importance.

8. **Answer** D
   Explanation Although the information is found within the project management plan, the communications management plan is the best answer because it directly answers the question.

9. **Answer** C
   Explanation The question states that all stakeholders received the information, so the issue is not that this stakeholder did not receive it. The problem presented here illustrates that there is something missing in the communications management plan. The best answer is to review the communications management plan in order to prevent future problems and find any instances of similar problems.

10. **Answer** A
    Explanation The project status needs to be known by many people. Therefore, it is best to present this information n in writing so that it can be transmitted to many people at once. It is also formal in that it is an official report of the project. Therefore, formal written communication is the best answer.

11. **Answer** B
Explanation Did you realize the project manager is part of the communication channels? Therefore, there are actually four stakeholders to begin with and six channels of communication. The question is asking how many total channels of communication you have with a team of five people. The formula is $[N \times (N-1)]/2$ or $(5 \times 4)/2 = 10$.

12. **Answer** D
Explanation Remember that nonverbal communication represents 55 percent of all communication. The choice including paralingual communication (pitch and tone), as well as physical mannerisms, is the best choice.

13. **Answer** B
Explanation Because of the differences in culture and the distance between team members, formal written communication is needed.

14. **Answer** D
Explanation Courtesy and consideration is not a "rule" for effective meetings. Since there is no indication that the meeting was not scheduled in advance or that there isn't a purpose, these cannot be the best answers. "Discussed at random" implies no agenda. If an agenda is issued beforehand, people will follow the outline and should not need random discussions.

15. **Answer** B
Explanation The key word is quickly. The status report is too detailed for a quick look. The forecast report only looks into the future. The progress report summarizes project status, and would be the most helpful for a quick review.

16. **Answer** A
Explanation Questions like this drive people crazy. There are many choices that are reasonably correct. Look for the most immediate need. Here, the team member is in a manufacturing environment. That means communications will most likely be blocked by noise. It is best for the project manager to ask the team member to repeat back what he says, to ensure the team member correctly heard what the project manager communicated.

17. **Answer** D
Explanation This is another question with more than one right answer. Would asking for something in writing be the best way to communicate? In this particular situation, asking for the concern to be in writing might alienate the stakeholders. The issue log is where the issue should be listed, but the situation does not say if the project manager knows what the stakeholders' concern is. Therefore, using the issue log cannot be the best choice. Why not make a presentation to all the stakeholders regarding the status of the project? The project manager already knows stakeholders A and B have the concern, not all the stakeholders. This problem would likely require informal verbal communication to discover the real problem. Arranging a meeting with the concerned stakeholders is therefore the best choice.

18. **Answer** A
Explanation It seems like all of these are good ideas, but having the stakeholders review the list of project requirements helps discover errors and changes, and could therefore be considered the best choice.

19. **Answer** B
Explanation Since there is no information about the sponsor or his needs in this situation, focusing on his needs cannot be best. The statement that successor activities should have been

watched, rather than the predecessors, is not a correct statement. A project manager should watch both predecessor and successor activities. Attendance at the party and the issue at hand are not related. Often forgotten in communications management plans are the bosses of team members (functional management in a matrix organization). Including the bosses of team members in communications planning, requirements gathering, risk management, and other areas of project management helps make the project better. In addition, it helps the functional managers manage their resources effectively. If the functional manager of the team member assigned to the predecessor activity had been included in the project planning processes, he would have known when the team member was needed to do work for the project and the impact, if any, of delay. The communications management plan should also have included a method to communicate potential delays.

20. **Answer** D
Explanation Working with people from different cultures with different cultural values and beliefs necessitates an understanding of both basic definitions and areas of cultural impact. As project managers, we need to have good communication skills and a willingness to adapt to other cultures.

21. **Answer** B
Explanation Many of these choices could be done, but ask yourself, "What is the most effective thing to do?" The party may well generate lessons learned, and recording them would certainly be a good idea, but the question asked what to do first. There is a more immediate issue—the manager. Meeting with all the stakeholders could be useful, but there is only one stakeholder, the manager, who definitely has an issue. Besides, a good project manager would be holding regular meetings with the stakeholders already. Making sure the manager has a copy of the communications management plan might be a good idea, as the manager apparently is not communicating with the project manager. However, this would not be enough to ensure the manager does communicate.

The manager is, in effect, saying he is not getting the information he needs. His lack of needed information is causing him to suggest more meetings. However, too many meetings are a problem on projects. A great project manager does not just add meetings, but solves the real problem in the best way.

A goal of information distribution is to get information to those who need it. The project manager may decide to adjust the information distribution process by changing the format of a report or sending existing reports to the manager with the issue, rather than adding meetings. Therefore, the correct choice is to review the information distribution methods on the project.

22. **Answer** A
Explanation Team members' reporting on what they are doing may best be done outside of meetings. The main purpose of status meetings is to exchange project information.

23. **Answer** D
Explanation This issue should be over, but since there were so many meetings and arguments about the requirements being removed, it is unlikely the issue will be dropped by the stakeholders. However, as it has not come up again and the project was started six months ago, spending time in a meeting is excessive. The other choices are easier, have less impact on the project, and are therefore things that could be done.

24. **Answer** D
Explanation The pitch and tone of voice (paralingual communication) is not relevant here, as the project manager could not even hear all that was being said. There were no issues recognized after the conversation, so none could be added to the issue log. This issue is not related to communications requirements, so that choice cannot be best. Saying, "I am not sure I properly heard what you said," during the conversation or repeating the message back to the team member would have prevented this problem. Giving and requesting feedback during the communication is the best option.

25. **Answer** A
Explanation Stakeholders have an impact throughout the project, but they must be identified and involved at the beginning of the project, in order to determine their requirements and expectations. If this effort is not done early, the results may be expensive changes and/or dissatisfaction later in the project.

26. **Answer** D
Explanation Once again, it is important to look for the choice that would solve the real problem. There is no reason to think that training, management oversight, or a need for more processes are factors contributing to the number of changes. The root cause is that stakeholders were missed and, as a result, their requirements were not found. Those stakeholders are now requesting changes to accommodate their needs.

27. **Answer** A
Explanation Stakeholders can be identified throughout the project. However, the earlier stakeholders are identified, the better for the project. If all of the stakeholders' needs and requirements are taken into account before plans are finalized and project work is begun, fewer changes will be needed later in the project, when they will be more costly.

28. **Answer** D
Explanation This situation describes the need to "compare." A trend report shows performance over time. A forecasting report looks only to the future. A status report is generally static (relating to a moment in time). The only choice that compares project results is a variance analysis.

29. **Answer** B
Explanation The project manager cannot avoid the stakeholder, because he has a stake in the project. The project manager can say "No," but this does not solve the root cause of the problem. There may be some good ideas within those changes. The only choice that deals with the problem is getting the stakeholder involved in the project as soon as possible.

Changes generally arise due to lack of input at the beginning of the project. If the project manager begins effective communication with this stakeholder early, there is a much better chance his changes will be discovered during the planning process, when they will have less of an impact on the project.

30. **Answer** A
Explanation When we talk about contracts, everything we do is more formal than in other project activities. Records are also important in procurement, thus the need for written communication.

CHAPTER ELEVEN Risk Management

Quicktest

- Risk management process
- Definition of risk management
- Threats
- Opportunities
- Inputs to risk management
- Risk register
- Risk management plan
- Risk response strategies
  - Avoid
  - Mitigate
  - Transfer
  - Exploit
  - Share
  - Enhance
  - Accept
- Reserves (contingency and management)
- Reserve analysis
- Probability and impact matrix
- Monte Carlo analysis
- Expected monetary value
- Contingency plans
- Fallback plans
- Watchlist
- Workarounds
- Revised project management plan and project documents
- Risk categories
- Types of risk
- Risk response owner
- Residual risks
- Secondary risks
- Common risk management errors
- Assumptions analysis
- Documentation reviews
- Information gathering techniques
- SWOT analysis
- Checklist analysis
- Diagramming techniques
- Variance and trend analysis
- Risk data quality assessment
- Risk audit
- Risk reassessments
- Risk urgency assessment
- Risk triggers
- Risk tolerance
- Risk threshold
- Uncertainty
- Decision tree
- Risk averse
- Risk factors
- Status meetings
- Closure of risks

Let's start this chapter with a story. There was a series of hurricanes in the state of Florida in the United States, a relatively frequent occurrence there. A project manager had been working on a hardware/software installation when one of the hurricanes came. Not long after the hurricane was over, he was telling people about what a great job his team did and how quickly they recovered from the disaster. Would you have been proud of yourself if you were the project manager? Before you answer, consider the following information.

The activity the team was working on required three days to complete. The project manager had warning that the hurricane was coming. Instead of being excited about how quickly his team was able to recover from the hurricane, the project manager—and his boss—should have questioned the wisdom of his decision to go ahead with the implementation at the scheduled time when everyone knew there was a hurricane coming. A project manager's work should not focus on dealing with problems; it should focus on preventing them. Had the project manager performed risk management on his project, he would have considered the possibility that a hurricane may occur during hurricane season and worked with his team as part of the project planning effort to identify possible actions to take if a hurricane was forecast for implementation weekend. Then, when one actually was forecast, the team would have reacted according to the plan, probably moving the implementation to another weekend and avoiding the damage and rework that resulted from the disaster. This is the value of risk management.

Think about your own projects. How would it feel if you could say, "No problem; we anticipated this, and we have a plan in place that will resolve it," whenever a problem occurs? How good would you look to your boss and sponsor? How much time and money would you save that would have otherwise been spent addressing the problem? How much less stress would you have in your life? Performing risk management helps prevent many problems on projects and helps make other problems less likely. And when you eliminate uncertainties, the estimates for work can decrease. This is another way risk management saves time and money on a project. These are the benefits of risk management, and they are the reason risk management is a required part of proper project management.

Rita's Process Chart—Risk Management

Where are we in the project management process?

INITIATING

- Select project manager
- Determine company culture and existing systems
- Collect processes, procedures, and historical information
- Divide large projects into phases
- Understand the business case
- Uncover initial requirements, assumptions, and risks
- Assess project and product feasibility within the given constraints
- Create measurable objectives
- Develop project charter
- Identify stakeholders
- Develop stakeholder management strategy

PLANNING

(This is the only process group with a set order)

- **Determine how you will do planning—part of all management plans**
- Determine detailed requirements
- Create project scope statement
- Assess what to purchase
- Determine team
- Create WBS and WBS dictionary
- Create activity list
- Create network diagram
- Estimate resource requirements
- Estimate time and cost
- Determine critical path
- Develop schedule
- Develop budget
- Determine quality standards, processes, and metrics
- Create process improvement plan
- **Determine all roles and responsibilities**
- Plan communications
- **Perform risk identification, qualitative and quantitative risk analysis, and risk response planning**
- **Go back—iterations**
- Prepare procurement documents
- Create change management plan
- **Finalize the "how to execute and control" parts of all management plans**
- **Develop realistic and final PM plan and performance measurement baseline**
- Gain formal approval of the plan
- Hold kickoff meeting

EXECUTING

- Execute the work according to the PM plan
- Produce product deliverables (product scope)
- Request changes
- Implement only approved changes
- Continuously improve
- Follow processes
- Perform quality assurance
- Perform quality audits
- Acquire final team
- Manage people
- Evaluate team and project performance
- Hold team-building activities
- Give recognition and rewards
- Use issue logs
- Facilitate conflict resolution
- Release resources as work is completed
- Send and receive information
- Hold meetings
- Select sellers

MONITORING & CONTROLLING

- **Take action to control the project**
- Measure performance against the performance measurement baseline
- **Measure performance against other metrics determined by the project manager**
- **Determine variances and if they warrant a corrective action or change request**
- **Influence the factors that cause changes**
- **Request changes**
- Perform integrated change control
- Approve or reject changes
- Inform stakeholders of the results of change requests
- Update the PM plan and project documents
- Manage configuration
- Create forecasts
- Gain acceptance of interim deliverables from the customer
- Perform quality control
- Report on project performance and solicit feedback
- **Perform risk assessments and audits**
- **Manage reserves**
- Administer procurements

CLOSING

- Confirm work is done to requirements
- Complete procurement closure
- Gain final acceptance of the product
- Complete financial closure
- Hand off completed product
- Solicit feedback from the customer about the project
- Complete final performance reporting
- Index and archive records
- Update lessons learned knowledge base

If you do not practice risk management on your real-world projects, this may be a difficult chapter for you. The exam asks questions on this topic at a sophisticated level, and you need to understand how risk management activities are an integral part of a project manager's daily work. The everyday impact of risk management on projects and the project manager is an incredibly important concept that you need to get your mind around before you take the exam. Through risk management, the project changes from being in control of the project manager to the project manager being in control of the project.

As you read this chapter, remember the basic, yet very important, concepts discussed next. Make sure you are prepared to deal with exam questions that test your knowledge of such concepts at an expert level.

If you find you want additional training in risk management, please consider our online or instructor-led risk management courses or the book *Risk Management, Tricks of the Trade® for Project Managers*, by Rita Mulcahy, the first edition of which won PMI's Professional Development Product of the Year award. Information on how to use the book to help prepare for the PMP exam is included on the free Web site associated with the book.

The exam also tests your knowledge of the process of risk management. This process is very logical. You may be given a situation on the exam and then asked which risk management process is being described in the situation. In other words, the question will ask "Where is the project manager in the story?" You need to understand which actions you and your team should take in each part of the process. Also expect questions on the exam that require you to analyze the situation and determine what should be done next.

We cannot stress the value of risk management enough. This chapter will provide the overview of this topic that you need for the exam. You should realize, however, there are more tools and techniques for real-world risk management than are covered here. If you are like many project managers and do not currently practice risk management on your projects, we encourage you to seek more knowledge or training about risk than you will get in this book. Risk management can greatly impact the efficiency and effectiveness of your projects and reduce stress for you and your team.

The following should help you understand how each part of risk management fits into the overall project management process:

The Risk Management Process	Done During
Plan Risk Management	Planning process group
Identify Risks	Planning process group
Perform Qualitative Risk Analysis	Planning process group
Perform Quantitative Risk Analysis	Planning process group
Plan Risk Responses	Planning process group
Monitor and Control Risks	Monitoring and controlling process group

Defining the Concepts The following are some of the basic risk management terms and concepts you need to understand for the exam.

Risk Management PAGE 273

Risk management includes risk management planning, risk identification, the qualitative and quantitative analysis of risks, risk response planning, and monitoring and controlling the risk responses. Through risk management, you work to increase the probability and impact of opportunities on the project (positive events), while decreasing the probability and impact of threats to the project (negative events).

Be careful! Risks are identified and managed starting in initiating and are continually kept up-to-date or added to while the project is underway. The project manager and the team look at what has happened on the project, the current status of the project, and what is yet to come and reassess the potential threats and opportunities.

Threats and Opportunities

A risk event is something identified in advance that may or may not happen. If it does happen, it can have positive or negative impacts on the project. Project managers often just focus on threats—what can go wrong and negatively impact the project. Do not forget that there can also be positive impacts—good risks, called opportunities! Opportunities can include such things as:

- If we can combine orders for the ZYX equipment to buy more than 20 items at once, the cost will be 20 percent less per item than planned.
- If we provide a training class to improve efficiency, work package number 3.4 could be completed two days faster than expected.
- If we can obtain a resource with more experience and a higher level of productivity in May, work on the critical path activity 4.7 could be done 10 percent faster.

Up to 90 percent of the threats identified and investigated in the risk management process can be eliminated. How much better off would you be if that happened? Would it benefit the project? How about your customer?

Uncertainty

Uncertainty is a lack of knowledge about an event that reduces confidence in conclusions drawn from the data. The work that needs to be done, the cost, the time, the quality needs, the communications needs, etc., can be uncertain. The investigation of uncertainties may help identify risks.

Risk Factors

When looking at risk, one should determine the following:

- The probability that a risk event will occur (how likely)
- The range of possible outcomes (impact or amount at stake)
- Expected timing for it to occur in the project life cycle (when)
- The anticipated frequency of risk events from that source (how often)

Risk Averse

Someone who does not want to take risks is said to be risk averse.

Risk Tolerances and Thresholds[1]

Risk tolerance is the degree or level of risk that is acceptable to a person or an organization. A risk threshold is the specific point at which risk becomes unacceptable (e.g., "We can accept the risk of a delay, as long as the potential delay will be no longer than two weeks."). Risk tolerances and thresholds vary depending on the individual or organization and the risk area. For example, an organization may have more tolerance for cost-related risks than for risks that affect customer satisfaction or their reputation in the marketplace. Risk areas can include any project constraints (scope, time, cost, quality, etc.), as well as reputation, customer satisfaction, and other intangibles.

Inputs to and Outputs of Risk Management Have you realized that there are inputs to the risk management effort as a whole and inputs to each individual risk management process? Be careful to read questions on the exam carefully. Is a question really asking you to identify an input to the overall risk management process, or should you just be thinking about what is needed before you can begin the Plan Risk Responses process? Risk management is a very step-by-step, process-oriented part of project management, so expect to see risk management input and output questions on the exam. But you should not need to memorize the inputs and outputs. As you go through this chapter, keep in mind that many of the inputs to each individual risk management process are the outputs of the processes that came before it.

Remember, inputs are merely, "What do I need to do this well?" or "What do I need before I can begin…?" Outputs are merely, "What will I have when I am done with…?"

The next exercise will help you understand what the inputs to the overall risk management effort are. You might be thinking, "Wait! The *PMBOK® Guide* does not describe inputs to the entire risk management process—just inputs to each part of the process." Although that is correct, inputs to the entire process are still on the exam. If you know Rita's Process Chart, you should not need to spend much time studying these inputs.

Exercise Test yourself! Explain why each of the following inputs to risk management are needed before you can adequately perform the risk management process. This is an important test. The following answer table is what you should know for the exam.

	Inputs to Risk Management	Why Is This Input Needed?
1	Project background information	
2	Historical records from previous projects	
3	Past lessons learned	
4	Company processes and procedures	
5	Organizational risk tolerances	
6	Organizational risk thresholds	
7	Company culture	
8	Project charter	
9	Project scope statement	
10	Team	
11	Work breakdown structure	

	Inputs to Risk Management	Why Is This Input Needed?
12	Network diagram	
13	Time and cost estimates	
14	Communications management plan	
15	Staffing management plan	
16	Procurement management plan	
17	Stakeholders	

Answer There can be many answers. Here are some possible ones.

	Inputs to Risk Management	Why Is This Input Needed?
1	Project background information	Correspondence from before the project was approved, articles written about similar projects, and other such information will help identify risks.
2	Historical records from previous projects	These records (part of organizational process assets) may have information about risks from past, similar projects.
3	Past lessons learned	Lessons learned (part of organizational process assets) tell you what teams would do differently if they could do their projects again. They help you identify, mitigate, and manage risks on your project.
4	Company processes and procedures	Company processes and procedures for project management and risk management (part of organizational process assets), or the lack of such standardized procedures, may help identify additional risks.
5	Organizational risk tolerances	Knowing the degree of risk the organization is willing to accept and the areas where there is the most and least tolerance (part of enterprise environmental factors) helps identify the impact of risks, rank risks, and determine which risk response strategies to use.

	Inputs to Risk Management	Why Is This Input Needed?
6	Organizational risk thresholds	Knowing the point at which risk becomes unacceptable (part of enterprise environmental factors) helps identify the impact of risks and which risk response strategies to use.
7	Company culture	A company's culture (and other components of enterprise environmental factors) can add risk and should be considered when identifying risks.
8	Project charter	The project charter indicates the initial, high-level risks identified on the project and helps you see if the overall project objectives and constraints are generally risky or not. The charter also helps identify risks based on what is and what is not included in the project.
9	Project scope statement	The project scope statement documents the project and product scope and deliverables. This information can help you assess how complex the project will be and what level of risk management effort is appropriate. The project scope statement also contains information about boundaries, constraints, and assumptions, which can indicate risks for the project.
10	Team	The project manager cannot identify all the risks alone. Taking a group approach and sharing risk management responsibilities make the risk management process more accurate and timely.
11	Work breakdown structure	The WBS is needed because risks must be specific, not general. They should be identified at the work package level in addition to the project level.
12	Network diagram	The network diagram is the only place where paths that converge into one activity can be easily seen. Such path convergence makes the activity riskier than if there was no path convergence. The network diagram also helps determine the critical path and any near-critical paths. The "tighter" the schedule, the more risk the project has.
13	Time and cost estimates	Knowing the estimates helps you determine the risk of the project not meeting the schedule and cost objectives. Initial estimates are an input to risk management, and detailed estimates are an output of risk management. The final budget and schedule cannot be determined without including risk reserves.

	Inputs to Risk Management	Why Is This Input Needed?
14	Communications management plan	Are there a lot of people to communicate with? Where in the project are communications so important that communication errors can actually add risk to the project? Is your communications management plan effective? Since the number one problem many people have on projects is poor communication, there is a strong connection between planning communications and decreasing risk.
15	Staffing management plan	The staffing management plan (part of the human resource plan) describes what resources are available, their skill sets, and how they will be moved on and off the project. Knowing this information will help you identify risks related to resources.
16	Procurement management plan	How many contracts will there likely be on the project? What is the level of expertise of those handling the contracts? Was the project manager involved before any contracts were signed? If not, the project will have more risk and is likely to cost more. Contracts are a way to mitigate or transfer risks in risk response planning.
17	Stakeholders	Stakeholders will view the project from different perspectives and thus will be able to see risks that the team cannot. Stakeholders are involved in many aspects of risk management.

The Risk Management Process PAGE 273 It is very important to understand the risk management process for the exam. You must MEMORIZE what happens when and know how risk management, done well, can change the way projects are managed and how it can change what happens in a typical day on a project. On large, properly managed projects where risk management has been an integral part of planning, the following occurs:

- There are no longer huge fires to put out every day—they were eliminated with risk response plans.
- Risks are brought up in every meeting to be addressed before they happen.
- If a risk event does occur, there is a plan in place to deal with it, meaning no more hectic meetings to develop a response.

As a result, the project manager has time for efforts such as:

- Monitoring and controlling the various aspects of the project, looking for deviations and trends to find them early.
- Implementing a reward system.
- Keeping stakeholders informed of project progress.
- Staying ahead of the project.

The six sequential risk management processes are:

1. Plan Risk Management
2. Identify Risks
3. Perform Qualitative Risk Analysis
4. Perform Quantitative Risk Analysis
5. Plan Risk Responses
6. Monitor and Control Risks

Although the processes are done in sequence, remember that they are done often during the course of the project, starting in initiating all the way through the end of the project. Risks can be identified any time, as can the responses for what to do about the new risks. So if a risk is uncovered after the initial risk identification process, it must be analyzed, responses must be planned, etc. The risk management process is very iterative.

Plan Risk Management PAGE 276

Process: Plan Risk Management
Process Group: Planning
Knowledge Area: Risk Management

The project manager, sponsor, team, customer, other stakeholders, and experts may be involved in the Plan Risk Management process to define how risk management will be structured and performed for the project. Since risk management is so critical to the success of a project, wouldn't it be wise to think about how you will approach risk management before you do it? Plan before you act. Risk management efforts should be appropriate to the size and complexity of the project, as well as the experience and skill level of the project team. Successful risk management cannot be done with just a standardized checklist of risks from past projects. Although such a checklist can be helpful in creating a plan and identifying risks, the risk management effort needs to happen for each project.

The Plan Risk Management process answers the question of how much time should be spent on risk management based on the needs of the project. It also answers questions such as who will be involved and how the team will go about performing risk management. Company procedures and templates related to risk, such as standard probability and impact matrices, are identified as part of this process and then adapted to the needs of the project.

Outputs of Plan Risk Management PAGE 279 When you have completed risk management planning, you should, of course, have a risk management plan.

Risk Management Plan

The risk management plan may include:

- **Methodology** This section of the plan defines how you will perform risk management for the particular project. Remember to adapt the methods to the needs of each project. Low-priority projects will likely warrant less of a risk management effort than high-priority projects.
- **Roles and responsibilities** This section answers the question of "Who will do what?" Did you realize that non-team members may have roles and responsibilities regarding risk management?
- **Budgeting** This section includes the cost of the risk management process. Yes, there is a cost of doing risk management, but risk management saves the project time and money overall by avoiding or reducing threats and taking advantage of opportunities.
- **Timing** This section of the plan talks about when to do risk management for the project. Risk management should start as soon as you have the appropriate inputs and should be repeated throughout the life of the project, since new risks can be identified as the project progresses and the degree of risk can change over the course of a project.
- **Risk categories** See the following discussion for an explanation of risk categories.

- **Definitions of probability and impact** Would everyone who rates the probability of a risk a 7 in qualitative risk analysis mean the same thing? A person who is risk averse might think of 7 as very high, while someone who is risk prone might think of 7 as a low figure. The definitions and the probability and impact matrix help standardize these interpretations and also help compare risks between projects.
- **Stakeholder tolerances** What if the stakeholders have a low risk tolerance for cost overruns? That information would be taken into account to rank cost impacts higher than if the low tolerance was in another area. Tolerances should not be implied, but uncovered in project initiating and clarified or refined continually.
- **Reporting formats** This section of the plan describes any reports related to risk management that will be created and what they will include.
- **Tracking** The tracking section of the plan describes how the risk process will be audited, and how information will be documented regarding what happens with risk management activities.

Risk Categories

How can you help ensure areas of risk are not forgotten on your projects? How about creating a standard list of risk categories? These categories are broad, common areas or sources of risk that the company or similar projects have experienced. They can include things like technology changes, lack of resources, or cultural issues. Companies and project management offices should have standard lists of risk categories that all projects can use to help identify risks. When leading risk identification efforts, you should make sure each category is considered.

There are many ways to classify or categorize risk, such as:

- **External** Regulatory, environmental, government, market shifts
- **Internal** Time, cost, or scope changes; inexperience; poor planning; people; staffing; materials; equipment
- **Technical** Changes in technology
- **Unforeseeable** Only a small portion of risks (some say about 10 percent) are actually unforeseeable

A better method to use is to create specific categories of risk that may occur on your company's projects. Rita's risk research has shown over 300 potential categories of risk. These include risks caused by or generated by:

- The customer
- Lack of project management effort (yes, a lack of project management effort can add risk)
- Lack of knowledge of project management by the project manager and stakeholders
- The customer's customers
- Suppliers
- Resistance to change
- Cultural differences

Another way to categorize risks is by source. In other words, "Where do risks come from?" The following are some examples:

- **Schedule** "The hardware may arrive earlier than planned, allowing work package XYZ to start three days earlier."
- **Cost** "Because the hardware may arrive later than planned, we may need to extend our lease on the staging area at a cost of $20,000."
- **Quality** "The concrete may dry before winter weather sets in, allowing us to start successor work packages earlier than planned."
- **Scope** "We might not have correctly defined the scope for the computer installation. If that proves true, we will have to add work packages at a cost of $20,000."

- **Resources** "Stephanie is such an excellent designer that she may be called away to work on the new project everyone is so excited about. If that occurs, we will have to use someone else and our schedule will slip between 100 and 275 hours."
- **Customer satisfaction (stakeholder satisfaction)** "There is a chance the customer will not tell us they are unhappy with the XYZ deliverable, causing at least a 20 percent increase in time to rework customer testing."

Expect the phrases "sources of risk" and "risk categories" to be used interchangeably on the exam. Risk categories or sources of risks can be organized in an organizational chart or WBS-like format called a risk breakdown structure, also referred to as an RBS.

Types of Risk In addition to risk categories, risks can be classified under two main types:

- **Business Risk** Risk of a gain or loss
- **Pure (Insurable) Risk**[2] Only a risk of loss (i.e., fire, theft, personal injury, etc.)

Identify Risks PAGE 282

Process: Identify Risks
Process Group: Planning
Knowledge Area: Risk Management

In this process, risks for the project are identified. This effort should involve all stakeholders and might even involve literature reviews, research, and talking to nonstakeholders. Sometimes the core team will begin the process and then other team members will become involved, making Identify Risks an iterative process.

When you get a question about who should be involved in risk identification, the best answer is everyone! Everyone has a different perspective of the project and can provide thoughts on opportunities and threats.

Smart project managers begin looking for risks as soon as a project is first discussed. In fact, the *PMBOK® Guide* lists high-level risks as an output of the creation of the project charter in integration management. However, the major risk identification effort occurs during planning, since the scope baseline (the project scope statement, WBS, and WBS dictionary) is an important input to risk identification.

Because risk identification primarily occurs during project initiating and planning, the exam has often said that the major part of risk identification happens at the onset of the project. But keep in mind that smaller numbers of risks may also be identified later in the project. Risks should be continually reassessed. For the exam, understand that risk identification is done during such activities as integrated change control, when working with resources, and when dealing with project issues.

The following are some risk identification tools and techniques.

Documentation Reviews PAGE 286 What is and what is not part of the documentation, including the charter, contracts, and planning documentation, can help identify risks. Those involved in risk identification might look at this documentation, as well as lessons learned, articles, and other documents, to help uncover risks. This technique used to be a trick for risk management and has proven to be so beneficial that it has now become standard practice.

Information Gathering Techniques PAGE 286 Another way to identify risks is to use one of the following techniques. Many of these techniques are also used to collect requirements for the project (see the Scope Management chapter).

- **Brainstorming** Brainstorming is usually done in a meeting where one idea helps generate another.
- **Delphi technique**[3] This technique is used to achieve consensus among experts who participate anonymously. A request for information is sent to the experts, their responses are compiled, and the results are sent back to them for further review until consensus is reached. This technique can also be used for estimating time and cost.

- **Interviewing** Also called expert interviewing on the exam, this technique consists of the team or project manager interviewing project participants, stakeholders, or experts to identify risks on the project or a specific element of work.
- **Root cause analysis**[4] In root cause analysis, the identified risks are reorganized by their root causes to help identify more risks.

Strengths, Weaknesses, Opportunities, and Threats (SWOT) Analysis[5]

This analysis looks at the project to identify its strengths and weaknesses and thereby identify risks (opportunities and threats).

Checklist Analysis PAGE 287

This technique looks at the checklist of risk categories that we discussed in the Plan Risk Management section of this chapter. The checklist is used to help identify specific risks within each category.

Assumptions Analysis PAGE 287

Analyzing what assumptions have been made on the project and whether they are valid may lead to the identification of more risks.

Diagramming Techniques PAGE 287

Some of the tools described in the Quality Management chapter can also be used to analyze the root causes of issues. These include cause and effect diagrams and flowcharts. When used as part of risk identification, they help identify additional risks for the project.

Outputs of Identify Risks PAGE 282

The Identify Risks process results in the creation of the risk register.

Risk Register[6]

The risk register is where most of the risk information is kept. Think of it as one document for the whole risk management process that will be constantly updated with information as Identify Risks and the later risk management processes are completed. The risk register becomes part of the project documents and is included in historical records that will be used for future projects.

TRICKS OF THE TRADE® Notice that an updated risk register is the only output of several of the risk management processes. Read exam questions carefully, as the risk register contains different information depending on when in the risk management process the question is referencing. For example, if the project has just started and you are in the Identify Risks process, the risk register will contain the identified risks and potential responses, not the response plans actually selected for the project, which come later.

At this point in the risk management process, the risk register includes:

- **List of risks**
- **List of potential responses** Though risk response planning occurs later, one of the things experienced risk managers know is that it is not always logical to separate work on each part of risk management. There will be times when a response is identified at the same time as a risk. These responses should be added to the risk register as they are identified, and analyzed later as part of risk response planning.
- **Root causes of risks** The root causes of risks are documented. This information is valuable in later efforts to reassess risk on the project and for historical records to be used for future projects.
- **Updated risk categories** You will notice a lot of places where historical records and company records are updated throughout the project management process. Make sure you are aware that lessons learned and communicating information to other projects does not just happen at the end of the project. As part of the risk identification effort, the project provides feedback to the rest of the company regarding new categories of risk to add to the checklist.

A tricky question for the exam might ask, "When in the risk management process are responses documented?" The answer is both during Identify Risks (as potential responses) and during Plan Risk Responses (as selected response plans)!

Perform Qualitative Risk Analysis[7] PAGE 289

Process: Perform Qualitative Risk Analysis
Process Group: Planning
Knowledge Area: Risk Management

In a later part of the risk management effort, you will determine what you are going to do about risks. But would you want to do something about all risks identified? Of course not. It would be too expensive, and you would not have enough time. You need to analyze the risks, including their probability and potential impact on the project, to determine which ones warrant a response. The Perform Qualitative Risk Analysis process involves doing this analysis and creating a short list of the previously identified risks. The short-listed risks may then be further analyzed in the Perform Quantitative Risk Analysis process, or they may move into the Plan Risk Responses process.

Remember that qualitative risk analysis is a subjective analysis of the risks identified. To perform this analysis, the following are determined:

- The probability of each risk occurring, using a standard scale such as Low, Medium, High or 1 to 10
- The impact (amount at stake, or consequences, positive or negative) of each risk occurring, using a standard scale such as Low, Medium, High or 1 to 10

The following are tools you can use to perform qualitative risk analysis.

Probability and Impact Matrix PAGE 291 Because qualitative risk analysis is based on subjective evaluation, the rating of any one risk can vary depending on the bias of the person doing the rating and how risk averse they are (e.g., one person's score of a 3 might be another person's 7). Therefore, organizations frequently have a standard rating system to promote a common understanding of what each risk rating means. This standard is shown in a probability and impact matrix.

A probability and impact matrix might look like the following image:

Probability										
10										
9										
8										
7										
6										
5										
4										
3										
2										
1										
	1	2	3	4	5	6	7	8	9	10
	Impact									

This matrix may be used to sort or rate risks to determine which ones warrant an immediate response (and will therefore be moved on through the risk process) and which ones should be put on the watchlist (described later). The matrix may be standardized within the company or department, or it may be customized to the needs of the project. Such a matrix results in a consistent evaluation of low, medium, or high (or some other scale) for the project and for all projects. Use of a standardized matrix makes the risk rating process more repeatable between projects.

Different matrices can be used for cost, time, and scope if the thresholds for each type of risk are different.

Risk Data Quality Assessment PAGE 293

This assessment answers the question of "How accurate and well understood is the risk information?" Before you can use the risk information collected so far on the project, you must analyze the precision of the data. In other words, you assess the accuracy and reliability of the data and determine whether more research is needed to understand the risk before a qualitative assessment can be done. Imagine, for example, a risk given to you anonymously on a notepad. Smart project managers might allow for anonymous contributions during risk identification, but all of the identified risks must be defined well enough to perform a qualitative assessment.

A risk data quality assessment may include determining the following for each risk:

- Extent of the understanding of the risk
- Data available about the risk
- Quality of the data
- Reliability and integrity of the data

Risk Categorization PAGE 293

Risk categorization examines the questions of, "What will we find if we regroup the risks by categories? By work packages?" Think about how useful it would be to not only have a subjective assessment of the total amount of risk on the project, but also to group the risks by cause to know which work packages, processes, people, or other potential causes have the most risk associated with them. Such data will be helpful in risk response planning, allowing you to eliminate many risks at once by eliminating one cause.

You can learn more about these concepts in the book *Risk Management, Tricks of the Trade® for Project Managers*, by Rita Mulcahy.

Risk Urgency Assessment PAGE 293

In addition to creating a short list of risks, qualitative risk analysis includes noting risks that should move more quickly through the process than others. Reasons for this could include the fact that the risk may occur soon or will require a long time to plan a response. Urgent risks may then move, independently, right into risk response planning while the rest continue through quantitative risk analysis, or they may simply be the first ones for which you plan a response in risk response planning. A project manager may consider both the urgency of the risk and the risk's probability and impact rating (from the probability and impact matrix) to determine the overall severity of the risk.

Outputs of Perform Qualitative Risk Analysis PAGE 293

This process results in updates to the risk register.

Risk Register Updates

The risk register is updated to add the results of qualitative risk analysis, including:

- **Risk ranking for the project compared to other projects** Qualitative risk analysis can lead to a number to be used to rank the project in comparison to other projects (e.g., this project has a risk score of 8.3). This ranking allows you to redo qualitative risk analysis after you have completed risk response planning and PROVE the value of your efforts. You can report, "The project now has a risk score of 4.8." Think how this will help you prove the value of project management!
- **List of prioritized risks and their probability and impact ratings**
- **Risks grouped by categories** (As previously explained)
- **List of risks for additional analysis and response** These are the risks that will move forward into quantitative risk analysis and/or response planning.
- **List of risks requiring additional analysis in the near term**

- **Watchlist (non-critical or non-top risks)** These risks are documented for later review during risk monitoring and controlling.
- **Trends** Qualitative risk analysis may be redone in planning or while the project work is being done. The project manager should know if risk is increasing, decreasing, or staying the same, so trends can be analyzed.

Qualitative risk analysis can also be used to:
- Compare the risk of the project to the overall risk of other projects.
- Determine whether the project should be selected, continued, or terminated.
- Determine whether to proceed to the Perform Quantitative Risk Analysis or Plan Risk Responses processes (depending on the needs of the project and the performing organization).

Perform Quantitative Risk Analysis PAGE 294

Process: Perform Quantitative Risk Analysis
Process Group: Planning
Knowledge Area: Risk Management

The Perform Quantitative Risk Analysis process involves numerically analyzing the probability and impact (the amount at stake or the consequences) of risks moved forward from qualitative risk analysis. Quantitative risk analysis also looks at how risks could affect the objectives of the project. The purpose of quantitative risk analysis is to:
- Determine which risk events warrant a response.
- Determine overall project risk (risk exposure).
- Determine the quantified probability of meeting project objectives (e.g., "We only have an 80 percent chance of completing the project within the six months required by the customer," or "We only have a 75 percent chance of completing the project within the $80,000 budget.").
- Determine cost and schedule reserves.
- Identify risks requiring the most attention.
- Create realistic and achievable cost, schedule, or scope targets.

Many people get confused between qualitative and quantitative risk analysis. Remember that qualitative risk analysis is a subjective evaluation, even though numbers are used for the rating. In contrast, quantitative risk analysis is a more objective or numerical evaluation; the rating of each risk is based on an attempt to measure the actual probability and amount at stake (impact). Therefore, while the rating for a risk in qualitative risk analysis might be a 5, it might be stated as a $40,000 added cost impact in quantitative risk analysis.

As a project manager, you should always do qualitative risk analysis, but quantitative risk analysis is not required for all projects and may be skipped in favor of moving on to risk response planning. You should proceed with quantitative risk analysis only if it is worth the time and money on your project. For some projects, you may have a subset of risks identified that require further quantitative analysis. But why spend time quantitatively assessing risks for a low-priority or short-term project or when the effort will provide minimal return?

There are a lot of terms on the exam that are mentioned in the *PMBOK® Guide*. One of these is "risk assessment" (not to be confused with "risk urgency assessment"). Risk assessment refers to the technique of identifying risks through quantitative risk analysis.

The Perform Quantitative Risk Analysis process can include a lot of calculation and analysis. Luckily the details of these efforts are not a focus of the exam. You need to know the following actions are part of quantitative risk analysis but not how to do them beyond what is explained in this chapter:
- Further investigate the highest risks on the project.
- Determine the type of probability distribution that will be used, such as triangular, normal, beta, uniform, or log normal distributions.

- Perform sensitivity analysis to determine which risks have the most impact on the project.
- Determine how much quantified risk the project has through expected monetary value analysis or Monte Carlo analysis (described later in this section).

Determining Quantitative Probability and Impact Quantitative probability and impact can be determined in various ways, including the following:

- Interviewing
- Cost and time estimating
- Delphi technique
- Use of historical records from previous projects
- Expert judgment
- Expected monetary value analysis (described next)
- Monte Carlo analysis (described later in this section)
- Decision trees (described later in this section)

Expected Monetary Value Analysis

To evaluate a risk, you can look at the probability or the impact, but calculating the expected monetary value is a better measure to determine an overall ranking of risks. The formula for expected monetary value (EMV) is simply probability (P) times impact (I).

$$EMV = P \times I$$

Questions on the exam can ask, "What is the expected monetary value of the following?" Expected monetary value can also appear in questions in conjunction with decision trees (described later in this section).

Exercise Do not think of this as another formula you need to memorize—it is too easy. Test yourself! Complete the following chart, and you will understand this calculation for the exam without memorization.

Work Package	Probability	Impact	Expected Monetary Value
A	10%	$20,000	
B	30%	$45,000	
C	68%	$18,000	

Answer See the answers in the following table. Does it feel better now that you know something on the exam is easy?

Work Package	Probability	Impact	Expected Monetary Value
A	10%	$20,000	$2,000
B	30%	$45,000	$13,500
C	68%	$18,000	$12,240

Monte Carlo Analysis (simulation technique)

Imagine if you could prove to the sponsor that even if the project was done 5,000 times, there is only low probability that the end date they desire will be met? Would this be valuable? This type of data is what simulation techniques like Monte Carlo analysis are all about. A Monte Carlo analysis uses the network diagram and estimates to "perform" the project many times and to simulate the cost or schedule results of the project. (See also the discussion of this topic in the Time Management chapter.)

This technique can be extremely valuable, but there have traditionally been only one or two questions about Monte Carlo analysis on the exam. It is mentioned as a choice a little more frequently, however.

You do not need to know how to perform this calculation for the exam. Simply know the following. Monte Carlo analysis:

- Is usually done with a computer-based program because of the intricacies of the calculations.
- Evaluates the overall risk in the project.
- Determines the probability of completing the project on any specific day, or for any specific cost.
- Determines the probability of any activity actually being on the critical path.
- Takes into account path convergence (places in the network diagram where many paths converge into one activity).
- Translates uncertainties into impacts to the total project.
- Can be used to assess cost and schedule impacts.
- Results in a probability distribution.

Decision Tree[8] PAGE 299 AND A PICTURE ON PAGE 300

If you have to choose between many alternatives, you should analyze how each choice benefits or hurts the project before making the decision. Decision trees can help you in this type of analysis. They are models of real situations and are used to make informed decisions about things like, "Which option should I choose?" or "How will I solve this problem?" by taking into account the associated risks, probabilities, and impacts.

There have traditionally been only one or two questions about decision trees on the exam, but they drive people crazy. So let us help you understand them. You should know what a decision tree is and be able to calculate a simple one from provided data. The exam could also ask you to calculate the expected monetary value (or just "value") of a path or the value of your decision.

Know the following about decision trees for the exam:

- A decision tree takes into account future events in making a decision today.
- It calculates the expected monetary value (probability times impact) in more complex situations than the expected monetary value example previously presented.
- It involves mutual exclusivity (previously explained in the Quality Management chapter).

Some examples of decision trees have the costs occurring only at the end of the project, while others have costs occurring early or in the middle of the project. Because a decision tree models all the possible choices to resolve an issue, costs can appear anywhere in the diagram, not just at the end. On the exam, don't get confused when you look at examples of decision trees. Pay attention to the data provided in the question in order to correctly interpret the answer.

The following exercise shows a picture of a decision tree. The box represents a decision to be made, and the circles represent what can happen as a result of the decision.

Exercise A company is trying to determine if prototyping is worthwhile on the project. They have come up with the following impacts (see the diagram) of whether the equipment works or fails. Based on the information provided in the diagram, what is the expected monetary value of your decision?

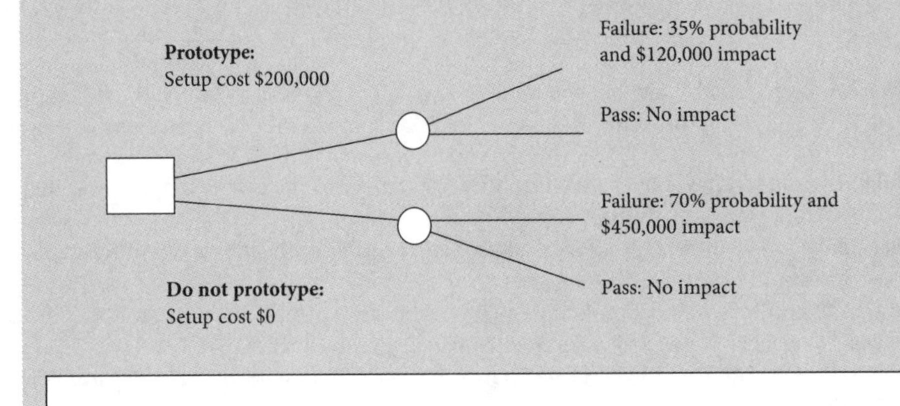

Answer If you just look at the setup cost of prototyping, it would seem like an unwise decision to spend money on prototyping. However, the analysis proves differently. Taking into account only one future event, the decision is that it would be cheaper to do the prototyping. The answer is $242,000, which is the expected monetary value of the decision to prototype.

Prototype	35% × $120,000 = $42,000 $42,000 + $200,000 = $242,000
Do Not Prototype	70% × $450,000 = $315,000

Exercise You need to fly from one city to another. You can take airline A or B. Considering the data provided, which airline should you take, and what is the expected monetary value of your decision?

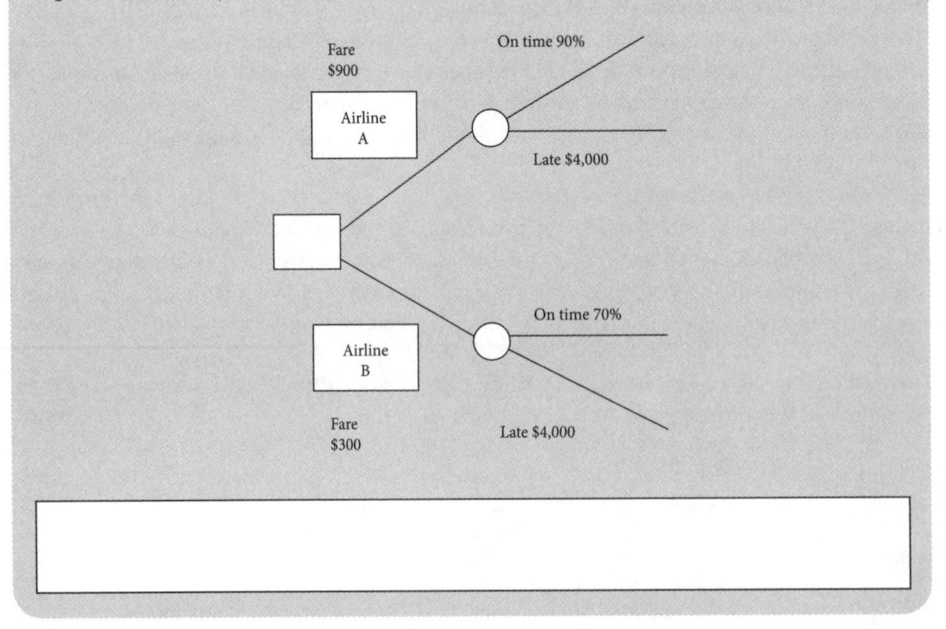

Answer If you just look at the cost of the airfare, you would choose airline B because it is cheaper. However, the airlines have different on-time-arrival rates. If the on-time-arrival rate for airline A is 90 percent, it must be late 10 percent of the time. We have a $4,000 impact for being late. The result is that we should choose airline A, with an expected monetary value of $1,300 as shown below.

Airline A	(10% × $4,000) + (90% × $0) + $900 $400 + $0 + $900 = $1,300
Airline B	(30% × $4,000) + (70% × $0) + $300 $1,200 + $0 + $300 = $1,500

Proving the Value of Project Management Project management saves time and money on projects. Getting your organization's executives to understand that fact can be difficult at times. How beneficial would it be if you could prove the value of project management?

Imagine you have just done the first calculation of the expected monetary value of all the risks that have made it through qualitative risk analysis or that you have completed a Monte Carlo analysis for the project. In either case, you calculate that you need a $98,000 contingency reserve on the project to accommodate risks. That number can be used in many ways. Let's try this example. The team moves on to the Plan Risk Responses process and therein eliminates some risks and reduces the probability or impact of others. The expected monetary value calculation or Monte Carlo analysis is then redone, showing a revised need for only a $12,000 reserve. You have just saved $86,000 and you have not even started the project yet! Can you imagine how much value information like that would have in gaining support for project management in the real world?

Outputs of Perform Quantitative Risk Analysis PAGE 300

The Perform Quantitative Risk Analysis process results in updates to the risk register.

Risk Register Updates

The risk register is updated to add the results of quantitative risk analysis, including:

- **Prioritized list of quantified risks** What are the risks that are most likely to cause trouble? To affect the critical path? That need the most contingency reserve?
- **Amount of contingency time and cost reserves needed** For example, "The project requires an additional $50,000 and two months of time to accommodate the risks on the project."
- **Possible realistic and achievable completion dates and project costs, with confidence levels, versus the time and cost objectives for the project** For example, "We are 95 percent confident that we can complete this project on May 25th for $989,000."
- **The quantified probability of meeting project objectives** For example, "We only have an 80 percent chance of completing the project within the six months required by the customer." Or, "We only have a 75 percent chance of completing the project within the $800,000 budget."
- **Trends in quantitative risk analysis** As you repeat quantitative risk analysis during project planning and when changes are proposed, you can track changes to the overall risk of the project and see any trends.

Plan Risk Responses PAGE 301

Process: Plan Risk Responses
Process Group: Planning
Knowledge Area: Risk Management

The Plan Risk Responses process involves figuring out "What are we going to do about each top risk?" In risk response planning, you find ways to reduce or eliminate threats, and you find ways to make opportunities more likely or increase their impact. The project's risk responses may include doing one or a combination of the following for each top risk:

- Do something to eliminate the threats before they happen.
- Do something to make sure the opportunities happen.
- Decrease the probability and/or impact of threats.
- Increase the probability and/or impact of opportunities.

For the remaining (residual) threats that cannot be eliminated:

- Do something if the risk happens (contingency plans).
- Do something if contingency plans are not effective (fallback plans).

Stop here for a moment to think about what we just described. In order to pass this exam, you will need to be able to envision a world that is not a reality for every project manager; you need to envision a world in which proper risk management is done. Think about the power of risk response planning. You eliminate problems (threats) while still in the planning process on your project. Had they not been eliminated, these problems could have caused stress, delays, and/or added cost to the project. Can you see the value of such efforts in your real world? This is what risk management is all about. If a person is causing a top risk, you can investigate the possibilities of removing that person from the project. If a work package is causing a large amount of risk, you might look at changing the work or removing it from the project. There are always options to respond to risks.

Risk management goes further than the examples just described, however. In addition to avoiding or eliminating risks, you and the team determine what to do about each of the residual risks (those that are not eliminated on the project) if the risks occur. You then assign the work involved in the responses to risk response owners—individuals who watch out for and implement preplanned responses.

If in reading this book, you have found yourself at points thinking, "I do not have time to do that," remember what project management, properly practiced, can do for you. As with many other areas of project management, risk management does not really take additional time; instead, it saves huge amounts of time on projects. When you have done risk management, your project will go smoother and faster, with significantly fewer complications, because avoidable problems were solved BEFORE they happened. You now have time to spend implementing reward systems, updating organizational process assets, creating lessons learned, preventing problems, assisting, coaching, and all the other items you might have thought you did not have time for.

So on the exam, assume all the major problems that could have been identified in advance as risks were determined before they occurred and that there was a plan put in place for each of these risks. With this in mind, the best answer to a question describing a major problem on the project would be the choice that talks about implementing the contingency plan, rather than the choice that talks about discussing possible solutions to the problem after it has occurred. Many people have said that these types of questions were the reason they failed the exam. They simply made the wrong choices in situational questions. Make sure you transition your mind into this way of thinking if it is unfamiliar to you.

Here are a couple of other points that can be tricky on the exam:

- Can you eliminate all risks on a project? Remember that risks can be eliminated, but the time and trouble involved in eliminating ALL the risks identified on a project would probably not be worthwhile.
- Qualitative risk analysis, quantitative risk analysis, and risk response planning do not end once you begin work on a project. As discussed at other points in this book, planning is iterative. You need to review risks throughout the project, including while the project work is being done or when checking results. When you identify new risks, you then need to spend time analyzing them and planning responses, if appropriate. In addition, risk ratings and response strategies for

existing risks can change later in the project as more information about the risks and the selected strategies becomes known. Therefore, you must also review ratings and response strategies for appropriateness over the life of the project. This is the iterative nature of risk management.

Now that you understand the philosophy of what a project manager is trying to do in the Plan Risk Responses process, let's look at the details you will need to know.

Risk Response Strategies (sometimes called Risk Mitigation Strategies) PAGE 303

When completing risk response planning, a thorough analysis must be done of the potential responses for each risk. The team may uncover many strategies for dealing with risks. Some strategies involve changing the planned approach to completing the project (e.g., changes to the WBS, quality management plan, resources, communications, schedule, or budget). Other strategies (called contingency responses) involve coming up with a plan to be implemented when and if a risk occurs. It is important to make sure all options are investigated.

The choices of response strategies for THREATS include:

- **Avoid** Eliminate the threat by eliminating the cause (e.g., remove the work package or person).
- **Mitigate** Reduce the probability or the impact of a threat, thereby making it a smaller risk and removing it from the list of top risks on the project. Options for reducing the probability are looked for separately from options for reducing the impact. Any reduction will make a difference, but the option with the most probability and/or impact reduction is often the option selected.
- **Transfer (Deflect, Allocate)** Make another party responsible for the risk by purchasing insurance, performance bonds, warranties, or guarantees or by outsourcing the work. Here is where the strong connection between risk and procurement (contracts) begins. In the world of properly practiced project management, you complete risk assessment before a contract is signed and transference of risk is included in the terms and conditions of the contract.

A response to certain risks such as fire, property damage, or personal injury (i.e., pure risks) is to purchase insurance. Insurance exchanges an unknown risk for a known risk. In the example of a risk of fire, the risk is unknown depending on the extent of the fire. But when insurance is purchased, the cost impact of a risk of fire becomes known; it is the cost of the insurance. Mitigating the risk by purchasing insurance does not eliminate all impacts. For example, there can still be schedule delays on the project caused by the fire.

If you were to outsource work to a third party as a response strategy, would the risk go away? Transferring a risk will leave some risk behind. For example, you outsource, but now there is a risk that if the third party has trouble, it could cause a schedule delay. So you still need to decide what to do about any such secondary risks.

The choices of response strategies for OPPORTUNITIES include:

- **Exploit (the reverse of avoid)** Add work or change the project to make sure the opportunity occurs.
- **Enhance (the reverse of mitigate)** Increase the likelihood (probability) and/or positive impacts of the risk event.
- **Share** Allocate ownership of the opportunity to a third party (forming a partnership, team, or joint venture) that is best able to achieve the opportunity.

A response strategy for both THREATS and OPPORTUNITIES is:

- **Accept** Do nothing and say, "If it happens, it happens." Active acceptance may involve the creation of contingency plans to be implemented if the risk occurs and the allocation of time and cost reserves to the project. Passive acceptance leaves actions to be determined as needed, if (after) the risk occurs. A decision to accept a risk must be communicated to stakeholders.

Whether responding to threats or opportunities:

- Strategies must be timely.
- The effort selected must be appropriate to the severity of the risk—avoid spending more money preventing the risk than the impact of the risk would have cost if it occurred.
- One response can be used to address more than one risk.
- More than one response can be used to address the same risk.
- A response can address a root cause of risk and thereby address more than one risk.
- Involve the team, other stakeholders, and experts in selecting a strategy.

Watch out for questions about communicating risk-related information on the exam! Your possible risk response strategies must be communicated to management, stakeholders, and the sponsor. These parties will need to know that you are in control of the project, even if there is a problem, and they may need to approve the resources to make the risk response strategies happen. Communicating about risk is essential in order to gain buy-in to the strategy.

Exercise Now let's see if you can apply what you have learned. Identify the type of risk response strategy (**avoid**, **mitigate the probability**, **mitigate the impact**, **transfer**, **exploit**, **enhance the probability**, **enhance the impact**, **share**, or **accept**) being described.

	Description of Strategy	Name of Risk Response Strategy
1	Remove a work package or activity from the project.	
2	Assign a team member to visit the seller's manufacturing facilities frequently to learn about a problem with delivery as early as possible.	
3	Move a work package to a date when a more experienced resource is available to be assigned to the project.	
4	Begin negotiation for the equipment earlier than planned so as to secure a lower price.	
5	Outsource a work package so as to gain an opportunity.	
6	Notify management that there could be a cost increase if a risk occurs because no action is being taken to prevent the risk.	
7	Remove a troublesome resource from the project.	
8	Provide a team member who has limited experience with additional training.	
9	Train the team on conflict resolution strategies.	
10	Outsource difficult work to a more experienced company.	
11	Ask the client to handle some of the work.	
12	Prototype a risky piece of equipment.	

Answer

	Description of Strategy	Name of Risk Response Strategy
1	Remove a work package or activity from the project.	Avoid
2	Assign a team member to visit the seller's manufacturing facilities frequently to learn about a problem with delivery as early as possible.	Mitigate the impact
3	Move a work package to a date when a more experienced resource is available to be assigned to the project.	Exploit
4	Begin negotiation for the equipment earlier than planned so as to secure a lower price.	Enhance the impact
5	Outsource a work package so as to gain an opportunity.	Share
6	Notify management that there could be a cost increase if a risk occurs because no action is being taken to prevent the risk.	Accept
7	Remove a troublesome resource from the project.	Avoid
8	Provide a team member who has limited experience with additional training.	Mitigate the probability
9	Train the team on conflict resolution strategies.	Mitigate the impact
10	Outsource difficult work to a more experienced company.	Transfer
11	Ask the client to handle some of the work.	Transfer
12	Prototype a risky piece of equipment.	Mitigate the probability

Outputs of Plan Risk Responses PAGE 305 The outputs of the Plan Risk Responses process are the updates to the risk register plus updates to the project management plan and project documents.

Project Management Plan Updates

The efforts spent in risk management will result in changes to the project management plan. Work packages or activities could be added, removed, or assigned to different resources, making planning an iterative process. Spend a moment now thinking about how risk response planning could change the schedule, cost, quality, and procurement management plans, as well as the human resource plan, the WBS, and the time and cost baselines for the project. This concept is critical for understanding the impact risk management has on projects, especially if you don't currently do risk management in your real world.

Project Document Updates

The other documents a project manager has created to help manage the project may also change. Can you imagine how risk response planning might affect the roles and responsibilities on a project, your stakeholder management strategy, or your quality metrics?

Risk Register Updates

The risk register is updated to add the results of risk response planning, including:

- **Residual risks**[9] These are the risks that remain after risk response planning. Residual risks are also risks that have been accepted and for which contingency plans and fallback plans can be created. Residual risks should be properly documented and reviewed throughout the project to see if their ranking has changed.
- **Contingency plans** Contingency plans are plans describing the specific actions that will be taken if the opportunity or threat occurs.
- **Risk response owners** A key concept in risk response planning is that the project manager does not have to do it all and neither does the team. Each risk must be assigned to someone who may help develop the risk response and who will be assigned to carry out the risk response or "own" the risk. The risk response owner can be a stakeholder other than a team member.
  Think about how the application of risk management can change real-world projects. The risk occurs; the risk response owner takes the prearranged and preapproved plan of action determined in project planning and informs the project manager. No meeting is needed—just action! This can be very powerful.
- **Secondary risks** Any new risks created by the implementation of selected risk response strategies should also be analyzed as part of risk response planning. Frequently, what is done to respond to one risk will cause other risks to occur. For example, if a portion of the project work is outsourced to a seller because the project team does not have the expertise to complete the work efficiently, there may be a secondary risk of the seller going out of business. This was not a risk to the project prior to outsourcing.
- **Risk triggers** These are events that trigger the contingency response. The early warning signs for each risk on a project should be identified so risk response owners know when to take action.
- **Contracts** A project manager must be involved before a contract is signed. Before the contract is finalized, the project manager should have completed a risk analysis and included contract terms and conditions required to mitigate or allocate threats and to enhance opportunities. Any contracts issued to deal with risks should be noted in the risk register.
- **Fallback plans** These plans are specific actions that will be taken if the contingency plan is not effective. Think how prepared you will feel if you have plans for what to do if a risk occurs and what to do if that original plan does not work.
- **Reserves**[10] **(contingency)** Having reserves for time and cost is a required part of project management. You cannot come up with a schedule or budget for the project without them. Reserves are covered in the Cost Management chapter, but let's look at them again here as well.

There can be two kinds of reserves for time and cost: contingency reserves and management reserves. Contingency reserves account for "known unknowns" (or simply "knowns"); these are items you identified in risk management. They cover the residual risks in the project. Management reserves account for "unknown unknowns" (or simply "unknowns"); these are items you did not or could not identify in risk management. Projects can have both kinds of reserves. As shown in the following diagram (also in the Cost Management chapter), contingency reserves are calculated and become part of the cost baseline. Management reserves are estimated (e.g., 5 percent of the project cost), and then these reserves are added to the cost baseline to get the project budget. The project manager has control of the cost baseline and can approve use of the contingency reserves, but management approval is needed to use management reserves.

Make sure you realize that reserves are not an additional cost to a project. The risk management process should result in a decrease to the project's projected time and cost. As risks are eliminated or their probability or impact reduced, there should be a reduction to the project's schedule and budget. Contingency reserves are for the prespecified opportunities and threats that remain after the risk management process is completed. No matter what you do, risks will remain in the project, and there should be a time or cost allotment for them, just as cost or time is allotted to work activities on the project.

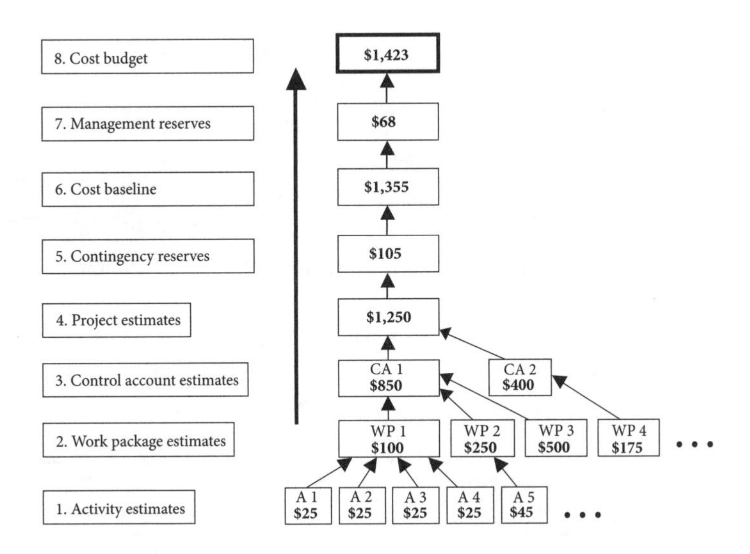

Let's try an example of calculating a contingency reserve in the next exercise.

Exercise Imagine you are planning the manufacture of an existing product's modifications. Your analysis has come up with the following information. What cost contingency reserve would you use?

Project Data	Cost Contingency Reserve Calculations
There is a 30 percent probability of a delay in the receipt of parts, with a cost to the project of $9,000.	
There is a 20 percent probability that the parts will cost $10,000 less than expected.	
There is a 25 percent probability that two parts will not fit together when installed, costing an extra $3,500.	
There is a 30 percent probability that the manufacture may be simpler than expected, saving $2,500.	
There is a 5 percent probability of a design defect, causing $5,000 of rework.	
Total Cost Contingency Reserve	

Answer You use the expected monetary value calculation (EMV = P × I) to determine the contingency reserve. The answer is $1,075 for the total cost contingency reserve. See the following table for the detailed calculations.

Project Data	Cost Contingency Reserve Calculations
There is a 30 percent probability of a delay in the receipt of parts, with a cost to the project of $9,000.	30% × $9,000 = $2,700 Add $2,700
There is a 20 percent probability that the parts will cost $10,000 less than expected.	20% × $10,000 = $2,000 Subtract $2,000
There is a 25 percent probability that two parts will not fit together when installed, costing an extra $3,500.	25% × $3,500 = $875 Add $875
There is a 30 percent probability that the manufacture may be simpler than expected, saving $2,500.	30% × $2,500 = $750 Subtract $750
There is a 5 percent probability of a design defect, causing $5,000 of rework.	5% × $5,000 = $250 Add $250
Total Cost Contingency Reserve	$1,075

Now let's try another exercise. If the risk management process is new to you, the following exercise should help you put it all together by looking at it in a chart form.

Exercise Create a flowchart of the risk process from Identify Risks through Plan Risk Responses.

Answer Creating this chart will help you check whether you have understood what you read in this chapter. Your flowchart could be different than the following depiction.

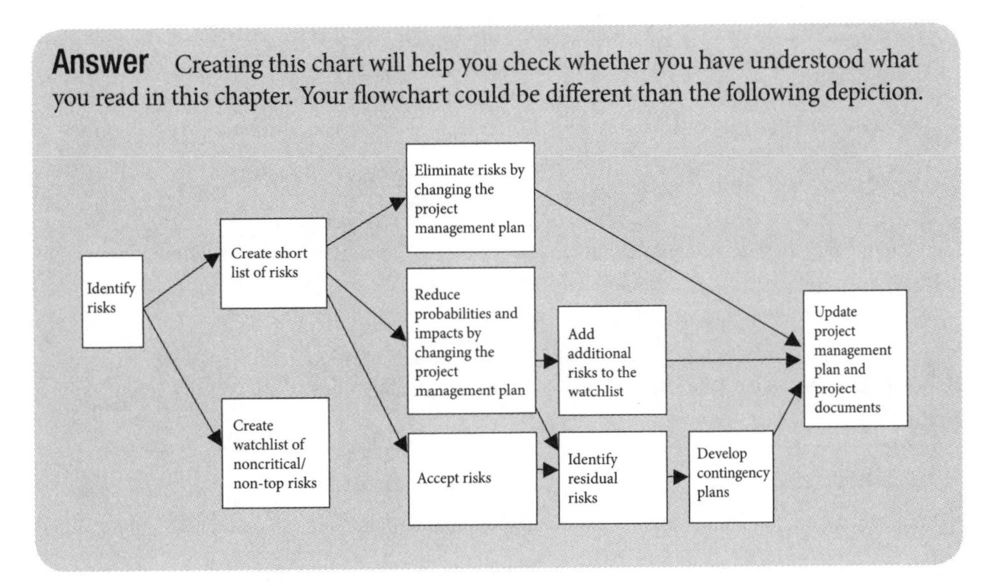

You are nearing the end of the Plan Risk Responses section! But first, let's look at what types of questions you may see in this area on the exam. The exam often asks questions such as:

> **Question** *What do you do with non-critical risks?*
> **Answer** *Document them in a watchlist, and revisit them periodically.*
>
> **Question** *Would you choose only one risk response strategy?*
> **Answer** *No, you can select a combination of choices.*
>
> **Question** *What risk management activities are done during the execution of the project?*
> **Answer** *Watching out for watchlisted (non-critical) risks that increase in importance, and looking for new risks.*
>
> **Question** *What is the most important item to address in project team meetings?*
> **Answer** *Risk.*
>
> **Question** *How would risks be addressed in project meetings?*
> **Answer** *By asking, "What is the status of risks? Are there any new risks? Is there any change to the order of importance?"*

Monitor and Control Risks PAGE 308

Process: Monitor & Control Risks
Process Group: Monitoring & Controlling
Knowledge Area: Risk Management

Risk-related questions on the exam are asked assuming the project manager has done proper project management, including assigning risk response owners, putting contingency plans in place, and taking other such actions. The exam also assumes the project is substantially less risky than it would have been if the project manager had not planned the project. If you do not have experience using risk management in the real world, these exam questions may be difficult. Try the next exercise. It will help you get your mind around what project management is like when it includes risk management.

Exercise Think about the previous paragraph. Because a project manager has completed risk management activities, he or she is no longer focusing on dealing with problems and figuring out what should be done. So what is the project manager doing?

Spend time really thinking through the actions involved in monitoring and controlling risks. Once you have completed your own list of actions, look at our list to make sure you do them all or at least understand what they are and why they are helpful to the project. You could include things on your list that are not on ours, but check each one of those items to determine if they are accurate additions to your list.

Actions Involved in Monitoring and Controlling Risks	Included Below?

Answer As you read over the answers, make sure you understand what each means. Realize that with risk management and proper project management, you are not doing things like "figuring out what work needs to be done on the project" or "determining who will do a piece of work." Those efforts were already done in project planning. You are not even spending much time solving problems, because you already have a plan in place for the major problems. Many people learn project management, but they learn it in a way that never seems real to them, so they do not use it. But even well-trained and experienced project managers do not always do enough to control risk. Read this list over very carefully and make sure you understand each of the actions. This is not a time for memorization; you are simply assessing what you know and do not know so that you can better understand these concepts and correctly answer situational questions on the exam.

The following is our list of actions involved in monitoring and controlling risks:

- Look for the occurrence of risk triggers.
- Monitor residual risks.
- Identify new risks and then analyze and plan for them. (**REMEMBER:** Risks can be identified anytime during the project, along with plans for how to handle the newly identified risks.)
- Evaluate the effectiveness of the risk management plan—"Are the risk management processes working?"
- Develop new risk responses—"That plan no longer seems like it will work based on new information. Let's plan a different response."
- Collect and communicate risk status—"Four identified risks occurred last month, and all risk response plans were implemented successfully. Next month we expect eight other risks to potentially occur. Risk reserves are still considered adequate for covering the identified risks on this project."
- Communicate with stakeholders about risks—"Remember that one of the major risks on the project could occur next week."
- Determine if assumptions are still valid.
- Ensure proper risk management procedures are being followed.
- Revisit the watchlist to see if additional risk responses need to be determined—"This change to the product scope might increase the impact of risk X, currently on our watchlist. Let's analyze it."
- Recommend corrective actions to adjust to the severity of actual risk events—"This risk did not have the impact we expected, so let's adjust the contingency plan we are in the middle of implementing and change what we will do if the risk reoccurs."
- Look for any unexpected effects or consequences of risk events—"We did not expect this risk to damage the construction site if the risk occurred. We need to decide how to fix the damage after we finish implementing the already agreed-upon contingency plan."
- Reevaluate risk identification and qualitative and quantitative risk analysis when the project deviates from the baseline—"The project cost is over the cost baseline (or over the schedule baseline). This implies we missed some major risks. Let's hold a risk identification session."
- Update risk management and response plans.
- Look at the changes, including recommended corrective actions, to see if they lead to identifying more risks—"We keep having to take corrective action related to this problem. Let's look at the root cause and identify any risks for the remaining part of the project that relate to the problem."
- Make changes to the project management plan and project documents when new risk responses are developed.
- Create a database of risk data that may be used throughout the organization on other projects.
- Perform variance and trend analysis on project performance data.
- Use contingency reserves and adjust for approved changes.

Other work that will be part of the Monitor and Control Risks process includes:

Workarounds PAGE 445 If the project is deviating from the baselines, the team may take corrective action to bring it back in line. Recommendations for such corrective actions may include workarounds. Whereas contingency responses are developed in advance, workarounds are unplanned responses developed to deal with the occurrence of unanticipated events or problems on a project. Project managers who do not perform risk management spend a lot of their time creating workarounds.

Risk Reassessments PAGE 310 Questions always seem to come up on the exam that require you to know the team needs to periodically review the risk management plan and risk register and adjust the documentation as required. Reassessing risk is a good topic for a team meeting or even a separate meeting. Many of the actions in the previous exercise relate to this. Remember, the results of such reassessments may include newly identified risks, additional qualitative or quantitative risk analysis, and further risk response planning.

Risk Audits[11] PAGE 310 Imagine having a team of auditors descend upon you, asking you to prove you have identified all the risks that can be or should be identified on your project, that you have plans for each of the major risks, and that risk response owners are prepared to take action. This is a risk audit. It is arranged by the project manager and results in identification of lessons learned for the project and for other projects in the organization. Risk audits are evidence of how seriously risk should be taken on a project.

Reserve Analysis PAGE 311 Reserve analysis while the work is being done is simply a matter of checking to see how much reserve remains and how much might be needed. It is like checking the balance in your bank account. Reserves must be guarded throughout the project life cycle.

Now let's talk about a concept that can be tricky on the exam, especially for those who are not experienced in using risk management. People wanting to change the project in response to problems that have occurred may suggest using the reserves instead of adding cost or time to the project. It is important to know that a contingency reserve may only be used to handle the impact of the specific risk it was set aside for. So, if the change is part of the risk response plan that was previously accounted for in the budget, the reserve designated for that response may be used. If it is not, the project manager must take preventive or corrective action, fast track, crash, or otherwise adjust the project to accommodate or make up for the impact of the problem and its resulting changes. Under certain circumstances, usually determined by the performing organization, management reserves may be used for problems that had not previously been identified as risks.

Asking for additional reserve can indicate that the project manager has not properly planned and managed the project. This is not an acceptable thing to do. The project should be done for what was agreed to in project planning. If identified risks do not occur, the associated time or cost reserves should be returned to the company, rather than used to address other issues on the project. Reserves are not a free amount of time or cost that can be used at will by the project manager for any needs! If you are inexperienced with risk management, make sure you understand how reserves are used and protected.

See the free tip about status meetings on our Web site, www.rmcproject.com.

Status Meetings PAGE 311 Do you use "go around the room" type status meetings on your projects? Are they an effective use of everyone's time? If you have 30 people in a room and each person gets a few minutes to report status on activities that do not directly impact others in the meeting, most people in the room will consider the meeting a waste of time. Such status can often be collected through other means, like reports or quick one-on-one conversations between the project manager and the team member. Instead of "go around the room" meetings, think of status meetings as team meetings. Risk should be a major point of discussion at such meetings to keep the focus on risks, to continue to identify new risks, and to make sure response plans remain appropriate.

Closing of Risks That Are No Longer Applicable The time when each identified risk can logically occur will eventually pass. Closing of risks allows the team to focus on managing the risks that are still open. The closing of a risk will likely result in the associated risk reserve being returned to the company.

Outputs of Monitor and Control Risks PAGE 311 As with the previous risk management processes, updates to the risk register are a result of Monitor and Control Risks, along with the other outputs listed here.

Risk Register Updates

The Monitor and Control Risks process will add the following to the risk register:

- Outcomes of the risk reassessments and risk audits
- Updates to previous parts of risk management, including the identification of new risks
- Closing of risks that are no longer applicable
- Details of what happened when risks occurred
- Lessons learned

Change Requests, Recommended Preventive and Corrective Actions

The Monitor and Control Risks process will uncover changes needed to the project. As noted earlier, the corrective actions may include workarounds.

Project Management Plan Updates

Risk monitoring and control can result in updates to the schedule, cost, quality, and procurement management plans, as well as the human resource plan, the WBS, and the time and cost baselines for the project.

Project Document Updates

Risk monitoring and control might also affect the roles and responsibilities on a project, the stakeholder management strategy, and the quality metrics.

Organizational Process Assets Updates

The risk process will lead to the creation of risk templates, such as a risk register including project risks and risk responses, checklists, and other data to be used as historical records for future projects.

TRICKS OF THE TRADE® Common Risk Management Errors

The exam may describe situations where the wrong thing is being done as a way of testing whether you realize it is wrong. The following is a list of some of the common risk management errors people make.

- Risk identification is completed without knowing enough about the project.
- Project risk is evaluated using only a questionnaire, interview, or Monte Carlo analysis and thus does not provide specific risks.
- Risk identification ends too soon, resulting in a brief list (20 risks) rather than an extensive list (hundreds of risks).
- The processes of Identify Risks through Perform Quantitative Risk Analysis are blended, resulting in risks that are evaluated or judged as they come to light. This decreases the number of total risks identified and causes people to stop participating in risk identification.
- The risks identified are general rather than specific (e.g., "communications" rather than "poor communication of customer's needs regarding installation of system XYZ could cause two weeks of rework").
- Some things considered to be risks are not uncertain; they are facts, and are therefore not risks.
- Whole categories of risks (such as technology, cultural, marketplace, etc.) are missed.
- Only one method is used to identify risks (e.g., only using a checklist) rather than a combination of methods. A combination helps ensure that more risks are identified.
- The first risk response strategy identified is selected without looking at other options and finding the best option or combination of options.
- Risk management is not given enough attention during project executing.
- Project managers do not explain the risk management process to their team during project planning.
- Contracts are signed long BEFORE risks to the project are discussed.

This list is from from RMC's online course titled "Common Risk Management Errors." To learn more about this course, visit www.rmcproject.com.

Exercise

The Risk Management Process There can be many questions about the process of risk management on the exam. The following exercise tests if you understand what you have read.

Recreate the risk management process, including the outputs, on the following form. Check your answers against the following table when you are done. Even with one reading of this chapter, you should get most of the actions and outputs correct. The second and third times you read the chapter, you should be almost 100 percent accurate. This exercise is about remembering key parts of risk management, not memorization. Create the chart three times, and you should know it well enough for the exam.

Plan Risk Management	Identify Risks	Perform Qualitative Risk Analysis	Perform Quantitative Risk Analysis	Plan Risk Responses	Monitor and Control Risks
Actions					
Outputs					

Answer

Plan Risk Management	Identify Risks	Perform Qualitative Risk Analysis	Perform Quantitative Risk Analysis	Plan Risk Responses	Monitor and Control Risks
Actions					
Answer the questions of: How will you perform risk management on the project? What risk management policies or procedures exist for use on the project?	Identify "all" the risks on the project Involve the stakeholders	Qualitatively determine which risk events warrant a response Assess the quality of the risk data Complete a risk urgency assessment Subjectively determine the probability and impact of all risks Determine if you will go to quantitative risk analysis or go directly to risk response planning Document the watchlist (non-top risks) Determine the overall risk ranking for the project	Numerically evaluate the top risks Quantitatively determine which risks warrant a response Determine initial reserves Create realistic time and cost objectives Determine the probability of meeting project objectives	Decrease project risk Determine secondary and residual risks Calculate final reserves Determine risk response owners (if not already done) Create contingency and fallback plans	Respond to risk triggers Monitor residual risks Create workarounds Evaluate effectiveness of plans Look for additional risks; then qualify, quantify, and plan responses for them Revisit the watchlist Update plans Communicate risk status Close risks Recommend changes, including corrective and preventive actions

Plan Risk Management	Identify Risks	Perform Qualitative Risk Analysis	Perform Quantitative Risk Analysis	Plan Risk Responses	Monitor and Control Risks
Outputs					
Risk management plan	Risk register including: ► List of risks ► List of potential risk responses ► Root causes of risks ► Updated risk categories	Risk register including: ► Risk ranking of the project as compared to other projects ► List of prioritized risks ► Risks by category ► Risks needing additional analysis and response ► Watchlist ► Trends	Risk register including: ► Prioritized list of quantified risks ► Initial reserves ► Project completion dates and costs ► Probability of achieving project objectives ► Trends	Updates to the project management plan and project documents Risk register including: ► Residual and secondary risks ► Contingency and fallback plans ► Risk response owners ► Triggers ► Final reserves ► Contracts	Risk register updates including: ► Risk reassessment and risk audit outcomes ► New risks ► Closed risks ► Details of risk occurences ► Lessons learned Workarounds Change requests, including recommended corrective and preventive actions Updates to the project management plan, project documents, and organizational process assets

Practice Exam

1. All of the following are factors in the assessment of project risk EXCEPT:
   A. Risk events.
   B. Risk probability.
   C. Amount at stake.
   D. Insurance premiums.

2. If a project has a 60 percent chance of a US $100,000 profit and a 40 percent chance of a US $100,000 loss, the expected monetary value (EMV) for the project is:
   A. $100,000 profit.
   B. $60,000 loss.
   C. $20,000 profit.
   D. $40,000 loss.

3. Assuming that the ends of a range of estimates are +/- 3 sigma from the mean, which of the following range estimates involves the LEAST risk?
   A. 30 days, plus or minus 5 days
   B. 22 to 30 days
   C. Optimistic = 26 days, most likely = 30 days, pessimistic = 33 days
   D. Mean of 28 days

4. Which of the following risk events is MOST likely to interfere with attaining a project's schedule objective?
   A. Delays in obtaining required approvals
   B. Substantial increases in the cost of purchased materials
   C. Contract disputes that generate claims for increased payments
   D. Slippage of the planned post-implementation review meeting

5. If a risk has a 20 percent chance of happening in a given month, and the project is expected to last five months, what is the probability that this risk event will occur during the fourth month of the project?
   A. Less than 1 percent
   B. 20 percent
   C. 60 percent
   D. 80 percent

6. If a risk event has a 90 percent chance of occurring, and the consequences will be US $10,000, what does US $9,000 represent?
   A. Risk value
   B. Present value
   C. Expected monetary value
   D. Contingency budget

7. Risks will be identified during which risk management process(es)?
   A. Perform Quantitative Risk Analysis and Identify Risks
   B. Identify Risks and Monitor and Control Risks
   C. Perform Qualitative Risk Analysis and Monitor and Control Risks
   D. Identify Risks

8. What should be done with risks on the watchlist?
   A. Document them for historical use on other projects.
   B. Document them and revisit during project monitoring and controlling.
   C. Document them and set them aside because they are already covered in your contingency plans.
   D. Document them and give them to the customer.

9. All of the following are ALWAYS inputs to the risk management process EXCEPT:
   A. Historical information.
   B. Lessons learned.
   C. Work breakdown structure.
   D. Project status reports.

10. Risk tolerances are determined in order to help:
    A. The team rank the project risks.
    B. The project manager estimate the project.
    C. The team schedule the project.
    D. Management know how other managers will act on the project.

11. All of the following are common results of risk management EXCEPT:
    A. Contract terms and conditions are created.
    B. The project management plan is changed.
    C. The communications management plan is changed.
    D. The project charter is changed.

12. Purchasing insurance is BEST considered an example of risk:
    A. Mitigation.
    B. Transfer.
    C. Acceptance.
    D. Avoidance.

13. You are finding it difficult to evaluate the exact cost impact of risks. You should evaluate on a(n):
    A. Quantitative basis.
    B. Numerical basis.
    C. Qualitative basis.
    D. Econometric basis.

14. Outputs of the Plan Risk Responses process include:
    A. Residual risks, fallback plans, and contingency reserves.
    B. Risk triggers, contracts, and a risk list.
    C. Secondary risks, process updates, and risk response owners.
    D. Contingency plans, project management plan updates, and change requests.

15. Workarounds are determined during which risk management process?
    A. Identify Risks
    B. Perform Quantitative Risk Analysis
    C. Plan Risk Responses
    D. Monitor and Control Risks

16. During which risk management process is a determination to transfer a risk made?
    A. Identify Risks
    B. Perform Quantitative Risk Analysis
    C. Plan Risk Responses
    D. Monitor and Control Risks

17. A project manager has just finished the risk response plan for a US $387,000 engineering project. Which of the following should he probably do NEXT?
    A. Determine the overall risk rating of the project.
    B. Begin to analyze the risks that show up in the project drawings.
    C. Add work packages to the project work breakdown structure.
    D. Hold a project risk reassessment.

18. A project manager asked various stakeholders to determine the probability and impact of a number of risks. He then analyzed assumptions. He is about to move to the next step of risk management. Based on this information, what has the project manager forgotten to do?
    A. Evaluate trends in risk analysis.
    B. Identify triggers.
    C. Provide a standardized risk rating matrix.
    D. Create a fallback plan.

19. A project manager has assembled the project team, identified 56 risks on the project, determined what would trigger the risks, rated them on a risk rating matrix, tested their assumptions, and assessed the quality of the data used. The team is continuing to move through the risk management process. What has the project manager forgotten to do?
    A. Simulation
    B. Risk mitigation
    C. Overall risk ranking for the project
    D. Involvement of other stakeholders

20. You are a project manager for the construction of a major new manufacturing plant that has never been done before. The project cost is estimated at US $30,000,000 and will make use of three sellers. Once begun, the project cannot be cancelled, as there will be a large expenditure on plant and equipment. As the project manager, it is MOST important to carefully:
    A. Review all cost proposals from the sellers.
    B. Examine the budget reserves.
    C. Complete the project charter.
    D. Perform an identification of risks.

21. Your team has come up with 434 risks and 16 major causes of those risks. The project is the last in a series of projects that the team has worked on together. The sponsor is very supportive, and a lot of time was invested in making sure the project work was complete and signed off by all key stakeholders.

    During project planning, the team cannot come up with an effective way to mitigate or insure against a risk. It is not work that can be outsourced, nor can it be deleted. What would be the BEST solution?
    A. Accept the risk.
    B. Continue to investigate ways to mitigate the risk.
    C. Look for ways to avoid the risk.
    D. Look for ways to transfer the risk.

22. A project manager is quantifying risk for her project. Several of her experts are offsite, but wish to be included. How can this be done?
    A. Use Monte Carlo analysis using the Internet as a tool.
    B. Apply the critical path method.
    C. Determine options for recommended corrective action.
    D. Use the Delphi technique.

23. An experienced project manager has just begun working for a large information technology integrator. Her manager provides her with a draft project charter and immediately asks her to provide an analysis of the risks on the project. Which of the following would BEST help in this effort?
    A. An article from *PM Network* magazine
    B. Her project scope statement from the project planning process
    C. Her resource plan from the project planning process
    D. A conversation with a team member from a similar project that failed in the past

24. You have been appointed as the manager of a new, large, and complex project. Because this project is business-critical and very visible, senior management has told you to analyze the project's risks and prepare response strategies for them as soon as possible. The organization has risk management procedures that are seldom used or followed, and has had a history of handling risks badly. The project's first milestone is in two weeks. In preparing the risk response plan, input from which of the following is generally LEAST important?
    A. Project team members
    B. Project sponsor
    C. Individuals responsible for risk management policies and templates
    D. Key stakeholders

25. You were in the middle of a two-year project to deploy new technology to field offices across the country. A hurricane caused power outages just when the upgrade was near completion. When the power was restored, all of the project reports and historical data were lost with no way of retrieving them. What should have been done to prevent this problem?
    A. Purchase insurance.
    B. Plan for a reserve fund.
    C. Monitor the weather and have a contingency plan.
    D. Schedule the installation outside of the hurricane season.

26. A system development project is nearing project closing when a previously unidentified risk is discovered. This could potentially affect the project's overall ability to deliver. What should be done NEXT?
    A. Alert the project sponsor of potential impacts to cost, scope, or schedule.
    B. Qualify the risk.
    C. Mitigate this risk by developing a risk response plan.
    D. Develop a workaround.

27. The cost performance index (CPI) of a project is 0.6 and the schedule performance index (SPI) is 0.71. The project has 625 work packages and is being completed over a four-year period. The team members are very inexperienced, and the project received little support for proper planning. Which of the following is the BEST thing to do?
    A. Update risk identification and analysis.
    B. Spend more time improving the cost estimates.
    C. Remove as many work packages as possible.
    D. Reorganize the responsibility assignment matrix.

28. While preparing your risk responses, you identify additional risks. What should you do?
    A. Add reserves to the project to accommodate the new risks, and notify management.
    B. Document the risk items, and calculate the expected monetary value based on the probability and impact of the occurrences.
    C. Determine the risk events and the associated costs, then add the cost to the project budget as a reserve.
    D. Add a 10 percent contingency to the project budget and notify the customer.

29. You have just been assigned as the project manager for a new telecommunications project as it is entering its second phase. There appear to be many risks on this project, but no one has evaluated them to assess the range of possible project outcomes. What needs to be done?
    A. Plan Risk Management
    B. Perform Quantitative Risk Analysis
    C. Plan Risk Responses
    D. Monitor and Control Risks

30. During project executing, a team member identifies a risk that is not in the risk register. What should you do?
    A. Get further information on how the team member identified the risk, because you already performed a detailed analysis and did not identify this risk.
    B. Disregard the risk, because risks were identified during project planning.
    C. Inform the customer about the risk.
    D. Analyze the risk.

31. During project executing, a major problem occurs that was not included in the risk register. What should you do FIRST?
    A. Create a workaround.
    B. Reevaluate the Identify Risks process.
    C. Look for any unexpected effects of the problem.
    D. Tell management.

32. The customer requests a change to the project that would increase the project risk. Which of the following should you do before all the others?
    A. Include the expected monetary value of the risk in the new cost estimate.
    B. Talk to the customer about the impact of the change.
    C. Analyze the impacts of the change with the team.
    D. Change the risk management plan.

33. Which of the following is a chief characteristic of the Delphi technique?
    A. Extrapolation from historical records from previous projects
    B. Expert opinion
    C. Analytical hierarchy process
    D. Bottom-up approach

34. A project has had some problems, but now seems under control. In the last few months, almost all the reserve has been used up and most of the negative impacts of events that had been predicted have occurred. There are only four activities left, and two of them are on the critical path. Management now informs the project manager that it would be in the performing organization's best interest to finish the project two weeks earlier than scheduled, in order to receive an additional profit. In response, the project manager sends out a request for proposal for some work that the team was going to do, hoping to find another company that might be able to do the work faster. The project manager can BEST be said to be attempting to work with:
    A. Reserve.
    B. Opportunities.
    C. Scope verification.
    D. Threats.

35. Monte Carlo analysis is used to:
    A. Get an indication of the risk involved in the project.
    B. Estimate an activity's length.
    C. Simulate possible quality issues on the project.
    D. Prove to management that extra staff is needed.

36. A project team is creating a project management plan when management asks them to identify project risks and provide some form of qualitative output as soon as possible. What should the project team provide?
    A. Prioritized list of project risks
    B. Risk triggers
    C. Contingency reserves
    D. Probability of achieving the time and cost objectives

37. A project manager is creating a risk response plan. However, every time a risk response is suggested, another risk is identified that is caused by the response. Which of the following is the BEST thing for the project manager to do?
    A. Document the new risks and continue the Plan Risk Responses process.
    B. Make sure the project work is better understood.
    C. Spend more time making sure the risk responses are clearly defined.
    D. Get more people involved in the Identify Risks process, since risks have been missed.

38. A watchlist is an output of which risk management process?
    A. Plan Risk Responses
    B. Perform Quantitative Risk Analysis
    C. Perform Qualitative Risk Analysis
    D. Plan Risk Management

39. During the Identify Risks process, a project manager made a long list of risks identified by all the stakeholders using various methods. He then made sure all the risks were understood and that triggers had been identified. Later, in the Plan Risk Responses process, he took all the risks identified by the stakeholders and determined ways to mitigate them. What has he done wrong?
    A. The project manager should have waited until the Perform Qualitative Risk Analysis process to get the stakeholders involved.
    B. More people should be involved in the Plan Risk Responses process.
    C. The project manager should have created workarounds.
    D. Triggers are not identified until the Identify Risks process.

40. Which of the following MUST be an agenda item at all team meetings?
    A. Discussion of project risks
    B. Status of current activities
    C. Identification of new activities
    D. Review of project problems

Answers

1. **Answer** D
   Explanation Insurance premiums are not factors in assessing project risk. They come into play when you determine which risk response strategy you will use.

2. **Answer** C
   Explanation Expected monetary value is calculated by EMV = Probability × Impact. We need to calculate both positive and negative values and then add them.

   0.6 × $100,000 = $60,000.
   0.4 × ($100,000) = ($40,000)
   Expected Monetary Value = $60,000 – $40,000 = $20,000 profit

3. **Answer** C
   Explanation This one drove you crazy, didn't it? Reread the question! When you look at the ranges of each choice, you will see that 30 days, plus or minus 5 days = a range of 10 days. The range of 22 to 30 days = a range of 8 days. An optimistic estimate of 26 days, most likely estimate of 30 days, and pessimistic estimate of 33 days represents a range of 7 days. The estimate with the smallest range is the least risky, and therefore the correct choice. Did you realize the words +/- 3 sigma are extraneous? Practice reading questions that are wordy and have extraneous data.

4. **Answer** A
   Explanation Cost increases and contract disputes for payments will not necessarily interfere with schedule. If a "post-implementation" review meeting slips, it may not interfere with the project schedule. Delays in obtaining required approvals is the only choice that always causes a time delay, and is therefore the most likely to threaten the project schedule.

5. **Answer** B
   Explanation Don't feel too silly if you got this wrong. Many people miss this one. No calculation is needed. If there is a 20 percent chance in any one month, the chance in the fourth month must therefore be 20 percent.

6. **Answer** C
   Explanation Expected monetary value is calculated by multiplying the probability times the impact. In this case, EMV = 0.9 × $10,000 = $9,000.

7. **Answer** B
   Explanation This is a tricky question. Risks are identified during the Identify Risk process, naturally, but newly emerging risks are identified in the Monitor and Control Risks process.

8. **Answer** B
   Explanation Risks change throughout the project. You need to review risks at intervals during the project to ensure non-critical risks have not become critical.

9. **Answer** D
   Explanation Project status reports can be an input to risk management. However, when completing risk management for the first time, you would not have project status reports. Therefore, project status reports are not always an input to risk management.

10. **Answer** A
    Explanation If you know the tolerances of the stakeholders, you can determine how they might react to different situations and risk events. You use this information to help assign levels of risk on each work package or activity.

11. **Answer** D
    Explanation Since a contract can only be created after risks are known (a contract is a tool to transfer risks), this cannot be the exception. The project management plan could change to include a modified WBS and new work packages related to mitigating risk. The communications management plan could change as a way to address a risk. A change to the charter is a fundamental change to the project and may require a major adjustment to all aspects of the project management plan. It is not a common result of risk management efforts.

12. **Answer** B
    Explanation To mitigate risk, we either reduce the probability of the event happening or reduce its impact. Acceptance of risk means doing nothing (if it happens, it happens). Avoidance of risk means we change the way we will execute the project so the risk is no longer a factor. Transference is passing the risk off to another party. Many people think of using insurance as a way of decreasing impact. However, purchasing insurance transfers the risk to another party.

13. **Answer** C
    Explanation If you cannot determine an exact cost impact to the event, use qualitative estimates such as Low, Medium, High, etc.

14. **Answer** A
    Explanation A risk list, process updates, and change requests are not outputs of the Plan Risk Responses process. Residual risks, fallback plans, and contingency reserves are all outputs of the Plan Risk Responses process, making this the correct answer.

15. **Answer** D
    Explanation A workaround refers to determining how to handle a risk that occurs but is not included in the risk register. The project must be in the Monitor and Control Risks process if risks have occurred.

16. **Answer** C
    Explanation Transference is a risk response strategy.

17. **Answer** C
    Explanation This situation is occurring during project planning. Planning must be completed before moving on. Determining the risk rating of the project is done during Perform Qualitative Risk Analysis, and should have already been done. Project risk reassessment occurs during Monitor and Control Risks, the next step in the risk management process after Plan Risk Responses. But the question does not ask what is next in the risk management process, just what is next. Adding work packages to the WBS, as part of iterations, comes next in project planning.

18. **Answer** C
    Explanation The project manager is in the Perform Qualitative Risk Analysis process. Activities of this process include assumptions testing (risk data quality assessment), and probability and impact matrix development. It appears the project manager has not yet completed the matrix. Trend analysis, identification of triggers, and development of fallback plans will occur later in risk management.

19. **Answer** D
    Explanation The process the project manager has used so far is fine, except the input of other stakeholders is needed in order to identify more risks.

20. **Answer** D
    Explanation A review of cost proposals could be done, but it is not a pressing issue based on the situation provided. Examining the budget reserves could also be done, but not until risk planning is completed. It is always important to carefully complete a project charter, but there are other issues needing detailed attention in this situation. Since this project has never been done before, and there will be a large cost outlay, it would be best for the project manager to spend more time on risk management. Risk identification is the most proactive response and would have the greatest positive impact on the project.

21. **Answer** A
    Explanation This question relates real-world situations to risk types. Did you realize that the entire first paragraph is extraneous? Based on the question, you cannot remove the work to avoid it, nor can you insure or outsource it to transfer the risk. This leaves acceptance as the only correct choice.

22. **Answer** D
    Explanation The Delphi technique is most commonly used to obtain expert opinions on technical issues, the necessary project or product scope, or the risks.

23. **Answer** D
    Explanation Did you realize this situation is taking place during project initiating? The scope statement and resource plan are created in project planning, and so are not yet available. Therefore, we are left with deciding if the magazine article or a conversation with a team member who worked on a similar project provides the greater value. Since the information gained in conversing with the team member provides input more specific to your company, it is the best choice.

24. **Answer** B
    Explanation Team members will have knowledge of the project and the product of the project and will thus have a lot to contribute to risk responses. Those responsible for risk templates will be able to provide the templates from past projects (historical records) and therefore will be very important. Key stakeholders will know more about the technical working of the project to help plan "What are we going to do about it?" so they are not likely to be the least important. The sponsor may have the least knowledge of what will work to solve the problems. Sponsors need to be involved in the project and help identify risks. They may even approve the response plans created by others, but they would not generally be major contributors to response plans.

25. **Answer** C
    Explanation The risk is the loss of data due to a power outage. Purchasing insurance is not related to "mitigating" the problem. It transfers the risk. Creating a reserve fund is acceptance of the risk, and would help address the cost factors after the power failure, but would not reduce the probability or impact of it. Avoiding the hurricane by scheduling the installation at a different time mitigates the power outage risk, but could have a large negative impact on the project schedule and so is not the best choice. The better choice of the mitigation options is to monitor the weather and know when to implement the contingency plan.

26. **Answer** B
Explanation A workaround is an unplanned response to an event that is occurring. This risk discussed in the question has been identified, but it is not occurring at this time, so there is no need to take the action of creating a workaround. You need to analyze the problem before talking to the sponsor. You cannot mitigate the risk until you qualify it. Qualifying the risk will help you determine how to proceed.

27. **Answer** A
Explanation This project has deviated so far from the baseline that updated risk identification and risk analysis should be performed.

28. **Answer** B
Explanation When new risks are identified, they should go through the risk management process. You need to determine the probability and impact of the risks and then try to diminish their impact through the Plan Risk Responses process. Only after these efforts should you consider adding reserves for time and/or cost. Any reserves should be based on a detailed analysis of risk. Calculating the expected monetary value of the risks is an important part of the risk management process, and the best choice presented here.

29. **Answer** A
Explanation Did you notice this project has already begun? Risk management is a required element of project management. You must complete risk management, starting with the Plan Risk Management process.

30. **Answer** D
Explanation First, you want to determine what the risk entails and the impact to the project, then determine what actions you will take regarding the risk.

31. **Answer** A
Explanation Following the right process is part of professional and social responsibility. Because an unidentified problem or risk occurred, it is important to reevaluate the Identify Risks process as well as to look for unexpected effects of the problem. However, they are not your first choices. You might need to inform management, but this is reactive, not proactive, and not the first thing you should do. Since this is a problem that has occurred, rather than a problem that has just been identified, the first thing you must do is address the risk by creating a workaround.

32. **Answer** C
Explanation This is a recurring theme. First, you should evaluate the impact of the change. Next, determine options. Then go to management and the customer.

33. **Answer** B
Explanation The Delphi technique uses experts and builds consensus; therefore, expert opinion is the chief characteristic.

34. **Answer** B
Explanation The wording of this question can be confusing. Reserve is mentioned in the situation, but the project manager is not dealing with reserves in the actions he is taking. Scope verification involves meeting with the customer to gain formal acceptance, so that cannot be the best choice. The project manager is trying to make something good happen, not dealing with a negative impact, or threat, which may or may not occur. The project manager is working to make a positive impact on the project more likely to occur. Therefore, he is working with an opportunity.

35. **Answer** A
Explanation A Monte Carlo analysis could indicate that an estimate for an activity needs to change, but not what the activity estimate should be. Monte Carlo is a simulation, but it does not specifically address quality. It does not deal directly with staff or resource needs either. Project risk can be assessed using Monte Carlo analysis. By considering the inputs to the PERT estimates and the network diagram, you can obtain a better overview of the overall project risk.

36. **Answer** A
Explanation This question essentially asks, "What is an output of Perform Qualitative Risk Analysis?" Risk triggers and contingency reserves are parts of the Plan Risk Responses process. The probability of achieving time and cost objectives is determined during the Perform Quantitative Risk Analysis process. A prioritized list of risks is an output of Perform Qualitative Risk Analysis.

37. **Answer** A
Explanation Did you realize this question describes secondary risks? Identifying secondary risks is an important part of completing the Plan Risk Responses process. With that in mind, the best thing to do is to document the newly identified risks and continue the Plan Risk Responses process.

38. **Answer** C
Explanation A watchlist is made up of low-priority risks that, in the Perform Qualitative Risk Analysis process, were determined to be of too low priority or low impact to move further in the risk management process.

39. **Answer** B
Explanation Stakeholders should be included in the Identify Risks process. Workarounds are created later in the risk process, as unidentified risk events occur. Plan Risk Responses must include the involvement of all risk response owners and possibly other stakeholders.

40. **Answer** A
Explanation Risk is so important that it must be discussed at all team meetings.

CHAPTER TWELVE Procurement Management

Quicktest

- Procurement management process
- Procurement management plan
- Contract types
  - FP, FPIF, FPAF, FPEPA, purchase order, T&M, CR, cost, CPF/CPPC, CPFF, CPIF, CPAF
- How project management is different with each contract type
- Advantages/ disadvantages of each contract type
- Contract change control system
- Termination
- Breach
- What is a contract
- Project manager's role in procurement
- Procurement documents: RFP, IFB, RFQ
- Procurement administration
- Noncompetitive forms of procurement
- Types of procurement statements of work
- Procurement performance review
- Claims administration
- Make-or-buy
- Formal acceptance
- Inputs to procurement management
- Records management system
- Bidder conferences
- Risk and contract type
- Waiver
- Financial closure
- Final contract performance reporting
- Conflict with procurement manager
- Procurement audit
- Product verification
- Source selection criteria
- Weighting system
- Screening system
- Incentives
- Special provisions
- Standard contract
- Terms and conditions
- Negotiation objectives/ tactics
- Privity
- Qualified seller lists
- Advertising
- Centralized/ decentralized contracting
- Contract interpretation
- Price
- Profit
- Cost
- Target price
- Sharing ratio
- Ceiling price
- PTA
- Letter of intent
- Presentations
- Lessons learned
- Procurement file
- Nondisclosure agreement
- Teaming agreement
- What makes a legal contract
- Force majeure

As with the Risk Management chapter, let's start this chapter with a story. There was once a very experienced student in an RMC class who was upset about a situation at work. He said he had arranged a meeting with a seller, and the seller did not show up. He then rescheduled the meeting, and the seller still did not show up. When the instructor asked what kind of contract he was working with, the student had to contact his office to find out he had a fixed price contract. The instructor then asked him where in the contract it said the seller had to attend such meetings. After some investigation, the student determined it was not listed in the contract. So was the seller's absence from the meeting wrong? Why would a seller attend such a meeting if he was not getting paid for it?

Think about what procurement management means on a project. We are not talking about the role of an attorney or a contracting or procurement office. We are talking about the project manager's role. The basic knowledge and skills of a project manager should include being able to help create, read, and manage contracts.

For some people, procurement management is one of the hardest knowledge areas on the exam. If you have worked with contracts before, you might have to fine-tune your knowledge and learn the terms for what you already do. You might also have to understand the project manager's role a little better, but you should score well on these questions. If you are like many other people, however, you may have little experience in procurement. Regardless of your real-world experience, the PMP exam will test you as if you were an expert. This chapter will walk you through the procurement process and suggest ways you can most effectively study this topic and prepare for the exam.

To help you better understand procurement, we will start with an overview of the process. Do not just read the description provided! Instead, IMAGINE what it would take to make this happen in your real world. Make sure you understand the overview and can generally describe the procurement process yourself before you continue reading the chapter.

Rita's Process Chart—Procurement Management

Where are we in the project management process?

INITIATING

- Select project manager
- Determine company culture and existing systems
- Collect processes, procedures, and historical information
- Divide large projects into phases
- Understand the business case
- Uncover initial requirements, assumptions, and risks
- Assess project and product feasibility within the given constraints
- Create measurable objectives
- Develop project charter
- Identify stakeholders
- Develop stakeholder management strategy

PLANNING

(This is the only process group with a set order)

- **Determine how you will do planning—part of all management plans**
- Determine detailed requirements
- Create project scope statement
- **Assess what to purchase**
- Determine team
- Create WBS and WBS dictionary
- Create activity list
- Create network diagram
- Estimate resource requirements
- Estimate time and cost
- Determine critical path
- Develop schedule
- Develop budget
- Determine quality standards, processes, and metrics
- Create process improvement plan
- **Determine all roles and responsibilities**
- Plan communications
- Perform risk identification, qualitative and quantitative risk analysis, and risk response planning
- **Go back—iterations**
- **Prepare procurement documents**
- Create change management plans
- **Finalize the "how to execute and control" parts of all management plans**
- **Develop realistic and final PM plan and performance measurement baseline**
- Gain formal approval of the plan
- Hold kickoff meeting

EXECUTING

- Execute the work according to the PM plan
- Produce product deliverables (product scope)
- **Request changes**
- Implement only approved changes
- Continuously improve
- Follow processes
- Perform quality assurance
- Perform quality audits
- Acquire final team
- Manage people
- Evaluate team and project performance
- Hold team-building activities
- Give recognition and rewards
- Use issue logs
- Facilitate conflict resolution
- Release resources as work is completed
- Send and receive information
- Hold meetings
- **Select sellers**

MONITORING & CONTROLLING

- **Take action to control the project**
- Measure performance against the performance measurement baseline
- **Measure performance against other metrics determined by the project manager**
- **Determine variances and if they warrant a corrective action or change request**
- **Influence the factors that cause changes**
- **Request changes**
- Perform integrated change control
- Approve or reject changes
- Inform stakeholders of results of change requests
- **Update the PM plan and project documents**
- Manage configuration
- Create forecasts
- Gain acceptance of interim deliverables from the customer
- Perform quality control
- Report on project performance and solicit feedback
- Perform risk assessments and audits
- Manage reserves
- **Administer procurements**

CLOSING

- **Confirm work is done to requirements**
- **Complete procurement closure**
- Gain final acceptance of the product
- Complete financial closure
- Hand off completed product
- Solicit feedback from the customer about the project
- Complete final performance reporting
- **Index and archive records**
- **Update lessons learned knowledge base**

TRICKS OF THE TRADE® If you have little or no experience working with contracts, you should obtain from your company some sample contracts, requests for proposals, and the resulting proposals and look at them before reading on. It might also be valuable to get in contact with your contracts, procurement, or legal department. The exam assumes that you have a close working relationship with these departments, that as a project manager you have specific involvement in the procurement process even if you do not lead that process, and that the procurement process cannot occur without your involvement. You have an opportunity to build an extremely worthwhile relationship with these other departments when you ask, "What should I know about contracts?" Plus you can improve your working relationship by explaining the project management process to them. Try it!

The following should help you understand how each part of procurement management fits into the overall project management process:

The Procurement Management Process	Done During
Plan Procurements	Planning process group
Conduct Procurements	Executing process group
Administer Procurements	Monitoring and controlling process group
Close Procurements	Closing process group

An Overview of the Procurement Management Process Let's start with a summary of the procurement management process. The rest of this chapter will discuss this process in more detail. Know that there can be multiple procurements on projects and that this process is done for every procurement on the project.

Procurement is a formal process to obtain goods and services. In addition to contracts, outputs of the procurement management process include the procurement management plan, procurement statement of work (SOW), procurement documents, change requests, additional procurement documentation, and lessons learned. Private companies have a lot of flexibility in their procurement practices. Because government entities are spending public funds, however, they normally have to comply with laws, rules, and regulations that specifically govern each step of the procurement process. Private companies that use public funds from the government may also be required to comply with some or all of these regulations.

In most companies, there is a department that handles and controls procurements. This department is often called the procurement, contracting, purchasing, or legal department (for simplicity, we'll call it the "procurement department"). Managing procurements requires legal knowledge, negotiation skills, and an understanding of the procurement process. Although project managers are not often expected to take the lead in legal matters, negotiations, or managing the procurement process, they must be familiar with all of these aspects.

When a project is planned, the scope is analyzed to determine whether internal resources can do everything or if any of the work will be outsourced (a make-or-buy decision). If one or more procurements are needed, the procurement department gets involved in the project to manage the procurement process. Project managers must understand what these procurement experts will need from them, provide the experts with that information, and then work with the procurement department throughout the life of the procurements.

Once the decision has been made to procure goods or services from an outside source, the project manager will facilitate creating a plan for how the procurement process will proceed (a procurement management plan) and will create a description of the work to be done by the seller (a procurement statement of work).

The procurement manager will determine what type of contract and procurement document should be used. The most common procurement documents are Request for Proposal (RFP), Invitation for Bid (IFB), and Request for Quotation (RFQ). The type of procurement document used is connected to the contract type selected and the form of the procurement statement of work. As you will see later in this chapter, the different types of contracts require project managers to focus their management activities in different areas.

The procurement department may review the scope of the work for completeness (always a good idea), and the project manager might add scope related to project management activities (e.g., specific reporting and attendance at meetings), resulting in the finalized procurement statement of work. This procurement statement of work is then combined with the contract terms to form the finalized procurement documents (RFP, RFQ, etc.), which are sent to prospective sellers.

At this point, the sellers take action and the buyer waits for the response. The prospective sellers will review the procurement documents and determine whether they are interested in submitting a bid or proposal to try to win the work. They may have the opportunity to participate in a bidder conference or a preproposal meeting. As part of the procurement process, prospective sellers may also have the opportunity to submit questions in writing relating to the procurement documents. They need to submit these questions to the buyer before the submission deadline for bids or proposals.

The prospective sellers will carefully review the buyer's statement of work and all the terms of the proposed contract contained in the procurement documents. This review helps the sellers get a full understanding of what the buyer wants. It also helps the sellers assess the risks involved in the project. If the scope is incomplete or unclear, if a prospective seller is aware of the buyer having a history of poorly managing projects, or if any other risks are identified, a prospective seller may decide not to submit a bid or will adjust the price, time, or both submitted to the buyer to account for these risks. When a fixed price is required, sellers should include these risks in the total detailed cost estimate, as well as other costs such as overhead, and then add profit to come up with a total cost estimate. In any case, the risk of the project is formally or informally assessed before sending the bid or proposal to the buyer. (Do you see the increased risk for the seller caused by unclear requirements if the seller does not get completely defined data before bidding on the work?)

The time that prospective sellers need to prepare a response to the procurement documents can be substantial (sometimes taking months), and the buyer's project manager must plan this time into the project schedule.

In most cases, procurement is competitive; there will be multiple sellers who can do the work and who are invited to submit a response to the procurement documents. Public organizations may be required by law to follow certain procurement practices and make a selection from the prospective sellers in a certain way. Because private companies may buy from anyone they want, competitive bidding is not required by law, though they might have internal policies that must be followed regarding procurement practices. A private company need not even obtain a bid; it can simply issue a purchase order to obtain goods or services. On occasion, work might be so specialized that there is only one potential seller (a noncompetitive bidding situation).

Organizations may use several different methods to select a seller. As noted in the previous paragraph, these methods may be dictated by law or internal policies. If a buyer receives competing submissions from many prospective sellers, the buyer might ask for presentations from all of the candidates to help select a seller. Another option is to shorten the list of prospective sellers first and then request presentations. If presentations will not add value for the buyer, the buyer may just move into negotiations with the preferred seller or sellers. All terms and conditions in the proposed contract, the entire procurement statement of work, and any other components of the procurement documents can be negotiated. Negotiations can take a lot of time, and they require the involvement of the project manager.

At the end of negotiations, one or more sellers are selected, and a contract is signed. The procurement management plan created earlier may also be updated.

Notice the procurement process does not end when the contract is entered into. Once the contract is signed, the procurement must be administered. This involves making sure all the requirements of the contract, even ones that seem unimportant, are met. It also means keeping control of the contract and making approved changes. As the procurement work is being completed, questions may arise, such as, "What is and what is not in the contract?" or, "What does a particular piece of the contract really mean?" The procurement department will help the project manager resolve these issues.

As stated in the previous paragraph, administering the procurement involves keeping control of the contract and making approved changes. Let's step out of the overview for a moment and imagine that work has started on the procurement. You find that a change is needed, only to realize that there is no plan in place describing how the change should be submitted, who should review it, who can approve the change, and how the cost, time, and other impacts of the change will be evaluated. You could spend more time figuring out how you will make the change than doing the work the change calls for. This is the reason for the contract change control system. This system for how changes will be handled is included in the contract so everyone is prepared for the amount of work it will take to make changes, in addition to completing the work described in the change.

Once the procurement work is complete, the procurement will be closed. This includes the completion of a procurement audit to determine lessons learned. Since there can be many different procurements involved with any one project, the process of closing a procurement can occur many times on a project. For example, in a project to renovate a house, a seller may be contracted to paint the house, another may be contracted to install new landscaping, and still another may be contracted to install the plumbing. Each of these procurements is closed as it is completed. Because there is only one project, the overall project is closed just once, upon completion of all the project work, unless the project is managed in phases. In that case, the Close Project or Phase process occurs at the end of each phase, after procurements completed in that phase have been closed out. Make sure you understand the difference between closing individual procurements and closing the project or project phase. During procurement closure, final reports are submitted, lessons learned are documented, and final payment is made.

Stop! Do you understand what you have just read? Can you now describe the procurement process to someone else? Be sure this overview makes sense to you before continuing to read this chapter.

Buyers and Sellers In the real world, the company or person who provides services and goods can be called a "contractor," "subcontractor," "designer," "vendor," etc. The *PMBOK® Guide* uses only one term, "seller," but the exam may use any of these terms to describe the seller. The company or person who purchases the services is called the "buyer." Many companies are a buyer in one procurement and a seller in another.

TRICKS OF THE TRADE® Be careful to read the questions carefully to see if the situation described in the question is from the buyer's or seller's point of view. If no point of view is mentioned, assume you are the buyer. Make sure you get your mind around being a buyer before you take this exam. The issues and impacts of many situations are completely different if you are a buyer than if you are a seller.

TRICKS OF THE TRADE® The exam also assumes the seller is not supplying people to adjunct the buyer's team, meaning that the seller remains external to the project team.

Tricks for Answering Procurement Questions Keep in mind the following general rules, especially if you find a question with an answer that is not immediately apparent:

- Contracts require formality.
- All product and project management requirements for the procurement work should be specifically stated in the contract.
- If it is not in the contract, it can only be done if a formal change order to the contract is issued.
- If it is in the contract, it must be done or a formal change order must be approved by both parties.
- Changes must be submitted and approved in writing.
- Contracts are legally binding; the seller has no choice but to perform as agreed in the contract.
- Contracts should help diminish project risk.
- Most governments back all contracts that fall within their jurisdiction by providing a court system for dispute resolution.

Remembering these pointers can help you get about four more questions right!

NOTE TO STUDENTS OUTSIDE OF THE UNITED STATES: The exam has had very few references to international contracts. Be aware that government contracting specialists in the United States wrote many of the questions on the PMP exam. PMI's process for procurement management closely follows what is done in the United States, but it is different from the way procurement is handled in other parts of the world. In many regions, the contract is an informal document and the relationship between the parties is more important than the contract. If you are not from the United States, a key trick is to take a more formal approach to the procurement process when answering questions. The contract is most important. It must be followed, and everything provided in it must be done. Study this chapter carefully.

The Project Manager's Role in Procurement You might ask yourself, "If there is a procurement manager, why would a project manager need to be involved in procurements?" This is an important question, and you must fully understand the answer before you take the exam. Here are a few more tricks to help you.

First, remember that it is the project manager's project. There are certain things that cannot be done effectively without the project manager. This fact is so important that a large percentage of the questions on the exam have focused on testing whether you know what you should do. Here is a quick summary. Do not memorize it; instead, make sure you understand it.

- Know the procurement process so you know what will happen when.
- Understand what contract terms and conditions mean so you can read and understand contracts.
- Make sure the contract contains all the scope of work and all the project management requirements, such as attendance at meetings, reports, actions, and communications deemed necessary to minimize problems and miscommunications with the seller(s).
- Identify risks, and incorporate mitigation and allocation of risks into the contract to decrease project risk.
- Help tailor the contract to the unique needs of the project while it is being written.
- Include the time required to complete the procurement process into the schedule for the project so the project schedule is realistic.
- Be involved during contract negotiations to protect the relationship with the seller.
- Protect the integrity of the project and the ability to get the work done by making sure the procurement process goes as smoothly as possible.
- Help make sure all the work in the contract is done, such as reporting, inspections, and legal deliverables, including the release of liens and ownership of materials, not just the technical scope.
- Do not ask for something that is not in the contract without making a corresponding change to the contract.
- Work with the procurement manager to manage changes to the contract.

TRICKS OF THE TRADE® The second thing to remember is that project managers must be assigned on both the buyer's and seller's sides before a contract is signed! Many companies that sell their services make a huge but common mistake by not having the project manager involved in the bidding and proposal process. Instead, only marketing and sales are involved until after the contract is signed. The project manager is then handed a project with a contract that may include unrealistic time or cost constraints. The project starts out in trouble.

Not including the project manager early in the procurement process is such a mistake that the exam will test you to see if you know when the project manager should be involved, and why. For example, the project manager is often uniquely capable of answering many of the technical and project management questions that arise during bidder conferences (described later in this chapter). If these questions are answered incorrectly or incompletely, there may be an inadvertent change in the specification or the scope of the contract that was never intended by the buyer.

Centralized/Decentralized Contracting Although this topic is not in the *PMBOK® Guide*, you may see it on the exam. When working with a procurement manager, you should know what authority the procurement manager has and how the procurement department is organized (similar to knowing if you are in a matrix form of organization, as described in the Project Management Framework chapter). In a centralized contracting environment, there is one procurement department, and a procurement manager may handle procurements on many projects. The project manager contacts the department when he or she needs help or to ask questions. In a decentralized contracting environment, a procurement manager is assigned to one project full-time and reports directly to the project manager. The form of contracting environment will impact the procurement manager's availability and authority.

Try the following exercise. If you do well, you do not have to study this topic much.

Exercise Identify the advantages and disadvantages of each type of buyer's contracting environment.

Centralized Contracting	
Advantages	Disadvantages

Decentralized Contracting	
Advantages	Disadvantages

Answer

Centralized Contracting	
Advantages	Disadvantages
Because they are part of a department that focuses on procurements, centralized contracting can result in procurement managers with higher levels of expertise.	One procurement manager may work on many projects, so this individual must divide his or her attention among many projects.
A procurement department will provide its employees with continuous improvement, training, and shared lessons learned.	It may be more difficult for the project manager to obtain contracting help when needed.
Standardized company practices allow efficiency and help improve understanding.	
Individuals in this department have a clearly defined career path in procurement.	

Decentralized Contracting	
Advantages	**Disadvantages**
The project manager has easier access to contracting expertise because the procurement manager is a member of the team.	There is no "home" department for the procurement manager to return to after the project is completed.
The procurement manager has more loyalty to the project.	It is more difficult to maintain a high level of contracting expertise in the company, because there is no procurement department with a focus on improving expertise.
	There may be duplication of expertise and inefficient use of procurement resources in projects across the organization.
	There may be little standardization of procurement practices from one project to the next.
	There may not be a career path as a procurement manager in the company.

In a centralized contracting environment, the procurement manager is involved with many projects at the same time and reports organizationally to the head of the procurement department, not to the project manager. There is generally more contracting expertise in this type of environment, as that expertise is managed and shared between many procurement experts. Procurement processes and even contract language will be standardized between projects, making it easier for a project manager to understand the contract terms and processes. However, each project is just one of many the procurement manager has to deal with. This can lead to issues of commitment, accessibility, and authority.

In a decentralized contracting environment, the procurement manager is hired to work for the project and reports only to the project manager. There is no procurement department. The procurement manager will be more accessible to the project manager, will be more loyal, and will understand the project better. In a decentralized contracting environment, there may be little standardization of procurement processes and contract language because there is not a procurement department to regulate standards, improve knowledge, and increase professionalism in procurement management.

The Procurement Management Process[1] PAGE 313

Project managers often come to procurement managers saying, "I need a seller NOW!" Procurement managers would like to say, "There is a procurement process designed to obtain the best seller at the most reasonable price. That process includes waiting time for the sellers to look at your needs and to respond. The process can take from one to three months for this type of procurement. Why didn't you manage your project well enough to account for this time in your schedule?" This is one of the reasons project managers must understand the procurement process and a reason procurement concepts are tested on the exam. Not only does the project manager need to be involved along the way, assisting the procurement department with project input, he or she also needs to plan for the amount of time procurements take. The remainder of this chapter will follow the procurement process from start to finish. You need to learn what each step includes and when it occurs in the procurement management process and the project management process.

Many questions relating to the procurement process are similar to those in risk management and the project management process as a whole. You must know what happens when, how procurement management works on a properly managed project, and how it relates to the project life cycle. The four sequential procurement management processes are:

1. Plan Procurements
2. Conduct Procurements
3. Administer Procurements
4. Close Procurements

Inputs to the Procurement Management Process (or "What do you need before you begin the procurement process?")

- **Enterprise environmental factors** These factors are company culture and existing systems your project will have to deal with or can use. For procurement, this includes marketplace conditions and what services are available to be purchased.
- **Organizational process assets** The organizational process assets that are used in procurement can include procurement procedures, standard contracts, lessons learned from past projects, and lists of prequalified sellers.
- **Procurement manager assigned** This assignment may come later in the process, depending on the amount of procurement involved.
- **The scope baseline (Project scope statement, WBS, and WBS dictionary)** The scope baseline helps those involved in the procurement process understand the scope of the project.
- **Risk register** The risk register provides an understanding of risks uncovered to date. Remember, risk analysis of the project should be done before contracts are signed.
- **Any procurements already in place on the project** The project manager must manage the interface between multiple sellers and multiple procurements on one project.
- **Identification of resources not available within the performing organization** This helps determine what services (if any) need to be procured.
- **The project schedule** The schedule will help determine when the procurements are needed.
- **Initial cost estimates for work to be procured** An internal cost estimate for each procurement should be created before the procurement process starts to be used for comparison with sellers' prices.
- **Cost baseline for the project** As with the cost estimate for each procurement, knowing the cost baseline for the project will help to make sure the procurement fits within the baseline costs.

Exercise So you think you read it well? Try to recreate what you just read, and see what you forgot. Then spend time thinking about these items to make sure you do not forget them on the exam.

What Are the Inputs to the Procurement Management Process?

What Are the Inputs to the Procurement Management Process?

Plan Procurements PAGE 316

Process: Plan Procurements
Process Group: Planning
Knowledge Area: Procurement Management

The Plan Procurements process answers the questions of "What goods and services do we need to buy for this project, how will we purchase them, and who are potential sellers to use?" In addition to creating a procurement management plan, this process involves putting together the procurement documents that will be sent to prospective sellers describing the buyer's need, how to respond, and the criteria the buyer will use to select a seller. The Plan Procurements process includes the following activities:

- Performing make-or-buy analysis
- Creating a procurement management plan
- Creating a procurement statement of work for each procurement
- Selecting a contract type for each procurement
- Creating the procurement documents
- Determining the source selection criteria

Make-or-Buy Analysis[2] PAGE 321 The company needs to make a decision about whether to do the project work themselves or outsource some or all of the work. The costs involved in managing the procurement should be considered as part of the decision, in addition to the direct costs of the product or service to be procured. The cost savings of purchasing a product or service may be outweighed by the cost of managing the procurement.

One of the main reasons to "buy" is to decrease risk to the project's constraints. It is better to "make" if:

- You have an idle plant or workforce.
- You want to retain control.
- The work involves proprietary information or procedures.

Expect to see questions on the exam that refer to this decision, or even questions that require you to calculate buy-or-lease situations, such as:

> **Question** *You are trying to decide whether to lease or buy an item for your project. The daily lease cost is $120. To purchase the item, the investment cost is $1,000 and the daily cost is $20. How long will it take for the lease cost to be the same as the purchase cost?*
>
> **Answer** *Let D equal the number of days when the purchase and lease costs are equal.*
> *$120D = $1,000 + $20D*
> *$120D - $20D = $1,000*
> *$100D = $1,000*
> *D = 10*

This calculation helps a project manager decide whether it is better to buy or lease. The calculation says that the costs are the same after 10 days. Therefore, if you are planning to use the item for fewer than 10 days, you should lease. If you are planning to use it for more than 10 days, it would be cheaper to buy the item. These costs are then included in the project cost estimate.

Procurement Management Plan PAGE 324 Once the decisions have been made about what to procure from outside sources, the project manager can create a plan to manage those procurements. Like other management plans, the procurement management plan describes how the procurement process will be planned, executed, and controlled. The concept of management plans has been discussed in almost every chapter. Does it make sense to you? Make sure you understand the purpose and content of management plans for the exam.

Procurement Statement of Work PAGE 325 The project manager also needs to determine the scope of work to be done on each procurement. This can be achieved by breaking down the project scope baseline into the work the project team will do and the work that will be purchased from a seller(s). The work to be done on each procurement is called the "procurement statement of work." It must be as clear, complete, and concise as possible, and it must describe all the work and activities the seller is required to complete.

Wait—did you read that last sentence too fast? We'll say it again. The procurement statement of work must be as clear, complete, and concise as possible, and it must describe all the work and activities the seller is required to complete. Yes, all the work. This includes all meetings, reports, and communications. If such activities are not included, the cost of adding them later is typically more than the cost of adding them at the beginning of the procurement. Does this make you think about the amount of work required to create a complete procurement statement of work?

What does the word "complete" mean? It depends on what you are buying. If you are buying expertise (such as software design or legal services), your procurement statement of work will include your functional and/or performance requirements (in addition to required meetings, reports, and communications). If you are buying the construction of a building, your requirements will be extremely specific, outlining things like the type of wood to be used, the process that must be followed, and even a work schedule. If you are hiring staff that you will direct (e.g., a programmer to be added to the team), your procurement statement of work will likely contain more details of what you want the person to create or achieve. Ask yourself, "If I were the seller, how comfortable would I be signing a legally binding contract to complete this work for a certain price?" Put yourself in the seller's shoes and make sure the scope of work is descriptive enough.

Remember that a contract is a document used to manage a procurement activity. It does not just sit in a drawer. Therefore, both parties to the contract should always be asking, "What does the contract say?" Contract problems are not easy to resolve. It is best to prevent problems by having a complete procurement statement of work. If the procurement statement of work is not complete, the seller will need to constantly request clarification or ask for change orders that can get expensive. The project manager and procurement manager could be constantly dealing with issues of whether a specific piece of work is contained within the original cost or time submitted by the seller.

Types of Procurement Statements of Work

The procurement statement of work may be revised during contract negotiation, but it should be finalized (excluding changes) by the time the contract is signed. There are many types of procurement statements of work. Your choice will depend on the nature of the work and the type of industry.

- **Performance** This type conveys what the final product should be able to accomplish, rather than how it should be built or what its design characteristics should be (e.g., "I want a car that will go from zero to 120 kilometers per hour in 4.2 seconds").

- **Functional** This type conveys the end purpose or result, rather than the specific procedures or approach. Functional procurement statements of work may include a statement of the minimum essential characteristics of the product (e.g., "I want a car with 23 cup holders" [yes, that is supposed to be a ridiculous example]).
- **Design** This type conveys precisely what work is to be done (e.g., "Build it exactly as shown on these drawings").

Performance and functional procurement statements of work are commonly used for information systems, information technology, high-tech, research and development, and projects that have never been done before. Design procurement statements of work are most commonly used in construction and equipment purchasing.

A procurement statement of work can include drawings, specifications, technical and descriptive wording, etc. No matter what it contains, however, the procurement statement of work becomes part of the contract.

Contract Types PAGE 322

There are many different types of contracts that can be used to acquire goods and services on a project. The procurement manager will select the contract type based on the following considerations:

- What is being purchased (a product or a service)
- The completeness of the statement of work
- The level of effort and expertise the buyer can devote to managing the seller
- Whether the buyer wants to offer the seller incentives
- The marketplace or economy
- Industry standards for the type of contract used

There are sometimes different names for the same type of contract. This can make it very difficult to learn the contract types. So here is a trick. Start out thinking that there are just three main categories of contract types, as shown in the following list. Then, when the exam asks a question relating to contract type, first see if knowing which category the contract is in helps you answer the question. In most cases, it does.

The three broad categories of contracts are:[3]

- Fixed price (FP)
- Time and material (T&M)
- Cost reimbursable (CR)

You must understand the contract types and be able to recognize the differences between them. You should be able to answer situational questions describing what you would do differently depending on the contract type. There may also be questions that require you to pick the most appropriate contract type based on a particular situation. Think through this section carefully!

Fixed Price (FP, or Lump Sum, Firm Fixed Price) PAGE 322

A fixed price contract is used for acquiring goods or services with well-defined specifications or requirements and when there is enough competition to determine a fair and reasonable fixed price before the work begins. This is the most common type of contract. If the costs are more than the agreed-upon amount, the seller must bear the additional costs. Therefore, the buyer has the least cost risk in this type of contract (assuming the scope is well defined). The seller is most concerned with the procurement statement of work (SOW) in a fixed price contract.

Sellers in some industries may not have the detailed accounting records of past project activities required to accurately estimate future projects. Buyers may not have the expertise to prepare a complete procurement statement of work. In such cases, a fixed price contract is inappropriate.

Because many companies are not knowledgeable about contracts, they often ask the seller to provide a fixed price, even when the scope of work is incomplete. Think for a minute about the consequences of doing this:

- The seller is forced to accept a high level of risk.
- The seller needs to add a huge amount of reserves to their price to cover their risks, and the buyer, therefore, pays more than they otherwise might have.
- The seller can more easily try to increase profits by cutting scope or claiming that work the buyer wants is outside the contract and thus requires a change. The buyer will not be able to state with certainty if something is within the scope of the work or outside of it (and, therefore, needs a change order and additional payment to the seller) if there is not a complete procurement statement of work.

If a fixed price contract is used when it shouldn't be and the seller realizes they will not be able to make any profit on the project, there is a risk the seller may try to take their best people off the project, try to cut work that is specifically mentioned in the contract, cut out work that is not mentioned in the contract but is needed, decrease quality, or take any other actions to save themselves money, all because the wrong contract type was used.

Example: Fixed Price Contract
Contract = $1,100,000.

Fixed Price Incentive Fee (FPIF) In a FPIF contract, profits (or financial incentives) can be adjusted based on the seller meeting specified performance criteria such as getting the work done faster, cheaper, or better. The final price is calculated by a formula based on the relationship of final negotiated costs to the total target cost. (See more on incentives later in this section.) A variation on a FPIF is a FPIF successive target contract, in which the target for the incentive is changed after the first target is reached.

Example: Fixed Price Incentive Fee Contract
Contract = $1,100,000. For every month early the project is finished, an additional $10,000 is paid to the seller.

You may need to calculate these incentives for the exam, so make sure you understand the exercises at the end of the contract types discussion (page 438 in this book).

Fixed Price Award Fee (FPAF) In a FPAF contract, the buyer pays a fixed price plus an award amount (a bonus) based on performance. This is very similar to the FPIF contract, except the total possible award amount is determined in advance and apportioned out based on performance. For example, the buyer might say there is a maximum $50,000 award fee available. It will be apportioned out at the rate of $5,000 for every month production exceeds a certain amount. This is a type of incentive contract. In many instances, the award paid is judged subjectively. Therefore, procedures must be in place in advance for giving out the award, and a board must be established to help make the decision fairly.

The cost to administer the award fee program versus the potential benefits must be weighed in the decision to use this type of contract.

Example: Fixed Price Award Fee Contract
Contract = $1,100,000. For every month performance exceeds the planned level by more than 15 percent, an additional $5,000 is awarded to the seller, with a maximum award of $70,000.

Fixed Price Economic Price Adjustment (FPEPA) If there are uncertainties about future economic conditions (future prices) for contracts that exist for a multi-year period, a buyer might choose a fixed price contract with economic price adjustment. Future costs of supplies and equipment that the seller might be required to provide under contract might not be predictable. Think "economy" whenever you see this on the exam, and you should remember it. A similar type of contract is called fixed price with prospective price redetermination.

Example: Fixed Price Economic Price Adjustment Contract
Contract = $1,100,000, but a price increase will be allowed in year two based on the U.S. Consumer Price Index report for year one.
Or:
Contract = $1,100,000, but a price increase will be allowed in year two to account for increases in specific material costs.

Purchase Order A purchase order is the simplest type of fixed price contract. This type of contract is normally unilateral (signed by one party) instead of bilateral (signed by both parties; most other contract types are bilateral). It is usually used for simple commodity procurements. Purchase orders become contracts when they are "accepted" by performance (e.g., equipment is shipped by the seller—a unilateral PO). Though unilateral purchase orders are most common, some companies will require the seller's signature on a purchase before the buyer will consider the purchase order official. In that case, it is the signature that forms the "acceptance" needed to make a contract.

Example: Purchase Order
Contract = 30 linear meters of wood at $9 per meter.

Time and Material (T&M) or Unit Price PAGE 324

In this type of contract, the buyer pays on a per-hour or per-item basis. Time and material contracts are frequently used for service efforts in which the level of effort cannot be defined when the contract is awarded. It has elements of a fixed price contract (in the fixed price per hour) and a cost reimbursable contract (in the material costs and the fact that the total cost is unknown).

If you were going to have to pay someone on a contract basis for every hour they worked, no matter how productive they were and no matter what they were doing, would you want to do this for a long period of time? Remember, the seller's profit is built into the rate, so they have no incentive to get the work done quickly or efficiently. For this reason, a time and material contract is best used for work valued at small dollar amounts and lasting a short amount of time. To make sure the costs do not become higher than budgeted, the buyer may put a "Not to Exceed" clause in the contract and thus limit the total cost they are required to pay. With a time and material contract, the buyer has a medium amount of cost risk compared with cost reimbursable and fixed price contracts.

Example: Time and Material Contract
Contract = $100 per hour plus expenses or materials at cost. *Or:* Contract = $100 per hour plus materials at $5 per linear meter of wood.

Cost Reimbursable (CR) PAGE 323

A cost reimbursable contract is used when the exact scope of work is uncertain and, therefore, costs cannot be estimated accurately enough to effectively use a fixed price contract. This type of contract provides for the buyer to pay the seller allowable incurred costs to the extent prescribed in the contract.

A cost reimbursable contract requires the seller to have an accounting system that can track costs by project. With a cost reimbursable contract, the buyer has the most cost risk because the total costs are unknown. Research and development or information technology projects in which the scope is unknown are typical examples of cost reimbursable contracts.

The following are common forms of cost reimbursable contracts.

Cost Contract A cost contract is one in which the seller receives no fee (profit). It is appropriate for work performed by nonprofit organizations.

Example: Cost Contract
Contract = Cost. There is no profit.

Cost Plus Fee (CPF) or Cost Plus Percentage of Costs (CPPC) A CPF or CPPC contract requires the buyer to pay for all costs plus a percentage of costs as a fee. This type of cost reimbursable contract is not allowed for US federal acquisitions or procurements under federal acquisition regulations and is bad for buyers everywhere. Can you figure out why? Sellers are not motivated to control costs because they will earn a profit on every cost without limit.

Example: Cost Plus Fee or Cost Plus Percentage of Costs Contract
Contract = Cost plus 10 percent of costs as fee.

Cost Plus Fixed Fee (CPFF) A cost plus fixed fee contract provides for payment to the seller of actual costs plus a negotiated fee that is fixed before the work begins. The fee does not vary with actual costs, thus the seller does not have an incentive to increase or inflate costs. The fee may be adjusted as a result of changes to the procurement statement of work.

Example: Cost Plus Fixed Fee Contract
Contract = Cost plus a fee of $100,000.

Cost Plus Incentive Fee (CPIF) A cost plus incentive fee contract provides for the seller to be paid for actual costs plus a fee that will be adjusted based on whether the specific performance objectives stated in the contract are met. In this type of contract, an original estimate of the total cost is made (the target cost) and a fee for the work is determined (a target fee). The seller then gets a percentage of the savings if the actual costs are less than the target costs or shares the cost overrun with the buyer. The ratio is usually 80 percent to the buyer and 20 percent to the seller. See more on incentives later in this section.

Example: Cost Plus Incentive Fee Contract
Contract = $500,000 target cost plus $50,000 target fee. The buyer and seller share any cost savings or overruns at 80% to the buyer and 20% to the seller.

You will need to know how to calculate the total payment or profit on a CPIF contract for the exam. See the exercise at the end of the contract types discussion (page 438 of this book).

Cost Plus Award Fee (CPAF) In a cost plus award fee contract, the buyer pays all costs and a base fee plus an award amount (a bonus) based on performance. This is similar to the CPIF contract, except the incentive is a potential award, rather than a potential award or penalty. The award amount in a CPAF contract is determined in advance and apportioned out depending on performance. This is a type of incentive contract. In some instances, the award given out is judged subjectively. Therefore, procedures must be in place in advance for giving out the award, and a board is established to help make the decision fairly.

As with a FPAF contract, the cost to administer an award fee contract vs. the potential benefits must be weighed in the decision to use this type of contract.

Example: Cost Plus Award Fee Contract
Contract = Cost plus a base fee plus $5,000 for every month production exceeds 100,000 units. Maximum award available is $50,000.

Though the buyer initially proposes the contract type, the final contract type is subject to negotiation with the seller. The best contract type meets the needs of the particular procurement, results in reasonable seller risk, and provides the seller with the greatest incentive for efficient performance.

Expect the exam to ask questions like, "You do not have a finalized scope; which contract type is best?" or "You do not have a complete scope of work and have a fixed price contract. What problems can you expect to run into?" The exam tests whether you know what to do in different situations, not just if you know definitions.

Incentives

Sellers are usually focused on the profits to be made on a project. The buyer may be focused on total cost, performance, schedule, or a combination of these concerns. Incentives are used to bring the seller's objectives in line with the buyer's. The buyer will provide an additional fee if the seller meets some cost, performance, or schedule objectives. Incentives, therefore, are designed to motivate the seller's efforts toward things that might not have been emphasized otherwise and to discourage seller inefficiency and waste in the areas in which the incentives are designated. Think of an incentive as a bonus for the seller.

Can you see how incentives can change the focus of the project? If there is an incentive for cost savings, then the work is to complete the project AND to look for cost savings. If the incentive is for some increased level of performance (the system can handle more capacity than contracted for, for example), then the work is to complete the project AND to look for ways to increase performance. The seller gains profit from both activities.

When Are Payments Made?

Each contract, no matter what type is used, will state when payments are to be made to the seller. Payments may be made as work is completed, as costs are incurred, according to a payment schedule, or only after the successful completion of the contract. The project manager must know when payments will be made in order to plan for the time required to review and make these payments. The project manager must also ensure the funds will be available to make the payments as scheduled.

TRICKS OF THE TRADE®

Advantages and Disadvantages of Each Contract Type

A trick on the exam is to realize that, in the real world, buyers must select the appropriate type of contract for what they are buying. The following exercise will test whether you really understand the different types of contracts and will help you select the appropriate type of contract on the exam.

Exercise In the following table, write the advantages and disadvantages of each form of contract from the perspective of the BUYER.

Fixed Price Contract	
Advantages	Disadvantages

Time and Material Contract	
Advantages	Disadvantages

Cost Reimbursable Contract	
Advantages	**Disadvantages**

Answer There can be more answers than listed here. Did you identify and understand these?

Fixed Price Contract	
Advantages	**Disadvantages**
An FP contract is less work for the buyer to manage.	If the seller underprices the work, they may try to make up profits on change orders.
The seller has a strong incentive to control costs.	The seller may try to not complete some of the procurement statement of work if they begin to lose money.
Companies have experience with this type of contract.	This contract type requires more work for the buyer to write the procurement statement of work.
The buyer knows the total price before the work begins.	FP can be more expensive than CR if the procurement statement of work is incomplete and the seller needs to add to the price for the increased risk.

Time and Material Contract	
Advantages	**Disadvantages**
This type of contract is quick to create.	There is profit for the seller in every hour billed.
The contract duration is brief.	The seller has no incentive to control costs.
This is a good choice when you are hiring "bodies," or people to augment your staff.	This contract type is appropriate only for small projects.
	T&M contracts require a great deal of day-to-day oversight from the buyer.

Cost Reimbursable Contract	
Advantages	**Disadvantages**
This contract type allows for a simpler procurement statement of work.	This contract type requires auditing the seller's invoices.
It usually requires less work to define the scope for a CR contract than for a FP contract.	CR requires more work for the buyer to manage.
CR is generally a lower cost than FP because the seller does not have to add as much for risk.	The seller has only a moderate incentive to control costs.
	The total price is unknown.

Exercise Name the most appropriate contract type to use in the situation described. Your choices are FP, FPIF, FPAF, FPEPA, Purchase Order, T&M, CR, CPF or CPPC, CPFF, CPIF, or CPAF contracts.

	Situation	Type of Contract to Use
1	You need work to begin right away.	
2	You want to buy expertise in determining what needs to be done.	
3	You know exactly what needs to be done.	
4	You are buying a programmer's services to augment your staff.	
5	You need work done, but you don't have time to audit invoices on this work.	
6	You need to rebuild a bridge as soon as possible after a storm.	
7	The project requires a high level of expertise to complete and you want to have the best performance possible in the finished product.	
8	You need to hire a contractor to perform research and development.	
9	The scope of work is complete, but the economy is currently unpredictable.	
10	You are buying standard commodities.	

Answer The answers are below. Also try to think of other situations in which you would use each type of contract.

	Situation	Type of Contract to Use
1	You need work to begin right away.	T&M
2	You want to buy expertise in determining what needs to be done.	CR
3	You know exactly what needs to be done.	FP

	Situation	Type of Contract to Use
4	You are buying a programmer's services to augment your staff.	T&M
5	You need work done, but you don't have time to audit invoices on this work.	FP
6	You need to rebuild a bridge as soon as possible after a storm.	FPIF
7	The project requires a high level of expertise to complete and you want to have the best performance possible in the finished product.	CPIF or CPAF
8	You need to hire a contractor to perform research and development.	CR
9	The scope of work is complete, but the economy is currently unpredictable.	FPEPA
10	You are buying standard commodities.	Purchase order

Risk and Contract Type

The exam may ask questions that correlate risk with the different types of contracts. The following diagram shows the amount of risk the buyer and seller have with each contract type. Use the diagram to better understand the different contract types and to help answer questions such as:

> **Question** *Who has the risk in a cost reimbursable contract—the buyer or seller?*
> **Answer** *The buyer. If the costs increase, the buyer pays the added costs.*
>
> **Question** *Who has the cost risk in a fixed price contract—the buyer or seller?*
> **Answer** *The seller. If costs increase, the seller pays the costs and makes less profit.*

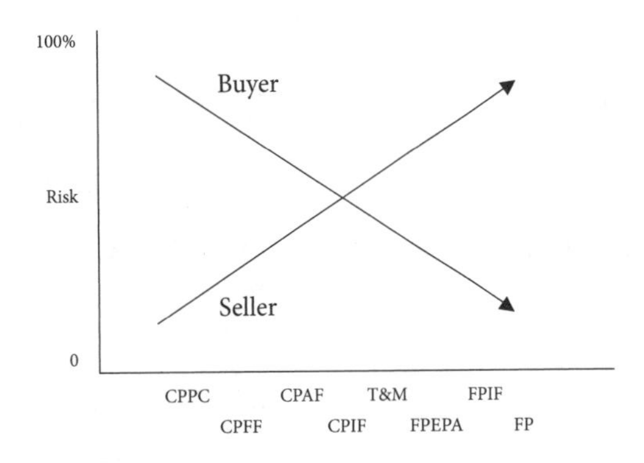

There are many sample questions within this chapter and at the end of the chapter. Take the time to answer all the questions in the chapter to increase and test your understanding of procurements.

Other Terms to Know

Remember, profit and cost are different. Profit is the amount of money the seller has left over after costs are paid. Be careful on the exam to read the questions carefully. It's also a matter of perspective. Are the questions referring to the buyer's cost or the seller's cost? The following list provides definitions of terms you should understand for the exam.

- **Price** This is the amount the seller charges the buyer.
- **Profit (fee)** This is planned into the price the seller provides the buyer. Sellers usually have an acceptable profit margin in mind. However, how much profit they actually receive is based on many factors, including the contract terms and the seller's ability to manage the project.

- **Cost** This is how much an item costs the seller to create, develop, or purchase. A buyer's costs can include a seller's costs and profits.
- **Target price**[4] This term is often used to compare the end result (final price) with what was expected (the target price). Target price is a measure of success. Watch for similar terms. Target cost plus target fee equals target price. (Remember, we are thinking about procurements from the buyer's point of view!)
- **Sharing ratio**[4] Incentives are usually expressed as a ratio, e.g., 90/10. This sharing ratio describes how the cost savings or cost overrun will be shared, the first number being the amount the buyer will keep and the second number being the amount the seller will keep (buyer/seller).
- **Ceiling price**[4] This is the highest price the buyer will pay. Keep in mind that answers to calculations on the exam can change when a ceiling price is mentioned.
- **Point of total assumption (PTA)**[5] This only relates to fixed price incentive fee contracts and refers to the amount above which the seller bears all the loss of a cost overrun. Costs that go above the PTA are assumed to be due to mismanagement. Sellers will sometimes monitor their actual costs against the PTA to make sure they are still receiving a profit for completing the project.

Formula: Point of Total Assumption

$$\text{PTA} = \frac{(\text{Ceiling price} - \text{Target price})}{\text{Buyer's share ratio}} + \text{Target cost}$$

Incentives Calculations

Now that you understand the concepts, it is time to work through some examples. You may see up to three questions on the exam requiring you to use these types of calculations.

As you do the following exercises, notice the terms "cost," "fee," and "price." These terms all have different meanings, as defined previously.

Exercise

Cost Plus Incentive Fee Calculation In this cost plus incentive fee contract, the cost is estimated at $210,000 and the fee at $25,000. The project is complete, and the buyer has agreed that the costs were, in fact, $200,000. Because the seller's costs came in lower than the estimated costs, the seller shares in the savings: 80 percent to the buyer and 20 percent to the seller. Calculate the final fee and final price.

Target cost	$210,000
Target fee	$25,000
Target price	$235,000
Sharing ratio	80/20
Actual cost	$200,000

Final Fee	
Final Price	

Answer Remember, you may have to calculate both the final fee and the final price for the exam.

Final Fee	\$210,000 – \$200,000 = \$10,000 \$10,000 × 20% = \$2,000 \$25,000 target fee + \$2,000 = \$27,000 fee
Final Price	\$200,000 + \$27,000 = \$227,000

Exercise

Fixed Price Incentive Fee Calculation Now try the following exercise from the seller's perspective. In this fixed price incentive fee contract, the target cost is estimated at \$150,000 and the target fee at \$30,000. The project is over, and the buyer has agreed that the costs were, in fact, \$210,000. Because the seller's costs came in higher than the estimated costs, the seller shares in the added cost: 60 percent to the buyer and 40 percent to the seller. Calculate the final fee, the point of total assumption, and the final price. Note the ceiling price.

Target cost	\$150,000
Target fee	\$30,000
Target price	\$180,000
Sharing ratio	60/40
Ceiling price	\$200,000
Actual cost	\$210,000

Final Fee	
Point of Total Assumption	
Final Price	

Answer In this case, the actual cost is higher than the target cost, so the seller receives less fee, or profit. Instead of receiving \$30,000 in fee, the seller receives only \$6,000. The actual cost plus fee comes to \$216,000, but this is higher than the ceiling price. The result is that the seller is paid \$200,000 when the costs were \$210,000 and the point of total assumption was \$183,333; therefore, the seller suffers the effects of the inability to control the project and loses money on it.

Final Fee	\$150,000 – \$210,000 = (\$60,000) overage (\$60,000) × 40% = (\$24,000) \$30,000 + (\$24,000) = \$6,000
Point of Total Assumption	[(\$200,000 – \$180,000)/60%] + \$150,000 (\$20,000/0.6) + \$150,000 \$33,333 + \$150,000 = \$183,333
Final Price	\$210,000 + \$6,000 = \$216,000 However, this amount is above the ceiling price of \$200,000. Therefore, the final price is \$200,000.

Exercise

Fixed Price Incentive Fee Calculation Try this one. For this exercise, you are again the seller in the procurement. In this fixed price incentive fee contract, the target cost is $9,000,000 and the target fee is $850,000. The project is done, and the buyer has agreed that the costs were, in fact, $8,000,000. Because the seller's costs came in lower than the estimated costs, the seller shares in the savings: 70 percent to the buyer and 30 percent to the seller. Calculate the final fee and final price.

Target cost	$9,000,000
Target fee	$850,000
Target price	$9,850,000
Sharing ratio	70/30
Ceiling price	$12,500,000
Actual cost	$8,000,000

Final Fee	
Final Price	

Answer In this case, the actual cost is lower than the target cost, so the seller receives more fee, or profit. Instead of receiving $850,000 in fee, the seller receives $300,000 more for a total of $1,150,000. The fee added to the cost totals $9,150,000. Since that is less than the ceiling price, the seller gets paid that amount. Therefore, the seller gains because of their ability to control the project.

Final Fee	$9,000,000 – $8,000,000 = $1,000,000 $1,000,000 × 30% = $300,000 Original fee of $850,000 + $300,000 = $1,150,000
Final Price	$8,000,000 + $1,150,000 fee = $9,150,000

Putting It All Together

After going through all these pages, you should start to feel like you understand the different types of contracts (or you have a big headache). Try the next exercise to help you put it all together.

You can also use the questions on *PM FASTrack®* to test your knowledge of contract types.

WAIT! We've heard people say they love the exercises in this book, but they always jump straight to the answers. Don't do that to yourself. The exercises are designed to increase your knowledge as you do them; you can learn through mistakes. Skipping to the answers means you will get 40 percent less value out of this book.

Exercise Answer the questions in the following table for each contract type.

	Question	Cost Reimbursable	Time and Material	Fixed Price
1	Generally, what is being bought? (Product or service)			
2	How might the costs to the buyer be stated in the contract?			
3	How might the profit be stated in the contract?			
4	What is the cost risk to the buyer? (High, medium, low, none)			
5	How important is a detailed procurement statement of work? (High, medium, low, none)			
6	What industry uses this type the most for its contracts?			
7	How much negotiation is usually required to sign the contract after receipt of the seller's price? (High, medium, low, none)			
8	What level of effort and expertise will the buyer need to devote to managing the seller? (High, medium, low, none)			
9	How are costs billed to the buyer?			

	Question	Cost Reimbursable	Time and Material	Fixed Price
10	How much auditing of the seller's costs will the buyer need to do? (High, medium, low, none)			

Answer You cannot expect to have gotten all the answers to these questions right, because some of the questions were difficult to understand. Wait until you see some of the convoluted questions on the actual exam!

Let's try to make sense of this exercise. Review the answers in the following table.

	Question	Cost Reimbursable	Time and Material	Fixed Price
1	Generally, what is being bought? (Product or service)	Service (some products may be included)	Service	Products
2	How might the costs to the buyer be stated in the contract?	Costs are variable, but the fee is fixed	Hourly rate or price per unit	As a set currency amount (e.g., $1 million)
3	How might the profit be stated in the contract?	Listed separately and known to the buyer	Included in the hourly rate and may be unknown to the buyer	Included in the price and unknown to the buyer
4	What is the cost risk to the buyer? (High, medium, low, none)	High; increases in costs are reimbursed by the buyer	Medium; though the costs are not fixed, this contract type is used for small purchases	Low; increases in costs are borne by the seller
5	How important is a detailed procurement statement of work? (High, medium, low, none)	Low; the procurement statement of work only needs to describe the performance or requirements, since the seller provides the expertise of how to do the work. The buyer pays all costs, so there is less need to finalize the scope.	Low; this type traditionally has very little scope and may only describe skill sets required.	High; the procurement statement of work must be complete so the seller knows exactly what work needs to be done in order to come up with an accurate price to do the work.

	Question	Cost Reimbursable	Time and Material	Fixed Price
6	What industry uses this type the most for its contracts?	IT, research and development; when the work has never been done before, such as it often is in these industries, the seller cannot fix a price. Therefore, this is the best form to use.	When you are hiring people for an hourly rate, you are usually hiring services such as legal, plumbing, programming, etc.	Complete scope of work is most common in the construction industry; in fact, they do not often even have cost records by project, making it impossible for them to have cost reimbursable contracts.
7	How much negotiation is usually required to sign the contract after receipt of the seller's price? (High, medium, low, none)	High; all estimated costs are looked at to calculate the fee to be fixed	Low or none	None
8	What level of effort and expertise will the buyer need to devote to managing the seller? (High, medium, low, none)	High	Medium	Low
9	How are costs billed to the buyer?	Actual costs as incurred, profit at project completion or apportioned, as allowed in the contract	Hourly or per-unit rate (which includes all costs and profit)	Fixed price (which includes profit) according to a payment schedule as work is completed and as allowed in the contract
10	How much auditing of the seller's costs will the buyer need to do? (High, medium, low, none)	High; all costs must be audited, and there will be a large number of costs	None; there may be an audit of work hours completed against those billed, but that will take little effort	Low; since the overall contract costs are fixed, auditing usually focuses on making sure work is completed, not looking at detailed costs and receipts

Procurement Documents (Bid Documents) Once the contract type is selected and the procurement statement of work has been created, the buyer can put together the procurement document, which describes the buyer's needs to sellers. The following are some of the different types of procurement documents:[6]

- **Request for Proposal (RFP, sometimes called Request for Tender)** RFPs request a detailed proposal on how the work will be accomplished, who will do it, résumés, company experience, price, etc.
- **Invitation for Bid (IFB, or Request for Bid, RFB)** IFBs usually just request a total price to do all the work.
- **Request for Quotation (RFQ)** RFQs request a price quote per item, hour, meter, or other unit of measure.

NOTE: The *PMBOK® Guide* lists **Request for Information (RFI)** as one of the types of procurement documents, but in reality, it does not belong in this category. A procurement document is an attempt to procure something, while an RFI is simply looking for information. An RFI might be used before procurement documents are created. The information received could help identify which companies are qualified to handle the procurement. Buyers can also use RFIs to collect information on what work is possible for later inclusion in RFPs or IFBs. Remember that the purpose of an RFI is to get information, whereas the purpose of a procurement document (e.g., RFP, IFB, and RFQ) is to buy something.

To provide the seller with as clear a picture as possible of what needs to be done to win the work and what the work involves, procurement documents may include the following:

- Information for sellers
  - Background information about why the buyer wants the work done
  - Procedures for trying to win the work (if there will be a bidder conference, when the responses are due, how the winner will be selected, etc.)
  - Guidelines for preparing the response (maximum length, topics to address in the response, etc.)
  - The exact format the response should be in (forms to fill out, whether e-mail submissions are allowed, etc.)
  - Source selection criteria—the criteria the buyer will use to evaluate responses from the sellers (number of years in business, quality of the response, price, etc.)
  - Pricing forms (forms to adequately describe the price to the buyer)
- Procurement statement of work
- Proposed terms and conditions of the contract (legal and business)

Note that the proposed contract is included in the procurement documents. Do you know why? Because the terms and conditions of the contract are also work that needs to be done and have costs associated with them (warranties, ownership, etc.). The seller must be aware of all the work that needs to be completed to adequately understand and price the project.

Well-designed procurement documents can have the following effects on the project:

- Easier comparison of sellers' responses
- More complete responses
- More accurate pricing
- Decreased number of changes to the project

Once they have reviewed the documents, sellers may make suggestions for changes to the procurement documents, including the procurement statement of work and the project management requirements contained in the documents, before the contract is signed. When approved, these changes are issued by the buyer as addenda to the procurement documents.

Try the next exercise to help you better understand these concepts.

Exercise Test yourself! In the space provided below, write the contract type (FP, CR, T&M) and the type of procurement statement of work (Performance, Functional, or Design) that applies next to the procurement document to be used.

Procurement Document	Contract Type	Procurement Statement of Work
Request for Proposal (RFP)		
Invitation for Bid (IFB)		
Request for Quotation (RFQ)		

Answer This is a general approach to promote understanding. In the world of contracts, an infinite variety of procurement documents and contract types exist. The exam keeps things simple by just focusing on a few types.

Procurement Document	Contract Type	Procurement Statement of Work
Request for Proposal (RFP)	CR	Performance or Functional
Invitation for Bid (IFB)	FP	Design
Request for Quotation (RFQ)	T&M	Any

Source Selection Criteria PAGE 327 Source selection criteria are included in the procurement documents to give the seller an understanding of the buyer's needs and to help the seller decide whether to bid or make a proposal on the work. When the buyer receives the sellers' responses during the Conduct Procurements process, source selection criteria become the basis for the buyer to use in evaluating the bids or proposals.

If the buyer is purchasing a commodity such as linear meters of wood, the source selection criteria may just be the lowest price. If the buyer is procuring construction services, the source selection criteria may be price plus experience. If the buyer is purchasing services only, the source selection criteria will be more extensive. In the latter case, such source selection criteria may include:

- Number of years in business
- Financial stability
- Understanding of need
- Price or life cycle cost (see the definition of life cycle cost in the Cost Management chapter)
- Technical ability
- Quality of past performance
- Ability to complete the work on time
- Project management ability (Shouldn't you require your sellers or vendors to use the project management techniques you have learned? How about asking for a WBS, network diagram, and risk analysis?)

The following are some additional terms a project manager should be familiar with when working with procurements.

Nondisclosure Agreement For many procurements, there is a great need for confidentiality. Perhaps the buyer does not want the general public or their competitors to know they are pursuing the procurement. Perhaps the seller will need to send the buyer information they want to keep confidential.

In these and many other cases, there may be a confidentiality or nondisclosure agreement signed before procurement information is released or at any other time when it may be appropriate to protect those interests. This is an agreement between the buyer and prospective sellers identifying the information or documents they will hold confidential and control, and who in the organization will gain access to the confidential information. With a nondisclosure agreement in place, the buyer can talk more openly about their needs without fear that the public or one of the buyer's competitors will gain access to the information. Like any agreement, a nondisclosure agreement has consequences if violated.

Teaming Agreement (could be called a Joint Venture) Often two sellers believe that their chance of winning work from a buyer will be enhanced if they join forces for one procurement. In this case, they will sign a teaming agreement with each other to address the legal and business aspects of the arrangement. The agreement must clearly define what role each seller will take. The buyer's project manager and procurement manager might want to review the teaming agreement to see if there are any legal ramifications or risks to the project.

Watch out for this term on the exam, as the *PMBOK® Guide's* definition of a teaming agreement is closer to what should really be called a master services agreement or a retainer contract. In this type of agreement, there is a contract in place between the buyer and seller for a type of service as needed (such as to provide information technology services). When specific work is needed, the buyer and seller work to create the scope of work and then initiate a project under the existing terms of the master services agreement.

Standard Contract The contract terms and conditions are most commonly created by the buyer, who may have even put their terms and conditions into a standard format that is used over and over for similar procurements. These types of standard contracts need no further legal review if used as they are. If they are signed without changes, they are legally sufficient. You should understand standard contracts, but also realize the project manager's role in special provisions (described next).

Special Provisions (Special Conditions) The project manager must be able to read and understand standard terms and conditions and to determine what needs to be added, changed, or removed from the standard provisions. By doing so, the project manager can make sure the resulting contract addresses the particular needs of the project. The project manager (again, remember that you are the buyer's project manager for the exam, unless it says otherwise) meets with the procurement manager to discuss the needs of the project and to determine the final contract terms and conditions. Additions, changes, or deletions are sometimes called special provisions and can be a result of:

- Risk analysis
- The requirements of the project
- The type of project
- Administrative, legal, or business requirements

Terms and Conditions Let's start out with a story. A project manager needed his team members trained to use some equipment. He contacted a seller to do the work and then proceeded to have his procurement department send the seller a contract. Meanwhile, he arranged for the team members to fly in from around the world for the training. In the contract the project manager's procurement department sent, there were terms and conditions that said the project manager's company would have the rights to create derivative works and make copies of any handouts from class. Those handouts were proprietary and already copyrighted. The seller could not and would not sign such a contract.

The class had to be cancelled at the last minute, after many people were already on planes to attend the training. Whose fault was this? It was the project manager's fault. He should have made sure the procurement department understood what they were buying and also should have taken a look at the contract before it was sent to make sure any inappropriate language was removed. Creating a contract requires the involvement of both the project manager and the procurement manager. Do you do this on your real-world projects?

Another reason it is important to understand contract language is to be able to enforce it. Remember, if it is in the contract, it must be done unless both sides agree and a change is issued!

Here's another story. One day, the head of a company called the project manager to ask where the seller's reports were. The project manager did not know what reports the company head was asking about; she had not confirmed they were received from the seller. It turned out that those reports seemed minor to the project manager when she finally read the contract, but they had major legal significance to the company. Not receiving them cost the buyer's company an extra $50,000. The lesson? Know what is in your contracts and why.

In another situation (hopefully you're not tired of stories yet), a seller didn't submit testing information required in the contract to the buyer, and the buyer's project manager did not notice it was not received. After four weeks, the company head asked for the testing information and found out it had not been received. The project manager then asked the seller to send the information. The seller argued, "You did not receive the testing reports for four weeks, and you did not say anything. You have therefore waived your rights to ever get them." They refused to give the reports without a change to the contract and additional payment. This issue went to a court of law to resolve. The court found in favor of the seller. The lesson? Read the contract, and enforce all that is there.

Terms and conditions (either standard or special) in a contract differ based on what you are buying. If you are buying work that includes equipment, you will need terms that describe when ownership of the equipment will be transferred to the buyer and terms that require insurance for damages in transit. If you are buying professional services, you will need terms requiring professional liability insurance or errors and omissions insurance to cover errors. The needed terms are usually determined by the procurement manager. However, the project manager should be generally familiar with most common terms.

The following are some general categories of the terms and conditions that can make up standard and special provisions. You do not need to know specific examples (e.g., the standard content of a confidentiality clause). Instead, you should be generally familiar with what all of these concepts mean. Don't get overwhelmed! You do not need to memorize these terms; just be familiar with the impact they have on you as the project manager. The exam will often simply use these terms in sentences such as, "There was a force majeure," and you have to know what it means. Conversely, the exam could use the definition of "There was a huge flood that caused the seller to not be able to perform," and you will have to know that this is a force majeure. You need to understand the situation and be able to determine what the appropriate action is.

- **Acceptance** How will you specifically know if the work is acceptable?
- **Agent** Who is an authorized representative of each party?
- **Arbitration** This method to resolve disputes uses private third parties to render a decision on the dispute. Arbitration is paid for by the parties and is used because it is usually faster and cheaper than the courts.
- **Assignment** Assignment refers to the circumstances under which one party can assign its rights or obligations under the contract to another.
- **Authority** Who has the power to do what?
- **Bonds** These are the payment or performance bonds, if any, that must be purchased. For example, a payment bond would protect the buyer from claims of nonpayment by the seller.

- **Breach/Default** This occurs when any obligation of the contract is not met. Watch out—a breach on the seller's part cannot be fixed by a breach on the buyer's part (e.g., not completing an item in the procurement statement of work [seller's breach] cannot be handled by the buyer stopping ALL payments [buyer's breach]).
  A breach is an extremely serious event. The exam may present situations in which seemingly little things in the contract are not done. The response to a breach must always be to issue a letter formally notifying the other party of the breach. The project manager must understand the legal implications of their actions. If he or she does not watch out for and send an official notice of breach, the project manager's company could lose its right to claim breach later.
- **Changes** How will changes be made? What forms will be used? What are the timeframes for notice and turnaround?
- **Confidentiality** What information must not be made known or given to third parties?
- **Dispute resolution** How will any disputes regarding the contract be settled? Some options for dispute resolution are to use the courts or an arbitrator.
- **Force majeure** This is a situation that can be considered an act of God, such as a fire or freak electrical storm, and is an allowable excuse for either party not meeting contract requirements. If a force majeure occurs, it is considered to be neither party's fault. It is usually resolved by the seller receiving an extension of time on the project. (See also Risk of loss.) Who pays for the cost of the items destroyed in a fire or other force majeure? Usually the risk of loss is borne by the seller and is hopefully covered by insurance.
- **Incentives** What benefits can the seller receive for aligning with the buyer's objectives of time, cost, quality, risk, and performance?
- **Indemnification (liability)** Who is liable for personal injury, damage, or accidents?
- **Independent contractor** This term means the seller is not an employee of the buyer.
- **Inspection** Does anyone have a right to inspect the work during execution of the project? Under what circumstances?
- **Intellectual property** Who owns the intellectual property (patents, trademarks, copyrights, processes, source code, books, etc.) used in connection with or developed as part of the contract? This may include warranties of the right to use certain intellectual property in performance of the contract.
- **Invoicing** When will invoices be sent? What supporting documents are required? To whom are they sent?
- **Liquidated damages** These are estimated damages for specific defaults, described in advance.
- **Management requirements** Examples of management requirements are attendance at meetings, approval of staff assigned to the project, etc.
- **Material breach** This breach is so large that it may not be possible to complete the work under the contract.
- **Notice** To whom should certain correspondence be sent?
- **Ownership** Who will own the tangible items (materials, buildings, equipment, etc.) used in connection with or developed as part of the contract?
- **Payments** When will payments be made? What are the late payment fees? What are reasons for nonpayment? Watch out for payment management questions. For example, as a response to inaccurate invoices, the buyer cannot stop ALL payments; this would be a breach. They can, however, stop payments on disputed amounts.
- **Procurement statement of work** If it is not a separate document, this will be included as part of the contract.
- **Reporting** What reports are required? At what frequency? From and to whom?
- **Retainage** This is an amount of money, usually 5 percent or 10 percent, withheld from each payment. This money is paid when all the final work is complete. It helps ensure completion.
- **Risk of loss** This allocates the risk between the parties to a contract in the event goods or services are lost or destroyed during the performance of a contract.

- **Site access** This describes any requirements for access to the site where the work will be performed.
- **Termination** Termination is stopping the work before it is completed.
- **Time is of the essence** This phrase means delivery dates are strictly binding. The seller is on notice that time is very important and that any delay is a material breach.
- **Waivers** Waivers are statements saying that rights under the contract may not be waived or modified other than by express agreement of the parties. A project manager must realize that he or she can intentionally or unintentionally give up a right in the contract through conduct, inadvertent failure to enforce, or lack of oversight. Therefore, a project manager must understand all aspects of the contract to enforce it, even if a procurement manager is available to administer the contract.
- **Warranties** These are promises of quality for the goods or services delivered under the contract, usually restricted to a certain time period.
- **Work for hire** This means the work provided under the contract will be owned by the buyer.

Letter of Intent Negotiating a contract and getting final signatures can take time. In some instances, the seller may need to start hiring people or ordering equipment and materials before the contract is signed in order to meet the contract requirements. If the contract is not signed in time, the seller may ask the buyer to provide a letter of intent. A letter of intent is NOT a contract, but simply a letter, without legal binding, that says the buyer intends to hire the seller. It is intended to give the seller confidence that the contract will be signed soon and to make them comfortable with taking the risk of ordering the equipment or hiring the staff that will eventually be needed.

Privity Sometimes the exam throws in terms that only procurement experts use. This is one of them. Privity simply means a contractual relationship. The following explains privity and shows you how questions on this topic may be asked.

> **Question** *Company A hires company B to do some work for them. Company B subcontracts to company C. The project manager for company A is at the job site and tells company C to stop work. Generally, does company C have to listen?*
>
> **Answer** *No. Companies C and A have no contractual relationship. A needs to talk to B, who needs to talk to C.*

You may not be familiar with the term, but you might be familiar with the situation just described. Can you see how this would be an important issue for a project manager to understand? Any directive the project manager from company A may give to company C can cause huge liability for company A. For example, company A may have to pay delay claims to company B plus the costs of delay to company C if company C stopped work at company A's direction.

Noncompetitive Forms of Procurement Most of this chapter talks about competitive forms of procurement in which there is more than one seller interested in and capable of doing the work. Competition can result in decreased price and the selection of a better seller for the buyer. But what if there is only one seller who can do the work, or you want to work with a company you have worked with before without a competitive procurement? Do you have to go through the whole procurement process? No. There is no reason you must go through the whole procurement process unless the procurement is for a government and there are laws requiring it or if the performing organization has rules regarding a bidding process for all procurements. Generally, private companies can hire anyone they want to, using any methods they choose. Regardless of whether the procurement is competitive, however, you must still have a procurement statement of work.

When would you award work to a company without competition?

- The project is under extreme schedule pressure.
- A seller has unique qualifications.
- There is only one seller who can provide the goods or service.
- A seller holds a patent for the item you need.
- Other mechanisms exist to ensure the seller's prices are reasonable.

If you do not use a competitive process, you are entering into one of the following types of noncompetitive procurements:

- **Single Source** In this type of procurement, you contract directly with your preferred seller without going through the procurement process. This might be a company you have worked with before and, for various reasons, you do not want to look for another.
- **Sole Source** In this type of procurement, there is only one seller. This might be a company that owns a patent.

If you are using one of these noncompetitive forms, you may save time compared with competitive forms by not having to go through the procurement process before bids or proposals are received, but you will still have to spend time in negotiations after the proposal or bid is received to finalize the contract.

TRICKS OF THE TRADE® The exam will frequently present situations and ask you questions about those situations. In procurement, tricky questions can address concepts you may not have dealt with before, such as describing the work that would need to be done to negotiate a contract when there is no competition. The following exercise will help.

Exercise Test yourself! What types of issues might occur in a noncompetitive procurement that would not be as significant in a competitive environment?

For Single Source—There Is a Preferred Seller

For Sole Source—There Is Only One Seller

Answer

For Single Source—There Is a Preferred Seller

- **Scope** More work will be needed to document all the items received without cost in the past to make sure you get them now. Only what is in the contract will be received.
- **Scope** There could be a tendency for the buyer's organization to say, "The seller knows us and we know them; we do not have to spend so much time determining our requirements and completing a procurement statement of work. They know what we want."
- **Quality** The seller may never be asked to prove they have the experience, cash flow, and manpower to complete the new work.
- **Cost** Time will need to be spent to compare previous cost to the new cost to check if it is reasonable.
- **Schedule** Now that the seller knows they have you as a longer-term customer, they may not be as responsive to your needs.
- **Customer satisfaction** Now that the seller knows they have you as a longer-term customer, they may not be as responsive to your needs.
- **Risk** The risk can be weighted more toward the buyer unless the previous issues are investigated and addressed.

For Sole Source—There Is Only One Seller

- **Risk** What if the seller owns a patent and goes out of business?
- **Risk** If the seller owns a patent and goes bankrupt, who owns the patent?
- **Quality** You may have to take what you get rather than request a certain quality level.
- **Cost** Multiple-year agreements may be required for the purchase of items to prevent a price increase in the future.
- **Schedule** The seller has little incentive to agree to a schedule.
- **Scope** You may have to change the work specified in the project to "take what you can get," rather than "ask for what you want."
- **Customer satisfaction** The seller has little incentive to be concerned with the buyer's needs and desires.
- **Risk** The overall risk can be weighted more toward the buyer unless the previous issues are investigated and resolved.

Make sure you read questions on the exam carefully. They might ask what to watch out for or what needs to be negotiated in noncompetitive procurements. They may simply ask about the procurement process. Do you understand how your efforts during the procurement process are different when there are not multiple companies to go to for the goods or service?

Conduct Procurements PAGE 328

Process: Conduct Procurements
Process Group: Executing
Knowledge Area: Procurement Management

This process involves getting the procurement documents that were created in the Plan Procurements process to the sellers, answering the sellers' questions, having them prepare responses, and reviewing the responses to select a seller.

Before you can send procurement documents to prospective sellers, you of course need to know who those sellers are. A buyer may use techniques such as advertising or Internet searches to find possible sellers, or send the procurement documents to a select list of prequalified sellers.

Advertising PAGE 332 To attract sellers, an advertisement may be placed in newspapers, in magazines, on the Internet, or in other types of media. NOTE: The US government is required to advertise most of its procurements.

Qualified Seller List (Prequalified Seller List) PAGE 330 The process of finding prospective sellers can take months. Another option, especially if a buyer purchases the same type of service often, is to find, investigate, and check the credentials of prospective sellers in advance. This will speed up the purchase and help make sure the sellers' qualifications are well researched before they are awarded procurements. This information may be part of organizational process assets, or the project team can develop it. If such a list is in place, the procurement documents for specific projects are then sent only to the prequalified sellers.

Bidder Conferences (Contractor Conferences, Vendor Conferences, Pre-Bid Conferences)[7] PAGE 331 Once the prospective sellers have been identified and have received the procurement documents, the buyer controls who can talk to the sellers and what can be said. This control allows the buyer to maintain the integrity of the procurement process and to make sure all sellers are bidding or proposing on the same work.

To make sure all the sellers' questions are answered, the buyer may invite the sellers to attend a meeting in which they can tour the buyer's facilities (if relevant to the project) and ask questions about the procurement. The questions and answers are documented and sent to all prospective bidders to make sure they all have the same information. The questions and answers asked during the bidder conference are also added to the procurement documents as addenda.

Getting answers to questions can be important, because many procurement documents will include a provision saying that by submitting the bid or proposal, the seller warrants that the bid covers all the work. The bidder conference is also an opportunity for the buyer to discover anything missing in the procurement documents.

A bidder conference can be key to making sure the pricing in the seller's response matches the work that needs to be done and is, therefore, the lowest price. Bidder conferences benefit both the buyer and seller. Many project managers do not attend these meetings or realize their importance. The exam often asks what things the project manager must watch out for in a bidder conference. The answers include:

- Collusion
- Sellers not asking questions in front of the competition
- Making sure all questions and answers are put in writing and issued to all potential sellers by the buyer as addenda to the procurement documents; this ensures that all sellers are responding to the same procurement statement of work

Seller Proposal (or Price Quote or Bid) This is a seller's response to the procurement documents. A proposal is usually the response to a request for proposal (RFP), a price quote is usually the response to a request for quote (RFQ), and a bid is usually the response to an invitation for bid (IFB). The proposal (or price quote or bid) represents an official offer from the seller.

Keep in mind that sellers may have many RFPs or IFBs sent to them. They need time to review them and determine which they are interested in responding to. To ensure the best sellers will be interested, the procurement documents should be as complete and straightforward as possible.

Once the seller decides to respond, they need to form a team, evaluate the buyer's needs, attend the bidder conference, and create a response. This can sometimes take a month or more. The buyer's project manager should allow for this time and the time for the rest of the procurement process in the project schedule.

Proposal Review After receiving the proposals, the buyer (represented by an evaluation committee) uses the source selection criteria identified in the Plan Procurements process to assess the potential sellers' ability and willingness to provide the requested products or services. The criteria are measurable and therefore provide a basis to quantitatively evaluate proposals and minimize the influence of personal prejudices. To select a seller:

- The buyer may simply select a seller and ask them to sign a standard contract.
- The buyer may ask a seller to make a presentation and then, if all goes well, move on to negotiations.
- The buyer may narrow down ("short-list") the list of sellers to a few.
- The buyer may ask the short-listed sellers to make presentations, and then ask the selected seller(s) to go on to negotiations.
- The buyer can negotiate with more than one seller.
- The buyer can use some combination of presentations and negotiations.

The choice of methods depends on the importance of the procurement, the number of interested sellers, and the type of work to be performed.

The sellers' proposals are usually reviewed, compared, or selected by the evaluation committee using one or a combination of the formal, structured processes discussed next.

Weighting System[8] This allows the buyer's evaluation committee to select a seller by weighting the source selection criteria according to the evaluation criteria. The buyer can then compare sellers to choose the one that best meets the criteria. There are no calculations on the exam regarding weighting systems. The following example is shown for information purposes to help you understand the concept better.

Seller A			
	A	B	C
Criteria	Weight	Rating for this category on a 1 to 100 scale	Category score (column A times B)
Number of years in business	5 percent	50	2.5
Understanding of need	25 percent	80	20
Price or life cycle cost (see definition in the Cost Management chapter)	10 percent	90	9
Technical ability	25 percent	40	10
Ability to complete the work on time	20 percent	30	6
Project management ability	15 percent	30	4.5
Total score for this seller			52

Independent Estimates The buyer may compare the seller's proposed cost with an estimate created in-house or with outside assistance. This allows the buyer to discover significant differences between what the buyer and seller intend in the procurement statement of work. The buyer must have their own estimates to check reasonableness and cannot rely solely on the seller's cost estimates.

Screening System A screening system eliminates sellers who do not meet the minimum requirements of the source selection criteria.

Past Performance History The buyer may consider their past history with the prospective sellers in determining which seller to award the procurement to.

Presentations In many cases, some of the sellers will be asked to make presentations of their proposals to the buyer so the buyer can select the most appropriate seller. This is often a formal meeting of the buyer's and seller's teams. It provides the seller with an opportunity to present their proposal, team, and approach to completing the work. The buyer has an opportunity to see the team they may hire and to ask questions to assess the team's competency, knowledge, and ability. Presentations are used most often for procurements that have cost reimbursable contracts, but they can be used in other situations (e.g., when there is a lot to assess, and when the way the seller is going to do the work is of prime importance).

Negotiations PAGE 332 Don't get worried about this topic. You do not have to be an expert negotiator to pass the exam. You do need to know some things about negotiations, however, because the exam assumes the project manager is involved, although not necessarily leading the negotiations. The procurement manager generally leads the negotiations.

Remember that procurement may or may not involve negotiations. For example, negotiations are not usually needed in a fixed price contract because the scope is complete and the lowest bidder is selected based on price. If negotiations are needed, they cover only parts of the proposed contract.

If a cost reimbursable or time and material contract is used, there will likely be negotiations to finalize the contract price and other issues. After the contract is signed, however, there will be negotiations in all contract types whenever there are proposed changes to any part of the contract. A key thing to remember is that project managers are involved in contract negotiations. Yes, this is a basic requirement. Just as the buyer's project manager must be involved before the procurement statement of work is finalized with the seller, the buyer's and seller's project managers must be involved in negotiations, because they are responsible for facilitating project management and technical issues on the project. The project manager must be involved in any issues that affect the key objectives of the project or how the project will be managed. Without the project manager's involvement in negotiations, it is common for a contract to be signed that the project manager later discovers cannot be completed.

The exam typically has only one or two questions about contract negotiations, and one of these questions usually deals with the reason the project manager must be involved.

Objectives of Negotiations

It is important for everyone involved in negotiations to understand that the objectives of the negotiations are to:

- Obtain a fair and reasonable price.
- Develop a good relationship with the seller.

The second item surprises most people, because they think of negotiations as win-lose. In a win-win situation, the buyer gets the work completed and the seller makes a reasonable profit. What is wrong with that? If negotiations turn from a win-win situation (preferable) to a win-lose situation, the seller will be less concerned with completing the work than with recovering what was lost in the negotiations. If negotiations are win-lose (in favor of the buyer), the buyer's project manager will have to spend time making sure the seller does not add extra costs, propose unnecessary work, or initiate other activities to "win" back what the seller lost during the negotiations. Many projects go bad because of how negotiations were handled, not because of project problems themselves.

Negotiation Tactics

This topic is often included on the exam, though it is not covered in the *PMBOK® Guide*. You should be familiar with the following types of negotiation tactics. Do not memorize them. Simply be able to pick the negotiation tactic being used in a situation.

- **Attacks** "If your organization cannot manage the details of its own operations, perhaps it should get out of the business!"
- **Personal insults** "If you do not understand what you are doing, perhaps you should find another job!"
- **Good guy/bad guy** One person is helpful to the other side, while another is difficult to deal with.
- **Deadline** "We have a flight leaving at 5 p.m. today and must finish negotiations before that time."
- **Lying** Lying may be obvious or hidden.
- **Limited authority** "I can't agree to shorten the schedule by six months. I have only been authorized to offer three months." Limited authority statements may or may not be true.
- **Missing man** "Only my boss can agree to that request, and he isn't here. Why don't we agree to only do ____? I can agree to that."
- **Fair and reasonable** "Let's be fair and reasonable. Accept this offer as it stands."
- **Delay** "Let's revisit this issue the next time we get together." This may also take the form of never actually getting down to negotiating until the last day of a planned visit.
- **Extreme demands** "We planned to give you a computer manufactured in 1988 to meet the requirement to deliver 'a computer' in the contract."
- **Withdrawal** This can either be an emotional withdrawal or a physical withdrawal and can show a lessening of interest.
- **Fait accompli** This is a done deal. "These government terms and conditions must be in all our contracts."

Main Items to Negotiate

The main items to address while negotiating a contract can be vastly different, depending on what is being purchased. To achieve a signed contract, the following are usually negotiated in order. See if the order makes sense to you.

- Scope
- Schedule
- Price

There are other things that need to be negotiated, however. These include:

- Responsibilities
- Authority
- Applicable law—If you are working with a seller from a different state, country, or region, you need to agree upon whose law will apply to the contract.
- Project management process to be used
- Payment schedule

Many people new to procurement management do not realize that price may not be the primary selection criteria or the major concern while negotiating. Often price is not a factor at all. Schedule may be more important, and a buyer might sacrifice cost to gain speed. Perhaps the procurement is to solve a problem rather than to complete specific work activities. In that case, the negotiations might involve detailed discussions of the feasibility of the proposed solution.

When negotiations are complete, the procurement contract is awarded to the selected seller.

What Is a Contract? When you think of the word "contract," what comes to mind? If you are like many others, you will think of all the legal words such as indemnification, intellectual property, and other legal fine print. People often think of only the preprinted or standard contracts (boilerplate contracts) supplied to them from the contracting or legal departments. They are only partially correct.

The word "contract" actually refers to the entire agreement between both parties. Therefore, it includes boilerplate language (with the terms and conditions previously described), but it also includes business terms regarding payments, reporting requirements, marketing literature, the proposal, and the procurement statement of work—all the requirements of the project.

What is the purpose of a contract?

- To define roles and responsibilities
- To make things legally binding
- To mitigate or allocate risk

Many project managers and business professionals think that the only relevant part of a contract is the procurement statement of work, because they are most familiar with that aspect of the contract. However, the procurement statement of work does not include all the requirements. In fact, some of the boilerplate language can be more important than the procurement statement of work. For example, think of a project to develop new software. Who owns the resulting program? Who owns the resulting program if it contains modules or pieces of programs previously used and planned for future reuse? How does the buyer protect their rights and ensure all source code is delivered? The ownership clause in a contract for such services might be more important than the procurement statement of work itself.

A contract is a legally binding document. Therefore, all terms and conditions in the contract must be met. Neither the buyer nor the seller can choose to not conform or to not do something required in the contract. Changes to the contract are made formally in writing.

What Do You Need to Have a Legal Contract?

- **An offer**
- **Acceptance**
- **Consideration** (Something of value, not necessarily money)
- **Legal capacity** (Separate legal parties, competent parties)
- **Legal purpose** (You cannot have a contract for the sale of illegal goods or services)

A contract, offer, or acceptance may be verbal or written, though written is preferred.

Try out this story. You need plumbing work done on your home. You contact a plumber who sends you a price with a notice that says, "If you want me to do the work on your home, send me a copy of the design drawings." Three weeks later, that plumber shows up at your home to start work. You are surprised, as you signed a contract with another plumber. The plumber says you also have a contract with him because you sent the drawings. Is the plumber right? Yes; acceptance can be an action, or it can be verbal. You have a difficult situation on your hands, and you will likely have to pay this plumber something. The trick is to avoid these situations by understanding contracts.

Administer Procurements PAGE 335

Process: Administer Procurements
Process Group: Monitoring & Controlling
Knowledge Area: Procurement Management

The Administer Procurements process involves managing the relationship between the buyer and seller and assuring that both parties perform as required by the contract. The exam tends to ask situational questions focusing on what happens after the contract is signed, so the Administer Procurements process is an important area on the exam.

While the work is underway, the buyer's needs may change and, as a result, the buyer may issue a change order to the contract. The impacts of contract changes are then negotiated by the two parties. If you do not have experience working with contracts, you should be aware of the concept of constructive changes. These changes occur when the buyer, through actions or inactions, gets in the seller's way of performing the work according to the contract. This can include over-inspection, failing to cooperate, and other situations unlikely to be on the exam. The buyer can also cause the seller to file a claim for damages if the buyer fails to uphold their end of the contract (e.g., failing to review documents on time). A project that spends too much time dealing with changes should be reevaluated and possibly renegotiated or terminated and a new contract should be negotiated, depending on the desires of both parties.

The buyer usually can terminate the contract at any time for convenience or for seller's default. Project managers need to be particularly sensitive to constructive changes. Such changes often happen during the course of managing a procurement. A simple direction to the contractor to perform certain work that may seem minor, if it is outside the scope of the contract, can result in a constructive change and cost the company a lot of money.

In the real world, and for the exam, you should understand the following about the Administer Procurements process. (These points are described in more detail later in this chapter.)

- What the project manager should be doing at any point in time
- What problems and issues to watch out for under the different contract types that might affect the management of the project
- That all work and legal requirements in the contract must be accomplished, however small and however seemingly unimportant
- That the project manager must help uphold all parts of the contract, not just the project scope

Now let's go into detail with the following exercise. What specific work actions do you think must be done during the Administer Procurements process? (Do not just look at the answers! Do the exercise once, and you will not have to do it again. Look at the answers, and you will have to spend three times as long to learn this information.)

Exercise Describe the specific actions involved in the Administer Procurements process.

Answer Be careful while reading over the following list. Do you understand what each of these actions is and how long it might take? Go slowly, and imagine what it would take to handle each one for a multimillion dollar construction project. Imagine you are building an office building and you are the project manager for the building's owner. Actions during this process may include:

- Review invoices (Were they submitted in the right form? Do they have all required supporting information? Are the charges allowable under the contract?)
- Complete integrated change control
- Document (Record everything—every phone call with the seller, every e-mail, every requested change, every approved change, etc.)
- Manage changes
- Authorize payments to the seller
- Interpret what is and what is not in the contract
- Interpret what the contract means
- Resolve disputes
- Make sure only authorized people are communicating with the seller

- Work with the procurement manager regarding requested and approved changes and contract compliance
- Hold procurement performance review meetings with your team and the seller
- Report on performance (your own performance and the seller's performance)
- Monitor cost, schedule, and technical performance against the contract, including all of its components (terms and conditions, procurement statement of work, etc.)
- Understand the legal implications of actions taken
- Control quality according to what is required in the contract
- Review claims filed by the seller asserting damages against the buyer
- Authorize the seller's work to start at the appropriate time, coordinating the seller's work with the project's work as a whole
- Correspond with the seller and with others
- Manage interfaces among all the sellers on the project
- Send copies of changes to the appropriate parties
- Verify that the correct scope is being done
- Perform inspections and audits
- Identify risks for future work
- Reestimate risks, costs, and schedule
- Monitor and control risk

Now the hard part. The exam will require you to know that management efforts, issues, and potential trouble spots are different under each form of contract, meaning there will be different things you will need to do depending on the type of contract you have. Be wary; not only does this apply to the real world, but there could be up to seven questions on the exam that require you to understand this concept. So let's try an exercise.

Exercise Hopefully, you have built a strong working relationship with the seller and are working well together. But what if the seller has financial troubles, changes owners, or did not include major pieces of the work in their estimate? The good relationship can go bad in an instant. Describe the specific things you must watch out for (spend your time managing) during the Administer Procurements process for each of the three main forms of contracts, regardless of what the relationship is like between the buyer and seller. Think about your real-world experience.

Fixed Price Contract

Time and Material Contract

Cost Reimbursable Contract

TRICKS OF THE TRADE® **Answer** This is not a complete list! Think of what other actions may be taken.

Fixed Price Contract
Watch for the seller cutting scope.
Watch for the seller cutting quality.
Make sure the seller's costs are real costs that have been incurred, not just future costs (unless there is an agreement stating otherwise).
Watch for overpriced change orders.
Check for scope misunderstandings.

Time and Material Contract
Provide day-to-day direction to the seller.
Attempt to get concrete deliverables.
Make sure the project length is not extended.
Make sure the number of hours spent on work is reasonable.
Watch for situations when switching to a different form of contract makes sense (e.g., you determine the procurement statement of work under a T&M contract and then switch to a fixed price contract for completion of the project).

Cost Reimbursable Contract
Audit every invoice.
Make sure all the costs are applicable and chargeable to your project.
Make sure the seller's work is progressing efficiently.
Watch for the seller adding resources to your project that do not add value or perform real work.
Watch for resources being shifted from what was said in the original proposal (e.g., more experienced people are proposed and less experienced people are used, but you are charged at the higher rate).
Watch for seller charges that were not part of the original plan.
Reestimate the cost of the project.

Conflict This is an important topic that can be addressed in tricky questions on the exam. As we have already discussed, in most projects that use a contract, someone other than the project manager controls the contract. This person may be called the procurement manager or contract administrator and, in many cases, IS THE ONLY ONE WITH AUTHORITY TO CHANGE THE CONTRACT. We have also already said that the contract includes the procurement statement of work. Can you see the potential for conflict between the procurement manager and the project manager? The project manager may want to initiate a change to the procurement statement of work (an area seemingly under his or her control), but cannot do so without the procurement manager's approval. The project manager might want to change the sequence of work, but if that sequence is specifically defined in the contract, it cannot be changed without the procurement manager's signature and approval. This adds another layer to the project manager's management activities that you may not have seen if you do not work with procurements in your real world.

Contract Change Control System[9] Procurements, like all projects, have changes. To handle these changes, a contract change control system is established. This system includes change procedures, forms, dispute resolution processes, and tracking systems and is specified in the contract. These procedures must be followed, and all changes should be made formally. Changes may be requested throughout the procurement process and are handled as part of the project integrated change control efforts, along with all other project changes. As with projects that do not involve contracts or purchase orders, any changes need to be analyzed for their impacts to the rest of the project.

Sometimes exam questions ask how project control is different in a procurement environment. These types of questions can be particularly difficult for those with little procurement experience. Let's look at this concept together. Some possible answers include:

- The seller will have a different company culture and different procedures than the buyer's organization.
- The buyer and seller have different objectives. The seller's objective is to generate revenue, and the buyer's objective is to complete the work.
- It is not as easy to "see" problems on the project because the procurement work is being done in a different location.
- There is a greater reliance on reports to determine if a problem exists.
- There is a greater reliance on relationships between the buyer's and seller's project managers to deal with issues that are not covered in the wording of the contract.

In instances in which there are many changes, it might be best to terminate the contract and start fresh through negotiating a new contract with the existing seller or finding a new seller. This is a drastic step to be done only when the existing contract no longer serves the purposes of defining all the work, roles, and responsibilities. Realize that contracts can be terminated, as described later in this chapter.

Procurement Performance Review PAGE 338 During the Administer Procurements process, the buyer's project manager analyzes all available data to verify that the seller is performing as they should. This is called a procurement performance review. Often the seller is present to review the data and, most importantly, to talk about what the buyer can do differently to help progress the work. The purpose of this review is to determine if changes are needed to improve the buyer/seller relationship and the processes being used, in addition to determining how the work is progressing. Formal changes to the contract may be requested as a result of this meeting.

Claims Administration PAGE 339 One of the frequently occurring activities during the Administer Procurements process is the handling of claims. A claim is an assertion that the buyer did something that has hurt the seller and the seller is asking for compensation. Another way of looking at claims is that they are a form of seller change requests. Claims can get nasty. Imagine a seller that is not making as much profit as they had hoped, issuing claims for every action taken by the buyer. Imagine the number of claims that can arise if you are working with a fixed price contract and an incomplete procurement statement of work.

Claims are usually addressed through the contract change control system. The best way to settle them is through negotiation or the use of the dispute resolution process specified in the contract. Many claims are not resolved until after the work is completed.

Records Management System PAGE 339 A contract is a formal, legal document, so thorough records relating to the contract must be kept. Record-keeping can be critical if actions taken or situations that occurred during a procurement are ever in question after the work is completed, such as in the case of unresolved claims or legal actions. Records may also be necessary to satisfy insurance requirements. For many projects, every e-mail, every payment, and every written and verbal communication must be recorded, kept, and stored. On other projects, information about the weather and the number of people on the buyer's property each day may be recorded. Whatever information is appropriate for the particular industry and project is kept.

On large or complex projects, a records management system can be quite extensive, with one person assigned just to manage these records. A records management system can include indexing systems, archiving systems, and information retrieval systems.

Contract Interpretation When working on projects that involve procurements, project managers frequently need to interpret the contract to answer questions like, "What does the contract really say?" and, "Who is responsible for what part of the procurement statement of work?"

Contract interpretation is never easy and frequently requires a lawyer's assistance. However, the exam may describe a simple situation about a conflict over interpretation of a contract and ask you to determine the correct answer.

TRICKS OF THE TRADE® Contract interpretation is based on an analysis of the intent of the parties to the contract and a few guidelines. One such guideline is that the contract supersedes any memos, conversations, or discussions that may have occurred prior to the contract signing. Therefore, if a requirement is not in the contract, it does not have to be met, even if it was agreed upon prior to signing the contract. The following is an exercise on intent.

Exercise In each row, circle the item on the left side or the right side that would "win" in a dispute over contract interpretation.

Contract language	*Or*	A memo drafted by one of the parties describing proposed changes after the contract is signed
Contract language	*Or*	A memo signed by both parties before the contract is signed that describes what was agreed to during negotiations
Contract terms and conditions	*Or*	Procurement statement of work
Common definition	*Or*	The intended meaning (without supplying a definition)
Industry use of the term	*Or*	Common use of the term
Special provisions	*Or*	General provisions
Typed-over wording on the contract	*Or*	A handwritten comment on the contract that is also initialed
Numbers	*Or*	Words
Detailed terms	*Or*	General terms

Answer The correct answers (in bold) show more clearly the intent of the parties to the contract.

Contract language	*Or*	A memo drafted by one of the parties describing proposed changes after the contract is signed
Contract language	*Or*	A memo signed by both parties before the contract is signed that describes what was agreed to during negotiations
Contract terms and conditions	*Or*	**Procurement statement of work**
The answer for the previous row depends on the Order of Precedence Clause in the contract that describes which terms and conditions take precedence over the others in the event of a conflict between them.		
Common definition	*Or*	The intended meaning (without supplying a definition)
Industry use of the term	*Or*	Common use of the term
Special provisions	*Or*	General provisions
Typed-over wording on the contract	*Or*	**A handwritten comment on the contract that is also initialed**
Numbers	*Or*	**Words**
Detailed terms	*Or*	General terms

Termination Many people who are new to procurement do not realize the contract can be terminated before the work is complete. The contract should have provisions for termination. Termination can be done for cause or for convenience. The buyer may terminate a contract for cause if the seller breaches the contract (i.e., does not perform according to the contract). This illustrates another reason the contract should clearly identify all the work required by the buyer (how can you terminate a seller for not completing work if the work was not in the contract?). The buyer can also terminate the contract before the work is complete because they no longer want the work done (termination for convenience). Sellers need to realize this can happen. It is rare to allow the seller to terminate a contract, but it could be appropriate on some projects. In any case, termination automatically puts the procurement into the closing process group, and there can be extensive negotiations on what costs the buyer will pay for. In a termination for convenience, the seller is paid for work completed and work in process. If the contract is terminated for default, the seller is generally paid for completed work but not for work in process. They may also be subjected to claims from the buyer for damages. In any case, termination is a serious issue, and one that has lasting effects on the project. Termination negotiations can be drawn out long after the work has stopped, thereby supporting the need to document details of the project on an ongoing basis.

Close Procurements PAGE 341

Process: Close Procurements
Process Group: Closing
Knowledge Area: Procurement Management

Closing procurements consists of tying up all the loose ends, verifying that all work and deliverables are accepted, finalizing open claims, and paying withheld retainage for each of the procurements on the project. The buyer will provide the seller with formal notice that the contract has been completed. There may be some continuing obligations, such as warranties, that will continue after the procurement is closed, however. Be prepared for up to six questions about this topic on the exam. The Close Procurements process is part of the closing process group.

Procurements are closed:

- When a contract is completed.
- When a contract is terminated before the work is completed.

All procurements must be closed out, no matter the circumstances under which they stop, are terminated, or are completed. Closure is a way to accumulate some added benefits such as lessons learned. It provides value to both the buyer and the seller and should not be omitted under any circumstances.

Procurements are closed through negotiated settlements between the buyer and the seller. You will see situational questions on the exam asking whether a procurement or contract is closed.

TRICKS OF THE TRADE® One of the things some people find confusing is the difference between the Close Project or Phase process and procurement closure. This is a question that often seems to come up on the exam. The answer is easy, though, if you think of project closure as closing out a project or phase and procurement closure as closing out a procurement. Depending on what choices the exam gives you, the answer could be:

- There may be many procurements in one project, so there will be many procurement closures, but project closure only happens at the end of the project or phase. All procurements must be closed before the final project closure. Therefore, upon completion of the contract for each procurement, the project manager performs a procurement audit and closes out the procurement. When the project as a whole is completed later, the project manager closes out the project.
- Procurement closure needs to happen before final project closure.
- To make it a little more confusing, there can be questions that ask about the frequency of project closure and procurement closure. Read these questions carefully, as the way the questions are

written will help you interpret the answer. For projects that are managed by phases, such as a design phase, testing phase, and installation phase, the Close Project or Phase process occurs at the end of each project phase. Therefore, project closure may be done at the end of each project phase and at the end of the project as a whole. Make sure you understand this for the exam. In contrast, procurement closure is done at the completion of each contract.

- Procurement closure requires more record keeping and must be done more formally than is generally required for project closure, to protect the legal interests of both parties.

Make sure you remember these points for the exam.

Now let's think about the real world. What do you think needs to be done at the end of the procurement in order to say the procurement is indeed finished? Wouldn't it be substantially similar to what needs to be done when you close out a project in the Close Project or Phase process?

Exercise Describe what work must be done during procurement closure.

Answer As you read the answer, think about how similar the Close Procurements process is to the Close Project or Phase process. Procurement closure includes all of the following:

- **Product verification** This involves checking to see if all the work was completed correctly and satisfactorily. Was the product of the procurement the same as what was requested? Did the product of the procurement meet the buyer's needs?
- **Negotiated settlement** The final settlement of all claims, invoices, and other issues may be handled through negotiations or through the dispute resolution process previously set up in the contract.
- **Financial closure** Financial closure is making final payments and completing cost records.
- **Procurement audit** This is a structured review of only the procurement process. Do not think of this as an audit of costs, but as a lessons learned of the procurement process that can help improve other procurements. Normally this

is done by the procurement manager and project manager, but companies that want to improve their processes may also involve the seller. Remember, this is only talking about how the whole procurement process went. Issues that might be discussed include: How can we handle negotiations better? How can we make the bidding process easier for sellers?

- **Updates to records** This involves making sure all records of the project are complete and are accessible in the records management system. This information could include whatever has been recorded to date on the project. These records will become part of the procurement file (described later in this discussion).
- **Final contract performance reporting** Think of this as creating a final report. First you need to analyze and document the success and effectiveness of the procurement and the seller, and then turn that into a final report.
- **Lessons learned** Procurement lessons learned are received from everyone involved in the project, even the seller, and become part of the lessons learned for the project. They often include a discussion of what went right, what went wrong, and what can be done better next time. Lessons learned are created as a result of the procurement audit. These then become part of the organizational process assets. These lessons learned are related to the project as a whole, not any specific procurement. Lessons learned are documented and disseminated throughout the organization. Could you imagine being able to access files from every project manager that has gone before you in your company, describing what they would do differently the next time? How valuable would that be? Thus, lessons learned provide input to help improve how the organization handles procurements in the future.
- **Procurement file** Creating the procurement file involves putting all e-mails, letters, conversation records, payment receipts, reports, etc., related to the procurement into an organized file. This file will be stored for use as historical records and will help protect the project in case of arguments or legal action regarding what was done and not done on the contract. The project manager, with the help of the procurement manager, decides what documents need to be kept. The file could include:
  - Contract
  - Changes (approved and rejected)
  - Submittals from the seller
  - Seller performance reports
  - Financial information
  - Inspection results
  - Lessons learned
- **Other** Procurement closure could also include the following activities:
  - Arranging for storage of procurement records and drawings
  - Creating and delivering legal documents, such as release of lien documents and formal acceptance letters
  - Returning property used for the procurement to its owner

Formal Acceptance and Closure Once closure is completed and the seller has received formal sign-off that the products of the procurement are acceptable from the buyer, the procurement is closed. Expect questions on the exam that provide you with situations and require you to determine whether the procurement is closed. In gaining formal acceptance, the seller is also working to measure customer satisfaction. Often a formal customer satisfaction survey may be included in a seller's closure records.

Exercise

The Procurement Process Now that you know so much about procurement, test your knowledge by completing the following chart. Notice the word "Actions." You need to know for the exam, among other things, what needs to be done during each step, and the outputs. This is one of the most important exercises in this chapter, because of the number of questions on the exam that ask about the procurement process.

Recreate the procurement management process, including the outputs, on the following form. Even with one reading of this chapter, you should get most of the key actions and outputs correct. When you have read the chapter two or three times, you should be almost 100 percent accurate. This exercise is about remembering key parts of procurement management, not memorization. Create the chart three times, and you should know it well enough for the exam.

Plan Procurements	Conduct Procurements	Administer Procurements	Close Procurements
Key Actions			

Key Outputs			

Answer The following actions and outputs are the ones you should give the most focus to in preparing for the exam.

TRICKS OF THE TRADE® Here is a trick for understanding the process without memorizing the whole thing—know only the outputs! If a question describes some activity and that activity is after the procurement documents are created and before the contract is signed, then it must be taking place as part of the Conduct Procurements process. If it is taking place after the contract is signed but before the work is substantially done, it must be occurring during the Administer Procurements process.

Plan Procurements	Conduct Procurements	Administer Procurements	Close Procurements
Key Actions			
► Make a make-or-buy decision ► Create a procurement management plan ► Create the procurement statement of work ► Select the appropriate contract type ► Create terms and conditions, including standard and special conditions ► Create procurement documents ► Create source selection criteria	► Find potential sellers through advertising or the Internet ► Send procurement documents ► Hold a bidder conference ► Answer sellers' questions ► Seller makes a decision to bid/propose ► Seller creates the proposal ► Receive the proposals ► Compare the proposals to source selection criteria using a weighting or screening system to pick/shortlist the sellers ► Receive presentations from seller(s) ► Compare to independent estimates ► Hold negotiations	► Understand the legal implications of your actions ► Hold procurement performance reviews ► Request changes and administer claims ► Manage interfaces among sellers ► Report performance ► Monitor performance against the contract ► Review cost submittals ► Make payments ► Perform inspections and audits ► Maintain records of everything	► Perform a procurement audit ► Reach a negotiated settlement ► Create lessons learned ► Complete final contract performance reporting ► Verify the product ► Issue formal acceptance ► Update records ► Create a procurement file ► Perform financial closure
Key Outputs			
► Procurement management plan ► Procurement statement of work ► Procurement documents ready	► Signed contract	► Substantial completion ► Change requests ► Project management plan updates	► Formal acceptance ► Closed procurements

Exercise Here is another exercise to review what we discussed in this chapter. You must understand the project manager's role in procurements to pass the exam. After reading this chapter, how would you describe the project manager's role?

Answer

As the project manager, you should:

- Know the procurement process so you know what will happen when.
- Understand what contract terms and conditions mean so you can read and understand contracts.
- Make sure the contract contains all the scope of work and all the project management requirements, such as attendance at meetings, reports, actions, and communications deemed necessary to minimize problems and miscommunications with the seller(s).
- Identify risks and incorporate mitigation and allocation of risks into the contract to decrease project risk.
- Help tailor the contract to the unique needs of the project while it is being written.
- Include the time required to complete the procurement process in the schedule for the project so the project schedule is more realistic.
- Be involved during contract negotiations to protect the relationship with the seller.
- Protect the integrity of the project and the ability to get the work done by making sure the procurement process goes as smoothly as possible.
- Help make sure all the work in the contract is done, such as reporting, inspections, and legal deliverables, including the release of liens and ownership of materials, not just the technical scope.
- Do not ask for something that is not in the contract without making a corresponding change to the contract.
- Work with the procurement manager to manage changes to the contract.

That is the procurement process! Was a lot of this new to you? If you are inexperienced in working with procurements, reread this chapter and try to visualize how the different topics are applied to a large project. The visualization will help you understand the process in a real way, so you know what proper project management is and what your involvement in the procurement process should be.

Practice Exam

1. Once signed, a contract is legally binding unless:
   A. One party is unable to perform.
   B. One party is unable to finance its part of the work.
   C. It is in violation of applicable law.
   D. It is declared null and void by either party's legal counsel.

2. With a clear procurement statement of work, a seller completes work as specified, but the buyer is not pleased with the results. The contract is considered to be:
   A. Null and void.
   B. Incomplete.
   C. Complete.
   D. Waived.

3. All of the following statements concerning procurement documents are incorrect EXCEPT:
   A. Well-designed procurement documents can simplify comparison of responses.
   B. Procurement documents must be rigorous with no flexibility to allow consideration of seller suggestions.
   C. In general, procurement documents should not include selection criteria.
   D. Well-designed procurement documents do not include a procurement statement of work.

4. A project manager for the seller is told by her management that the project should do whatever possible to be awarded incentive money. The primary objective of incentive clauses in a contract is to:
   A. Reduce costs for the buyer.
   B. Help the seller control costs.
   C. Synchronize objectives.
   D. Reduce risk for the seller by shifting risk to the buyer.

5. All the following statements about change control are incorrect EXCEPT:
   A. A fixed price contract will minimize the need for change control.
   B. Changes seldom provide real benefits to the project.
   C. Contracts should include procedures to accommodate changes.
   D. More detailed specifications eliminate the causes of changes.

6. A routine audit of a cost reimbursable (CR) contract determines that overcharges are being made. If the contract does not specify corrective action, the buyer should:
   A. Continue to make project payments.
   B. Halt payments until the problem is corrected.
   C. Void the contract and start legal action to recover overpayments.
   D. Change the contract to require more frequent audits.

7. The primary objective of contract negotiations is to:
   A. Get the most from the other side.
   B. Protect the relationship.
   C. Get the highest monetary return.
   D. Define objectives and stick to them.

8. A seller is working on a cost reimbursable (CR) contract when the buyer decides he would like to expand the scope of services and change to a fixed price (FP) contract. All of the following are the seller's options EXCEPT:
   A. Completing the original work on a cost reimbursable basis and then negotiating a fixed price for the additional work.
   B. Completing the original work and rejecting the additional work.
   C. Negotiating a fixed price contract that includes the work.
   D. Starting over with a new contract.

9. Bidder conferences are part of:
   A. Plan Procurements.
   B. Administer Procurements.
   C. Conduct Procurements.
   D. Communications Management.

10. All of the following MUST be present to have a contract EXCEPT:
    A. A procurement statement of work.
    B. Acceptance.
    C. The address of the seller.
    D. Buyers' signatures.

11. Which of the following BEST describes the project manager's role in the procurement process?
    A. The project manager has only minor involvement.
    B. The project manager should be the negotiator.
    C. The project manager should provide an understanding of the risks of the project.
    D. The project manager should tell the contract manager how the contracting process should be handled.

12. What is one of the KEY objectives during contract negotiations?
    A. Obtain a fair and reasonable price.
    B. Negotiate a price under the seller's estimate.
    C. Ensure that all project risks are thoroughly delineated.
    D. Ensure that an effective communications management plan is established.

13. Which of the following activities occurs during the Plan Procurements process?
    A. Make-or-buy decisions
    B. Answering sellers' questions about the bid documents
    C. Advertising
    D. Proposal evaluation

14. Which of the following is the BEST thing for a project manager to do in the Conduct Procurements process?
    A. Evaluate risks.
    B. Select a contract type.
    C. Update the project schedule.
    D. Answer sellers' questions about the procurement documents.

15. The sponsor is worried about the seller deriving extra profit on the cost plus fixed fee (CPFF) contract. Each month he requires the project manager to submit CPI calculations and an analysis of the cost to complete. The project manager explains to the sponsor that extra profits should NOT be a worry on this project because:
    A. The team is making sure the seller does not cut scope.
    B. All costs invoiced are being audited.
    C. There can only be a maximum 10 percent increase if there is an unexpected cost overrun.
    D. The fee is only received by the seller when the project is completed.

16. In a fixed price (FP) contract, the fee or profit is:
    A. Unknown.
    B. Part of the negotiation involved in paying every invoice.
    C. Applied as a line item to every invoice.
    D. Determined with the other party at the end of the project.

17. A project performed under a cost reimbursable contract has finally entered the Close Procurements process. What MUST the buyer remember to do?
    A. Decrease the risk rating of the project.
    B. Audit seller's cost submittals.
    C. Evaluate the fee she is paying.
    D. Make sure the seller is not adding resources.

18. The sponsor and the project manager are discussing what type of contract the project manager plans to use on the project. The sponsor points out that the performing organization spent a lot of money hiring a design team to come up with the design. The project manager is concerned that the risk for the buyer be as small as possible. An advantage of a fixed price contract for the buyer is:
    A. Cost risk is lower.
    B. Cost risk is higher.
    C. There is little risk.
    D. Risk is shared by all parties.

19. As part of the records management system, you are trying to make sure all records from the procurement are documented and indexed. Which of the following do you NOT have to worry about?
    A. Proposal
    B. Procurement statement of work
    C. Terms and conditions
    D. Negotiation process

20. You are in the middle of a complex negotiation when the other party says, "We need to finish in one hour because I have to catch my plane." That person is using which of the following negotiation strategies?
    A. Good guy, bad guy
    B. Delay
    C. Deadline
    D. Extreme demands

21. Which of the following is an advantage of centralized contracting?
    A. Increased expertise
    B. Easier access
    C. No home for the procurement manager
    D. More loyalty to the project

22. With which type of contract is the seller MOST concerned about project scope?
    A. Fixed price
    B. Cost plus fixed fee
    C. Time and material
    D. Purchase order

23. Your company has an emergency and needs contracted work done as soon as possible. Under these circumstances, which of the following would be the MOST helpful to add to the contract?
    A. A clear procurement statement of work
    B. Requirements as to which subcontractors can be used
    C. Incentives
    D. A force majeure clause

24. During what part of the procurement process does procurement negotiation occur?
    A. Plan Procurements
    B. Close Procurements
    C. Administer Procurements
    D. Conduct Procurements

25. The project team is arguing about the prospective sellers who have submitted proposals. One team member argues for a certain seller while another team member wants the project awarded to a different seller. What part of the procurement process is the team in?
    A. Plan Procurements
    B. Administer Procurements
    C. Negotiate Contracts
    D. Conduct Procurements

26. The project team seems to like to argue; they have argued about everything. Luckily the project manager set in place a reward system and team-building sessions that will help and encourage the team to cooperate more. The latest thing they are arguing about is whether they should complete a work package themselves or outsource the work to someone else. What part of the procurement process must they be in?
    A. Conduct Procurements
    B. Plan Procurements
    C. Administer Procurements
    D. Claims Administration

27. A project manager is in the middle of creating a request for proposal (RFP). What part of the procurement process is he in?
    A. Conduct Procurements
    B. Plan Procurements
    C. Administer Procurements
    D. Make-or-Buy Analysis

28. Your program manager has come to you, the project manager, for help with a bid for her newest project. You want to protect your company from financial risk, and you have limited scope definition. What is the BEST type of contract to choose?
    A. Fixed price (FP)
    B. Cost plus percentage of cost (CPPC)
    C. Time and material (T&M)
    D. Cost plus fixed fee (CPFF)

29. Negotiations between two parties are becoming complex, so Party A makes some notes that both parties sign. However, when the work is being done, Party B claims they are not required to provide an item they both agreed to during negotiations, because it was not included in the subsequent contract. In this case, party B is:
    A. Incorrect, because both parties must comply with what they agreed on.
    B. Correct, because there was an offer.
    C. Generally correct, because both parties are only required to perform what is in the contract.
    D. Generally incorrect, because all agreements must be upheld.

30. Your project has just been fast tracked and you are looking to quickly bring in a subcontractor to complete networking. There is no time to issue a request for proposal (RFP), so you choose to use a company you have used many times before for software development. A PRIMARY concern in this situation is:
    A. Collusion between subcontractors.
    B. The subcontractor's qualifications.
    C. The subcontractor's evaluation criteria.
    D. Holding a bidder conference.

31. The project manager and project sponsor are discussing the project costs and whether it is better to have their own company do part of the project or hire another company to do the work. If they asked for your opinion, you might say it would be better to do the work yourself if:
    A. There is a lot of proprietary data.
    B. You have the expertise but you do not have the available manpower.
    C. You do not need control over the work.
    D. Your company resources are limited.

32. After much excitement and hard work, the procurement statement of work for the project is completed. Even after gaining agreement that the procurement statement of work is complete, the project manager is still unsure of whether it actually addresses all the buyer's needs. The project manager is about to attend the bidder conference. He asks you for advice on what to do during the session. Which of the following is the BEST advice you can give him?
    A. You do not need to attend this session. The procurement manager will hold it.
    B. Make sure you negotiate project scope.
    C. Make sure you give all the sellers the opportunity to ask questions.
    D. Let the project sponsor handle the meeting so you can be the good guy in the negotiation session.

33. A seller is awarded a contract to build a pipeline. The contract terms and conditions require a work plan to be issued for the buyer's approval prior to commencing work, but the seller fails to provide one. Which of the following is the BEST thing for the buyer's project manager to do?
    A. File a letter of intent.
    B. Develop the work plan and issue it to the seller to move things along.
    C. Issue a default letter.
    D. Issue a stop work order to the seller until a work plan is prepared.

34. Close Procurements is different from Close Project or Phase in that Close Procurements:
    A. Occurs before Close Project or Phase.
    B. Is the only one to involve the customer.
    C. Includes the return of property.
    D. May be done more than once for each contract.

35. You have just started administering a procurement when management decides to terminate the contract. What should you do FIRST?
    A. Go back to the Plan Procurements process.
    B. Go back to the Conduct Procurements process.
    C. Finish the Administer Procurements process.
    D. Go to the Close Procurements process.

36. The project team is arguing about the prospective sellers who have submitted proposals. One team member argues for a certain seller while another team member wants the project to be awarded to a different seller. The BEST thing the project manager should remind the team to focus on in order to make a selection is the:
    A. Procurement documents.
    B. Procurement audits.
    C. Source selection criteria.
    D. Procurement management plan.

37. The performing organization is trying to decide whether to split the procurement department and assign procurement responsibilities to departments directly responsible for the projects. A procurement professional might not want this split to occur because he or she would lose ___________ in a decentralized contracting environment.
    A. Standardized company project management practices
    B. Loyalty to the project
    C. Experience
    D. Access to others with similar expertise

38. Your project team member delivers a project deliverable to the buyer. However, the buyer refuses the deliverable, stating it does not meet the requirement on page 300 of the technical specifications. You review the document and find that you agree. What is the BEST thing to do?
    A. Explain that the contract is wrong and should be changed.
    B. Issue a change order.
    C. Review the requirements and meet with the responsible team member to review the WBS dictionary.
    D. Call a meeting of the team to review the requirement on page 300.

39. What type of contract do you NOT want to use if you do not have enough labor to audit invoices?
    A. Cost plus fixed fee (CPFF)
    B. Time & material (T&M)
    C. Fixed price (FP)
    D. Fixed price incentive fee (FPIF)

40. A new project manager is about to begin creating the procurement statement of work. One stakeholder wants to add many items to the procurement statement of work. Another stakeholder only wants to describe the functional requirements. The project is important for the project manager's company, but a seller will do the work. How would you advise the project manager?
    A. The procurement statement of work should be general to allow the seller to make his own decisions.
    B. The procurement statement of work should be general to allow for clarification later.
    C. The procurement statement of work should be detailed to allow for clarification later.
    D. The procurement statement of work should be as detailed as necessary for the type of project.

Answers

1. **Answer** C
   Explanation Once signed, a contract is binding. Generally, the inability to perform, get financing, or one party's belief that the contract is null and void does not change the fact that the contract is binding. If, however, both sides agree to terminate the contract, the contract can move into the Close Procurements process.

2. **Answer** C
   Explanation If the seller completes the work specified in the procurement statement of work, the contract is considered complete. That does not mean the same thing as the procurement being closed. The Close Procurements process must still occur. However, in this situation, the contract work is completed.

3. **Answer** A
   Explanation Often the seller is required to inform the buyer of anything that is missing or unclear in the procurement documents. It is in the buyer's best interest to discover missing items, since it will save the buyer money and trouble to correct the problem early. Procurement documents must contain terms and conditions and selection criteria, as well as documentation of all the work that is to be done (which includes the procurement statement of work). This is so the seller can price the project and know what is most important to the buyer. Well-designed procurement documents can simplify comparison of responses. This is an important point for the real world and is the best answer.

4. **Answer** C
   Explanation Incentives are meant to bring the objectives of the seller in line with those of the buyer, so both are progressing toward the same objective.

5. **Answer** C
   Explanation There are always good ideas (changes) that can add benefit to the project, regardless of the contract type. Although detailed specifications may reduce the need for changes, they do not eliminate the causes. Contracts should include procedures to accommodate changes.

6. **Answer** A
   Explanation Halting all payments would be a breach of contract on the buyer's part. Voiding the contract and beginning legal action is too severe and cannot be done unilaterally. Changing the contract to require more frequent audits does not solve the problem presented. A choice that said, "Halt payments on the disputed amount" would probably be the best answer, but it is not offered. The best choice available is to continue to make the payments.

7. **Answer** B
   Explanation As a project manager, you want to develop a good relationship during negotiations that will last throughout the project.

8. **Answer** D
   Explanation The seller can try to negotiate change or simply continue the original contract and refuse requests to complete additional work, but the seller cannot unilaterally decide to start over with a new contract. Both parties have to agree to this option through negotiations.

9. **Answer** C
   Explanation Expect questions on the exam that require you to know in what part of the procurement process activities are done.

10. **Answer** C
    Explanation Many people miss the fact that a contract includes a procurement statement of work. To have a contract, you must also have acceptance. One set of signatures is not enough; you must have sign-off (i.e., acceptance) from both parties, not just from the buyer. The address of the seller is not required, and therefore is the exception.

11. **Answer** C
    Explanation The project manager knows the project risks. He or she needs to make sure provisions are included in the contract to address these risks.

12. **Answer** A
    Explanation Thorough risk identification and an effective communications management plan are good ideas, but not key objectives of contract negotiation. Negotiations should be win/win, so negotiating a price below the seller's estimate is not the best choice. A fair and equitable price will help to create a good working atmosphere. Otherwise, you will pay later, through change orders.

13. **Answer** A
    Explanation Answering sellers' questions, advertising, and proposal evaluation occur during the Conduct Procurements process. Make-or-buy decisions are made earlier, in the Plan Procurements process.

14. **Answer** D
    Explanation Risk analysis is done before the procurement process begins, as procurement is a risk mitigation and transference tool. Selecting a contract type is part of Plan Procurements. Changes to the project schedule may be an output of the Administer Procurements process. During the Conduct Procurements process, the project manager answers questions submitted by the sellers.

15. **Answer** B
    Explanation Cutting scope decreases profits on this type of contract, so that would not be a way for the seller to generate extra profits. CPFF contracts generally do not limit fee increases, and the fee in a CPFF contract is usually paid out on a continuous basis during the life of the project. One of the ways to change the profit in a cost plus fixed fee contract is to invoice for items not chargeable to the project. Therefore, all invoiced costs should be audited.

16. **Answer** A
    Explanation The fee or profit is known to the seller, but this question is asked from the buyer's perspective. The buyer does not know what profit the seller included in the contract.

17. **Answer** B
    Explanation Although a reserve might be decreased for the project overall when one of its procurements enters closure, the risk rating of the project is generally not affected. Evaluation of the fee should have been done during the Conduct Procurements process. Making sure the seller does not add resources may be a concern during the Administer Procurements process, but it is not common during Close Procurements. Auditing the seller's cost submittals is part of the procurement audit and is a required aspect of the Close Procurements process.

18. **Answer** A
    Explanation If you had trouble with this one, you need to remember that the questions are asked from the buyer's perspective unless otherwise noted. The seller has the most cost risk in a fixed price contract, and the buyer's risk is lower.

19. **Answer** D
Explanation To answer this question, you need to know what a records management system is and that it would not be used to keep track of negotiations. The negotiation process is not a document. The proposal, procurement statement of work, and the contract terms and conditions are all records that need to be documented and indexed.

20. **Answer** C
Explanation Putting a time limit on the negotiation is an example of a deadline negotiation strategy.

21. **Answer** A
Explanation Centralized contracting usually means it is more difficult to get access to the procurement manager, and the procurement manager has less loyalty to the project. The fact that the procurement manager has no home when he or she is not working on a project is a disadvantage of decentralized contracting. Increased expertise of the procurement manager is an advantage of centralized contracting.

22. **Answer** A
Explanation In a fixed price contract, the seller has the cost risk and therefore wants to completely understand the procurement statement of work before bidding.

23. **Answer** C
Explanation If you follow the proper project management process, you ALWAYS have good definition of scope. In this situation, you are in a time crunch. Both good scope definition and incentives are required to make it happen. Which provides the better answer? Along with good scope definition, you need the seller to share your need for speed. Incentives bring the seller's objectives in line with the buyer's and thus would be the MOST helpful. Good scope definition alone does not ensure speed.

24. **Answer** D
Explanation Negotiation occurs during the Conduct Procurements process.

25. **Answer** D
Explanation Selected sellers are an output of the Conduct Procurements process.

26. **Answer** B
Explanation Did you notice that much of this question is irrelevant? Did you also notice that the words "make-or-buy decision" were not used in the question? Instead, the question used the definition of make-or-buy. Watch out for this on the exam. A make-or-buy decision is needed before the rest of the procurement process can occur. Therefore, the situation must be taking place in one of the early steps of the procurement process. Plan Procurements is the correct choice.

27. **Answer** B
Explanation The procurement documents are created during the Plan Procurements process. The request for proposal is one of those documents, so the project manager is in the Plan Procurements process.

28. **Answer** D
Explanation Of the options given, the only contract that limits fees for large projects with limited scope definition is cost plus fixed fee.

29. **Answer** C
Explanation Party B is only required to deliver what is defined in the contract.

30. **Answer** B
    Explanation Although you have used this contractor before, how can you be sure the company is qualified to do the new work, since it is not exactly like the previous work? This is the risk you are taking.

31. **Answer** A
    Explanation It is generally better to do the work yourself if using an outside company means you have to turn over proprietary data to the other company.

32. **Answer** C
    Explanation The project manager should attend the bidder conference, although the procurement manager may lead it. Did you select negotiating scope? Sellers may ask questions about scope during the conference, but negotiations occur after the seller is selected. Allowing ample opportunity for all of the prospective sellers to ask questions is one of the many challenges of a bidder conference. They may not want to ask questions while their competitors are in the room.

33. **Answer** C
    Explanation Any time a seller does not perform according to the contract, the project manager must take action. The preferred choice might be to contact the seller and ask what is going on, but that choice is not available here. Therefore, the best choice is to let the seller know they are in default.

34. **Answer** A
    Explanation The customer may be involved in lessons learned and procurement audits, and would certainly be involved in formal acceptance. Both Close Procurements and Close Project or Phase involve the return of property. Close Procurements is done once for each procurement, at the end of the contract. All procurements are closed before the project is closed.

35. **Answer** D
    Explanation If the contract is terminated, the procurement needs to enter closure. The results of the procurement and its documentation are archived as historical records in the Close Procurements process.

36. **Answer** C
    Explanation The source selection criteria is the primary tool for evaluating potential sellers and should be used by the team in order to make a selection.

37. **Answer** D
    Explanation The change would not impact the organization's overall project management practices, only procurement. Loyalty to the project would be gained, not lost, in a decentralized environment, as the procurement manager is part of the project team. In a decentralized procurement environment, there is less focus on maintaining the skill or expertise of the contracting function, and access to other procurement professionals with comparable expertise would be reduced.

38. **Answer** C
Explanation This question is written from the perspective of the seller. The contract could be wrong, or the customer could be wrong, but this should have been discovered earlier if proper project management was followed. A seller cannot issue a change order (although they could request one). Did you select calling a meeting of the team? If so, remember that project management is not about making every decision with ALL the team members. The best choice involves reviewing the requirements documentation and meeting with the appropriate team member. If such a problem has arisen, it could mean something was wrong in the WBS dictionary or in how the team member completed the work.

39. **Answer** A
Explanation If you got this question wrong, reread it. You need to audit invoices in all contract types, so how do you choose? Look for the answer that is BEST. In this case, it would be the choice that requires the greatest effort.

A T&M contract should be used for low dollar and short duration contracts (remember that a T&M contract has no incentive to finish), so it does not have a high level of risk. FP and FPIF contracts cannot be best, because the risk to the buyer is limited. The buyer is still only going to pay the contracted price. In a CPFF contract, the buyer pays all costs. The seller could be charging the buyer for costs that should not be allocated to the buyer. Because of the size and dollar amount of this type of contract, and because the risk to the buyer is great, a CPFF contract requires the most auditing. In this case, you would not want to use a CPFF contract.

40. **Answer** D
Explanation When the seller has more expertise than the buyer, the procurement statement of work should describe performance or function rather than a complete list of work. In any case, the procurement statement of work should be as detailed as possible.

CHAPTER THIRTEEN Professional and Social Responsibility

Quicktest

- Ethical application of project management
- PMI-isms in professional and social responsibility
- Responsibility
  - Make decisions based on the best interests of the company
  - Accept only assignments you are qualified for
  - Protect proprietary information
  - Report unethical behavior and violations
- Respect
  - Maintain an attitude of mutual cooperation
  - Respect cultural differences
  - Negotiate in good faith
  - Deal with conflict directly
  - Do not use your position to influence others
- Fairness
  - Act impartially without bribery
  - Look for and disclose conflicts of interest
  - Do not discriminate
  - Do not use your position for personal or business gain
- Honesty
  - Understand the truth
  - Be truthful in all communications

Although there is not a chapter dedicated to professional and social responsibility in the *PMBOK® Guide*, this is an important part of a project manager's job. A project manager who fails to uphold the standards of the profession can have damaging impacts to the project and the organization, as well as to the profession as a whole. If someone with a PMP certification does not act professionally and ethically, it diminishes the credibility of the certification and the practice of project management. For this reason, concepts related to professional and social responsibility will be tested throughout the exam. It is part of everything a project manager does, from project initiating to closing.

To study this topic, read and make sure you understand the concepts discussed in this chapter; do not waste your time memorizing the information. Be honest with yourself about what you know and do not know, and identify gaps in your knowledge. These gaps do not make you an unethical project manager. We all have gaps we need to fill.

In addition, you should review and understand PMI's Code of Ethics and Professional Conduct, available at PMI's Web site (www.pmi.org), since many questions relate directly to that code. The Code of Ethics and Professional Conduct breaks professional and social responsibility down into the following categories:

- Responsibility
- Respect
- Fairness
- Honesty

Do these four categories seem difficult? If asked if we are responsible, respectful, fair, and honest, we of course say yes. But have there been times when you did not complete all your responsibilities? How many times have you been disrespectful or unfair? Hopefully we do the right thing most of the time, but none of us are perfect. This chapter will discuss some important points about the previously listed categories, but it will also address two other important topics not specifically covered in the Code of Ethics and Professional Conduct that can help you on the exam: the ethical application of project management, and PMI-isms in professional and social responsibility.

Rita's Process Chart—Professional and Social Responsibility

Where are we in the project management process?

INITIATING

- Select project manager
- Determine company culture and existing systems
- Collect processes, procedures, and historical information
- Divide large projects into phases
- Understand the business case
- Uncover initial requirements, assumptions, and risks
- Assess project and product feasibility within the given constraints
- Create measurable objectives
- Develop project charter
- Identify stakeholders
- Develop stakeholder management strategy

PLANNING
(This is the only process group with a set order)

- Determine how you will do planning—part of all management plans
- Determine detailed requirements
- Create project scope statement
- Assess what to purchase
- Determine team
- Create WBS and WBS dictionary
- Create activity list
- Create network diagram
- Estimate resource requirements
- Estimate time and cost
- Determine critical path
- Develop schedule
- Develop budget
- Determine quality standards, processes, and metrics
- Create process improvement plan
- Determine all roles and responsibilities
- Plan communications
- Perform risk identification, qualitative and quantitative risk analysis, and risk response planning
- Go back—iterations
- Prepare procurement documents
- Create change management plan
- Finalize the "how to execute and control" parts of all management plans
- Develop realistic and final PM plan and performance measurement baseline
- Gain formal approval of the plan
- Hold kickoff meeting

EXECUTING

- Execute the work according to the PM plan
- Produce product deliverables (product scope)
- Request changes
- Implement only approved changes
- Continuously improve
- Follow processes
- Perform quality assurance
- Perform quality audits
- Acquire final team
- Manage people
- Evaluate team and project performance
- Hold team-building activities
- Give recognition and rewards
- Use issue logs
- Facilitate conflict resolution
- Release resources as work is completed
- Send and receive information
- Hold meetings
- Select sellers

MONITORING & CONTROLLING

- Take action to control the project
- Measure performance against the performance measurement baseline
- Measure performance against other metrics determined by the project manager
- Determine variances and if they warrant a corrective action or change request
- Influence the factors that cause changes
- Request changes
- Perform integrated change control
- Approve or reject changes
- Inform stakeholders of results of change requests
- Update the PM plan and project documents
- Manage configuration
- Create forecasts
- Gain acceptance of interim deliverables from the customer
- Perform quality control
- Report on project performance and solicit feedback
- Perform risk assessments and audits
- Manage reserves
- Administer procurements

CLOSING

- Confirm work is done to requirements
- Complete procurement closure
- Gain final acceptance of the product
- Complete financial closure
- Hand off completed product
- Solicit feedback from the customer about the project
- Complete final performance reporting
- Index and archive records
- Update lessons learned knowledge base

The Ethical Application of Project Management Are you honest? Most people are essentially honest, but we all have our moments. For example, have you ever agreed to and started work on a project without being reasonably sure the end date could be met? Is that honest? Is it ethical? People often do this in their real world without ever labeling it as being dishonest or unethical. For the exam, however, you need to understand that part of professional and social responsibility is the ethical application of project management in the real world.

Did you know it is unethical to provide a project schedule that you do not believe to be accurate? It is also unethical to waste company resources because you have not properly planned a project. And it is unethical to manage a project without a project charter or a WBS. These are serious issues in the real world, and they are serious for the exam.

So why is the lack of such project management activities unethical? Think about the impact project management tools such as a charter or WBS have on a project. Not having a project charter hurts your project and, at the least, causes increased costs and wasted time. Not having a WBS means that some of the scope will likely be missed and, when it is discovered later, that work will be more costly than including it in the project from the beginning. Does this sound realistic? If not, you may not fully understand the benefits of these tools and should review them again in this book. To pass the exam, think about what you should be doing in your real world, not what you are doing (if there is a discrepancy). Project managers must understand the project management process in order to do the right thing!

Some organizations do not give their project managers the authority needed to get projects done. Imagine a situation where the project manager only has the authority to write reports and transmit them to others. This lack of authority means no one is directing the integration of the work. As a result, the project will likely be late and people working on the project will waste valuable time in rework. This is not an acceptable situation. In order to uphold the standards of the project management profession, project managers have a professional responsibility to obtain the authority necessary to manage the project.

Now let's think about unrealistic project completion deadlines or milestones. Have you ever been given an unrealistic schedule constraint? Many project managers with unrealistic deadlines just implement the project the best they can and wait to see what happens regarding the timeline. But professional and social responsibility requires project managers to handle unrealistic schedule problems upfront. This may mean saying, "Assign the project to someone else!" or "You have requested that the project be completed within six months. Our analysis makes us very certain that we can meet that due date only if we adjust the scope, cost, or quality on this project. If we cannot make any changes, the project will be completed in eight months."

Professional and social responsibility may also mean saying, "I am sorry you do not want to support my efforts in planning the project and want me to start producing work right away. As part of my PMP certification, however, I am ethically bound to do project management correctly for the best interests of the project and the company. This means I must have a project charter and at least a high-level work breakdown structure." Project managers are REQUIRED to do the right thing and stand up for the right process!

Did you notice the attitude illustrated in the previous statements? Do you have such an attitude? Being assertive and in control as a project manager is required. For the exam, make sure you understand this assertive, proactive attitude and what it means for how a project manager should act and what a project manager should and should not be doing. Attitude is extremely important, and the expectation for project managers to be assertive and in control applies to project managers in every country and culture.

PMI-isms in Professional and Social Responsibility We discussed PMI-isms and their impact on the exam in the first chapter of this book. You need to be aware of PMI-isms related to professional and social responsibility as well. There are often questions on the exam that talk about the relationship of a PMP certification holder to PMI and how that person should promote PMI within his or her organization. The exam can also include questions that assume you are involved with PMI as a chapter member or chapter officer. These types of questions are relatively easy if you maintain the PMI focus described in the following points:

- You will not get involved with PMI to promote your own business.
- You have a duty of loyalty to PMI. When acting on behalf of a PMI chapter, you will keep the best interest of PMI in mind, not your own best interest.
- When contracting for services for the chapter, you will provide equal access for all to submit proposals and not keep the work for your own company or your friends.
- You will not let anyone cheat on the application for the PMP exam.
- You will not let anyone copy PMP exam prep materials or perform other illegal behavior.
- You will not disclose questions on the PMP exam.
- You will promote PMI and the PMP exam within your organization.

Categories of Professional and Social Responsibility Now that we've discussed the concepts of the ethical application of project management and PMI-isms in professional and social responsibility, let's look at the four categories in PMI's Code of Ethics and Professional Conduct. Read the following list, and make a note in the right-hand column of any areas where you have had problems in the past. The topics you have had difficulty with are the ones you should think about a little more. Remember that ethics is a messy topic and no one is perfect. This simple checklist will help shorten your study time and keep you more focused on what you need to know for the exam.

Responsibility—Ownership of Decisions and Actions	Areas Where I Have Had a Problem
Make decisions based on the best interests of the company and the team, as well as society, rather than your own best interest.	
Only take on assignments you are qualified to complete.	
If you are given a project to manage that is beyond your qualifications or experience, make sure the sponsor knows of any gaps in your qualifications before accepting the assignment.	
Do what you say you will do—including completing projects on time.	

Responsibility—Ownership of Decisions and Actions	Areas Where I Have Had a Problem
Acknowledge your own errors.	
Respect confidentiality requirements and protect proprietary information—including obeying copyright laws.	
Uphold laws.	
If you witness or are aware of unethical behavior, report it to management and to those the behavior affects.	
Report violations of PMI's Code of Ethics and Professional Conduct when you have factual proof of the violation. If you know someone has been retaliated against because he or she reported such violations, pursue disciplinary action.	
Respect—The Appropriate Treatment of People and Resources	**Areas Where I Have Had a Problem**
Maintain an attitude of mutual cooperation.	
Respect cultural differences.	
Do not gossip or say things that could damage another person's reputation.	
Engage in good faith negotiations.	

Respect—The Appropriate Treatment of People and Resources	Areas Where I Have Had a Problem
Respect others.	
Be direct in dealing with conflict.	
Do not use your power or position to influence others for your own personal benefit.	

Fairness—Being Objective and Making Impartial Decisions	Areas Where I Have Had a Problem
Act impartially without favoritism, nepotism, bribery, or prejudice, and frequently stop to reexamine your actions to make sure you are being impartial.	
Continuously look for conflicts of interest and disclose them.	
Do not discriminate against others.	
Honor your duty of loyalty to those companies and organizations with whom you are affiliated.	
Do not use your position for personal or business gain.	

Honesty—Understanding the Truth and Taking Action Based on Truth	Areas Where I Have Had a Problem
Try to understand the truth.	
Be truthful in all communications, including making sure the information you are using or sending out is truthful.	
Work to create an environment where others tell the truth.	
Do not deceive others.	

Now let's take a more detailed look at some of the points in each category.

Responsibility—Ownership of Decisions and Actions

- **Make decisions based on the best interests of the company, rather than your own best interest** This one sounds simple, doesn't it? Watch out; if a question on this topic was asked directly, everyone would get it right, but most questions are not asked directly on the exam. For example, what about an instance where you discover the project is suffering because you have not created a project management plan, and you feel that if you tell management of the problem, you will look bad or lose your job? In such situations, the correct answer is to deal with the issue hurting the project and put the project's needs before your own. This is an easy rule to remember, but it can be difficult to apply.

- **Only accept assignments you are qualified to complete** Can you imagine saying to your boss, "I cannot take that assignment, because it requires the control of cost on the project and I am not qualified to manage costs"? Do you think your boss would accept that? Probably not. It is smart to make sure you can handle a job before it is assigned to you, but there are times when the expectations presented on the exam seem a lot more complex in the real world.

- **Protect proprietary information** When was the last time you made a copy of an article or made a copy of a music CD and gave that copy to others? Did you know that such materials are considered proprietary items and that these actions could be violating copyright laws? How about taking excerpts from this book, or any book, and putting them in a company report or in the material used for a training class without written permission of the copyright owner? These actions are also likely violations of copyright laws, as well as violations of PMI's Code of Ethics and Professional Conduct. This is an area many people have misconceptions about and it is a concept that is frequently tested on the exam, so we'll explain it in more detail. Make sure you understand the concept of protecting proprietary information.

International copyright laws give the owner of the copyright the exclusive rights to make copies of the work and to prepare derivative works based on the work. It is illegal to infringe upon these rights—that is, to use the copyrighted work in certain ways without the owner's permission. For example, without the copyright owner's permission, no one may copy or reproduce any part of a book, create new material based on or incorporating any part of a book, or sell or distribute copies of a book except in limited instances covered by the Fair Use Doctrine[1]. A copyright notice is not required on the document for something to be considered copyrighted.

The fact that copyright laws are international means that people can be prosecuted for copying works by authors outside their country. Because of recent business and legal events in many countries, the exam tests whether you know what is ethical regarding copyrighted materials. Assume all documents, software, applications, articles, books, training materials, and every other work created by someone else is considered proprietary information and copyrighted. The general rule is to not copy without written permission from the author.

When you are working with copyrighted materials, you should be mindful of the following issues:
- If you need another copy of software, does the software license give you permission to simply make a copy, or does it require you to purchase another copy?
- If you are a contractor asked to create a copyrightable work, who owns the copyright—you or the company that hired you to create it?
- If you are an employee and create a work, do you own the copyright or does your employer?

These are some basic issues confronting project managers who deal with copyrighted works. A project manager should ask questions before taking any action that could result in copyright infringement.

- **Report unethical behavior and violations** What would you do if someone in your company told you that he or she does not follow a certain company procedure? The correct answer is to report the person to those responsible for the policy.

  Do you agree with this answer? Many people find questions like this annoying or frustrating, so let's look at why the ethical choice is to report the violation. You are probably not the one who created the policy and are therefore not the best person to explain the reasons behind the policy. If you attempt to explain it to the person, you could misrepresent the policy and cost the company time and money. It is best to leave such things to those responsible for them. Does it seem more logical now? Questions on the exam may require the project manager to immediately report violations of policies, laws, or ethics to a manager or supervisor.

  The easier types of questions on this topic involve someone violating PMI's Code of Ethics and Professional Conduct or cheating on their application to become a PMP certificate holder. Review questions related to reporting unethical behavior carefully before answering them.

Respect—The Appropriate Treatment of People and Resources

- **Maintain an attitude of mutual cooperation** Many people have issues they are not even aware of regarding respect and professional responsibility. For example, think about your interactions with resource managers on a project. Are you in the habit of going to them and asking for the immediate assignment of the resources you need for your project? This action is contrary to the concepts of respect and maintaining an attitude of mutual cooperation.

Put yourself in the shoes of a resource manager for a moment. Resource managers are usually compensated for how well they do their own work, not how well they support projects. They have their own needs and responsibilities, yet many project managers treat resource managers as if they exist only to serve the project. A project manager has an ethical responsibility to provide resource managers with advance notice of what resources the project needs and the impact to the project if those resources are not available. The project manager must also provide a realistic schedule, so the resource managers know when their resources will be used on the project. That information enables the resource managers to better manage project work with their other work. This scenario is an example of both mutual cooperation and the ethical application of project management in the real world. For exam questions related to this concept, you will need to know the proper use of project management tools, techniques, and practices.

Now let's look at the team. Do you consider the reputation of each of your team members to be in your hands? How well the project goes will reflect on their careers. If a team member believes the project will be unsuccessful, the individual will remove him- or herself from as much work on the project as possible so it does not tarnish the team member's reputation. The project manager has a duty to team members that includes making sure there is a realistic schedule so they know when they really need to complete work on the project, providing a reward system, asking their opinions, asking them to contribute to the development of the project management plan, and providing formal and informal training as needed for them to effectively work on the project. Team members also need to help control the project. Do you truly treat them as members of your team, or do you treat them as servants? This is another example of the ethical application of project management in the real world.

How you choose to communicate with others also falls under this topic. Would your team members or stakeholders be surprised if you asked them what the best way is to communicate with them about various topics? Should you call them, e-mail them, or send a letter? Such actions should be commonplace. Not only does asking these types of questions show respect for the other person, but it also helps effectively plan communications.

- **Respect cultural differences** Another part of respect as it relates to professional and social responsibility has to do with cultural differences. Cultural differences can mean differences in language, cultural values, nonverbal actions, and cultural practices. If you do not plan how to handle these differences and do not monitor and control their impacts, they can easily impede the project.

  One major cause of cultural differences is ethnocentrism[2]. This is the tendency for people to look at the world primarily from the perspective of their own culture. So individuals take the viewpoint that their own group is the center of everything.

  But cultural differences do not only occur between people from different countries; they may also occur between individuals from the same country. People from different regions or areas of a country may have cultural differences. Project managers need to take actions to diminish the negative impacts and enhance the positive impacts of cultural differences. Such actions include:
  - Embrace diversity. Cultural differences can make a project more fun.
  - Prevent culture shock, the disorientation that occurs when you find yourself working with other cultures in a different environment. Training and advance research about the different cultures will help prevent culture shock.
  - Expect cultural differences to surface on the project.
  - Use clear communication to the appropriate people and in the right format, as outlined in the Communications Management chapter, to prevent cultural differences from becoming a problem.
  - Uncover cultural differences when identifying stakeholders, including differences in work ethics and practices.
  - Ask for clarification whenever a cultural difference arises.

- Discuss the topic of cultural differences at team meetings as needed.
- Follow practices in use in other countries when appropriate, as long as they do not violate laws.

- **Engage in good faith negotiations** What about engaging in good faith negotiations? Many people skip over this section because they believe it is an easy concept. But think about the real world. Have you seen someone negotiating without ever intending to enter a contract or negotiating a provision in a contract they have no intention of honoring? What about someone presenting information as a fact when the person knows at the time the information is untrue? These are examples of not negotiating in good faith.

- **Be direct in dealing with conflict** The topic of conflict is discussed in the Human Resource Management chapter, but it is also part of professional and social responsibility. In dealing with conflicts, it is inappropriate and unproductive to complain or talk about the conflict or about others involved in the conflict behind their backs. Do you see this happening in the real world? Although such behavior is very common in the real world, a project manager has a professional responsibility to deal directly and openly with the other party and say to the person, "What you have done has caused a problem. Can we discuss it?" This can be easier said than done. Imagine that the person causing the problem is powerful or uninterested, or that the person is your boss. Regardless of the situation, questions on the exam expect you to address the conflict directly and openly.

- **Do not use your power or position to influence others for your own benefit** Have you ever said to yourself, "How do I get this person to do what I want?" This could be a violation of professional and social responsibility if you are trying to influence others to do what you want, rather than what is right or most appropriate in a given situation. Project managers cannot use their power or position to pressure others for their own benefit.

Fairness—Being Objective and Making Impartial Decisions

- **Act impartially without bribery** In many countries, bribery is punishable as a crime and can result in jail time. So what is bribery? Is it bribery if someone asks you to pay a fee in order to bring machinery through a city? How about if someone requests a payment for police protection?

  In many countries, fees for services such as protection and bringing machinery through a town, or fees for issuing permits and other official documents, are allowable and are not considered bribes. Payments to convince a government official to select your company for a project are bribes, however. Many companies have policies or codes of business conduct to help prevent bribes or other illegal activity.

  What about other "payments"? Would it be appropriate to accept a free automobile or a free weekend holiday for you and your family? These "gifts" are probably not allowable. Thomas Donaldson, in *The Ethics of International Business*, suggests a practice is permissible if you can answer "No" to both of the following questions:

  1. Is it permissible to conduct business successfully in the host country without undertaking the practice?
  2. Is the practice a clear violation of a fundamental international right?

  Fundamental rights include the right to food, a fair trial, non-discriminating treatment, minimal education, physical safety, and freedom of speech.

  There will be few questions on this area on the exam, but if you feel you need more help, see the exercise later in this chapter.

- **Continuously look for conflicts of interest and disclose them** A conflict of interest is a situation that requires a person to make a decision or take action that could help one person or organization while hurting another person or organization to which they have a duty of loyalty. For example, "If I help my friend, I hurt my company," or "If I help this organization, I hurt my own company." Because the exam does not always ask questions that are direct and clear, you might have a question with entire paragraphs devoted to describing the details of a situation, when all you really need to understand is that it is a conflict of interest. So what do you do when there is a conflict of interest? You should disclose it to those affected and let them decide how to proceed. If something appears to be a conflict of interest, it should be handled as if it actually is a conflict of interest.

  What does it mean to "continuously look for conflicts of interest"? This practice involves more effort than simply noticing conflicts of interest when they arise; it involves frequently sitting down and reviewing the project for areas that have the potential to create such conflicts. You need to be proactive in this effort.

- **Do not discriminate against others** Discrimination seems to be all around us. People discriminate against those from different economic backgrounds (rich and poor), against those who are from a different area of the country or world, and against those who are a different race, religion, gender, etc. Professional and social responsibility requires us to treat others fairly and not discriminate. In some cultures, this may be hard, as certain discriminatory practices are the cultural norm and are commonly accepted. Make sure you understand how project management should be done, rather than what is common in your real world.

- **Do not use your position for personal or business gain** Most people realize that someone in government should not use their position to make him- or herself wealthy. But what about people who join organizations (such as PMI), not to help promote the organization's mission, but to gain business from other members of the organization? It is a violation of professional and social responsibility to use your position for personal interest or business gain.

Honesty—Understanding the Truth and Taking Action Based on Truth

- **Try to understand the truth** The truth is not always easy to find, especially when you are running around managing projects. Someone may tell you something that they perceive to be the truth, but there might be more to what is really going on. We often simply accept what people tell us and do not spend time seeking the whole truth. When you think of the many activities on a project and the different people involved, you can see how important it is to accurately understand a situation.

- **Be truthful in all communications, and create an environment where others tell the truth** Do you ever hide the fact that a project is in trouble? Do you say that you can accomplish some piece of work or a whole project when you are not really sure if you can? If so, you might have some issues with truthful communication. If we stretch the truth or outright lie, our team members will start to do it, too, and we have not fostered an environment where others tell the truth. As a result, the project and those involved in it, including the project manager, suffer.

  If everyone starts being untruthful, how will you know what information you can trust? Imagine you provide a schedule to the team that you know to be unreasonable or unrealistic and do not inform the team. They quickly realize the schedule is unreasonable and, as a result, do not cooperate with you or tell you what is really going on. When you take the exam, you need to understand the consequences of such actions. The consequences of being untruthful are less accurate information from others and poor cooperation.

Exercise Let's try to put it all together. Look at the following situations and determine what to do.

1. Your management has told you that you will receive part of the incentive fee from the customer if you can bring the project in early. While finalizing a major deliverable, your team informs you that the deliverable meets the requirements in the contract, but will not provide the functionality the customer needs. If the deliverable is late, you know the project will not be completed early. What action should you take?

2. You are asked to make a copy of a magazine article and include it in the internal training and support materials for the new software the project is creating. You see the article has a copyright notice. What is the best thing to do?

3. Your company is in competition to win a major project for the government of country X. You are told you must make a large payment to the foreign minister in order to be considered for the project. What is the best thing to do?

4. You provide a cost estimate for the project to the project sponsor. He is unhappy with the estimate, because he thinks the cost should be lower. He asks you to cut 15 percent off the project estimate. What should you do?

5. In reviewing the draft of the monthly project update report published by the project management office, you notice another project manager is exaggerating his project's status. You know this project manager is being untruthful because a deliverable due to your project is estimated to be delivered in two weeks. He is reporting the delivery has already taken place. What do you do?

6. You have three sellers bidding on some of your project work. You have worked with one of the sellers (X) before and know they do excellent work. The project manager from company X calls to ask for clarification on the RFP you sent out last week so they can better address your needs. What do you do?

7. As stated in situation 5, a project manager is exaggerating his project's status. You notified him of the inaccuracy, but he still did not change his monthly update. What do you do now?

8. You and a friend from college regularly attend your alma mater's sports games together. Your company has hired the firm your friend works for to do some work on your project. Your friend is not in the division that is working on your project, nor is she involved with any of the work. Your friend calls excitedly and says that due to her efforts this year, she has gotten two tickets to the division football game from her boss. She wants you to go with her. Should you go?

9. You have been asked to do a presentation about your project's status to senior management in your company and to the external customer. The day before the meeting, a delay in delivery of some critical materials has caused a two-month delay in the critical path. You do not have time to work out a plan to get the project back on track before the presentation. You feel sure the delay can be made up and don't want to scare the customer unnecessarily, nor do you want the extra work that will be required if you present the information now. What should you do?

10. You have successfully guided your project team through four of five phases of your project. Testing went especially well due to a subject matter expert's earlier input, which helped avoid a critical threat from occurring. At the quarterly senior management review, they specifically comment about how great you are doing with the project so far, especially with testing, and congratulate you. How do you respond?

Answers The answers depend on the exact wording of the choices, but generally:

1. Review the situation with the customer; review what is required in the contract.
2. Ask the copyright owner for permission.
3. Refuse to make the payment; it is a bribe.
4. Look for options such as schedule compression, reestimating, or changing scope.
5. Hold the project manager accountable by notifying him of the discrepancy and reporting accurately on your own project.
6. Either provide ALL sellers the additional information or do not provide the information to the project manager from company X.
7. Report the other project manager's dishonesty to both your boss and his.
8. No, because this could be perceived as a conflict of interest, which must be avoided.

9. You should present the current status of the project, without downplaying or minimizing the effect of the delay. You cannot bury the bad news in an effort to avoid conflict. You need to present the information, along with your planned approach for coming up with possible solutions to the problem, and provide the customer with a timeline for when they should expect an update.
10. You need to give credit to the subject matter expert and let senior management know the expert's input really helped ensure the testing process went smoothly. You cannot take credit for the good work of others, nor can you pass blame down to others.

Professional and social responsibility can seem easy at first but can quickly get complicated. This is an important topic to understand, not just for the exam but also in the real world. Unethical and unprofessional behavior hurts the project, the organization, and the profession. As project managers, and especially as PMP certification holders, we have a responsibility to uphold the standards of the profession and prove the value project management brings to all who benefit from successful project results.

Practice Exam

1. A project manager is being considered for a particular project that will deal exclusively with global virtual teams. He only has experience with local teams. What should he do when discussing the opportunity with the sponsor?
   A. Since he has managed many projects and teams, it does not make any difference that the new project involves global virtual teams. He should tell the sponsor he has the relevant experience.
   B. He should avoid any conversation regarding the types of teams involved so the sponsor does not know he lacks experience in this area.
   C. The project manager should point out to the sponsor that he has not had experience with global virtual teams, but discuss why he thinks he is a good fit for the project anyway.
   D. The project manager should point out to the sponsor that he has not had experience with global virtual teams and therefore must decline the assignment.

2. A project manager gathered data to perform earned value calculations on his project. He used the results to report to management that the project is under budget and on schedule. After reporting this information, he discovered the base figures he used in the calculations were incorrect, as they came from an old copy of the project file that had not been updated. What should he do now?
   A. He should contact management to make them aware of the error, give the correct information, and explain how he made the mistake.
   B. He should contact management and tell them to expect some changes in the next reporting period, and that things are starting to look gloomy.
   C. He should use the correct figures to calculate the information when it is time for the next report and ignore the fact that he reported incorrect information.
   D. He should tell management that the data he received from team members was incorrect and thus the report was not accurate.

3. A project manager is working with a vendor on a project when she learns one of the sellers has bribed a subcontractor to work on this project instead of fulfilling previous commitments to other projects. What should she do?
   A. She should report the offense to management and the project managers of the affected projects.
   B. She should not do anything because this is the vendor's problem. The project manager herself didn't do anything wrong.
   C. She should report this to other subcontractors so they know they could get more money from the vendor.
   D. She should resign from the project so as to remove herself from this type of activity, but keep it to herself rather than cause problems.

4. You are in the middle of a new product development project for your publicly traded company when you discover the previous project manager made a US $3,000,000 payment that was not approved in accordance with your company policies. Luckily, the project cost performance index (CPI) is 1.2. What should you do?
   A. Contact your manager.
   B. Put the payment in an escrow account.
   C. Bury the cost in the largest cost center available.
   D. Ignore the payment.

5. While staffing a project in another country, the project leader from that country comes to you with a suggested team consisting of members of the project leader's family. Your FIRST course of action should be to:
   A. Inquire if hiring only through family lines is common practice in the project leader's country.
   B. Review the resumes of the individuals to see if they are qualified.
   C. Ask the project leader to provide additional names of people unrelated to him/her.
   D. Use a different project leader to prevent problems later in the project.

6. When checking the calendar of a team member to schedule a meeting, you see she has scheduled a meeting with a key stakeholder that you were not informed of. The BEST approach would be to:
   A. Avoid mentioning it to the team member but continue to watch her activities.
   B. Notify your boss about the problem.
   C. Address the concern with the team member's boss.
   D. Address the concern with the team member.

7. Your employee is three days late with a report. Five minutes before the meeting where the topic of the report is to be discussed, she hands you the report. You notice some serious errors in it. What should you do?
   A. Cancel the meeting and reschedule when the report is fixed.
   B. Go to the meeting and tell the other attendees there are errors in the report.
   C. Allow the employee to do the presentation and remain silent as the other attendees find the errors.
   D. Cancel the meeting and rewrite the report yourself.

8. A manager has responsibility for a project that has the support of a senior manager. From the beginning, you have disagreed with the manager as to how the project should proceed and what the deliverables should be. You and she have disagreed over many issues in the past. Your department has been tasked with providing some key work packages for the project. What should you do?
   A. Provide the manager with what she needs.
   B. Inform your manager of your concerns to get her support.
   C. Sit down with the manager at the beginning of the project and attempt to describe why you object to the project, and discover a way to solve the problem.
   D. Ask to be removed from the project.

9. A large, complex construction project in a foreign country requires coordination to move needed equipment through crowded city streets. To ensure the equipment is transported successfully, your contact in that country informs you that you will have to pay the local police a fee for coordinating traffic. What should you do?
   A. Do not pay the fee because it is a bribe.
   B. Eliminate the work.
   C. Pay the fee.
   D. Do not pay the fee if it is not part of the project estimate.

10. A major negotiation with a potential subcontractor is scheduled for tomorrow when you discover there is a good chance the project will be cancelled. What should you do?
    A. Do not spend too much time preparing for the negotiations.
    B. Cut the negotiations short.
    C. Only negotiate major items.
    D. Postpone the negotiations.

11. You've been assigned to take over managing a project that should be half complete according to the schedule. After an extensive evaluation, you discover the project is running far behind schedule, and the project will probably take twice the time originally estimated by the previous project manager. However, the sponsor has been told the project is on schedule. What is the BEST course of action?
    A. Try to restructure the schedule to meet the project deadline.
    B. Report your assessment to the sponsor.
    C. Turn the project back to the previous project manager.
    D. Move forward with the schedule as planned by the previous project manager and report at the first missed milestone.

12. You are halfway through a major network rollout. There are 300 locations in the United States with another 20 in England. A software seller has just released a major software upgrade for some of the equipment being installed. The upgrade would provide the customer with functionality they requested, which was not available at the time the project began. What is the BEST course of action under these circumstances?
    A. Continue as planned; your customer has not requested a change.
    B. Inform the customer of the upgrade and the impacts to the project's timeline and functionality if the upgrade is implemented.
    C. Implement the change and adjust the schedule as necessary because this supports the customer's original request.
    D. Implement the change on the remaining sites and continue with the schedule.

13. You are a project manager for one of many projects in a large and important program. At a high-level status meeting, you note that another project manager has reported her project on schedule. Looking back on your project over the last few weeks, you remember many deliverables from the other project that arrived late. What should you do?
    A. Meet with the program manager.
    B. Develop a risk control plan.
    C. Discuss the issue with your boss.
    D. Meet with the other project manager.

14. You have always been asked by your management to cut your project cost estimate by 10 percent after you have given it to them. The scope of your new project is unclear and there are over 30 stakeholders. Management expects a 25 percent reduction in downtime as a result of the project. Which of the following is the BEST course of action in this situation?
    A. Replan to achieve a 35 percent improvement in downtime.
    B. Reduce the estimates and note the changes in the risk response plan.
    C. Provide an accurate estimate of the actual costs and be able to support it.
    D. Meet with the team to identify where you can find 10 percent savings.

15. Your employee is three days late with a report. She walks into a meeting and hands you a copy of the report five minutes before the topic is to be discussed. You notice some serious errors in the report. How could this have been prevented?
    A. Require periodic updates from the employee.
    B. Coach and mentor the employee.
    C. Make sure the employee was competent to do the work.
    D. Cancel the meeting earlier because you did not have a chance to review the report.

16. You are in the middle of a project when you discover that a software seller for your project is having major difficulty keeping employees due to a labor dispute. Many other projects in your company are also using the company's services. What should you do?
    A. Attempt to keep the required people on your project.
    B. Tell the other project managers in your company about the labor problem.
    C. Contact the company and advise that you will cancel the company's work on your project unless the labor dispute is settled.
    D. Cease doing business with the company.

17. All of the following are responsibilities of a project manager EXCEPT:
    A. Maintain the confidentiality of customer confidential information.
    B. Determine the legality of company procedures.
    C. Ensure that a conflict of interest does not compromise the legitimate interest of the customer.
    D. Provide accurate and truthful representations in cost estimates.

18. Although your company is not the lowest bidder for a project, the client has come to expect good performance from your company and wants to award the contract to you. To win the contract, the client asks you to eliminate your project management costs. The client says your company has good project processes, and project controls unnecessarily inflate your costs. What should you do under these circumstances?
    A. Eliminate your project management costs and rely on experience.
    B. Remove costs associated with project team communications, meetings, and customer reviews.
    C. Remove meeting costs but not the project manager's salary.
    D. Describe the costs incurred on past projects that did not use project management.

19. You are the project manager for one part of a new program in your organization. You are four months into a three-year project when your project team makes significant discoveries on your project. What is the BEST thing to do?
    A. Make certain the discoveries are included in the project lessons learned.
    B. Make certain the discoveries are reported in the monthly status report.
    C. Make certain you mention the discoveries at the senior management meeting in two months.
    D. At the weekly meeting, make certain you tell the other project managers involved in this program about the discoveries.

20. You have just discovered an error in the implementation plan that will prevent you from meeting a milestone date. The BEST thing you can do is:
    A. Develop options to meet the milestone date.
    B. Change the milestone date.
    C. Remove any discussion about dates in the project status report.
    D. Educate the team about the need to meet milestones.

21. While testing the strength of concrete poured on your project, you discover that over 35 percent of the concrete does not meet your company's quality standards. You feel certain the concrete will function as it is, and you don't think the concrete needs to meet the quality level specified. What should you do?
    A. Change the quality standards to meet the level achieved.
    B. List in your reports that the concrete simply "meets our quality needs."
    C. Ensure the remaining concrete meets the standard.
    D. Report the lesser quality level and try to find a solution.

22. You are the project manager for a new international project, and your project team includes people from four countries. Most of the team members have not worked on similar projects before, but the project has strong support from senior management. What is the BEST thing to do to ensure that cultural differences do not interfere with the project?
    A. Spend a little more time creating the work breakdown structure and making sure it is complete.
    B. As the project manager, make sure you choose your words carefully whenever you communicate.
    C. Ask one person at each team meeting to describe something unique about their culture.
    D. Carefully encode all of the project communications.

23. A project has a tight budget when you begin negotiating with a seller for a piece of equipment. The seller has told you the equipment price is fixed. Your manager has told you to negotiate the cost with the seller. What is your BEST course of action?
    A. Make a good faith effort to find a way to decrease the cost.
    B. Postpone negotiations until you can convince your manager to change his mind.
    C. Hold the negotiations, but only negotiate other aspects of the project.
    D. Cancel the negotiations.

24. A PMP-certified project manager is contacted by PMI and asked to provide information regarding another project manager who has been reported to be involved in unethical activities. The PMP-certified project manager knows his information would support the accusations, and the other project manager in question is a friend. He decides the best thing to do would be to not respond, and therefore neither confirm nor deny the accusations. Would this be the right thing to do?
    A. Yes. It would be a safe thing to do to just ignore the request and stay out of it.
    B. No. If he knows something, he is required by the Code of Ethics and Professional Conduct to cooperate.
    C. No. It would be better to deny the charges against his friend to maintain the relationship.
    D. Yes. It is expected that project managers will support each other in the field.

25. A project manager discovers a defect in a deliverable that is due to the customer under contract today. The project manager knows the customer does not have the technical understanding to notice the defect. The deliverable meets the contract requirements, but it does not meet the project manager's quality standard. What should the project manager do in this situation?
    A. Issue the deliverable and get formal acceptance from the customer.
    B. Note the problem in the lessons learned so future projects do not encounter the same problem.
    C. Discuss the issue with the customer.
    D. Inform the customer that the deliverable will be late.

26. Your company wants to open a plant in a country where the law stipulates that women can earn only 50 percent of what men earn. Under these circumstances, what should you recommend to your company?
    A. Do not open the plant.
    B. Your company should meet with government officials and try to get a waiver that equalizes the rate between men and women.
    C. Do not hire women.
    D. Provide the women you hire with extra work to increase their salary.

27. Three students from another country are working as interns on a project. The project manager has arranged for some games to play as team-building activities to help create a close-knit sense of team with the group members. At the event where the activities are taking place, the three students refuse to participate, claiming the behavior involved is unacceptable in their country and they would be very uncomfortable participating. What should the project manager do?
    A. He should tell the students they need to become familiar with how things are done in this country and they must play along.
    B. He should excuse the students from playing and arrange to discuss with them alternative team-building activities they would be more comfortable with.
    C. He should report the students to their functional manager and request they be removed from the project since their attitude will have a negative impact on the project.
    D. He should tell the students they are excused from the activities and to not attend any team-building activities in the future.

28. A project manager discovers an urgent need for outsourced resources on the project. He knows he has the money to cover the cost of these resources. He goes to the procurement manager and explains the situation, insisting a contract be drawn up today so he can obtain resources and circumvent the standard procedure. Is this the correct process to follow?
    A. Yes. For urgent needs, it is not necessary to follow the organization's procedure regarding procurement.
    B. Yes. Urgent needs from projects should always be dealt with immediately as directed by the project manager.
    C. No. The procurement manager has a process to follow when creating contracts that helps protect the company and its projects.
    D. No. The procurement manager should be checking in with the project manager to see if he is in need of a contract, rather than making the project manager come and ask for one.

29. The engineering department wants the project objective to be a 10 percent improvement in throughput. The information technology department wants no more than 5 percent of its resources to be used on the project. Management, who is also your boss, wants the project team to decrease tax liability. The BEST thing you can do is:
    A. Put a plan together that meets all the objectives.
    B. Have these people get together and agree on one objective.
    C. Include the engineering and information technology objectives but hold further meetings regarding management's objective.
    D. Include only management's objective.

30. You are finalizing the monthly project status report due now to your manager when you discover that several project team members are not reporting actual hours spent on project activities. This results in skewed project statistics. What is the MOST appropriate action to take?
    A. Discuss the impacts of these actions with team members.
    B. Report the team members' actions to their functional managers.
    C. Continue reporting information as presented to you.
    D. Provide accurate and truthful representations in all project reports.

Answers

1. **Answer** C
   Explanation There are many issues that will be different in this project than those the project manager has experience with. It is unethical to overtly or indirectly mislead the sponsor about his qualifications. On the other hand, the project manager may have so many skills that would benefit the project that his lack of experience with global teams might not be a major problem. The project manager must make sure the sponsor is aware of the gaps in his qualifications, so the sponsor has the correct information on which to base his decision.

2. **Answer** A
   Explanation Although things may be gloomy, this is not a new development, since the report was based on old data. It is unethical for the project manager not to admit his mistake, or to blame someone else for his error. The ethical thing to do is to acknowledge and take responsibility for the error.

3. **Answer** A
   Explanation It is the responsibility of the project manager to report unethical behavior to management and those affected. Not reporting this knowledge to the appropriate people is unethical.

4. **Answer** A
   Explanation Putting the payment in an escrow account or burying the cost hides it. Ignoring the payment is not an option. Project managers must deal with potentially unethical situations like the situation described. This payment must be brought to the attention of the project manager's manager.

5. **Answer** A
   Explanation Ask yourself, what is the root problem? Your first action would be to find out whether working with family members is a common practice in that country, as there is nothing inherently illegal in this activity. Then, you would review qualifications. You may find it is not necessary to ask the project leader to provide additional names, or to consider using a different project leader.

6. **Answer** D
   Explanation Not mentioning the issue to the team member is withdrawal. Notifying your boss or the team member's boss would not be appropriate until you learn the root cause of the problem. Always look for the choice that deals with and solves the problem. In this case, the best course of action is to address your concern with the team member directly.

7. **Answer** A
   Explanation Allowing the employee to deliver the inaccurate report is penalizing and embarrassing her. The only choice that does not involve decreasing the employee's morale or wasting the time of the other attendees is to cancel the meeting, and reschedule when you and the employee have identified and addressed the root cause of the problem with the report.

8. **Answer** A
   Explanation We assume that proper project management was followed and your opinion was considered during project initiating. Therefore, you need to provide the work as approved by management.

9. **Answer** C
   Explanation This is fee for service paid to a government official. It is not a bribe.

10. **Answer** D
    Explanation Postponing the negotiations is the most ethical choice and demonstrates good faith. Why spend time in negotiations if it may be wasted time?

11. **Answer** B
    Explanation It is not possible to turn the project back to the previous project manager, as the previous project manager may have left the company, or he may be busy with new projects. That is a form of withdrawal. Moving ahead without addressing the situation also withdraws from the problem, and withdrawal is not the best choice. There are two problems described here; the project is behind schedule, and the sponsor does not know it. There seem to be two possible right answers; restructuring the schedule, and reporting the situation to the sponsor. You should work to get the project on schedule. However, looking only at restructuring the schedule excludes other possibilities, such as cutting scope, which might more effectively deal with the schedule problem. You do not know if the project completion date is critical. What if the sponsor would agree to change the due date? The best choice in this situation is to inform the sponsor of the revised completion time estimate, and discuss options.

12. **Answer** B
    Explanation Professional and social responsibility includes looking after the customer's best interests. Therefore, ignoring the newly available upgrade cannot be best. In this case, the schedule and scope are already approved and all changes must go through the integrated change control process. Therefore, implementing the change on any of the sites without following the process is not acceptable. The best option is to inform the customer of the available upgrade and the impacts to the project's timeline and functionality if the upgrade is implemented.

13. **Answer** D
    Explanation You should confront the situation by discussing it with the other project manager. You can then find out if the other project is really on schedule and thereby confirm or deny your information. Meeting with the program manager or with your boss would be the next step if meeting with the other project manager validates your concern. You might also develop a risk response plan to deal with the risk to your project. First, though, you need to meet with the other project manager regarding those late deliverables.

14. **Answer** C
    Explanation This is a common problem on projects. If your estimates are accurate, you are ethically bound to stand by them. Management's only option to cut cost is to support the project manager in looking for alternatives related to all project constraints.

15. **Answer** D
    Explanation Both requiring updates from the employee and cancelling the meeting could have prevented the outcome, but cancelling the meeting is the only one that would ensure you were not sitting in a meeting with a document that had not been reviewed.

16. **Answer** B
    Explanation Attempting to keep the required people on your project puts your interests over those of your company, so it cannot be the best choice. There is no indication that the labor dispute has caused any problems, so there is no need to cancel this work or to cease doing business with the company. The best choice would be to inform others in your company about the labor dispute.

17. **Answer** B
    Explanation The project manager is neither empowered nor competent to determine the legality of company procedures.

18. **Answer** D
    Explanation Describing the costs on past projects incurred due to project management processes not being used addresses the real problem by giving the client information they may not have. An alternate choice is to explain that project management and its associated costs are reasons for the company's past performance and success. Project management activities are not optional.

19. **Answer** D
    Explanation The sooner such discoveries are made known to other project managers, the better you can improve the capabilities of colleagues in your company. It is part of a project manager's professional and social responsibility to build such capabilities. The discoveries should also be documented in the project lessons learned and the status report, especially if that report has a wider distribution.

20. **Answer** A
    Explanation Educating the team on the importance of milestones is not addressing the real problem. Changing the milestone date is unethical. Avoiding mention of the due date in the status report violates the rule to report honestly. Only developing and reporting options to meet the milestone date solves the problem.

21. **Answer** D
    Explanation Changing the quality standards or stating that the concrete "meets our quality needs" are unethical. Ensuring that the remaining concrete meets the existing quality standards withdraws from the problem and is therefore not the best solution. The only possible choice is to report the lesser quality level. That choice would involve quality and other experts to find a resolution.

22. **Answer** C
    Explanation Since this is an issue involving everyone, everyone should be involved in the solution. Spending extra time with the team on creating the WBS is generally a good idea, but it does not specifically address cultural issues. The best choice is to ask one person at each team meeting to describe something unique about their culture. This will lead to better understanding among people of different cultures, and help to avoid potential culture-related problems.

23. **Answer** A
    Explanation There is always a way to decrease costs on the project. The best choice is to attempt to find a way to decrease the cost.

24. **Answer** B
    Explanation Ignoring the request from PMI or lying for the project manager do not support PMI's request for information and are unethical actions. PMI's Code of Ethics and Professional Conduct requires PMP-certified project managers to report unethical behavior and violations of the code. The PMP-certified project manager is obligated to cooperate with PMI in collecting information.

25. **Answer** C
Explanation Issuing the deliverable as it is does not protect the best interests of the customer. Simply noting the issue in lessons learned does not solve the problem. Informing the customer that the deliverable will be late will cause a default of contract. Although the deliverable meets the contractual requirements, it is best to bring the problem to the customer's attention so an option that does no harm can be found.

26. **Answer** A
Explanation Working under these rules would be a clear violation of the fundamental right to nondiscriminating treatment. You should recommend that your company not open the plant in that location.

27. **Answer** B
Explanation Insisting that the team members participate is forcing them to do something that is unacceptable in their culture. Requesting their removal from the project penalizes the team members for expressing their cultural preferences, which is not a valid reason to remove them. Excluding them from all future team building does not show respect for their culture, and would have a negative impact on the project. Excusing them from playing, and discussing alternative activities for the whole team with which they would be more comfortable is best because it demonstrates respect for cultural differences.

28. **Answer** C
Explanation Procrastination or a lack of planning on the part of the project manager does not create an emergency situation for the procurement manager. Circumventing the process is not ethical. Projects may not always come first, and the project manager does not have authority over the procurement manager. It is not a common practice, nor is it logical, for a procurement manager to regularly check with a project manager to inquire if he or she is in need of a contract. The project manager should show respect for the procurement manager and the processes in place to protect the organization, and allow sufficient time for the contract to be completed.

29. **Answer** C
Explanation Did this one catch you? All the objectives should be met, but they must be quantifiable. Management's objective cannot be measured and, therefore, needs more work. You need to have more discussions with management so you can make their objective quantifiable. Then you will be able to create a plan that meets all the objectives.

30. **Answer** D
Explanation The project manager's responsibility is to provide truthful project information. He or she should thereafter discuss the impacts of their actions with the team members. If that does not work, the next step is to report it to their functional managers. In the meantime, the project manager must report the status as accurately as possible.

CHAPTER FOURTEEN The PMP Exam: Tips for Passing the Exam the First Time

Are you worried you might fail the exam? It is natural to be worried, but here is something that may help increase your confidence: RMC has spent years counseling people who have failed the exam, and we have addressed all the reasons they failed in this book. This chapter serves as a review of some of the key things you need to know. Take this opportunity to find any remaining gaps in your knowledge so you are prepared to pass the exam on your first try.

TRICKS OF THE TRADE® Putting It All Together

Many people studying for the exam study each topic individually and never put it all together. Rita's Process Chart is one trick designed to help you connect the ideas in this book. If you worked through the accompanying games in chapter 3, you should understand the overall project management process and know the efforts involved in it. Now let's look at additional information and exercises to help you put all the concepts together.

There are some themes that appear throughout the *PMBOK® Guide*. There are also some terms that are repeated in most knowledge areas. These are not necessarily the most important topics to know, but understanding them will help you see how each concept relates to the overall project management process. Because they appear so often in the process, you may frequently see these concepts on the exam. Hopefully you also use them regularly as you manage projects in your real world.

The following are some of the frequently occurring concepts you need to understand for the exam:

Organizational Process Assets How many times have you seen the term "organizational process assets" in preparing for the exam? Do you understand what it really means? Organizational process assets are an organization's existing processes, procedures, and historical information. With this definition in mind, can you see why they are inputs to many of the individual project management processes from initiating to closing? Remember that organizational process assets are a PMI-ism. They are considered to be inputs even when they are not specifically listed in this book or in the *PMBOK® Guide*. Similarly, updates to the organizational process assets are outputs of many processes. These updates can provide valuable templates, records, lessons learned, and other information for future projects.

Enterprise Environmental Factors Enterprise environmental factors are inputs to nearly as many processes as organizational process assets are. As noted earlier in this book, think of enterprise environmental factors as company culture and existing systems that the project will have to deal with or can make use of. Remember that enterprise environmental factors are a PMI-ism. Like organizational process assets, they are considered to be inputs even when they are not specifically listed in this book or in the *PMBOK® Guide*. Updates to these factors are outputs of many processes as well. Enterprise environmental factors updates provide valuable historical data regarding the company's culture or its systems for the benefit of future projects.

Management Plans for Each Knowledge Area Planning is a key step in addressing the knowledge areas of scope, time, cost, quality, human resource, communications, risk, and procurement management. Some knowledge areas have a designated planning process (i.e., Plan Quality, Develop Human Resource Plan, Plan Communications, Plan Risk Management, and Plan Procurements) that results in the management plan for that knowledge area. Scope, time, and cost management do not have their own planning processes, however. Instead, the scope management plan, schedule management plan, and cost management plan are created as part of the Develop Project Management Plan process in integration management. All management plans become part of the project management plan.

Project Management Plan The project management plan is discussed in the Integration Management chapter and throughout this book. This plan contains the blueprint for the project. Thus, it is an input to many executing and monitoring and controlling processes, as well as the two closing processes on a project. Work is compared against the plan to ensure that the correct work is being accomplished. Because the plan is the blueprint for the project, it needs to be maintained and kept up to date when there are changes. Therefore, project management plan updates are an output of most of the executing and monitoring and controlling processes (see the Project Management Plan Updates and Project Document Updates discussion for more on this topic).

Baselines Baselines help the project manager control the project. This is an important concept for the exam. The knowledge areas of scope, time, and cost have baselines, which combine to create the performance measurement baseline for the project. How well the project is performing in terms of scope, time, and cost is then measured against these baselines. Changes to the project management plan that are approved in the Perform Integrated Change Control process result in changes to the appropriate baseline.

- **Scope baseline** This baseline includes the WBS, WBS dictionary, and project scope statement. It is an input to the processes of Define Activities, Estimate Costs, Determine Budget, Plan Quality, Identify Risks, and Plan Procurements.
- **Schedule baseline** This is a version of the project schedule. It is an input to the Plan Quality process.
- **Cost baseline** The cost baseline includes all budgets, but it does NOT include management reserves. It is an input to the Plan Quality and Plan Procurements processes.

Project Management Plan Updates and Project Document Updates Updates to the project management plan and project documents are frequent outputs of the project management processes, including most executing processes and almost all of the monitoring and controlling processes. Do you know why? The project documentation needs to be updated to reflect adjustments, actions, and changes on the project. These updates ensure everyone has a common understanding of the project as it progresses and allow the project manager to reliably use the documentation to measure and control the project.

Is it clear to you what is included in the project management plan and what is included in the project documents? The project management plan includes the individual management plans for each knowledge area (i.e., scope, time, cost, quality, human resource, communications, risk, and procurement management), the baselines for the project, the requirements management plan, the change management plan, the configuration management plan, and the process improvement plan. Therefore, updates to the project management plan include updates to any of these components.

Project documents include the other documentation that can be used to manage a project, such as the requirements traceability matrix, the stakeholder register, the activity list, quality checklists, the risk register, the change log, resource calendars, the issue log, etc.

Project Scope Statement The project scope statement is created during the Define Scope process. It spells out the deliverables of the project. This document is used to create the WBS. It is also an input to time, cost, quality, risk, and procurement management planning.

Work Performance Information Work performance information comes out of the Direct and Manage Project Execution process. It is information about the status of the deliverables being produced on the project. This information is then used (is an input) in most monitoring and controlling processes.

Expert Judgment Expert judgment is the most common tool and technique of project management. This term refers to using the knowledge and experience of someone who has done the types of things you are about to do. Although it is not often discussed in this book, it is used throughout the project in every process group, including in every integration management process (i.e., Develop Project Charter, Develop Project Management Plan, Direct and Manage Project Execution, Monitor and Control Project Work, Perform Integrated Change Control, and Close Project or Phase). Expert judgment is particularly valuable in planning a project and is a tool and technique of many of the individual planning processes.

Change Requests Change requests include recommended corrective and preventive actions and defect repair. They are outputs of the planning process of Plan Procurements; the executing processes of Direct and Manage Project Execution, Perform Quality Assurance, Manage Project Team, Manage Stakeholder Expectations, and Conduct Procurements; and all the monitoring and controlling processes except the Perform Integrated Change Control process. Change requests are inputs to Perform Integrated Change Control, where they are reviewed. Approved change requests are then inputs to Direct and Manage Project Execution, where the changes are implemented.

Understanding Inputs and Outputs What about other inputs and outputs? Many people who have not had good project management training stress over memorizing the inputs and outputs. Do you realize how many inputs and outputs there are, and how much time you could waste focusing on memorization? Since the exam will test your ability to apply knowledge, such memorization would prove to be a waste of your valuable time, and it does not benefit you in the real world. If you know Rita's Process Chart and understand project management, you can use logic to identify most of the key inputs and outputs that could be on the exam, rather than relying on memorization. For example, if you know what a WBS is, you should understand that you need information about scope and requirements to create the WBS. Therefore, the project scope statement and requirements documentation (both of which are created prior to the WBS in the planning process) are major inputs. If you understand the integrated change control process, you should know that it results in updates to project documents and components of the project management plan affected by approved changes. The following exercises will give you some additional help with inputs and outputs.

TRICKS OF THE TRADE® **Exercise** The following are the most important project management processes for which you should know the inputs and outputs. Enter the inputs and outputs for each process, including any real-world inputs and outputs that you can think of that are not in the *PMBOK® Guide*. When you are finished, check your answers with the *PMBOK® Guide* and the rest of this book.

Project Management Process	Key Inputs	Key Outputs
Define Activities		
Sequence Activities		
Close Project or Phase		
Plan Procurements		
Develop Project Management Plan		
Collect Requirements		
Direct and Manage Project Execution		
Estimate Activity Resources		
Develop Schedule		
Define Scope		

Project Management Process	Key Inputs	Key Outputs
Verify Scope		
Identify Stakeholders		
Conduct Procurements		

Exercise Here is one more TRICK to getting more familiar with the project management processes. For each of the processes listed, fill in the appropriate information in the columns.

Project Management Process	Knowledge Area	Process Group	What Does It Mean?	What Knowledge Area Process Comes Before?	What Knowledge Area Process Comes After?
Define Activities					
Sequence Activities					
Plan Procurements					
Develop Project Management Plan					
Collect Requirements					

Project Management Process	Knowledge Area	Process Group	What Does It Mean?	What Knowledge Area Process Comes Before?	What Knowledge Area Process Comes After?
Direct and Manage Project Execution					
Develop Schedule					
Define Scope					
Verify Scope					
Identify Stakeholders					
Conduct Procurements					
Monitor and Control Project Work					
Perform Integrated Change Control					

Answer As you read the answers to this exercise, notice the words, "Whatever needs to be done." They are repeated often and are meant to hint at all the soft, interpersonal activity needed, as well as the project management and technical activity needed.

Project Management Process	Knowledge Area	Process Group	What Does It Mean?	What Knowledge Area Process Comes Before?	What Knowledge Area Process Comes After?
Define Activities	Time management	Planning	Whatever needs to be done to create an activity list from each work package	None	Sequence Activities
Sequence Activities	Time management	Planning	Whatever needs to be done to create a network diagram	Define Activities	Estimate Activity Resources
Plan Procurements	Procurement management	Planning	Whatever needs to be done to create the procurement statement of work, procurement documents, and the procurement management plan	None	Conduct Procurements
Develop Project Management Plan	Integration management	Planning	Whatever needs to be done to create a project management plan that is bought into, approved, realistic, and formal	Develop Project Charter	Direct and Manage Project Execution
Collect Requirements	Scope management	Planning	Whatever needs to be done to finalize and document detailed requirements and determine how they will be managed	None	Define Scope
Direct and Manage Project Execution	Integration management	Executing	Producing work according to the project management plan	Develop Project Management Plan	Monitor and Control Project Work

Project Management Process	Knowledge Area	Process Group	What Does It Mean?	What Knowledge Area Process Comes Before?	What Knowledge Area Process Comes After?
Develop Schedule	Time management	Planning	Whatever needs to be done to create a bought into, approved, realistic, and formal schedule and schedule baseline	Estimate Activity Durations	Control Schedule
Define Scope	Scope management	Planning	Whatever needs to be done to create the project scope statement	Collect Requirements	Create WBS
Verify Scope	Scope management	Monitoring and controlling	Meeting with the customer to gain formal acceptance of interim deliverables	Create WBS	Control Scope
Identify Stakeholders	Communications management	Initiating	Identifying and documenting information about the stakeholders on the project	None	Plan Communications
Conduct Procurements	Procurement management	Executing	Whatever needs to be done to select a seller based on the seller responses and obtain a signed contract	Plan Procurements	Administer Procurements
Monitor and Control Project Work	Integration management	Monitoring and controlling	Whatever needs to be done to measure performance against the project management plan and request changes	Direct and Manage Project Execution	Perform Integrated Change Control
Perform Integrated Change Control	Integration management	Monitoring and controlling	Whatever needs to be done to evaluate the impact to the project constraints and approve or reject change requests	Monitor and Control Project Work	Close Project or Phase

Formulas to Know for the Exam

Although we do not suggest you memorize a lot of information to prepare for the exam, the following formulas are some of the items you do need to memorize, as well as understand. There will not be a lot of questions requiring you to use these formulas, but it will be helpful to be able to apply these at a moment's notice. If you are not comfortable with math, you should be happy to hear that you can know none of these formulas and still pass the exam! The most important formulas are those relating to earned value, as earned value is a key component of monitoring and controlling.

Formulas to Know for the Exam

Title	Formula	*PMP® Exam Prep* Chapter Reference
PERT expected activity duration (EAD)	$\frac{P + 4M + O}{6}$	Time Management
Standard deviation of an activity (SD)	$\frac{P - O}{6}$	Time Management
Variance of an activity	$\left[\frac{P - O}{6}\right]^2$ *Also stated as standard deviation squared*	Time Management
Range of an activity duration	EAD +/– SD	Time Management
Total float	LS – ES, or LF – EF	Time Management
Cost Variance (CV)	EV – AC	Cost Management
Schedule Variance (SV)	EV – PV	Cost Management
Cost Performance Index (CPI), or Cumulative CPI (CPI^C)	$\frac{EV}{AC}$ or $\frac{EV^C}{AC^C}$	Cost Management
Schedule Performance Index (SPI)	$\frac{EV}{PV}$	Cost Management
Estimate at Completion (EAC)	AC + Bottom-up ETC	Cost Management
Estimate at Completion (EAC)	$\frac{BAC}{CPI^C}$	Cost Management
Estimate at Completion (EAC)	AC + (BAC – EV)	Cost Management
Estimate at Completion (EAC)	$AC + \frac{(BAC - EV)}{(CPI^C \times SPI^C)}$	Cost Management
To Complete Performance Index (TCPI)	$\frac{(BAC - EV)}{(BAC - AC)}$	Cost Management
Estimate to Complete (ETC)	EAC – AC	Cost Management
Variance at Completion (VAC)	BAC – EAC	Cost Management
Communication channels	$\frac{N(N - 1)}{2}$	Communications Management
Expected Monetary Value	EMV = P × I	Risk Management
Point of Total Assumption (PTA)	$\frac{\text{Ceiling price} - \text{Target price}}{\text{Buyer's share ratio}} + \text{Target Cost}$	Procurement Management

Before You Take the Exam

Many people fail the exam because their preparation was faulty. You can avoid that mistake. Read the following tips slowly, and honestly assess how each item applies to you.

If you purchased this book directly from RMC, you should have received tips about how to use the *PMBOK® Guide* along with this book to help prepare for the exam.

- Know the material thoroughly, but do not approach the exam assuming it tests the memorization of facts. The exam tests knowledge, application, and analysis! You must understand how to use the concepts and processes in the real world, and how they work in combination with each other in the context of a large project.
- Have real-world experience using all the major project management tools and techniques. If you do not have this experience now, try to get it. If you cannot get this experience before you take the exam, make sure you can visualize how the tools and processes would be used on real projects. This visualization will help you see the potential challenges of using project management tools and techniques in the real world and help you prepare for the situational questions on the exam.
- As noted throughout this book, make sure you are thinking in terms of large projects when studying for and taking the actual exam.
- Read the *PMBOK® Guide*.
- Understand the areas PMI emphasizes (PMI-isms, explained in Chapter 1 and throughout this book).
- Be familiar with the types of questions you can expect on the exam, as explained in Chapter 1, but do not get caught off guard if you see new types of questions on the exam.
- Be prepared to see ambiguous and wordy questions on the exam that might be multiple paragraphs long. Practice interpreting these types of questions.
- If you have *PM FASTrack®*, practice being able to pick an answer from what appears to be two or three "right" answers.
- Decide in advance what notes you will write down when you are given a piece of scrap paper at the actual exam. You can use it as a download sheet for formulas or gaps in your project management knowledge.
- Deal with your stress BEFORE you take the exam. There is a free tip for nervous test takers on our Web site, www.rmcproject.com. In addition, if you are a nervous test taker, using *PM FASTrack®* can give you an opportunity to practice stress control during the exam simulation.
- Plan and use your strategy for taking the exam. This may mean, "I will take a 10-minute break after every 50 questions because I get tired quickly," or "I will answer all the questions as quickly as possible and then take a break and review my answers."
- Expect that there will be questions you cannot answer or even understand. This happens to everyone. Be prepared so you do not get annoyed or, worse yet, doubt your abilities during the exam.
- Visit the exam site before your exam date to determine how long it will take to get there and to see what the testing room looks like. This is particularly helpful if you are a nervous test taker.
- Do not expect the exam site to be quiet. A student from one of RMC's PMP Exam Prep courses had a band playing outside the testing center for three hours. Others have had someone taking an exam that required intensive typing, and thus more noise, right next to them. Many testing sites will have earplugs or headphones available.
- Do not overstudy. Getting completely comfortable with all the material in this book is just not possible. It is not worth studying for hundreds of hours. It is a waste of time and will not help you on the exam.
- Take the night off before the exam to do something relaxing and get a little extra sleep. DO NOT STUDY! You will need time to process all you have learned so you can remember it when you take the exam.

TRICKS OF THE TRADE® Tricks for Taking and Passing the PMP Exam

We have talked about what you should do and know before you take the exam. Now what about on the big day? The following are some tips for taking—and passing—the exam.

1. You must bring your authorization letter from PMI to the test site, as well as two forms of ID with exactly the same name you entered on the exam application.
2. Make sure you are comfortable during the exam. Wear layered clothing and bring a sweater to sit on in case the chairs are uncomfortable.
3. Bring snacks! Bring lunch! You will not be able to bring snacks into the exam room, but have them accessible outside the exam room in case you get hungry. You do not need the distraction of hunger pains when taking the exam.
4. You will be given scratch paper and pencils (and possibly earplugs or headphones) and have the chance to do a 15-minute computer tutorial, if your exam is given on computer, to become familiar with the computer and its commands. NOTE: The testing center will require you to exchange your used scratch paper if you need more during the exam.
5. When you are given scratch paper, create your "download sheet" by writing down anything you are having trouble remembering. This will free up your mind to handle questions once the information you are concerned about is written down.
6. Some test sites provide physical calculators. At other locations, the calculators are online or on the computer and appear with every question that requires a calculation.
7. When you take the exam, you will see one question on the screen at a time. You can answer a question and/or mark it to return to it later. You will be able to move back and forth through questions during the exam.
8. The exam does not adapt to your answers. This means 200 questions are selected when your exam starts, and those 200 do not change.
9. Use deep-breathing techniques to help relax. This is particularly helpful if you are very nervous before or during the exam and when you notice yourself reading the same question two or three times. Breathing techniques can be as simple as breathing deeply five times, to provide more oxygen to your brain.
10. Smile when taking the exam. Smiling relieves stress and makes you feel more confident.
11. Use all the exam time. Do not leave early unless you have reviewed each question twice.
12. Remember your own unique test-taking quirks and how you plan to deal with them while taking the exam.
13. Control the exam; do not let it control you. How would you feel if you read the first question and had no idea of the answer? The second question? And the third question? This can happen because you are just not ready to answer questions and your level of stress is not allowing you to think. So what do you do? If you do not immediately know the answer to the question, use the Mark for Review function and come back to it later. This will mean your first pass through the exam will generally be quick.
14. Control your frustration and maintain focus on each question. You might very well dislike or disagree with some of the questions on this exam. You might also be surprised at how many questions you mark for review. Make sure you stay focused on the current question. If you are still thinking about question 20 when you reach question 120, there will have been 100 questions that you have not looked at closely enough.
15. Answer each question from PMI's perspective, not the perspective you have acquired from your real-world or life experience. Many people who failed the exam tried to answer questions from their real-world perspective. Since these people did not use all aspects of project management in their real world, they got many questions wrong on the exam. If approaching it from PMI's perspective does not give you an answer, rely on your training. If this still does not help you answer the question, only then should you rely on your real-world experience.

16. First identify the actual question in the words provided (it is often the last sentence), and then read the rest of the text. Note the topics discussed in the question and the descriptors (e.g., "except," "includes," "not an example of"). This should help you understand what the question is asking and reduce the need to reread questions. Determine what your answer should be, and then look at the answers shown.
17. One of the main reasons people answer incorrectly is they do not read all four choices. Do not make the same mistake! Make sure you read the question and all four choices when you take the exam. This will help you select the BEST answer. If you find yourself forgetting to read all the options, start reading the choices backwards (choice D first, then C, etc.).
18. Quickly eliminate answers that are highly implausible. Many questions have only two plausible options and two obviously incorrect options.
19. There may be more than one "correct" answer to each question, but only one "BEST" answer. Make sure you are looking for the BEST answer.
20. Be alert to the fact that the answer to one question is sometimes given away in another question. Write down things you do not understand as you take the exam. Use any extra time at the end of the exam to go back to these questions.
21. Attempts have been made to keep all choices the same length. Therefore, do not follow the old rule that the longest answer is the right one.
22. A concerted effort has been made to use "distracters"—choices that distract you from the correct answer. These are plausible choices that less knowledgeable people will pick. Distracters make it appear as though some questions have two or more right answers. To many people, it seems as though there are only shades of differences between the choices. As noted earlier, make sure you look for the BEST answer for such questions, and think about the situation from PMI's perspective.
23. Look for words like "first," "last," "next," "best," "never," "always," "except," "not," "most likely," "less likely," "primary," "initial," "most," etc. Make certain you clearly read the question and take note of these words, or you will answer the question incorrectly!
24. Watch out for choices that are true statements but do not answer the question.
25. Watch out for choices that contain common project management errors. They are intentionally there to determine if you really know project management. You can combat this aspect of the exam prior to taking it by looking for errors in your knowledge and correcting those errors as you go through this book. (See the "Common Project Management Errors and Pitfalls" list at the end of this chapter.)
26. Options that represent broad, sweeping generalizations tend to be incorrect, so be alert for "always," "never," "must," "completely," and so forth. Alternatively, choices that represent carefully qualified statements tend to be correct, so be alert for words such as "often," "sometimes," "perhaps," "may," and "generally."
27. When a question asks you to fill in a blank space, the correct answer may not be grammatically correct when inserted in the sentence.
28. Look for the "rah, rah" project management answer (e.g., "The project manager is so important," "The WBS is so useful").
29. You will have multiple chances to indicate that you have completed the exam. The exam will not be scored until you indicate you are ready, or your time is up. You will receive a printed summary of your test results. If you pass, the computer will print out a certificate, and you will officially be certified. If you do not pass, PMI will send you information on retaking the exam. You will have to pay an additional fee to retake the exam.
30. Now it is time to make sure YOU ARE AWAKE! Are you ready for something very important? A major reason people get questions wrong on the exam is that they do not realize the following:
    a. "Rules" are meant to be broken. Rules, such as what to do when there is a conflict, can change depending on the situation. This drives people crazy who expect the exam to just test facts. You need to be able to read and understand the situations on the exam and then be able to figure out the best thing to do *in that situation*. Most of the questions are situational.

b. Assume proper project management was done. For example, assume there is a charter, a WBS, and management plans on the projects described on the exam, even if the question does not say so. If you answer the question thinking about real-world projects that do not use proper project management, you might miss the correct answer.
c. Notice where you are in the story. If the situation described in the question is taking place in project planning, your answer may be different than if it occurred in project executing.
d. Be prepared for questions with multiple problems. A question may describe a situation with various problems and ask you to determine which one to address first. The following silly example illustrates where people with less experience can have a difficult time with these types of questions. Imagine an exam question describes a fire at a manufacturing facility and asks you what you should do first. Would you pick a choice like "find out what caused the fire"? Although that problem will need to be solved eventually, it is not the right choice. The right answer is to get out of the building. After everyone is safe, then you might look for the cause of the fire. The following tips will help you pick the right answer for questions that ask what you should do and for many other questions where there seems to be more than one problem.
   › Determine the immediate problem to address.
   › Deal with the root cause first.
   › Deal with the problem with the greatest NEGATIVE impact first.
   › Solve the problem that occurred the earliest.
   › Look for a proactive solution.

Common Project Management Errors and Pitfalls

As mentioned at other points in this book, common errors in project management are often listed as choices on the exam. Here is a summary of some of the major errors even highly experienced project managers make. Make sure you understand why these items are errors so you can avoid them on the exam.

Common errors include:

- Focusing primarily on asking for percent complete.
- Holding "go around the room" type status meetings.
- Spending most of your time babysitting team members by constantly checking on them.
- Asking team members to cut 10 percent off their estimates.
- Thinking a bar (Gantt) chart is a project management plan.
- Not attempting to obtain finalized requirements.
- Not getting real resource commitments.
- Not having a rewards and recognition system.
- Not focusing on quality.
- Not having a change control system.
- Not having management plans.
- Not measuring against the project management plan, or even creating metrics.
- Not spending time finding and eliminating root causes of problems or deviations.
- Not implementing corrective actions to keep the project in line with the project management plan.
- Not reevaluating the effectiveness of the project management plan.
- Not reevaluating the accuracy or completeness of scope, schedule, or cost.
- Not keeping the project management plan and project documents updated to reflect changes to the project.
- Ignoring resource managers' needs to have their people do their own departments' work.
- Not realizing the project can affect the reputation of team members.

- Not realizing the project manager has some human resource responsibilities to the project team, such as creating project job descriptions and adding letters of recommendation to team members' human resource files.
- Blaming unrealistic schedules on management instead of realizing a realistic timeline is the project manager's responsibility.

A Day in the Life Exercise

The following exercise is one last opportunity to test yourself to see if you really understand what a project manager does.

Exercise Many people do not practice proper project management on their real-world projects. This may be because they have not received the training needed, or because they do not understand the project management process or its value. A lack of experience in properly managing large projects can affect you dramatically on the exam. This exercise is designed to help you uncover what you might be doing incorrectly on your projects so differences between your real-world experience and the world of proper project management do not get in your way on the exam. In the following table, list which activities a project manager should spend the most, medium, and least amount of time on during a typical day.

Most	Medium	Least

Answer There are any number of correct answers to this question. Let's first review what should NOT be on your "Most" list, and then we will look at what efforts a project manager should focus on during the course of a day. Think through the items listed here and identify whether you have any misconceptions about what you should be doing as a project manager. If you do, you need to clarify and fix these misconceptions before you take the exam.

Items that should NOT be on your "Most" list:

- Dealing with problems (rather than preventing them)
- Schedule- or schedule-management-related topics
- Meetings
- Babysitting
- Completing work activities

The following items should have been included in your "Most" list:

- Using project management tools, such as a charter, WBS, project management plan, etc.
- Measuring
- Recommending and taking corrective and preventive actions
- Doing risk management and implementing risk responses
- Coaching and mentoring
- Communicating
- Looking for possible changes

Conclusion

You have reached the end of this book! Congratulations!

As noted Chapter 1, in order to really retain the information you've learned, you need to review it several times. Therefore, read through the book again, focusing on the areas where you have identified gaps in your knowledge. You will find in a second pass through the book that you understand some topics differently than you did the first time, and other concepts will stand out to you that you previously missed. In particular, make sure you review the PMI-isms presented in Chapter 1 and Rita's Process Chart and the project management process exercises in Chapter 3. Having a solid understanding of the project management process and the material presented in this book will not only help you pass the exam (you can use logic instead of having to memorize information), it will also enable you to apply what you have learned to your real-world projects.

Thank you for taking this journey with us. We hope you will come back to RMC Project Management after you have earned your PMP. We can help you continue your training and earn PDUs to maintain your certification through our advanced instructor-led and e-Learning courses and products. So good luck, and we look forward to seeing you after you pass the exam!

Notes

The following notes provide the historical background of many of the terms in this book. You do not need to know this information for the exam. It is simply provided for your interest and reference.

CHAPTER TWO

1. **Project Management Office** The development of departments within organizations to manage projects dates back to the beginning of project management as a discipline. [Frank Parth, Cynthia Snyder, and Cynthia Stackpole, *Introduction to IT Project Management* (Vienna, VA. Management Concepts, 2007), 22.]

2. **Management By Objectives (MBO)** The ideas from Peter Ferdinand Drucker's book, *The Practice of Management*, became known as management by objectives (MBO). [Stuart Crainer, *The Management Century: A Critical Review of 20th Century Thought and Practice* (San Francisco: Jossey-Bass Publishers, 2000), 120.]

3. **Constraints** Dr. Martin Barnes was the first to describe what he called the "iron triangle" of time, cost, and output in his course "Time and Money in Contract Control" in 1969, laying the foundations for what has become known as the "triple constraint" (time, cost, and scope constraints). [Patrick Weaver, "The Origins of Modern Project Management," (Lecture, Fourth Annual PMI College of Scheduling Conference, Vancouver, Canada, April 15-17, 2007).]

4. **Stakeholder** The first use of the word "stakeholder" in management literature was in 1963 in an international memorandum at the Stanford Research Institute. [Robert Y. Cavana and Arun A. Elias, "Stakeholder Analysis for Systems Thinking and Modelling" (Paper presented at ORSNZ, New Zealand, December 2000).]

5. **Stakeholder Management** The concept of stakeholders became central to management when R. Edward Freeman published his book in 1984, *Strategic Management: A Stakeholder Approach.* [Robert Y. Cavana and Arun A. Elias, "Stakeholder Analysis for Systems Thinking and Modelling" (Paper presented at ORSNZ, New Zealand, December, 2000).]

6. **Matrix** These categories were defined in 1971 by Jay R. Galbraith to help organizations improve their management efficiency. [Jay R. Galbraith, "Matrix Organization Designs: How to Combine Functional and Project Forms," *Business Horizons,* Vol. 14, Iss. 1 (1971), 29-40.]

7. **Project Expediter** The concept of the project expediter was first invented in the Soviet Union, in order to help projects get through the tangle of Soviet bureaucracy. [Karl W. Ryavec, *Soviet Society and the Communist Party* (Amherst: University of Massachusetts Press, 1978), 54.]

8. **Project Life Cycle** Dr. Russell Archibald, a founder of PMI, was one of the theorists who refined the concept of the project life cycle. [R. Max Wideman, *The Role of the Project Life Cycle (Life Span) in Project Management* (Vancouver: AEW Services, 2004), 2.]

9. **Lessons Learned** The organization of formal systems to integrate experience into corporate management is a fairly recent development. J. G. March and J. P. Olsen published a paper in 1975 that became the basis of "organizational learning." [Keith F. Snider, "Integrating Individual and Organizational Learning: Agency Lessons Learned Systems and the Case Method in Teaching Public Procurement," in Proceedings of the Third Annual Public Procurement Conference, 2008.]

CHAPTER FOUR

1. **Project Charter** While the concept of the project charter is very old, it was refined as part of the Six Sigma methodology. [Penelope Przekop, *Six Sigma for Business Excellence* (New York: McGraw Hill, 2003), 61.]

2. **Business Case** This term has been in wide use for decades; business cases were being written and studied in the 1920s as part of the scientific management movement. After Harvard Business School began using them as a teaching method, they became widely popular in the 1950s. [Michael Davis, *Ethics and the University* (New York: Routledge, 1999), 145.]

3. **Benefit Measurement Methods** Benefit measurement first evolved as a cost benefit analysis method. After a series of studies on productivity improvements and information technology in the 1990s, it became an important project management tool. [Sonia Mountain, "New Corporate Systems; Adding Value or Keeping with the Times?" (Paper presented at the ATEM NZ Conference, Wellington, New Zealand, 1994), 9.]

4. **Constrained Optimization Methods** Constrained optimization as a pure mathematical technique dates back to the 18th century French mathematician Lagrange. In the 1920s, students of the economist Alfred Marshall began applying optimization techniques to economic planning. The use of constrained optimization in project management has evolved from these techniques. [William Lazonick, *Business Organization and the Myth of the Market Economy* (Cambridge: Cambridge University Press, 1991), 292.]

5. **Present Value, Net Present Value, Internal Rate of Return, Cost Benefit Analysis, Opportunity Cost, Sunk Costs, Law of Diminishing Returns, Depreciation** These key terms are borrowed from economics. The investment of time and money in a project should be reviewed as carefully as the investment of time or money in any business venture. [Colin Haslam and Alan Neale, *Economics in a Business Context* (London: Thomson, 2000), xx.]

6. **Law of Diminishing Returns** This is one of the fundamental principles of modern economics, developed by David Ricardo and Thomas Malthus in 1815. It has been applied to many fields of social science in the two centuries since its discovery. [Mark Skousen, *The Making of Modern Economics: The Lives and Ideas of the Great Thinkers* (Armonk, NY: M.E. Sharpe, 2001), 100.]

7. **Statement of Work** The first clearly defined statement of work in the modern sense was published by the US government in 1908, which issued requirements for an airplane prototype to be purchased by the US Army. [Michael G. Martin, *Delivering Product Excellence with the Statement of Work* (Vienna, VA: Management Concepts, 2003), 4.]

8. **Corporate Knowledge Base** The concept of the knowledge base dates back to the 19th century. It has been applied in different contexts to different fields, including computer science, education, and management science. [William H. Inmon, Bonnie K. O'Neil, and Lowell Fryman. *Business Metadata: Capturing Enterprise Knowledge* (Burlington, MA: Morgan Kaufman, 2008), 93.]

9. **Project Management Plan** The integration of various project management techniques into a formal process began in the 1950s with projects coordinated for the US Department of Defense by the RAND Corporation and Booz Allen Hamilton. [Lauren Keller Johnson, Richard Luecke, and Robert Daniel Austin. *The Essentials of Project Management* (Harvard: Harvard Business School Publishing, 2006), xv.]

10. **Baseline** The use of the baseline as a statistical tool dates to the 19th century. The word has been redefined in the context of management science, although it still generally refers to measurement using numerical or statistical methods. [Harold Kerzner, *Project Management: A Systems Approach to Planning, Scheduling and Controlling* (Hoboken, NJ: Wiley, 2001), 1014.]

11. **Configuration Management System** Configuration management was first developed in the 1950s by NASA. The technique was then borrowed by the US Department of Defense, before it was refined by private corporations in the 1960s. It was originally intended to manage large, complex projects like the design and launch of rockets. [Frank B. Watts, *Engineering Documentation Control Handbook* (Norwich, NY: William Andrew Publishing, 2000), 10.]

12. **Work Authorization System** The concept of a refined work authorization system evolved from the PERT methodology of the 1960s and quickly spread from the US federal government to private corporations. [Gregory A. Garrett and Rene G. Rendon, *U.S. Military Program Management: Lessons Learned and Best Practices* (Vienna, VA: Management Concepts, 2007), 133.]

13. **Integrated Change Control Processes** The concept of integrated change control was refined at NASA, where an Integrated Change Control Board was organized in the late 1970s. [Gale Research Company, *Acronyms, Initialisms and Abbreviations Dictionary* (Farmington Hills, MI: Gale Research Company, 1980), 1512.]

14. **Change Control Board** The change control board was an important part of the change control process from its earliest days in the 1970s. [John A. Burgess, *Design Assurance for Engineers and Managers* (Boca Raton, FL: CRC Press, 1984), 96.]

CHAPTER FIVE

1. **Nominal Group Technique** This technique was invented by researchers Andre Delbecq and Andrew Van de Ven in 1971 to overcome the hesitations some participants might feel in a face-to-face meeting. [Charles M. Judd and Harry T. Reis, *Handbook of Research Methods in Social and Personality Psychology* (Cambridge, MA: Cambridge University Press, 2000), 181.]

2. **Mind Maps** While similar techniques have been used for centuries, the modern mind-mapping technique was developed by British consultant Tony Buzan. Buzan first conceived of the mind map in the 1970s and has continually refined the technique. [Tony Buzan, *How to Mind Map* (New York: Thorsons, 2002).]

3. **Affinity Diagrams** The affinity diagram is also called the KJ Method, after Jiro Kawakita, a Japanese anthropologist who devised the affinity diagram in the 1960s. This method has been popularized in the United States as part of the Six Sigma methodology. [Kaliym A. Islam and Edward A. Trolley, *Developing and Measuring Training the Six Sigma Way: A Business Approach to Training and Development* (San Francisco: Wiley and Sons, 2006) 99.]

4. **Requirements Tracebility Matrix** The requirements traceability matrix was developed in the software industry and was adopted as standard procedure by the US Department of Defense in 1988. [Deborah A. Cerino, Judith A. Clapp, and Wendy W. Peng, *Software Quality Control, Error Analysis, and Testing* (Park Ridge, NJ: Noyes Data Corporation, 1995), 45.]

5. **Project Scope Statement** The concept of the project scope statement is very old, but the term itself dates to IT projects of the 1970s. [Blackman, *The Design of Real Time Applications* (Hoboken, NJ: Wiley, 1975), 236.]

6. **Work Breakdown Structure (WBS)** The work breakdown structure was developed as part of the PERT methodology. Although it was not mentioned by name in the 1959 paper that introduced PERT, the term was in widespread use by 1961. [Gregory T. Haugan, *The Work Breakdown Structure in Government Contracting* (Vienna, VA: Management Concepts, 2003), 8.]

7. **Verify Scope** Scope verification entered the project management lexicon in the 1980s, as the concept of scope management was developed. [E. Balagurusamy, and J.A.M. Howe, *Expert Systems for Management and Engineering* (Chichester, U.K.: Ellis Horwood, 1990), 306.]

CHAPTER SIX

1. **Network Diagrams** Also called a PERT chart. The network diagram was developed in the 1950s as part of the PERT methodology. [Robert T. Futrell, Donald F. Shafer, and Linda Shafer, *Quality Software Project Management* (Upper Saddle River, NJ: Prentice Hall PTR, 2002), 501.]

2. **Precedence Diagramming Method** The precedence diagramming method was developed as a "noncomputer" alternative to the critical path method in 1961 by Dr. John Fondahl. [Patrick Weaver, "The Origins of Modern Project Management" (Lecture, Fourth Annual PMI College of Scheduling Conference, Vancouver, Canada, April 15-17, 2007).]

3. **Arrow Diagramming Method (ADM)** James E. Kelley and Morgan Walker began devising the algorithms that became the Activity-on-Arrow scheduling method in 1956 and 1957 for E.I. du Pont de Numours. [Patrick Weaver, "A Brief History of Scheduling: Back to the Future" (Lecture, myPrimavera06, Canberra, Australia, April 4-6, 2006).]

4. **GERT** The GERT method was developed by Alan Pritzker in 1966 for the RAND Corporation to improve work scheduling. [Peter W. G. Morris, *The Management of Projects* (London: Telford, 1994), 79.]

5. **Mandatory, Discretionary, External Dependency** The use of these terms in project management dates to the 1980s. They were popularized as part of the Six Sigma methodology. [*Reshaping School Mathematics: A Philosophy and Framework for Curriculum* (Washington, DC: National Academies Press, 1990), 34.]

6. **Analogous Estimating** This type of top-down estimation is very ancient. The term itself derives from mathematical theory, and its use in project management dates to the 1990s. [American Mathematical Society, *20 Lectures Delivered at the International Congress of Mathematicians* (Providence, RI: American Mathematical Society, 1974), 111.]

7. **Regression Analysis** Regression analysis was first developed by the British scientist Sir Francis Galton as part of his research into human heredity in 1886. [Michael Patrick Allen, *Understanding Regression Analysis* (New York: Plenum Press, 1997), 2.]

8. **Heuristics** Heuristics are as old as human language. Modern computer-assisted heuristics can be traced to the work of theorist Claude Shannon in the 1950s. [Bruce Abramson, *Digital Phoenix: Why the Information Economy Collapsed and How It Will Rise Again* (Cambridge, MA: MIT Press, 2005), 86.]

9. **Three-Point Estimating** The three-point estimate is part of the PERT methodology developed by Booz Allen Hamilton, Inc., in 1958. [Christopher D. McKenna, *The World's Newest Profession: Management Consulting in the Twentieth Century* (New York: Cambridge University Press, 2006), 294.]

10. **PERT** In 1957, a team from the US Navy Special Projects Office, Bureau of Ordinance, and the consulting firm Booz Allen Hamilton developed the concept of PERT. [Patrick Weaver, "A Brief History of Scheduling: Back to the Future" (Lecture, myPrimavera06, Canberra, Australia, April 4-6, 2006).]

11. **Standard Deviation (SD)** The term "standard deviation" was invented in 1893 by the mathematician Karl Pearson, although the technique was used by earlier mathematicians such as Gauss. [Theodore M. Porter, *Karl Pearson: The Scientific Life in a Statistical Age* (Princeton: Princeton University Press, 2004), 237.]

12. **Critical Path Method** The Critical Path Method was developed in 1956 when E. I. du Pont de Numours was trying to find a use for its UNIVACI computer. James E. Kelley and Morgan Walker presented the Critical Path Method to the public at a conference in 1959. [Patrick Weaver, "A Brief History of Scheduling: Back to the Future" (Lecture, myPrimavera06, Canberra, Australia, April 4-6, 2006).]

13. **Near-Critical Path** This concept was developed as part of the critical path method. [Patrick Weaver, "A Brief History of Scheduling: Back to the Future" (Lecture, myPrimavera06, Canberra, Australia, April 4-6, 2006).]

14. **Float** The concept of float is part of the critical path methodology. [Rocco Martino, *Project Management* (Springfield, MO: Management Development Institute, 1968), xiii.]

15. **Schedule Compression** Schedule compression and the terms of "fast tracking" and "crashing" are part of the critical path methodology. [Charles Heath and James L. Riggs, *Guide to Cost Reduction Through Critical Path Scheduling* (Englewood Cliffs, N.J.: Prentice Hall, 1966), 118.]

16. **Monte Carlo Analysis** The Monte Carlo method was first used in 1930 by Enrico Fermi to calculate the properties of the neutron. It was also used by scientists working on the Manhattan Project during World War II; the development of the electronic computer allowed the Monte Carlo method to be refined in the 1950s. [Jeffrey Seth Rosenthal, *Struck By Lightning: The Curious World of Probabilities* (Washington, DC: Joseph Henry Press, 2006), 186.]

17. **Resource Leveling** This concept was first developed in the construction industry and rapidly spread into other areas of management science in the 1980s. [Thomas J. Driscoll, Stephen B. Hurlbut, and Jon M. Wickwire, *Construction Scheduling: Preparation, Liabilities, and Claims* (New York: Aspen Publishers, 2003), 423.]

18. **Critical Chain Method** The critical chain method was introduced by the Israeli business consultant Eliyahu Goldratt in 1997, to increase emphasis on resources. [Eliyahu Goldratt, *Critical Chain* (Great Barrington, MA: North River Press, 1997).]

19. **Milestone Charts** Milestone charts were developed in the 1940s. [Patrick Weaver, "The Origins of Modern Project Management" (Lecture, Fourth Annual PMI College of Scheduling Conference, Vancouver, Canada, April 15-17, 2007).]

20. **Bar Charts** The bar chart was first developed by Karol Adamiecki in 1896, but was popularized and refined during the 1910s by management consultant Henry Gantt. [Peter W. G. Morris, *The Management of Projects* (London: Telford; New York: American Society of Civil Engineers [distributor] 1994), 18.]

CHAPTER SEVEN

1. **Life Cycle Costing** The modern conception of life cycle costing can be traced to 1965, when the Logistics Management Institute published a document outlining the basics of the concept. [B. S. Dhillon, *Medical Device Reliability and Associated Areas* (Boca Raton, FL: CRC Press, 2000), 172.]

2. **Value Analysis** Value analysis was first developed by L. D. Miles, a researcher for General Electric, in 1947. He was trying to develop a new method to scientifically predict the best way to reduce costs while improving the value of projects. [D. H. Stamatis, *TQM Engineering Handbook* (Boca Raton, FL: CRC Press, 1997), 306.]

3. **Cost Risk** Peter Simon et al. *Project Risk Analysis and Management Guide* (High Wycombe, UK: APM Publishing, 2004), 163. Cost-risk analysis is a field of study first developed in the 1970s that seeks to estimate exact figures for the amount of these risks, mainly using Monte Carlo simulations.

4. **Bottom-Up Estimating** This is an old practice, but time-consuming. Parametric estimating was developed to solve some of bottom-up estimation's difficulties. [John C. Goodpasture, *Quantitative Methods in Project Management* (Boca Raton, FL: J. Ross Publishing, 2004), 89.]

5. **Rough Order of Magnitude Estimate (ROM)** This type of estimating has been around for a very long time, although the title is fairly new. The RAND Corporation developed parametric estimating in order to refine their ROM estimates. [RAND Corporation, *The Rand Paper Series* (Santa Monica, CA: RAND Corporation, 1988), 17.]

6. **Contingency Reserve and Management Reserve** These concepts have been part of financial planning for decades; Samuel Paul suggested integrating reserve analysis techniques into project management in 1982. [Peter W. G. Morris, *The Management of Projects* (London: Telford; New York: American Society of Civil Engineers [distributor] 1994), 18.]

7. **Funding Limit Reconciliation** This term was recently invented. The process it describes, however—the checking of costs against the budget set for the project—has been a part of project management since its very beginning. [United States Department of Defense, *Financial Management in the Department of Defense* (Washington, DC: United States Department of Defense, 1954), 21.]

8. **S-Curve** The application of the S-curve to corporate planning can be traced to Iowa State University's B. Ryan and N. C. Gross, who were projecting the adoption of corn varieties by farmers in 1943. [Hendrik Van den Berg and Joshua J. Lewer, *International Trade and Economic Growth* (Armonk, NY: M.E. Sharpe, 2007), 118.]

9. **Earned Value Measurement** The earned value technique was developed by the US Department of Defense in the 1960s as an alternative to PERT methodology. It began to spread into the corporate world in the 1980s. [Wayne F. Abba, "Earned Value Management: Reconciling Government and Commercial Practices," *PM Magazine,* Vol. Jan/Feb (1997), 58-63.]

10. **Cost Performance Index (CPI)** This is a standard accounting term. Its use in project management is derived from US Department of Defense contracts of the 1950s. [Edited by Cecil Hamilton Chilton and the staff of Chemical Engineering, *Cost Engineering in the Process Industries.* (New York: McGraw-Hill, 1960), 337.]

CHAPTER EIGHT

1. **Plan-Do-Check-Act Cycle** This concept was invented in 1939 by Walter Shewhart of Bell Laboratories in order to better integrate knowledge and practice. It was popularized by W. Edwards Deming. [Thomas Pyzdek, *Quality Engineering Handbook* (Boca Raton, FL: CRC, 2003), 372.]

2. **Gold Plating** This term is commonplace in contracting, and was already the subject of criticism in a 1962 paper analyzing US defense contracts. [Peter W. G. Morris, *The Management of Projects* (London: Thomas Telford, 1997), 58.]

3. **Marginal Analysis** Marginal analysis was utilized by early economists such as David Ricardo, but was revived as a theory in 1934 by economist Joan Robinson. [Kenneth Ewart Boulding and W. Allen Spivey, *Linear Programming and the Theory of the Firm* (New York: Macmillan, 1960), 2.]

4. **Kaizen** Masaaki Imai made the term "Kaizen" famous in his book published in 1986, *Kaizen: The Key to Japan's Competitive Success.* [American Society for Quality Glossary, s.v. "Kaizen," http://www.asq.org/glossary/k.html (accessed October 14, 2008)].

5. **Just in Time (JIT)** JIT systems were refined by Japanese corporations during the 1980s, although the process may have originated from the observations of Taiicho Ohno, who studied the stocking systems of US supermarkets during the 1950s. [Ian Inkster, *The Japanese Industrial Economy: Late Development and Cultural Causation* (New York: Routledge, 2001), 106.]

6. **Total Quality Management (TQM)** Ways to implement total quality management can be traced to quality gurus such as Philip B. Crosby, W. Edwards Deming, Armand V. Feigenbaum, Kaoru Ishikawa and Joseph M. Juran. Source: American Society for Quality Glossary, s.v. "Total quality management (TQM)," http://www.asq.org/glossary/t.html (accessed October 14, 2008).

7. **CISG** The CISG is in constant change; the courts of many nations interpret the CISG in different ways, and periodic conventions have met to reconcile differing interpretations. [Lookovsky, Joseph M. *Understanding the CISG in the USA.* (The Hague, Netherlands: Kluwer Law International, 2004), 34.]

8. **ISO 9000** The ISO introduced the ISO 9000 standards in 1987, just as the European Union was being formed. The adoption of ISO 9000 standards by the EU led to its widespread adoption throughout the world. [Paul A. Nee, *ISO 9000 in Construction* (Hoboken, NJ: Wiley, 1996), 5.]

9. **Cost Benefit Analysis** Cost-benefit analysis was fully developed as a technique by the US Army Corps of Engineers in the 1930s. The technique spread throughout the US federal government, and was integrated into corporate planning after World War Two. [Michael Power, *Accounting and Science: Natural Inquiry and Commercial Reason* (Cambridge: Cambridge University Press, 1996), 41.]

10. **Cost of Quality (COQ)** This concept was developed and refined as part of the Six Sigma methodology. [William Truscott, *Six Sigma: Continual Improvement for Businesses: A Practical Guide* (Amsterdam; Boston, MA: Butterworth-Heinemann, 2003), 26.]

11. **Costs of Conformance and Cost of Noncomformance** These concepts, and many of the other concepts in this chapter such as cost of quality, were refined as part of the Six Sigma methodology in the 1980s. [William Truscott, *Six Sigma: Continual Improvement for Businesses A Practical Guide* (Amsterdam; Boston, MA: Butterworth-Heinemann, 2003), 26.]

12. **Control Charts** Walter Shewhart came up with the idea of a production control chart in 1924. [Stuart Crainer, *The Management Century: A Critical Review of 20th Century Thought and Practice* (San Francisco: Jossey-Bass Publishers, 2000), 82.]

13. **Rule of Seven** This is a common statistical rule of thumb; if seven runs of data produce results on the same side of the target value, then the mean is assumed to have changed. [Christopher Chatfield, *Statistics for Technology: A Course in Applied Statistics* (London; New York: Chapman and Hall, CRC Press, 1983), 301.]

14. **Assignable Cause/Special Cause Variation** This concept was first developed in 1924 by the researcher Walter Shewhart. It was later refined by the TQM and Six Sigma movements. [William C. Johnson and Richard J. Chvala, *Total Quality in Marketing* (Delray Beach, FL: St. Lucie Press, 1996), 43.]

15. **Benchmarking** The modern benchmarking process originated at Xerox in the 1980s. Dr. Robert Camp was instrumental in developing and popularizing the benchmarking process. [James L. Heskett, W. Earl Sasser, and Leonard A. Schlesinger, *The Value Profit Chain: Treat Employees Like Customers and Customers Like Employees* (New York: Free Press, 2003), 103.]

16. **Design of Experiments (DOE)** Experimental design has been a central concern of scientists for centuries. The application of scientific methods to management problems is an important part of the revolution in management science since World War II. [Jiju Antony, *Design of Experiments for Engineers and Scientists* (Oxford: Butterworth-Heinemann, 2003), 29.]

17. **Flowcharting** The flowchart was first invented by Frank Gilbreth in 1921 to better document processes, and quickly adopted throughout the management industry. It was refined during the 1940s by researchers at Procter and Gamble, as well as by Princeton's John von Neumann. [Mark R. Lehto and James R. Buck, *Introduction to Human Factors and Ergonomics for Engineers* (New York : Lawrence Erlbaum, 2008), 100.]

18. **Perform Quality Assurance** In the late 1950s, the idea that quality assurance must be strictly followed in developing new products was revolutionary for early quality theorists. [Kaoru Ishikawa, *What Is Total Quality Control? The Japanese Way* (New Jersey: Prentice Hall, Inc., 1985), 19-20.]

19. **Process Analysis** While process analysis is an old concept, it has been refined as part of the Six Sigma methodology. [George Eckes, *Six Sigma for Everyone* (Hoboken, NJ: Wiley, 2003), 49.]

20. **6 Sigma** In the late 1980s, Mikel Harry, an engineer at Motorola, developed the concept of Six Sigma, which became a key method of doing business for Motorola. [George Eckes, *The Six Sigma Revolution: How General Electric and Others Turned Process Into Profits* (New York: John Wiley and Sons, Inc., 2001), 5.]

21. **Cause and Effect Diagram (Fishbone Diagram, Ishikawa Diagram)** The cause and effect diagram is sometimes referred to as the "Ishikawa diagram" because it was developed by Kaoru Ishikawa. [American Society for Quality Glossary, s.v. "Cause and effect diagram," http://www.asq.org/glossary/c.html (accessed October 14, 2008).]

22. **Histogram** Although the word "histogram" was first coined in 1892, the earliest known histogram appeared in 1786. These tools were well-known and used throughout the 19th century. [Yannis Ioannidis, *The History of Histograms (Abridged)* (Athens, Greece: University of Athens, 2003), 1.]

23. **Pareto Chart** The Pareto chart was defined in 1950 by Joseph M. Juran. It is based on the Pareto principle, which was named after the 19th century economist Vilfredo Pareto. [American Society for Quality Glossary, s.v. "Pareto chart," http://www.asq.org/glossary/p.html (accessed October 14, 2008).]

24. **Run Chart** The run chart (or run-sequence plot) is one of the oldest visual tools in statistics. The introduction of spreadsheet computer programs in the 1970s led to their wide use in corporate management. [John M. Chambers, William Cleveland, Beat Kleiner, and Paul Tukey, *Graphical Methods for Data Analysis* (Belmont, CA: Wadsworth Publishing, 1983), 95.]

25. **Scatter Diagram** The scatter diagram, or scatter plot, was invented by Sir Francis Galton in 1908 as part of his research on human heredity. [A. Reza Hoshmand, *Design of Experiments for Agriculture and the Natural Sciences* (Boca Raton, FL: Chapman and Hall/CRC, 2006), 269.]

CHAPTER NINE

1. **Responsibility Assignment Matrix** The RAM was first developed by IT project managers in the 1970s; it spread into wider use over the next decade. [M. D. Wadsworth, *Electronic Data Processing Project Management Controls* (New York: Prentice Hall, 1972), 43.]

2. **Organizational Breakdown Structure** After the work breakdown structure became a common tool in the industry during the 1980s, the concept of the organizational breakdown structure also became widespread. [Peter W. G. Morris, *The Management of Projects* (London: Telford: American Society of Civil Engineers [distributor], 1994), 264.]

3. **Staffing Management Plan** The staffing management plan was refined in the 1970s for industries like education and health care. The concept was imported into project management later in the decade. [Duncan Boldy, *Operational Research Applied to Health Services* (New York: St. Martin's Press, 1981), 217.]

4. **Halo Effect** This was first demonstrated with objective data by Edward Thorndike in 1920, who was studying the ratings of officers in the US Army. Thorndike's findings were quicly applied to business. [Neil J. Salkind and Kristin Rasmussen, *Encyclopedia of Educational Psychology* (Thousand Oaks, CA: Sage Publications, 2008), 458-459.]

5. **Forming, Storming, Norming, Performing** Psychologist Bruce Tuckman described the phases of team development as Forming, Storming, Norming, and Performing in 1965. He later added the final stage of Adjourning, also referred to as Mourning. [Mindtools, Ltd. "Forming, Storming, Norming, Performing: Helping New Teams Perform Effectively, Quickly." http://www.mindtools.com/pages/article/newLDR_86.htm.)]

6. **Expectancy Theory** Expectancy theory was developed in 1964 by Victor Vroom of the Yale School of Management to explain the motivations of employees. [Ronald R. Sims, *Managing Organizational Behavior* (Westport, CT: Greenwood Press, 2002), 62.]

7. **Fringe Benefits** In 1942, the US War Labor Board approved employee benefits like health insurance to allow employers to attract new employees. The term "fringe benefit," first used around this time, took several years to gain wide acceptance. [Nelson Lichtenstein, *Labor's War at Home: The CIO in World War II* (New York: Cambridge University Press, 1982), 240.]

8. **Motivation Theory** Modern motivation theory has its roots in the work of pioneering economists like Adam Smith, who asserted that money was the root of all motivation. 20th century psychologists began developing new concepts as part of modern management theory. [Patrick J. Montana and Bruce H. Charnov, *Management* (Happauge, NY: Barron's, 2000), 238.]

9. **McGregor's Theory of X and Y** Douglas McGregor introduced this theory in 1960. He hoped to persuade managers to trust their employees, and therefore to act according to Theory Y. [Donald Clark, "A Time Capsule of Training and Learning," 2008, http://www.skagitwatershed.org/~donclark/hrd/history/xy.html]

10. **Maslow's Hierarchy of Needs** Abraham Maslow introduced this theory in his 1943 article "A Theory of Human Motivation." While later researchers have questioned Maslow's results, the hierarchy of needs has become accepted wisdom. [Christopher D. Green, "Classics in the History of Psychology," 2004, http://psychclassics.yorku.ca/Maslow/motivation.htm]

11. **David McClelland's Theory of Needs** McClelland first developed this theory at Harvard in the 1960s as part of his research into political power and motivation theory. [Ellen Weisbord, Bruce H. Charnov, and Jonathan Lindsey, *Managing People in Today's Law Firm* (Westport, CT: Quorum Books, 1995), 35.]

12. **Herzberg's Theory** Frederick Herzberg refined his theory in a series of papers between 1959 and 1968. He hoped to help create a new kind of workplace based on employee satisfaction. [Robert B. Denhardt, Janet Vinzant Denhardt, and Maria Pilar Aristgueta, *Managing Human Behavior in Public and Nonprofit Organizations* (Thousand Oaks, CA: Sage Publications, 2001), 150.]

CHAPTER TEN

1. **Interactive, Push, Pull Communication** These categories have been in use in communication theory for decades. Their use has been popularized by the explosion of the Internet and the replacement of early "pull" technologies like static Web sites by "push" technologies like RSS feeds and e-mail updates. [National Association of Women Deans, Administrators and Counselors, *National Association of Women Deans, Administrators and Counselors* (1958), 61.]

2. **Variance Report** This is an accounting term. The use of this concept in project management dates to the 1970s. [Harold Kerzner, *Project Management: A Systems Approach to Planning, Scheduling, and Controlling* (New York: Van Nostrand Reinhold, 1979), 447.]

3. **Earned Value Report** Earned value management techniques were first developed and used by the US government in the 1960s. [David I. Cleland and Lewis R. Ireland, *Project Manager's Portable Handbook* (New York: McGraw-Hill Professional, 2004), 389.]

CHAPTER ELEVEN

1. **Risk Thresholds** The concept of a "risk threshold" became widely popular as a business term in the 1960s. It originated as a medical term, and spread into business through engineering. [Max H. O'Connell, *Aircraft Noise* (Brooks City, Texas: U.S. Air Force School of Aerospace Medicine, 1960), 2.]

2. **Pure (Insurable) Risk** This term was invented in Britain in the 19th century, when the first modern insurance companies were taking shape there. [J. M. Ross, ed. *The Globe Encyclopaedia of Universal Knowledge* (Edinburgh, U.K.: Grange Publishing, 1877), 506.]

3. **Delphi Technique** The Delphi Technique is named after the Greek Oracle of Delphi, who foretold the future. This technique was created by the RAND Corporation in the late 1960s to better examine problems with a strong emotional or political element. [H. J. Strauss and L. H. Zeigler, "The Delphi Technique and Its Uses in Social Science Research," *Journal of Creative Behavior,* Vol. 9: 253-259.]

4. **Root Cause Analysis** Root cause analysis was first developed in the 1950s by the US Department of Energy, in order to investigate industrial (and specifically nuclear) accidents. The methodology was refined by the health care industry, and became popular in management science in the 1980s. [B. S. Dhillon, *Reliability Technology, Human Error, and Quality in Health Care* (Boca Raton, FL: CRC Press, 2008), 45.]

5. **Strengths, Weaknesses, Opportunities, and Threats Analysis (SWOT)** SWOT analysis was developed by Albert Humphrey of Stanford University to improve long-range planning techniques. Humphrey and his colleagues introduced SWOT in 1964, and the first prototype project using SWOT was completed in 1973. [Regina Fazio Maruca, *The Way We Work: An Encyclopedia of Business Culture* (Westport, CT: Greenwood Press, 2008), 244.]

6. **Risk Register** The concept of the risk register began in the United Kingdom as a medical tool in the 1960s, before it was adopted as a project management tool. [Fred Grundy, *The New Public Health; An Introduction to Personal Health and the Welfare Services for Health Visitors, Social Workers and Midwives* (London: H.K. Lewis, 1968), 63.]

7. **Qualitative Risk Analysis** In its simplest form—thinking carefully about the risks of any project—qualitative risk analysis is as old as humanity. In its modern sense, qualitative risk analysis and the terms in this section have been developed over the last few decades, and the term itself first appeared in the 1970s. [Tom Kendrick, *Identifying and Managing Project Risk: Essential Tools for Failure-Proofing Your Project* (New York: AMACOM, 2003), 165.]

8. **Decision Tree** The concept of the decision tree is very old; an excellent early example is the system invented by Carl Linnaeus in the 1730s to classify species by kingdom, phylum, class, etc. [Michael J. A. Berry and Gordon Linoff, *Data Mining Techniques for Marketing, Sales, and Customer Relationship Management, Second Edition* (Indianapolis, IN: Wiley Publishing, 2004), 166.]

9. **Residual Risks** Residual risk was defined as a business term during the scientific management movement after the First World War. By 1922, it was familiar to many managers and business owners. [Fred Emerson Clark, *Principles of Marketing* (New York: The Macmillan Company, 1922), 361.]

10. **Reserves (Contingency)** The concept of the contingency reserve has been used in creating business and government budgets for over a century. It was popularized during the scientific management movement of the 1920s. [Actuarial Society of America, *Transactions* (New York: Actuarial Society of America, 1907), 109.]

11. **Risk Audits** The concept of the risk audit evolved to deal with serious problems like epidemics or disaster management. The concept spread in the 1990s to apply to project management. [Alan E. Boyle, *Environmental Regulation and Economic Growth* (Oxford: Oxford University Press, 1994), 42.]

CHAPTER TWELVE

1. **Procurement Management** Procurement management as a discipline dates to the 1930s, when the federal government massively increased spending and began organizing a number of large, long-term projects. [*Design-Build for the Public Sector*, ed. Michael C. Loulakis (New York: Aspen Publishers, 2003), 61.]

2. **Make-or-Buy Analysis** This process relies heavily on the research of consultant Michael Porter, who introduced analytical tools for make-or-buy analysis in the 1980s. [Chris Argyris, Derek F. Channon, and Cary L. Cooper, *The Concise Blackwell Encyclopedia of Management* (Malden, MA: Blackwell Business, 1998), 681.]

3. **Fixed Price, Time and Material, Cost Reimbursable Contracts** Contract law has distinguished between these types of contracts for a long time. The term "fixed price contract" appears in legal documents from 1845. The contract types were defined by the US government to streamline military procurement in the late 19th century. [U.S. Office of the Federal Register, *Code of Federal Regulations* (Washington, DC: US National Archives, 1901), 15.]

4. **Target Price, Sharing Ratio, Ceiling Price** The terms "target price," "sharing ratio," and "ceiling price" are standard terms. Their usage was popularized in RFPs issued by the US government after World War II. [A. Michael Agapos, *Government-Industry and Defense: Economics and Administration* (Tuscaloosa, AL: University of Alabama Press, 1975), 164.]

5. **Point of Total Assumption (PTA)** The term "total assumption" has a long history, having been used in government contracts and debates since the 19th century. The PTA is a newer term, and was introduced by the US government. [John W. Langford, *Logistics: Principles and Applications* (New York: SOLE Press/McGraw-Hill, 2007), 207.]

6. **RFP, IFB, RFQ** These terms were first used in the 19th century. The US government pioneered procurement law, with the first such law in 1795. Corporations adopted many later refinements of procurement by the US federal government. [Margaret M. Worthington, Louis P. Goldsman, Frank M. Alston. *Contracting with the Federal Government* (New York: John Wiley, 1998), 1.]

7. **Bidder Conferences** These conferences became common after the concept was introduced at the 1959 conference of the American Society for Quality Control. [American Society for Quality Control, *National Convention Transactions, 1959* (Milwaukee, WI: American Society for Quality Control, 1959), 438.]

8. **Weighting System** The concept of a weighting system has a long history in economics. The application of this term to project management and specifically contracting is fairly recent. [Michael Greer, *The Project Manager's Partner: A Step-by-Step Guide to Project Management* (Amherst, MA: Human Resource Development Press, 2001), 108.]

9. **Contract Change Control System** When the concept of change control was introduced in the 1970s, it was quickly adapted to contracts, since many of the companies that used change control for IT projects were also government contractors. [Philip A. Metzger, *Managing a Programming Project* (New York: Prentice-Hall, 1973), 84.]

CHAPTER THIRTEEN

1. **Fair Use Doctrine** For more information, see this Web page maintained by the Library of Congress: http://www.copyright.gov/fls/fl102.html. This is a doctrine in US law that allows limited use of copyrighted materials.

2. **Ethnocentrism** The term was coined in 1906 by US anthropologist William Graham Sumner. He argued that scientists had to recognize and see past ethnocentrism to effectively observe the world. The concept has been explored intensively by scientists for the last century. [Neuliep, James William. *Intercultural Communication: A Contextual Approach* (Los Angeles, CA: Sage Publications, 2009), 183.]

Index